Communications
in Computer and Information Science   1512

More information about this series at https://link.springer.com/bookseries/7899

Jeffrey Nichols · Arthur 'Barney' Maccabe ·
James Nutaro · Swaroop Pophale ·
Pravallika Devineni · Theresa Ahearn ·
Becky Verastegui (Eds.)

Driving Scientific and Engineering Discoveries Through the Integration of Experiment, Big Data, and Modeling and Simulation

21st Smoky Mountains Computational Sciences
and Engineering, SMC 2021
Virtual Event, October 18–20, 2021
Revised Selected Papers

 Springer

Editors
Jeffrey Nichols (iD)
Oak Ridge National Laboratory
Oak Ridge, TN, USA

Arthur 'Barney' Maccabe (iD)
Oak Ridge National Laboratory
Oak Ridge, TN, USA

James Nutaro (iD)
Oak Ridge National Laboratory
Oak Ridge, TN, USA

Swaroop Pophale (iD)
Oak Ridge National Laboratory
Oak Ridge, TN, USA

Pravallika Devineni (iD)
Oak Ridge National Laboratory
Oak Ridge, TN, USA

Theresa Ahearn (iD)
Oak Ridge National Laboratory
Oak Ridge, TN, USA

Becky Verastegui (iD)
Oak Ridge National Laboratory
Oak Ridge, TN, USA

ISSN 1865-0929   ISSN 1865-0937 (electronic)
Communications in Computer and Information Science
ISBN 978-3-030-96497-9   ISBN 978-3-030-96498-6   (eBook)
https://doi.org/10.1007/978-3-030-96498-6

This Springer imprint is published by the registered company Springer Nature Switzerland AG
The registered company address is: Gewerbestrasse 11, 6330 Cham, Switzerland

Preface

The Smoky Mountains Computational Sciences and Engineering Conference (SMC 2021) organized by the Oak Ridge National Laboratory (ORNL) took place during October 18–20, 2021. This year, like last year, we had a virtual venue due to the COVID-19 pandemic. The conference focused on four major areas—theory, experiment, modeling and simulation, and data—with the main theme being accelerated node computing and integrated instruments for science. Over the past year, the U.S. Department of Energy National Laboratories conducted a series of "Town Hall" meetings aimed at collecting community input on the opportunities and challenges facing the scientific community as high-performance computing (HPC) and other technologies converge, as well as how this convergence will integrate large-scale simulation, advanced data analysis, data-driven predictive modeling, theory, and high-throughput experiments. Reflecting the focus of these meetings, SMC 2021 featured four distinct tracks for submission: Advanced Computing Methods, Advanced Computing Applications, Advanced Computing Systems and Software, and Deploying Advanced Computing Platforms, along with a scientific Data Challenge (SMCDC 2021).

We issued a call for papers (CFP) inviting scientists to share research breakthroughs in HPC, edge computing, large data sets, modeling and simulation, instruments, and the convergence of new technologies and discuss ideas to contribute to our program via peer-reviewed papers. SMC 2021's Program Committee consisted of 70 leading experts who helped advertise the CFP, then reviewed papers for the main program and our scientific data challenge competition. Using a single-blind review process, the Program Committee accepted 20 of the 71 submissions to the main program and five submissions were accepted as posters. All papers were peer-reviewed by at least three experts, and the majority had five reviewers. SMCDC 2021 accepted eight of the 17 submissions making the overall acceptance rate of the conference 35%.

The accepted papers, which are compiled in the SMC 2021 conference proceedings, describe the most important directions for research, development, and production, as well as elucidating experiences and advocating for investment in areas related to the conference theme. These important areas were defined by the following sessions:

Session 1. Advanced Computing Methods: Instruments from Edge to Supercomputers. In this session participants discussed applications that embrace data-driven and first-principle methods, focusing on the convergence of AI and high-performance modeling and simulation applications. Topics included experiences, algorithms, and numerical methods with an emphasis on applications to edge computing. Specific topics ranged from mixed-precision algorithms, data reduction methods, and scientific libraries and frameworks for integrating HPC and AI. Participants also discussed how simulation can be used to train AI models and integrating AI models into simulation applications while quantifying errors.

Session 2. Advanced Computing Applications: Use Cases that Combine Multiple Aspects of Data and Modeling.
Participants discussed multi-domain applications that use federated scientific instruments with data sets and large-scale compute capabilities, including sensors, actuators, instruments for HPC systems, data stores, and other network-connected devices. This session centered on applications that focus on integration across domains and scientific datasets that combine AI and HPC with edge computing.

Session 3. Advanced Computing Systems and Software: Connecting Instruments from Edge to Supercomputer.
This session included topics related to programming systems and software technologies for novel computing processors such as neuromorphic, automata, advanced FETs, carbon nanotube processors, and other types of accelerators that meet the SWaP constraints to be deployed at the edge. In this session the latest ideas and findings in the programming and software ecosystems for these rapidly changing and emerging fields were presented.

Session 4. Deploying Advanced Computing Platforms: On the Road to a Converged Ecosystem.
Topics in this session included industry experience and plans for deploying both hardware and software infrastructure needed to support emerging AI and/or classical simulation workloads; for combining on-premises and cloud resources; and for connecting distributed experimental, observational, and data resources and computing facilities using edge technologies. This session focused on how emerging technologies can be co-designed to support compute and data workflows at scale for next-generation HPC and AI systems.

The Smoky Mountain Poster Session. For this session, the SMC 2021 Program Committee highlighted accepted papers that provided novel contributions to the main themes of the conference proceedings.

The Smoky Mountain Data Challenge. Scientific data sponsors developed challenges based on eminent ORNL data sets from scientific simulations and instruments in physical and chemical sciences, electron microscopy, bioinformatics, neutron sources, urban development, and other areas for the SMC Data Challenge (SMCDC 2021) competition. Students and data analytics experts submitted papers describing their strategies and solutions to a series of increasingly difficult challenge questions. Overall, 55 teams registered for the competition and a peer review process selected 17 finalists, all of whom presented lighting talks at SMC 2021. Finally, seven papers were selected to be included in the proceedings based on their merit and scores from the SMCDC judges.

SMC 2021 had an excellent lineup of speakers eager to engage with our attendees. In addition to the paper presentations there were four invited talks, covering related important topics, along with a keynote from Sarah Tariq, VP of Autonomous Driving Software at NVIDIA.

SMC 2021 would not have been possible without our authors, the Program Committee, the Session Chairs, and the scientific community, who once again came together in our shared mission to discuss solutions to the most complex problems in energy science and computing.

October 2021

Jeffrey Nichols
Arthur 'Barney' Maccabe
James Nutaro
Swaroop Pophale
Pravallika Devineni
Theresa Ahearn
Becky Verastegui

Organization

General Chair

Jeffrey Nichols   Oak Ridge National Laboratory, USA

Conference Organizers

Theresa Ahearn   Oak Ridge National Laboratory, USA
Becky Verastegui   Oak Ridge National Laboratory, USA

Media and Communications

Scott Jones   Oak Ridge National Laboratory, USA
Elizabeth Rosenthal   Oak Ridge National Laboratory, USA

Program Committee Chairs

James Nutaro   Oak Ridge National Laboratory, USA
Swaroop Pophale   Oak Ridge National Laboratory, USA
Arthur 'Barney' Maccabe   Oak Ridge National Laboratory, USA

Data Challenge Chair

Pravallika Devineni   Oak Ridge National Laboratory, USA

Steering Committee

Jeff Nichols   Oak Ridge National Laboratory, USA
Arthur 'Barney' Maccabe   Oak Ridge National Laboratory, USA
Kate Evans   Oak Ridge National Laboratory, USA
Theresa Ahearn   Oak Ridge National Laboratory, USA
Becky Verastegui   Oak Ridge National Laboratory, USA
Pravallika Devineni   Oak Ridge National Laboratory, USA
Suzanne Parete-Koon   Oak Ridge National Laboratory, USA
Gina Tourassi   Oak Ridge National Laboratory, USA

Session Chairs

Scott Atchley   Oak Ridge National Laboratory, USA
David Bernhold   Oak Ridge National Laboratory, USA
Neena Imam   Oak Ridge National Laboratory, USA
Olga Kuchar   Oak Ridge National Laboratory, USA

Teja Kuruganti	Oak Ridge National Laboratory, USA
Olga Ovchinnokova	Oak Ridge National Laboratory, USA
Juan Restrepo	Oak Ridge National Laboratory, USA
Arjun Shankar	Oak Ridge National Laboratory, USA

Program Committee

Kate Evans	Oak Ridge National Laboratory, USA
Vincent Paquit	Oak Ridge National Laboratory, USA
Jonathan Beard	ARM Research, USA
Vassil Alexandrov	STFC Hartree Centre, UK
Bernd Mohr	Jülich Supercomputing Center, Germany
Aric Hagberg	Los Alamos National Laboratory, USA
Cj Newburn	NVIDIA, USA
Jibo Sanyal	Oak Ridge National Laboratory, USA
Jim Ang	Pacific Northwest National Laboratory, USA
Kody Law	University of Manchester, UK
Steven Hamilton	Oak Ridge National Laboratory, USA
Bronson Messer	Oak Ridge National Laboratory, USA
Thomas Schulthess	ETH Zurich/CSCS, Switzerland
Andreas Herten	Forschungszentrum Jülich GmbH, Germany
John Levesque	HPE, USA
Jeff Hittinger	Lawrence Livermore National Laboratory, USA
David Brown	Lawrence Berkeley National Laboratory, USA
Laura Pullum	Oak Ridge National Laboratory, USA
Tjerk Straatsma	Oak Ridge National Laboratory, USA
James Stewart	Sandia National Laboratories, USA
Stan Tomov	University of Tennessee, USA
Vivek Sarkar	Georgia Institute of Technology, USA
Cerlane Leong	A*STAR, Singapore
Debbie Bard	Lawrence Berkeley National Laboratory, USA
Subhashish Mitra	Stanford University, USA
Suhas Somnath	Oak Ridge National Laboratory, USA
Amy Rose	Oak Ridge National Laboratory, USA
Manuel Arenaz	Appentra Solutions S.L., Spain
Roxana Rositoru	Arm Ltd., UK
James Sexton	IBM, USA
Stuart Slattery	Oak Ridge National Laboratory, USA
Mitsuhisa Sato	RIKEN AICS/University of Tsukuba, Japan
Christian Terboven	RWTH Aachen University, Germany
Rio Yakota	Tokyo Institute of Technology, Japan
Oscar Hernandez	NVIDIA, USA
Veronica Vergara	Oak Ridge National Laboratory, USA
Valerie Taylor	Argonne National Laboratory, USA
Esteban Meneses	Costa Rica Institute of Technology, Costa Rica
Norbert Eicker	Jülich Supercomputing Centre, Germany

Dirk Pleiter	KTH Royal Institute of Technology, Sweden
Matt Baker	Oak Ridge National Laboratory, USA
Shantenu Jha	Rutgers University, USA
Mathias Mueller	RWTH Aachen University, Germany
Jony Castagna	STFC Hartree Centre, UK
Sadaf Alam	Swiss National Supercomputing Centre (CSCS), Switzerland
Patrick Bridges	University of New Mexico, USA
Piotr Luszczek	University of Tennessee, Knoxville, USA
Nick Wright	Lawrence Berkeley National Laboratory, USA
Brice Goglin	Inria, France
Kathryn Mohror	Lawrence Livermore National Laboratory, USA
Ian Karlin	Lawrence Livermore National Laboratory, USA
Matt Leininger	Lawrence Livermore National Laboratory, USA
Chris Zimmer	Oak Ridge National Laboratory, USA
Woong Shin	Oak Ridge National Laboratory, USA
Phil Roth	Oak Ridge National Laboratory, USA
Hartwig Anzt	University of Tennessee, Knoxville, USA
Sean Smith	NCI, Australia
Joseph Schuchart	University of Tennessee, Knoxville, USA
Goekcen Kestor	Pacific Northwest National Laboratory, USA

Data Challenge Program Committee

Andy Berres	Oak Ridge National Laboratory, USA
Cassandra Oduola	Microsoft, USA
Sajal Dash	Oak Ridge National Laboratory, USA
Piyush Sao	Oak Ridge National Laboratory, USA
Jacob Bond	General Motors, USA
Jordan Chipka	Telemetry Sports, USA
Drahomira Herrmannova	Oak Ridge National Laboratory, USA
Chathika Gunaratne	Oak Ridge National Laboratory, USA
Rutuja Gurav	University of California, Riverside, USA
Saheli Ghosh	PayPal Inc., USA
Tania Lorido	University of Deusto, Spain
Ivy Peng	Lawrence Livermore National Laboratory, USA
Abhishek Biswas	Oak Ridge National Laboratory, USA
Hassina Bilheux	Oak Ridge National Laboratory, USA
Seung-Hwan Lim	Oak Ridge National Laboratory, USA
Melissa Allen	Oak Ridge National Laboratory, USA
Ramakrishnan Kannan	Oak Ridge National Laboratory, USA
Maxim Ziatdinov	Oak Ridge National Laboratory, USA
Rama K. Vasudevan	Oak Ridge National Laboratory, USA
Arnab Kumar Paul	Oak Ridge National Laboratory, USA
Richard Riedel	Oak Ridge National Laboratory, USA
Jean-Christophe Bilheux	Oak Ridge National Laboratory, USA

Guojing Cong   Oak Ridge National Laboratory, USA
Hao Lu   Oak Ridge National Laboratory, USA
Kuldeep Kurte   Oak Ridge National Laboratory, USA

Contents

**Deploying Advanced Computing Platforms: On the Road to a
Converged Ecosystem**

Scientific Data Challenges

Computational Applications: Converged HPC and Artificial Intelligence

Randomized Multilevel Monte Carlo for Embarrassingly Parallel Inference

Ajay Jasra[1], Kody J. H. Law[2(✉)], Alexander Tarakanov[2], and Fangyuan Yu[1]

[1] Computer, Electrical and Mathematical Sciences and Engineering Division,
King Abdullah University of Science and Technology,
Thuwal 23955, Kingdom of Saudi Arabia
{ajay.jasra,fangyuan.yu}@kaust.edu.sa

[2] Department of Mathematics, University of Manchester, Manchester M13 9PL, UK

Abstract. This position paper summarizes a recently developed research program focused on inference in the context of data centric science and engineering applications, and forecasts its trajectory forward over the next decade. Often one endeavours in this context to learn complex systems in order to make more informed predictions and high stakes decisions under uncertainty. Some key challenges which must be met in this context are robustness, generalizability, and interpretability. The Bayesian framework addresses these three challenges, while bringing with it a fourth, undesirable feature: it is typically far more expensive than its deterministic counterparts. In the 21st century, and increasingly over the past decade, a growing number of methods have emerged which allow one to leverage cheap low-fidelity models in order to precondition algorithms for performing inference with more expensive models and make Bayesian inference tractable in the context of high-dimensional and expensive models. Notable examples are multilevel Monte Carlo (MLMC), multi-index Monte Carlo (MIMC), and their randomized counterparts (rMLMC), which are able to provably achieve a dimension-independent (including $\infty-$dimension) canonical complexity rate with respect to mean squared error (MSE) of 1/MSE. Some parallelizability is typically lost in an inference context, but recently this has been largely recovered via novel *double randomization* approaches. Such an approach delivers independent and identically distributed samples of quantities of interest which are unbiased with respect to the *infinite resolution target distribution*. Over the coming decade, this family of algorithms has the potential to transform data centric science and engineering, as well as classical machine learning applications such as deep learning, by scaling up and scaling out fully Bayesian inference.

Keywords: Randomization methods · Markov chain Monte Carlo · Bayesian inference

1 Introduction

The Bayesian framework begins with a statistical model characterizing the causal relationship between various variables, parameters, and observations. A canonical example in the context of inverse problems is

© Springer Nature Switzerland AG 2022
J. Nichols et al. (Eds.): SMC 2021, CCIS 1512, pp. 3–21, 2022.
https://doi.org/10.1007/978-3-030-96498-6_1

$$y \sim N(G_\theta(u), \Gamma_\theta), \quad u \sim N(m_\theta, C_\theta), \quad \theta \sim \pi_0,$$

where $N(m, C)$ denotes a Gaussian random variable with mean m and covariance C, $G_\theta : U \to \mathbb{R}^m$ is the (typically nonlinear) parameter-to-observation map, $\theta \in \mathbb{R}^p$ is a vector of parameters with π_0 some distribution, and the data is given in the form of *observations* y [52,53]. Nothing precludes the case where U is a function space, e.g. leading to a Gaussian process prior above, but to avoid unnecessary technicalities, assume $U = \mathbb{R}^d$. The objective is to *condition* the prior knowledge about (u, θ) with the observed data y and recover a *posterior distribution*

$$p(u, \theta|y) = \frac{p(u, \theta, y)}{p(y)} = \frac{p(y|u, \theta)p(u|\theta)p(\theta)}{\int_{U \times \mathbb{R}^p} p(y|u, \theta)p(u|\theta)p(\theta)dud\theta}.$$

Often in the context above one may settle for a slightly simpler goal of identifying a point estimate θ^*, e.g. $\theta^* = \text{argmax}_\theta p(\theta|y)$ (which we note may require an intractable integration over U) and targeting $p(u|y, \theta^*)$ instead.

In the context described above, one often only has access to an *approximation* of the map G_θ, and potentially an approximation of the domain U, which may in principle be infinite dimensional. One example is the numerical solution of a system of differential equations. Other notable examples include surrogate models arising from reduced-physics or machine-learning-type approximations [46] or deep feedforward neural networks [44]. For the sake of concreteness the reader can keep this model in mind, however it is noted that the framework is much more general, for example the parameters θ can encode the causal relationship between latent variables via a graphical model such as a deep belief network or deep Boltzmann machine [4,42].

A concise statement of the general problem of Bayesian inference is that it requires exploration of a posterior distribution Π from which one cannot obtain independent and identically distributed (i.i.d.) samples. Specifically, the aim is to compute quantities such as

$$\Pi_\theta(\varphi) := \int_U \varphi(u)\Pi_\theta(du), \quad \varphi : U \to \mathbb{R}, \tag{1}$$

where $\Pi_\theta(du) = \pi_\theta(u)\nu_\theta(du)$, $\nu_\theta(du)$ is either Lebesgue measure $\nu_\theta(du) = du$, or one can simulate from it, $\pi_\theta(u) = \gamma_\theta(u)/\nu_\theta(\gamma_\theta)$, and given u one can evaluate $\gamma_\theta(u)$ (or at least a non-negative unbiased estimator). Markov chain Monte Carlo (MCMC) and sequential Monte Carlo (SMC) samplers can be used for this [49]. Considering the example above with $U = \mathbb{R}^d$, we may take $\nu(du) = du$ and then

$$\gamma_\theta(u) = |\Gamma_\theta|^{-1/2}|C_\theta|^{-1/2} \exp(-\frac{1}{2}|\Gamma_\theta^{-1/2}(y - G_\theta(u))|^2 - \frac{1}{2}|C_\theta^{-1/2}(u - m_\theta)|^2), \tag{2}$$

where $|A|$ denotes the determinant for a matrix $A \in \mathbb{R}^n$. Note we have used a subscript for θ, as is typical in the statistics literature to denote that everything is conditional on θ, and note that the θ-dependent constants are not necessary here, per se, but it is customary to define the un-normalized target as the joint on

(u, y), such that $Z_\theta := \nu_\theta(\gamma_\theta) = p(y|\theta)$. Also note that in (2), u would be referred to as a *latent variable* in the statistics and machine learning literature, and so this setup corresponds to a complex *physics-informed (via G_θ) unsupervised learning model*. Labelled data problems like regression and classification [43], as well as semi-supervised learning [39,56], can also be naturally cast in a Bayesian framework. In fact, if $G_\theta(u)$ is point-wise evaluation of u, i.e. $G_\theta^i(u) = u(x^i)$, for *inputs* or *covariates* x^i associated to labels y^i, and one allows U to be an infinite-dimensional (reproducing kernel) Hilbert space, then standard Gaussian process (GP) regression has this form. In infinite-dimensions there is no Lebesgue density, so (2) does not make sense, but the marginal likelihood and posterior can both be computed in closed form thanks to the properties of GP [47]. Alternatively, if u are the parameters of a deep feedforward neural network [44] $f_\theta(\cdot; u)$, and $G_\theta^i(u) = f_\theta(x^i; u)$ with Gaussian prior on u, then one has a standard Bayesian neural network model [4,44].

1.1   The Sweet and the Bitter of Bayes

Three challenges which are elegantly handled in a Bayesian framework are (a) robustness, (b) generalizability, and (c) interpretability [1,51]. Uncertainty quantification (UQ) has been a topic of great interest in science and engineering applications over the past decades, due to its ability to provide a more robust model [1,16]. A model which can extrapolate outside training data coverage is referred to as generalizable. Notice that via prior knowledge (1) and the physical model, (2) has this integrated capability by design. Interpretability is the most heavily loaded word among the three desiderata. Our definition is that the model (i) can be easily understood by the user [7], (ii) incorporates all data and domain knowledge available in a principled way [7,26], and (iii) enables inference of causal relationships between latent and observed variables [45]. The natural question is then, "Why in the age of data doesn't everybody adopt Bayesian inference for all their learning requirements?"

The major hurdle to widespread adoption of a fully Bayesian treatment of learning is the computational cost. Except for very special cases, such as GP regression [47], the solution cannot be obtained in closed form. Point estimates, Laplace approximations [50], and variational methods [5,37] have therefore taken center stage, as they can yield acceptable results very quickly in many cases. In particular, for a strongly convex objective function, gradient descent achieves exponential convergence to a local minimizer, i.e. MSE $\propto \exp(-N)$ in N steps. Such point estimates are still suboptimal from a Bayesian perspective, as they lack UQ. In terms of computation of (1), Monte Carlo (MC) methods are able to achieve exact inference in (1) in general [40,49]. In the case of i.i.d. sampling, MC methods achieve the canonical, dimension-independent convergence rate of MSE $\propto 1/N$, for N-sample approximations, without any smoothness assumptions and out-of-the-box[1]. Quadrature methods [15] and quasi-MC [8] are able to

---

[1] This is the same rate achieved by gradient descent for general non-convex smooth objective functions. In fact, the success of deep neural networks for learning high-dimensional functions has been attributed to this dimension-independence in [55].

achieve improvements over MC rates, however the rates depend on the dimension and the smoothness of the integrand.

A curse of dimensionality can still hamper application of MC methods through the constant and the cost of simulation, meaning it is rare to achieve canonical *complexity* of cost $\propto 1/\text{MSE}$ for non-trivial applications. Usually this is manifested in the form of a penalty in the exponent, so that cost $\propto \text{MSE}^{-a}$, for $a > 2$. A notable exception is MLMC [18,22] and MIMC [21] methods, and their randomized counterparts rMLMC [48,54] and rMIMC [11], which are able to achieve dimension-independent canonical complexity for a range of applications. These estimators are constructed by using a natural telescopic sum identity and constructing coupled increment estimators of decreasing variance. As an added bonus, the randomized versions eliminate discretization bias *entirely*, and deliver estimates with respect to the limiting *infinite-resolution distribution*.

In the context of inference problems, i.i.d. sampling is typically not possible and one must resort to MCMC or SMC [49]. This makes application of (r)MLMC and (r)MIMC more complex. Over the past decade, there has been an explosion of interest in applying these methods to inference, e.g. see [3,14,24,25,32] for examples of MLMC and [30,34] for MIMC. A notable benefit of MC methods is easy *parallelizability*, however typically MLMC and MIMC methods for inference are much more synchronous, or even serial in the case of MCMC. A family of rMLMC methods have recently been introduced for inference [23,31,35], which largely recover this lost parallelizability, and deliver i.i.d. samples that are unbiased with respect to the limiting infinite resolution target distribution *in the inference context*. In other words, the expectation of the resulting estimators are free from any approximation error. The first instance of rMLMC for inference was [9], and the context was different to the above work – in particular, consistent estimators are constructed that are free from discretization bias.

The rest of this paper is focused on these novel parallel rMLMC methods for inference, which are able to achieve the gold standard of Bayesian posterior inference with canonical complexity rate $1/\text{MSE}$. In the age of data and increasing parallelism of supercomputer architecture, these methods are prime candidates to become a staple, if not the defacto standard, for inference in data-centric science and engineering applications. Section 2 describes some technical details of the methods, Sect. 3 presents a specific motivating example Bayesian inverse problem and some compelling numerical results, and Sect. 4 concludes with a call to action and roadmap forward for this exciting research program.

2   Technical Details of the Methodology

The technical details of the methodology will be sketched in this section. The idea is to give an accessible overview and invitation to this exciting methodology. The interested reader can find details in the references cited. With respect to the previous section, the notation for θ will be suppressed – the concerned reader should imagine either everything is conditioned on θ or it has been absorbed into $u \leftarrow (u, \theta)$. Subsection 2.1 sketches the MLMC idea, and some of the challenges, strategies for overcoming them, and opportunities in the context of inference. Subsection 2.2 sketches the rMLMC idea, and some of the challenges, strategies for overcoming them, and opportunities in the context of inference. Finally Subsect. 2.3 briefly sketches MIMC.

2.1 Multilevel Monte Carlo

As mentioned above, for problems requiring approximation, MLMC methods are able to achieve a *huge speedup* in comparison to the naive approach of using a single fixed approximation, and indeed in some cases canonical complexity of cost $\propto 1/\text{MSE}$. These methods leverage a range of successive approximations of increasing cost and accuracy. In a simplified description, most MLMC theoretical results rely on underlying assumptions of

(i) a hierarchy of targets Π_l, $l \geq 0$, of increasing cost, such that $\Pi_l \to \Pi$ as $l \to \infty$;

(ii) a coupling Π^l s.t. $\forall A \subset U$,

$$\int_{A \times U} \Pi^l(du, du') = \Pi_l(A), \quad \text{and} \quad \int_{U \times A} \Pi^l(du, du') = \Pi_{l-1}(A);$$

(iii) the coupling is such that

$$\int |\varphi(u) - \varphi(u')|^2 \Pi^l(du, du') \leq C h_l^\beta, \tag{3}$$

and the cost to simulate from Π^l is proportional to $C h_l^{-\zeta}$, for some $h_l > 0$ s.t. $h_l \to 0$ as $l \to \infty$, and $C, \beta, \zeta > 0$ independent of l.

Now one leverages the telescopic sum

$$\Pi(\varphi) = \underbrace{\sum_{l=0}^{L} \Delta_l(\varphi)}_{\text{approximation}} + \underbrace{\sum_{l=L+1}^{\infty} \Delta_l(\varphi)}_{\text{bias}}, \tag{4}$$

where $\Delta_l(\varphi) = \Pi_l(\varphi) - \Pi_{l-1}(\varphi)$, $\Pi_{-1} \equiv 0$, by approximating the first term, $\Pi_L(\varphi)$, using i.i.d. samples from the couplings Π^l, $l = 0, \ldots, L$. The second term is the bias $= \Pi(\varphi) - \Pi_L(\varphi)$. This allows one to optimally balance cost with more samples on coarse/cheap levels, and a decreasing number of samples as l increases, to construct a multilevel estimator $\widehat{\Pi}(\varphi)$ that achieves a given mean square error (MSE),

$$\mathbb{E}(\widehat{\Pi}(\varphi) - \Pi(\varphi))^2 = \text{variance} + \text{bias}^2,$$

more efficiently than a single level method. A schematic is given in Fig. 1(a).

The MLMC estimator is defined as

$$\widehat{Y} = \sum_{l=0}^{L} \frac{1}{N_l} \sum_{i=1}^{N_l} Y_l^i, \tag{5}$$

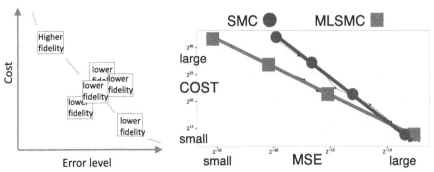

(a) Few high fidelity (high-cost) simulations are combined with many at low-fidelity (low cost).

(b) MSE vs Cost: MLSMC vs SMC for elliptic PDE, illustrating the large gain in efficiency (smaller Cost for a given MSE). [3]

Fig. 1. Synopsis of MLMC methods: a family of models, including coarse-resolution approximation of differential equations, surrogates, etc. (a) can be combined in the MLMC framework to yield improved complexity cost $\propto 1/\text{MSE}$ (b).

where $Y_l^i = \varphi(U_l^i) - \varphi(U_{l-1}^i)$ and $(U_l, U_{l-1})^i \sim \Pi^l$ for $l \geq 1$, $Y_0^i = \varphi(U_0^i)$, $U_0^i \sim \Pi_0$, and L and $\{N_l\}_{l=0}^L$ are chosen to balance the bias and variance. In particular, $L \propto \log(\text{MSE})$ and $N_l \propto h_l^{(\beta+\zeta)/2}$. In the canonical regime where $\beta > \zeta$ one achieves the canonical complexity of cost $\propto 1/\text{MSE}$. If $\beta \leq \zeta$, there are penalties. See [18] for details. Note that for the theory above, controlling the bias requires only $\alpha > 0$ such that

$$\left| \int \varphi(u) - \varphi(u')\Pi^l(du, du') \right| \leq Ch_l^{\alpha},$$

however it is clear that Jensen's inequality provides $\alpha \geq \beta/2$, which is suitable for the purposes of this exposition. There are notable exceptions where one can achieve $\alpha > \beta/2$, e.g. Euler-Maruyama or Milstein simulation of SDE [17], and this of course provides tighter results.

Note that the assumptions above can be relaxed substantially if one sacrifices a clean theory. In particular, the models Π_l need not be defined hierarchically in terms of a small parameter h_l corresponding to "resolution", as long as h_l^{β} and $h_l^{-\zeta}$ in assumption (iii) above can be replaced with V_l and C_l, respectively, such that $V_l \to 0$ as $C_l \to \infty$ in some fashion. Indeed in practice one need not ever consider the limit and can work with a finite set of models within the same framework, as is advocated in the related multifidelity literature (see e.g. [46]).

MLMC for Inference. In the context of inference, it is rare that one can achieve i.i.d. samples from couplings Π^l. As described in Sect. 1, one more often only has access to (unbiased estimates of) the un-normalized target and must resort to MCMC or SMC. In the canonical regime $\beta > \zeta$ the theory can proceed in a similar fashion provided one can obtain estimators $\hat{Y}_l^N$ such that for some $C, \beta > 0$ and $q = 1, 2$

$$\mathbb{E}\left[\hat{Y}_l^N - (\Pi_l(\varphi) - \Pi_{l-1}(\varphi))\right]^q \leq C \frac{h_l^{\beta q/2}}{N}. \tag{6}$$

In the sub-canonical regime, the situation is slightly more complex.

Achieving such estimates with efficient inverse MC methods has been the focus of a large body of work. These methods can be classified according to 3 primary strategies: importance sampling [2,3,24,36,41], coupled algorithms [14,20,25,28,33], and approximate couplings [29,30,34]. See e.g. [32] for a recent review. Importance sampling estimators are the simplest, and they proceed by expressing the desired increment in terms of expectation with respect to one of the levels. Its applicability is therefore limited to cases where the importance weights can be calculated or estimated. Coupled algorithms attempt to achieve the required rates by coupling two single level algorithms targeting the coarse and fine targets, respectively. These are in some sense the most natural, and in principle the most general, but it can be deceptively tricky to get them to work correctly. Approximate coupling is the most straightforward strategy and can also be quite versatile. In this case, one abandons exactness with respect to coarse and fine marginals, and aims only to achieve well-behaved weights associated to a change of measure with respect to an approximate coupling.

2.2   Randomized Multilevel Monte Carlo

Randomized MLMC (rMLMC) is defined similarly to (5) except with a notable difference. Define a categorical distribution $\mathbf{p} = (\mathbf{p}_0, \mathbf{p}_1, \dots)$ on $\mathbb{Z}_+$ and let $L^i \sim \mathbf{p}$, and $Y_{L^i}^i$ as above. The single term estimator [48] is defined as

$$Z^i = \frac{Y_{L^i}^i}{\mathbf{p}_{L^i}}. \tag{7}$$

Notice that, as a result of (4),

$$\mathbb{E}Z^i = \sum_{l=0}^{\infty} \mathbf{p}_l \mathbb{E}\left(\frac{Y_l^i}{\mathbf{p}_l}\right) = \Pi_0(\varphi) + \sum_{l=1}^{\infty} \Pi_l(\varphi) - \Pi_{l-1}(\varphi) = \Pi(\varphi),$$

i.e. this estimator is free from discretization bias. The corresponding rMLMC estimator is given by

$$\hat{Z} = \frac{1}{N} \sum_{i=1}^{N} Z^i = \sum_{l=0}^{\infty} \frac{1}{N\mathbf{p}_l} \sum_{i; L_i = l} Y_l^i. \tag{8}$$

It is easy to see that $\mathbb{E}\#\{i; L_i = l\} = N\mathbf{p}_l$ and $\#\{i; L_i = l\} \to N\mathbf{p}_l$ as $N \to \infty$, and the optimal choice level of distribution is analogous to level selection above, $\mathbf{p}_l \propto N_l$, with N_l as in (5). Despite the infinite sum above, this estimator does not incur infinite cost for finite N, because only finitely many summands are non-zero. Furthermore, $\mathbf{p}_l \to 0$, so higher levels are simulated rarely and the expected cost is also typically finite. See [48] for further details and other variants.

rMLMC for Inference. In the inference context, one typically does not have access to *unbiased* estimators of Y_{L^i}, and rather $\mathbb{E}(\hat{Y}_l^N) \neq \Pi_l(\varphi) - \Pi_{l-1}(\varphi)$. In the finite L case, one can get away with this provided (6) holds, however rMLMC methods rely on this property. In the work [9], SMC is used to construct unbiased estimators of increments with respect to the *un-normalized* target (a well-known yet rather remarkable feature of SMC methods [13]), and subsequently a ratio estimator is used for posterior expectations, which are hence biased (for finite N) but consistent (in the limit $N \to \infty$) with respect to the infinite-resolution ($L = \infty$) target. Subsequently it has been observed that another inner application of the methodology presented above in Sect. 2.2 allows one to *transform a consistent estimator into an unbiased estimator* [31, 35].

In particular, suppose one can couple two estimators $\hat{Y}_l^N$ and $\hat{Y}_l^{N'}$, with $N' > N$, that marginally satisfy (6), and such that the resulting estimator satisfies, for $q = 1, 2$,

$$\mathbb{E}\left[\hat{Y}_l^N - \hat{Y}_l^{N'}\right]^q \leq C \frac{h_l^{\beta q/2}}{N}. \tag{9}$$

Introduce inner levels N_k, $k \geq 1$, such that $N_k \to \infty$ as $k \to \infty$, and another categorical distribution $\mathsf{p} = (\mathsf{p}_0, \mathsf{p}_1, \dots)$ on $\mathbb{Z}_+$. Now let $K^i \sim \mathsf{p}$, $L^i \sim \mathsf{p}$ and simulate $\hat{Y}_{L^i}^{N_{K^i}}, \hat{Y}_{L^i}^{N_{K^i-1}}$ as above. The resulting *doubly-randomized* single term estimator is given by

$$Z^i = \frac{1}{\mathsf{p}_{L^i}\mathsf{p}_{K^i}} \left(\hat{Y}_{L^i}^{N_{K^i}} - \hat{Y}_{L^i}^{N_{K^i-1}}\right). \tag{10}$$

Now, as above,

$$\mathbb{E}\left[\frac{1}{\mathsf{p}_{K^i}} \left(\hat{Y}_l^{N_{K^i}} - \hat{Y}_l^{N_{K^i-1}}\right)\right] = \Pi_l(\varphi) - \Pi_{l-1}(\varphi),$$

and hence $\mathbb{E}Z^i = \Pi(\varphi)$. Furthermore, the estimators (10) can be simulated i.i.d. In other words, the embarrassingly parallel nature of classical MC estimators is restored, as well as all the classical results relating to i.i.d. random variables, such as the central limit theorem.

The work [35] leverages such a doubly randomized estimator for online particle filtering in the framework of [28]. The work [31] uses a so-called *coupled sum* variant in the framework of MLSMC samplers [3]. Both of these estimators suffer from the standard limiting MC convergence rate with respect to the inner randomization, which is sub-canonical. In other words the cost to achieve an estimator at level K is $\mathcal{O}(N_K)$ and the error is $\mathcal{O}(N_K^{-1})$. As a result, it is not possible to achieve finite variance and finite cost, and one must settle for finite variance and finite cost *with high probability* [48]. In practice, one may truncate the sum at finite $K_{\max}$ to ensure finite cost, and accept the resulting bias.

rMLMCMC. An alternative incarnation of the inner randomization can be used in the context of MCMC, relying on the unbiased MCMC introduced in [27], which is based on the approach of [19]. In [27] one couples a pair of MCMCs

(U_n, U_n') targeting the same distribution Π in such a way that they (i) have the same distribution at time n, $U_n \overset{\mathcal{D}}{\sim} U_{n+1}'$, (ii) meet in finite time $\mathbb{E}(\tau) < \infty$, $\tau = \inf\{n; U_n = U_n'\}$, and (iii) remain identical thereafter. An unbiased estimator is then obtained via

$$\widehat{X} = \varphi(U_{n^*}) + \sum_{n=n^*+1}^{\infty} \varphi(U_n) - \varphi(U_n')$$

$$= \varphi(U_{n^*}) + \sum_{n=n^*+1}^{\tau} \varphi(U_n) - \varphi(U_n').$$

It is clear that in expectation the sum telescopes, giving the correct expectation $\mathbb{E}\widehat{X} = \mathbb{E}(\varphi(U_\infty)) = \Pi(\varphi)$. Such estimators can be simulated i.i.d., which removes the fundamental serial roadblock of MCMC, and the finite meeting time ensures finite cost. Variations of the approach allow similar efficiency to a single MCMC for a single CPU implementation, i.e. without leveraging parallelization. As above, with parallel processors, the sky is the limit.

In order to apply such technology to the present context, one couples a pair of coupled chains $(U_{n,l}, U_{n,l-1}, U_{n,l}', U_{n,l-1}')$ such that

$$U_{n,l}, U_{n,l-1} \overset{\mathcal{D}}{\sim} U_{n+1,l}', U_{n+1,l-1}',$$

yielding a foursome that is capable of delivering finite-cost unbiased estimators of $\Pi_l(\varphi) - \Pi_{l-1}(\varphi)$. Indeed we are also able to achieve estimates of the type in (6), and therefore (for suitable β) rMLMC estimators *with finite variance and finite cost*. Note that only the intra-level pairs need to meet and remain faithful. Ultimately, the i.i.d. estimators have the following form. Simulate $L^i \sim \mathbf{p}$ as described in Sect. 2.2, and define $Z^i = \widehat{Y}_{L^i}^i / \mathbf{p}_{L^i}$, where

$$\widehat{Y}_l^i = \varphi(U_{n^*,l}) - \varphi(U_{n^*,l-1})$$

$$+ \sum_{n=n^*+1}^{\tau_l} \varphi(U_{n,l}) - \varphi(U_{n,l}') - \sum_{n=n^*+1}^{\tau_{l-1}} \left(\varphi(U_{n,l-1}) - \varphi(U_{n,l-1}') \right), \quad (11)$$

with $\tau_\ell = \inf\{n; U_{n,\ell} = U_{n,\ell}'\}$, for $\ell = l, l-1$. The final estimator is

$$\widehat{Z} = \frac{1}{N} \sum_{i=1}^{N} Z^i. \tag{12}$$

2.3 Multi-index Monte Carlo

Recently, the hierarchical telescopic sum identity that MLMC is based upon has been viewed through the lense of sparse grids, for the case in which there are multiple continuous spatial, temporal, and/or parametric dimensions of approximation [21]. In other words, there is a hierarchy of targets Π_α, where α is a multi-index, such that $\Pi_\alpha \to \Pi$ as $|\alpha| \to \infty$. Under a more complex set of assumptions, one can appeal instead to the identity

$$\Pi(\varphi) = \sum_{\alpha \in \mathcal{I}} \Delta_\alpha(\varphi) + \sum_{\alpha \notin \mathcal{I}} \Delta_\alpha(\varphi), \quad \mathcal{I} \subset \mathbb{Z}_+^d,$$

where d−fold multi-increments Δ_α are used instead, i.e. letting $e_j \in \mathbb{R}^d$ denote the jth standard basis vector and $\delta_j \Pi_\alpha := \Pi_\alpha - \Pi_{\alpha - e_j}$, then $\Delta_\alpha := \delta_d \circ \cdots \circ \delta_1 \Pi_\alpha$ (for any multi-index α' with $\alpha'_i < 0$ for some $i = 1, \ldots, d$, $\Pi_{\alpha'} := 0$). The first term is approximated again using coupled samples and the second is the bias. Under suitable regularity conditions, this MIMC method *yields further huge speedup* to obtain a given level of error [18,21]. Some preliminary work in this direction has been done recently [30,34]. Forward randomized MIMC (rMIMC) has recently been done as well [11].

3   Motivating Example

3.1   Example of Problem

The following particular problem is presented as an example. This example is prototypical of a variety of inverse problems involving physical systems in which noisy/partial observations are made of the solution of an elliptic PDE and one would like to infer the diffusion coefficient. For example, the solution to the PDE v could represent pressure of a patch of land, subject to some forcing f (sources/sinks), and the diffusion coefficient $\hat{u}(u)$ then corresponds to the subsurface permeability [52,53], a highly desirable quantity of interest in the context of oil recovery. Let $D \subset \mathbb{R}^d$ with $\partial D \in C^1$ convex and $f \in L^2(D)$. Consider the following PDE on D:

$$-\nabla \cdot (\hat{u}(u)\nabla v) = f, \quad \text{on } D, \tag{13}$$
$$v = 0, \quad \text{on } \partial D, \tag{14}$$

where the diffusion coefficient has the form

$$\hat{u}(x; u) = \bar{u} + \sum_{j=1}^{J} u_j \sigma_j \phi_j(x), \tag{15}$$

Define $u = \{u_j\}_{j=1}^J$, and the state space will be $\mathsf{X} = \prod_{j=1}^J [-1, 1]$. Let $v(\cdot; u)$ denote the weak solution of (1) for parameter value u. The prior is given by $u_j \sim U[-1, 1]$ (the uniform distribution on $[-1, 1]$) i.i.d. for $j = 1, \ldots, J$. It will be assumed that $\phi_j \in C(D)$, $\|\phi_j\|_\infty \le 1$, and there is a $u_* > 0$ such that $\bar{u} > \sum_{j=1}^J \sigma_j + u_*$. Note that under the given assumptions, $\hat{u}(u) > u_*$ uniformly in u. Hence there is a well-defined (weak) solution $v(\cdot; u)$ that is bounded in $L^\infty(D)$ and $L^2(D)$ uniformly in u, and its gradient is also bounded in $L^2(D)$ uniformly in u [10,12].

Define the following vector-valued function

$$G(u) = [\langle g_1, v(\cdot; u)\rangle, \dots, \langle g_m, v(\cdot; u)\rangle]^\mathsf{T}, \tag{16}$$

where $g_i \in L^2(D)$ for $i = 1, \dots, m$. We note that pointwise evaluation is also permissible since $u \in L^\infty(D)$, i.e. g_i can be Dirac delta functions, however for simplicity we restrict the presentation to $L^2(D)$. It is assumed that the data take the form

$$y = G(u) + \xi, \quad \xi \sim N(0, \theta^{-1} \cdot \boldsymbol{I}_m), \quad \xi \perp u, \tag{17}$$

where $\perp$ denotes independence. The unnormalized density $\gamma_\theta : \mathsf{X} \to \mathbb{R}_+$ of u for fixed $\theta > 0$ is given by

$$\gamma_\theta(u) = \theta^{m/2} \exp\left(-\frac{\theta}{2}\|G(u) - y\|^2\right). \tag{18}$$

The normalized density is

$$\eta_\theta(u) = \frac{\gamma_\theta(u)}{I_\theta},$$

where $I_\theta = \int_\mathsf{X} \gamma_\theta(u) du$, and the quantity of interest is defined for $u \in \mathsf{X}$ as

$$\varphi_\theta(u) := \nabla_\theta \log\left(\gamma_\theta(u)\right) = \frac{m}{2\theta} - \frac{1}{2}\|G(u) - y\|^2. \tag{19}$$

To motivation this particular objective function, notice that γ_θ is chosen such that the marginal likelihood, or "evidence" for θ, is given by $p(y|\theta) = I_\theta$. Therefore the MLE ($\lambda = 0$) or MAP are given as minimizers of $-\log I_\theta + \lambda R(\theta)$, where $R(\theta) = -\log p(\theta)$. Assuming $R(\theta)$ is known in closed form and differentiable, then a gradient descent method requires

$$\nabla_\theta \log I_\theta = \frac{1}{I_\theta} \int_\mathsf{X} \nabla_\theta \gamma_\theta(u) du = \frac{1}{I_\theta} \int_\mathsf{X} \underbrace{\nabla_\theta \log\left(\gamma_\theta(u)\right)}_{\varphi_\theta(u)} \gamma_\theta(u) du = \eta_\theta(\varphi_\theta(u)).$$

$$\tag{20}$$

Stochastic gradient descent requires only an unbiased estimator of $\eta_\theta(\varphi_\theta(u))$ [38], which the presented rMLMC method delivers.

Numerical Approximation. The finite element method (FEM) is utilized for solution of (14) with piecewise multi-linear nodal basis functions. Let $d = 1$ and $D = [0, 1]$ for simplicity. Note the approach is easily generalized to $d \geq 1$ using products of such piecewise linear functions described below following standard FEM literature [6]. The PDE problem at resolution level l is solved using FEM with piecewise linear shape functions on a uniform mesh of width $h_l = 2^{-l}$, for $l \geq 0$. Thus, on the lth level the finite-element basis functions are $\{\psi_i^l\}_{i=1}^{2^l-1}$ defined as (for $x_i = i \cdot 2^{-l}$):

$$\psi_i^l(x) = \begin{cases} (1/h_l)[x - (x_i - h_l)] & \text{if } x \in [x_i - h_l, x_i], \\ (1/h_l)[x_i + h_l - x] & \text{if } x \in [x_i, x_i + h_l]. \end{cases}$$

To solve the PDE, $v^l(x) = \sum_{i=1}^{2^l-1} v_i^l \psi_i^l(x)$ is plugged into (1), and projected onto each basis element:

$$-\left\langle \nabla \cdot \left(\hat{u} \nabla \sum_{i=1}^{2^l-1} v_i^l \psi_i^l \right), \psi_j^l \right\rangle = \langle f, \psi_j^l \rangle,$$

resulting in the following linear system:

$$\boldsymbol{A}^l(u)\boldsymbol{v}^l = \boldsymbol{f}^l,$$

where we introduce the matrix $\boldsymbol{A}^l(u)$ with entries $A_{ij}^l(u) = \langle \hat{u} \nabla \psi_i^l, \nabla \psi_j^l \rangle$, and vectors $\boldsymbol{v}^l, \boldsymbol{f}^l$ with entries $v_i^l = \langle v, \psi_i^l \rangle$ and $f_i^l = \langle f, \psi_i^l \rangle$, respectively.

Define $G^l(u) = [\langle g_1, v^l(\cdot; u)\rangle, \ldots, \langle g_m, v^l(\cdot; u)\rangle]^\mathsf{T}$. Denote the corresponding approximated un-normalized density by

$$\gamma_\theta^l(u) = \theta^{m/2} \exp \left\{ -\frac{\theta}{2} \|G^l(u) - y\|^2 \right\}, \tag{21}$$

and the approximated normalized density by $\eta_\theta^l(u) = \gamma_\theta^l(u)/I_\theta^l$, where $I_\theta^l = \int_X \gamma_\theta^l(u) du$. Furthermore, define

$$\varphi_\theta^l(u) := \nabla_\theta \log \left(\gamma_\theta^l(u) \right) = \frac{m}{2\theta} - \frac{1}{2} \|G^l(u) - y\|^2. \tag{22}$$

It is well-known that under the stated assumptions $v^l(u)$ converges to $v(u)$ as $l \to \infty$ in $L^2(D)$ (as does its gradient), uniformly in u [6,10], with the rate $h_l^{\beta/2}$, $\beta = 4$. In a forward UQ context, this immediately provides (3) for Lipschitz functions of v, with $\beta = 4$. Furthermore, continuity ensures $\gamma_\theta^l(u)$ converges to $\gamma_\theta(u)$ and $\varphi_\theta^l(u)$ converges to $\varphi_\theta(u)$ uniformly in u as well. See also [2,3] for further details. This allows one to achieve estimates of the type (6) in the inference context.

3.2 Numerical Results

This section is for illustration purposes and reproduces results from [23], specifically Sect. 4.1.2 and Fig. 5. The problem specified in the previous section is considered with forcing $f(x) = 100x$. The prior specification of $u = (u_1, u_2)$ is taken as $J = 2$, $\bar{u} = 0.15$, $\sigma_1 = 1/10$, $\sigma_2 = 1/40$, $\phi_1(t) = \sin(\pi x)$ and $\phi_2(t) = \cos(2\pi x)$. For this particular setting, the solution v is continuous and hence point-wise observations are well-defined. The observation function $G(x)$ in (16) is chosen as $g_i(v(u)) = v(0.01 + 0.02(i - 1); u)$ for $i \in \{1, \ldots, m\}$ with $m = 50$. The FEM scheme in Sect. 3.1 is employed with mesh width of $l \leftarrow l + l_0$, where $l_0 = 3$. Using a discretization level of $l = 10$ to approximate $G(x)$ with $G_l(x)$, $x = (0.6, -0.4)$ and $\theta = 1$, observations $y \in \mathbb{R}^m$ are simulated from (17).

The estimators $\widehat{Y}_{L^i}^i$ are computed using a reflection maximal coupling of pCN kernels, as described in [23]. The left panel of Fig. 2 illustrates that averaging single term estimators (11) as in (12) yields a consistent estimator that converges at the canonical Monte Carlo rate of $1/\text{MSE}$.

Consider now inference for θ in the Bayesian framework, under a prior $p(\theta)$ specified as a standard Gaussian prior on $\log \theta$. A stochastic gradient ascent algorithm is initialized at $\theta^{(0)} = 0.1$ to compute the maximum a posteriori probability (MAP) estimator $\theta_{\text{MAP}} \in \arg\max p(\theta) I_\theta$, simulated by subtracting $\nabla_\theta R(\theta)$ from the estimator of (20) given by Z^i defined above and in (11). The right panel of Fig. 2 displays convergence of the stochastic iterates to θ_{MAP}. An estimator following [31], of the type in (10), is also shown here, using the algorithm in [3] instead of coupled MCMC. The plot shows some gains over [31] when the same learning rates are employed.

Parallel Implementation. An example is now presented to illustrate the parallel improvement of these methods on multiple cores. These results are borrowed from [35] for (online) filtering of partially observed diffusions. In particular, an estimator of the form (10) is constructed, in which each $\hat{Y}_{L^i}^{N_{K^i}}$ is a coupled particle filter increment estimator at resolution L^i and with K^i particles, for $i = 1, \ldots, N$, and these estimators are then averaged as in (12). The parallel performance is assessed with up to $1000(\leq N)$ MPI cores on the KAUST supercomputer Shaheen. A Python notebook that implements the unbiased estimator both on a single core and multiple cores can be found in the following Github link: https://github.com/fangyuan-ksgk/Unbiased-Particle-Filter-HPC-.

To demonstrate the parallel scaling power, various numbers of processors $M \in \{1, 5, 10, 20, 50, 100, 500, 1000\}$ are used, with $N = 10^3 M$. The serial computation time to obtain the estimator on a single core is recorded, as well as the parallel computation time on M cores. The parallel speedup is defined as the ratio of cost for serial implementation and the cost for parallel implementation, and the parallel efficiency is given by the ratio of parallel speedup and the number of parallel cores M.

The results are shown in Fig. 3, which shows almost perfect strong scaling for up to 1000 MPI cores, for this level of accuracy. It is important to note that there will be a limitation to the speedup possible, depending upon the accuracy level. In particular, the total simulation time is limited by the single most expensive sample required. Therefore, it will not be possible to achieve $\text{MSE} \propto \varepsilon^2$ in $\mathcal{O}(1)$ time, even with arbitrarily many cores.

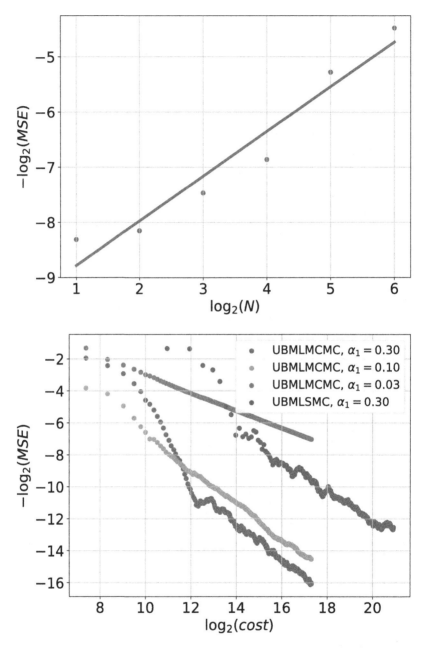

Fig. 2. Elliptic Bayesian inverse problem of Sect. 3.2 Left: accuracy (minus MSE) against number of single term samples N. The samples were simulated in serial on a laptop, but can all be simulated in parallel. Right: convergence of stochastic gradient iterates $\theta^{(n)}$ to the maximum a posteriori probability estimator θ_{MAP}. The learning rates considered here are $\alpha_n = \alpha_1/n$. The red curve corresponds to the unbiased MLSMC algorithm of [31] for comparison. (Color figure online)

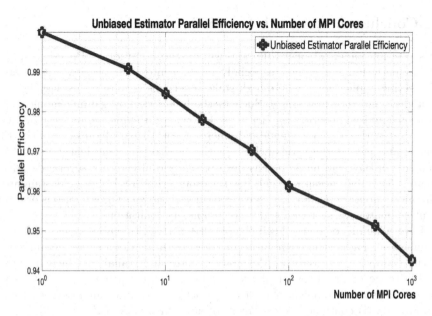

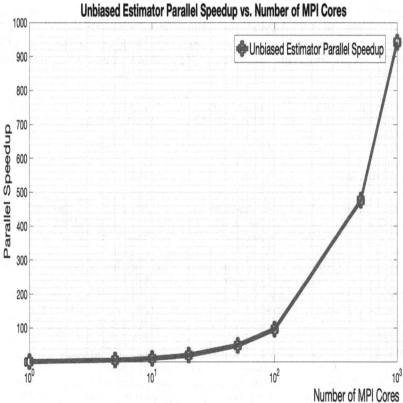

Fig. 3. Parallel Speedup and Parallel Efficiency against number of MPI cores for the unbiased particle filter from [35].

4   Conclusion and Path Forward

This position paper advocates for the widespread adoption of Bayesian methods for performing inference, especially in the context of complex science and engineering applications, where high-stakes decisions require robustness, generalizability, and interpretability. Such methods are rapidly gaining momentum in science and engineering applications, following an explosive interest in UQ, in concert with the data deluge and emerging fourth paradigm of data-centric science and engineering. Meanwhile, in the field of machine learning and AI the value of Bayesian methods has been recognized already for several decades. There it is widely accepted that the Bayesian posterior is the gold standard, but the community has largely converged on variational approximations or even point estimators as surrogates, due to complexity limitations.

Here a family of embarrassingly parallel rMLMC simulation methods are summarized. The methods are designed for performing exact Bayesian inference in the context where only approximate models are available, which includes a wide range of problems in physics, biology, finance, machine learning, and spatial statistics. Canonical complexity is achieved. Important priorities going forward are: (i) continued development of novel instances of this powerful class of algorithms, (ii) adaptation to specific large scale application contexts across science, engineering, and AI, and (iii) automation of the methods and the design of usable software to enable deployment on a large scale and across applications in science, engineering, and AI, ideally by practitioners and without requiring an expert.

Acknowledgements. KJHL and AT were supported by The Alan Turing Institute under the EPSRC grant EP/N510129/1. AJ and FY acknowledge KAUST baseline support.

References

1. Baker, N., et al.: Workshop report on basic research needs for scientific machine learning: core technologies for artificial intelligence. Technical report, USDOE Office of Science (SC), Washington, DC (United States) (2019)
2. Beskos, A., Jasra, A., Law, K.J.H., Marzouk, Y., Zhou, Y.: Multilevel sequential Monte Carlo with dimension-independent likelihood-informed proposals. SIAM/ASA J. Uncertain. Quant. **6**(2), 762–786 (2018)
3. Beskos, A., Jasra, A., Law, K.J.H., Tempone, R., Zhou, Y.: Multilevel sequential Monte Carlo samplers. Stoch. Processes Appl. **127**(5), 1417–1440 (2017)
4. Bishop, C.M.: Pattern Recognition and Machine Learning. Springer, New York (2006)
5. Blei, D.M., Kucukelbir, A., McAuliffe, J.D.: Variational inference: a review for statisticians. J. Am. Stat. Assoc. **112**(518), 859–877 (2017)
6. Brenner, S., Scott, R.: The Mathematical Theory of Finite Element Methods, vol. 15. Springer, New York (2007). https://doi.org/10.1007/978-0-387-75934-0
7. Bundy, A., et al.: Explainable AI: The Basics (2019)

8. Caflisch, R.E., et al.: Monte Carlo and quasi-Monte Carlo methods. Acta Numerica **1998**, 1–49 (1998)
9. Chada, N., Franks, J., Jasra, A., Law, K.J.H., Vihola, M.: Unbiased inference for discretely observed hidden Markov model diffusions. SIAM JUQ (2020, to appear)
10. Ciarlet, P.G.: The finite element method for elliptic problems. SIAM (2002)
11. Crisan, D., Del Moral, P., Houssineau, J., Jasra, A.: Unbiased multi-index Monte Carlo. Stoch. Anal. Appl. **36**(2), 257–273 (2018)
12. Dashti, M., Stuart, A.M.: Uncertainty quantification and weak approximation of an elliptic inverse problem. SIAM J. Numer. Anal. **49**(6), 2524–2542 (2011)
13. Del Moral, P.: Feynman-Kac formulae. Springer, New York (2004). https://doi.org/10.1007/978-1-4684-9393-1
14. Dodwell, T.J., Ketelsen, C., Scheichl, R., Teckentrup, A.L.: A hierarchical multilevel Markov chain Monte Carlo algorithm with applications to uncertainty quantification in subsurface flow. SIAM/ASA J. Uncertain. Quant. **3**(1), 1075–1108 (2015)
15. Gerstner, T., Griebel, M.: Dimension-adaptive tensor-product quadrature. Computing **71**(1), 65–87 (2003)
16. Ghanem, R., Higdon, D., Owhadi, H.: Handbook of Uncertainty Quantification, vol. 6. Springer, Cham (2017). https://doi.org/10.1007/978-3-319-12385-1
17. Giles, M.B.: Multilevel Monte Carlo path simulation. Oper. Res. **56**(3), 607–617 (2008)
18. Giles, M.B.: Multilevel Monte Carlo methods. Acta Numer. **24**, 259–328 (2015)
19. Glynn, P.W., Rhee, C.-H.: Exact estimation for Markov chain equilibrium expectations. J. Appl. Probab. **51**(A), 377–389 (2014)
20. Gregory, A., Cotter, C.J., Reich, S.: Multilevel ensemble transform particle filtering. SIAM J. Sci. Comput. **38**(3), A1317–A1338 (2016)
21. Haji-Ali, A.-L., Nobile, F., Tempone, R.: Multi-index Monte Carlo: when sparsity meets sampling. Numerische Mathematik **132**(4), 767–806 (2015). https://doi.org/10.1007/s00211-015-0734-5
22. Heinrich, S.: Multilevel Monte Carlo methods. In: Margenov, S., Waśniewski, J., Yalamov, P. (eds.) LSSC 2001. LNCS, vol. 2179, pp. 58–67. Springer, Heidelberg (2001). https://doi.org/10.1007/3-540-45346-6_5
23. Heng, J., Jasra, A., Law, K.J.H., Tarakanov, A.: On unbiased estimation for discretized models. arXiv preprint arXiv:2102.12230 (2021)
24. Hoang, V.H., Schwab, C., Stuart, A.M.: Complexity analysis of accelerated MCMC methods for Bayesian inversion. Inverse Probl. **29**(8), 085010 (2013)
25. Hoel, H., Law, K.J.H., Tempone, R.: Multilevel ensemble Kalman filtering. SIAM J. Numer. Anal. **54**(3), 1813–1839 (2016)
26. The Alan Turing Institute. The AI revolution in scientific research (2019)
27. Jacob, P.E., O'Leary, J., Atchadé, Y.F.: Unbiased Markov chain Monte Carlo methods with couplings. J. Roy. Stat. Soc.: Ser. B (Stat. Methodol.) **82**(3), 543–600 (2020)
28. Jasra, A., Kamatani, K., Law, K.J.H., Yan, Y.: Multilevel particle filters. SIAM J. Numer. Anal. **55**(6), 3068–3096 (2017)
29. Jasra, A., Kamatani, K., Law, K.J.H., Zhou, Y.: Bayesian static parameter estimation for partially observed diffusions via multilevel Monte Carlo. SIAM J. Sci. Comput. **40**(2), A887–A902 (2018)
30. Jasra, A., Kamatani, K., Law, K.J.H., Zhou, Y.: A multi-index Markov chain Monte Carlo method. Int. J. Uncertain. Quant. **8**(1) (2018)

31. Jasra, A., Law, K.J.H., Lu, D.: Unbiased estimation of the gradient of the log-likelihood in inverse problems. Stat. Comput. **31**(3), 1–18 (2021). https://doi.org/10.1007/s11222-021-09994-6
32. Jasra, A., Law, K.J.H., Suciu, C.: Advanced multilevel Monte Carlo methods. Int. Stat. Rev. **88**(3), 548–579 (2020)
33. Jasra, A., Law, K.J.H., Xu, Y.: Markov chain simulation for multilevel Monte Carlo. Found. Data Sci. **3**, 27 (2021)
34. Jasra, A., Law, K.J.H., Xu, Y.: Multi-index sequential Monte Carlo methods for partially observed stochastic partial differential equations. Int. J. Uncertain. Quant. **11**(3) (2021)
35. Jasra, A., Law, K.J.H., Yu, F.: Unbiased filtering of a class of partially observed diffusions. arXiv preprint arXiv:2002.03747 (2020)
36. Jasra, A., Law, K.J.H., Zhou, Y.: Forward and inverse uncertainty quantification using multilevel Monte Carlo algorithms for an elliptic nonlocal equation. Int. J. Uncertain. Quant. **6**(6) (2016)
37. Jordan, M.I., Ghahramani, Z., Jaakkola, T.S., Saul, L.K.: An introduction to variational methods for graphical models. Mach. Learn. **37**(2), 183–233 (1999)
38. Kushner, H., Yin, G.G.: Stochastic Approximation and Recursive Algorithms and Applications, vol. 35. Springer, New York (2003). https://doi.org/10.1007/b97441
39. Lawrence, N., Jordan, M.: Semi-supervised learning via Gaussian processes. Adv. Neural Inf. Process. Syst. **17**, 753–760 (2004)
40. Metropolis, N., Ulam, S.: The Monte Carlo method. J. Am. Stat. Assoc. **44**(247), 335–341 (1949)
41. Del Moral, P., Jasra, A., Law, K.J.H., Zhou, Y.: Multilevel sequential Monte Carlo samplers for normalizing constants. ACM Trans. Model. Comput. Simul. (TOMACS) **27**(3), 1–22 (2017)
42. Murphy, K.P.: Machine Learning: A Probabilistic Perspective. MIT Press, Cambridge (2012)
43. Neal, R.: Regression and classification using Gaussian process priors. Bayesian Stat. **6**, 475 (1998)
44. Neal, R.M.: Bayesian Learning for Neural Networks, vol. 118. Springer (2012)
45. Pearl, J., et al.: Causal inference in statistics: an overview. Stat. Surv. **3**, 96–146 (2009)
46. Peherstorfer, B., Willcox, K., Gunzburger, M.: Survey of multifidelity methods in uncertainty propagation, inference, and optimization. SIAM Rev. **60**(3), 550–591 (2018)
47. Rasmussen, C.E., Williams, C.K.I.: Gaussian Processes for Machine Learning (2006)
48. Rhee, C.-H., Glynn, P.W.: Unbiased estimation with square root convergence for SDE models. Oper. Res. **63**(5), 1026–1043 (2015)
49. Robert, C., Casella, G.: A short history of Markov chain Monte Carlo: subjective recollections from incomplete data. Stat. Sci. **26**, 102–115 (2011)
50. Rue, H., Martino, S., Chopin, N.: Approximate Bayesian inference for latent Gaussian models by using integrated nested Laplace approximations. J. Roy. Stat. Soc.: Ser. B (Stat. Methodol.) **71**(2), 319–392 (2009)
51. Stevens, R., Taylor, V., Nichols, J., Maccabe, A.B., Yelick, K., Brown, D.: AI for science. Technical report, Argonne National Lab. (ANL), Argonne, IL (United States) (2020)
52. Stuart, A.M.: Inverse problems: a Bayesian perspective. Acta Numerica **19**, 451–559 (2010)

53. Tarantola, A.: Inverse problem theory and methods for model parameter estimation. SIAM (2005)
54. Vihola, M.: Unbiased estimators and multilevel Monte Carlo. Oper. Res. **66**(2), 448–462 (2018)
55. Weinan, E., Han, J., Zhang, L.: Integrating machine learning with physics-based modeling. Arxiv preprint. https://arxiv.org/pdf/2006.02619.pdf (2020)
56. Zhu, X., Ghahramani, Z., Lafferty, J.D.: Semi-supervised learning using Gaussian fields and harmonic functions. In: Proceedings of the 20th International Conference on Machine Learning (ICML-03), pp. 912–919 (2003)

Maintaining Trust in Reduction: Preserving the Accuracy of Quantities of Interest for Lossy Compression

Qian Gong[1]([⊠]), Xin Liang[2], Ben Whitney[1], Jong Youl Choi[1], Jieyang Chen[1], Lipeng Wan[1], Stéphane Ethier[3], Seung-Hoe Ku[3], R. Michael Churchill[3], C. -S. Chang[3], Mark Ainsworth[4], Ozan Tugluk[4], Todd Munson[5], David Pugmire[1], Richard Archibald[1], and Scott Klasky[1]

[1] Oak Ridge National Laboratory, Oak Ridge, TN 37830, USA
gongq@ornl.gov
[2] Missouri University of Science and Technology, Rolla, MO 65409, USA
[3] Princeton Plasma Physics Laboratory, Princeton, NJ 08540, USA
[4] Brown University, Providence, RI 02912, USA
[5] Argonne National Laboratory, Lemont, IL 60439, USA

Abstract. As the growth of data sizes continues to outpace computational resources, there is a pressing need for data reduction techniques that can significantly reduce the amount of data and quantify the error incurred in compression. Compressing scientific data presents many challenges for reduction techniques since it is often on non-uniform or unstructured meshes, is from a high-dimensional space, and has many Quantities of Interests (QoIs) that need to be preserved. To illustrate these challenges, we focus on data from a large scale fusion code, XGC. XGC uses a Particle-In-Cell (PIC) technique which generates hundreds of PetaBytes (PBs) of data a day, from thousands of timesteps. XGC uses an unstructured mesh, and needs to compute many QoIs from the raw data, f.

One critical aspect of the reduction is that we need to ensure that QoIs derived from the data (density, temperature, flux surface averaged momentums, etc.) maintain a relative high accuracy. We show that by compressing XGC data on the high-dimensional, nonuniform grid on which the data is defined, and adaptively quantizing the decomposed coefficients based on the characteristics of the QoIs, the compression ratios at various error tolerances obtained using a multilevel compressor (MGARD) increases more than ten times. We then present how to mathematically guarantee that the accuracy of the QoIs computed from the reduced f is preserved during the compression. We show that the error in the XGC density can be kept under a user-specified tolerance over 1000 timesteps of simulation using the mathematical QoI error control theory of MGARD, whereas traditional error control on the data to be reduced does not guarantee the accuracy of the QoIs.

Keywords: Lossy compression · Error control · Quantities of interest · XGC simulation data

© Springer Nature Switzerland AG 2022
J. Nichols et al. (Eds.): SMC 2021, CCIS 1512, pp. 22–39, 2022.
https://doi.org/10.1007/978-3-030-96498-6_2

1   Challenges in Lossy Compression for Physics Simulations

Storage and I/O capacities have not increased as rapidly as computational power over the last decade. Storage constraints influence how many files can be output, their frequency, and how long the output files can be kept in short-term storage like parallel file systems. With the exascale computing era approaching, there has been an urgent call for general and reliable reduction techniques that achieve large compression ratios for scientific applications. The compression of scientific data is challenging in several aspects. First, most scientific data are stored in 32- or 64-bit floating-point format. As the low-order bits of floating-point numbers are essentially random, lossless compression algorithms can only achieve limited compression ratios on most scientific data [10]. Second, compression algorithms targeting scientific data must provide guaranteed and quantifiable error bounds so that scientists can use the reduced data in their investigations and trust the results. Recently, several lossy compression algorithms for scientific data have been proposed based on prediction (SZ [11]), block transformation (ZFP [12]), multilevel decomposition (MGARD [13–15]), and machine learning (VAPOR [16]). This paper concerns the problem of compression under constraints on the errors incurred in quantities of interest (QoI), so we limit our study to error-bounded lossy compressors (i.e., MGARD, SZ, and ZFP).

Ideally, lossy compressors should be flexible with regard to the structure of the data, generalize to arbitrarily high dimensions, and allow control of errors both in the original degrees of freedom and in downstream QoIs. Scientific data usually resides on high-dimensional, underlying uniform, nonuniform, or unstructured grids [1,4,9,22]. Compressing data in the same high-dimensional space where it is defined can make more of the data's spatial correlations visible to the compression algorithm, resulting in higher compression ratios. Similarly, compression algorithms should make use of as much of the data's spatial structure as possible. Compression nonuniform or unstructured data as though it were defined on a uniform grid risks obscuring redundancies and patterns in the data, resulting in lower compression ratios. A third design goal is the control of errors incurred by compression algorithms. A natural starting point is to bound the error in the 'raw' data—i.e., the difference between the original dataset and the reduced dataset output by the compression algorithm. Often, though, scientists are less concerned with the pointwise error in the raw data than with the change to the QoIs computed from the data. The mathematics required to relate errors in the raw data to errors in QoIs is nontrivial, especially for QoIs that are nonlinear and/or obtained by complex post-processing. Empirical approaches can provide estimates for, but not guaranteed bounds on, QoI errors by extrapolating from previously encountered datasets and QoIs.

In this paper we focus our attention on XGC [1,2], a leadership-class application in the fusion community which simulates high-dimensional data (five phase space dimensions + time) on an unstructured mesh and whose output is used to compute many simple and complicated, linear and nonlinear QoIs. XGC is a full-f gyrokinetic particle-in-cell (PIC) code which specializes in simulating kinetic transport in edge tokamak plasmas, where strong particle and energy sources and sinks drive the plasma away from thermal equilibrium. The code represents particles as samples with specific positions, velocities and weights [21] and solves the gyrokinetic equations for a 5-dimensional particle distribution function f. XGC can run in parallel on supercomputers such as the Oak Ridge Leadership Computing Facility's (OLCF) Summit [20], fully utilizing all of the CPUs and GPUs. Although the parallel code enables fusion scientists to model more complicated tokamak experiments at finer resolution and for longer timescales, the data generated is too large for permanent storage on the parallel file system at OLCF. To give an idea of the scale, a simulation modelling ITER-scale [6] problems will typically contain trillions of particles and run for thousands of timesteps and can each day produce over 200 petabytes of data [5], which would, if stored in its entirety, fill 80% of the storage capacity of Summit's parallel file system.

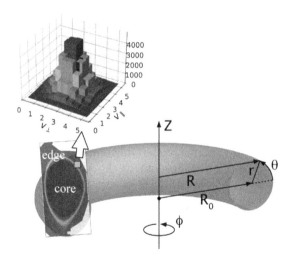

Fig. 1. Coordinates of the XGC 5D distribution function $f(\phi, \theta, r, v_{\parallel}, v_{\perp})$ in a tokamak device. To reduce the particle data, the output routine in XGC discretizes the 3D space $\{\phi, \theta, r\}$ into cross-sections uniformly spaced across the toroidal direction ϕ and groups the particles on each cross-section into histograms in 2D velocity space $v = \{v_{\parallel}, v_{\perp}\}$.

Direct compression of the XGC simulation data at such enormous scale is unrealistic due to the extreme compression ratio required. Instead, compression is preceded by a discretization and binning step in the XGC output routine. As shown in Fig. 1, XGC discretizes the 3D space $x = \{r, z, \phi\}$ into radial-poloidal cross-sections (RZ planes) [7]. An unstructured mesh is used to model the common geometry of the RZ planes, and XGC groups the particles on each plane into volumes around the nodes of the mesh. The particles at each mesh node are further sorted into bins in the 2D Cartesian velocity space $v = \{v_{\parallel}, v_{\perp}\}$ [8].

The code then outputs a particle distribution histogram defined on this five-dimensional, nonuniform, unstructured grid, reducing the output size from hundreds of petabytes to hundreds of terabytes per run. This histogram data must be further reduced by compression techniques before being written to storage.

To shed light on the relationship between compression errors and downstream QoIs, we investigate in this paper the impacts of errors in the histogram data on five physical quantities specified by XGC scientists. The QoIs we consider are density (n), parallel temperature $(T_{\parallel})$, perpendicular temperature $(T_{\perp})$, flux surface averaged density $(n0\_avg)$, and flux surface averaged temperature $(T0\_avg)$. The density, n, is computed by integrating f over the mesh nodes,

$$n(x,t) = \int \frac{f(x,v,t)}{\text{vox}(x)} \, dv_{\parallel} \, dv_{\perp}, \tag{1}$$

where t represents the timestep and $\text{vox}(x)$ is the volume of the mesh node at x. $T_{\parallel}$ and $T_{\perp}$ are integrals of parallel and perpendicular kinetic energy, mv^2,

$$T_{\perp}(x,t) = \frac{1}{2} \int \frac{mv_{\perp}^2 f(x,v,t)}{n(x,t)} \, dv_{\parallel} \, dv_{\perp},$$

$$T_{\parallel}(x,t) = \frac{1}{2} \int \frac{m(v_{\parallel} - u_{\parallel})^2 f(x,v,t)}{n(x,t)} \, dv_{\parallel} \, dv_{\perp},$$

where m is the mass of atomic particles corresponding to f and $u_{\parallel}$ is the parallel flow, computed using $u_{\parallel}(x,t) = \int v_{\parallel} f(x,v,t)/n(x,t) \, dv_{\perp} \, dv_{\parallel}$. Finally, the flux surface averaged density and temperature are computed by averaging the density and temperature over a thin volume between toroidal magnetic flux surface contours. For brevity, we omit the equations for the flux surface averaged quantities [3]. These five physical quantities represent different types of QoIs. Among these, density is a linear function of f, $T_{\perp}$ and $T_{\parallel}$ are nonlinear quantities, and $n0\_avg$ and $T0\_avg$ represent QoIs that are smoothed over the space. Throughout the paper, we measure the error using the Normalized Root Mean Square Error (NRMSE), defined as follows:

$$\text{NRMSE}(u, \tilde{u}) = \frac{\sqrt{\sum_{i=0}^{N}(u_i - \tilde{u}_i)^2/N}}{\max(u) - \min(u)},$$

where u is the original data, $\tilde{u}$ is the reconstructed data, and N is the number of degrees of freedom in u. To ensure the integrity of scientific discovery, the downstream analysis of XGC requires that f and the above five physical quantities have errors no larger than 10^{-3}.

In this paper, we demonstrate the use of compression accounting for high dimension, various grid structures, and error control for different types of QoIs. Our application driver is data generated by XGC. We show that higher compression quality can be achieved when compressing in high dimension, allowing high-dimensional correlations to be utilized. We next show that the compression quality can be further improved when the decorrelation and quantization steps of the compression algorithm are adapted to the nonuniform grid structure and to characteristics of QoIs to be preserved. Lastly, we show the importance of mathematically guaranteed error control for derived QoIs and how to achieve this control using MGARD.

The rest of the paper is organized as follows. In Sect. 2, we introduce the three error-controlled compressors that are evaluated in this work. In Sect. 3, we demonstrate the impact of utilizing high-dimensional decorrelation. In Sect. 4, we show how the grid can be leveraged to improve compression ratios using MGARD. In Sect. 5, we demonstrate how to adaptively compress the data for desired QoIs and how to guarantee the accuracy of the QoIs computed from the reduced data. In Sect. 6, we discuss future work. We conclude the paper in Sect. 7.

2 Background of Error-Controlled Lossy Compression

Compression techniques have been extensively studied as a direct way to reduce data size. Traditional lossless compressors [23–25] can recover full precision data but usually suffer from low compression ratios on floating-point scientific data [10]. Although lossy compressors widely used in the image processing community [32,33] are able to trade off precision for higher compression ratios, they are not preferred in the scientific computing community as the errors are difficult to quantify. Hence, error-controlled lossy compression [11–15] was proposed as an alternative to significantly reduce the size of scientific data with guaranteed error control on the reconstructed data.

There are two popular categories of error-controlled lossy compressors, namely prediction- and transform-based models. The models differ in the method used to decorrelate the original data. Prediction-based models decorrelate the data using prediction or approximation techniques such as curve fitting, while transform-based models use domain transforms such as discrete cosine and wavelet transforms. After the decorrelation stage, data is quantized and then encoded for the actual byte reduction. In this paper, we focus on three error-controlled lossy compressors – SZ, ZFP, and MGARD – as they are recognized as the state of the art according to recent studies [26–28].

SZ leverages a general prediction-based lossy compression pipeline. Specifically, it first performs data decorrelation based on a multi-algorithm predictor, followed by error-controlled linear-scaling quantization and lossless encoding. ZFP is a transform-based lossy compression method. It splits d-dimensional data into blocks of size 4^d and compresses each independently. Data in a block is aligned to the same exponent, converted to a fixed-point format, and then decorrelated using a customized invertible transform. The transform coefficients are ordered by energy and encoded using embedded encoding. MGARD provides another elegant method for reducing scientific data. Due to the space limit, here we only sketch the key steps of the algorithm. MGARD decomposes the original data into a sequence of multilevel components using L^2 projection and multilinear interpolation. The multilevel coefficients encoding the multilevel components are then quantized adaptively based on the target error metric. A more detailed introduction is available in [28] and the full mathematical treatment can be found in [14].

The unique features of MGARD include compression over nonuniform coordinate space, compression optimized for QoI preservation, and compression with mathematically guaranteed error control on certain linear QoIs. SZ and ZFP make predictions and transformations based on the assumption that the data are defined on a uniformly spaced d-dimensional Cartesian grid. MGARD does not rely on this assumption in its decorrelation step. Rather, it carries out the requisite projections and interpolations using the actual distances between mesh nodes and quantizes the multilevel coefficients using their actual volumes in the multilevel subgrid space. Moreover, MGARD can adaptively improve the compression quality of certain QoIs by tuning a smoothness parameter s. This parameter controls the bin widths used to quantize the multilevel coefficients, allowing more aggressive quantization of coefficients that will have little impact on the accuracy of the QoI. The smoothness parameter s can be further combined with the operator norm of the QoI to provide guaranteed error control [14] as follows:

$$|\mathcal{Q}(u) - \mathcal{Q}(\tilde{u})| \leq \Upsilon_s(\mathcal{Q})\Big(\sum_{l=0}^{L} 2^{2sl} \sum_{x \in \mathcal{N}_l^*} \text{vol}(x)\,|\texttt{u\_mc}\,[x] - \tilde{\texttt{u}}\_\texttt{mc}\,[x]|^2\Big)^{1/2} \quad (2)$$

where $\mathcal{Q}$ is the target bounded linear operator, $\Upsilon_s(\mathcal{Q})$ is its operator norm, $\text{vol}(x)$ is the volume of the level l element centered at x, $\mathcal{N}_l^*$ is the collection of nodes in level l but not level $l-1$, and $\texttt{u\_mc}\,[x]$ and $\tilde{\texttt{u}}\_\texttt{mc}\,[x]$ are the original and quantized multilevel coefficients at node x, respectively.

We conclude this section with a concrete description of the dataset used in our experiments. The particle distribution function f output by XGC comprises a velocity histogram at each node of each unstructured RZ plane mesh. SZ, ZFP, and MGARD all require data to be given on Cartesian grids or very particular triangulation/tetrahedration mesh structure [15], so none of the three can compress the XGC output in its original format. To enable the application of the compressors, we unroll the meshes in 2D unstructured RZ planes by radius, as the magnetic field in a tokamak tends to expand the plasmas outward along the major diameter. The spacing of the 1D grid is determined by the edge lengths of each unstructured mesh. This conversion changes the distribution function f from 5D to 4D: $\{\phi, \text{mesh nodes}, v_\perp, v_\parallel\}$. We conduct our experiments using a coarse resolution XGC dataset with 1000 simulation timesteps, each containing $\{8, 16395, 39, 39\}$ double-precision floating-point values. With the exception of the resolution, the dataset was generated using the same parameters and settings as high-resolution production runs. Throughout the paper, we always perform compression on f rather than on any QoI computed from f. We reduce f with a prescribed NRMSE tolerance, record the compression ratio, and compute the achieved NRMSE in either f or a QoI. The reported NRMSE is this observed error rather than the initial prescribed tolerance. If a figure calls for the compression ratio at an achieved NRMSE that is not exactly observed in our experiments, we compute an estimate by linearly interpolating the compression ratios at the neighboring measurements.

3   Error-Controlled Lossy Compression in High-Dimensional Space

This section demonstrates how the compression of f can be improved by utilizing data correlations in high-dimensional space. In our first experiment, we apply SZ, ZFP, and MGARD to the 700th timestep of f, an array with dimensions $\{8, 16395, 39, 39\}$. ZFP currently supports 1D, 2D, 3D, and 4D input, and MGARD supports input of arbitrary dimension, so these compressors can be applied to the dataset without modification. SZ currently supports 1D, 2D, and 3D input, so we interpret the dataset as an array with dimensions $\{8 \times 16395, 39, 39\}$ when applying SZ. Whether compressing in 3D or 4D, we must also decide how to handle the spacing between the data values. SZ and ZFP always interpret their input as an array defined on a uniform Cartesian grid. Because this experiment is focused on the impact of dimensionality, not spacing, we also use uniform node spacing in MGARD. Figure 2a shows the compression ratios achieved by each compressor. When the NMRSE level is low, e.g. 10^{-6}, the compression ratios of the three methods are similar, as the tight error bound does not provide enough flexibility for the algorithms to reduce the data. When the NMRSE is at the range of $[10^{-5}, 10^{-4}]$, ZFP 4D achieves better compression ratios than SZ 3D and worsen compression ratios than MGARD 4D. When the measured NRMSE keeps increasing, SZ 3D obtains better compression ratios than ZFP 4D but still worsen compression ratios than MGARD 4D. In our second experiment, we investigate the effect of dimension on the compression ratio achieved by MGARD. The results are shown in Fig. 2b. When compressing in 4D plus time, we use timesteps 700 to 770. Across all tested NRMSE levels, the compression ratio increases with the dimension used for compression.

4   Error-Controlled Lossy Compression on Nonuniform Grids

In this section, we demonstrate that compressing using nonuniform grid can improve the accuracy of QoIs computed from the reduced data. We begin with a description of the nonuniform grid used. XGC uses an unstructured mesh, shown in Fig. 3a, to model the complex RZ plane geometry and a nonuniform Cartesian grid, shown in Fig. 3b, to discretize the velocity space. As described in Sect. 2, we unroll the unstructured mesh into a nonuniform 1D grid to allow compression of the data by existing methods. The result is a Cartesian grid with coordinates $\{\phi, \text{mesh nodes}, v_\perp, v_\parallel\}$ which is nonuniform in all coordinates except ϕ. SZ and ZFP do not support nonuniform grids, so we only use MGARD for

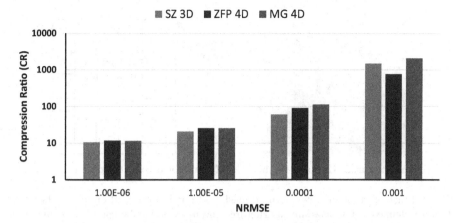

a Compression ratios at which f meets various NRMSE levels when f is compressed on a uniform Cartesian grid with SZ 3D, ZFP 4D, and MGARD 4D. The color of each bar indicates the compressor used. The horizontal position indicates the achieved NRMSE in f. The height indicates the achieved compression ratio.

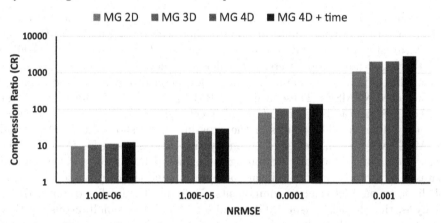

b Compression ratios achieved when f is compressed on a uniform Cartesian grid with MGARD 2D, MGARD 3D, MGARD 4D, and MGARD 4D plus time.

Fig. 2. Illustration of the improvement in compression ratios achieved by compressing f in high-dimensional space. a shows the compression ratios achieved when compressing the 700th timestep of f with SZ, ZFP, and MGARD using the highest dimension supported by each compressor. b shows the compression ratios achieved using MGARD in 2D, 3D, 4D, and 4D plus time.

the experiments in this section. Within MGARD, the nonuniform grid spacing impacts the decorrelation, where the central operations of L^2 projection and multilinear interpolation depend on the grid, and the quantization, where errors are prorated according to the spacing at each node.

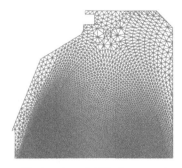

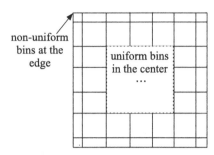

a Unstructured RZ plane mesh.   b Nonuniform velocity space grid.

Fig. 3. Illustration of the unstructured mesh and nonuniform grid on which the XGC data are defined. XGC uses an unstructured mesh to model the complex geometry of radial-poloidal planes and Cartesian bins to model the discretized velocity space. The nodes of the 2D unstructured RZ plane mesh are linearized to a 1D nonuniform grid and combined with the velocity space for compression.

In our first experiment, we establish a baseline by measuring the QoI errors when compressing using uniform grid spacing. We apply MGARD 4D to the 700th timestep of the XGC data with a variety of error tolerances, yielding a collection of reduced datasets with different achieved compression ratios. For each reduced dataset, we compute the five QoIs described in Sect. 1 and calculate the achieved NRMSEs. These achieved NRMSEs are generally different, so that the compression ratios at which the QoIs meet a given NRMSE level are likewise generally different. The results of the experiment are shown in Fig. 4a. At all NRMSE levels tested, the achieved compression ratio is lowest for $T_{\parallel}$. This is the consequence of $T_{\parallel}$ generally exhibiting the highest NRMSE for a given reduced dataset, as a result of its non-linear computation and the complicated structure of the large parallel velocity components. To ensure the fidelity of downstream analysis, the physicists using XGC require that all QoIs simultaneously satisfy appropriate error bounds. If the prescribed NRMSE tolerance is the same for all QoIs, the results of this experiment suggest that the achievable compression ratio will be determined by the error in $T_{\parallel}$.

Our second experiment is identical to the first except that we compress using nonuniform grid spacing. Providing the spacing information to MGARD allows the quantizer to adjust the error bound used for a node according to the volume of the corresponding element. Larger elements result in tighter error bounds; see Eq. (2). Accordingly, the coefficients that represent variations over small regions will be compressed more heavily than the coefficients that represent variations over large regions. We expect that this adaptive, nonuniform error quantization will benefit the errors observed in the QoIs. The results of the experiment are shown in Fig. 4b. Using nonuniform grid spacing in the compression lifts the compression ratios at which all five QoIs meet the NRMSE levels, and the benefit increases as the NRMSE grows larger.

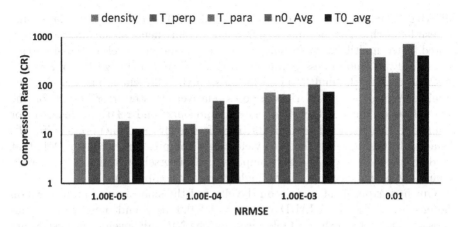

a Compression ratios at which the QoIs meet various NRMSE levels when f is compressed on a uniform Cartesian grid with MGARD 4D. The color of each bar indicates the QoI. The horizontal position indicates the achieved NRMSE in the QoI. The height indicates the achieved compression ratio.

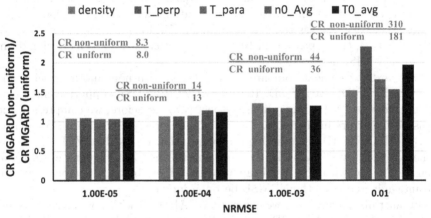

b Ratios of compression ratios at which NRMSE levels are met when using nonuniform spacing to those at which the levels are met when using uniform spacing. The compression ratios given above each group of bars are those at which all of the QoIs meet the NMRSE level.

Fig. 4. Comparison between using uniform and nonuniform spacing when compressing the 700th timestep of f with MGARD 4D. a shows the results obtained using uniform spacing; b compares those results with those obtained using nonuniform spacing.

5   Error-Controlled Lossy Compression for QoIs

In this section we show how adapting MGARD's compression algorithm (specifically, the quantization stage) to a QoI can reduce the error incurred in that QoI at a given compression ratio. This adaptive quantization is a unique feature of

MGARD. The multilinear decomposition of MGARD decorrelates the data using a mesh hierarchy. The low and high frequency components of the data are represented by the multilevel coefficients on the coarse and fine levels of the hierarchy, respectively. A smoothness parameter s can be used to change the bin widths used to quantize the multilevel coefficients on the different levels. $s = 0$ is the baseline. When $s < 0$, MGARD imposes relatively tighter error bounds on the coarse level coefficients (low frequency components) and relatively looser error bounds on the fine level coefficients (high frequency components); see Eq. (2). As a result, taking $s < 0$ tends to yield larger compression ratios for QoIs that are determined by low frequency components. Conversely, taking $s > 0$ generally benefits QoIs that are sensitive to high frequency components.

Our first experiment focuses on the effect of the smoothness parameter s on the errors. We apply MGARD with $s = -1, 0, 1$ to f and measure the compression ratios at which the QoIs meet various NRMSE levels. The results are shown in Fig. 5. For all five QoIs, taking $s = -1$ leads to the best results, with the average quantities $n0\_avg$ and $T0\_avg$ benefiting most from that choice of smoothness parameter. This outcome may be explained by the relative insensitivity of the QoIs considered to the high frequency components of the data; as seen in Sect. 1, all can be written as convolutions with functions that are not highly oscillatory. As was the case with nonuniform compression in the experiment in Sect. 4, the improvement from adaptive quantization is more significant at higher NRMSE levels.

Our next experiment compares MGARD 4D with nonuniform spacing and $s = -1$, ZFP 4D, and SZ 3D. Recall that ZFP and SZ support compression in up to four and three dimensions, respectively. As before, we compress f and measure the errors in the QoIs. The results are presented in Fig. 6. As seen in Fig. 6a, MGARD 4D achieves higher compression ratios than ZFP 4D at the same NRMSE level. MGARD 4D also outperforms SZ 3D in this example, as seen in Fig. 6b, with the discrepancy being larger. In both comparisons, the advantage increases as the NRMSE becomes larger.

In our third experiment, we compare MGARD 4D with nonuniform spacing and $s = -1$ to MGARD 2D with uniform spacing and $s = 0$, the baseline configuration. The results are shown in Fig. 7. For each configuration and each of four NRMSE levels, we measure the maximum compression ratio at which all five QoIs meet the prescribed error level. These maximum compression ratios for MGARD 4D with nonuniform spacing and $s = -1$ are improved $1.24\times$, $1.47\times$, $4.62\times$, and $21.6\times$ over the baseline at NRMSE levels 10^{-5}, 10^{-4}, 10^{-3}, and 10^{-2}, respectively. The degree of improvement increases with the NRMSE level and is more significant for the average quantities $n0\_avg$ and $T0\_avg$.

Most state-of-the-art compression algorithms, with the exception of MGARD in certain linear cases, only support error bounds set on the 'raw' data. If users want the errors in QoIs to stay below a certain threshold, they have to estimate the corresponding error bound on the raw data through empirical studies. Empirical relations, though, may not continue to hold as the data distribution changes. Our fourth experiment concerns the relationship between the error bound on the

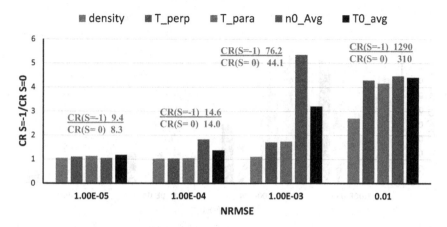

a Ratios of compression ratios at which NRMSE levels are met when using $s = -1$ to those at which the levels are met when using $s = 0$.

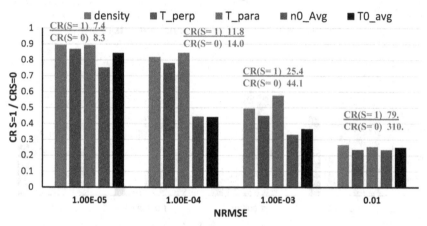

b Ratios of compression ratios at which NRMSE levels are met when using $s = 1$ to those at which the levels are met when using $s = 0$.

Fig. 5. Illustration of the effect of the smoothness parameter s when compressing the 700th timestep of f with MGARD 4D with nonuniform spacing. For $s = -1, 0, 1$, we compress f and measure the compression ratios at which the QoI meet various NRMSE levels. a shows the ratios of the compression ratios obtained when using $s = -1$ to those obtained when using $s = 0$; b shows the ratios of the compression ratios obtained when using $s = 1$ to those obtained when using $s = 0$.

raw data and the measured error in QoIs. We apply MGARD to each of the 1000 timesteps of f with an NRMSE tolerance of 10^{-4}. We then compute the NRMSE of f and two QoIs, density n and parallel temperature $T_{\|}$. The results are shown in Fig. 8. The error in f stays below the prescribed error bound, but the errors in density and temperature rise above 10^{-4} and 10^{-3} over time. It is not entirely

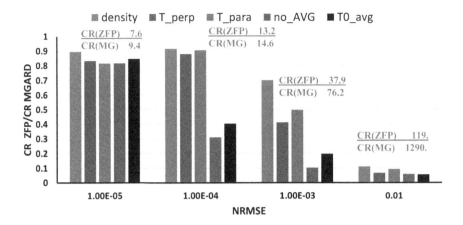

a Ratios of compression ratios at which NRMSE levels are met when using ZFP 4D to those at which the levels are met when using MGARD 4D with nonuniform spacing and $s = -1$.

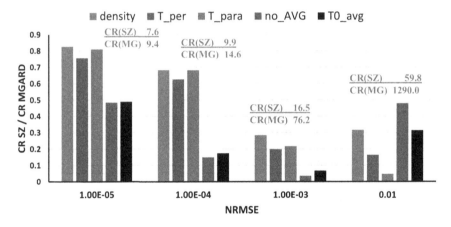

b Ratios of compression ratios at which NRMSE levels are met when using SZ 3D to those at which the levels are met when using MGARD 4D with nonuniform spacing and $s = -1$.

Fig. 6. Comparison between MGARD, SZ, and ZFP on the 700th timestep of f. Each compressor is used with its best settings: for MGARD, 4D, nonuniform spacing, and $s = -1$; for ZFP, 4D and uniform spacing; and for SZ, 3D and uniform spacing. a compares ZFP to MGARD; b compares SZ to MGARD.

unexpected to observe these increased errors in the QoIs, since the distribution functions become more complicated as the turbulence builds up, but it does make empirical error control challenging. The data generated by many scientific experiments and simulations, including XGC, would be costly or even impossible to reproduce if the errors in QoIs were later found to be unacceptable, so

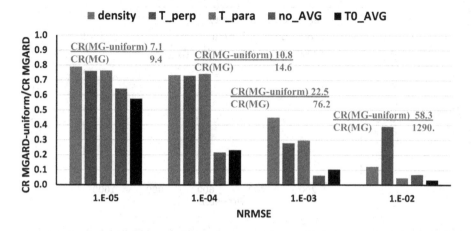

Fig. 7. Illustration of the improvement in compression ratios due to compressing f in high-dimensional, nonuniform space and catering the error quantization to the characteristics of the QoIs. `CR(MG-uniform)` is obtained with MGARD 2D using uniform spacing and $s = 0$. `CR(MG)` is obtained with MGARD 4D using nonuniform spacing and $s = -1$.

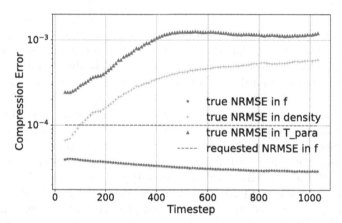

Fig. 8. Illustration of the error in f, density n, and parallel temperature $T_{\parallel}$ when compressing 1000 timesteps of f using MGARD with an NRMSE tolerance of 10^{-4}. The NRMSE of f stays relatively flat over the simulation, but the NRMSE of density and temperature increase as the turbulence builds up. The compression ratio of f ranges from $25\times$ to $50\times$ and rises over time.

compressors should mathematically guarantee that the errors in QoIs will respect user-specified tolerances.

MGARD allows error bounds set on scalar, linear QoIs $\mathcal{Q}$. To enable this, the operator norm $\Upsilon_s(\mathcal{Q})$ is first computed using a procedure developed in [14]. $\Upsilon_s(\mathcal{Q})$ represents the maximum growth from the compression error $\|f - \tilde{f}\|_s$ to

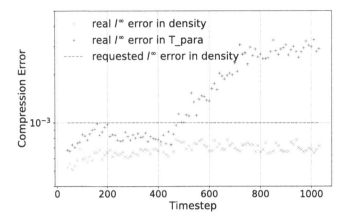

Fig. 9. Illustration of the error in density n and parallel temperature $T_\parallel$ when compressing 1000 timesteps of f using MGARD with an error bound set on density. The L^∞ error in density remains under the requested threshold and is relatively flat. The L^∞ error in $T_\parallel$, which is a nonlinear QoI that MGARD cannot control, rises above the requested error tolerance. The compression ratio ranges from 16.5× to 19.5× and decreases over time.

the QoI error $|\mathcal{Q}(f) - \mathcal{Q}(\tilde{f})|$. By reducing f using an error bound of $\epsilon/\Upsilon_s(\mathcal{Q})$, MGARD can then ensure that the error in $\Upsilon_s(\mathcal{Q})$ is no more than ϵ. Our final experiment is identical to the timestep experiment described above except that we set the error bound on density rather than on f. We compute the operator norm $\Upsilon_s(\mathcal{Q})$ for density, set $\epsilon = 10^{-3}$, then use $\epsilon/\Upsilon_s(\mathcal{Q})$ to compress f in the 2D velocity space and compute density and parallel temperature from the reduced data. To measure the error, here we use the relative L^∞ norm, another commonly used error metric, which is given by $\|f - \tilde{f}\|_{L^\infty}/[\max(f) - \min(f)]$ (and likewise for the QoIs). Note that by keeping the relative L^∞ error smaller than ϵ we guarantee that the NRMSE of the density field will be smaller than ϵ as well. The results are shown in Fig. 9. The density is successfully preserved to within the error tolerance at every timestep. We also plot the error in a nonlinear QoI, $T_\parallel$, which MGARD cannot control. As expected, bounding the error in density does not guarantee that the error in $T_\parallel$ will stay below the requested error tolerance.

6   Future Work

State-of-the-art compressors that support compression on arbitrary unstructured meshes do not exist. To enable the compression of XGC data, we convert the unstructured 2D RZ plane to nonuniform 1D grid, potentially lowering the compression efficacy. In the previous work [15], we develop compression algorithms for data defined on meshes formed by particular types of triangulations/tetrahedrations. We plan to expand that work to support data defined on arbitrary unstructured meshes.

Furthermore, the different error trend of f and QoIs, as shown in Fig. 8, suggests that empirically error control for QoIs is unreliable. In our previous work on MGARD, we develop algorithms that guarantee the preservation of certain linear QoIs, but the error control for complicated nonlinear QoIs (e.g., $T_\parallel$ in Fig. 9) remains to be understood and developed. Our future work will include formulating new theories to provide guaranteed error bounds for multiple and nonlinear QoIs.

This work does not discuss the throughput performance of lossy compressors as the trade-offs between throughput and reduction ratios is not the focus of the paper. Our evaluations in this paper were conducted using sequential implementations, but compression techniques can be accelerated on different hardware [29–31]. Due to the page limit, we leave the evaluation on accelerated lossy compression to the future work.

7 Conclusion

Lossy compression can be used to reduce the cost of scientific data transmission and storage. To ensure that the lossy compression does not weaken the integrity of downstream analysis, the compression must be able to control the uncertainties in both 'raw' data and derived QoIs. In this paper we focus on the data generated by XGC, which is high in dimension, nonuniform in spacing, and can be used to compute many simple and complex, linear and nonlinear QoIs. Choosing the particle distribution function f and its five derived QoIs as the example, we show that the better compression quality can be achieved when high-dimensional data correlation is utilized, and the decorrelation and quantization steps of the compression algorithm are adapted to the nonuniform grid structure and to the characteristics of QoIs. We discuss the importance of having mathematically guaranteed error control for linear and nonlinear QoIs. We demonstrate that we can conserve the accuracy of linear QoI (i.e., density) over 1000 timesteps of XGC simulation using the QoI error control theory of MGARD, whereas the empirical studies with error control on 'raw' data cannot guarantee the error in QoIs.

Acknowledgement. This research was supported by the ECP CODAR, Sirius-2, and RAPIDS-2 projects through the Advanced Scientific Computing Research (ASCR) program of Department of Energy, and the LDRD project through DRD program of Oak Ridge National Laboratory.

References

1. Chang, C.-S., et al.: Spontaneous rotation sources in a quiescent tokamak edge plasma. Phys. Plasmas **15**(6), 062510 (2008)
2. Chang, C.-S., et al.: Compressed ion temperature gradient turbulence in diverted tokamak edge. Phys. Plasmas **16**(5), 056108 (2009)

3. Hager, R., et al.: Gyrokinetic study of collisional resonant magnetic perturbation (RMP)-driven plasma density and heat transport in tokamak edge plasma using a magnetohydrodynamic screened RMP field. Nucl. Fusion **59**(12), 126009 (2019)

4. Jesse, S., et al.: Using multivariate analysis of scanning-Rochigram data to reveal material functionality. Microsc. Microanal. **22**(S3), 292–293 (2016)

5. https://www.olcf.ornl.gov/2021/02/18/scientists-use-supercomputers-tostudy-reliable-fusion-reactor-design-operation (2021, Online)

6. Rebut, P.-H.: ITER: the first experimental fusion reactor. Fusion Eng. Des. **30**(1–2), 85–118 (1995)

7. Ku, S.-H., et al.: Full-f gyrokinetic particle simulation of centrally heated global ITG turbulence from magnetic axis to edge pedestal top in a realistic tokamak geometry. Nucl. Fusion **49**(11), 115021 (2009)

8. Dominski, J., et al.: Spatial coupling of gyrokinetic simulations, a generalized scheme based on first-principles. Phys. Plasmas **28**(2), 022301 (2021)

9. Wolfram Jr, et al.: Global to Coastal Multiscale Modeling via Land-river-ocean Coupling in the Energy Exascale Earth System Model (E3SM). No. LA-UR-20-24263. Los Alamos National Lab. (LANL), Los Alamos, NM (United States) (2020)

10. Ratanaworabhan, P., et al.: Fast lossless compression of scientific floating-point data. In: Data Compression Conference, DCC 2006 (2006)

11. Liang, X., et al.: Error-controlled lossy compression optimized for high compression ratios of scientific datasets. In: 2018 IEEE International Conference on Big Data (Big Data). IEEE (2018)

12. Lindstrom, P.: Fixed-rate compressed floating-point arrays. IEEE Trans. Vis. Comput. Graph. **20**(12), 2674–2683 (2014)

13. Ainsworth, M., et al.: Multilevel techniques for compression and reduction of scientific data-the multivariate case. SIAM J. Sci. Comput. **41**(2), A1278–A1303 (2019)

14. Ainsworth, M., et al.: Multilevel techniques for compression and reduction of scientific data-quantitative control of accuracy in derived quantities. SIAM J. Sci. Comput. **41**(4), A2146–A2171 (2019)

15. Ainsworth, M., et al.: Multilevel techniques for compression and reduction of scientific data-the unstructured case. SIAM J. Sci. Comput. **42**(2), A1402–A1427 (2020)

16. Choi, J., et al.: Generative fusion data compression. In: Neural Compression: From Information Theory to Applications-Workshop ICLR (2021)

17. https://github.com/CODARcode/MGARD/blob/master/README_MGARD_GPU.md

18. https://github.com/LLNL/zfp

19. https://github.com/szcompressor/SZ

20. Hines, J.: Stepping up to summit. Comput. Sci. Eng. **20**(2), 78–82 (2018)

21. Faghihi, D., et al.: Moment preserving constrained resampling with applications to particle-in-cell methods. J. Comput. Phys. **409**, 109317 (2020)

22. Jackson, M., et al.: Reservoir modeling for flow simulation by use of surfaces, adaptive unstructured meshes, and an overlapping-control-volume finite-element method. SPE Reservoir Eval. Eng. **18**(02), 115–132 (2015)

23. Alted, F.: Blosc, an extremely fast, multi-threaded, meta-compressor library (2017)

24. Burtscher, M., et al.: FPC: a high-speed compressor for double-precision floating-point data. IEEE Trans. Comput. **58**(1), 18–31 (2008)

25. https://facebook.github.io/zstd/. Accessed 2021

26. Chen, J., et al.: Understanding performance-quality trade-offs in scientific visualization workflows with lossy compression. In: 2019 IEEE/ACM 5th International Workshop on Data Analysis and Reduction for Big Scientific Data (2019)

27. Lu, T., et al.: Understanding and modeling lossy compression schemes on HPC scientific data. In: 2018 IEEE International Parallel and Distributed Processing Symposium (IPDPS). IEEE (2018)

28. Liang, X., et al.: MGARD+: optimizing multi-grid based reduction for efficient scientific data management. IEEE Trans. Comput. (2021, to appear)

29. Chen, J., et al.: Accelerating Multigrid-Based Hierarchical Scientific Data Refactoring on GPUs. arXiv preprint arXiv:2007.04457 (2020)

30. Tian, J., et al.: cuSZ: an efficient GPU-based error-bounded lossy compression framework for scientific data. In: Proceedings of the ACM International Conference on Parallel Architectures and Compilation Techniques (2020)

31. Lindstrom, P., et al.: cuZFP. https://github.com/LLNL/zfp/tree/develop/src/cuda_zfp

32. Wallace, G.K.: The JPEG still picture compression standard. IEEE Trans. Consum. Electron. **38**(1), xviii–xxxiv (1992)

33. Rabbani, M.: JPEG2000: image compression fundamentals, standards and practice. J. Electron. Imaging **11**(2), 286 (2002)

Applying Recent Machine Learning Approaches to Accelerate the Algebraic Multigrid Method for Fluid Simulations

Thorben Louw$^{(\boxtimes)}$ and Simon McIntosh-Smith$^{(\boxtimes)}$

Department of Computer Science, University of Bristol, Bristol BS8 1UB, UK
{thorben.louw.2019,S.McIntosh-Smith}@bristol.ac.uk

Abstract. In this work, we describe our experiences trying to apply recent machine learning (ML) advances to the Algebraic Multigrid (AMG) method to predict better prolongation (interpolation) operators and accelerate solver convergence. Published work often reports results on small, unrepresentative problems, such as 1D equations or very small computational grids. To better understand the performance of these methods on more realistic data, we create a new, reusable dataset of large, sparse matrices by leveraging the recently published Thingi10K dataset of 3D geometries, along with the FTetWild mesher for creating computational meshes that are valid for use in finite element method (FEM) simulations. We run simple 3D Navier-Stokes simulations, and capture the sparse linear systems that arise.

We consider the integration of ML approaches with established tools and solvers that support distributed computation, such as HYPRE, but achieve little success. The only approach suitable for use with unstructured grid data involves inference against a multi-layer message-passing graph neural network, which is too memory-hungry for practical use, and we find existing frameworks to be unsuitable for efficient distributed inference. Furthermore, the model prediction times far exceed the complete solver time of traditional approaches. While our focus is on inference against trained models, we also note that retraining the proposed neural networks using our dataset remains intractable.

We conclude that these ML approaches are not yet ready for general use, and that much more research focus is required into how efficient distributed inference against such models can be incorporated into existing HPC workflows.

Keywords: HPC-AI · AMG · GNN

1 Introduction

In this paper, we describe our experience applying recently proposed machine learning (ML) models to predict better interpolation operators for the algebraic

This work was funded by the Engineering and Physical Sciences Research Council (EPSRC) via the Advanced Simulation and Modelling of Virtual Systems (ASiMoV) project, EP/S005072/1.

© Springer Nature Switzerland AG 2022
J. Nichols et al. (Eds.): SMC 2021, CCIS 1512, pp. 40–57, 2022.
https://doi.org/10.1007/978-3-030-96498-6_3

multigrid (AMG) method, with the aim of reducing the number of iterations the method takes to converge. Our interest lies in speeding up the solution of large, sparse linear systems which arise during fluid simulations.

A common criticism of recent ML-based approaches to solving partial differential equations (PDEs) or accelerate scientific simulations is that they are typically demonstrated on small 1D or 2D structured grids. Yet industrial and scientific simulations currently solve problems many orders of magnitude larger, and existing tools are designed to support *unstructured* 3D meshes. To be useful, ML acceleration approaches must be shown to work on these inputs. In this work, we use the 10,000 3D geometries in the Thingi10K dataset, run a simple 3D Navier-Stokes FEM fluid simulation on each, and capture the sparse matrices which result, to create a new dataset of sparse linear systems for evaluating such ML approaches.

In 2020, Luz et al. reported using a graph neural network (GNN) approach for accelerating AMG that is able to deal with unstructured data [24]. Since they found good generalization to domains outside of their original training regime, we use their implementation as a basis for our work.

Machine learning models such as the one in [24] learn good values for parameters in a process called *training*. Training is much more computationally demanding than *inference* against a trained model, so it attracts the bulk of research attention today. However, the researcher wanting to use or deploy a trained model for inference is left with a significant amount of software engineering effort to make their model to run well, and this is not often discussed.

A disconnect exists between the way high-performance computing (HPC) tools are designed to scale in over the distributed compute nodes in a supercomputer – typically using implementations of the Message Passing Interface (MPI) to communicate over fast interconnects and are invoked via workload managers such as Slurm – and the support for serving machine learning models in the dominant ML frameworks, which favor a cloud-like distributed computing setup. Model serving frameworks load trained, optimized models and make them available to clients through an interface such as gRPC. They optimize for latency and throughput, dynamically batching requests and scaling compute resources to match demand, and allow optimized models to make use of acceleration hardware, using hardware-specific frameworks such as NVIDIA's TensorRT that optimizes models to make use of TensorCores on NVIDIA accelerators. Alternatively, one might wish to simply load a model locally in an application by integrating modern machine learning frameworks directly in source code. Even so, the post-training optimization process can involve serializing to a model interchange format like ONNX [25], sparsification, data-type reduction and quantization, and running models through deep learning (DL) compilers such as TVM [5] to optimize computation and data movement. This difficulty is reflected in the growth of a software engineering trend called "MLOps" (Machine Learning Operations), which recognizes that the devising and training models is only a small part of the overall effort in making these models useful [22,26].

Our attempt at using the approach in [24] with our dataset fails: the message-passing graph neural network (GNN) model and the graph neural network framework used for the implementation do not scale to support the size of matrices in our dataset. An inference against the model – one small part of the problem setup phase – runs longer than a traditional solver takes to complete the whole solution, and uses huge amounts of memory even for modest problem sizes. In addition, the model does not generalize well to even the smaller sparse matrices in our dataset. We find that support for distributed exact inference using large graphs in GNN frameworks today is limited, and difficult to integrate into our workflow. The GNN nature of the model makes it difficult to optimize, and support in the common ONNX interchange format is lacking.

The structure of the rest of this paper is as follows: we give an overview of AMG in Sect. 2.1 and discuss our evaluation dataset in Sect. 2.2. We review of the recently proposed ML acceleration approaches for AMG in Sect. 3 with special focus on the approaches of Greenfeld et al. [16] and Luz et al. [24]. We discuss our results in Sect. 4 before concluding with some thoughts on future work.

Our contributions in this work are

- A new dataset of 30,000 sparse linear systems representative of the fluid mechanics simulations arising from FEM simulation complex 3D geometries. The dataset is easy to modify for different problems and boundary conditions, and useful for practically evaluating suggestions for ML-accelerated solvers.
- Findings from our experience with the model from Greenfeld et al. [16], which demonstrate that much simpler models can also learn good interpolation operators, with corresponding benefits for integrating them into applications
- A description of our experience trying to apply a Graph Neural Network such as the one in [24] to larger, 3D fluid dynamics problems.

2   Background

2.1   Overview of Algebraic Multigrid

In this section we give a very brief the AMG concepts which are important for contextualizing the ML methods which follow. A thorough overview of AMG is available in [29].

In this setting, we are interested in solving linear systems of the familiar form:

$$A\mathbf{x} = \mathbf{b} \tag{1}$$

where $A \in \mathbb{R}^{n \times n}$ is a very sparse matrix. These systems frequently arise in scientific domains when solving partial differential equations (PDEs) that are discretized on a computational grid, and then solved using techniques such as FEM, or the Finite Difference Method (FDM) or Finite Volume Method (FVM).

For example, in a typical fluid dynamics solver, such linear systems are solved at each timestep when calculating the next grid values for the velocity and pressure fields.

In real-world problems these linear systems are both very large (many millions of rows), and extremely sparse, encouraging the use of specialized solvers which take advantage of these properties. Iterative *relaxation* methods are used, which improve on an initial guess until the solution converges (i.e. until the residual $e_i = \|A x_i - \mathbf{b}\|$ becomes sufficiently small).

Many relaxation methods have been developed over the last few decades, including the well-known class of Krylov subspace methods such as the Conjugate Gradient (CG) method and Generalized Minimal Residual Method (GMRES).

Relaxation methods are known to be good at reducing high-frequency errors (associated with eigenvectors of A that have large eigenvalues), but poor at reducing the smooth or low-frequency errors, and can need many iterations to converge.

Multigrid methods improve on this situation by creating a hierarchy of coarser (smaller) grid levels. At each level, residual errors after applying smoothing at the fine grid level are projected to the next coarsest grid using a problem- and level-specific 'restriction operator' R, before applying smoothing (relaxation) at the coarser grid level. This process is repeated, resulting in smaller and smaller linear systems, until eventually a system is small enough to solve directly. The coarsest grid error is then interpolated back from coarse to fine grid levels using problem- and level-specific 'prolongation operators' P and added back to the post-smoothing guess as a correction, until finally a few relaxations are applied to the finest system. This entire process forms one "V-cycle", several iterations of which are performed until the residual converges.

Coarse-grid correction smooths out the low-frequency errors, while relaxations at the finest grid level smooth out the high-frequency errors, resulting in rapid convergence.

In the original Geometric Multigrid context, the problem geometry ('grid') is available to the solver, but the Algebraic Multigrid method [28] extends this multilevel idea to general linear systems in a 'black-box' fashion, using only the entries of the matrix A and the target vector $\mathbf{b}$ as inputs. Coarsening strategies in AMG use algebraic properties of the nodes in the matrix (such as the strength-of-connection or energy-based properties) rather than the problem geometry to select coarse nodes, and heuristic methods to select the weights in the prolongation operator.

AMG's black-box approach may be less efficient than approaches which can exploit the problem geometry, but it has an important software engineering advantage: easily re-usable, optimized libraries for the solution of general linear systems from different domains can be created which use standard matrix-vector interfaces. Examples of such libraries in the HPC world are HYPRE's Boomer-AMG solver [11] and ML [13], which have developed parallel versions of AMG algorithms that support distributed sparse matrices for very large systems, and scale well over thousands of nodes.

Coarsening Strategies. Several algorithms have been proposed to identify which nodes of the grid are "coarse" (to be included in the next grid level), and which are "fine". This split is used to create the next grid level, but also forms vital information in the construction of the operators which interpolate values back between the coarse and fine grids.

Examples are the "classical" Ruge-Stüben coarsening [28], Cleary-Luby-Jones-Plassman (CLJP) [6], and parallel coarsenings which lead to lower operator complexity, such as Parallel Modified Independent Set (PMIS) and HMIS [7]. The aggressiveness of the coarsening influences the size of the next-coarsest grid (and thus the run-time of the final algorithm), but also impacts the subsequent choice of interpolation operators.

Interpolation and the Construction of the Prolongation Operator. Between two grid levels, the error propagation matrix is given by

$$M = S^{\sigma_2}(I - P[P^T A P]^{-1} P^T A)S^{\sigma_1} \tag{2}$$

where the S terms represent error propagation matrices of the pre- and post-smoothing relaxation sweeps.

The asymptotic convergence rate of AMG is determined by the spectral radius of this error propagation matrix $\rho(M)$. After the pre- and post-smoother are chosen, $\rho(M)$ depends only on P. While a good P is one that results in a small spectral radius for M, it should also be sparse for computational efficiency.

We note that the restriction operator which maps from fine to coarse grids is often chosen such that $R = P^T$.

The methods we consider in Sect. 3 will aim to improve on the weights in a candidate P.

Use of AMG as a Preconditioner. The multilevel nature of AMG means that each iteration is much more expensive to execute than an iteration of a single-level Krylov solver. As a result, instead of being used as a standalone solver, AMG is frequently used as a preconditioner to improve the convergence of Krylov subspace methods. In this task, only a few AMG iterations are run to get an approximate solution, and the setup cost of AMG (including building P) becomes more important than the cost of AMG iterations to solve the system.

2.2 A Dataset of Sparse Systems from 3D Unstructured Meshes

To evaluate the usefulness of newly proposed methods, we build a large dataset of sparse matrices captured from simple FEM fluid simulations on a diverse set of geometries. Our search for existing open datasets of geometries to leverage as a starting point led us to Zhou and Jacobson's 2016 Thingi10K dataset [38], which contains 10,000 3D printing models. Similar sources of 3D shape datasets exist in the ModelNet [34] and ShapeNet [4] datasets. However, Thingi10K was chosen since it has already been used as an evaluation set for the FTetWild mesher [19], which transforms "triangle soup" input meshes into high quality tetrahedral meshes that are valid for use with FEM simulations.

To generate our dataset, we use the FEniCS [23] framework with the 10,000 high quality versions of the Thingi10K meshes after FTetWild processing, and implement a simple 3D Navier-Stokes simulation using P2-P1 (Taylor-Hood) finite elements with a time-varying pressure condition, and Dirichlet boundary conditions. At each timestep, the solver must solve three large linear systems representing the velocity update, pressure correction, and velocity correction steps. After a few timesteps, we capture these linear systems to files, giving us 30,000 test matrices.

This process can be re-run with a variety of boundary and initial conditions, different PDEs with various coefficients, different FTetWild triangle densities, and different solvers (e.g. finite volume method simulations) to easily generate many other candidate sparse linear systems to evaluate the accuracy of acceleration methods.

An example of a mesh from the Thingi10K dataset is shown in Fig. 1. Here we show Item 47251 ("Living Brain Right Part"). The geometry is transformed using FTetWild then used as the basis for a simple FEM simulation with 438,897 degrees of freedom. We show a rendering of the original mesh (252,204 faces), and a visualization of the corresponding sparse matrix from the velocity update step of our simulation. The square matrix is challenging at 2,995,242 rows, but is also 99.997% sparse. While this is still orders of magnitude smaller than problem sizes in industrial applications, it is more representative of the problems we wish to solve than the small test problems used in [24] (64–400,000 rows).

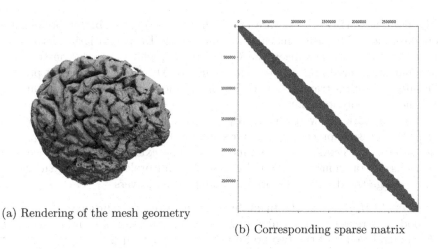

(a) Rendering of the mesh geometry

(b) Corresponding sparse matrix

Fig. 1. Item 47251 *Living Brain Right Part* from the Thingi10K dataset, with a visualisation of the corresponding sparse matrix from a FEM fluid simulation using this geometry.

Figure 2 gives an overview of the matrix sizes and sparsity of the matrices in the dataset (using the default FTetWild triangle density). As we will discuss in

Sect. 3.2, these sparse matrices are also much larger than those used in benchmark datasets for common graph neural network frameworks.

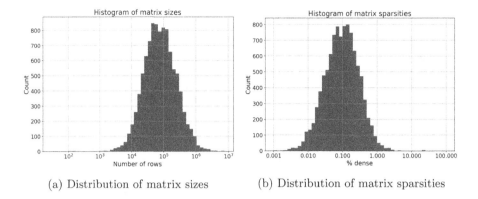

(a) Distribution of matrix sizes   (b) Distribution of matrix sparsities

Fig. 2. Distribution of matrix sizes and sparsities in the dataset (velocity projection step only)

3   Overview of the Recently Proposed Methods

The earliest work we are aware of which tries to predict better prolongation operators for AMG using machine learning is the Deep Multigrid Method proposed by Katrutsa, Daulbaev and Oseledets [21], which they demonstrate only on small structured grid problems for PDEs in 1D. The method is not practical because it requires training a new deep neural network for every new matrix A. We did not apply it in our work.

For our work, we were specifically attracted to the approaches in Luz et al. [24] and the work preceding it in Greenfeld et al. [16], which try improving on the values in a candidate P produced by some existing method. Since these methods use previously computed coarsening and prolongation sparsities, they can leverage the decades of work in existing AMG solvers.

Learning to Minimize $\rho(M)$. In all three of these works, the problem of predicting a good P is recast as a learning problem where the aim is to minimize $\rho(M)$, the spectral radius of the two-grid error matrix from Eq. 2.

Any algorithm that tries to minimise $\rho(M)$ directly faces a difficult time: evaluating $\rho(M)$ means inverting the large $(P^T A P)^{-1}$ term in Eq. 2, and subsequently performing a very expensive ($\mathcal{O}(n^3)$) eigen-decomposition with n extremely large. To make matters worse, neither TensorFlow nor PyTorch (the two dominant DL frameworks today) currently support sparse matrix inversion, and converting to dense representations is infeasible for problems of this size.

Instead, Katrutsa, Daulbaev and Oseledets approximate the spectral radius using Gelfand's formula [21], and develop an efficient, unbiased stochastic estimator for this approximation. It still requires evaluating norms of M, and thus computing the expensive $(P^T A P)^{-1}$ term.

In contrast, both [24] and [16] choose a proxy loss function: they minimize the upper bound for the spectral radius given by the Frobenius norm $\|M\|_F^2$. To avoid the large cost of evaluating the $(P^T A P)^{-1}$ term directly, they restrict their training data distribution to specially synthesized block-circulant, block-diagonalized matrices, where the norm is the sum of the small diagonal blocks' norms. This allows efficient and stable calculation of the loss function, but severely restricts the distribution of input matrices available for training.

3.1   Deep Residual Feed-Forward Network for 2D Structured Grid Problems (Greenfeld et al. [16])

Our interest is in methods that work for 3D *unstructured* grids, but in this section we briefly discuss the work of Greenfeld et al. [16]. Their neural network model is for a 2D structured grid discretized using a 3×3 stencil. However, it lays important groundwork for the unstructured grid method which follows.

Input and Output. The proposed deep neural network aims to improve on values in a candidate prolongation matrix as determined by an existing interpolation algorithm, by only using information local to each coarse point. The same network is used to predict P at all levels of the grid.

In addition to inference against the model, there is non-trivial pre- and post-processing to assemble the inputs and interpret the neural network's outputs.

As input, for each coarse point in the grid, we pass to the network the equivalent point in the fine grid and its four nearest neighbors, using the 3×3 stencil of each of these 5 points, resulting in 45 real values which are concatenated and flattened to build an input in $\mathbb{R}^{45}$.

The output of the network is fixed to be in $\mathbb{R}^4$ and represents the weightings of the coarse point to the fine grid points to the north, south, east and west. Remaining directions' weightings are then solved algebraically. In the specific problem formulation the authors choose, the sparsity of the columns in P is fixed to allow at most 9 non-zeros, and the maximum distance to which coarse points can contribute to fine points is fixed at 1.

Despite its limitations, this network is more flexible than earlier proposals for PDE solvers such as the one in Tang [30]: it works for grids of any size without re-training, as long as the stencil size of the problem is the same. The authors also show some generalization capability when used with different boundary conditions and distributions of coefficients for the underlying PDE.

However, this approach involves very tight integration with the problem being solved, and means training entirely different networks for different discretizations (consider that when using a 3D 27-point stencil instead of a 2D 9-point stencil, the concatenated, flattened inputs will be in $\mathbb{R}^{189}$ instead of $\mathbb{R}^{45}$), and needs an entirely different formulation to use longer-range interpolation strategies. It is also limited to structured grids. So we look to another proposal to tackle the unstructured problems of interest in our dataset.

3.2 Graph Neural Networks for Unstructured Problems (Luz et al. [24])

Seeking to extend the work of Greenfeld et al. to unstructured problems, Luz et al. develop an approach in [24] which uses the Graph Neural Network shown in Fig. 3.

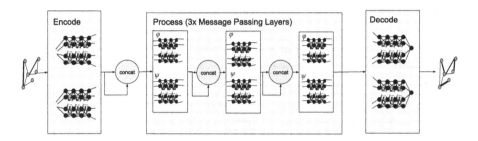

Fig. 3. The graph neural network used in [24].

GNNs are a recent kind of machine learning model that can deal with general unstructured input. A common unifying framework for reasoning about graph networks is presented by Bataglia et al. in [1], who also developed the DeepMind GraphNets library that Luz et al. used for the implementation of this model.

Luz et al. learn to predict P using a non-recurrent encode-process-decode architecture, in which

- the *encode* block learns a representation of the input edge and node features in a higher-dimensional latent space ($\mathbb{R}^{64}$). It has two 4-layer dense feed-forward neural networks to learn this function for edges and nodes independently.
- the *process* block consists of 3 message-passing layers. In graph networks, message passing layers (Gilmer et al. [14]) are a graph generalization of spatial convolution, and are essential for learning representations. Message passing layers produce a "message" for each edge by evaluating some learned function ϕ, taking as input the edge feature and the node features of the edge's incident nodes. Then, for each node, we aggregate the messages from its edges using another learned function ψ which takes as input the sum reduction of the incoming messages. In graph neural networks, the learnable functions ϕ and ψ are implemented using some choice of neural network. Luz, et al. use 4-layer dense feed-forward networks, but also choose to concatenate each message layer's input with the previous layer's input[1].

---

[1] Plus we note that a bug in the original authors' implementation results in a superfluous concatenation of the encoded input with itself before being fed to any message passing layers.

– the *decode* block translates the high-dimensional latent node and edge representations back into a single real value per edge using two independent 4-layer feed-forward networks.

This model has 286,146 learnable parameters.

In addition to the model, there are non-trivial pre-processing and post-processing tasks to translate between the sparse tensors in the problem domain and the data structure (a "GraphsTuple") used by the GraphNets framework.

Similar to the Greenfeld et al. model in Sect. 3.1, to prepare the input to the network we need: the list of coarse nodes from an existing coarsening method, a candidate prolongation matrix from an existing method, and the sparse matrix A. These are transformed into a GraphsTuple structure in which nodes are one-hot encoded to indicate whether they are coarse or fine, and edge values are concatenated with a one-hot encoding indicating whether they are included in the candidate P's sparsity pattern. Note that the size of the graph structure depends on both the size and the sparsity of A.

The output from the graph network is another GraphsTuple, from which the final P must be reconstructed. The original coarse nodes list is used to select the columns of P, and the baseline P is used to re-impose the sparsity pattern (i.e. only selecting those edge values from the graph network output).

The current implementation uses the DeepMind GraphNets library, which in turn is based on the Sonnet library that builds on the well-known TensorFlow ML framework, allowing the implementation to use TensorFlow's optimised kernels for sparse and dense Tensor operations on various devices, and benefiting from TensorFlow's extensive ecosystem of tooling. However, we note that other graph network libraries exist which are more actively maintained and report better performance, such as DGL [31].

4   Results

4.1   For the Model in Greenfeld et al.

Faster Training with Simpler Models. The authors of [16] choose a 100-wide, 100-deep residual feed-forward network with over 10^6 trainable parameters to learn the $f : \mathbb{R}^{45} \to \mathbb{R}^4$ mapping, without justifying why such an expressive network might be necessary (although they state in their conclusions that future work should consider simpler models). The network as proposed in [16] took almost a day to train on a high-end (Intel Xeon 8168 48-core) CPU, or several hours on a GPU – a prohibitive upfront cost for a method so tightly integrated with the specific problem being solved, considering that the problem sizes in [16] only take seconds to solve using a traditional solver.

Pursuing simpler, shallower neural network models is attractive because they would not only allow for a faster forward pass and much less computation during inference, but also consume less memory, and require fewer weights to be loaded from a serialized description of the model.

We retrained two much simpler network architectures: a simple 4-layer encoder-decoder network (layer widths 100, 50, 30, 50 with ReLu activations) with 12,998 learnable parameters and a shallow 2-layer multi-layer perceptron (layer widths 20, 10 with ReLu activations) with 1,038 learnable parameters. Layer widths were chosen to result in networks with approximately two and three orders of magnitude fewer learnable parameters than that proposed in [16], respectively.

Informed by results showing that incorporating large learning rates aids rapid learning convergence (Wilson et al. [32]), we also introduced an exponentially decaying learning rate schedule with a large initial value ($\epsilon = 0.1$, decay rate 0.95) to replace the authors' approach of only setting a small initial learning rate ($\epsilon = 1.2 \times 10^{-5}$). When used with the common "early-stopping" technique [27], these changes can reduce training from hours to minutes on a CPU, yet we still achieve very good prediction accuracy. The simple networks continue to outperform the classical Ruge-Stüben interpolation the authors of [16] use as a baseline comparison, although not as well as the original network, and the simplest network's results do not generalize to larger matrix sizes (see Table 1).

Table 1. Performance of simpler network architectures applied to the work in [16], indicating the percentage of cases where the model's predicted P resulted in convergence in fewer AMG V-cycles than a baseline Ruge-Stüben solver to solve the 2D FEM problem.

Grid size	Original from [16]	4 layer enc-dec	2-layer MLP
32×32	83%	93%	96%
64×64	92%	90%	88%
128×128	91%	88%	78%
256×256	84%	82%	78%
512×512	81%	86%	68%
1024×1024	83%	80%	52%

Integration and Parallelization. The design of the model in [16] allows it to be used in a parallel, distributed-memory setting. Gathering the stencil of surrounding nodes uses mostly local values and communication patterns very similar to those required during coarsening and classical interpolation, and allows extensive re-use of values already in a distributed node's memory. Similarly, since the network considers each input in isolation, it is possible to have several distributed instances of the model to query (e.g. one per compute node), and we can batch inputs to the network for efficient computation. Finally, the simplest network we found has a very light computational profile (two layers of matrix multiplication and activation function computation) and not many weights to load during model deserialization, making it feasible to use the model on the same compute nodes where the coarsening and interpolation work happen. Models are agnostic to the size of the input grid, making them re-usable. Even though a different model may be needed for each problem (distribution, boundary conditions), having pre-trained model weights for a variety of problem settings available for download in a 'model zoo' might be feasible.

4.2   For the Model in Luz et al.

Scalability of Inference. First, we try to evaluate how well a model trained as described in [24] copes with the matrices in our dataset without modification.

A problem quickly becomes apparent: as shown in Fig. 4, when performing inference on a single node, the execution time of the forward pass of the graph network quickly becomes problematic for larger matrices, e.g. taking almost 5 min for a medium-sized $800,445 \times 800,445$ matrix in our test set on a 48-core Intel Skylake CPU. This inference represents only the first level of the grid's setup of P – in a real problem setting, subsequent levels still would need to make inferences in serial (for progressively smaller graphs) during the problem setup phase. For comparison the single-core pyAMG [2] solver using a classical direct framework for this same problem takes just 71.1s for the whole problem setup phase and 50.5s for the iterations, i.e. the traditional approach using a single core can solve the whole system in less time than just a small portion of the setup phase takes using the GNN model.

The time complexity of the GNN inference is linear in the size of the input network. Wu [35] derives the time complexity of similar message-passing Graph Convolutinal Network (GCN) layers as $\mathcal{O}(Kmd + Knd^2)$ with K the number of layers in the network, m the number of edges and n the number of nodes d is a fixed constant denoting the size of the hidden features. This is borne out by the linear scaling seen in Fig. 4, where deviation from the ideal slope is attributable to the slightly different sparsities of the matrices affecting the number of edges in the graph.

While the runtime is already problematic, a bigger problem is the memory usage of this network. In the default implementation, modest compute nodes with only 16GiB of RAM (or smaller GPUs) run out of memory at inputs of about $20,000$ nodes. The largest matrix we were able to use as input ($800,000$ nodes) on a more powerful compute node used approximately 400GiB of RAM to perform the query.

As with run-time, the memory required for inference in this network also grows linearly with the size of the network. Specifically, for the message passing layers we look to a result in Wu [35] which demonstrates the memory complexity for graph convolutional layers as $O(Knd + Kd^2)$, with K the number of layers in the network, n the number of nodes and d a fixed constant denoting the size of the hidden features. However, since the network architecture in [24] also *concatenates* outputs of each message passing layer as inputs to the next layer, this size of the latent space grows with each layer, with each edge feature consisting of 384

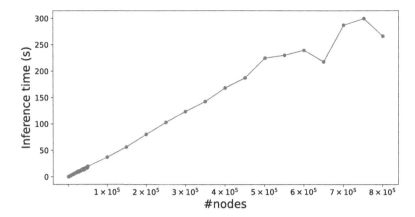

Fig. 4. Inference time against the graph network model in seconds on a 48 core Intel Xeon (Skylake) 8168 (2.7 GHz) CPU, for increasing graph sizes (excluding input and output processing). The largest problem size for which inference succeeded had 800,445 nodes and 49,609,863 edges. Larger problems ran out of memory (using in excess of 391 GiB of RAM)

`float64`'s after the last message passing layer! Luz et al. perform an ablation study which shows that omitting this concatenation slightly hurts the accuracy of the network.

Memory usage for exact inference in Graph Neural Networks today is known to be problematic [35]. Intermediate layers store the values for all nodes, making memory usage highly sensitive to the size of input graphs. The typical approach is to resort to stochastic sampling of a limited number of nodes or edges in a neighborhood [17], but our problem setting for predicting P makes this impossible (we need the edge values of all elements of P in our output). For exact inference against large networks on GPUs, it is possible to loop over the nodes and edges per layer in batches, and copy intermediate layer values back to CPU memory. But this approach requires a manual, device-specific implementation that reduces portability [8], and still assumes that the data fits in CPU memory.

Our situation is not unusual: we see other recent works reporting out-of-memory errors (OOMs) on modest network sizes (e.g. the performance comparison of various frameworks in [31]), and note that benchmarks for GNNs typically use small (<20,000 node) problem sizes, focus on training times and report single-node inference [10,33]. This unrepresentative state of affairs is being addressed by initiatives such as the recent Open Graph Benchmark dataset [18].

Of course, we can use further tricks to squeeze more performance from a single node, such as using mixed precision (`float32` accumulation and `float16` weights in the network) or reduced precision datatypes for the intermediate vectors instead of the `float64` widths used by Luz et al. (although we note that these are not supported by the versions of the frameworks used in their original implementation), and possibly reducing the dimensionality of the latent space (not tested in the authors' ablation study). Skillful application of techniques such as inducing sparsity in the model through pruning, and the use of a DL compiler such as TVM [5] may reduce the computation and memory usage to allow for much larger single-node inferences. In addition, alternative frameworks like DGL have much better memory use owing to their use of fused message passing kernels that do not store the intermediate message values [31]. However, even with such mitigations, scaling to the large problem sizes with billions of nodes as required by industrial-scale problems is not feasible on a single inference node.

Distributed Inference. Industrial use cases involving billion-scale graphs, such as that reported by Ying et al. [37] on 18-billion edge graphs at Pinterest, have led to the development of large-scale frameworks. A survey of leading GNN frameworks (PyTorch Geometric [12], DGL [31], GraphNets [1], Spektral [15], Angel [20], Graph-Learn [36]) shows widespread support for distributed *training*, especially using data-parallel rather then model-parallel techniques, but distributed *inference* (where a single large input graph is distributed over many nodes) remains poorly supported. Our survey found support for distributed inference in recent versions of DGL, Angel, and Graph-Learn but the heavyweight process for initializing the servers and workers, determining graph partitions, and loading the distributed data efficiently (from shared storage) to build the distributed graph is overkill given that we only need to make a single inference during the AMG problem setup phase per multigrid level. We have not re-implemented the model in these frameworks as part of our work.

Model Input and Output Processing. In our integrations with scalable solvers such as HYPRE, we face the problem that the large sparse matrix A is partitioned over distributed compute nodes' memories. The transformation from this sparse matrix into a single "GraphsTuple" input for inference against the model using some standard serving framework can easily be implemented in a parallel, distributed fashion, but the interface between this distributed representation and the model framework is awkward: when using a serving framework, e.g. by initiating a request using the gRPC framework, we still need to send the whole graph, and by implication have gathered it into a single originating node's memory. Similarly, the response must be unmarshalled, the sparsity pattern of P re-imposed, and the resulting elements of P repartitioned to their distributed locations to continue with solver setup.

Testing Small-Graph Generalization Without Retraining. Despite training on a limited class of matrices that allow for cheap evaluation of the loss function, Luz et al. show some generalization capability of this network to other distributions and even different PDEs problems without retraining, including to a simple 2D FEM problem.

However, we note that the inputs to the network are also shaped by the coarsening strategies and interpolation methods used (they are used in the pre-processing and post-processing stages to impose a sparsity pattern). The authors of [24] choose classical Ruge-Stüben direct interpolation with the CLJP [6] coarsening and no Krylov acceleration as their baseline – a choice which sets the bar for comparison quite low (it produces many more iterations and deeper hierarchies than a more aggressive coarsening and longer-range interpolation).

Classical AMG is designed for Hermitian positive definite matrices, and our FEM simulations are not guaranteed to produce these. Before testing how well a pre-trained model can generalize to our dataset, it is important to establish whether a baseline (non-ML) classical Ruge-Stüben solver, as configured with the coarsening and interpolation [24] used during training, can solve our systems. As a test, we use those "velocity projection" matrices with fewer than 25,000 rows, comprising 1,624 matrices from the dataset.

The solver is configured as in [24] to perform V-cycles using CLJP coarsening, a classical algebraic strength metric with $\theta = 0.25$, a single symmetric sweep of Gauss-Seidel pre- and post-smoothing, and a limit of 12 on the maximum number of levels. With this solver configuration, only 69.2% of the linear systems in the sampled dataset converge in under 500 iterations. Better results can be expected by using other options, such as smoothed aggregation coarsening with GMRES acceleration.

In contrast, when using the model from [24] to predict values of P, we find that only 17.7% of these systems converge in under 500 iterations. Even in cases where both the model and the baseline converge, the model's predictions result in fewer iterations to convergence only 1.2% of the time. It has not been able to generalize to the PDE and shapes in our dataset, even for the smallest matrices.

Infeasibility of Retraining or Fine-Tuning with Our Dataset. Lastly, we note that the prohibitive cost of evaluating the loss function on large matrices means we cannot use our dataset to retrain or fine-tune the network as it is currently proposed. Since TensorFlow does not currently support sparse inversion of matrices, the large $P^T A P$ matrices must be converted to dense matrices before matrix inversion, for which they are infeasibly large.

5   Conclusion

To date, the work of Luz, et al. [24] remains the only work we are aware of in this domain that supports unstructured grid problems. The proposed model has appealing 'black box' properties that mean the solver implementation is separated from the problem discretization, and the model can be used to complement the decades of work optimizing AMG solvers. However, we find that the model (as currently implemented) cannot scale usefully to even moderately sized matrices in our dataset. Although the situation may be improved by more optimization and re-implementation in a more performant framework, single-node inference cannot scale to the billions of nodes required for current applications. Yet unfortunately the current heavyweight setup for distributed graph inference frameworks is not suitable for this problem either: the nature of AMG means that inferences are infrequent (once per level per linear system) and necessarily sequential (cannot be batched for all the levels). But our work with the proposal from Greenfeld et al. shows that there may be hope for simpler models to achieve good results on these problems, and these simpler networks are currently more amenable to deployment for inference in a distributed setting.

Computation for the coarsening and the classical interpolation must be carried out *in addition* and strictly prior to invoking the ML methods we considered, i.e. the run-time for the setup phase is guaranteed to be substantially longer. This only pays off if the cost of the additional inferences is recovered by run-time savings from substantially fewer iterations. For the small subset of our dataset with reasonable run-times, this was not the case.

Our hope had been to extend this approach to testing some of the very large models we are considering (with billions of degrees of freedom), but given the limitations of scaling the Graph Neural Network approach with existing implementations, we terminated our investigation early. Future work is required before these methods are ready for general application to real-world problems.

Future Work. We are investigating the use of DLPack [9], a proposal for an in-memory tensor structure that allows no-copy tensor sharing between DL networks. It already has support in PyTorch, TensorFlow, DGL and PetSc, potentially enabling easier integration of traditional HPC and DL tools.

Re-implementing the model of Luz et al. in a more actively developed framework such as DGL will allow more scope for optimization using techniques such as reduced precision and weight quantization, and can allow evaluating whether stochastic neighborhood sampling can be made to work with this problem and relieve memory pressure.

Adapting the model in [24] for smoothed aggregation and longer-range interpolation, and perhaps combining it with preconditioners for FEM such as AMGe [3], may prove to be more successful for the problems in our dataset.

Lastly, we are considering a hybrid of the approaches in [16] and [24], in which the distance-4 neighborhoods for each point are gathered at their distributed nodes and passed to local, simpler graph networks which operate only on the small subgraphs, allowing the GNN approach to scale better.

A   Dataset

Code and instructions for reproducing our dataset and training the models can be found at https://github.com/UoB-HPC/scaling-ml-approaches-to-amg.

References

1. Battaglia, P.W., et al.: Relational inductive biases, deep learning, and graph networks. arXiv preprint arXiv:1806.01261 (2018)
2. Bell, W., Olson, L., Schroder, J.: PyAMG: algebraic multigrid solvers in Python (2011). https://github.com/pyamg/pyamg. Accessed 01 June 2021
3. Brezina, M., et al.: Algebraic multigrid based on element interpolation (AMGE). SIAM J. Sci. Comput. **22**(5), 1570–1592 (2001)
4. Chang, A.X., et al.: ShapeNet: an information-rich 3D model repository. arXiv preprint arXiv:1512.03012 (2015)

5. Chen, T., et al.: TVM: end-to-end optimization stack for deep learning, pp. 11–20. arXiv preprint arXiv:1802.04799 (2018)
6. Cleary, A.J., Falgout, R.D., Henson, V.E., Jones, J.E.: Coarse-grid selection for parallel algebraic multigrid. In: Ferreira, A., Rolim, J., Simon, H., Teng, S.-H. (eds.) IRREGULAR 1998. LNCS, vol. 1457, pp. 104–115. Springer, Heidelberg (1998). https://doi.org/10.1007/BFb0018531
7. De Sterck, H., Yang, U.M., Heys, J.J.: Reducing complexity in parallel algebraic multigrid preconditioners. SIAM J. Matrix Anal. Appl. **27**(4), 1019–1039 (2006)
8. DGL v0.6.1 user guide: exact inference against large graphs. https://docs.dgl.ai/en/0.6.x/guide/minibatch-inference.html (2018). Accessed 01 June 2021
9. DLPack: Open in memory tensor structure. https://github.com/dmlc/dlpack (2017). Accessed 06 June 2021
10. Dwivedi, V.P., Joshi, C.K., Laurent, T., Bengio, Y., Bresson, X.: Benchmarking graph neural networks (2020)
11. Falgout, R.D., Yang, U.M.: *hypre*: a library of high performance preconditioners. In: Sloot, P.M.A., Hoekstra, A.G., Tan, C.J.K., Dongarra, J.J. (eds.) ICCS 2002. LNCS, vol. 2331, pp. 632–641. Springer, Heidelberg (2002). https://doi.org/10.1007/3-540-47789-6_66
12. Fey, M., Lenssen, J.E.: Fast graph representation learning with PyTorch geometric. arXiv preprint arXiv:1903.02428 (2019)
13. Gee, M., Siefert, C., Hu, J., Tuminaro, R., Sala, M.: ML 5.0 smoothed aggregation user's guide. Technical Report SAND2006-2649, Sandia National Laboratories (2006)
14. Gilmer, J., Schoenholz, S.S., Riley, P.F., Vinyals, O., Dahl, G.E.: Neural message passing for quantum chemistry. In: ICML 2017, pp. 1263–1272. PMLR (2017)
15. Grattarola, D., Alippi, C.: Graph neural networks in TensorFlow and Keras with Spektral [application notes]. IEEE Comput. Intell. Mag. **16**(1), 99–106 (2021)
16. Greenfeld, D., Galun, M., Kimmel, R., Yavneh, I., Basri, R.: Learning to optimize multigrid PDE Solvers. In: 36th ICML 2019 June, pp. 4305–4316, February 2019
17. Hamilton, W.L., Ying, R., Leskovec, J.: Inductive representation learning on large graphs. arXiv preprint arXiv:1706.02216 (2017)
18. Hu, W., et al.: Open graph benchmark: Datasets for machine learning on graphs. arXiv preprint arXiv:2005.00687 (2020)
19. Hu, Y., Schneider, T., Wang, B., Zorin, D., Panozzo, D.: Fast tetrahedral meshing in the wild. ACM Trans. Graph. **39**(4) (2020). https://doi.org/10.1145/3386569.3392385
20. Jiang, J., Yu, L., Jiang, J., Liu, Y., Cui, B.: Angel: a new large-scale machine learning system. Natl. Sci. Rev. **5**(2), 216–236 (2018)
21. Katrutsa, A., Daulbaev, T., Oseledets, I.: Deep Multigrid: learning prolongation and restriction matrices. arXiv preprint arXiv:1711.03825 (2017)
22. Katsiapis, K., et al.: Towards ML engineering: a brief history of tensorflow extended (TFX). arXiv preprint arXiv:2010.02013 (2020)
23. Logg, A., Mardal, K.A., Wells, G.: Automated solution of differential equations by the finite element method: The FEniCS Book, vol. 84. Springer, Heidelberg (2012). https://doi.org/10.1007/978-3-642-23099-8
24. Luz, I., Galun, M., Maron, H., Basri, R., Yavneh, I.: Learning algebraic multigrid using graph neural networks. In: PMLR, pp. 6489–6499, November 2020
25. Open neural network exchange: The open standard for machine learning interoperability. https://www.onnx.ai. Accessed 04 June 2021
26. Paleyes, A., Urma, R.G., Lawrence, N.D.: Challenges in deploying machine learning: a survey of case studies. arXiv preprint arXiv:2011.09926 (2020)

27. Prechelt, L.: Early stopping—But when? In: Montavon, G., Orr, G.B., Müller, K.-R. (eds.) Neural Networks: Tricks of the Trade. LNCS, vol. 7700, pp. 53–67. Springer, Heidelberg (2012). https://doi.org/10.1007/978-3-642-35289-8_5
28. Ruge, J.W., Stüben, K.: Algebraic multigrid. In: Multigrid Methods, pp. 73–130. SIAM (1987)
29. Stüben, K.: A review of algebraic multigrid. J. Comput. Appl. Math. **128**(1), 281–309 (2001). https://doi.org/10.1016/S0377-0427(00)00516-1. Numerical Analysis 2000. Vol. VII: Partial Differential Equations
30. Tang, W., et al.: Study on a Poisson's equation solver based on deep learning technique. In: 2017 IEEE EDAPS, pp. 1–3. IEEE (2017)
31. Wang, M., et al.: Deep graph library: A graph-centric, highly-performant package for graph neural networks. arXiv preprint arXiv:1909.01315 (2019)
32. Wilson, A.C., Roelofs, R., Stern, M., Srebro, N., Recht, B.: The marginal value of adaptive gradient methods in machine learning. arXiv preprint arXiv:1705.08292 (2017)
33. Wu, J., Sun, J., Sun, H., Sun, G.: Performance analysis of graph neural network frameworks. In: Proceedings - ISPASS 2021, pp. 118–127 (2021). https://doi.org/10.1109/ISPASS51385.2021.00029
34. Wu, Z., et al.: 3D shapeNets: a deep representation for volumetric shapes. In: Proceedings of the IEEE CVPR, pp. 1912–1920 (2015)
35. Wu, Z., Pan, S., Chen, F., Long, G., Zhang, C., Philip, S.Y.: A comprehensive survey on graph neural networks. IEEE Trans. Neural Netw. Learn. Syst. **32**, 4–24 (2020)
36. Yang, H.: AliGraph: a comprehensive graph neural network platform. In: Proceedings of the 25th ACM SIGKDD International Conference on Knowledge Discovery & Data Mining, pp. 3165–3166 (2019)
37. Ying, R., He, R., Chen, K., Eksombatchai, P., Hamilton, W.L., Leskovec, J.: Graph convolutional neural networks for web-scale recommender systems. Proceedings of the 24th ACM SIGKDD International Conference on Knowledge Discovery & Data Mining, July 2018. https://doi.org/10.1145/3219819.3219890
38. Zhou, Q., Jacobson, A.: Thingi10K: a dataset of 10,000 3D-printing models. arXiv preprint arXiv:1605.04797 (2016)

Building an Integrated Ecosystem of Computational and Observational Facilities to Accelerate Scientific Discovery

Suhas Somnath[✉], Rama K. Vasudevan, Stephen Jesse, Sergei Kalinin,
Nageswara Rao, Christopher Brumgard, Feiyi Wang, Olga Kuchar,
Arjun Shankar, Ben Mintz, Elke Arenholz, J. Robert Michael,
and Sarp Oral

Oak Ridge National Laboratory, Oak Ridge, TN 37831, USA
somnaths@ornl.gov

Abstract. Future scientific discoveries will rely on flexible ecosystems that incorporate modern scientific instruments, high performance computing resources, parallel distributed data storage, and performant networks across multiple, independent facilities. In addition to connecting physical resources, such an ecosystem presents many challenges in logistics and accessibility, especially in orchestrating computations and experiments that span across leadership computing systems and experimental instruments. Past efforts have typically been application-specific or limited to interfaces for computing resources. This paper proposes a general framework for integrating computation resources and instrument operations, addressing challenges in code development/execution, data staging and collection, software stack, control mechanisms, resource authorization and governance, and hardware integration. We also describe a demonstration use case wherein a Bayesian optimization algorithm running on an edge computing resource guides a scanning probe microscope to autonomously and intelligently characterize a material sample. This science edge ecosystem framework will provide a blueprint for federating multi-institutional, disparate resources and orchestrating scientific workflows across them to enable next-generation discoveries.

1 Introduction

Recent advances in edge computing and networking, combined with autonomy empowered in part by artificial intelligence, promise a scientific discovery continuum that seamlessly spans across distributed computational resources and multi-modal, multi-domain experiments. A science ecosystem for such a continuum with tighter integration across computational resources and scientific experimental facilities requires both broad and deep knowledge of complex workflows and potential performance bottlenecks. Indeed, it requires a sound strategy to design, implement, test and deploy solutions that combine diverse aspects of computation, theory and experiments in a synergistic manner.

© Springer Nature Switzerland AG 2022
J. Nichols et al. (Eds.): SMC 2021, CCIS 1512, pp. 58–75, 2022.
https://doi.org/10.1007/978-3-030-96498-6_4

To understand the complex requirements of such an ecosystem, we outline science workflows executed by composing and automating complex scientific computations and experiments that support collaborations among researchers. These workflows enable scientists to remotely execute codes, collect measurements and steer experiments [8]. Department of Energy's (DOE) science workflows often require large computations executed as batch jobs at remote supercomputer facilities, such as Argonne Leadership Computing Facility (ALCF) and Oak Ridge Leadership Computing Facility (OLCF), and experiments conducted at science facilities such as the Advanced Photon Source (APS), Spallation Neutron Source (SNS) and Center for Nanophase Materials Sciences (CNMS).

The productivity of current workflows, however, continues to be impeded by the "stop-and-go" steps needed to utilize these geographically distributed resources. The current trend has been to mitigate these impediments by introducing or enhancing the computing capabilities at the instrument edge to: (i) locally execute smaller jobs that do not need remote supercomputers, and (ii) close the latency gap between computations and instruments in collecting measurements and steering experiments. These systems range from specialized edge AI computational systems (e.g., NVIDIA EGX-AI [3]), to multi-core, hybrid memory systems, to generic micro Data Centers (mDC) [23]. This development signals a paradigm shift from "flops provided at a distance" to "edge-core continuum computation" with enhanced diversity and heterogeneity of computing platforms. Furthermore, DOE facilities are spread within and across distant geographical sites, which adds to the challenge as campus-area and wide-area networks are now an integral part of the ecosystem. Indeed, computations that span heterogeneous, distributed computing platforms and experimental facilities require an effective science ecosystem (consisting of diverse hardware and software) to make them transparently available to scientists that use them and facility providers that federate them.

At Oak Ridge National Laboratory (ORNL), we are building a science ecosystem with a system-of-systems (SoS) architecture to enable "self-driven" experiments and smart laboratories for DOE future science discovery. This paper outlines this concerted effort in building this ecosystem, and describes example CNMS use-cases involving automated microscopy via edge computations.

This paper is organized as follows. We provide a brief outline of the past efforts in connecting science facilities in Sect. 2. We outline our vision for ORNL Science Edge ecosystem in Sect. 3. We describe the main resources in the ecosystem such as scientific instruments and computational resources in Sect. 4. An architecture and framework for our ecosystem is described in Sect. 5. Use cases using CNMS as an example are described in Sect. 6, followed by conclusions.

2   Background and Context: Connecting Science Facilities

In the past decade, ORNL and other laboratories have piloted workflows that connected experimental and computational facilities. In 2015 and 2016, several DOE laboratories have offered data-transfer and analysis related demonstrations at the Supercomputing Conference [6] to show the feasibility of connecting light sources and neutron sources to computing facilities. The DOE Experimental and Observational Science Data ("EOD") report on experimental and observational data [11] provided a rich background of requirements and opportunities to connect experimental and observational facilities. In recent years, the National Energy Research Scientific Computing Center (NERSC) Superfacility project [2], and the Swiss Supercomputer's FireCrest API [13] have focused on building APIs around a facility to enable easy access from a remote user or observational facility into a computational facility. Following suit, the Shanghai Synchrotron Facility has taken steps [40] towards setting up the linkage between its beamlines and an accompanying big data science center. There are a host of policy considerations that affect how to implement and deploy such end-to-end workflows that go from edge to Exascale [33]. In prior work we have shown that a data backplane [35] can provide the backdrop on which facilities can communicate. Cross-facility workflows from CNMS to computing resources have also enhanced the end-to-end campaign [25]. Initial work in defining a federated ecosystem also defined a federated software stack [27] that provides a software framework to interconnect a variety of computing and experimental resources. Advancing the central and important idea of integrated research infrastructures, DOE's Office of Science's (SC) Advanced Scientific Computing and Research (ASCR) office has been exploring and identifying the core components of a Distributed Computing and Data Ecosystem [32] and the underpinnings of an Integrated Research Infrastructure (IRI). The light source facilities supported by the Basic Energy Sciences (BES) office in DOE SC are similarly exploring how to establish an end-to-end pipeline that couples the light sources to computing and data facilities. The ever-increasing scales of experimental and observational data collections rely on such connections to computational and data facilities to enable rapid analysis and feedback to experimentalists.

Although past and ongoing work has established the benefits and feasibility of ecosystems spanning diverse research facilities, aside from API building efforts, the end-to-end pipelines continue to be developed independently in a bespoke manner by a few committed individuals. The API design and development efforts take a first necessary step at a scope of a facility interface. However, the ability to flexibly compose an ecosystem of instruments, edges, data resources, network components, and computing resources so that they can be dynamically instantiated and co-scheduled, remains an unrealized goal. Our work here provides the next step by identifying the components of an ecosystem for science discovery over the edge-to-exascale continuum and presents an early use case at CNMS. The use case scenario focuses on the instrument-to-edge interface, as well as the upcoming broader edge-to-exascale interface.

3   Overview of the ORNL Federated Science Edge Ecosystem

The ORNL ecosystem will enable workflows that couple experiments, computation, and data analytics to automate experiments on microscopes at the CNMS, beamline data analysis at SNS, phenotyping studies at the Advanced Plant Phenotyping Laboratory (APPL), and dynamic monitoring and steering of additive manufacturing at the Manufacturing Demonstration Facility (MDF). The design pattern that unites these end-to-end workflows is a set of composable architectural elements that provide instrument-to-edge connectivity, edge-to-ecosystem plug-ins that ultimately connect to exascale computing through scalable computational and storage resources.

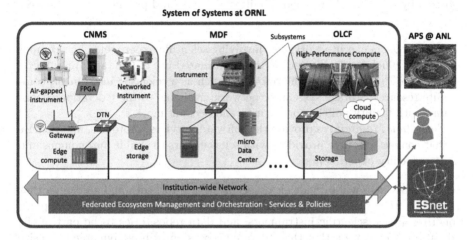

Fig. 1. Overview of the interconnected ecosystem consisting of scientific instruments, high-performance and edge computing resources, edge and central data storage resources, local area and wide area networks, and the ecosystem software that enables cross-facility and automated experiments.

Figure 1 provides an overarching view of the ecosystem with various distributed components that will collectively enable cross-facility and semi-autonomous or autonomous experiments. For our ecosystem, we define a system-of-systems (SoS) as a collection of component systems that are operated and managed independently to fulfill their own purpose [26]. This definition provides a simple framework that allows independent development and/or acquisition of systems. Such an approach will enable rapid integration of new systems through well defined inter-system interfaces, be capable of interfacing with systems beyond ORNL, while providing significant flexibility for the intra-system architecture.

Our ecosystem will build on existing capabilities at CNMS, SNS, APPL and MDF (facilities are represented as systems in Fig. 1), existing networking, existing resource provisioning and management infrastructure and connect these to the next-generation OLCF, which is expected to have significant AI computational and data storage capabilities. We will strategically deploy a continuum of edge computing and storage hardware in proximity to the scientific instruments to suit the requirements of each scientific application. These existing and upcoming heterogeneous hardware components will be interconnected and federated via a collection of standardized and transparent services (communication, coordination, and orchestration), protocols and policies to enable autonomous and semi-autonomous capabilities for a wide range of applications including electron microscopy, neutron imaging, 3D printing and the electric grid. This being said, this federated ecosystem should enable cross-facility and autonomous experiments without impeding the use of these resources for traditional or other use-cases. The main components in the federated ecosystem can broadly be categorized by roles based on responsibilities for using and providing the resources [27]:

- *Science Users* execute workflows involving scientific experiments and computations, which are facilitated by the coordinated use of federated resources.
- *Resource Providers* make the resources, such as a scientific instrument, compute resource, storage system, or network, available to the federation consistent with facility policies for security and accounting.
- *Federation Maintainers* provide the software, services, protocols, and policies that connect resource providers with science users to enable autonomous and cross-facility experiments.

The ecosystem will provide clear specification, protocols, and guidelines that will allow other facilities, within and beyond ORNL to opt in their computational resources, scientific instruments, and data repositories to be part of the federation. We envision that this federated ecosystem will be dynamic in its size and membership with partners joining and leaving the federation.

The subsequent sections of this article will be organized along the two primary roles in the federation - Resource Providers and Federation Maintainers, to provide a comprehensive view of and the challenges in building such a federated ecosystem.

4   Resources

This section describes the primary components that will make up the federated ecosystem such as the scientific instruments, high performance computing and storage resources, edge computing and storage resources, and network.

4.1   Instrument Interfaces

To fully realize the future scientific ecosystem, we need to support automated and integrated instrument access. For scientific instruments, or generally any resource, to become part of the (opt-in) ecosystem, they would need to implement standardized software interfaces that bridge the custom nature of the resource with the rest of the federation. Each resource would need to implement and run a persistent process that communicates with the federation's resource management to make the resource discoverable and publish the current state and performance of the resource. Resources would provide standardized interfaces to any existing provisioning or scheduling mechanisms and policies that provide access to the resource. An open-source resource provisioning system and workload manager, such as Slurm, may be deployed onto resources in the absence of such provisioning mechanisms. The federation would also need application interfaces and networking protocols for granular control of crucial components in instruments (e.g. motors and sensors), monitoring of status variables and signals, and transmitting data from detectors. We will use proven and open-source control toolkits for distributed control systems of scientific instruments such as Experimental Physics and Industrial Control System (EPICS) [1] or BlueSky [9] wherever possible and already in use, such as in custom-made experimental facilities like accelerators and telescopes. Such fine-grained access and control of instruments is expected to be a challenge for commercial scientific instruments, for example microscopes or 3D printers, which typically limit access and control via proprietary or ad-hoc software and hardware interfaces, obfuscate access to data streams, and write data into proprietary file formats. In such cases, adapter software will be written to interface the instrument with the rest of the ecosystem.

Virtual Design and Test Environment. Assessing the design options of the ecosystem as well as the development and testing of its software would require allocations of significant resources and coordination among the sites. It is impractical and ineffective, particularly during early development, to carry out these tasks over production facilities due to the expense and potential for disruptions and damage. We will explore the use of digital twins that replicate the ecosystem by emulating its hosts, networks and instrument systems to design the ecosystem designs and software stack [31].

4.2   Compute

Computational resources, whether at the scientific edge locations or the supercomputing center, will be organized to provide a continuum of resources for various levels of data access, control latency, and computational power. As an example, we envision that FPGAs will augment scientific experiments to drive and enhance detectors and sensors, providing a very-low-latency control and feedback loop. Microcontrollers or small scale computers can accelerate data acquisition from instruments. AI computing systems, such as NVIDIA DGX systems [3], are being deployed at several ORNL edge locations to improve GPU-intensive near-real-time analysis and AI-driven experiment steering. mDCs are being explored as alternate edge compute resources. Further away from the edges, institutional computing resources such as the Compute and Data Environment for Science (CADES) with ubiquitous resources are the succeeding link in the chain of increased computational capabilities. Finally, the large-scale supercomputers, such as Summit and Frontier at OLCF, will provide the computational power needed for processing the experimental data, training large AI models, or running large-scale first-principle simulations to guide or validate measurements. All these computing resources, like the experimental resources, will be made available through the federation's resource management system.

4.3 Storage

Like the compute capability, the storage will be distributed and hierarchically organized to support the data access latency, throughput, and capacity requirements. Edge compute systems, such as the NVIDIA DGX systems [3] will be equipped with multiple fast non-volatile memory express (NVMe) storage drives in RAID configuration to support very-low latency and high-throughput applications such as training deep learning models, near-real-time data analysis and AI applications that steer autonomous experiments. Spectra Logic BlackPearl systems [5] with petabyte-scale storage capacities will be coupled with these DGX systems for hosting databases, longer-term storage of raw measurement data, subsequent analysis products, machine learning models, and telemetry data from instruments at the individual facility level. Note that the federation will not preclude or limit other facilities from using each other's DGX or BlackPearl systems. On the other end of the spectrum, CADES and OLCF will provide storage systems on the orders of multi-hundred petabytes to low exabytes but entail higher access latency. Future plans include evaluating other storage technologies and augmenting the edge locations with more capable storage systems, perhaps providing direct data processing capabilities on the storage systems themselves, such as Fungible DPU storage devices [7]. The federation's scientific data management system, described in Sect. 5.6, will logically unify these distributed data repositories in to a cohesive and user-friendly data ecosystem.

4.4 Network

The network will also be distributed and composed of multiple local-area and campus-area segments in different security zones. These subnets will be connected to each other via Data Transfer Nodes (DTNs) to form a science DMZ [14]. One particular challenge is to build seamless network transport mechanisms to provide correct authentication and authorization controls over these various zones and firewalls. Another challenge is integrating devices or instruments that are intentionally air-gapped into our ecosystem. We have reported earlier on "Data Gateway" devices that provide secure data transfer and ingest capabilities via performant transport mechanisms (e.g., Globus) for bulk data [35]. We will develop a more generic networking bridge system to provide necessary control and data interfaces between the air-gapped instruments and the rest of the ecosystem without introducing significant communication latency or overriding security protocols. Though initial use-cases are within ORNL, we plan on leveraging ESNet [24] to facilitate efficient multi-institutional and autonomous workflows as shown in Fig. 1.

5   Federation Services and Policies

Seamlessly coordinating, orchestrating, and scheduling compute resources across a federated ecosystem, especially on-demand, is anticipated to be a significant challenge to support the scientific experiments. This section describes the control and data planes that will be developed and deployed to connect all the aforementioned resources into an interconnected ecosystem (Fig. 2).

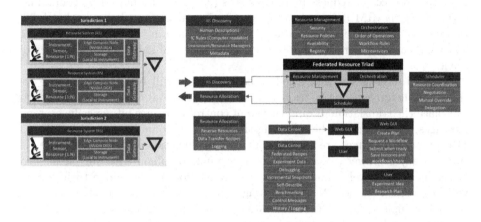

Fig. 2. Architectural overview of the software services and policies that enable the federated science ecosystem

5.1   Resource Management

The Resource Manager (RM) will be one of the most important services in the federation crucial for enabling workflows to run across facilities. The RM will be responsible for discovering, managing, and making available the federation of heterogeneous and distributed resources, via a standardized interface. The RM would also continuously update the status of individual resources by listening to "heartbeat" messages that indicate instantaneous availability and performance metrics. When it does not hear from resources, the RM will mark resources as unavailable, and alert the user or automatically provision alternate resources to ensure the proper functioning of any running experiments. Crucially, the RM will also provide workflows a standardized interface to provisioning or reserving resources by managing the heterogeneity in the types of resources (computational, experimental, data repository, etc.) and existing provisioning, authentication, authorization mechanisms and policies associated with each resource. Furthermore, the RM would also be capable of elastically provisioning additional resources, as needed, during a running workflow. Since it serves as an interface to the resource's provisioning and identity management services, the RM would also hide or display resources depending on whether the current user has access to the underlying resource.

5.2   Command and Control

Per experiment, the federation would spawn a central controller process (CCP) that communicates with and orchestrates actions via similar resource controller processes (RCP) running on each resource. These RCPs would also set up and configure all necessary daemons including data streaming daemons on the appropriate resources. The CCP will be configurable with logic and policies that will enable it to make autonomous decisions. For example, the CCP could decide to swap resources or request more resources (e.g. compute nodes) by communicating with the RM if the performance of a resource drops below a threshold in order to maintain a minimum level of performance in the running workflow. The CCP can also alert the end user if it is incapable of handling an unexpected event.

Control messages within a federated ecosystem will be challenging due to the highly heterogeneous instruments and computational resources. In an effort to isolate the translation of our ecosystem control messages into specific system messages, we will create the following three types of common control messages: 1) *Command* messages are used to control a single action within a system (e.g., turn on, adjust power). As most systems are not compliant with our messaging layer, these low level commands require translation and a bridge to interface with a specific resource. 2) *Task* messages are the first level of control abstraction for a single system; a task is created and assigned without the user needing to know or understand the lower level commands and subsequent system translations necessary to accomplish the task. 3) *Objective* messages allow the user to create broad goals without needing to know which specific systems are necessary to accomplish the goals. By providing these three different levels of control messages, the complex issue of interfacing with heterogeneous systems is isolated to the translation of our ecosystem command messages into the specific system messages.

5.3   Workflows

Autonomous or semi-autonomous experiments spanning multiple heterogeneous resources and policy zones will necessitate complex workflows. At a minimum, workflows in the federation will need to be capable of dynamic steering, managing distributed and heterogeneous resources. Significant efforts will be required to simplify the process of composing and executing such complex workflows via user-friendly graphical user interfaces (GUIs) and application programming interfaces (APIs) such that they are accessible to the average end user. The current paradigm of specifying tuples of computational application and computational resource may need to be replaced by a larger or more abstract tuple that expresses the requirements from the resource (e.g. computational architecture, required software stack, latency or time to solution, constraints, contingency plans or redundancy strategy/policy). This may provide the CCP and RM with the ability to swap comparable resources or even scale resources intelligently.

Some of the challenges that will need to be addressed are: 1) exception handling and graceful maintenance workflow's progress; 2) declarative specification of control and data flows; 3) declarative policies on authentication, resource allocation, usage, and data storage; 4) automatic scheduling, orchestration, and monitoring of workflows across federated resources; 5) alert system for human involvement, including workflow creator and resource administrator; and 6) auditability of the computations and data used for decisions that impact safety and physical scientific instruments.

Several workflows such as Pegasus [15], Fireworks [21], and Swift/T [43] have been used for relatively complex and dynamic workflows in the past. We will evaluate these workflows based on aforementioned requirements to decide the most appropriate options to adopt or adapt.

Resiliency. Resiliency of the workflows in the federation will be a major consideration to avoid potential damage to sensitive samples or the scientific instrument itself and to ensure that time sensitive phenomena are studied with the necessary temporal resolution. Several strategies could be taken to improve resiliency including: 1) requesting extra or alternate resources, 2) running identical critical computations on multiple resources, 3) caching any necessary (potentially large) data in close proximity to compute resources, 4) allowing for dynamic adjustment of compression rates when streaming data, 5) policies to guide the CCP to act autonomously, and 6) policies that prioritize the order in transfer of various data streams or files. Such resiliency strategies could be incorporated into the composition of the workflows.

5.4   Dashboard

We plan on developing a dashboard that can serve as the primary entry point to the federated ecosystem and provides all necessary capabilities to configure, launch, and monitor cross-facility experiments. This dashboard would display: 1) all available resources that the scientist is eligible to use; 2) the current state and expected availability of the resources; 3) all available digital twins, surrogate models, data analytics modules, visualization modules, and decision making algorithms; and 4) workflows associated with a given resource. Upon discovering the available tools, the user would be able to construct a workflow either graphically or using scripts on the dashboard. Upon launching a cross-facility workflow, the dashboard would be highly configurable to allow users to add or remove different widgets to monitor the instantaneous state and progress of the experiment. Similar to the workflows' inherent logging capabilities, the dashboard would also log its own user-defined configuration, along with the provenance of all data streams that provide data for a monitoring widget on the dashboard. We expect that the dashboard to the federation would be deployed as a web application given their sheer ubiquity and versatility. We are exploring candidates such as eSimMon [18].

5.5   Data Movement

The federated ecosystem will also need to efficiently and transparently move information between resources and users and at multiple timescales and priorities. The ecosystem will be supported by three classes of messaging and data movement planes:

Streaming Data: During experiments, there is a need to transfer a stream of small, but often rapidly generated, packets of data between heterogeneous resources, often with minimal latency. For example, real-time measurement data generated at a detector in an instrument might need to be streamed to data experiment steering algorithms running on edge compute resources. This data may eventually be accumulated and archived or discarded after its use. Consumers and producers of information can be configured to listen to specific activities or messages to trigger responsive actions for workflows. Given that experiments may have data from multiple simultaneous data producers and consumers flowing at different rates, the "publish/subscribe" messaging model is most ideal for such streaming data needs. We will evaluate several proven solutions such as ADIOS [30], MQTT [10], Apache Kafka [17], RabbitMQ [19], and adapt a candidate for use in the federation.

Command and Control Messages: Similar to streaming data, there is also a need to transmit important orchestration, status, and coordination messages across the federation. Example message types and uses cases include resource allocation, resource discovery such as instruments, schema negotiation, and instructions to start or stop measurements. These messages are expected to be much smaller in volume and quantity compared to the streaming data messages. However, unlike streaming data, it is absolutely critical that command and control messages be transmitted reliably and in a timely fashion. Though these messages could also be transmitted using the same technology or even the same logical pipes as the streaming data, guarantees regarding the reliability and timeliness of the data transmission will need to be established.

Bulk Data: Between experiments, there is a need to transport unprecedented volumes of bulk data across the federation swiftly and reliably. Examples of such data include accumulated raw measurement or simulation data from a recently completed experiment, training data for a digital twin, configuration for a machine learning model, and telemetry data of resources. Among the several existing protocols such as the (secure) file transport protocol (SFTP), and gridFTP, we plan on using Globus [28] (based on gridFTP) as the foundational technology to move bulk data within and beyond the federation due to its widespread availability, reliability, and high throughput.

5.6 Data Management

Given that (bulk) data would be stored at multiple locations with different underlying infrastructure, performance capabilities, access and retention policies as shown in Fig. 1, the ecosystem will need a scientific data management system (SDMS) to federate such data into a single, cohesive environment. The SDMS will need to allow facilities interested in being part of this ecosystem to opt in their data repositories seamlessly. These data will need to be accessible in a consistent and user-friendly manner, abstracting the underlying technologies and policies, via GUIs and APIs. Given the complexity of future scientific endeavors, the SDMS would need to enable geographically distributed and multi-disciplinary teams of experts in simulations, data analytics, instrument control, and mathematics to collaborate with data. We also expect the need to easily locate and collate data from multiple sources (e.g. simulations, experimental data from different instruments, and published data) and effortlessly combine and interoperate such data towards goals, such as the developing a digital twin. In other words, the federation will need data to comply with the Findable, Accessible, Interoperable, and Reusable (FAIR) data principles [42]. Futhermore, there is a need to capture rich context for data to unambiguously trace the provenance, quality, and applicability of data to tasks such as developing digital twins. We are evaluating several available SDMS such as iRODS [20], Rucio [12], and DataFed [35] against the aforementioned requirements.

5.7 Identity Management

Given that the ecosystem will federate resources managed by multiple facilities with differing cybersecurity policies, there is a need for a federated identity management system [34]. Federated identity in information technology is a means of linking a user's electronic identity across multiple separate identity management systems that have agreed to a common set of policies, practices, and protocols. Supporting ease of access relies on the techno-policy challenge of supporting seamless identity management (IdM) without requiring a user or a software component to register with a multifactor authentication provider. Well known as an outstanding problem in federating and distributing campaigns across multiple facilities, creating a decentralized trust structure is a key aspect of our ecosystem architecture. Our approach is to rely on DOE's OneID [4,32] federation to provide a trustworthy broker for trusting identity providers from each facility. The authorization framework is a policy and governance decision that is overlaid on the IdM structure. We plan on enabling such identity management for both web based and SSH based access of resources.

5.8 Policy and Governance

While resource allocation and cost policies for centralized compute and storage systems is a reasonably solved problem, cross-facility workflows over distributed and heterogeneous resources requires novel policies and a unique approach to governance. The distributed nature of ownership of the resources in the federation will need to be taken into account when developing policies and governance for the ecosystem. HPC facilities will need to develop new policies that will accommodate elastic provisioning of resources, preempting of running jobs to accommodate a cross-facility workflow, as well as cost models for both charging these cross-facility workflows as well as compensation for disrupting other computational jobs [33,41]. Similar to computational considerations, data acquisition, movement, and access across federated storage requires new approaches to stewardship and governance. Clearly, technical and administrative solutions to these challenges will be required prior to operationalization of the federated ecosystem.

6   Use Case: Autonomous Microscopy at CNMS

Extracting rich quantitative physical knowledge instead of low-level signals, automatically tuning and speeding up measurements while minimizing sample damage, fabricating designer materials atom-by-atom are just some of the many grand challenges in nanotechnology and material sciences; however, such efforts undoubtedly require a large degree of fast, intelligent control and automation. Automation is critical in two regimes where edge-compute capabilities combined with AI methodologies can offer tremendous leverage. The first is the extremely rapid measurement, feedback, and control of processes, which can be on the order of μs to ms, that far exceed the speed at which a human operator can react. The second is in the very large data regime within very large experimental parameter space where a single measurement is performed, which can be gigabytes (GB) in size. Here, information needs to be processed, compared with previous sets of data, and analyzed to provide informed guidance on how best to perform the next measurements, whether it be through adjustment of experimental parameters, deciding a new location on a sample to perform a measurement, or adjusting excitation signal to create a desired outcome (e.g., in the case of atomic fabrication). Notably, automating these processes is also critical for the eventual scalability of these enterprises.

6.1   Scanning Probe Microscopy

Automating experiments can also improve efficiency and minimize the time to scientific discovery. As an example, consider the acquisition of hysteresis loops on a ferroelectric sample, as shown in Fig. 3. Each sample pixel is associated with a spectra (hysteresis loop, shown in the yellow box), that takes several seconds to acquire. Sampling densely across a grid of points is generally wasteful because spatial correlations exist that can be exploited to improve the sampling efficiency. CNMS recently demonstrated [37] one solution to this problem where a surrogate model was trained on sparse observations and then used to formulate this challenge as a Bayesian optimization (BO) problem. The BO determined the next best location to sample to maximize a target metric, in this case, the area

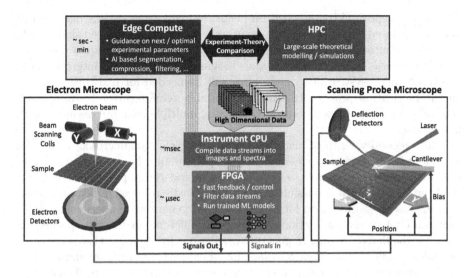

Fig. 3. Schematic depiction of edge and high-performance computing connected to multiple kinds of microscopes to enable automated experiments.

within hysteresis loops which is associated with energy storage in the material. The list of next measurement locations was then passed back to the instrument and the process repeated until a stopping criterion was reached. Given that the training of the surrogate model is computationally expensive, this was done on an edge compute device with GPUs. The measurement speed improved by roughly a factor of 2 given that several *ad-hoc* approaches were necessary for this automated experiment. For example, given that the instrument computer was airgapped, data was transmitted between the instrument and the edge compute device via a laptop on the network. However, the measurement speed could be sped up by a factor of 10 if our ecosystem was deployed instead.

6.2 Electron Microscopy

The automation of spectroscopy is also applicable to the sphere of electron microscopy. Common imaging modalities that could benefit from automation and adaptive sampling methods include techniques such as electron energy loss spectroscopy (EELS) [16] and convergent beam electron diffraction [36] on a scanning transmission electron microscopy (sometimes referred to as "4D STEM" [29]).

Besides minimizing measurement time, the combination of aforementioned automation with intelligent sampling or other methods such as compressed sensing has an added benefit of reducing the duration for which the sample is exposed to the (potentially harmful) electron beam, which in-turn reduces damage to sensitive samples. Reduced damage to sample naturally results in more interpretable spectral and structural information with higher information content.

The energy deposited by the electron beam that can cause sample damage can also be employed as a tool to fabricate or sculpt matter into desired shapes [22]. Methods to automate such process are necessary if these techniques are to be scaled to create larger structures and designer materials. The interconnected and modular ecosystem described above will be needed for real-time feedback on the fabrication process, training and running reinforcement learning models, and crafting complex workflows connecting multiple compute resources with microscopes.

More generally, for most materials imaging with electron microscopy, the goal is to identify the atomic species or structures present and then compare the structure with theoretical models so as to derive the underlying physics. Recently, it has been shown that it is possible to utilize atomically resolved images from electron microscopes directly to form physics-based generative models using HPCs that can explain the interactions between the different constituent species and then use the derived model to generate predictions for different thermodynamic variables [38, 39]; however, such connection of experiments with simulations currently takes place over the span of several months and is performed manually. The interconnected ecosystem described above is expected to enable scientists to co-schedule time on the instrument and HPC, construct a workflow that spans multiple facilities, establish data pipelines to stream experimental data to the HPC, perform and tune the necessary simulations on the HPC, and finally present physical models of the sample under the microscope to the user in near-real-time.

Combining the simulations with the instrument via the interconnected ecosystem, so as to "steer" the microscope towards acquiring data in the regions that have a higher likelihood of confirming or denying the specific hypothesis, can present a significant advance with benefits in terms of scientific productivity as well as enabling scientific discoveries that might not have been practical or possible. This approach will move the control of instruments away from simply maximizing information (in the strict theoretic sense), to maximize physical knowledge acquired, which is associated with confirming or refuting specific hypotheses. Regardless, in all cases there is a need to perform real-time image segmentation, determine the types of atoms and defects present, track them through time, analyze local crystallographic orientations and distortions, and compare the acquired statistics with those of models, all preferably in real-time. Accomplishing this requires the interconnected ecosystem, and will undoubtedly accelerate automation in microscopy and possibly lead to a dramatic change in the way materials science is conducted.

7   Conclusions

This paper describes our federated science ecosystem framework for integrating computational, experimental, and data resources that will facilitate a class of cross-facility, autonomous, and hitherto impossible experiments that can significantly accelerate scientific discovery. This federation will be realized through a transparent and standardized software stack for monitoring, controlling, and managing resources, moving and managing data, communicating between heterogeneous resources, identity management, workflows, dashboards, and corresponding policies and governance. We describe a recent use case wherein a scanning probe microscope was autonomously guided by Bayesian optimization algorithms running on edge computing resources. Aside from recent efforts to build APIs, especially for computational facilities, the ability to compose a flexible ecosystem of instruments, compute and data resources, and network components that can be dynamically co-scheduled and optimized, still remains open. This paper describes progress towards realizing this goal. Overall, our work will provide a blueprint for connecting multi-institutional computing and experimental systems, and orchestrating scientific workflows across them to enable next-generation science discoveries.

Acknowledgments. This research used resources of the Oak Ridge Leadership Computing Facility (OLCF) and Compute and Data Environment for Science (CADES) at the Oak Ridge National Laboratory (ORNL), and also supported by Robust Analytic Models for Science at Extreme Scales (RAMSES) project, all supported by the Office of Science of the U.S. Department of Energy under Contract No. DE-AC05-00OR22725. It is also supported by Laboratory Directed Research and Development (LDRD) project at ORNL. A portion of this work was conducted at and supported (RKV, SJ, SVK) by the Center for Nanophase Materials Sciences, ORNL, a US DOE Office of Science User Facility.

References

1. Experimental physics and industrial control system. epics.anl.gov
2. NERSC Superfacility. https://www.nersc.gov/research-and-development/superfacility/
3. NVIDIA DGX Systems for Enterprise AI
4. OneID: modernizing digital identities. https://computing.llnl.gov/newsroom/oneid-modernizing-digital-identities
5. Spectra logic BlackPearl models
6. Supercomputing 2016 Data Transfer Demonstrations
7. Best DPU platform 2021 (2021)
8. Workshop on Autonomous Discovery in Science and Engineering Report (2021)
9. Allan, D., Caswell, T., Campbell, S., Rakitin, M.: Bluesky's ahead: a multi-facility collaboration for an a la carte software project for data acquisition and management. Synchrotron Radiat. News **32**(3), 19–22 (2019)
10. Banks, A., Briggs, E., Borgendale, K., Gupta, R.: MQTT version 5.0 (2019). https://mqtt.org/mqtt-specification/. Accessed 26 May 2021
11. Bethel, E.W., Greenwald, M. (eds.): Report of the doe workshop on management, analysis, and visualization of experimental and observational data - the convergence of data and computing, May 2016
12. CERN. Rucio scientific data management (2021). https://rucio.cern.ch. Accessed 26 May 2021
13. Cruz, F.A., Martinasso, M.: FirecREST: RESTful API on Cray XC systems. CoRR, abs/1911.13160 (2019)

14. Dart, E., Rotman, L., Tierney, B., Hester, M., Zurawski, J.: The science DMZ: a network design pattern for data-intensive science. Sci. Program. **22**(2), 173–185 (2014)
15. Deelman, E., et al.: Pegasus: a workflow management system for science automation. Future Gener. Comput. Syst. **46**, 17–35 (2015)
16. Egerton, R.F.: Electron Energy-Loss Spectroscopy in the Electron Microscope. Springer, Boston (2011). https://doi.org/10.1007/978-1-4419-9583-4
17. Apache Software Foundation. Kafka protocol guide (2017). https://kafka.apache.org/protocol. Accessed 26 May 2021
18. Galbreath, Z., Major, B., Harris, C.: eSimMon, February 2019
19. VMWare Inc., RabbitMQ (2021). https://www.rabbitmq.com. Accessed 26 May 2021
20. iRODS Consortium. Open source data management software (2021). https://irods.org. Accessed 26 May 2021
21. Jain, A., et al.: Fireworks: a dynamic workflow system designed for high-throughput applications. Concurr. Comput.: Pract. Exp. **27**(17), 5037–5059 (2015)
22. Jesse, S., et al.: Atomic-level sculpting of crystalline oxides: toward bulk nanofabrication with single atomic plane precision. Small **11**(44), 5895–5900 (2015)
23. Lee, W., Kim, S., Kim, T., Kim, H.: Micro-datacenter management architecture for mobile wellness information. In: 2014 International Conference on IT Convergence and Security (ICITCS), pp. 1–4 (2014)
24. Leighton, J.F. ESnet: the energy sciences network (1996)
25. Lingerfelt, E.J., et al.: BEAM: a computational workflow system for managing and modeling material characterization data in HPC environments. Proc. Comput. Sci. **80**, 2276–2280 (2016). In: International Conference on Computational Science 2016, ICCS 2016, 6–8 June 2016, San Diego, California, USA
26. Maier, M.W.: Architecting principles for systems-of-systems. Syst. Eng.: J. Int. Counc. Syst. Eng. **1**(4), 267–284 (1998)
27. Naughton, T., et al.: Software framework for federated science instruments. In: Nichols, J., Verastegui, B., Maccabe, A.B., Hernandez, O., Parete-Koon, S., Ahearn, T. (eds.) SMC 2020. CCIS, vol. 1315, pp. 189–203. Springer, Cham (2020). https://doi.org/10.1007/978-3-030-63393-6_13
28. University of Chicago. Globus (2021). https://docs.globus.org. Accessed 26 May 2021
29. Ophus, C., Ercius, P., Sarahan, M., Czarnik, C., Ciston, J.: Recording and using 4D-stem datasets in materials science. Microsc. Microanal. **20**(S3), 62–63 (2014)
30. Podhorszki, N., et al.: The adaptable IO system (ADIOS) (2021). https://www.olcf.ornl.gov/center-projects/adios/. Accessed 26 May 2021
31. Rao, N.S.V., Al Najjar, A., Foster, I., Kettimuthu, R., Liu, Z.: Virtual framework for science federations with instruments access and control. In: Workshop on Autonomous Discovery in Science and Engineering report (2021)
32. Shankar, M., Lancon, E.: Background and roadmap for a distributed computing and data ecosystem (2019)
33. Shankar, M., Somnath, S., Alam, S., Feichtinger, D., Sala, L., Wells, J.: Policy Considerations When Federating Facilities for Experimental and Observational Data Analysis (chap. 18), pp. 387–409. World Scientific (2020)
34. Shim, S.S.Y., Bhalla, G., Pendyala, V.: Federated identity management. Computer **38**(12), 120–122 (2005)

35. Stansberry, D., Somnath, S., Shutt, G., Shankar, M.: A systemic approach to facilitating reproducibility via federated, end-to-end data management. In: Nichols, J., Verastegui, B., Maccabe, A.B., Hernandez, O., Parete-Koon, S., Ahearn, T. (eds.) SMC 2020. CCIS, vol. 1315, pp. 83–98. Springer, Cham (2020). https://doi.org/10.1007/978-3-030-63393-6_6

36. Steeds J.W.: Convergent beam electron diffraction. In: Hren, J.J., Goldstein, J.I., Joy, D.C. (eds.) Introduction to Analytical Electron Microscopy, pp. 387–422. Springer, Boston (1979). https://doi.org/10.1007/978-1-4757-5581-7_15

37. Vasudevan, R.K., et al.: Autonomous experiments in scanning probe microscopy and spectroscopy: choosing where to explore polarization dynamics in ferroelectrics. ACS Nano **15**(7), 11253–11262 (2021)

38. Vlcek, L., Maksov, A., Pan, M., Vasudevan, R.K., Kalinin, S.V.: Knowledge extraction from atomically resolved images. ACS Nano **11**(10), 10313–10320 (2017)

39. Vlcek, L., et al.: Thermodynamics of order and randomness in dopant distributions inferred from atomically resolved imaging. NPJ Comput. Mater. **7**(1), 1–9 (2021)

40. Wang, C., et al.: Deploying the big data science center at the shanghai synchrotron radiation facility: the first superfacility platform in China. Mach. Learn.: Sci. Technol. **2**(3), 035003 (2021)

41. Wang, D., Jung, E.-S., Kettimuthu, R., Foster, I., Foran, D.J., Parashar, M.: Supporting real-time jobs on the IBM Blue Gene/Q: simulation-based study. In: Klusáček, D., Cirne, W., Desai, N. (eds.) JSSPP 2017. LNCS, vol. 10773, pp. 83–102. Springer, Cham (2018). https://doi.org/10.1007/978-3-319-77398-8_5

42. Wilkinson, M.D., et al.: Addendum: the FAIR guiding principles for scientific data management and stewardship. Sci. Data **6**, 6 (2019)

43. Wozniak, J.M., Armstrong, T.G., Wilde, M., Katz, D.S., Lusk, E., Foster, I.T.: Swift/T: large-scale application composition via distributed-memory dataflow processing. In 2013 13th IEEE/ACM International Symposium on Cluster, Cloud, and Grid Computing, pp. 95–102. IEEE (2013)

Advanced Computing Applications: Use Cases that Combine Multiple Aspects of Data and Modeling

Fast and Accurate Predictions of Total Energy for Solid Solution Alloys with Graph Convolutional Neural Networks

Massimiliano Lupo Pasini[1]([✉]), Marko Burčul[2], Samuel Temple Reeve[1], Markus Eisenbach[3], and Simona Perotto[4]

[1] Computational Sciences and Engineering Division, Oak Ridge National Laboratory, Oak Ridge, TN 37831, USA
`lupopasinim@ornl.gov`
[2] Department of Automation and Control Engineering, Politecnico di Milano, 20133 Milan, Italy
[3] National Center for Computational Sciences, Oak Ridge National Laboratory, Oak Ridge, TN 37831, USA
[4] Department of Mathematics, Politecnico di Milano, 20133 Milan, Italy

Abstract. We use graph convolutional neural networks (GCNNs) to produce fast and accurate predictions of the total energy of solid solution binary alloys. GCNNs allow us to abstract the lattice structure of a solid material as a graph, whereby atoms are modeled as nodes and metallic bonds as edges. This representation naturally incorporates information about the structure of the material, thereby eliminating the need for computationally expensive data pre-processing which would be required with standard neural network (NN) approaches. We train GCNNs on ab-initio density functional theory (DFT) for copper-gold (CuAu) and iron-platinum (FePt) data that has been generated by running the LSMS-3 code, which implements a locally self-consistent multiple scattering method, on OLCF supercomputers Titan and Summit. GCNN outperforms the ab-initio DFT simulation by orders of magnitude in terms of computational time to produce the estimate of the total energy for a given atomic configuration of the lattice structure. We compare the predictive performance of GCNN models against a standard NN such as dense feedforward multi-layer perceptron (MLP) by using the root-mean-squared errors to quantify the predictive quality of the deep learning (DL) models. We find that the attainable accuracy of GCNNs is at least an order of magnitude better than that of the MLP.

This manuscript has been authored in part by UT-Battelle, LLC, under contract DE-AC05-00OR22725 with the US Department of Energy (DOE). The US government retains and the publisher, by accepting the article for publication, acknowledges that the US government retains a nonexclusive, paid-up, irrevocable, worldwide license to publish or reproduce the published form of this manuscript, or allow others to do so, for US government purposes. DOE will provide public access to these results of federally sponsored research in accordance with the DOE Public Access Plan (http://energy.gov/downloads/doe-public-access-plan).

© Springer Nature Switzerland AG 2022
J. Nichols et al. (Eds.): SMC 2021, CCIS 1512, pp. 79–98, 2022.
https://doi.org/10.1007/978-3-030-96498-6_5

1   Introduction

Understanding and predicting the properties of materials with different atomic structures is critical for improved application performance and new technologies. There are of course many features that control material properties beyond the atomic level, from the mesoscale to macroscale. However, due to the combinatorial complexity of elements, crystal structures, and atomic disorder [1–3], there are still significant opportunities in materials discovery from information at the atomic scale. While many computational approaches have been developed to accurately model and predict the behavior of materials at the atomic scale from the electronic structure, including density functional theory (DFT) [4,5], quantum Monte Carlo (QMC) [6,7], and *ab-initio* molecular dynamics (MD) [8,9], these techniques come with very high computational cost, even for relatively small numbers of atoms and/or small timescales [10]. To alleviate this cost, several techniques have been developed ranging from direct approximations of electronic structures methods to empirical models, which trade predictive accuracy for computational effort. For example, cluster expansion builds the total energy as a linear combination of contributions from interactions of different atom clusters, with input from smaller direct electronic structure calculations [11–13]. Classical MD starts from a larger scale approximation which ignores electrons entirely and fits an interatomic interaction model with DFT, or other quantum simulation algorithms [14,15]. These models use empirical functional forms to represent bonding or approximate electronic effects. Quite importantly, MD is orders of magnitude faster than DFT for most atomic systems; however, MD models are difficult to develop even for a small number of elements and generally are not transferable from the dataset on which they were trained.

In spite of these issues, MD interatomic models built from DFT are widely used as surrogate models that do not require training from data. The one to one mapping between the high and low fidelity systems is a strength of the approach. Indeed, rather than a generic fitting procedure for the surrogate model parameters matching various output quantities of interest, forces and energies on each atom in each system can be used to train the MD model to match DFT. This force matching approach represents a significant advance for the field [16] and is now standard for training MD models, particularly as the increasing size of the systems modeled leads to more complex, multi-dimensional optimizations.

As the power of data-driven and machine learning (ML) approaches in science continues to grow, ML surrogate models can also provide significant benefits. Neural networks (NN) are attractive as a general mathematical form which include non-linear interactions and, once trained, can be orders of magnitude faster than full physics simulations. There are many examples of NN surrogates for electronic structure calculations [17–21], as well as classical MD models [22–25]. This has advanced classical MD significantly beyond the original empirical models. Critical features of these approaches include high accuracy (particularly when resolving atomic dynamics) and preservation of translational and rotational invariances.

However, complex NNs require significant effort to translate the atomic structure dataset into a form understood by the DL model. This data pre-processing inevitably leads to some loss of information originally contained in the raw DFT simulations and also requires additional effort to be performed.

The DL community has recently developed graph convolutional neural networks (GCNNs) [26,27] which directly map the atomic input to graph structures, with atoms as graph nodes and chemical bonds as edges. This direct connection between the high-fidelity training data and the surrogate model is compelling as a DL equivalent of classical MD models. GCNNs not only reduce the cumbersome and expensive data pre-processing, but also, by abstracting the representation of the lattice structure using adjacency matrices, GCNNs can naturally be trained on lattices of different structures and sizes. Previous work with GCNN models in materials science includes crystal graph convolutional neural networks (CGCNN) [28] and material graph network (MEGNet) [29]. The focus of these efforts was on using GCNNs for prediction of material properties across broad classes of crystalline materials, sourced from the Materials Project and the Open Quantum Materials Database (OQMD) [2,3]. This work showed significant flexibility of the DL model, simultaneously handling many materials across different properties, with good accuracy relative to the original DFT results. In this work, we focus on improving the predictive accuracy of DL models using GCNNs for chemically disordered binary solid solution alloys. Although the approach consists in training GCNN on DFT data, our goal is not to necessarily use GCNN as a replacement for DFT. Instead, we aim to use GCNN models to construct well educated initial guesses that could be used as starting point for DFT simulations, enabling the numerical study of large scale atomic structures that otherwise would not be computationally affordable.

In particular, we use open source DFT datasets, published on OLCF Data Constellation, to predict the total energy of copper-gold (CuAu) and iron-platinum (FePt) alloys with DL models. We train GCNNs on these datasets and compare their predictive performance with respect to multi-layer perceptron (MLP) architectures previously used. We show that GCNNs attain higher accuracy than MLPs and reduce the root mean squared error (RMSE) on validation data by an order of magnitude on both datasets. GCNNs also outperform the base-line DFT simulation by orders of magnitude in terms of computational time to produce the estimate of the total energy for a given atomic configuration of the lattice structure.

2   Physical System - Solid Solution Binary Alloys

The material systems on which we focus in this work are solid solution binary alloys, where two constituent elements are randomly placed on a fixed underlying crystal lattice. We consider two binary alloy systems, each with 32 atoms and with periodic boundary conditions considered within the DFT calculations. The first system is the CuAu [30] alloy arranged in a 2 × 2 × 2 supercell and a face-centered cubic (FCC) structure, while the second system is the FePt alloy [31] arranged in a 2 × 2 × 4 supercell with a body-centered cubic (BCC) structure.

For both CuAu and FePt datasets, each data point in the dataset provides the information about the atomic positions on a lattice. Denoting the total number of atoms in a configuration N_{atoms}, each input data point is represented as a $N_{atoms} \times 4$ matrix, where the first three columns provide the (x, y, z) coordinates of an atom and the fourth column provides the proton number that uniquely characterizes the atomic element located at a specific lattice point. The total energy is a single scalar for every configuration.

Figure 1 shows the local numbering of atoms inside a FCC or a BCC unit cell. For the atoms in CuAu arranged in $2 \times 2 \times 2$ FCC unit cells, the atoms are numbered starting from the $(x = 0, y = 0, z = 0)$ unit cell. The counting traverses through the unit cells in the x-direction first, then the y-direction, and the z-direction last. For example, atoms 1 to 4 are from unit cell $(0, 0, 0)$, atoms 5 to 8 are from unit cell $(1, 0, 0)$, atoms 9 to 12 are from unit cell $(0, 1, 0)$, and so on. Within a unit cell, the order of counting follows the local numbering of atoms. The numbering of atoms for FePt follows the same manner, with a difference that the atoms are arranged in a supercell having $2 \times 2 \times 4$ BCC unit cells, each unit cell only has two atoms.

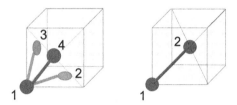

Fig. 1. A face-centered cubic (FCC) unit cell for CuAu (left) and a body-centered cubic (BCC) unit cell for FePt (right). The local numbering of atoms in the unit cell for each structure is shown.

For each of these two alloys, 32,000 configurations with different chemical compositions between the two atom species (Cu and Au for the first system, and Fe and Pt for the second system) were chosen to construct the training dataset. More details about the dataset construction are presented in Sect. 4.

3   Graph Convolutional Neural Networks (GCNNs)

A graph G is usually represented in mathematical terms as

$$G = (V, \mathcal{E}) \tag{1}$$

where V represents the set of nodes and $\mathcal{E}$ represents the set of edges between these nodes [32]. An edge is defined as a pair $(u, v) \in \mathcal{E}$ where $u, v \in V$, $\mathcal{E} \in V \times V$, and the edge starts at node u and ends in node v. The topology of a graph can be described through the *adjacency matrix*, a square matrix, A, with as many rows and columns as the number of nodes in the graph, whose entries are associated with edges of the graph according to the following rule:

$$\begin{cases} A[u, v] = 1 & \text{iff} \quad (u, v) \in \mathcal{E} \\ A[u, v] = 0 & \text{otherwise.} \end{cases} \tag{2}$$

The degree of a node $u \in V$ is defined as:

$$d_u = \sum_{v \in V} A[u, v] \tag{3}$$

and it represents the number of edges incident to a node. The node degree is used in the GCNN when aggregating the information from the neighborhood of a node.

In order to take advantage of the topology of the graph with N nodes, the DL model has to consider the following properties as input features:

- The number of neighbors ($L < N$) for each atom
- The distance between atoms (i.e., bond length).

If the input structure is defined with respect to N nodes in the graph, MLPs cannot take advantage of the information about neighboring nodes, as the fully connectivity of the MLP architectures forces all nodes to communicate with each other. This approach is difficult to scale for graphs of increasing size because the number of interactions increases combinatorially with N. One solution is to change the representation of the input, so that the input is defined in terms of edges instead of being defined in terms of nodes. However, this representation increases the dimensionality in the input from N to $L \times N$ and this further increases the computational cost to train the MLP model.

GCNNs embed the interaction between nodes without increasing the size of the input by representing the local interaction zone as a hyperparameter that cuts-off the interaction of a node with all the other nodes outside a prescribed local neighborhood. The fact that GCNN can naturally distinguish between short-range and long-range interactions without expanding the dimensionality of the input results into a computational saving with respect to an MLP.

GCNNs [26,27] are DL models based on a message-passing framework, a procedure that combines the knowledge from neighboring nodes, which in our applications maps directly to the interactions of a central atom with its neighbors in the lattice structure. The typical GCNN architecture is characterized by three different types of hidden layers: graph convolutional layers, graph pooling layers, and fully connected layers. A schematic of a GCNN structure is provided in Fig. 6. The convolutional graph layers represent the central part of the architecture and their functionality is to transfer feature information between adjacent nodes (in this case atoms). Every node $u_i \in V$ is associated with a p-dimensional vector $h_i \in \mathbb{R}^p$ which contains the embedded nodal features for node u_i. Message passing is performed at each step of the training, and it requires performing in sequential the following operations:

1. Aggregate information from neighbors
2. Update hidden state information.

Through aggregation, the node u_i collects the hidden embedded features of its neighbors as shown in Fig. 2 as well as the information on the edges (if available). After the aggregation is completed, the node u_i updates its hidden state h_i at iteration $(t+1)$ according to the following formula:

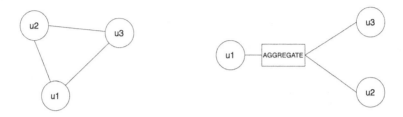

Fig. 2. Message passing on a simple graph with three nodes.

$$m_i^{t+1} = \sum_{j \in N(i)} m_j^t(h_j^t, e_{ij}^t) \tag{4}$$

where m_j^t is a message obtained from neighboring node u_j and the edge e_{ij} that connects them. Following, the nodal features h_i^{t+1} of the node u_j are updated at the $(t+1)$th step of the training as follows:

$$h_i^{t+1} = UPDATE(h_i^t, m_i^{t+1}) \tag{5}$$

where $UPDATE$ is a an arbitrarily differentiable function which combines aggregated messages m_i^{t+1} of node u_i neighbors with its nodal features h_i^t from the previous step t.

Through consecutive steps of message passing, the graph nodes gather information from nodes that are further and further away. As shown in Fig. 3 where k = 2, node u_1 gets the information from neighbors of its neighbors. The type of information passed through a graph structure can be either related to the topology of the graph or features assigned to the nodes. An example of a topological information is the node degree, whereas an example of nodal feature in the context of this work is the proton number of the atom located at the node. The aggregation function aims at collecting information from adjacent nodes in a graph can be defined as:

$$AGGREGATE(u_i) = W_{neighborhood}^{(k)} \sum_{v \in N(u_i)} h_v^{k-1} + b^{k-1} \tag{6}$$

and the function that updates the nodal features is defined as:

$$UPDATE(u_i) = \sigma(W_{self}^{(k)} h_i^{k-1} + AGGREGATE(u_i))$$

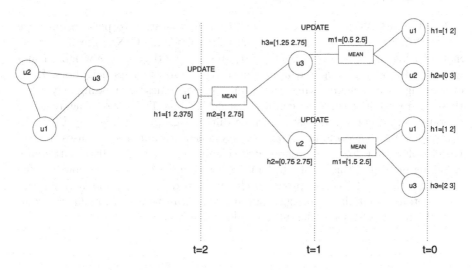

Fig. 3. Example of 2-iteration message passing where the aggregation function used is mean of neighbors hidden states. The update function is also mean of the current node hidden state and aggregated message from node neighbors.

where

$$W^{(k)}_{self}, W^{(k)}_{neighborhood} \in \mathbb{R}^{p \times p} \tag{7}$$

are the weights of one layer of GCNN and σ is an activation function (e.g., ReLU) that introduces nonlinearity to the model (Fig. 4).

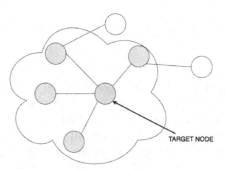

Fig. 4. Convolution performed on target node of a graph where the number of neighbors varies in size and nodes are unordered.

The most common types of graph convolution layers are:

1. graph isomorphism network (GIN);
2. graph attention network (GAT); and
3. principal neighborhood aggregation (PNA).

GIN [33] and GAT [34] use a single aggregating operation to perform message passing among adjacent nodes of a graph. In particular, GIN aggregates information using a sum, whereas GAT aggregates information using a weighted sum where each nodes is weighted according to the number of its neighbors. However, using a single aggregating operation to perform message passing may cause these aggregation schemes to confuse distinct graphs. Examples of aggregating operations that can fail in distinguishing different graphs are given in Fig. 5. In contrast, PNA [35] combines multiple aggregating techniques and uses degree-based scalers that depend on a node degree and accordingly amplify or attenuate incoming messages; this results in an increase of the discriminating power of the model, as the model is less prone to classify two different graphs as identical. More details about the PNA aggregation scheme can be found in [36]. We compare the results of these different graph layers in Sect. 6.

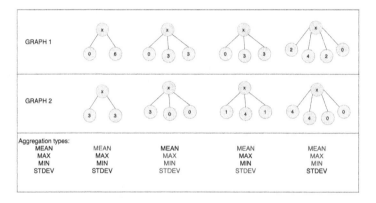

Fig. 5. Examples of different aggregation schemes failing to distinguish between different graph pairs.

The graph pooling layers are interlaced between successive graph convolutional layers and reduce the dimensionality of the graph by aggregating the information contained in adjacent nodes and edges of the graph (the atomic neighborhood for each atom). Fully connected (FC) layers are positioned at the end of the architecture to take the results of pooling and flatten them in order to match the dimensionality of the output. Batch normalizations are performed between consecutive convolutional layers along with a rectified linear unit (ReLU) activation function to avoid vanishing gradients.

The set of hyperparameters that fully characterize the architecture of the DL model are the radius to define the local neighborhood of a graph node, the maximum number of nodes allowed in a neighborhood, the number of neurons in a hidden convolutional layer (also referred to as size of a layer), and the number of hidden convolutional layers. Hyperparameter optimization is performed to identify the architecture of the NN with best predictive performance.

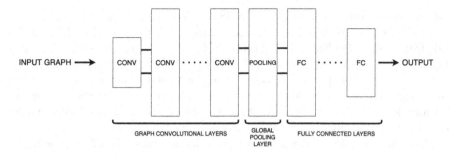

Fig. 6. High level overview of the GCNN architecture used.

Solid solution binary alloys consist of two types of atoms that randomly populate a crystal lattice. Studying the behavior of these materials is challenging due to the combinatoric complexity that quickly increases with the number of types and with the size of the lattice. Therefore, developing an accurate GCNN model that reliably estimates the material properties for each disordered configuration requires a large amount of data.

3.1   Software Implementation

We use the `Pytorch` framework [37] to implement the GCNN in Python. `Pytorch` is not only a robust NN toolkit, but also serves as a performance portability layer for running on heterogeneous computing architectures, e.g., CPU and GPU. This method enables running our GCNN on any local machine, as well as the Summit and coming Frontier supercomputers. In addition, there are many packages which are extensions to `Pytorch`: `Pytorch Geometric` [38, 39] is particularly relevant to this work for graph structures. The code used in this work is openly available and developed on GitHub [40]. The hyperparameter configurations for each neural network architecture have been identified by performing hyperparameter optimization using the `Ray Tune` library [41, 42].

4   Dataset Description

The dataset for each alloy comprises 32,000 configurations out of the 2^{32} available. The selection of the configurations is performed to ensure that every composition is adequately represented in the dataset. If the number of configurations for a specific composition is less than 1,000, then all those configurations are included in the dataset. For all other compositions, configurations are randomly selected up to the total of 32,000. Moreover, the splitting between the training, and validation sets is performed at the level of each composition, to ensure that all the compositions are adequately represented in both the training and validation portions of the dataset. For each selected configuration, we computed the total energy of the system at each atomic position using the locally self-consistent multiple scattering (LSMS) DFT approach, which exhibits linear scaling with respect to the number of atoms [43–45]. We used the LSMS-3 code from Oak Ridge National Laboratory [46]. These data are openly available through the OLCF Constellation [30,31], and describe material properties for atomic systems with chemical disorder. The chemical disorder makes the task of describing the material properties combinatorially complex, and the combinatorial complexity addressed by these datasets represents the main difference from other open source databases that only focus on ordered compounds [1–3].

Since different physical quantities have different units and different orders of magnitude, the inputs and outputs are respectively standardized (normalized) across all data points for each quantity, such that each quantity has a zero mean and unit standard deviation.

Raw input data is imported in the format of csv files and transformed into a `Python Data` object to handle the data through the `Pytorch Geometric` framework. The data object contains the following information:

1. **edge_index** $\in \mathbb{R}^{32 \times 2}$ contains index pairs of neighboring nodes
2. **pos** $\in \mathbb{R}^{32 \times 3}$ contains coordinates for each atom

Since `PyTorch Geometric` was built upon `PyTorch`, all of the primitive types are converted to `PyTorch` tensors. After loading the data, the total energy value for each configurations needs to be normalized using the min-max normalization defined as

$$e'_i = \frac{e_i - e_{\min}}{e_{\max} - e_{\min}} \tag{8}$$

where $e_{\min}$ and $e_{\max}$ minimum and maximum value of the total energy across all the nodes with the same index in the dataset, and use these values to perform the normalization. The range of values of the energy expressed in Rydberg is $[-1.22 \cdot 10^6, -1.41 \cdot 10^5]$ for CuAu and $[-1.12 \cdot 10^6, -1.16 \cdot 10^5]$ for FePt.

After standardizing the data, we extract the graph topology from the lattice structure. Since the connections between atoms in the lattice structure are not directly provided by the datasets, we created a procedure described in Algorithm 1 to calculate an approximation of the adjacency matrix that only considers local interactions between nodes of the graph with a maximum neighborhood radius and a maximum number of neighbors. The approximate adjacency matrix is then fed into the GCNN to characterize the structure of the graph convolutional layers that will perform successive aggregations of nodal features on adjacent nodes of the graph. The nodal feature for the first graph convolutional layer is the proton number, whereas the nodal features for successive convolutional layers are the result of convolutional operations that cannot be directly interpreted in terms of physical properties. Once the GCNN produces the prediction of the target quantity, a data post-processing is performed to remap the predicted quantities back to the physical space to restore their actual values and units.

Larger sizes of the local neighborhood lead to a higher computational cost to train the GCNN, as the number of regression coefficients to train at each hidden convolutional layer increases quadratically with the size of the local neighborhood. Moreover, a local interaction zone is also used in the LSMS-3 code to

input : nodes - list containing nodes of the graph with coordinate information
r - radius within to search for the neighbors of a node
mnnn - maximum number of node neighbors
output: adj - adjacency matrix
adj = [len(nodes), len(nodes)] initialize adjacency matrix with zeros
neighbors = {} dictionary of size n where key is index of a node and value is empty list
distances = [len(nodes), len(nodes)] matrix of node distances
i = 0 initalize index to zero
for i < len(nodes) **do**

> j ← i + 1
> **for** j < len(nodes) **do**
> > distances [i][j] = calculate_distance_in_3D (nodes [i],nodes [j])
> > **if** distances [i][j] <= r **then**
> > | neighbors [i].$append(j)$
> > **end**
>
> **end**

end

// Order neighbors for each node by their distance.
ordered_neighbors = order_candidate_neighbors_by_distance(neighbors, distances)
  // For each node find neighbors.

for node, neighbors in ordered_neighbors **do**
> neighbors = resolve_neighbor_conflicts (node, neighbors, adj, mnnn)
> adj [node, neighbors] = 1
> adj [neighbors, node] = 1

end

algorithm 1: Calculating graph adjacency matrix in 3D

generate the DFT training data; therefore, setting the size of the local neighborhood to a large value causes the GCNN model to overfit as the model reconstructs interatomic interactions that are not captured in the DFT data.

5   Use of Federated Instruments, Compute, and Storage

The workflow pipeline described in this work benefits from the entire ORNL computing and data storage infrastructure, and in turn benefits it by developing additional robust and accurate DL capabilities. We illustrate how the research described in this work integrates in the entire OLCF infrastructure of federated instruments, compute, and storage in Fig. 7. This research, part of the Artificial Intelligence for Scientific Discovery (AISD) Thrust of the Artificial Intelligence (AI) Initiative at ORNL, aims at developing and deplying fast and accurate surrogate models to accelerate the material design. As such, our GCNN take advantage of the existing ORNL resources:

– OLCF supercomputers
– OLCF data management
– OLCF-CADES edge computing.

The OLCF supercomputer Summit is used to quickly generate training data from large-scale ab-initio DFT simulations. The OLCF Constellation is used to permanently store the full results of the DFT simulations, enabling public access and citations through DOIs. The OLCF-CADES GPU-enabled edge computing clusters allow us to quickly train the GCNN model on the data downloaded from the OLCF Constellation, where eventually we can deploy the trained and validated model for scientific discovery. The outcome of this research, which strongly relies on the Oak Ridge Leadership Computing Facility, will provide strategically relevant AI capabilities to the other ORNL user facilities such as the Manufacturing Demonstration Facility (MDF) and the Spallation Neutron Source (SNS).

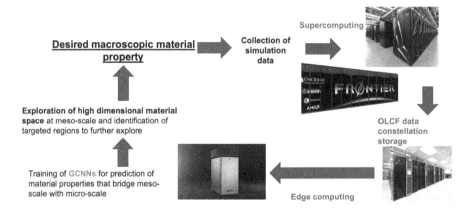

Fig. 7. Illustration of the OLCF infrastructure.

6   Numerical Results

We present numerical results to predict the total energy for the binary CuAu and FePt alloys using DL models by comparing the predictive performance of simple fully connected MLPs with GCNNs that use GIN, GAT, and PNA graph convolutional layers. The output of DFT calculations is considered as the exact reference that the DL model has to reconstruct. Therefore, the predictive performance of a DL model is tested by measuring the departure of quantities predicted by the DL models from the results produced by DFT calculations.

We used the `HyperOpt` search algorithm based on the Tree-Structured Parzen Estimator approach (TPE) inside the `Ray Tune` library to identify the NN architecture that minimizes the RMSE. Details about GCNN architectures resulting from the hyperparameter optimization are presented in Table 1.

Table 1. Hyperparameter setting for GCNNs with GIN, GAT, and PNA graph convolutional layers.

Hyperparameter	NN model		
	GCNN-GIN	GCNN-GAT	GCNN-PNA
Radius size	5	5	5
Maximum number of node neighbors	7	7	7
Hidden layer size	60	20	15
Number of convolutional layers	5	16	16

The DL models are trained using the Adam method [47] with an initial learning rate equal to 0.0001, with a total number of 200 epochs performed. The batch size for each step of an epoch is 64 data points. Early stopping is performed to interrupt the training when the validation loss function does not decrease for several consecutive epochs, as this is a symptom that further epochs are very unlikely to reduce the value of the loss function. The training set for each of the NN represents 80% of the total dataset; the validation set represents the remaining 20%.

6.1 Comparison Between Computational Times for First Principles Calculations and DL Models

The DFT calculations to generate the dataset to train the NN models were performed with the LSMS-3 code on the Titan supercomputer at Oak Ridge National Laboratory (ORNL), each calculation used 8 Titan nodes (each Titan node had 1 NVIDIA K20X GPU) for a hybrid MPI-CUDA parallelization. For more details about the hardware specifics of Titan we refer to [48]. Because ORNL's Titan supercomputer has been decommissioned as of this writing, we present here the computational time of the same calculations on ORNL's current supercomputer Summit [49]. Each calculation was performed on one Summit node, utilizing all 6 NVIDIA V100 GPUs on the node.

Our DL approach demonstrates significant time reductions for both CuAu and FePt cases when NN models are used in place of DFT calculations for one configuration. The first-principles LSMS calculations take about 260 wall-clock seconds for CuAu and 300 wall-clock second for FePt on average on a Summit node, whereas the NN models predict the physical quantities in about one wall-clock second. The training of the NN models takes about 4,000 wall-clock seconds on an NVIDIA V100 GPU.

Table 2. CuAu binary alloy - Average time in wall-clock seconds needed to estimate macroscopic physical properties on a random lattice configuration with first principles calculations, time for one single-tasking NN models evaluation, time for one multitasking NN evaluation, total wall-clock time to perform 10^6 DFT calculations and total wall-clock time to perform 32,000 DFT calculations, train the NN and evaluate the total energy for 10^6 configurations using the NN.

Computational approach	Compute resources	Wall-clock time(s)
1 DFT calculation	1 Summit node	263.7
MLP	1 NVIDIA-V100 GPU	0.9
GCNN	1 NVIDIA-V100 GPU	1.3
$\sim 10^6$ DFT calculations	1 Summit node	$2.63 \cdot 10^8$
32,000 DFT calc. + train NN + 10^6 NN pred	1 Summit node	$9.71 \cdot 10^6$

In Figs. 8 and 9 we show the trend of the training MSE and validation MSE with respect to different percentage of the entire CuAu and FePt datasets to train the GCNN model with PNA aggregation. The results show that using only 10% of the data for training increases the validation MSE of the GCNN model by two orders of magnitude with respect to the use of 90% of the dataset for training. Moreover, the fact that both training MSE and validation MSE reach plateau means that the neural network has been trained long enough to reach its expressive power on the dataset.

Table 3. FePt binary alloy - Average time in wall-clock seconds needed to estimate macroscopic physical properties on a random lattice configuration with first principles calculations, time for one single-tasking NN models evaluation, time for one multitasking NN evaluation, total wall-clock time to perform 10^6 DFT calculations and total wall-clock time to perform 32,000 DFT calculations, train the NN and evaluate the total energy for 10^6 configurations using the NN.

Computational approach	Compute resources	Wall-clock time(s)
1 DFT calculation	1 Summit node	303.2
MLP	1 NVIDIA-V100 GPU	0.9
GCNN	1 NVIDIA-V100 GPU	1.3
$\sim 10^6$ DFT calculations	1 Summit node	$3.03 \cdot 10^8$
32,000 DFT calc. + train NN + 10^6 NN pred	1 Summit node	$1.10 \cdot 10^7$

Tables 2 and 3 compare the computational time to compute the total energy for 10^6 configurations using the LSMS code, with the time needed for the scenario where the total energy is calculated just for $32,000$ configurations with LSMS to generate the dataset, train the NN model on this dataset, then use the NN model to predict the total energy for 10^6 alloy configurations. This comparison is of relevance for the possible use of surrogate DL models in Monte Carlo simulations to predict the thermodynamic properties of a solid solution alloy, in which the

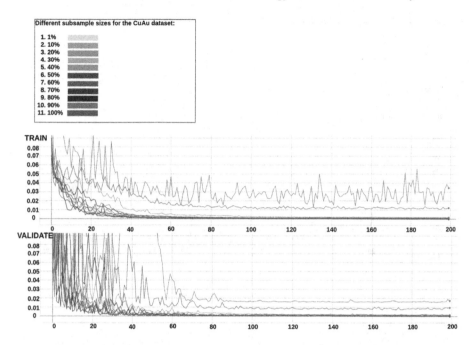

Fig. 8. Training and validation MSE at different epochs for training a GCNN model with PNA aggregation policy on the CuAu dataset using different percentages of the dataset for training.

number of Monte Carlo samples required would at least be of the order of 10^6 for sufficient sampling. In this case, it is clear that using DL surrogate models for accurate predictions of total energy significantly reduces the computational time needed to predict material properties that would be otherwise unattainable given limited computational resources. Although the reduction of computational time has been achieved by sacrificing accuracy with respect to the DFT itself, we point out that our goal is not to use a GCNN surrogate model to compete against ab-initio calculations, but rather facilitating the use of DFT in Monte Carlo (MC) simulations to determine the thermodynamic properties of large scale lattices for solid solution alloys.

6.2 Comparison Between Statistical Models for Predictive Performance

Numerical results obtained by training the NN models on CuAu and FePt datasets are presented in Tables 4 and 5 respectively. The metric used to measure the predictive performance of the models is the RMSE and it shows that GCNNs attain a higher accuracy than MLPs for the prediction of total energy for both CuAu and FePt. The GCNNs, and their natural mapping to the atomic input data, is indeed better to predict system properties. Moreover, these results show

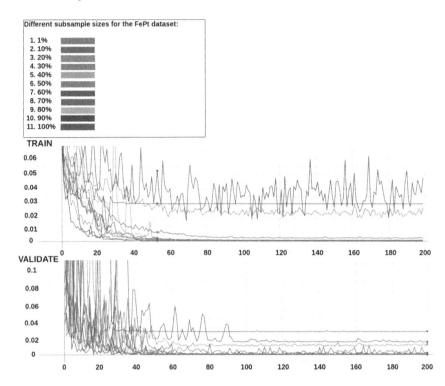

Fig. 9. Training and validation MSE for training of a GCNN model with PNA aggregation policy on the FePt dataset using different percentages of the dataset for training.

Table 4. Validation root mean squared error (RMSE) for neural networks that predict total energy for randomly sampled configurations of CuAu. The name of each training method refers to whether it is a multi-layer perceptron (MLP) or graph convolutional neural network (GCNN). Graph isomorphism network (GIN), graph attention network (GAT), and principal neighborhood aggregation (PNA) layers are used to perform the aggregation of neighboring nodes.

NN model	RMSE - Total Energy
MLP	6.65×10^{-3}
GCNN - GIN	5.10×10^{-3}
GCNN - GAT	7.14×10^{-3}
GCNN - PNA	2.52×10^{-4}

that PNA outperforms the other aggregation techniques by an order of magnitude. The results are in line with what expected by the DL theory, since the PNA layer has more expressive power than GIN and GAT. We also notice that MLP and GCNN-PNA attain lower accuracy on the FePt dataset than on the CuAu dataset (while the other two aggregations result in similar accuracy both

Table 5. Validation root mean squared error (RMSE) for neural networks that predict total energy for randomly sampled configurations of FePt alloy. The name of each training method refers to whether it is a multi-layer perceptron (MLP) or graph convolutional neural network (GCNN). Graph isomorphism network (GIN), graph attention network (GAT), and principal neighborhood aggregation (PNA) layers are used to perform the aggregation of neighboring nodes.

NN model	RMSE - Total Energy
MLP	1.22×10^{-2}
GCNN - GIN	5.97×10^{-3}
GCNN - GAT	6.73×10^{-3}
GCNN - PNA	8.01×10^{-4}

datasets). This is partially due to the fact that the FePt binary alloy is a hard ferromagnetic metal, making it more difficult for the DFT to converge during self-consistent iterations. As the data for FePt is less accurate than the data for CuAu, so also is the attainable accuracy of the models trained on it.

7 Conclusions

We trained GCNNs on ab-initio DFT data that produce fast and accurate predictions of the total energy for solid solution binary alloys CuAu and FePt. GCNN architectures use graph representations to directly map to the topology of the atomic structure, which enables GCNNs to attain higher accuracy than dense MLPs. Numerical results show that DL models outperform ab-initio DFT calculations in terms of computational time to provide estimates of the total energy for specific lattice configurations by compromising the accuracy within a tolerable margin of error. A comparison between MLPs and GCNNs in terms of predictive performance shows that GCNNs outperform MLPs on both datasets by reducing the RMSE by at least an order of magnitude. Our goal is not to necessarily replace DFT with a GCNN surrogate model, but rather integrate the two approaches to run large-scale Monte Carlo (MC) simulations for thermodynamic properties of solid solution alloys. Future work will combine two MC procedures in sequence: the first MC procedure will use a GCNN model to generate an educated initial guess, which can then be used as starting point for a new MC run where DFT is called directly. Combining the two MC runs is expected to drastically reduce the total number of calls to the DFT code substantially reducing the computational time with respect to running DFT with uninformed initial guesses.

Acknowledgements. Massimiliano Lupo Pasini thanks Dr. Vladimir Protopopescu for his valuable feedback in the preparation of this manuscript.

This work was supported in part by the Office of Science of the Department of Energy and by the Laboratory Directed Research and Development (LDRD) Program of Oak Ridge National Laboratory. This research is sponsored by the Artificial Intelligence Initiative as part of the Laboratory Directed Research and Development Program of Oak Ridge National Laboratory, managed by UT-Battelle, LLC, for the US Department of Energy under contract DE-AC05-00OR22725. This work used resources of the Oak Ridge Leadership Computing Facility, which is supported by the Office of Science of the U.S. Department of Energy under Contract No. DE-AC05-00OR22725.

References

1. Curtarolo, S., et al.: AFLOW: an automatic framework for high-throughput materials discovery. Comput. Mater. Sci. **58**, 218–226 (2012)
2. Jain, A., et al.: Commentary: the materials project: a materials genome approach to accelerating materials innovation. APL Mater. **1**(1), 1–11 (2013)
3. Saal, J.E., Kirklin, S., Aykol, M., Meredig, B., Wolverton, C.: Materials design and discovery with high-throughput density functional theory: the Open Quantum Materials Database (OQMD). JOM **65**(11), 1501–1509 (2013). https://doi.org/10.1007/s11837-013-0755-4
4. Nityananda, R., Hohenberg, P., Kohn, W.: Inhomogeneous electron gas. Resonance **22**(8), 809–811 (2017). https://doi.org/10.1007/s12045-017-0529-3
5. Kohn, W., Sham, L.J.: Self-consistent equations including exchange and correlation effects. Phys. Rev. **140**, A1133–A1138 (1965)
6. Nightingale, M.P., Umrigar., J.C.: Self-Consistent Equations Including Exchange and Correlation Effects. Springer (1999)
7. Hammond, B.L., Lester, W.A., Reynolds, P.J.: Monte Carlo Methods in Ab Initio Quantum Chemistry. World Scientific, Singapore (1994)
8. Car, R., Parrinello, M.: Unified approach for molecular dynamics and density-functional theory. Phys. Rev. Lett. **55**, 2471–2474 (1985)
9. Marx, D., Hutter, J.: Ab Initio Molecular Dynamics, Basic Theory and Advanced Methods. Cambridge University Press, New York (2012)
10. Aarons, J., Sarwar, M., Thompsett, D., Skylaris, C.K.: Perspective: methods for large-scale density functional calculations on metallic systems. J. Chem. Phys. **145**(22), 220901 (2016)
11. Sanchez, J.M., Ducastelle, F., Gratias, D.: Generalized cluster description of multicomponent systems. Phys. A Stat. Mech. Appl. **128**, 334–350 (1984)
12. De Fontaine, D.: Cluster approach to order-disorder transformations in alloys. Phys. A Stat. Mech. Appl. **47**, 33–176 (1994)
13. Levy, O., Hart, G.L.W., Curtarolo, S.: Uncovering compounds by synergy of cluster expansion and high-throughput methods. J. Am. Chem. Soc. **132**(13), 4830–4833 (2010)
14. Alder, B.J., Wainwright, T.E.: Phase transition for a hard sphere system. J. Chem. Phys. **27**(5), 1208–1209 (1957)
15. Rahman, A.: Correlations in the motion of atoms in liquid argon. Phys. Rev. **136**(2A), A405–A411 (1964)
16. Ercolessi, F., Adams, J.B.: Interatomic potentials from first-principles calculations: the force-matching method. Europhys. Lett. **26**(8), 583–588 (1994)
17. Brockherde, F., Vogt, L., Tuckerman, M.E., Burke, K., Müller, K.R.: Bypassing the Kohn-Sham equations with machine learning. Nat. Commun. **8**(872), 1–10 (2017)
18. Wang, C., Tharval, A., Kitchin, J.R.: A density functional theory parameterised neural network model of zirconia. Mol. Simul. **44**(8), 623–630 (2018)

19. Sinitskiy, A.V., Pande, V.S.: Deep neural network computes electron densities and energies of a large set of organic molecules faster than density functional theory (DFT). https://arxiv.org/abs/1809.02723
20. Custódio, C.A., Filletti, É.R., França, V.V.: Artificial neural networks for density-functional optimizations in fermionic systems. Sci. Rep. **9**(1886), 1–7 (2019)
21. Ryczko, K., Strubbe, D., Tamblyn, I.: Deep learning and density functional theory. Phys. Rev. A **100**, 022512 (2019)
22. Behler, J., Parrinello, M.: Generalized neural-network representation of high-dimensional potential-energy surfaces. Phys. Rev. Lett. **98**(14), 146401 (2007)
23. Schütt, K., et al.: SchNet: a continuous-filter convolutional neural network for modeling quantum interactions. In: Guyon, I., et al. (eds.) Advances in Neural Information Processing Systems 30, pp. 991–1001. Curran Associates Inc. (2017)
24. Smith, J.S., Isayev, O., Roitberg, A.E.: ANI-1: an extensible neural network potential with DFT accuracy at force field computational cost. Chem. Sci. **8**(4), 3192–3203 (2017)
25. Zhang, L., Han, J., Wang, H., Car, R., Weinan, E.: Deep potential molecular dynamics: a scalable model with the accuracy of quantum mechanics. Phys. Rev. Lett. **120**(14), 143001 (2018)
26. Scarselli, F., Gori, M., Tsoi, A.C., Hagenbuchner, M., Monfardini, G.: The graph neural network model. IEEE Trans. Neural Netw. **20**(1), 61–80 (2009)
27. Defferrard, M., Bresson, X., Vandergheynst, P.: Convolutional neural networks on graphs with fast localized spectral filtering. In: Lee, D., Sugiyama, M., Luxburg, U., Guyon, I., Garnett, R. (eds.) Advances in Neural Information Processing Systems, vol. 29. Curran Associates Inc. (2016)
28. Xie, T., Grossman, J.C.: Crystal graph convolutional neural networks for an accurate and interpretable prediction of material properties. Phys. Rev. Lett. **120**(14), 145301 (2018)
29. Chen, C., Ye, W., Zuo, Y., Zheng, C., Ong, S.P.: Graph networks as a universal machine learning framework for molecules and crystals. Chem. Mater. **31**(9), 3564–3572 (2019)
30. Pasini, M.L., Eisenbach, M.: CuAu binary alloy with 32 atoms - LSMS-3 data, February 2021. https://doi.org/10.13139/OLCF/1765349
31. Pasini, M.L., Eisenbach, M.: FePt binary alloy with 32 atoms - LSMS-3 data, February 2021. https://doi.org/10.13139/OLCF/1762742
32. Murty, U.S.R., Bondy, J.A.: Graphs and subgraphs. In: Graph Theory with Applications. North-Holland
33. Xu, K., Hu, W., Leskovec, J., Jegelka, S.: How powerful are graph neural networks? arXiv:1810.00826 [cs, stat], February 2019
34. Kipf, T.N., Welling, M.: Graph attention networks. arXiv:1609.02907 [cs, stat], February 2017. arXiv: 1710.10903
35. Corso, G., Cavalleri, L., Beaini, D., Liò, P., Veličković., P.: Principal neighbourhood aggregation for graph nets. arXiv:2004.05718 [cs, stat], December 2020
36. Hamilton, W.L.: Graph representation learning. Synth. Lect. Artif. Intell. Mach. Learn. **14**(3), 1–159 (2020)
37. Paszke, A., et al.: PyTorch: an imperative style, high-performance deep learning library. In: Wallach, H., Larochelle, H., Beygelzimer, A., d' Alché-Buc, F., Fox, E., Garnett, R. (eds.) Advances in Neural Information Processing Systems 32, pp. 8024–8035. Curran Associates Inc. (2019)
38. Fey, M., Lenssen, J.E.: Fast graph representation learning with PyTorch geometric. In: ICLR Workshop on Representation Learning on Graphs and Manifolds (2019)

39. PyTorch Geometric. https://pytorch-geometric.readthedocs.io/en/latest/
40. Pasini, M.L., Reeve, S.T., Zhang, P., Choi, J.Y.: HydraGNN. Comput. Softw. (2021). https://doi.org/10.11578/dc.20211019.2
41. Liaw, R., Liang, E., Nishihara, R., Moritz, P., Gonzalez, J.E., Stoica, I.: Tune: a research platform for distributed model selection and training. arXiv preprint arXiv:1807.05118 (2018)
42. Ray Tune: Hyperparameter Optimization Framework. https://docs.ray.io/en/latest/tune/index.html
43. Eisenbach, M., Larkin, J., Lutjens, J., Rennich, S., Rogers, J.H.: GPU acceleration of the locally self-consistent multiple scattering code for first principles calculation of the ground state and statistical physics of materials. Comput. Phys. Commun. **211**, 2–7 (2017)
44. Wang, Y., Stocks, G.M., Shelton, W.A., Nicholson, D.M.C., Szotek, Z., Temmerman, W.M.: Order-N multiple scattering approach to electronic structure calculations. Phys. Rev. Lett. **75**, 2867–2870 (1995)
45. Yang, Y., et al.: Quantitative evaluation of an epitaxial silicon-germanium layer on silicon. Nature **542**(7639), 75–79 (2017)
46. Eisenbach, M., Li, Y.W., Odbadrakh, O.K., Pei, Z., Stocks, G.M., Yin, J.: LSMS. https://github.com/mstsuite/lsms
47. Kingma, D.P., Ba, J.: Adam: a method for stochastic optimization. arXiv:1412.6980 [cs], January 2017
48. OLCF Supercomputer Titan. https://www.olcf.ornl.gov/for-users/system-user-guides/titan/
49. OLCF Supercomputer Summit. https://www.olcf.ornl.gov/olcf-resources/compute-systems/summit/

Transitioning from File-Based HPC Workflows to Streaming Data Pipelines with openPMD and ADIOS2

Franz Poeschel[1,4](✉) [iD], Juncheng E[5] [iD], William F. Godoy[3] [iD],
Norbert Podhorszki[3] [iD], Scott Klasky[3] [iD], Greg Eisenhauer[6] [iD], Philip E. Davis[7],
Lipeng Wan[3] [iD], Ana Gainaru[3] [iD], Junmin Gu[2] [iD], Fabian Koller[4] [iD],
René Widera[4] [iD], Michael Bussmann[1,4] [iD], and Axel Huebl[2,4](✉) [iD]

[1] Center for Advanced Systems Understanding (CASUS), 02826 Görlitz, Germany
f.poeschel@hzdr.de
[2] Lawrence Berkeley National Laboratory (LBNL), Berkeley, CA 94720, USA
axelhuebl@lbl.gov
[3] Oak Ridge National Laboratory (ORNL), Oak Ridge, TN 37830, USA
[4] Helmholtz-Zentrum Dresden-Rossendorf (HZDR), 01328 Dresden, Germany
[5] European XFEL GmbH (EU XFEL), 22869 Schenefeld, Germany
[6] Georgia Institute of Technology (Georgia Tech), Atlanta, GA 30332, USA
[7] Rutgers University (Rutgers), New Brunswick, NJ 08901, USA

Abstract. This paper aims to create a transition path from file-based IO to streaming-based workflows for scientific applications in an HPC environment. By using the openPMP-api, traditional workflows limited by filesystem bottlenecks can be overcome and flexibly extended for in situ analysis. The openPMD-api is a library for the description of scientific data according to the Open Standard for Particle-Mesh Data (openPMD). Its approach towards recent challenges posed by hardware heterogeneity lies in the decoupling of data description in domain sciences, such as plasma physics simulations, from concrete implementations in hardware and IO. The streaming backend is provided by the ADIOS2 framework, developed at Oak Ridge National Laboratory. This paper surveys two openPMD-based loosely-coupled setups to demonstrate flexible applicability and to evaluate performance. In loose coupling, as opposed to tight coupling, two (or more) applications are executed separately, e.g. in individual MPI contexts, yet cooperate by exchanging data. This way, a streaming-based workflow allows for standalone codes instead of tightly-coupled plugins, using a unified streaming-aware API and leveraging high-speed communication infrastructure available in modern compute clusters for massive data exchange. We determine new challenges in resource allocation and in the need of strategies for a flexible data distribution, demonstrating their influence on efficiency and scaling on the Summit compute system. The presented setups show the potential for a more flexible use of compute resources brought by streaming IO as well as the ability to increase throughput by avoiding filesystem bottlenecks.

© Springer Nature Switzerland AG 2022
J. Nichols et al. (Eds.): SMC 2021, CCIS 1512, pp. 99–118, 2022.
https://doi.org/10.1007/978-3-030-96498-6_6

Keywords: High performance computing · Big Data · Streaming · RDMA

1 The Need for Loosely-Coupled Data Pipelines

Scientists working with massively scalable simulations on high-performance compute (HPC) systems can currently observe an increasing IO bottleneck threatening the performance of their workflows. As GPU hardware has reshaped the compute landscape found in the TOP500 list[1], state-of the art HPC codes have become able to exploit the compute power of thousands of GPUs in parallel. When storage systems cannot keep pace with this development, workflows must be adapted to continue exploiting advancements made in compute performance. This paper explores streaming IO as a scalable alternative to persistent IO.

This section first gives an overview on the performance of state-of-the-art supercomputers as well as on typical scientific workflows for massive data processing. Section 2 proposes streaming IO as an approach at keeping these workflows scalable on recent systems. Section 3 discusses the challenge of streaming data distribution. Finally, Sect. 4 builds and examines two prototypical streaming data processing pipelines and evaluates the data distribution patterns previously discussed.

1.1 The IO Bottleneck – A Challenge for Large-Scale IO

Hoping to bring forward more detailed scientific insights, recent supercomputer systems strive to enable simulation sizes that are impossible to fit on smaller clusters. Applications that use a large percentage of resources on such a system are challenged to near-perfect parallel weak scaling. While from the perspective of the compute system, achieving this goal – while demanding – has been proven possible by applications such as PIConGPU [3], storage systems on recent systems are far less scalable:

Table 1. System performance: OLCF Titan to Frontier. The last column shows the storage size needed by a full-scale simulation that dumps all GPU memory in the system 50 times.

system	compute performance [PFlop · s^{-1}]	parallel FS bandwidth [TiByte · s^{-1}]	FS capacity [PiByte]	example storage requirements [PiByte]
Titan	27	1	27	5.3
Summit	200	2.5	250	21.1
Frontier	>1500	5–10	500–1000	80–100

---

[1] https://www.top500.org/.

Table 1 shows that the full-scale peak compute performance increases by a factor of $\sim$7.4 from Titan (2013) to Summit (2018) and by a further factor of >7.5 from Summit to Frontier (planned 2021). Conversely, the parallel bandwidth increases from Titan to Summit by merely 2.5 and the parallel bandwidth of Frontier is planned at 2–4 times that figure. For the storage capacity, the increase from Titan to Summit goes by a factor of 7.8, keeping up with the increase in compute performance. The storage capacity for Frontier, however, is planned at 2–4 times that of Summit, falling behind the pace of the peak compute performance. The table shows that full-scale applications that write regular data dumps will use significant portions of the system storage.

Large-scale capability application runs perceive this as an *IO wall*: At full scale, the theoretical maximum parallel filesystem (PFS) throughput per node on Titan (NVidia Tesla K20x) is 56 MByte $\cdot$ s^{-1}, and 95 MByte $\cdot$ s^{-1} on Summit (NVidia Tesla V100). Summit compute nodes are further equipped with 1.6 TiB of non-volatile memory (NVM). While envisioned as a burst-buffer for the PFS, draining of NVM data dumps during parallel application runs can lead to a competition for network resources.

Traditional methods for further processing of simulation data reach their limits due to the PFS bandwidth. Simulations intending to scale up to full capability cannot continue to rely on file-based IO and must explore alternative methods for further processing of data.

1.2 From Monolithic Frameworks to Loosely-Coupled Pipelines

Multi PB-scale data output does not solely pose a technical challenge, as from a domain scientist's perspective this raw data also provides a relatively low informational density, necessitating data extraction through adequate analysis.

An example is the particle-in-cell simulation PIConGPU [3,9], developed at the Helmholtz-Zentrum Dresden-Rossendorf. It produces massive amounts of raw data that requires further processing and extraction of information. As depicted in Fig. 1, PIConGPU provides a number of tightly-coupled *plugins* to perform simple analysis tasks on raw data.

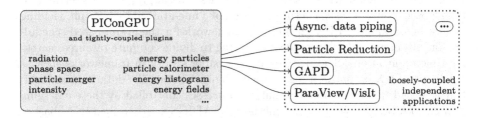

Fig. 1. Tight and loose coupling in the example of PIConGPU

In the context of this work, the *tightly-coupled* approach is defined as a data analysis routine built into the data producer, which cannot be used as a standalone application. It brings the advantage of trivial data access at the expense of flexibility. While a tightly-coupled plugin can benefit from using the same address space as the actual simulation, it also comes with a list of downsides.

The development of such plugins is highly application specific, requiring more development resources, and the software stack of all plugins, including potentially very large frameworks with incompatible dependencies and compiler constraints, needs to compile and link at once. The heavy investment of developing a plugin only pays off for algorithms that scale well with the simulation size. As shown in [14], algorithms that require communication between the processes can sometimes run faster separately at smaller scale even with the additional cost of data movement. An example analysis in large 3D PIConGPU runs that does not benefit from proportionally scaled-up parallel analysis is the extraction of a distributed 2D simulation slice followed by a 2D Hilbert transform, often used to find the position of a laser pulse.

This paper defines *loose coupling* as a workflow wherein multiple discrete stages in a computational data processing pipeline are performed by different independent applications, usually launched as different processes on the system. Loose coupling does not require combining several heterogeneous stages of a simulation/analysis/visualization/aggregation workflow into a monolithic integrated application, which is indeed often impossible due to contradicting dependency requirements in complex software stacks.

This paper's approach at creating loosely-coupled workflows in an efficient and scalable manner is data streaming, introduced in Sect. 2.

1.3 Related Work

SIMEX platform [6,7] implements the openPMD standard [11] through HDF5 files and uses loose coupling to integrate "some of most advanced simulation tools [...] to mimic an entire light source beamline". Similarly, Mayes et al. [19] (LUME) integrates single simulation modules with openPMD into a file-based loosely-coupled pipeline for unified particle accelerator and lightsource modeling. Wan et al. [22] investigate layout reorganization of parallel PIC simulation data to increase file IO performance, including downstream processing and data loads on finely chunked, distributed data. An established framework for loose coupling in the domain of Big Data is the JVM-based Apache Spark [24]. DASK [4] is a Python-based framework for "scalable analytics". Its approach is to couple multiple loosely-coupled tasks via the definition of a fine-grained task-graph, yielding an acyclic dataflow. FLUX [2] builds a framework for the graph-based scheduling for jobs in an HPC environment, allowing to divide compute resources across multiple applications. The position of this paper's work in frameworks such as DASK or FLUX is that of a means for exchange of scientific data between arbitrarily scaled, parallel compute/analysis processes controlled by these emerging frameworks. Staging (streaming) methods in ADIOS are described in Abbasi et al. [1] and were recently redesigned into a scalable publish/subscribe abstraction that supports various coupling use-cases [17]. Both Ascent (part of the Alpine project [15]) as well as the SENSEI [18] project build in-situ visualization and analysis algorithms, running alongside simulations to avoid bottlenecks in bandwidth and storage incurred by post-hoc processing. ADIOS is an available data transport method. Compared to these frameworks, openPMD initially standardizes data organization and self-describing meta-data as frequently needed for analysis, coupling and interpretation in the respective domain-science [11]; it can be implemented directly on a variety of data transports/libraries and formats, yet also provides a scalable reference implementation, openPMD-api [13].

2   Building a System for Streaming IO

The considerations in Subsect. 1.2 already hint at the largest challenge in loose coupling compared to tight coupling: Instead of reducing the raw simulation data by mode of analysis within the simulation by using a tightly-coupled plugin, transfer of massive amounts of data into a reading application becomes necessary, rendering relevant the IO bottleneck discussed in Subsect. 1.1. This section presents *data streaming* (sometimes also referred to as *staging*) as a means to implement highly-scalable loosely-coupled data processing pipelines.

2.1   Loosely Coupled Data Processing Pipelines Built via Streaming

Data streaming in this work refers to a form of IO between two (or more) applications that bypasses persistent storage media, using instead scalable high-speed communication infrastructure such as Infiniband. In such workflows, data is sometimes held (staged) in a temporary location, e.g. RAM or NVM.

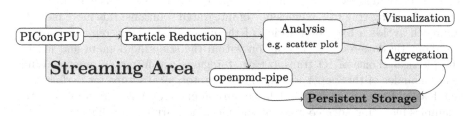

Fig. 2. An envisioned complex, loosely-coupled workflow: PIConGPU is the data producer, a domain-specific particle reduction can conserve relevant ensemble properties, the analysis step might filter and bin, and aggregation might create a temporal integration from high-frequency data. At various sections of the workflow, visualization or data dumps might be generated from subscribers.

Such methods are interesting from two perspectives: For the scientist working in a loosely-coupled setup, persistent storage of intermediate raw data is in general not necessary, and from the perspective of the IO system, it is not feasible. In consequence, our response to the IO wall lies in streaming-based loosely-coupled workflows that allow to forgo persistent storage infrastructure bound by parallel bandwidths and filesystem capacities. An example for a loosely-coupled scientific data processing pipeline, consisting of multiple simulations, is depicted in Fig. 2, demonstrating a multi-stage pipeline that avoids writing unwanted intermediate results to permanent storage. The script `openpmd-pipe`, which allows for capturing a stream into a file, serves as basis for this paper's first benchmark in Sect. 4.1.

The IO system presented in this work focuses on the following criteria, driven by needs of domain scientists:

Efficiency. Naturally, any IO system prepared for the Exascale era needs to move massive amounts of data in a scalably efficient manner.

Expressiveness. Scientists need to express, transport and share their data and meta-data in a language that comes naturally within the problem's domain. Any need for manually dealing with low-level concepts should be avoided and needs of FAIR principles [23] should be considered as integral part.

Flexibility. The IO system should be usable on different systems and in different setups with different IO backends and configurations without altering the application code's data description. Optimization for system specifics should be exposed through runtime configuration.

Reusability. Current-day IO routines are often written in terms of persistent-storage based reading and writing. Upgrading to a streaming-aware IO description should be straightforward. The upgraded routine should allow for file-based as well for streaming-based IO.

2.2 Impact in an Increasingly Heterogeneous Compute Landscape

These properties in an IO system prepare scientific workflows for a trend towards heterogeneity in software and hardware, up to approaches such as federated computing. Keeping true to the efficiency of integrated solutions, this more modular approach avoids a fixed description of the concrete IO layer, replacing it with an idiomatic data-focused description within the scientific domain and leaving the physical choice of IO transport or storage as a runtime parameter. While the remainder of this paper focuses on two prototypical setups for performance and feasibility benchmarking, further more complex workflows are thinkable, two examples including edge computing and machine learning workflows.

For edge computing, such an IO framework, while still satisfying the needs of classical scientific simulation workflows, can serve as the communication layer in the complex communication patterns demanded between compute and edge nodes. Scientific software is thus generalized to unify traditional as well as upcoming workflows into one data description. Similarly, such an IO system makes it possible to schedule each compute part of a loosely-coupled simulation separately on heterogeneous systems, making use of available compute resources in a way best fit for each one. Hence, a GPU compute partition can be used for hardware-accelerated simulation codes, while a CPU-based post-processing transformation of the data can be scheduled on more fitting hardware.

An interesting application for machine learning is found in the computation of surrogate models for simulations. As argued before, scientific simulations create lots of data – in machine learning setups, the training of an accurate model additionally needs a rich set of input data. Both these facts combine into data requirements that can no longer be supported by file-based IO routines. An envisioned workflow supported by a flexible IO system consists of a long-running surrogate model training process being fed by dynamically launching instances of a scientific simulation via streaming methods, thus bypassing the filesystem.

2.3 OpenPMD and ADIOS2: Scientific Self-description and Streaming

In this paper, we explore a streaming-aware IO infrastructure that leverages scientific self-description of data through the Open Standard for Particle-Mesh Data (openPMD) [11]. We use ADIOS2 [8] to add a streaming backend implementation to the library openPMD-api [13].

The openPMD-api, developed openly in collaboration of Helmholtz-Zentrum Dresden-Rossendorf, the Center for Advanced Systems Understanding and Lawrence Berkeley National Laboratory, is an IO middleware library that assists domain-scientists with data description along the openPMD standard for FAIR particle-mesh data, used already in numerous physics simulations.[2]

In comparison to direct implementations of application codes against high-speed IO backends [10], using openPMD-api saves thousands of lines of code per application, reduces integration time for application developers, promotes sharing of best practices for IO library tuning options, provides a high-level interface to describe scientific data and conserves this standardized meta-data for analysis and coupling workflows. The *expressiveness* property from Subsect. 2.1 is thereby achieved. The ability to pick different backends and configurations for them at runtime brings *flexibility*. Implementing high-speed backends such as HDF5, ADIOS1 and ADIOS2 as depicted in Fig. 3 achieves *efficiency* (whereas a serial JSON backend serves for prototyping and learning purposes). Additional language bindings on top of the core C++ implementation ease integration into many established post-processing frameworks, such as Python bindings for parallel readers into ParaView, Dask and domain-specific analysis tools.

We leverage the benefits of the openPMD-api and make its interface aware of streaming, thus allowing scientists that already script their traditional data analysis routines for file-based IO to rapidly transition to streaming IO with a small number of changes, keeping in mind the goal of *reusability*.

The ADIOS2 (*adaptable IO system*) framework [8], developed by Oak Ridge National Laboratory, in collaboration with Kitware Inc., Lawrence Berkeley National Laboratory, Georgia Institute of Technology and Rutgers University, is a unified high-performance IO framework, located one logical layer of abstraction below the openPMD-api, and provides the backend implementation for streaming IO. It supersedes the earlier ADIOS1 framework [16] by creating a general IO-API based on the publisher/subscriber model, decoupling the data producers and consumers in a manner that allows for a flexible framework to incorporate various data movement *engines* specialized for different use cases (permanent storage, staging through local NVMes, streaming through RDMA, TCP and

---

[2] https://github.com/openPMD/openPMD-projects.

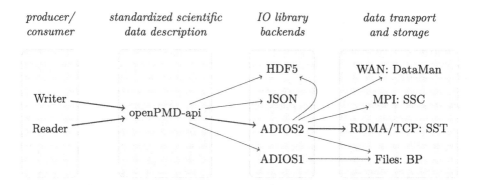

Fig. 3. IO software stack built by openPMD and ADIOS2 (Color figure online)

MPI, etc.). It provides *efficiency* at extreme-scale and *flexibility* by providing many specialized IO engines. ADIOS2 also supports *reusability* via the publish/subscribe API that allows for selecting an engine at runtime without any change to the user code.

The openPMD-api (0.14.0) uses mainly its BP3 and BP4 (*binary pack*) engines for file-based IO, SSC (*strong static coupler*) for strong coupling via MPI, and its SST (*sustainable staging transport*) engine for loose coupling [17] on which this paper focuses.

The purpose of SST is to enable very dynamic coupling workflows, allowing arbitrary numbers of readers to register to a stream while it keeps running. Between each writer and reader, communication between their respective parallel instances can go in arbitrary patterns up to full $m \times n$ meshes, opening connections only between instances that exchange data. The engine can pick from different low-level data transport implementations: The libfabric[3]-based RDMA (*remote direct memory access*) data transport for high scalability and use of technologies such as Infiniband, as well as the TCP data transport that uses network sockets for communication and that works as a fallback if libfabric is not available on the system.

The openPMD-api documentation[4] lists and explains a minimal example how to communicate between a writer and a reader with ADIOS2/SST (highlighted blue in Fig. 3). If not specified differently, this study uses the SST engine with the RDMA data transport, backed by libfabric 1.6.3a1.

3   Data Distribution Patterns

A writer for openPMD-formatted output will generally produce data in form of n-dimensional chunks that differ in size (location in the problem domain) and parallel instance of origin (location in the compute domain). A non-trivial

---

[3] https://ofiwg.github.io/libfabric/.

[4] https://openpmd-api.readthedocs.io/en/0.13.3/usage/streaming.html.

decision problem emerges concerning which data regions should be read by which instance of a reading code. This section determines properties that efficient data distributions should have and discusses a number of algorithms to achieve these properties.

3.1 Properties Found in a Performant Distribution Pattern

The SST engine of the ADIOS2 framework leaves some leeway for experimentation and optimization by theoretically allowing fully-connected communication patterns where each reading instances holds communication with each writing instance. For a performant pattern, we put forward a number of properties:

Locality. Rather than fully-connected "$m \times n$" style communication patterns, each instance's communication partners should bounded in number and located close within the system's topology. When carefully picking a local communication pattern, perfect IO weak scaling behaviour can ideally be achieved. Naturally, this point is subject to the communication infrastructure and the topology of a system.

Balancing. The distribution of data over parallel instances of a reading application should be as even as possible. Loose coupling serves as an opportunity to implement load balancing in a data processing pipeline.

Alignment. Access patterns should be congruent with the data layout in the backend. For ADIOS2, which generally organizes data in form of the chunks as they were written, this means that loaded chunks should coincide as much as possible with those that were written. Loading a chunk that must be pieced together from parts of several written chunks inhibits efficiency.

Read constraints. Applications often impose domain-specific constraints on the temporal and/or spatial order of data for processing. This can limit the sensible distribution patterns.

3.2 Chunk Distribution Algorithms

This subsection surveys a number of chunk distribution algorithms in the context of the properties as detailed in Subsect. 3.1. Pseudocode is found in the supplementary material [20]. Since the *read constraints* property depends on the data requirements within the problem domain, we do not further concern ourselves with it in this subsection.

Each of the following algorithms guarantees a complete distribution of data from writers to readers. Efficiency cannot generally be guaranteed and requires careful scheduling of applications and selection of a fitting distribution strategy.

Round Robin. The Round Robin approach at chunk distribution distributes the available data chunks over the parallel readers until none are left. It optimizes only for the *alignment* property, fully forgoing the properties of *locality* and *balancing*. It is interesting only in situations where its effects can be fully controlled by other means, such as knowledge on the way data is produced and consumed.

Slicing the Dataset into n-dimensional Hyperslabs. Since datasets have known sizes, one possibility is pre-assigning regions in form of hyperslabs in a dataset to reading ranks. This comes close to the conventional approach of explicitly selecting chunks to load. The available chunks are intersected with the hyperslab assigned to a rank to determine that rank's chunks to load.

This approach optimizes for the *balancing* property, mostly ignoring the other two properties. However, the *locality* property can be achieved if the distribution of parallel compute resources correlates with the problem domain, a condition often met in codes that do not use complex load balancing schemes. Similarly, the *alignment* property is achieved to some extent by the controlled number of cuts on the problem domain.

Since the achieved distribution is generally one that can be easily dealt with in reading analysis codes, this makes this rather simple approach interesting.

Binpacking. This approach tries to combine the advantages of the first two approaches. The rough proceeding is to calculate an ideal amount of data per rank, slice the incoming chunks such that this size is not exceeded and then distribute those size-fitted chunks across the reading ranks. The last step is non-trivial and an instance of the NP-complete bin-packing problem. Johnson [12] discusses algorithms to approximate the problem. For this paper, we adapt the Next-Fit algorithm to approximate the problem within a factor of 2, i.e. at most the double number of bins is used. For the purpose of chunk distribution, it is simple to modify such that each reading rank gets assigned at worst double the ideal amount. Later benchmarks in Subsect. 4.3 show that this worst-case behavior, while uncommon, does in practice occur.

Other than Round Robin, this algorithm has a guarantee on data *balancing*, and other than the approach that slices the dataset into hyperslabs, it guarantees that the incoming chunks are not arbitrarily subdivided, but instead at most sliced into fixed-sized subchunks, creating some notion of *alignment*. Both guarantees are weakened compared to those given by the earlier algorithms.

Distribution by Hostname. This algorithm serves to enrich the previous algorithms by some notion of data *locality*, making use of the information on topology of the writing and reading codes. Its schematics are sketched in Fig. 4.

It works in two phases: The first phase sorts chunks by node to readers on the same node. Specifically, the hostname is used for this step, and it can also be replaced with other layers in a system's topology, such as CPU sockets or host cohorts. A secondary distribution algorithm computes the chunk distribution within each single node.

After this, chunks may remain unassigned if a node is populated only by writers and no readers. To ensure a complete distribution, any of the preceding algorithms can be chosen as a fallback distribution for the leftover chunks.

As a result, this algorithm can be used to dynamically adapt to job scheduling: If nodes are populated by writers and readers at the same time, communication stays within a node. If however a job is scheduled to populate nodes only with either writers or readers, another strategy is automatically picked up.

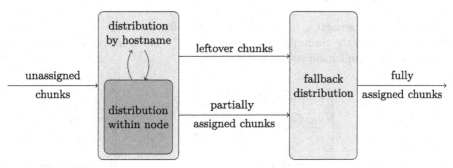

Fig. 4. Workflow for keeping a chunk distribution's *locality* property by keeping communication within the same node.

4 Evaluation for Two Streaming Setups

This section sees the construction and evaluation of two setups for streaming. The first setup uses streaming as a method for asynchronous IO, giving us a first insight into streaming performance characteristics. The second setup then constructs a data processing pipeline built from PIConGPU as data source and from GAPD, a GPU-accelerated diffraction simulation, as a data sink. It includes a study on the influence of chunk distribution strategies, of resource allocation, of streaming backend and of parallel scaling.

4.1 Streaming as Basis for an Asynchronous IO Workflow

The first setup demonstrates the potential that streaming has for exhausting idle compute resources. Data is streamed to a different process to be written to the filesystem in the background. The approach does not avoid the filesystem bottleneck, but instead provides asynchronous IO and hides the cost of IO if there is enough free memory to stage data.

In our evaluations, the data producer is the aforementioned particle-in-cell simulation code PIConGPU [3]. With the particle-in-cell algorithm being a computational method within the field of plasma physics, the raw output of PIConGPU is particle-mesh based and naturally expressible in openPMD.

For rapid setups of asynchronous IO pipelines via streaming, we developed the tool `openpmd-pipe`, which is an openPMD-api based Python script that redirects any openPMD data from source to sink. While this script performs the most simple transformation that any stage in a loosely-coupled pipeline might possibly do (none at all), it serves as an adaptor within a loosely-coupled pipeline: Further enabled workflows include (de)compressing a dataset or conversion between different backends, and capture of a stream into a file, used by the following setup. Within the context of openPMD, this builds expressivity comparable to using POSIX tee (by using the SST engine as a multiplexer) and to POSIX pipes (by using `openpmd-pipe` as an adaptor piece), motivating its name.

Figure 5 on the next page shows the setup for this first benchmark with `openpmd-pipe` on the Summit supercomputer [21]. (Software versions are documented in the supplementary materials [20].)

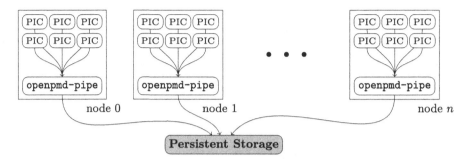

Fig. 5. Benchmark setup: Each node hosts 6 instances of PIConGPU, one per GPU. Those feed their data to one instance of `openpmd-pipe` which then asynchronously writes to the PFS.

Each compute node hosts six instances of PIConGPU, running a Kelvin Helmholtz simulation that is weakly scaled along the y axis. 9.14 GiB are produced per data output step and parallel process. Each node hosts one instance of `openpmd-pipe` to which each PIConGPU process on the same node sends data via SST. `openpmd-pipe` then writes that data to the parallel filesystem (Alpine).

This way, each node creates only one file on the parallel filesystem – a feature also supported natively by the ADIOS2 BP engine under the name of *aggregation*. Regular ADIOS2 BP output with node-level aggregation serves as the benchmarks's baseline. The baseline is referred to as "BP-only", while the setup shown in Fig. 5 is "SST+BP". Each benchmark runs for fifteen minutes and attempts to write data every 100 time steps in the simulation. The setup uses a feature in the ADIOS2 SST engine to automatically discard a step if the reader is not ready for reading yet.[5] This way, the simulation is never affected by actual file operations and IO granularity is automatically reduced if it becomes too slow.

Figure 6 on the facing page plots the throughput results. It shows the *perceived throughput* which we define through dividing the amount of data to be stored/sent by the time from starting the operation to its completion. Unlike the raw throughput, this includes latency time needed for communication and synchronization. It provides a good lower bound on the throughput while simplifying measurement in user code. When streaming, the time is measured between requesting and receiving data on the reader's side. Since the SST+BP setup performs IO in two phases, the throughput is shown for both of them.

The throughput is computed by average over each single data dump and over each parallel instance, scaled to the total amount of written data. Each benchmark is repeated three times and the plot shows each of those measurements.

---

[5] `"QueueFullPolicy" = "Discard"` The alternative is to block. A queue of steps can be held for some additional leeway, but it requires additional memory.

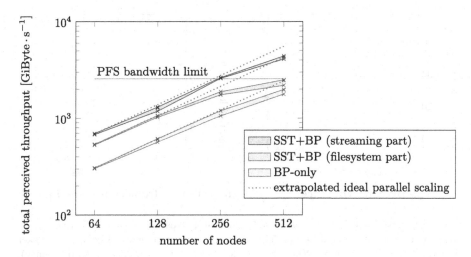

Fig. 6. Perceived total throughput. The file-based outputs (BP-only as well as SST+BP) are limited by the PFS bandwidth. At 512 nodes, the methods reach 4.15, 2.32, and 1.86 TiByte $\cdot$ s^{-1} on average, respectively.

The figure shows reasonable scaling behavior for both filesystem throughput as well as streaming throughput, with slight deviations from ideal scaling appearing at 512 nodes. At the time of running the benchmarks, the streaming example was not able to run without crashing on 1024 nodes.[6] At 4.0 to 4.3 TiByte $\cdot$ s^{-1}, the streaming throughput exceeds the PFS bandwidth (2.5 TiByte $\cdot$ s^{-1}) at 512 nodes. Since the first phase in the SST+BP setup already performs node-level data aggregation, the perceived BP throughput is higher than in the BP-only setup. At 512 nodes, the PFS bandwidth is approached (2.1 to 2.4 TiByte $\cdot$ s^{-1}).

Figure 7 on the next page plots the measured load/store times from the same benchmark. By computing the average numbers, the previous figure did not show any meaningful information on outliers. In parallel contexts, outliers can be serious hurdles for performance, hence Fig. 7 shows the data as boxplots (including each single measurement across all three repetitions of each benchmark). Results are shown for the streaming part of the SST+BP setup and for the BP-only setup. For BP-only, the median times range between 10 and 15 s with the worst outlier at 45 s. The median time for streaming is between 5 and 7 s with the worst outlier just above 9 s. A general trend is the increasing number of outliers at 256 nodes. At 512 nodes, longer load times become numerous enough to skew the median and no longer be outliers, explaining the observed decreasing throughput.

Finally, to compare overall performance between both approaches, we count the number of successfully written data dumps within the given time frame of

---

[6] After recent successful streaming setups at 1024 nodes, the likely cause for this were scalability issues in the metadata strategy used in the openPMD-api.

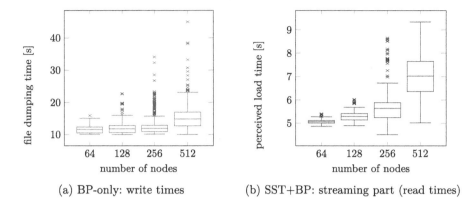

(a) BP-only: write times   (b) SST+BP: streaming part (read times)

Fig. 7. Perceived runtimes for file-based writes and streaming loads as boxplots. The box displays the interval containing 50% of sampled measurements. The upper whisker is at the largest value below "(upper quartile) + 1.5 · IQR" (inter quartile difference), lower whisker accordingly.

15 min. The BP-only setup blocks the simulation during IO. The number of successfully dumped simulation steps ranges from 22–23 on 64 nodes to 17–20 on 512 nodes. In contrast, the SST+BP setup can increase the number of data dumps as long as the IO time can be hidden within the simulation time. Hence, we observe 32–34 data dumps at 64 and at 128 nodes. Between 22 and 27 data dumps are written at 256 nodes and only 16–17 at 512 nodes. This is because outputs are dropped as soon as the IO time cannot be hidden behind the simulation time any more.

We examine the portion of the simulation time that the IO plugin requires in PIConGPU (first percentage: raw IO operation, second percentage: IO plugin including host-side data preparation and reorganization). For the BP-only setup those numbers range from (44%/54%) at 64 nodes to (55%/64%) at 512 nodes, explaining the slight drop in successfully dumped simulation steps. For the streaming side of the SST+BP setup, they range from (2.1%/27%) to (6.2%/32%), showing that raw IO is barely noticeable at low scale, while gaining some significance due to communication latencies between up to 3072 writers in our setup.

As the BP engine in ADIOS2 has a feature to write data synchronously to node-local NVM drives and drain them asynchronously to the parallel filesystem, enabling this feature is possible for both setups benchmarked so far. However, we consistently measure worse throughputs achieved by doing so, most peculiarly a significant decrease in the performance of the SST engine. As noted in Subsect. 1.1, asynchronous draining can compete for network resources with other parts of a parallel application, i.e. inter-node communication. Such an effect on MPI and the SST engine is a possible reason for this observed behavior.

4.2   A Staged Simulation-Analysis Pipeline: Setup

The next benchmark loosely couples a PIConGPU simulation with an X-ray scattering analysis code named GAPD [5]. GAPD is an "atom-based polychromatic diffraction simulation code for direct, kinematics-based simulations of X-ray/electron diffraction of large-scale atomic systems with mono-/polychromatic beams and arbitrary plane detector geometries" [5]. It takes into regard only particle data while ignoring mesh data produced by PIConGPU or similar simulations. Through scaling up to GPU clusters via MPI, GAPD is able to simulate diffraction patterns of systems up to 5 billion atoms.

Running this analysis is not only interesting from the perspective of extracting meaningful and interpretable data from the massive amounts of raw data produced by the simulation, it is also valuable as a means of reducing the amount of data to be processed via IO systems by several orders of magnitude down from the number of raw macroparticles to the number of points in reciprocal space.

GAPD is coupled with PIConGPU and configured to calculate the SAXS (Small-angle X-ray scattering) pattern from the input stream with the kinematical method [5]. If needed, the X-ray energy/wavelength, detection geometry can be adjusted in the input file whose configuration for the following benchmarks is found in the supplementary material along with software versions and an example for a created scatter plot [20]. This way, we commit ourselves to a realistic problem statement to be solved by simulation with PIConGPU and GAPD (scaled weakly to analyze scaling behavior) and aim to utilize the compute resources as fully as possible, avoiding waiting times introduced either by IO or asynchrony.

For reducing *IO-introduced* waiting times, IO should perform as fast as possible. To this end, the influence of chunk distribution strategies is shown. For reducing *asynchrony-introduced* waiting times, the setup will not block the simulation by performing IO. Again, ADIOS2 is configured to drop steps if the analysis has not finished yet, thus letting the pacing of the analysis determine the frequency of output. We demonstrate that this frequency can be tweaked by shifting the share of compute resources between writer and reader.

Codes must be scheduled carefully to allow for localized communication patterns. The Summit compute system hosts six GPUs per node, and the surveyed setup shares them equally between simulation and analysis, running three instances of PIConGPU and three instances of GAPD on each node. Distribution algorithms may or may not take the topology of the setup into account and we will show the impact of either.

Since GAPD only reads particle data, field data needs not be sent and does not influence the IO system, reducing the IO size per process to ∼3.1 GiB. The field data stays relevant for computing the next steps in the PIC simulation.

4.3   A Staged Simulation-Analysis Pipeline: Evaluation

We evaluate the following three distribution strategies, based on the algorithms discussed in Sect. 3.2:

(1) **Distribution by hostname:** Communication happens exclusively within a node. Distribution within a node is done via the Binpacking approach.

(2) **Binpacking:** Only the Binpacking algorithm runs and topology is ignored.

(3) **Slicing the dataset into hyperslabs:** The datasets are sliced into equal-sized hyperslabs which are distributed over the reading instances. Since PIConGPU uses no load balancing and data distribution in the problem space hence correlates with data distribution across the hardware, this approach keeps some notion of locality and avoids fully interconnected communication meshes.

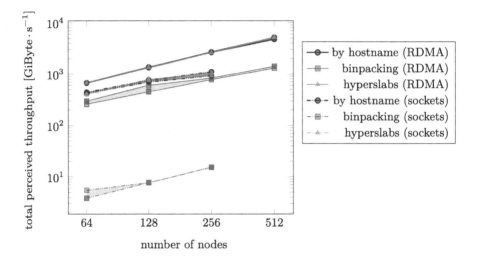

Fig. 8. Perceived total throughput. At 512 nodes, the RDMA-based methods reach 4.93, 1.35 and 5.12 TiByte $\cdot$ s^{-1} on average, respectively. The sockets-based methods reach 995, 15 and 985 GiByte $\cdot$ s^{-1}. The *by hostname* and *hyperslabs* strategy results overlap each other, for RDMA and sockets alike.

Figure 8 shows the perceived throughput. As in Sect. 4.1, the perceived throughput is defined by the time between write/load request and the end of the operation. This figure is subject to communication latencies, rendering the perceived throughput a lower bound for the actual throughput.

Again, each single benchmark is repeated three times and the plot shows the single measurements. The throughput is computed as the average over each parallel writer and each data exchange between writer and reader. The benchmark additionally shows the throughput observed with the sockets-based WAN implementation of the SST engine up until 256 nodes.

The RDMA tests show a reasonable quasi-linear parallel scaling behavior. The slightly higher peak bandwidth of 5.18 TiByte $\cdot$ s^{-1} compared to the bandwidths observed in Subsect. 4.1 can be related to the lower amount of data sent as well as to the different scheduling and communication patterns. Strategy *(2)* has a consistently worse performance than the other two strategies which clock out relatively similarly. The distinctive difference of strategy *(2)* is the number of communication partners that each parallel instance has, suggesting that controlling this number is important. Since no intra-host communication infrastructure is used, keeping communication strictly within one node in strategy *(1)* bears no measurable improvement over strategy *(3)*.

The WAN/sockets tests show similar tendencies, but at a consistently worse throughput than their RDMA-based counterparts. The worst throughput, with the Binpacking strategy, achieves throughputs between 400 and 970 GiByte · s^{-1}, correlating to loading times up to and above three minutes. We conclude that for scientific simulations, where data is usually written in bulk, sockets do not provide a scalable streaming solution.

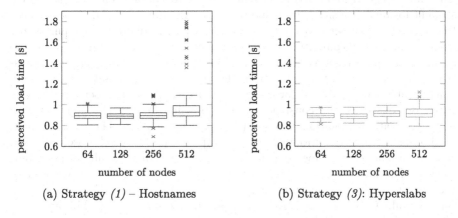

(a) Strategy *(1)* – Hostnames   (b) Strategy *(3)*: Hyperslabs

Fig. 9. Perceived data loading times for strategies *(1)* and *(3)* as boxplots.

Figure 9 plots the loading times for the two most promising strategies as boxplot. The median loading times are relatively consistent at 0.9 s for both strategies, explaining the good parallel scaling. The outliers observed for the Hostname strategy at 512 nodes all stem from the same single communication operation. Upon closer inspection, in that operation the Binpacking strategy (used within a node in strategy *(1)*) sent double the ideal amount of data to a single reader. This demonstrates that the worst-case behavior of the simple approximation algorithm can occur in practice. We conclude that for this setup, strategy *(3)* yields the best observed throughput and does not suffer from sporadic imbalances. Further heuristics should be explored for making the Binpacking algorithm more resistant against those.

With the setup chosen so far, GAPD takes around 5 min and 15 s to compute one scatter plot. Without blocking the simulation, this allows to create a scatter plot every 2000 steps in our experiments for the RDMA-based transport. Doing so via file-based loose coupling would require writing outputs of size 9.3 TiB per scatter plot at 512 nodes (after filtering the relevant data!). For the single data dump where the worst-case behavior of the Binpacking approach was observed, the respective scatter plot took roughly 10 min of computation due to the bad parallel load balancing.

For increasing the frequency of scatter plots, a benefit of loose coupling can be exploited: Dedicating five GPUs on a node to GAPD and only one to PIConGPU decreases the compute time for GAPD to roughly one minute, allowing it to run every 400 simulation steps. This is achieved only by changing the job script and without such a feature having been explicitly coded into either application, as would be necessary in a tightly-coupled monolithic application.

5   Summary and Outlook

The library openPMD-api has been extended to enable domain scientists a straight-forward transition from file-based to streaming IO. All data is scientifically self-describing and IO is performed flexibly, adapting to requirements from workflows and compute systems. Our benchmarks use streaming to exhaust available compute resources and to avoid bottlenecks caused by parallel filesystems. The achieved throughputs from the use of RDMA/Infiniband streaming reach double the bandwidth of the Summit PFS. In the first benchmark, this paper demonstrates the construction of a pipeline for asynchronous IO, and node-level data aggregation comes naturally with the setup. The second benchmark demonstrates the straightforward setup of a prototypical loosely-coupled simulation-analysis pipeline, avoiding to write intermediate results to persistent storage. The importance of data distribution is discussed and we respond to the challenge with flexibly interchangeable distribution algorithms, allowing to rapidly evaluate the best-performing strategy for a discrete setup. This approach allows for future extensibility towards setups with properties such as application-specific constraints or parallel load balancing that influence data distribution. Our experiments saw no benefits from using purely intra-node communication compared to inter-node communication. Backends with support for inter-process communication (IPC) techniques are a chance to exhaust potential from node-local communication, ideally to achieve near-perfect scaling at extreme scale. By substantiating that common technology like network sockets may not hold up to the challenge of streaming IO for HPC applications, this work employs efficient transport layers such as Infiniband successfully in an accessible manner for scientifically self-describing streaming data pipelines.

Acknowledgements. This research used resources of the Oak Ridge Leadership Computing Facility at the Oak Ridge National Laboratory, which is supported by the Office of Science of the U.S. Department of Energy under Contract No. DE-AC05-00OR22725. Supported by the Exascale Computing Project (17-SC-20-SC), a collaborative effort of two U.S. Department of Energy organizations (Office of Science and the National Nuclear Security Administration). Supported by EC through Laserlab-Europe, H2020 EC-GA 871124. Supported by the Consortium for Advanced Modeling of Particles Accelerators (CAMPA), funded by the U.S. DOE Office of Science under Contract No. DE-AC02-05CH11231. This work was partially funded by the Center of Advanced

Systems Understanding (CASUS), which is financed by Germany's Federal Ministry of Education and Research (BMBF) and by the Saxon Ministry for Science, Culture and Tourism (SMWK) with tax funds on the basis of the budget approved by the Saxon State Parliament.

References

1. Abbasi, H., Wolf, M., Eisenhauer, G., Klasky, S., Schwan, K., Zheng, F.: Datastager: scalable data staging services for petascale applications. Cluster Comput. **13**(3), 277–290 (2010). https://doi.org/10.1145/1551609.1551618

2. Ahn, D.H., Garlick, J., Grondona, M., Lipari, D., Springmeyer, B., Schulz, M.: Flux: a next-generation resource management framework for large HPC centers. In: 2014 43rd International Conference on Parallel Processing Workshops, pp. 9–17 (2014). https://doi.org/10.1109/ICPPW.2014.15

3. Bussmann, M., et al.: Radiative signatures of the relativistic Kelvin-Helmholtz instability. In: Proceedings of the International Conference on High Performance Computing, Networking, Storage and Analysis, SC 2013, pp. 5:1–5:12. ACM, New York (2013). ISBN 978-1-4503-2378-9, https://doi.org/10.1145/2503210.2504564

4. Rocklin, M.: Dask: parallel computation with blocked algorithms and task scheduling. In: Huff, K., Bergstra, J. (eds.) Proceedings of the 14th Python in Science Conference, pp. 130–136 (2015). https://dask.org

5. E, J.C., Wang, L., Chen, S., Zhang, Y.Y., Luo, S.N.: GAPD: a GPU-accelerated atom-based polychromatic diffraction simulation code. J. Synchrotron Radiat. **25**(2), 604–611 (2018). https://doi.org/10.1107/S1600577517016733

6. Fortmann-Grote, C., et al.: SIMEX: simulation of experiments at advanced light sources. In: 11th NOBUGS Conference, Copenhagen, pp. 29–34 (2016). https://doi.org/10.17199/NOBUGS2016.21

7. Fortmann-Grote, C., et al.: Simulations of ultrafast X–ray laser experiments. In: Proceedings of SPIE, Advances in X-ray Free-Electron Lasers Instrumentation IV, vol. 10237, p. 102370S (2017). https://doi.org/10.1117/12.2270552

8. Godoy, W.F., et al.: ADIOS 2: the adaptable input output system. A framework for high-performance data management. SoftwareX **12**, 100561 (2020). https://doi.org/10.1016/j.softx.2020.100561

9. Huebl, A.: PIConGPU: predictive simulations of laser-particle accelerators with manycore hardware. Ph.D. thesis, Technische Universität Dresden (2019). https://doi.org/10.5281/zenodo.3266820

10. Huebl, A., et al.: On the scalability of data reduction techniques in current and upcoming HPC systems from an application perspective. In: Kunkel, J.M., Yokota, R., Taufer, M., Shalf, J. (eds.) ISC High Performance 2017. LNCS, vol. 10524, pp. 15–29. Springer, Cham (2017). https://doi.org/10.1007/978-3-319-67630-2_2

11. Huebl, A., et al.: openPMD: a meta data standard for particle and mesh based data (2015). https://doi.org/10.5281/zenodo.591699, https://github.com/openPMD

12. Johnson, D.: Near-optimal bin packing algorithms. Ph.D. thesis, Massachusetts Institute of Technology (1973)

13. Koller, F., Poeschel, F., Gu, J., Huebl, A.: openPMD-api: C++ & Python API for scientific I/O with openPMD (2018). https://github.com/openPMD/openPMD-api. https://doi.org/10.14278/rodare.27

14. Kress, J., et al.: Comparing time-to-solution for in situ visualization paradigms at scale. In: 2020 IEEE 10th Symposium on Large Data Analysis and Visualization (LDAV), pp. 22–26 (2020). https://doi.org/10.1109/LDAV51489.2020.00009

15. Larsen, M., et al.: The alpine in situ infrastructure: ascending from the ashes of strawman. In: Proceedings of the In Situ Infrastructures on Enabling Extreme-Scale Analysis and Visualization, pp. 42–46 (2017). https://doi.org/10.1145/3144769.3144778

16. Liu, Q., et al.: Hello ADIOS: the challenges and lessons of developing leadership class I/O frameworks. Concurr. Comput.: Pract. Exp. **26**(7), 1453–1473 (2014). https://doi.org/10.1002/cpe.3125

17. Logan, J., et al.: Extending the publish/subscribe abstraction for high-performance I/O and data management at extreme scale. IEEE Data Eng. Bull. **43**, 35–46 (2020)

18. Loring, B., et al.: Improving performance of M-to-N processing and data redistribution in In Transit analysis and visualization. In: Frey, S., Huang, J., Sadlo, F. (eds.) Eurographics Symposium on Parallel Graphics and Visualization. The Eurographics Association (2020). ISBN 978-3-03868-107-6, https://doi.org/10.2312/pgv.20201073

19. Mayes, C.E., et al.: Lightsource unified modeling environment (LUME) - a start-to-end simulation ecosystem. In: IPAC (2021)

20. Poeschel, F., et al.: Supplementary material: transitioning from file-based HPC workflows to streaming data pipelines with openPMD and ADIOS2. https://doi.org/10.5281/zenodo.4906276

21. Vazhkudai, S.S., et al.: The design, deployment, and evaluation of the coral pre-exascale systems. In: SC18: International Conference for High Performance Computing, Networking, Storage and Analysis, pp. 661–672 (2018). https://doi.org/10.1109/SC.2018.00055

22. Wan, L., et al.: Improving I/O performance for exascale applications through online data layout reorganization. Under review (2021)

23. Wilkinson, M.D., et al.: The FAIR Guiding Principles for scientific data management and stewardship. Sci. Data **3**(1), 160018 (2016). ISSN 2052-4463, https://doi.org/10.1038/sdata.2016.18

24. Zaharia, M., et al.: Apache spark: a unified engine for big data processing. Commun. ACM **59**(11), 56–65 (2016). ISSN 0001-782, https://doi.org/10.1145/2934664

Understanding and Leveraging the I/O Patterns of Emerging Machine Learning Analytics

Ana Gainaru[1]([✉]), Dmitry Ganyushin[1], Bing Xie[1], Tahsin Kurc[2], Joel Saltz[2], Sarp Oral[1], Norbert Podhorszki[1], Franz Poeschel[4], Axel Huebl[3], and Scott Klasky[1]

[1] Oak Ridge National Laboratory, Oak Ridge, USA
`gainarua@ornl.gov`
[2] Stony Brook University, New York, USA
[3] Lawrence Berkeley National Laboratory (LBNL), Berkeley, USA
[4] Center for Advanced Systems Understanding, Görlitz, Germany

Abstract. The scientific community is currently experiencing unprecedented amounts of data generated by cutting-edge science facilities. Soon facilities will be producing up to 1 PB/s which will force scientist to use more autonomous techniques to learn from the data. The adoption of machine learning methods, like deep learning techniques, in large-scale workflows comes with a shift in the workflow's computational and I/O patterns. These changes often include iterative processes and model architecture searches, in which datasets are analyzed multiple times in different formats with different model configurations in order to find accurate, reliable and efficient learning models. This shift in behavior brings changes in I/O patterns at the application level as well at the system level. These changes also bring new challenges for the HPC I/O teams, since these patterns contain more complex I/O workloads. In this paper we discuss the I/O patterns experienced by emerging analytical codes that rely on machine learning algorithms and highlight the challenges in designing efficient I/O transfers for such workflows. We comment on how to leverage the data access patterns in order to fetch in a more efficient way the required input data in the format and order given by the needs of the application and how to optimize the data path between collaborative processes. We will motivate our work and show performance gains with a study case of medical applications.

This manuscript has been authored in part by UT-Battelle, LLC, under contract DE-AC05-00OR22725 with the US Department of Energy (DOE). The US government retains and the publisher, by accepting the article for publication, acknowledges that the US government retains a nonexclusive, paid-up, irrevocable, worldwide license to publish or reproduce the published form of this manuscript, or allow others to do so, for US government purposes. DOE will provide public access to these results of federally sponsored research in accordance with the DOE Public Access Plan (http://energy.gov/downloads/doe-public-access-plan).

© Springer Nature Switzerland AG 2022
J. Nichols et al. (Eds.): SMC 2021, CCIS 1512, pp. 119–138, 2022.
https://doi.org/10.1007/978-3-030-96498-6_7

Keywords: Emerging HPC applications · Deep learning methods · I/O patterns · I/O optimization · Data management

1 Introduction

Science facilities, such as the LCLS experiment (Linac Coherent Light Source) are forecast to produce over 1 TB of data per second [15] in the very near future. Trends suggest that these facilities will reach rates of up to 1 PB/s within the next 10 years [29]. Accordingly, to meet the resource demands of digital twins and surrogates for these facilities and experiments, high performance computing (HPC) has continued to advance infrastructure including hybrid compute nodes (e.g., CPU and GPU collocated nodes), high-speed network interconnects, and heterogeneous storage capabilities (e.g., Burst Buffer, parallel file systems, HPSS).

Beyond generating unprecedented amounts of data, more and more domain scientists actively employ ever-larger machine learning models in their applications and produce higher resolutions than ever before. The corresponding accumulation of varied and detailed data creates greater learning opportunities. This big data revolution started from early 2010 with the introduction of novel pattern recognition algorithms in the computing landscape. These algorithms were capable of parsing large, high-quality data sets and eventually led to an explosion of efficient machine learning algorithms optimized for modern accelerators architectures. The rapid succession of advances in many computing fields, such as computer vision, speech recognition, natural language processing, etc., has triggered a convergence of AI and HPC. This is the case for a wide range of scientific areas: bioinformatics, fusion energy science, medical research, computational fluid dynamics, lattice quantum chromodynamics using deep learning network and other machine learning algorithms for a large variety of projects, such as classifying galaxies types [5], analyzing medical images [10], reconstructing the 2D plasma profile [8] and predicting protein structure properties [42].

Clearly, over the past decade, there has been a significant advancement in AI and deep learning theories for HPC. But at the same time, at system level there is currently no consensus achieved on which software framework or methodology should be used for a given problem. In particular, the algorithms used, have typically been developed to accelerate the training of specific AI models for HPC platforms and currently have a strong experimental component. Each scientific application is using different machine learning models (or an ensemble of several models) in an ad-hoc manner, relying on trial-an-error to find the best model and model configurations or to understand the model's sensitivity to outliers.

In a quest to address the challenge from system level, several approaches have been proposed recently to automatically identify model architecture [26] and hyperparameters [23,35] best suited for a given problem. In specific, sensitivity analysis methods proposed to detect the parts of a model [1,39] are most relevant to optimizing training/inference processes. Similarly, outlier tolerance analysis [37] characterizes the robustness of a model and the ability to reuse the learned patterns to solve related problems. In general, all these methods, unfortunately, complicate the workflow behind an AI framework and the I/O life-cycle. AI frameworks currently include complex workflows where datasets are analyzed multiple times in different formats with different learning configurations. In addition, each machine learning instance uses parallel methods of training/inference splitting the computation using a mix of data parallel, model and layer parallel approaches creating chains of processes distributed across compute nodes with complex dependencies between them. These coupled processes share computational and I/O patterns that are currently not leveraged by the machine learning framework.

In this paper, we highlight the data patterns and lifecycle of AI frameworks and the performance impact these pattern have on emerging scientific applications that rely on AI frameworks for their studies. Optimizing the data lifecycle management is becoming critical as emerging HPC applications add another layer of difficulty by coupling multiple such applications each with its own data format and AI characteristics. By showcasing a testcase from the medical field, we illustrate the challenges brought by the way application use AI frameworks. We propose a workflow framework that uses a model abstraction to store additional metadata with each model allowing applications to collaboratively work on the same pieces of data. In addition, the framework is capable of keeping the relation of an application's domain decomposition to the initial data which allows querying capabilities on data objects. These features are essential to allow workflow management systems to optimize the data path between processes and applications for every moment of interest.

We summarize our contributions and the outline of the paper as follows:

- We discuss optimization opportunities in the context of machine learning methods, where a mix of methods are increasingly applied to improve the performance and scalability of the training and inference phases. We discuss optimization directions specific to emerging applications in their quest of incorporating ensembles of machine learning applications for enhancing and running their codes on accelerator applications (Sect. 2).
- We introduce an overview of our vision for a workflow framework that implements the discussed optimizations. The abstractions included in the framework can be used as a fundamental building block to prioritize and stream datasets between applications using different formats corresponding to the N to M patterns used by ensemble machine learning methods (Sect. 3).
- We discuss the advantages of our model abstraction and show early results. We position our vision in the context of state-of-art medical imagining processing, highlighting it's impact (Sect. 4).

2   Machine Learning Patterns

We highlight in this section the patterns within current machine learning frameworks and the way they are used by HPC applications. The section provides a

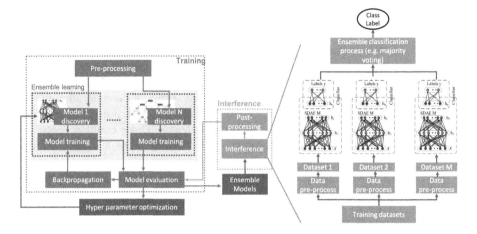

Fig. 1. Typical AI application workflow using ensemble learning for training and inference

high level overview of the machine learning process and the workflow of coupled AI applications, with a test cases in the medical field, followed by two sub-sections, each dedicated to the training and interference phases respectively. Each sub-section identifies opportunities for leveraging the data lifecycle patterns for each phase.

2.1 Overview

Machine learning frameworks provide a variety of configurations options for shaping the parameters of the model as well as for optimizing hardware allocations and other system related parameters [18]. For example, the Spark framework, an in-memory machine learning framework for data analytics and SQL databases, provides over one hundred parameters for tuning the performance [22]. Identifying the best configuration in the space defined by these parameters is challenging and manually tuning these configurations requires substantial knowledge of a specific framework. Automatic techniques for parameter tuning use performance models (e.g. for random forests [2], neural networks [23] or general machine learning frameworks [17,34]) and are currently implemented in one way or another by recent HPC applications.

The typical machine learning method used by current HPC applications follows the overall workflow in Fig. 1. All applications use a pre-processing step to transform the data into some initial representation. This pre-processing step can be a simple process, like data cleaning or it can include multiple data transformation steps, like data augmentation by creating more training samples by stretching or rotating images, or projecting the data to a different space. Given a prediction task, the model discovery phase often starts from well-known models that have been successful in similar task domains. Based on a user given output loss functions, the model is repeatedly adjusted and tuned through algorithms

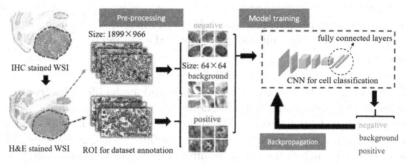

(a) CNN for training (modified from [19])

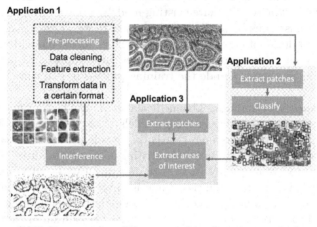

(b) Inference using different machine learning methods

Fig. 2. Example of applications from the medical field using machine learning frameworks for whole slide tissue images

for hyper-parameter search (like MENNDL [24]). The model is evaluated at each iteration and the process stops when the prediction accuracy does not improve.

Understating the mechanics behind how models work is not straightforward. Because of this, the adjustments and tuning made to the model are based on heuristics and can have different complexities in different applications. One such example is by adjusting only the hyper-parameters that appear to have a significant impact on the learned weights. More complex examples include growing the model or incorporating parts of other models that show good results in other similar tasks. In this context, there is a need to train and develop a series of model variants while exploring a large number of alternatives.

Current training methods maintain a large population of promising models that are evolved or combined to improve the accuracy of the machine learning process.

The sets of artifacts created during the data and model lifecycles (containing the model configurations and parameters as well as training logs) are useful to understand the model behaviors and to try out new models. There are currently solutions for storing and versioning such artifacts (like MODELHUB [20]). These solutions typically include model versioning systems, provenance management system to keep track of the problem generating a specific model, a querying language for searching through the model space and in some cases hosted services to store learned, explore and share existing models. Such solution are critical for learning from past runs or similar applications. However they lack a dynamic component and does not capture intermediate steps in the model formation. We believe the framework we propose in this paper can complement such versioning systems and allow them to guide the training process in real time.

Testcase: Medical Applications. The medical community has developed throughout the years various machine learning models to extract and classify imaging features from different image types (MRIs [14], whole slide tissue images [10,19], retina images [40] etc.). There are many existing imaging modalities: X-ray radiography, computed tomography (CT), MR imaging (MRI), ultrasound, digital pathology, etc. and new modalities, such as spectral CT, are being routinely invented. Even for commonly used imaging modalities, the information density has continued to increase (for example, the spatial resolution of clinical CT and MRI, the spatial and temporal resolution of ultrasound, etc.).

Figure 2 presents two example application workflows; one for training and one for inference. In the first case (Fig. 2a), the application uses convolutional neural networks (CNN) for training a model capable of predicting positive tests for Ki-67 that indicate high concentration of proteins in cells. In the pre-processing step the image is transformed to a required format that exposes the required phenomenon. After which each image is divided into patches of a fixed size which are used for the training process. The training phase may execute hyper-parameter and/or neural architecture searches in order to develop accurate and robust models. As mentioned previously, in such strategies, multiple candidate models are trained and evaluated concurrently; hence, the training and test datasets are processed multiple times.

Medical applications may employ a variety of analysis workflow patterns. One pattern involves execution of multiple machine/deep learning models targeted for different types of characterizations of the same dataset. For example, a model may detect and segment cells in high resolution tissue images while another model may segment and classify regions of tumor. Another pattern involves the use of ensemble models, where predictions from multiple models are combined to generate final predictions. Each model in the ensemble may be built from the same neural network architecture but trained with different hyper-parameters

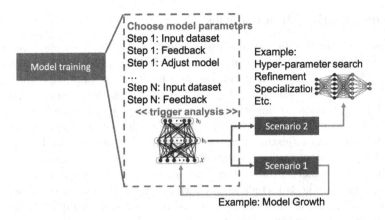

Fig. 3. Typical dynamic behavior during the training phase of an AI applications. Different analysis are triggered within the training process: Scenario 1 grows to model to incorporate more complex behaviors; Scenario 2 triggers new training phases starting from the current model for hyper-parameters searches or model specialization.

and subsets of training data or each model may be implemented using different neural network architectures. A third pattern employs multiple models which use output from other models in training and/or inference phases. Similarly to application 3 from Fig. 2b, some applications can optimize their search based on the output of others. For example, an application that identify nuclei in WSIs and segment their boundaries could feed information to an application identifying tumour cells so the second application could focus on the areas that have higher chances of returning positive results. Another direction is to couple two applications that identify tumour cells through different methods (for example, [19] using tests for Ki-67 and [33] relying on nuclei size or shapes) to coordinate and inform each others training or inference steps.

Within each application multiple models can be used for both training and inference phases by using strategies, such as evolutionary techniques [26] or reinforcement learning [12], where there are multiple variations of environments and alternative actions possible. When these workflow possibilities are combined with multiple image modalities and numerous disease types, a very large number of highly complex tasks associated with numerous applications are formed. In addition, there can be multiple synchronization points within an application with an application-defined frequency. Synchronization is a necessary step for both training (to merge potential models into one) and inference (by implementing majority voting or some other algorithm to combine the outputs of each model).

Medical applications rely on workflows of tightly coupled applications operating on the same datasets each implementing their own model, requiring synchronization within an application between multiple models and between applications.

2.2 Optimization Opportunities

Based on the overview in the previous section, we highlight specific opportunities for optimizing the training phase used by HPC applications. Note that the inference follows a very similar pattern and most of the opportunities applied to both training and inference. Figure 3 summarizes the typical behavior of one HPC application during the training phase as highlighted in the previous overview section. The process adjusts the model iteratively by parsing the input dataset. The adjustment process accounts for variance and bias in the model. Variance accounts for prediction errors related to randomness in the estimated model parameters due to the randomness in the data and training. Most model training methods include non-deterministic elements (for e.g. neural network start by randomly initializing a model and only take samples of the input datasets [28]; some tree-based models split nodes iteratively based on randomly selected thresholds [38]). In order to reduce prediction variance, machine learning methods rely on sampling more configurations for training.

Machine learning frameworks need to also deal with errors produced by models despite having been trained with enough data (called the bias of the model). Bias characterizes the model's inability to capture complex behaviors within the dataset. This is usually caused by models whose structures are too simple and a fix would require more complex models. Figure 3, Scenario 1 presents a solution for growing the model on-the-fly to deal with bias once an acceptable variance has been obtained. Once the model is adjusted, with new layers or different layer configuration (for neural networks) or with new trees or higher depths (for random forests [27,30]) for example, the process continue and the dataset is once parsed iteratively on the new model.

Partial models that show good prediction capabilities are good starting candidates for similar or related tasks within other applications. It is common practice to trigger additional analysis on partial models that fit a certain criteria [25,31]. These analysis usually include hyper-parameter searches starting with the partial model or refinement and specialization either by growing or pruning the partial model or by retraining it on a different dataset to focus on a subset problem. A good example for Scenario 2 Fig. 3 is the CANDLE application (Cancer Deep Learning Environment) [36] where the input data is split into regions and the training process is forked into alternative directions, each of which excludes one of the regions. This division allows the study of each regions impact on the training and creates similar models that are then combined.

The model lifecycle includes transitions and changes of the model in the quest to increase its accuracy as well as artifacts related to learned parameters and configurations. Through the life of the workflow of coupled applications, there are partial models that need to be shared and worked on collaboratively as well as many similar models that need to be identified and tested.

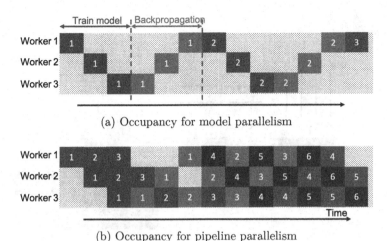

(a) Occupancy for model parallelism

(b) Occupancy for pipeline parallelism

Fig. 4. Occupancy for different types of parallelism

Each application is creating a large set of models and artifacts. There is currently no robust way of keeping track of similar models and artifacts during runtime to allow dynamic collaborative work on models.

Training approaches for machine learning frameworks are constantly being developed or adapted to take advantage of state of the art HPC architectures. The most used techniques to parallelize the training process are synchronous data-parallel and model-parallel training [41]. Data parallel refers to distributing the dataset among workers, in which case the model is either in shared memory or replicated among all processes involved in the training. Model parallel assumes a distribution of the model on the processes and each worker updates its own part of the model on the same images iteratively going through the entire dataset. As opposed to the all process synchronization required by data parallel techniques, the synchronization for model parallel is a one to one communication between workers in order to update the entire model in multiple steps. This process is illustrated in Fig. 4a. Other implementations of deep neural networks use layer-parallel training [11] by dividing the layers among the processing units. Similarly with model parallel each process updates the model in an incremental way without requiring a global synchronization.

More recent methods (pipeline parallelism) combine the data and model parallel methods to overcome the hardware efficiency limitations of model-parallel training. A general pipeline parallel setup involves layers split across stages, with each stage potentially replicated and running data parallel. The pipeline parses multiple batches in order to keep it full in steady state (Fig. 4b). One example of a AI framework using pipeline parallelism is PipeDream [13] that is able to automatically determine how to systematically split a given model across the available compute nodes in order to maximize the occupancy of all the workers.

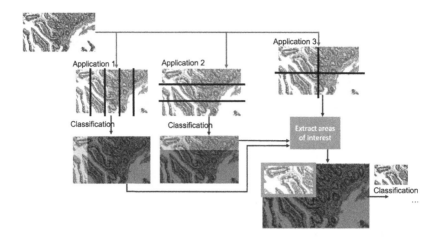

Fig. 5. Typical behavior of the inference step in emerging applications

At present all these methods exist at the same time, each being used by different frameworks within the HPC community. In the big data field, Spark [21] is one of the most used AI framework due to it's ease in usage partially because it hides the details of parallelism from the user, enabling performance portability across platforms.

In this context, the training process is divided not only between multiple applications but also within one application between multiple workers and tasks. Different frameworks use different computational patterns, adjusting the model at different levels. We propose in this paper a framework that allows each separate method to define model dependencies within and between applications by using abstractions that define moments of interest where optimizations can be applied. Multiple tasks within an applications need to share the same model in real time and similarly multiple applications can benefit from sharing partial models (as illustrated by the medical applications described in the previous section). The large dataset and the analysis results need to be staged from and to storage based on the needs of each framework.

> Large amounts of data need to be processed by multiple models repeatedly and transferred between different tasks or applications to evaluate if more efficient models provide better accuracy performance. There is currently no automatic way of moving data to and where is needed in an efficient way.

2.3   Automation Opportunities

The pre-processing step is usually a separate step that is independent of the AI method that follows. However, the relation between the domain decomposition

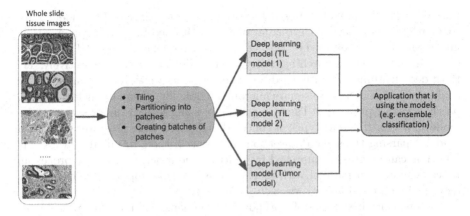

Fig. 6. Typical behavior for ensemble learning

and the machine learning technique can be exploited to optimize the data transfers between coupled applications. Figure 5 illustrates a representative example of domain decomposition between medical applications:

- Application 1 uses models for segmenting and classifying nuclei by dividing the input images in patches of approximately 120×120 square microns
- Application 2 trains and classifies models for characterizing spatial patterns of tumor infiltrating lymphocytes using patches of 50×50 square microns
- Application 3 uses models for segmenting and classifying tumor by using the same images divided into patches of 88×88 square microns.

In the current format all applications are running independently using the same input images read from storage. Identifying tumor cells (application 3) is done by investigating the patches that present a given pattern in the output given by the first two applications. Patches that do not contain nuclei for example will not contain any useful information for identifying tumor cells. In the current format, the applications are unable to filter out irrelevant patches without reading the full image. Ideally the I/O framework would be capable of prioritizing the data to only bring (or bring first) the pieces of data relevent to a given study. For example, in Fig. 5, application 3 only needs the top left patch of the input data (based on the outputs of applications 1 and 2) to output its classification.

> Querying capabilities are needed to be able to prioritize and filter data based on the needs of coupled applications.

Figure 6 presents a typical scenario for ensemble learning when multiple models are used to classify the same input data and the partial results are fed into a global decision process that combines them into one. One such example is the deep learning model used by the Stony Brook medical department to predict the distribution of lymphocyte cells at the resolution of 50×50 square micron (in this case TIL model 1 uses a Inception V4 network and TIL model 2 the VGG16 network). Each WSI in a dataset is partitioned into image patches. The image patches are processed by the deep learning model and labeled TIL-positive or TIL-negative, i.e., a patch has lymphocyte cells in it or not, respectively. The third deep learning model is used for segmenting and classifying tumor regions at the resolution of 88 × 88 square micron patches. The model predicts whether a patch is Tumor-positive or Tumor-negative by using several tumor segmentation models, one for different types of cancer (lung, pancreatic, prostate, etc.). Each model is parsing the same dataset, but pre-process them in different ways. The I/O time can be greatly improved by splitting the process into a pre-processing process running in parallel with multiple classification applications feeding the data in the required format for each.

Automating these types of workflows can be beneficial not only for the inference step, but also for training, especially in the context of hyper-parameter search. Training multiple models requires parsing the same data multiple times. By separating the I/O layer from the hyper-parameter process, our framework will be capable of reusing the data required by each model. In addition, it will allow the hyper-parameter process to investigate how different ways of partitioning the data influences the accuracy of the neural network. More specifically, it give the opportunity of extending the search to parameters outside the model.

> Automation through data streaming is key for medical applications that parse the same data even when pre-processed in different ways

3   Data Management Vision

The previous section has highlighted potential optimization areas for data management in AI frameworks. In current implementations, models are just another data object that is handled by the I/O middleware in the same way as any other variables and applications are ran independent of each other. Model and workflow management are left to the discretion of each user. However, the application training/inference cycle includes patterns that can be reused for different applications or task within the same coupled execution or for future studies.

Current solutions for managing data include frameworks that use self describing formats to store the data (like ADIOS [9] or DIMES [6]) including versioning and time step tracker which allows applications to access the state of a data at a given point in the simulation time in real time or postmortem. Workflow management systems, like [3,4] have been developed to run over data management systems and couple applications running in an HPC center (or geographically distributed). However, all these framework target general scientific applications and have not been designed for read intensive codes that frequently re-use data. Moreover, the data formats they expect are general and do not have any specific information on the model parameters and its evolution.

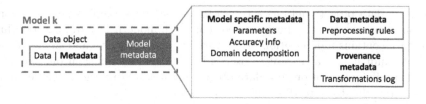

Fig. 7. Model metadata information is being attached to every data object adding information specific to the models being saved.

There has been increasing work on developing general-purpose systems for supporting machine learning, e.g. pushing predictive models into databases [7] and managing modeling lifecycles and serving predictive models in advanced ways [16,32]. Frameworks like MODELHUB [20] are able to support versioning as a first-class construct and offer the possibility to inspect models and their properties once they have been uploaded to the system. These solution offer ways of storing and using existing models for future similar tasks but lack the dynamic nature of coupled applications.

In this context, we propose in this paper a framework that separates the I/O layer from the ML process and bridges workflow management systems with ML frameworks by including model specific metadata capable of being queried similar to MODELHUB into general purpose I/O frameworks like ADIOS that are capable of real time data staging between coupled applications. We believe this is a required first step in facilitating efficient collaboration between coupled AI applications and allowing more complex optimizations specific to the needs of these applications (compression or priority transfers services based on the importance of different parts of the model or input data, workflow management systems specifically designed for AI coupled applications, etc.)

The proposed ML workflow framework has two main components:

– a **model object** that attaches model metadata as illustrated in Fig. 7 to every data object that is handled by the I/O framework
– **querying capabilities** that leverage the model metadata and **link them with actions** in order to allow similar models to be discovered and to identify important parts of the model or of the input data on-the-fly.

We detail each component in the next two sections and we present impact and early results.

3.1   Model Metadata

Pub/sub IO frameworks (e.g. ADIOS) operate on data objects and allow an application to publish data where other can subscribe to based on some given metadata. Our framework defines a model object in a similar way. In simple terms, a model object defines the state of the model at a certain moment of interest, which includes the chain of states recorded during the evolution of the model. A data object contains a collection of metadata keeping general information about the payload being stored. For more modern I/O frameworks this metadata contains a description of the variable, including size and shape of the variable, min/max, value ranges etc. and other general information. We add model specific information to a data object as illustrated in Fig. 7. These additions can be divided into three distinct parts:

- **Model specific metadata** contains information about the parameters and configurations used to create the model as well as performance information based on partial results. This section also contains information about the domain decomposition used for training the model. The information stored in this region can be used to stage the models between coupled applications based on different requirements.
- **Data metadata** includes information about the way the data needs to be pre-processed before it can be used by the ML application. The information can include tile size/shape, resolution information or a pointer to a function that needs to be called on the input data.
- **Provenance metadata** contains the evolution of a model through recorded moments of interest. These moments include the creation of the model, a split into other partial models due to hyper-parameter search, a growth triggered by an attempt to decrease the bias error etc.
- **[Optionally] Priority metadata** includes information about which parts of the models are more relevant to the inference phase. This information can be used to prioritize the transfers of certain parts of the model or for scheduling tasks based on the domain decomposition of the model.

Using the model object, the framework allows distributed applications and tasks to share the same model object and transform it collaboratively by updating its content. The framework can alter, delete model objects or trigger the creation of others through a pre-defined set of actions given by the ML application. Based on our observations, the actions required by medical applications need to include: pruning and growing a model object and forking it into others representing a different subset. The action list can be extended based on future functionalities that allow the interaction of our ML workflow framework with both versioning systems and ML applications.

Based on the patterns presented by hyper-parameter search algorithms, the ML workflow framework needs to keep track of all these actions. The evolution of the data is kept in the provenance metadata attached to the model object and allows applications to navigate through different states of a model and to search for different versions that fit a certain criteria.

The model metadata can be used by workflow frameworks as guidelines to stream data and start processes in an efficient manner and to prioritize the data transfers so the most relevant data is received first.

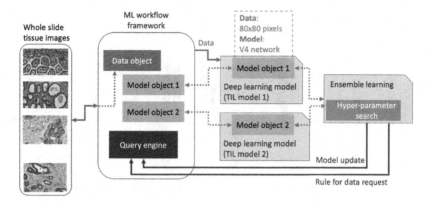

Fig. 8. ML workflow framework used by two deep learning model applications and an ensemble learning process

3.2 Add Query Capabilities over the Model Metadata

In order to take full advantage of the model object proposed in the previous section, the framework needs to have query capabilities over the model metadata. The query capabilities will operated on a model object metadata in the same way as modern I/O frameworks operate on data objects. ADIOS, for example can bring data that fits a certain criteria based on the metadata it stores for each variable. There are two classes of queries that are most relevant to the patterns of AI frameworks, namely: (i) Queries for models fitting certain criteria; (ii) Queries for domain decomposition information linked to a model.

Figure 8 shows the design of the ML workflow framework when used by two deep learning model applications and an ensemble learning process for both types of queries. By separating the I/O plane from the machine learning tasks, the deep learning models can set up the model object with information about how the pre-processing needs to be done (for example, in the Figure, TIL model 1 requires segmenting the input images into 80×80 pixel tiles). This information allows the framework prepare the input data in the format required by each application (and decrease the amount of redundant computation if possible). In addition, the queries for domain decomposition leverage the relation between the input data and the domain decomposition within a model to automatically detect which parts of the data are relevant to a given classification task. For example, given the applications in our previous examples (Fig. 5) the patch division will be captured in the model metadata. The input dataset used by this mode will always use the same decomposition (division in patches of the same size and shape in the example). Workflow frameworks can leverage this information to transform data on-the-fly in the required format or to prioritize the parts of the data relevant to a study.

Using our framework, the ensemble learning process can revert to previous states of a model or could decide to change the shape and/or growing the model to decrease the bias error. It can also allow to migrate and re-distribute

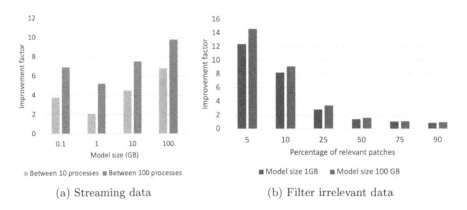

(a) Streaming data   (b) Filter irrelevant data

Fig. 9. Results for using the model abstraction to optimize data management in AI frameworks: (a) by streaming data between coupled application and (b) by only reading from storage the relevant patches

the machine learning process in an automatic way on the workers similarly to the pattern used by distributed training/inference of CNN or forest tree models. Being able to navigate through state of a model and searching for relevant moments combined with actions on how to handle the data in each case allows to implement flexible strategies for hyper-parameter search and to explore efficiently multiple evolutions of a model.

3.3 Positioning and Impact

By leveraging modern I/O frameworks, the model metadata together with the query capabilities, the proposed framework is capable of describing in a format way the common data patterns used by AI frameworks. Applications can use these concepts to describe their usecases and I/O. The framework can then use them to optimize the data movements when and where is needed. A typical usecase includes creating an initial model initialized with the domain decomposition and training it iteratively by pre-processing datasets corresponding to the domain decomposition and filtering out irrelevant patches. When a moment of interest is being reached the model object tags it and updates the metadata. Multiple applications/tasks can work on the same model at the same time updating the model metadata at each moment of interest (based on the parallel method used for example). Hyper-parameter search methods can start from a partial model (found using queries capabilities) and fork the model into others with different parameters automatically. The model history is stored in the metadata and can influence other applications dealing with similar tasks.

The formal descriptions of queries linked to model objects are used by the ML workflow framework in different ways to leverage the computational power and optimization possibilities given by the underlying large-scale architecture. For example, I/O frameworks can leverage the hints within model objects to stream data between coupled applications.

Figure 9 presents results on Summit when the framework is used for two types of tasks. In the first scenario, the training is optimized to stream the model from one process to multiple workers building on the same model and testing different configurations (like in the case of hyper-parameter search). Currently this is done through storage with one process writing the model and multiple others reading it. Figure 9a show the IO bandwidth improvement compared to the classical method if data streaming is used when the search investigates 10 or 100 different configurations. Using the hints provided in the model metadata, the IO management system would trigger this process automatically and could offer up to 9x speed-up in the IO time.

Figure 9a presents the IO improvement when the model abstraction is used to leverage on the fly filtering of the input dataset similarly to our previous example in Fig. 5. We simulate this scenario by hard coding in the workflow manager the domain distribution and patch prioritization. In our example, only 25% of the input image needs to be read from storage, corresponding to a 3.5x improvement in the IO bandwidth. The results account for the time the workflow manager needs to compute what parts of the data it needs to bring. While these results show great potential, the flexibility of an framework as the one proposed in this paper extends well beyond these two results.

> Separating the I/O and model plane from the deep learning application provides flexibility in how the optimizations can be implemented by the framework in many areas: data management, scheduling, compression, workflow management.

4   Conclusions

We argue in this paper for a framework specifically designed for machine learning models that can be leveraged to optimize the execution of individual and coupled AI applications based on the idea that the model and I/O needs to be disconnected from the machine learning application. We highlighted the data lifecycle and patterns within these applications and identified areas of potential improvements. The ML workflow framework targets these areas by providing a formal way of describing the model specific characteristics, how the model interacts with the data and how it needs to be handled in real time. We show results showing the potential benefits of such frameworks.

Acknowledgements. This research used resources of the Oak Ridge Leadership Computing Facility at the Oak Ridge National Laboratory, which is supported by the Office of Science of the U.S. Department of Energy under Contract No. DE-AC05-00OR22725. This work was partially funded by the Center of Advanced Systems Understanding (CASUS), which is financed by Germany's Federal Ministry of Education and Research (BMBF) and by the Saxon Ministry for Science, Culture and Tourism (SMWK) with tax funds on the basis of the budget approved by the Saxon State Parliament.

References

1. Baghban, A., Kahani, M., Nazari, M.A., Ahmadi, M.H., Yan, W.-M.: Sensitivity analysis and application of machine learning methods to predict the heat transfer performance of CNT/water nanofluid flows through coils. Int. J. Heat Mass Transf. **128**, 825–835 (2019)
2. Bei, Z., et al.: RFHOC: a random-forest approach to auto-tuning hadoop's configuration. IEEE Trans. Parallel Distrib. Syst. **27**(5), 1470–1483 (2016)
3. Cummings, J., et al.: EFFIS: an end-to-end framework for fusion integrated simulation. In: 2010 18th Euromicro Conference on Parallel, Distributed and Network-based Processing, pp. 428–434 (2010)
4. Deelman, E., et al.: The Pegasus workflow management system: translational computer science in practice. J. Comput. Sci. **52**, 101200 (2021). Funding Acknowledgments: NSF 1664162
5. Dieleman, S., Willett, K.W., Dambre, J.: Rotation-invariant convolutional neural networks for galaxy morphology prediction. Mon. Not. R. Astron. Soc. **450**(2), 1441–1459 (2015)
6. Docan, C., Parashar, M., Klasky, S.: Dataspaces: an interaction and coordination framework for coupled simulation workflows. Clust. Comput. **15**(2), 163–181 (2012)
7. Feng, X., Kumar, A., Recht, B., Ré, C.: Towards a unified architecture for in-RDBMS analytics. In: Proceedings of the 2012 ACM SIGMOD International Conference on Management of Data, SIGMOD 2012, pp. 325–336. Association for Computing Machinery, Scottsdale, Arizona, USA, May 2012 (2012)
8. Ferreira, D.R.: Applications of deep learning to nuclear fusion research (2018)
9. Godoy, W.F., et al.: ADIOS 2: the adaptable input output system. A framework for high-performance data management. SoftwareX **12**, 100561 (2020)
10. Gupta, R., et al.: Characterizing immune responses in whole slide images of cancer with digital pathology and pathomics. Curr. Pathobiol. Rep. **8**(4), 133–148 (2020)
11. Günther, S., Ruthotto, L., Schroder, J.B., Cyr, E.C., Gauger, N.R.: Layer-parallel training of deep residual neural networks (2019). arXiv 1812.04352
12. Hafiz, A.M.: Image classification by reinforcement learning with two-state Q-learning (2020)
13. Harlap, A., et al.: PipeDream: Fast and efficient pipeline parallel DNN training (2018)
14. Huo, Y., et al.: Consistent cortical reconstruction and multi-atlas brain segmentation. Neuroimage **138**, 197–210 (2016)
15. Jin, M., Homma, Y., Sim, A., Kroeger, W., Wu, K.: Performance prediction for data transfers in LCLS workflow. In: Proceedings of the ACM Workshop on Systems and Network Telemetry and Analytics, SNTA 2019, pp. 37–44. Association for Computing Machinery, New York, NY, USA (2019)
16. Kumar, A., McCann, R., Naughton, J., Patel, J.M.: Model selection management systems: the next frontier of advanced analytics. SIGMOD Rec. **44**(4), 17–22 (2016)
17. Li, M., Liu, Z., Shi, X., Jin, H.: ATCS: auto-tuning configurations of big data frameworks based on generative adversarial nets. IEEE Access **8**, 50485–50496 (2020)
18. Liang, C.-J.M., et al.: AutoSys: the design and operation of learning-augmented systems. In: 2020 USENIX Annual Technical Conference, July 2020, pp. 323–336. USENIX Association (2020)
19. Liu, Y., et al.: Predict Ki-67 positive cells in H&E-stained images using deep learning independently from IHC-stained images. Front. Mol. Biosci. **7**, 183 (2020)

20. Miao, H., Li, A., Davis, L.S., Deshpande, A.: ModelHub: deep learning lifecycle management. In: 2017 IEEE 33rd International Conference on Data Engineering (ICDE), pp. 1393–1394 (2017)
21. Mushtaq, H., Liu, F., Costa, C., Liu, G., Hofstee, P., Al-Ars, Z.: SparkGA: a spark framework for cost effective, fast and accurate DNA analysis at scale. In: Proceedings of the 8th ACM International Conference on Bioinformatics, Computational Biology, and Health Informatics. ACM-BCB 2017, pp. 148–157. Association for Computing Machinery, New York, NY, USA (2017)
22. n/a. Tuning Spark. https://spark.apache.org/docs/latest/tuning.html (Accessed 1 June 2021)
23. Neary, P.: Automatic hyperparameter tuning in deep convolutional neural networks using asynchronous reinforcement learning. In: 2018 IEEE International Conference on Cognitive Computing (ICCC), pp. 73–77 (2018)
24. Patton, R.M., et al.: Exascale deep learning to accelerate cancer research. CoRR, abs/1909.12291 (2019)
25. Potapov, A., Rodionov, S.: Genetic algorithms with DNN-based trainable crossover as an example of partial specialization of general search. In: Everitt, T., Goertzel, B., Potapov, A. (eds.) AGI 2017. LNCS (LNAI), vol. 10414, pp. 101–111. Springer, Cham (2017). https://doi.org/10.1007/978-3-319-63703-7_10
26. Real, E., et al.: Large-scale evolution of image classifiers (2017)
27. Saffari, A., Leistner, C., Santner, J., Godec, M., Bischof, H.: On-line random forests. In: 2009 IEEE 12th International Conference on Computer Vision Workshops, ICCV Workshops, pp. 1393–1400 (2009)
28. Scardapane, S., Wang, D.: Randomness in neural networks: an overview. WIREs Data Min. Knowl. Discov. 7(2), e1200 (2017)
29. Schwarz, N., Campbell, S., Hexemer, A., Mehta, A., Thayer, J.: Enabling scientific discovery at next-generation light sources with advanced AI and HPC. In: Nichols, J., Verastegui, B., Maccabe, A.B., Hernandez, O., Parete-Koon, S., Ahearn, T. (eds.) SMC 2020. CCIS, vol. 1315, pp. 145–156. Springer, Cham (2020). https://doi.org/10.1007/978-3-030-63393-6_10
30. Tarlow, D., Batra, D., Kohli, P., Kolmogorov, V.: Dynamic tree block coordinate ascent. In: ICML, pp. 113–120 (2011)
31. Tax, T.M.S., Mediano, P.A.M., Shanahan, M.: The partial information decomposition of generative neural network models. Entropy 19(9), 474 (2017)
32. Vartak, M., et al.: ModelDB: a system for machine learning model management. In: Proceedings of the Workshop on Human-In-the-Loop Data Analytics. HILDA 2016. Association for Computing Machinery (2016)
33. Vu, Q.D., et al.: Methods for segmentation and classification of digital microscopy tissue images. Front. Bioeng. Biotechnolo. 7, 53 (2019)
34. Wang, H., Rafatirad, S., Homayoun, H.: A+ tuning: architecture+application autotuning for in-memory data-processing frameworks. In: 2019 IEEE 25th International Conference on Parallel and Distributed Systems (ICPADS), pp. 163–166 (2019)
35. Wawrzyński, P., Zawistowski, P., Lepak, Ł.: Automatic hyperparameter tuning in on-line learning: classic momentum and adam. In: 2020 International Joint Conference on Neural Networks (IJCNN), pp. 1–8 (2020)
36. Wozniak, J.M., et al.: Scaling deep learning for cancer with advanced workflow storage integration. In: Proceedings of MLHPC 2018, Proceedings of MLHPC 2018: Machine Learning in HPC Environments, Held in Conjunction with SC 2018: The International Conference for High Performance Computing, Networking, Storage and Analysis, February 2019, pp. 114–123 (2019)

37. Xu, Z., Kakde, D., Chaudhuri, A.: Automatic hyperparameter tuning method for local outlier factor, with applications to anomaly detection. In: 2019 IEEE International Conference on Big Data (Big Data), pp. 4201–4207 (2019)
38. Yang, F., Chen, Z., Gangopadhyay, A.: Using randomness to improve robustness of tree-based models against evasion attacks. IEEE Trans. Knowl. Data Eng., 25–35 (2020)
39. Zhang, P.: A novel feature selection method based on global sensitivity analysis with application in machine learning-based prediction model. Appl. Soft Comput. **85**, 105859 (2019)
40. Zhang, S., Liang, G., Pan, S., Zheng, L.: A fast medical image super resolution method based on deep learning network. IEEE Access **7**, 12319–12327 (2019)
41. Zhang, Z., Yin, L., Peng, Y., Li, D.: A quick survey on large scale distributed deep learning systems. In: 2018 IEEE 24th International Conference on Parallel and Distributed Systems (ICPADS), pp. 1052–1056 (2018)
42. Zhou, J., Troyanskaya, O.G.: Deep supervised and convolutional generative stochastic network for protein secondary structure prediction (2014)

Secure Collaborative Environment for Seamless Sharing of Scientific Knowledge

Srikanth Yoginath$^{(\boxtimes)}$, Mathieu Doucet, Debsindhu Bhowmik, David Heise, Folami Alamudun, Hong-Jun Yoon, and Christopher Stanley$^{(\boxtimes)}$

Oak Ridge National Laboratory, Oak Ridge, TN, USA
{yoginathsb,doucetm,bhowmikd,heiseda,alamudunft,yoonh,stanleycb}@ornl.gov

Abstract. In a secure collaborative environment, tera-bytes of data generated from powerful scientific instruments are used to train secure machine learning (ML) models on exascale computing systems, which are then securely shared with internal or external collaborators as cloud-based services. Devising such a secure platform is necessary for seamless scientific knowledge sharing without compromising individual, or institute-level, intellectual property and privacy details. By enabling new computing opportunities with sensitive data, we envision a secure collaborative environment that will play a significant role in accelerating scientific discovery. Several recent technological advancements have made it possible to realize these capabilities. In this paper, we present our efforts at ORNL toward developing a secure computation platform. We present a use case where scientific data generated from complex instruments, like those at the Spallation Neutron Source (SNS), are used to train a differential privacy enabled deep learning (DL) network on Summit, which is then hosted as a secure multi-party computation (MPC) service on ORNL's Compute and Data Environment for Science (CADES) cloud computing platform for third-party inference. In this feasibility study, we discuss the challenges involved, elaborate on leveraged technologies, analyze relevant performance results and present the future vision of our work to establish secure collaboration capabilities within and outside of ORNL.

Keywords: Differential privacy · Secure multi-party computation · Secure sharing of scientific knowledge

© Springer Nature Switzerland AG 2022
J. Nichols et al. (Eds.): SMC 2021, CCIS 1512, pp. 139–156, 2022.
https://doi.org/10.1007/978-3-030-96498-6_8

1   Introduction

Scientific innovations and advancements are the result of sustained collaborative efforts among scientists spread across multiple disciplines and institutions around the world. However, an environment of stiff competition exists within a scientific community to establish a leading edge in their respective domains. While the former demands an open exchange of ideas, the latter persistently promotes guarding of ideas as intellectual properties. Without a significant mechanism to exchange shareable ideas while guarding non-shareable ones, the scientific community would either result in a slow innovation rate or suffer from losing hard-earned intellectual property.

In the era of artificial intelligence and big-data machine learning, institutions hosting large scientific instruments have an opportunity to play a significant role in hastening the innovation cycle. Dataset generation, either through sophisticated scientific instruments or using high-fidelity simulations and their subsequent analyses, are the core functionalities that are carried out in the process of scientific exploration, which over time leads to scientific innovations. A realization of long-term scientific goals involves several experiments that might be independent or follow-on, and which generally result in a reduction of exploration space. In this regard, insights from these complex, intermediary and, by themselves, insufficient experimental steps performed during the course of scientific exploration could be extremely helpful for the progress of domain science innovations. Sharing such insights could significantly reduce the scientific exploration space and experimental time of fellow researchers. Similarly, protecting certain technical details and capabilities, while being able to share the experimental insights with a peer researcher, is essential. With this approach, we not only participate actively in the progress of science but also protect the intellectual property of the enabling technology that helps to maintain a technical edge. Cryptographic techniques, like secure multi-party computation and differential privacy play a significant role in realizing such a secure sharing platform. In this paper, we bring together existing cryptographic methods to demonstrate the feasibility of a secure environment for unhindered exchange of information across research facilities to accelerate innovations. We highlight, discuss, and demonstrate secure information sharing use cases that utilize instruments from the Spallation Neutron Source (SNS), high performance computing facility Summit and ORNL's private cloud, CADES.

1.1   Background and Motivation

Apart from the need to identify the significant scientific insights in the generated data, a method is required to communicate such insights given relevant inputs. To achieve this, the data needs to be learned to generate a machine learning (ML) model. The expectation is that the ML model would impart additional insights on the input data through prediction or classification. Such insights would help the domain scientists to streamline their subsequent process of experimental exploration. Several technologies need to come together to realize secure sharing of scientific knowledge. At the hardware level, this task touches upon experimental facilities, high-performance computing (HPC) systems and commodity clouds. At the software level, we need software implementations of cryptographic techniques, ML models that support these techniques, scalable HPC implementations for training ML models and service-oriented architectures that support and securely expose the ML models to the outside world for secure inferences. Further, all of these wide-ranging technologies should interoperate to realize a secure collaborative environment. We designed our platform around two privacy computing capabilities: differential privacy and secure multi-party computation, which are described in further detail below.

Differential privacy (DP) employs a statistical strategy, where tunable noise is introduced either to the inputs, outputs, or at certain steps within an algorithm [1]. Using the TF_Privacy library [2,18], we utilize (ε, δ)-DP: $Pr[M(D) \in S] \leq e^{\varepsilon}Pr[M(D^{'}) \in S] + \delta$, where an algorithm (M) is run on adjacent inputs/databases $(D$ and $D^{'})$ to give any subset of outputs (S) and with ε and δ as privacy parameters (ε = upper bound on privacy loss, δ = probability for privacy guarantee to not hold). The addition of δ makes the method more generally applicable by relaxing the original ε-DP definition that only considers very strong, worst case conditions. Distinct advantages of (ε, δ)-DP are sequential composability and privacy guarantees through the calculated privacy loss. Algorithmic modules can be individually composed with (ε, δ)-DP and then sequentially constructed while maintaining privacy. With TF_Privacy, this allows us to introduce (ε, δ)-DP through the layers within the DL training models [2,3], which we also have demonstrated for DL training on medical data scenarios [5]. The quantified privacy loss of DP also sets the privacy guarantees, up to the privacy budget threshold. Overall, DP for ML model training protects both the model and training data from model inversion and membership inference attacks, respectively [4].

Secure multi-party computation (MPC) is an encryption scheme that allows two or more parties to jointly compute a function over their private inputs without revealing these inputs [8,9]. Here, we utilize the TF_Encrypted library [10, 19], which employs the SPDZ protocol [11] with additive secret sharing. Overall, MPC offers robust security to compute on an open resource, like Cloud, but can incur substantial communication overhead. We therefore leverage its capabilities for secure ML model inferencing, where practical performance is achieved.

The secure MPC computation involves two entities A and B. A has a trained model on certain data, called M. B holds another data D and wants to use model M to obtain some helpful insights on their data. However, both A and B consider their holdings M and D, respectively, as their intellectual property that provide them a leading edge in their respective domains. Secure MPC allows such interactions to happen using the encrypted model and data on an independent set of servers. TF_Encrypted [19] uses three servers S_0, S_1 and S_2 for this purpose and establishes secure communication MPC protocols over gRPC [21].

1.2   Organization

In Sect. 2, we discuss the possible use case scenarios for secure information sharing, with a detailed description of one particular case. In Sect. 3, we discuss the ML model development and training process with and without DP. We demonstrate how a trained ML model is securely shared among users, along with the relevant performance results in Sect. 4. We summarize, discuss our future work, and conclude the paper in Sect. 5.

2   Use Case Scenarios

Insights from physical experiments and computational simulations are known drivers of scientific innovations. Regardless of whether the data from the experiments and simulations are complementary or similar, they both contribute informative results. The advancements in ML-based technologies have provided a means by which significant insights from such datasets can be exposed through classification or prediction models. The advancements in web technologies have provided a means to share such models for inferencing across a wide community, and audiences, around the world.

Such exchange scenarios include (a) Experimental or computational scientists exchanging insights with their peers (b) Experimental scientists exchanging insights with computational scientists for validation purposes (c) Computational scientists exchanging insights with experimental scientists that could be helpful for the design of experiments (d) Real-time steering of simulations or experiments using insights from previous experiments or simulations, respectively (e) Multiple collaborating groups can come together to train ML models that can be shared without divulging any details of their datasets to each other.

As a more in-depth example, we consider a practical use case scenario for a scientific user facility that involves secure collaboration between instrument operators and facility users. A fundamental collaboration is required for data quality assessment of neutron scattering instruments. We will also see that the needs of this scenario brings together the experimental facilities, HPC and the Cloud infrastructure resources.

2.1   Data Quality Assessment from Small-Angle Neutron Scattering (SANS) Instrument

Experiments involving sophisticated instruments usually are a multi-institutional operation. Also, several types of instruments typically are hosted by an institutional facility, like SNS at ORNL, and such instruments are made available to experimental scientists either from academia or industry (outside users). These experimental processes are a collaborative effort between the outside users and instrument scientists at the facility. During such procedures, special scenarios can exist where a user would like to guard all data generated. Examples are industry partners that will generate proprietary data without intent to publish in the open literature, and scientific researchers working in a highly competitive area where the new, timely results are sensitive. However, to ensure the efficient use of the user's beamtime, including collection of the highest quality results, the instrument scientists need access to certain details on the collected data. Hence, a security concern arises, as the data generators would not want to freely share their datasets. Such a practical scenario can arise to create barriers and ultimately prohibit the full utilization of a scientific instrument.

To frame the challenge within a specific example, consider a company or industry partner is using the extended Q-range small-angle neutron scattering (EQ-SANS) instrument at SNS [12,13] to measure a series of proprietary pharmaceutical formulations, and the data needs to be protected during collection. However, the instrument scientists would like to assist, with their expertise, in evaluating how the experiment is progressing and inform the decision making (e.g. samples to prepare and run) during the data collection. If some samples are showing very low signal-to-noise, they may need to be measured for longer exposure times and/or prepared at higher concentration. If a sample appears to show unanticipated results, like sample aggregation, early detection and rectifying measures would be important. While these activities normally occur during a conventional data collection, the challenge here with a sensitive-data user is to maintain privacy of all data except the necessary information needed to properly assist in still performing an optimal experiment. Current practices with industry users that plan to generate sensitive data without publishing involve lengthy measures: the participating instrument scientists sign a non-disclosure agreement (NDA), and isolation approaches are employed at the instrument and with the data. A more efficient and versatile solution, which we propose, is to establish seamless data privacy computing methods within the experimental data collection and initial analysis phases, such that only pertinent, pre-defined and agreed upon information is shared. By incorporating privacy methods, we also envision the capability to train ML models using multitudes of instrument data that protects the training data privacy and can then inform on these sensitive data experiments in real-time without disclosing the raw data information. Next, we delineate these steps, and associated details, by training a privacy-enabled ML model on SANS data, utilizing DP, to then perform secure inferencing on the model using secure MPC. Of note, the dataset generated and used below is meant to serve as a starting point for the given scenario. The chosen classes were based on current data availability. For a real use case, we would include more classes, along with more training examples per class. Stemming from this particular scenario, the privacy tools can be extended to afford general data sharing and analytics among scientific user facility users with other collaborators and researchers where concerns over data sensitivity are encountered.

2.2 Data Collection

The SANS data were obtained from the EQ-SANS instrument at SNS. A series of standard calibration sample measurements, along with data from two unpublished scientific experiments (data generated by C.S.), were used to construct

agbeh   bkgd   gmp

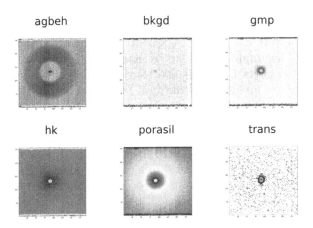

hk   porasil   trans

Fig. 1. Representative SANS detector images for the 6 classes. These specific sample classes generalize to some of the common scattering patterns obtained in experiments: peaks (agbeh), background/low intensity samples (bkgd), rod-like particles (gmp), globular particles (hk), strong intensity samples (porasil), and transmission measurements (trans).

the raw SANS detector image dataset. The standard samples included silver behenate (AgBeh), porous silica (Porasil) [14], hydrogenated water (H_2O), and deuterated water (D_2O). Scientific SANS data on a protein, hexokinase (HK), and self-assembled structures of the guanosine derivative, 2'-deoxyguanosine-5'-monophophate (dGMP), measured over multiple experiments also were included into the dataset. The HK and dGMP experiments also had background measurements, which were buffer and salt in H_2O/D_2O. The images for these background runs were combined with the H_2O and D_2O standard run images to form a background category (bkgd) in the dataset. In addition, a transmission mode measurement is made on every sample, and those detector images were included as a transmission category (trans) in the dataset.

The physical detector on the EQ-SANS instrument is 1×1 m in size and provides 192×256 (nearly square) pixel resolution. All measurements comprised a range of instrument settings, using 1.3 to 8 m sample-to-detector distance (SDD) and 1 to 20 Å wavelength neutrons, with a nominal 3.5 Å bandwidth at each setting. The detector images used to make the dataset were raw neutron counts, covering the entire time-of-flight (ToF) and exposure time measured for each sample, and summed for each detector pixel. Overall, the images were grouped into 6 classes, with each image assigned one of the following single labels: agbeh, bkgd, gmp, hk, porasil, trans (Fig. 1). These classes can be generally considered as scattering patterns of: peaks, background (or low intensity samples), rod-like particles, globular particles, strong intensity samples, and transmission (direct beam) mode measurements, respectively.

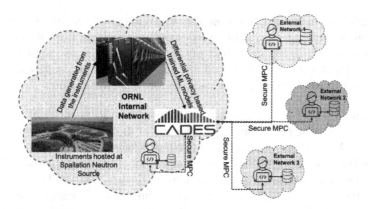

Fig. 2. Secure information sharing use case schematic involves data generated from the EQ-SANS instrument used to train ML models on Summit, an HPC platform, and finally securely shared among internal and/or external scientists through CADES, a Cloud platform.

2.3   ML Models and Privacy

We used a convolutional neural network (CNN) to train on collected data, which can be used to classify datasets from future experiments. The ML models that are built by the operators classify the new set of incoming data from the experiments to a certain category, which provides the operators necessary information for data quality assessment. By using secure sharing methods, the experimental scientists can ensure their data is protected from leakage while still gaining assistance and insights from the instrument operators.

Using DP, the ML models can be trained to ensure the information privacy of the ML model. However, training of the privacy models are more compute intensive than their non-privacy models. This, along with the resolution and volume of the incoming data, creates a demand for HPC resources. Once trained, these models can be shared with the external world, as shown in Fig. 2, through application services hosted in a community Cloud platform. DP protects the model and training data from model inversion and membership inference attacks. However, since DP does not inherently provide collaborative setups or secure a client's test data, we use secure MPC protocols. The secure MPC protocols that can be realized over public Cloud infrastructure ensures both data and model privacy, addressing the privacy concerns of both data and model owners.

3   Machine Learning Model Training

3.1   Model Setup

Data Pre-processing. Images were first center-cropped to remove white-space, resized to $n \times n$ ($n = 64, 128, 224$) and rescaled by the factor $1/255$. Horizontal and vertical flip image data augmentation was applied to avoid the training algorithm from learning on any characteristic detector patterns, like tubes turned off or top/bottom edges, for any subset of the data. The data was split into training/validation/testing (64%/16%/20%), where the test data paths were saved for each run to use the exact same samples for MPC inferencing.

Model. To demonstrate the use case with scientific user facilities data, we performed deep learning (DL) training, both without and with DP, on our generated dataset of SANS detector images comprised of 6 classes (see Fig. 3). For the CNN model training on the SANS detector images, VGG9 (for $n = 64$) and VGG16 (for $n = 128, 224$) models [22] were implemented with Keras in Tensorflow 2.4.1 [23]. For the standard, non-DP training, the runs used a learning rate = 0.008, batch size = 16, epochs = 40, with a stochastic gradient decent (SGD) optimizer. For DP training, the TF_Privacy library (v0.5.1) [18] was used. Similar settings to the standard training were used for comparison, along with the additional privacy hyperparameters. The only adjustments were to use a learning rate = 0.004, epochs = 35, and the TF_Privacy DPKerasSGDOptimizer. Privacy hyperparameters used were noise multiplier = 0.76, L2 norm clip = 1.0, and microbatches = 4. These settings were reached based on initial runs using typical values and ranges described in TF_Privacy, along with previous reported settings [2].

To consider (ε, δ)-DP for machine learning, as we do here with TF_Privacy, ε specifies an upper bound on the probability for a model output to vary if any single training sample is included or excluded. For many practical uses, ε between 0.1–10 is typically used [6,7]. The δ is set in the training and reflects the leak rate probability of the sample training inputs, where $\delta \leq 1/($training size$)$ is a typical range to target. Overall, we could continue to optimize across the privacy parameters for the DL training, but these results fully satisfy the (ε, δ)-DP conditions while also yielding reasonable accuracy. They also remain as similar to the non-DP training for best baseline comparison.

3.2 Model Training

With a VGG16 model architecture and images resized to 224×224 input size, the standard (no DP) training achieved ~99% accuracy after 40 epochs (Fig. 3). In comparison, the DP settings (see Methods for details) reached a plateau of ~88% accuracy by 35 epochs (see Fig. 3) and additionally provided a (ε, δ)-DP privacy guarantee of $(9.35, 1.79e^{-3})$-DP. The reduction in training accuracy is expected when adding DP, as this is part of the privacy-utility tradeoffs of the method. We also performed training runs using VGG16 and 128×128 input size, and a smaller network and input size (VGG9 and 64×64, respectively), for comparison and for MPC inferencing, described below. The corresponding accuracy curves are shown in Fig. 3b and c. The VGG16 model training with 128×128 input size and DP was trained for 35 epochs and also achieved $(9.35, 1.79e^{-3})$-DP. The VGG9 model training with DP was trained for 40 epochs and achieved $(10.11, 1.79e^{-3})$-DP.

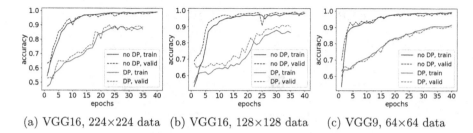

(a) VGG16, 224×224 data   (b) VGG16, 128×128 data   (c) VGG9, 64×64 data

Fig. 3. VGG training accuracy curves that compare without and with DP, and for different image input sizes. The privacy-utility balance is noticeable in all cases, where each DP training plateaus at a lower accuracy compared to no DP (specific DP settings used are listed in the main text).

We make the following observations on the model training with DP, compared to the non-DP case:

1. A lower learning rate was required to maintain a stable and monotonic accuracy growth (and commensurate loss function decay) due to the added noise and gradient clipping.
2. The ε increases with the number of training epochs, so we performed a series of runs with varying epochs to reach 35 for DP training of the VGG16 network, which yielded a reasonable privacy-utility balance. Fewer epochs did not reach sufficient accuracy and more epochs resulted in $\varepsilon > 10$.
3. We performed training runs with larger noise multiplier values (>0.67), but they often resulted in sub-optimal accuracy and, therefore, utility. This is reasonable, given the relatively small training size we are using for our example here. DP is best for generalizing over large data, so it is expected that utilizing larger, aggregated datasets would provide more utility along with capacity for higher privacy settings in real use cases.

Further, when performing inferencing on the test data, we observe a loss in accurately predicting certain classes (bkgd, gmp, hk). This can be seen by comparing the confusion matrix for non-DP and DP training (Fig. 4a, b, respectively).

3.3   Differential Privacy Cost

To assess training performance, we also varied image input size (from 64×64 up to 320×320) for non-DP and DP training with the VGG network (Fig. 5). Again, the 64×64 input used a smaller, VGG9, model while the other input sizes used the VGG16 model. We found a strong divergence in the DP training time, relative to the non-DP, for increasing input size. Also, the DP training failed at the highest input size (320×320) due to GPU device memory limitations.

At the input size used for the results shown above (with 224×224), DP training is ~2× slower compared to non-DP training. We observed that adjusting

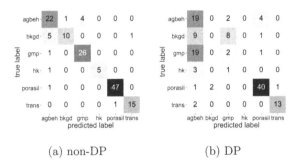

(a) non-DP   (b) DP

Fig. 4. Confusion matrix plots for VGG16 testing (224 × 224 data) that show accuracy is maintained in DP models for some classes (agbeh, porasil, trans) but with a discrepancy in accurately predicting certain other classes (bkgd, gmp, hk).

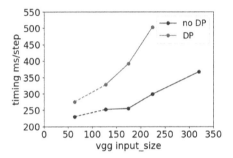

Fig. 5. Cost of training VGG network with DP. The DP training was observed to be almost 2× slower compared to non-DP training and could get much slower for increased privacy levels.

DP parameters for increased privacy levels (e.g. increasing noise multiplier) can impact training speed even further, with ∼5× slower training times compared to non-DP. With the incremental, step training time for the 224 × 224 input size and DP settings used here (503 ms for batch size = 16), 100K images with 40 epochs would require ∼35 h of training time on a single V100 GPU.

To frame these data volumes and compute timings within a possible SANS data collection, there are three high-throughput SANS instruments at ORNL: EQ-SANS at SNS, Bio-SANS and GP-SANS at the High Flux Isotope Reactor (HFIR) and each can operate at a rate of ∼10 min/sample and these facilities operate at up to ∼70% of the year. Given these trends, a large volume of over 100K images per year can be obtained by SANS experiments. Training CNN models with and without privacy over such a large volume of data would demand a significant amount of computational resources and such needs can be met using an HPC system like Summit.

4   Secure Inference

4.1   Secure MPC Setup

A secure MPC test setup was developed over CADES Cloud platform. To enable secure inference by an external entity on an internally hosted ML model, we used TF_encrypted, a python module that implements secure MPC protocols. The setup prescribed by TF_encrypted involves a ML model hosting server (M_s) and a client with test datasets (C_d) that do not see each other but they interact through three intermediate secure servers (S_1, S_2 and S_3). We developed containers to host model, intermediate secure servers and the data owner who performs inferences. Each of these containers were spawned on the virtual machine (VM) instances of CADES cloud. Three different setups were used in our experiments.

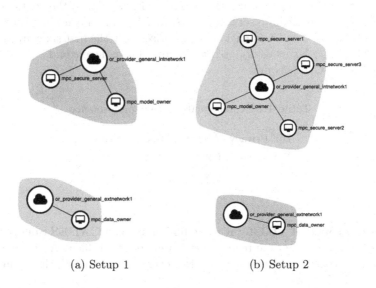

(a) Setup 1   (b) Setup 2

Fig. 6. Setup 1: single host for secure servers and Setup2: separate hosts for secure servers on CADES for secure MPC evaluation.

- **Setup 1:** Each VM instance involved in the experiments were of type *m1.2xlarge* supporting 16 virtual CPUs, 32 GB of memory and 40 GB of disk space. VM instances *mpc_model_owner* host container with M_s, *mpc_data_owner* hosts a container with C_d and *mpc_secure_server* hosts a container with secure servers S_1, S_2 and S_3 listening on different ports. Figure 6a represents this setup.
- **Setup 2:** Three VM instances (*mpc_secure_server1*, *mpc_secure_server2* and *mpc_secure_server3*) of type *m1.2xlarge* were used to host secure servers S_1, S_2 and S_3. Two VM instances (*mpc_model_owner* and *mpc_model_owner*) of

type *m1.large* supporting 4 virtual CPUs, 8 GB of memory and 80 GB of disk space, were used to host (M_s) and (C_d). Figure 6b represents this setup.

- **Setup 3:** Two VM instances (*mpc_model_owner* and *mpc_model_owner*) of type *m1.large* supporting 4 virtual CPUs, 8 GB of memory and 80 GB of disk space, were used to host (M_s) and (C_d). This setup was used to estimate baseline performance without secure MPC.

4.2   Secure MPC Performance

We performed 100 random inferences over Cloud-based secure MPC setup on CADES for both VGG models with and without differential privacy. At each inference cycle, the client sends an encrypted single image over the network to the intermediate secure servers. A model server executing as a service on a different VM instance interacts with the intermediate secure servers to fulfill the inference request of the client. To measure the performance, we polled the container M_s, container with intermediate servers $(S_1, S_2$ and $S_3)$ and a container hosting C_d using *docker stats*. The VGG9 network comprises only the first six convolutional layers and 3 dense layers as opposed to 13 convolution layers and 3 dense layers in the usual VGG16 network.

Table 1. Accuracy and Runtime performance

Diff-Privacy	Accuracy	Inference time
No	0.96	8.82 ± 0.43
Yes	0.66	8.3 ± 0.31

Secure Inference of VGG9 on 64 × 64 Data over CADES Setup 1. The accuracy and inference time readings are tabulated in Table 1. A high accuracy is observed for the model without DP. However, as anticipated, the accuracy of the DP model is lower.

In Fig. 7a and b we show the instantaneous CPU and memory utilization percentages in the *model_host*, *data_host* and the *secure_servers*. In Fig. 7c and d we show the cumulative incoming and outgoing network loads during inferencing ML models with DP and without DP.

From Fig. 7c and d, we see that the cumulative network loads remain similar for inferencing on ML models with and without DP. This is expected and we also observed similar trend in the CPU and memory utilization. Hence, we show CPU and memory utilization plots for inferencing models using DP, which is almost the same as the one without DP.

Instantaneous CPU utilization curves in Fig. 7a show regular spikes corresponding to consecutive inference activities. A very low (<10%) virtual CPU utilization and almost negligible amount of memory utilization can be observed in the *data_owner* and *model_owner*. However, the VM hosting the secure servers

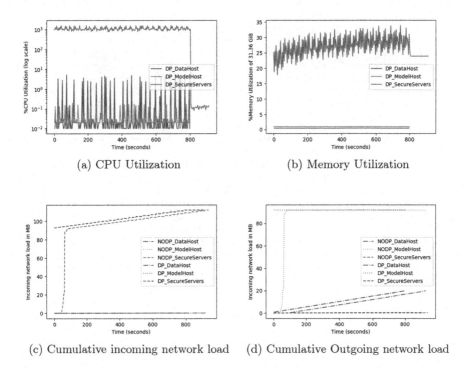

(a) CPU Utilization

(b) Memory Utilization

(c) Cumulative incoming network load   (d) Cumulative Outgoing network load

Fig. 7. Percent CPU, memory and network utilization in the data host, model host and the secure servers during secure MPC inference. The plots suggest that the secure servers are computationally intensive, while the model owners and data owners computationally lightweight.

(S_1, S_2 and S_3) appears to utilize almost all of 16 virtual CPU cores and around 30% (∼11 GB) of memory.

The cumulative outgoing network load in Fig. 7d suggest that the model is communicated once to the *secure_servers* by the *model_owner* and the *data_owner* consecutively sends data at regular intervals for inferencing. Further, the outgoing network load from the *secure_servers*, which is an inference label, is almost negligible. The cumulative incoming network load in Fig. 7c suggest the *secure_servers* receives the network traffic from both *data_owner* and *model_owner*. Hence, from the plots in Fig. 7, we can conclude that much of the computational tasks are carried out on secure servers. A single CPU VM instance with minimal memory 5% of their 32 GB of memory (<3 GB) should suffice the computational needs of the model host and the data host for VGG9 network inferencing data of dimension 64 × 64.

Observations. (a) Similar runtime performance and resource utilization is observed during secure inference of models with and without DP. (b) The secure servers are computationally intensive, while the model owners and data owners just communicate their encrypted model and data to the secure servers.

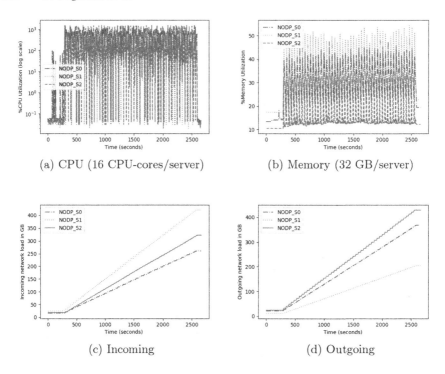

(a) CPU (16 CPU-cores/server)   (b) Memory (32 GB/server)

(c) Incoming   (d) Outgoing

Fig. 8. Percent CPU, memory and network utilization across secure servers S0, S1 and S2 during secure inference in a multi-node setup show that secure server computations are compute-, memory- and network-wise expensive.

Secure Inference of VGG16 on 128 × 128 Data over CADES Setup 2. This test used the VGG16 model without DP support, since the performance results were almost similar. The same experimental procedure of random image inferences was performed over CADES Setup 1. However, after two successful secure inferences, the execution stalled or significantly slowed down. This behavior of significant slow down could be due to page swapping due to lack of memory at the secure servers. The first run took around 200 s to complete and the next run took almost 37 s for completion.

Splitting the secure servers into three different containers and having a large resource allocation for each secure server overcomes this resource relevant problem. Hence, we use CADES Setup 2 to understand the CPU, memory and network resource utilization among the *secure_servers* with the larger ML model VGG16 working on a larger dataset input size 128 × 128.

We performed 50 random single image inferences over CADES Setup 2. In Fig. 8 instantaneous CPU and memory utilization percentages and cumulative network load plots among secure servers (S_0, S_1 and S_2) that are hosted as separate containers on three different VMs. The regular spikes seen in Fig. 8a in all the servers correspond to the relevant computations. With a maximum instantaneous percent utilization of 1600%, 1000% and 1600%, the servers seem to significantly utilize all virtual CPU-cores. As seen in Fig. 8b memory utilization of $S_1 > S_0 > S_2$, a maximum memory utilization of 47% (14.8 GiB), 54% (17 GiB) and 44% (10.6 GiB) was observed in servers S_0, S_1 and S_2, respectively. The cumulative network load measuring several hundreds of gigabytes were observed to be exchanged between the servers for just 50 inferences. These numbers indicate that the Tf_encrypted implementation of secure MPC is not only network-wise expensive but are also memory-wise and compute-wise expensive. Further the turn-around time for inferencing a single 128×128 data image over a CADES Setup 2 configuration was around 46 s on average. Comparing this runtime with our similar experiment on Setup 1, we can see almost a fourth of the 46 s corresponds to network communications between the servers hosted on different VMs.

Observations: (a) Secure MPC implementation of Tf_encrypted is compute-, memory- and network-wise expensive.

4.3 Secure MPC Cost

To estimate the cost of secure MPC, we used CADES Setup 3 to perform inference without secure MPC. We used Tensorflow Serving [20] to setup a SANS inference service at *model_owner*, which is accessed by the *data_owner* using the REST API for inference. In this setup, the *data_owner* sends the input data of dimension 128×128 for inference and the *model_owner* performs are the requisite computations and communicates the result to the *data_owner*. Hence, the network load is significantly low. We polled the container at the *model_owner* VM to obtain the runtime statistics using docker stats. We performed 100 random single image inferences over CADES Setup 3. Figure 9a shows the instantaneous CPU and memory utilization percentage. The cumulative network load mostly corresponds to the communication of input images to the *model_host*, which was around 106 MB. This is seen from plots in Fig. 9a with a maximum of 63% of CPU load, maximum of 6.4% (540 MB) of memory load. From these readings we can infer that the secure MPC inference operation is compute-, memory- and network-wise extremely expensive in comparison with the regular inference. Further, a regular inference is also extremely fast with a turn-around time of 0.24 s.

Figure 9b shows exactly how expensive in terms of runtime, CPU load, memory load and network load. The CPU and memory loads are over an order-of-magnitude expensive, with memory load closer to two orders-of-magnitude. Runtime performance is over two orders-of-magnitude slower. The network load with over four orders-of-magnitude is the most expensive of all. These numbers were obtained from the results from the experimental runs carried out for secure inference on CADES Setup 2 and regular inference on CADES Setup 3. A ratio of per inference runtimes were used to determine relative runtime cost. The maximum instantaneous CPU and memory utilization from these two experiments were used to determine relative CPU and memory cost. We aggregated the final cumulative incoming network load values of all the secure servers and divided

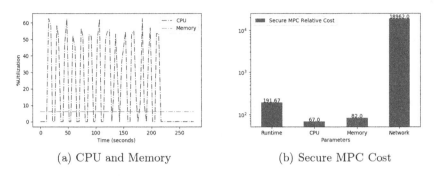

(a) CPU and Memory   (b) Secure MPC Cost

Fig. 9. Privacy cost in DP training and secure MPC inference.

them by the number of secure inferences performed (50) to obtain network load per secure inference. This network load for regular inference corresponds to the input data communicated by the *data_owner*, which was ∼1 MB. The ratio (network load per secure inference)/(network load per regular inference) was used to obtain relative network cost for secure inference.

5   Conclusion and Future Work

We started the paper highlighting the need for secure information exchange and its feasibility using existing technologies. We showcased a practical use case scenario of secure information exchange between EQ-SANS instrument operators at SNS and facility users at academic institutions or industry. The information exchange was formulated using a ML model, such that the privacy of the model and the data were preserved. To achieve this a secure ML model using DP algorithms and secure inference using MPC protocols were used. We performed training of a deep learning VGG network with and without DP on a Summit node. With the performance readings from the model training process and the expected data resolution and volume, we emphasized the need for an HPC facility to handle this compute-intensive model training process. We developed secure inference services using containers over VM instances from the CADES Cloud platform. A performance study of MPC-based secure inference involving multiple VM instances and containers were carried out and the results were presented. With these tasks, we implemented a full life-cycle iteration of a SANS use case scenario where privacy preserving algorithms were used. We successfully demonstrated its practical feasibility using ORNL resources namely, the SNS EQ-SANS instrument, Summit HPC and the CADES Cloud infrastructure. Performance of DP and secure MPC training and inference were recorded. The relative cost of privacy for training with DP and inference with secure MPC were presented. Despite the higher resource cost and significantly slower runtimes, the training with DP and inference with secure MPC for privacy were shown to be realistically feasible.

The presented SANS use case can be extended to other high-throughput SANS instruments at ORNL: Bio-SANS and GP-SANS HFIR. This work can also be extended to train an agent to automate the process of experimental setup using reinforcement learning to a certain extent. Further, this method can be used as a general template to achieve secure exchange of scientific knowledge amongst local and non-local researchers. In this regard, we are working on secure model and inference for a prediction class of supervised learning problems using data from the reflectometry instruments at SNS [15, 16]. We are also working on secure inference of an unsupervised learning class of problems with a convolutional variational auto-encoder model using molecular dynamics simulation data to identify and analyze the microstates in biomolecules [17].

Acknowledgements. This work was supported by the Laboratory Directed Research and Development (LDRD) program of Oak Ridge National Laboratory, under LDRD project 9831. A portion of this research at ORNL's Spallation Neutron Source was sponsored by the Scientific User Facilities Division, Office of Basic Energy Sciences, U.S. Department of Energy. C.S. acknowledges the EQ-SANS beamline staff: Changwoo Do, Carrie Gao, and William Heller, that also assisted in the calibration samples data collection over the time period. This research used resources of the Oak Ridge Leadership Computing Facility, which is a DOE Office of Science User Facility supported under Contract DE-AC05-00OR22725. This research used resources of the Compute and Data Environment for Science (CADES) at the Oak Ridge National Laboratory, which is supported by the Office of Science of the U.S. Department of Energy under Contract No. DE-AC05-00OR22725. We would like to acknowledge the timely support and assistance provided by Chris Layton and Daniel Dewey. We very much appreciate their help and support.

References

1. Dwork, C., Roth, A.: The algorithmic foundations of differential privacy. Found. Trends Theoret. Comput. Sci. **9**(3–4), 211–407 (2014)
2. Abadi, M., et al.: Deep learning with differential privacy. In: Proceedings of the 2016 ACM SIGSAC Conference on Computer and Communications Security (CCS 2016), pp. 308–318. Association for Computing Machinery, New York (2016)
3. Papernot, N., Song, S., Mironov, I., Raghunathan, A., Talwar, K., Erlingsson, Ú.: Scalable private learning with PATE. arXiv:1802.08908 (2018)
4. Shokri, R., Stronati, M., Song, C., Shmatikov, V.: Membership inference attacks against machine learning models. In: 2017 IEEE Symposium on Security and Privacy (SP), pp. 3–18. IEEE (2018)
5. Yoon, H.-J., et al.: Privacy-preserving knowledge transfer with bootstrap aggregation of teacher ensembles. In: Gadepally, V., et al. (eds.) DMAH/Poly - 2020. LNCS, vol. 12633, pp. 87–99. Springer, Cham (2021). https://doi.org/10.1007/978-3-030-71055-2_9
6. Lee, J., Clifton, C.: How much is enough? Choosing ε for differential privacy. In: Lai, X., Zhou, J., Li, H. (eds.) ISC 2011. LNCS, vol. 7001, pp. 325–340. Springer, Heidelberg (2011). https://doi.org/10.1007/978-3-642-24861-0_22
7. Hsu, J., et al.: Differential privacy: an economic method for choosing epsilon. In: 2014 IEEE 27th Computer Security Foundations Symposium, pp. 398–410 (2014)

8. Hazay, C., Lindell, Y.: Efficient Secure Two-Party Protocols. Information Security and Cryptography, Springer, Heidelberg (2010). https://doi.org/10.1007/978-3-642-14303-8

9. Evans, D., Kolesnikov, V., Rosulek, M.: A Pragmatic Introduction to Secure Multiparty Computation. NOW Publishers, Delft (2018)

10. Dahl, M., et al.: Private machine learning in tensorflow using secure computation. arXiv:1810.08130 (2018)

11. Damgård, I., Pastro, V., Smart, N., Zakarias, S.: Multiparty computation from somewhat homomorphic encryption. In: Safavi-Naini, R., Canetti, R. (eds.) CRYPTO 2012. LNCS, vol. 7417, pp. 643–662. Springer, Heidelberg (2012). https://doi.org/10.1007/978-3-642-32009-5_38

12. Zhao, J.K., Gao, C.Y., Liu, D.: The extended Q-range small-angle neutron scattering diffractometer at the SNS. J. Appl. Crystallogr. **43**, 1068–1077 (2010)

13. Heller, W., et al.: The suite of small-angle neutron scattering instruments at Oak Ridge National Laboratory. J. Appl. Cryst. **51**, 242–248 (2018)

14. Wignall, G.D., Bates, F.S.: Absolute calibration of small-angle neutron scattering data. J. Appl. Crystallogr. **20**, 28–40 (1987)

15. Doucet, M., et al.: Machine learning for neutron reflectometry data analysis of two-layer thin films. Mach. Learn.: Sci. Technol. **2**, 035001 (2021)

16. Maranville, B.B., et al.: reflectometry/refl1d: v0.8.13 (2020). https://github.com/reflectometry/refl1d

17. Bhowmik, D., Gao, S., Young, M.T., et al.: Deep clustering of protein folding simulations. BMC Bioinform. **19**, 484 (2018)

18. TensorFlow Privacy. https://github.com/tensorflow/privacy

19. TF_Encrypted: Encrypted Learning in Tensorflow. https://github.com/tf-encrypted

20. TF_Serving: Serving Models. https://www.tensorflow.org/tfx/guide/serving

21. gRPC: A high performance, open source universal RPC framework. https://grpc.io/

22. Simonyan, K., Zisserman, A.: Very deep convolutional networks for large-scale image recognition. arXiv:1409.1556 (2014)

23. Abadi, M., et al.: TensorFlow: large-scale machine learning on heterogeneous systems (2015). Software available from tensorflow.org

The Convergence of HPC, AI and Big Data in Rapid-Response to the COVID-19 Pandemic

Sreenivas R. Sukumar[1]([✉]), Jacob A. Balma[1], Christopher D. Rickett[1],
Kristyn J. Maschhoff[1], Joseph Landman[1], Charles R. Yates[2], Amar G. Chittiboyina[2],
Yuri K. Peterson[3], Aaron Vose[4], Kendall Byler[5], Jerome Baudry[5],
and Ikhlas A. Khan[2]

[1] Hewlett Packard Enterprise (HPE), Houston, USA
sreenivas.sukumar@hpe.com
[2] The University of Mississippi, Oxford, USA
[3] The Medical University of South Carolina, Charleston, USA
[4] MaxLinear Incorporated, Carlsbad, USA
[5] The University of Alabama in Huntsville, Huntsville, USA

Abstract. The "Force for Good" pledge of intellectual property to fight COVID-19 brought into action HPE products, resources and expertise to the problem of drug/vaccine discovery. Several scientists and technologists collaborated to accelerate efforts towards a cure. This paper documents the spirit of such a collaboration, the stellar outcomes and the technological lessons learned from the true convergence of high-performance computing (HPC), artificial intelligence (AI) and data science to fight a pandemic. The paper presents technologies that assisted in an end-to-end edge-to-supercomputer pipeline - creating 3D structures of the virus from CryoEM microscopes, filtering through large cheminformatics databases of drug molecules, using artificial intelligence and molecular docking simulations to identify drug candidates that may bind with the 3D structures of the virus, validating the binding activity using *in-silico* high-fidelity multi-body physics simulations, combing through millions of literature-based facts and assay data to connect-the-dots of evidence to explain or dispute the *in-silico* predictions. These contributions accelerated scientific discovery by: (i) identifying novel drug molecules that could reduce COVID-19 virality in the human body, (ii) screening drug molecule databases to design wet lab experiments faster and better, (iii) hypothesizing the cross-immunity of Tetanus vaccines based on comparisons of COVID-19 and publicly available protein sequences, and (iv) prioritizing drug compounds that could be repurposed for COVID-19 treatment. We present case studies around each of the aforementioned outcomes and posit an accelerated future of drug discovery in an augmented and converged workflow of data science, high-performance computing and artificial intelligence.

Keywords: Drug discovery · High performance computing · Artificial intelligence · Knowledge graphs

© Springer Nature Switzerland AG 2022
J. Nichols et al. (Eds.): SMC 2021, CCIS 1512, pp. 157–172, 2022.
https://doi.org/10.1007/978-3-030-96498-6_9

1 Background

1.1 Problem Statement

The average inception-to-approval time required for a new drug is over 12 years and costs over \$1 billion [1]. This is because drug discovery is a sequence of cumbersome needle-in-a-haystack search problems with life-critical consequences. These problems that can be cast as the search for – (i) relevant compounds (from a chemical space of 10^{60} potential synthesizable molecules) that modulate a given biological system and subsequently influence disease development and progression, (ii) the appropriate pose and active site interaction between a disease/symptom causing protein and over 10^6 drug ligands, (iii) evidence from over 10^6 research documents to explain the mechanism-of-action, (iv) similarity across 10^6 open-science proteins to understand the characteristics of the disease causing organism, (v) knowledge nuggets from assay and experimental data (over 10^8 medical facts) to list protein-protein and protein-molecule interactions, and (vi) safety and efficacy indicators in siloed public-health data sources with over 10^8 past patient records and trial data. This paper is organized to present results and lessons from collaborative research between scientists and technologists to accelerate the drug discovery process for COVID-19 and beyond.

1.2 Collaborative Response

In rapid-response mode, the aforementioned search problems were addressed by – (i) offering supercomputing cycles via the HPC COVID Consortium [2] to conduct molecular dynamics simulations at unprecedented scale (of Newtonian to quantum physics fidelity and resolution), (ii) inviting researchers to use the Cray Supercomputer on Microsoft Azure [3] free-of-charge for scale-out protein-ligand docking experiments, (iii) open-sourcing an AI model trained on supercomputers [4, 5] for virtual screening of novel drug molecule databases, (iv) building a knowledge graph by integrating 13 popular life science databases (over 150 billion facts, >30 terabytes on disk) and conducting hackathons for users to leverage such a resource [6], (v) rapidly prototyping a natural language platform on the CORD-19 corpus released by the White House [7], (vi) enabling federated privacy-preserving disease classification using swarm machine learning techniques [8], and (vii) providing reference architectures with storage and compute infrastructure to accelerate 3D reconstruction of viral protein targets from CryoEM microscopes [58], tools for open-science and privacy-protected AI model development, training and deployment, services for scientific data ingest, transform, indexing and visualization. While all of these efforts may appear unrelated, the value demonstrated by the end-to-end pipeline illustrated in Fig. 1 offers drug/vaccine researchers a variety of tools for virtual screening that extends beyond the COVID-19 pandemic.

1.3 HPC, AI and Big Data Case Studies

The focus for this paper is to present results and insights from specific workflows that applied HPC, AI and Big Data techniques to drug discovery. More specifically, given a database of possible drug ligands and the reconstructed CryoEM 3D protein structure of the COVID-19 virus, how can HPC, AI and Big Data be used to rank, prioritize and hypothesize potential drug ligands?

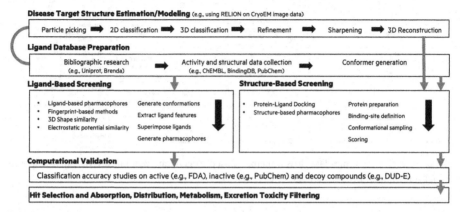

Fig. 1. The end-to-end computational workflows for in-silico drug discovery can now be augmented with simulations, artificial intelligence and Big Data methodologies. With Big data methods, scientists are able to query the "what-is" and "what-else". Artificial intelligence answers the "what-if" and high-performance simulations imagine the "what-could-be".

Collaborators from the University of Alabama at Huntsville (UAH), Medical University of South Carolina (MUSC) and National Center for Natural Products Research (NCNPR), at the University of Mississippi were respectively able to instantiate workflows that are illustrated in Fig. 2. In a paper published based on the results from the HPE-UAH collaboration [3], the authors describe the use of a Cray supercomputer to perform virtual screening of natural products and natural product derivatives against several conformations of three proteins of the COVID-19 virus. UAH researchers analyzed the common chemical features of the top molecules predicted to bind and describe the pharmacophores responsible for the predicted binding.

The AI collaboration with MUSC, resulted in the development and testing of a neural network model – PharML. As an alternative to approximating the rules of quantum mechanics (docking) or simulating the kinetics of the interaction through molecular dynamics or quantum chemistry based numerical methods, PharML builds an approximation using data from prior docking as well as assay information of known protein-ligand interactions. The AI model training requires a supercomputer. However, once trained and distributed in inferencing mode [9, 10] the predictions are orders of magnitude faster and cheaper. MUSC used the model to evaluate Food and Drug Administration (FDA) approved repurposable drug candidates for COVID-19. MUSC and HPE open-sourced this effort. PharML performed the best among other AI-driven methods [11] – by picking more anti-virals than its competitors and more predictions that were undergoing clinical trials for COVID-19.

Scientists from the NCNPR at Mississippi leveraged the Cray Graph Engine as a knowledge graph host for evaluating a rapid drug-repurposing methodology. Their approach extended the proven value of knowledge graphs for the drug repurposing

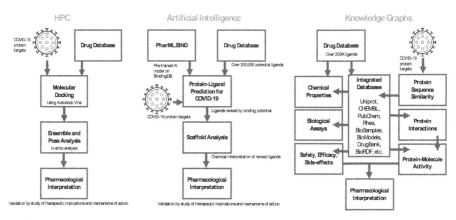

Fig. 2. The HPC, AI and data-driven methods used to generate hypotheses via rapid-response virtual screening of drug databases for COVID-19.

problem described in [12–15] by rapidly identifying targets with sequence similarity (compared to the universe of 4+ million known protein sequences of disease-causing organisms) to the COVID-19 target protein, and expanding target pool to improve odds of finding molecule(s) that modulate the disease target. When applied to COVID-19, this approach hypothesized the impact of Tetanus vaccine on COVID-19 severity [16] and was able to detect that the COVID-19 virus bore similarity to SARS, MERS and certain bat coronaviruses. By connecting the dots to known evidence of molecules and protein-protein interactions, this approach identified 86 molecules out of 196 in active clinical trials in just a few seconds across multiple COVID-19 protein targets. Connecting the dots manually or using other tools would otherwise take months.

2 Case Study 1: High Performance Computing

2.1 Problem Statement

The HPC approach to develop potent drug candidates utilizes the three-dimensional structure of the disease-specific protein to identify small molecules that exhibit the desired chemical features needed to bind, or 'dock', to the proteins of interest. These molecular docking calculations are physics-based simulations that estimate the binding free energy of a chemical and a protein, positioning a small molecule in the binding site of the virus target and evaluating interaction energy between the small molecule and its protein environment. More accurate but computationally expensive "ensemble docking", uses several structures of a target to give small drug molecules the opportunity to bind to different protein target conformations/poses. Can this approach, that has been successfully used in the discovery of new molecular effectors against a variety of targets [17, 18], and in particular to inhibit protein-protein complexes [19], help us prioritize drug candidates for COVID-19?

2.2 Methodology

We used the COCONUT v4 database [20] with 423,706 natural product candidates as the repository of drug molecules and the 3D structures for the spike protein, main protease, and papain-like protease of the COVID-19 virus from open-source molecular dynamics simulation coordinate files from [21]. These structures are representative conformations clustered from the trajectories of 100-ns restrained temperature replica exchange molecular dynamics simulations of the proteins [22] using GROMACS [23] and starting from the Protein Databank Bank entries 6Y2E (main protease), 6W41 (spike protein), and 6W9C (papain like protease). The ten most populated conformations from each set of clustered structures were used as an ensemble for molecular docking, with each structure being prepared as individual PDBQT files using MGLTools 1.5.6. The docking code used in this study was Auto Dock Vina 1.1.2 [24].

The molecular docking simulations using AutoDock Vina were performed on a 48-node HPE Cray XC50 single cabinet supercomputer located in the Microsoft Azure public cloud data center featuring 1920 physical Intel Skylake cores operating at 2.4 GHz with 192 GB ram per node and connected to a shared 612 TB Cray HPE ClusterStor-based file system.

2.3 Results

Several compounds from the COCONUT database after the pharmacophore analysis and interpretation have been identified as potential inhibitors of the three most significant targets in the COVID-19 proteome, CLpro, PLpro and the spike protein receptor-binding domain (ACE2). Among the results predicted to bind to the spike protein in a way that would disrupt its interaction with ACE2, polyphenols and in particular flavonoids, are seen in several computational hits. In particular, compounds based at least in part on scaffold similar to these of apigenin scaffolds are observed. Apigenin, interestingly, is hypothesized to regulate the expression of ACE2 [25]. Apigenin is found in many plants and is particularly abundant in the flowers of the chamomile plants. In addition to prekinamycin A, which has been reported in the literature to exhibit cytotoxicity to human leukemia cells [26], harunganin [CNP0334196], isolated from the Dragon's blood tree, *Harungana madagascariensis*, from Madagascar and several nearby countries in Africa, where the extracts have been used in traditional medicines to treat a variety of ailments such as dysentery, diarrhea, anemia, typhoid and heart ailments [27]. Compounds similar to beccamarin [28, 29] was also found to fit the pharmacophore. This compound is found in the bark of the ironwood tree, *Mesua beccariana*, whose extract has been used in traditional medicine to treat fever, renal diseases, poultice and dyspepsia in Malaysia. Beccamarin has recently been shown to inhibit the proliferation of the Raji (lymphoma), SK-MEL-28 (malignant melanoma cells) and HeLa (cervical cells) human cancer cell lines [30].

3   Case Study 2: Artificial Intelligence

3.1   Problem Statement

The theoretically inspired *in-silico* simulations presented in Case Study 1 are computationally intensive - requiring many hours to weeks to screen and predict binding potential between the viral target and a drug molecule database. Can artificial intelligence techniques such as deep learning help sift through the search space of multiple protein and drug databases faster and better? Can AI learn from past simulations and observational data to predict the probability of protein-drug interactions? Can such an AI model generalize to new/novel molecules in the chemical space of 10^{60} compounds? How does such a model perform as a hypothesis generation tool for drug repurposing?

3.2   Methodology

Our detailed approach is documented in [9], and our source code is available at [31]. The model from [31] was trained on a Cray supercomputer with 64 NVIDIA V100 GPUs. The results presented in this paper can be reproduced by using the published pre-trained PharML model in inferencing mode to screen public and private databases on a personal computer without the need for expensive computing resources – orders of magnitude faster and cheaper than simulation approaches. Our novelty is in designing a Molecular-Highway Graph Neural Network (MH-GNN) – a special kind of deep learning network that efficiently operates on molecular representations of both ligands and proteins, preserving the 3D shape, form, and atomic properties.

The MH-GNN architecture takes as input a loosely connected representation of the protein called a neighborhood graph. The neighborhood graph is defined as a set of nodes, defined by elements and their atomic number, and the set of edges representing the distance between different atoms that constitute the protein. This representation has been used in virtual molecule synthesis using deep learning prior to our work [32, 33]. The drug (or ligand) is also represented as a graph, independent of its location or orientation in 3D space as an N by N bond-matrix, where N is the number of atoms making up the drug compound. The neural network then maps and learns patterns between the neighborhood graphs of the protein and the bond matrix of the ligands. We build these neighborhood graphs from PDB structure files of proteins and utilize SDF format files to convert drug databases into graph representations.

For the results in this paper, we have used an ensemble of pre-trained MH-GNN models [9, 31]. That is, we train k MH-GNN models (each with 503,652 trainable parameters) which learns to predict a probability of binding for a protein and ligand pair. The models are trained on protein-ligand ground truth data available in BindingDB [34]. We then score and rank the binding potential using the k predictions. This ensemble technique using multiple models provides state-of-the-art accuracy [35] on BindingDB and ZINC [36] datasets.

3.3 Results

We conducted multiple experiments with different input data sizes and hyper-parameter sweeps of different MH-GNN models to ensure that our model generalizes well - particularly to unseen datasets of drug ligands and novel viral targets. The best model among the sweep was able to achieve 98.3% accuracy on the largest test set, containing 2,708,151 pairs from BindingDB in under 25 min – i.e., the model being trained on only 25% of the entire dataset, with the remainder reserved for validation and testing. Based on cross-validation experiments, we confirmed that the AI model generalizes as well as the alternative state-of-the-art methods derived from first principles. Our deep learning model also performs well when trained with adversarial inputs. On a decoy dataset DUD.E [37], the area-under the receiver-operating-characteristic curve for our approach (for the k ensemble models) varies between (0.67–0.74) compared to 0.71 from physics-based ground-truth results.

Encouraged by the results, we applied the PharML model to predict and identify potential drugs for COVID-19 using publicly available DrugBank [38] and ChEMBL [39] ligand databases and open 3D structures of the viral protein made available via the protein databank (PDB) [40]. Initially, we focused on the main protease (PDB: 6Y2E) as the COVID-19 viral target to predict ligands that have the highest probability of binding. Our approach, based on the weighted probability scores, identified and ranked 7 out of the ~800 approved drugs in the top-50 that are actively undergoing clinical trials for COVID-19. Compared to four competing techniques [11, 41–43] with a best hit-rate of 15% on antivirals, our approach achieved a hit rate of 25% despite being the only active-site agnostic method. We were then able to screen and rank potential compounds for many other viral target proteins (PDB: 6Y84, 6VSB, 6M3M, etc.) in a few hours (at 9 compounds a second on a single NVIDIA V100 GPU) as opposed to what would have taken days on expensive compute resources with competing methods. Across different viral targets, our ranked top-50 list also had 30% more compounds that satisfied the Lipinski rules [44]. While deep learning is often criticized for the lack of interpretability (black-box nature of predictions), the model appears to have learned the physics-driven and biologically observed rules governing the ligand-protein interaction purely from the BindingDB data without pharmacological inputs to the model design. The experimental results are summarized in Table 1 below.

The next set of experiments were conducted on 203,826 chemical structures of isolated natural products and their analogs provided to us by the collaborators at the University of Mississippi. Unlike ChEMBL or DrugBank structures, these chemical structures have minimal to no known overlap/similarity with structures used for training from BindingDB. PharML was then used to predict and rank potential natural products relevant to COVID-19. In the top-50 ranked natural product-based ligands against the PDB: 6Y2E viral target, PharML ranked 32 inflammation-treating substances, three angiotensin-converting enzyme inhibitors, and three androgen receptor ligands – all relevant to COVID-19 symptoms/treatment [45–47]. Further analysis of the top-50 natural candidates revealed that the identified 'hits' are related to ongoing clinical trials with colchicine, macro-carpal, and tanshinones. Several synthetic efforts to fine-tune the protein-ligand interactions with these privileged scaffolds are underway.

Table 1. Summary of results measured as accuracy, adversarial robustness, success rate and speed of an AI model to generate new hypotheses.

Database	# of molecules	Key result/differentiation
BINDINGDB	820,433 molecules 7493 targets	98.3% accuracy trained on 2,708,151 protein-ligand pairs used as training set
DUD.E	22846 molecules 102 targets 50 decoys/active site	ROC metrics comparable to docking PharML AUC: 0.669–0.741 DockAlign AUC: 0.717
CHEMBL	13,377 targets (8 COVID-19) 1,950,765 molecules	Success rate measured by number of molecules in clinical trials (~15% on antivirals and ~25% across targets)
FDA	~500 molecules 8 COVID-19 targets	More anti-viral drugs identified More drugs featured in clinical trials
NCNPR	8 COVID-19 targets 202,046 molecules	Ranked molecules for 8 COVID-19 targets in ~1 day

4   Case Study 3: Big Data

4.1   Problem Statement

While the HPC approach is scientifically well-founded, the AI approach is a black-box prediction for the drug repurposing use-case. Can Big Data tools augment the insights from HPC and AI with empirical evidence by - understanding the protein structures of the disease-causing organism, interpreting the interactions of the organism's protein structures with the human body, mining through properties of potential drug molecules, connecting the dots across curated literature to explain the mechanism-of-action, searching for evidence in assay data, analyzing for potential safety and efficacy using data from prior trials, and more? How can we help life-sciences researchers to: (a) understand the disease-causing organism by matching and comparing protein sequences to previously known or studied disease-causing organisms (over 4 million sequences), (b) handle and process multi-modal Big data (protein sequences, proteomic interactions, bio-chemical pathways, structured data from past clinical trials, etc.), (c) integrate and search for patterns connecting across the multiple multi-modal multi-terabyte datasets, (d) install, configure and run a plethora of tools (genetics, proteomics, molecular dynamics, data science etc.) to generate insights, and finally (e) verify and validate the scientific rigor for pharmacological interpretation?

4.2   Methodology

Our approach [48] leverages the design and implementation of a massively parallel database that (a) stores, handles, hosts and processes multi-modal data represented in the form of knowledge graphs, (b) provides interactive query and semantic-traversal capabilities for data-driven discovery, (c) accelerates domain-specific functions such as Smith-Waterman algorithm [59] to conduct protein similarity analysis, vertex-centric and whole-graph algorithms such as PageRank for graph-theoretic connectivity and relevance analysis, and (d) runs/executes a workflow of queries across multiple datasets to generate drug hypotheses in the order of seconds as opposed to months. We demonstrate the application of this technology using an integrated knowledge graph of multiple multi-modal life-science databases, conduct protein-sequence matching in parallel and present a novel rapid drug-repurposing methodology that is able to query across 4+ million proteins, 155+ billion facts while handling approximately 30 terabytes of data.

Our approach extends the proven value of knowledge graphs for the drug repurposing problem described in [12–15] by offering a generalizable Big Data platform to other biomedical discovery problems beyond the COVID-19 pandemic in the form of the Life-Sciences knowledge graph. The integrated Life-Sciences knowledge graph assembled to study potential drug repurposing candidates for COVID-19 was generated from a collection of publicly available databases commonly used in life sciences and systems biology research, bringing together a knowledge graph with over 150 billion facts (Table 2). To the best of our knowledge, no other graph database is able to host such a large dataset and offer interactive query capabilities.

Table 2. List of open- source databases integrated into a knowledge graph.

Dataset	Size	Source
UniProt (Mar 2020)	12.7 Terabytes	[49]
PubChemRDF (v1.6.3 beta)	13.0 Terabytes	[50]
ChEMBL-RDF (27.0)	81 Gigabytes	[51]
Bio2RDF (Release 4)	2.4 Terabytes	[52]
OrthoDB (v10)	275 Gigabytes	[53]
Biomodels (r31)	5.2 Gigabytes	[54]
Biosamples (v20191125)	112.8 Gigabytes	[55]
Reactome (r71)	3.2 Gigabytes	[56]

On this massive knowledge graph, our approach begins by first allowing researchers to understand the similarity/variability of the novel virus compared to other known viruses. If parts of the protein sequence that make up the novel virus have sequence over-laps of functional domains with other known viruses, the information in the integrated knowledge graph helps us extrapolate the search to identify potential drug candidates that are known to inhibit disease-causing activity of the known viruses. The typical work-flow for researchers conducting hypothesis-driven research would have been to perform searches in one of the databases, then construct queries for another database, and iter-ate. The effort of manually mapping the ontologies of various data sources and piecing together results from multiple query end points (or using yet another database to perform this translation), is a cumbersome process. In our case, all of the relevant databases are loaded in one environment, enabling seamless cross-database queries – and automated cross-database pattern search.

4.3 Results

The first query posed on the knowledge graph was to compute the similarity of all known protein sequences of known virus, bacteria and fungi in Uniprot to match protein-substructures of COVID-19. One interesting result while computing and comparing the well-studied COVID-19 protein sub-structure called the Spike protein (also discussed in Sect. 2) was the tetanus toxin, which has the Uniprot identifier P04958 and mnemonic TETX_CLOTE. The similarity query against the Spike protein returns TETX_CLOTE as one of the highest non-coronavirus matches based on the similarity score across all available protein sequences in Uniprot – serendipitously revealing potential cross-immunity for tetanus vaccines against COVID-19.

The next set of queries searched the existing published literature on proteins, compounds, chemical interactions and clinical trials as well as the protein structure information. For example, once we identified UniProt protein-substructures such as (P04958, P12821, P08183, P0A8V2, O43451, P47820, P12822, O00462, P35968, P47989, etc.) bearing sequence similarity with COVID-19 protein structures we are able to associate proteins in a host organism that are known to interact with the disease-causing protein structure. For example, for the protein-substructures listed above, some of the host organism protein structures identified were the angiotensin-converting enzyme, ATP-dependent translocase ABCB1, DNA-directed RNA polymerase subunit beta, maltase-glucoamylase, among others. At this step, we broadened the scope to include both animals and humans as host organisms. For these host-organism proteins, we then search for known small molecules in databases like CHEMBL, PubChem and/or Drugbank with documented evidence of protein-small molecule interaction. In our result set, several of the drugs currently under clinical trials [57] appear high in the list of compounds suggested by the knowledge graph. The Big Data system is able to look for patterns around prior evidence of efficacy and safety from open clinical trial datasets. Some of the drugs recommended by the Life-Sciences knowledge graph that were undergoing clinical trials include Baricitinib, Ribavirin, Ritonavir, Dexamethasone, Azithromycin and Lopinavir. Out of the 66 molecules recommended by our system based on Spike protein similarity, 20 drug molecules were already undergoing clinical trials as of June 2020. The Big Data system offers interactive exploratory analysis on the knowledge graph with typical query run-times (including multi-database joins and 4 million protein comparisons) of approximately one minute. A multi-database join query result for the COVID-19 Spike protein is illustrated in Fig. 3.

COVID-like proteins	➡ Known protein activity	➡ Protein target in organism	➡ Known protein-molecule interactions		
			GLUTAMIC ACID	DESIPRAMINE	
			CAPTOPRIL (3)	ERYTHROMYCIN (2)	
			ENALAPRIL (2)	SAQUINAVIR	
			CHLORPROPAMIDE	PIMOZIDE	PROTRIPTYLINE
			PROMETHAZINE (1)	TERFENADINE	CHLORZOXAZONE
			QUINIDINE	METERGOLINE	TRIFLUPROMAZINE
			FLURAZEPAM	FLUVOXAMINE (1)	RIFAMPIN
P04958		TETX_CLOTE	RITONAVIR (57)	VERAPAMIL (2)	ACARBOSE
P12821	Tetanus toxin	ACE_HUMAN	CAFFEINE	MICONAZOLE (5)	MIGALASTAT
P08183	Angiotensin-converting enzyme	MDR1_HUMAN	FLUOXETINE	DEXAMETHASONE (9)	ANDROGRAPHOLIDE
P0A8V2	ATP-dependent translocase ABCB1	RPOB_ECOLI	TAMOXIFEN	ETOPOSIDE (1)	SPIRAPRIL
O43451	DNA-directed RNA polymerase subunit beta	MGA_HUMAN	MAPROTILINE	RANITIDINE	BENAZEPRIL
P47820	Maltase-glucoamylase, intestinal	ACE_RAT	DOXEPIN	AMIODARONE (2)	ENALAPRILAT (2)
P12822	Beta-mannosidase	ACE_RABIT	MIDAZOLAM (3)	DIGOXIN	GEFITINIB
O00462	Vascular endothelial growth factor receptor 2	MANBA_HUMAN	CLOTRIMAZOLE (5)	HALOPERIDOL	NERATINIB
P35968	Xanthine dehydrogenase/oxidase	VGFR2_HUMAN	VINBLASTINE	ITRACONAZOLE	ERLOTINIB
P47989		XDH_HUMAN	CLOMIPRAMINE	LOVASTATIN	SUNITINIB
			BEPRIDIL	NELFINAVIR	ADENINE (1)
			CIMETIDINE	NICARDIPINE (3)	ALLOPURINOL
			MIBEFRADIL	AMITRIPTYLINE	CAFFEIC ACID
			NIFEDIPINE (2)	COLCHICINE (10)	
			KETOCONAZOLE	MORPHINE (2)	
			HYDROCORTISONE (7)	BUSPIRONE	
			ASTEMIZOLE	CHLORPROTHIXENE	
			PROCHLORPERAZINE		

Fig. 3. The results of comparing the COVID-19 Spike protein with other proteins in other sequenced viruses and bacteria reveals previously studied protein activity with organism-specific complexes that can then be linked to known protein-molecule interactions. We have listed the hypothesized drug names along with the number of active clinical trials for COVID-19 as of June 3, 2020 within parenthesis using this approach.

5   Lessons Learned

Thus far in this paper, we have presented HPC, AI and Big Data as independent workflows that aim to identify potential drug candidates targeting proteins of the COVID-19 virus. Several workflows were designed and executed that combined results from HPC, AI and Big Data. One such workflow was to generate ranked lists as output from HPC, AI and Big Data methods to understand the complementary features and robustness to molecular diversity and protein promiscuity using three scenarios. The scenarios utilize HPC, AI and Big Data to generate a list for each of the following experiments - same database of molecules on a specific viral target, multiple databases for a specific viral target and a specific database for multiple target proteins. This list was then used to evaluate compare the results using the different metrics in Table 3.

The analysis of these workflows posing different scenarios with the appropriate metrics revealed that HPC methods are best suited for unknown virus vs. novel molecule hypotheses (e.g. Spike protein vs. virtual molecule). Big Data methods were effective for drug repurposing when empirical richness of the drug molecule database was high (e.g. Spike protein vs. CHEMBL). AI methods were preferred for new molecule synthesis use-cases (e.g. Flu vs. virtual molecule). While conducting a prospective analysis based on the number of prioritized (top-ranked) molecules undergoing clinical trials as the figure of merit for the COVID-19 experiment, Big Data and AI methods outperformed simulation results.

Table 3. Experiment design to understand outputs from HPC, AI and Big Data methods

Scenarios	Purpose	Metrics
Database: NCNPR Target: Spike protein	Study similarity of the ranked list of drug molecules	Number of drug molecules in common
Database: NCNPR, CHEMBL, SWEETLEAD Target: Spike protein	Study robustness to molecule diversity	Number of molecules in active clinical trials
Database: CHEMBL Target: Spike, main protease	Evaluate robustness to protein-promiscuity	Number of molecules hypothesized across targets

These results revealed key science and technology insights discussed in the Sections below.

5.1 Scientific Gaps and Benefits

Converged HPC, AI and Big Data methods:

- Offered scientists and researchers a more holistic view for *in-silico* drug discovery that encompasses theory, experiment, simulation and data.
- Demonstrated the fusion of theoretical interpretability and empirical explainability at scales and speeds required in a rapid-response situation.
- Are complementary hypothesis generation approaches, each with its own logic to rank/prioritize and hypothesize drug molecules.
- Produced results with little overlap in the ranked list of results when treated as independent methods (both in the Top 50 and Top 100).
- Exposed blindspots and shortcomings of each method when used independently. For instance, the HPC approach did not leverage the empirical knowledge about known target proteins, the AI approach had a propensity to learn patterns about molecules better than viral proteins (due to sample bias in training data), and the Big Data approach was unable to overcome gaps in curation and experimental data collection.

5.2 Technology Gaps and Benefits

Converged HPC, AI and Big Data workflows:

- Significantly reduce the data gravity problem compared to the alternative of treating simulation, AI and knowledge graphs as three independent siloes of information.
- Reveal the dire need for foundational data infrastructure that is capable of ingesting, indexing and hosting multiple formats and shapes of scientific data (protein sequences, chemical structures, structured, tabular, graphs, 3D structures, 2D images, etc.).
- Need interfaces that allow the data infrastructure to feed different application codes (e.g. RELION for reconstructing 3D structure from the CryoEM microscopic images,

Auto-Dock Vina for protein-ligand docking, PharML for predicting binding potential, Cray Graph Engine for serving the knowledge graph) with query end-points are essential to answer questions posed by collaborating customers/scientists.
- Require specialized data science skillsets before domain scientists are able to iterate, interact and benefit from HPC, AI and Big Data components in the workflow.

6 Summary

Based on the experiments to date, we have run high-fidelity molecular dynamics models on HPC hardware. The AI model PharML is one of the best active-site agnostic "binding predictors" (with accuracy of >95%) between a viral protein and ligand trained on the largest possible public dataset (BindingDB). We are able to demonstrate the value of a massively parallel processing protein-sequence analytics engine embedded into a scalable graph database for interactive knowledge-graph traversal. This graph engine is able to compare 4+ million proteins and reason through 150 billion facts for every query in a few seconds. Bringing together the different technology components in rapid-response to the COVID-19 pandemic as a converged workflow on HPE supercomputers has revealed several lessons. These lessons have inspired a sense of purpose among engineers. Collaborating scientists have been able to envision the art of the possible with modern tools, frameworks, models and services that extend to broader impacts in pharmaceutical, life-sciences and public-health research. We have shown an early glimpse into the value and a future of AI infused into physics simulations, AI learning in parallel from ensemble physics simulations and data science techniques saving precious computational resources on focused/filtered problems with in-situ analysis to steer both AI and HPC methods.

References

1. http://phrma-docs.phrma.org/sites/default/files/pdf/rd_brochure_022307.pdf. Accessed 01 June 2021
2. https://covid19-hpc-consortium.org/. Accessed 01 June 2021
3. https://www.uah.edu/news/items/uah-boosts-search-for-covid-19-drugs-using-hpe-cray-sentinel-supercomputer. Accessed 01 June 2021
4. https://community.hpe.com/t5/advancing-life-work/introducing-pharml-bind-a-powerful-tool-to-advance-drug/ba-p/7086167. Accessed 01 June 2021
5. https://web.musc.edu/about/news-center/2020/05/15/musc-hpe-make-innovative-drug-discovery-software-open-source. Accessed 01 June 2021
6. https://www.hpe.com/us/en/insights/articles/How-supercomputers-are-identifying-Covid-19-therapeutics-2011.html. Accessed 01 June 2021
7. https://covid19.labs.hpe.com/. Accessed 01 June 2021
8. Warnat-Herresthal, S., et al.: Swarm learning for decentralized and confidential clinical machine learning. Nature **594**, 1–7 (2021)
9. Vose, A.D., Balma, J., Farnsworth, D., Anderson, K., Peterson, Y.K.: PharML.Bind: pharmacologic machine learning for protein-ligand interactions. arXiv preprint arXiv:1911.06105 (2019)
10. Balma, J., et al.: Deep learning predicts protein-ligand interactions. In: 2020 IEEE International Conference on Big Data (Big Data), pp. 5627–5629 (2020)

11. Beck, B.R., Shin, B., Choi, Y., Park, S., Kang, K.: Predicting commercially available antiviral drugs that may act on the novel coronavirus (SARS-CoV-2) through a drug-target interaction deep learning model. Comput. Struct. Biotechnol. J. **18**, 784–790 (2020)
12. Sadegh, S., et al.: Exploring the SARS-CoV-2 virus-host-drug interactome for drug repurposing. Nat. Commun. **11**(1), 1–9 (2020)
13. Zhou, Y., Hou, Y., Shen, J., Huang, Y., Martin, W., Cheng, F.: Network-based drug repurposing for novel coronavirus 2019-nCoV/SARS-CoV-2. Cell Discov. **6**(1), 1–18 (2020)
14. Gysi, D.M., et al.: Network medicine framework for identifying drug-repurposing opportunities for COVID-19. Proc. Natl. Acad. Sci. **118**(19), e2025581118 (2021)
15. https://github.com/Knowledge-Graph-Hub/. Accessed 01 June 2021
16. Rickett, C.D., Maschhoff, K.J., Sukumar, S.R.: Does tetanus vaccination contribute to reduced severity of the COVID-19 infection? Med. Hypotheses **146**, 110395 (2021)
17. Abdali, N., et al.: Reviving antibiotics: efflux pump inhibitors that interact with AcrA, a membrane fusion protein of the AcrAB-TolC multidrug efflux pump. ACS Infect. Dis. **3**(1), 89–98 (2017)
18. Velazquez, H.A., et al.: Ensemble docking to difficult targets in early-stage drug discovery: methodology and application to fibroblast growth factor 23. Chem. Biol. Drug Des. **91**(2), 491–504 (2018)
19. Kapoor, K., McGill, N., Peterson, C.B., Meyers, H.V., Blackburn, M.N., Baudry, J.: Discovery of novel nonactive site inhibitors of the prothrombinase enzyme complex. J. Chem. Inf. Model. **56**(3), 535–547 (2016)
20. Sorokina, M., Merseburger, P., Rajan, K., Yirik, M.A., Steinbeck, C.: COCONUT online: Collection of Open Natural Products database. J. Cheminform. **13**(1), 1–13 (2021)
21. https://coronavirus-hpc.ornl.gov/data/. Accessed 01 June 2021
22. Smith, M.D., Smith, J.C.: Repurposing therapeutics for COVID-19: supercomputer-based docking to the SARS-CoV-2 viral spike protein and viral spike protein-human ACE2 interface (2020). https://chemrxiv.org/engage/api-gateway/chemrxiv/assets/orp/resource/item/60c74980f96a00352b28727c/original/repurposing-therapeutics-for-covid-19-supercomputer-based-docking-to-the-sars-co-v-2-viral-spike-protein-and-viral-spike-protein-human-ace2-interface.pdf
23. Van Der Spoel, D., Lindahl, E., Hess, B., Groenhof, G., Mark, A.E., Berendsen, H.J.: GROMACS: fast, flexible, and free. J. Comput. Chem. **26**(16), 1701–1718 (2005)
24. Trott, O., Olson, A.J.: AutoDock Vina: improving the speed and accuracy of docking with a new scoring function, efficient optimization, and multithreading. J. Comput. Chem. **31**(2), 455–461 (2010)
25. Salehi, B., et al.: The therapeutic potential of apigenin. Int. J. Mol. Sci. **20**(6), 1305 (2019)
26. Abbott, G.L., et al.: Prekinamycin and an isosteric-isoelectronic analogue exhibit comparable cytotoxicity towards K562 human leukemia cells. MedChemComm **5**(9), 1364–1370 (2014)
27. Happi, G.M., et al.: Phytochemistry and pharmacology of Harungana madagascariensis: mini review. Phytochem. Lett. **35**, 103–112 (2020)
28. Ee, G.C.L., Teh, S.S., Mah, S.H., Rahmani, M., Taufiq-Yap, Y.H., Awang, K.: A novel cyclodione coumarin from the stem bark of Mesua beccariana. Molecules **16**(9), 7249–7255 (2011)
29. Karunakaran, T., Ee, G.C., Tee, K.H., Ismail, I.S., Zamakshshari, N.H., Peter, W.M.: Cytotoxic prenylated xanthone and coumarin derivatives from Malaysian Mesua beccariana. Phytochem. Lett. **17**, 131–134 (2016)
30. Teh, S.S., Cheng Lian Ee, G., Mah, S.H., Lim, Y.M., Rahmani, M.: Mesua beccariana (Clusiaceae), a source of potential anti-cancer lead compounds in drug discovery. Molecules **17**(9), 10791–10800 (2012)
31. https://github.com/jbalma/pharml. Accessed 01 June 2021

32. Zhavoronkov, A., et al.: Deep learning enables rapid identification of potent DDR1 kinase inhibitors. Nat. Biotechnol. **37**(9), 1038–1040 (2019)
33. Schwaller, P., et al.: Molecular transformer: a model for uncertainty-calibrated chemical reaction prediction. ACS Cent. Sci. **5**(9), 1572–1583 (2019)
34. Liu, T., Lin, Y., Wen, X., Jorissen, R.N., Gilson, M.K.: BindingDB: a web-accessible database of experimentally determined protein–ligand binding affinities. Nucl. Acids Res. **35**(Suppl_1), D198–D201 (2007)
35. Huang, K., Xiao, C., Glass, L., Sun, J.: MolTrans: molecular interaction transformer for drug target interaction prediction. arXiv preprint arXiv:2004.11424 (2020)
36. Irwin, J.J., Shoichet, B.K.: ZINC – a free database of commercially available compounds for virtual screening. J. Chem. Inf. Model. **45**(1), 177–182 (2005)
37. Mysinger, M.M., Carchia, M., Irwin, J.J., Shoichet, B.K.: Directory of useful decoys-enhanced (DUD-E): better ligands and decoys for better benchmarking. J. Med. Chem. **55**(14), 6582–6594 (2012)
38. Wishart, D.S., et al.: DrugBank: a knowledgebase for drugs, drug actions and drug targets. Nucl. Acids Res. **36**(Suppl_1), D901–D906 (2008)
39. Gaulton, A., et al.: ChEMBL: a large-scale bioactivity database for drug discovery. Nucl. Acids Res. **40**(D1), D1100–D1107 (2012)
40. https://www.rcsb.org/. Accessed 01 June 2021
41. Odhar, H.A., Ahjel, S.W., Albeer, A.A.M.A., Hashim, A.F., Rayshan, A.M., Humadi, S.S.: Molecular docking and dynamics simulation of FDA approved drugs with the main protease from 2019 novel coronavirus. Bioinformation **16**(3), 236 (2020)
42. Kandeel, M., Al-Nazawi, M.: Virtual screening and repurposing of FDA approved drugs against COVID-19 main protease. Life Sci. **251**, 117627 (2020)
43. Pant, S., Singh, M., Ravichandiran, V., Murty, U.S.N., Srivastava, H.K.: Peptide-like and small-molecule inhibitors against Covid-19. J. Biomol. Struct. Dyn. **39**, 1–10 (2020)
44. Lipinski, C.A.: Lead-and drug-like compounds: the rule-of-five revolution. Drug Discov. Today: Technol. **1**(4), 337–341 (2004)
45. Tay, M.Z., Poh, C.M., Rénia, L., MacAry, P.A., Ng, L.F.: The trinity of COVID-19: immunity, inflammation and intervention. Nat. Rev. Immunol. **20**, 1–12 (2020)
46. South, A.M., Diz, D.I., Chappell, M.C.: COVID-19, ACE2, and the cardiovascular consequences. Am. J. Physiol.-Heart Circulat. Physiol. **318**, H1084–H1090 (2020)
47. Wambier, C.G., Goren, A.: Severe acute respiratory syndrome coronavirus 2 (SARS-CoV-2) infection is likely to be androgen-mediated. J. Am. Acad. Dermatol. **83**(1), 308–309 (2020)
48. Rickett, C.D., Maschhoff, K.J., Sukumar, S.R.: Massively parallel processing database for sequence and graph data structures applied to rapid-response drug repurposing. In: 2020 IEEE International Conference on Big Data (Big Data), pp. 2967–2976. IEEE (2020)
49. UniProt Consortium: UniProt: the universal protein knowledgebase. Nucl. Acids Res. **46**(5), 2699 (2018)
50. Kim, S., et al.: PubChem 2019 update: improved access to chemical data. Nucl. Acids Res. **47**(D1), D1102–D1109 (2019)
51. Mendez, D., et al.: ChEMBL: towards direct deposition of bioassay data. Nucl. Acids Res. **47**(D1), D930–D940 (2019)
52. Belleau, F., Nolin, M.A., Tourigny, N., Rigault, P., Morissette, J.: Bio2RDF: towards a mashup to build bioinformatics knowledge systems. J. Biomed. Inform. **41**(5), 706–716 (2008)
53. Kriventseva, E.V., et al.: OrthoDB v10: sampling the diversity of animal, plant, fungal, protist, bacterial and viral genomes for evolutionary and functional annotations of orthologs. Nucl. Acids Res. **47**(D1), D807–D811 (2019)
54. Malik-Sheriff, R.S., et al.: BioModels—15 years of sharing computational models in life science. Nucl. Acids Res. **48**(D1), D407–D415 (2020)

55. Jupp, S., et al.: The EBI RDF platform: linked open data for the life sciences. Bioinformatics **30**(9), 1338–1339 (2014)

56. Fabregat, A., et al.: The reactome pathway knowledgebase. Nucl. Acids Res. **46**(D1), D649–D655 (2018)

57. Clinicaltrials.gov (2020). https://clinicaltrials.gov/ct2/results?cond=COVID-19. Accessed 6 Mar 2020

58. https://www.hpe.com/psnow/doc/a50000691enw?jumpid=in_lit-psnow-red. Accessed 01 June 2021

59. Okada, D., Ino, F., Hagihara, K.: Accelerating the Smith-Waterman algorithm with inter-pair pruning and band optimization for the all-pairs comparison of base sequences. BMC Bioinform. **16**(1), 1–15 (2015)

High-Performance Ptychographic Reconstruction with Federated Facilities

Tekin Bicer[1,3]($\boxtimes$), Xiaodong Yu[1], Daniel J. Ching[3], Ryan Chard[1],
Mathew J. Cherukara[3], Bogdan Nicolae[2], Rajkumar Kettimuthu[1],
and Ian T. Foster[1]

[1] Data Science and Learning Division, CELS, Argonne National Laboratory,
Lemont, IL 60439, USA
{tbicer,xyu,rchard,kettimut,foster}@anl.gov

[2] Mathematics and Computer Science Division, CELS, Argonne National
Laboratory, Lemont, IL 60439, USA
bnicolae@anl.gov

[3] X-ray Science Division, APS, Argonne National Laboratory,
Lemont, IL 60439, USA
{dching,mcherukara}@anl.gov

Abstract. Beamlines at synchrotron light source facilities are powerful scientific instruments used to image samples and observe phenomena at high spatial and temporal resolutions. Typically, these facilities are equipped only with modest compute resources for the analysis of generated experimental datasets. However, high data rate experiments can easily generate data in volumes that take days (or even weeks) to process on those local resources. To address this challenge, we present a system that unifies leadership computing and experimental facilities by enabling the automated establishment of data analysis pipelines that extend from edge data acquisition systems at synchrotron beamlines to remote computing facilities; under the covers, our system uses Globus Auth authentication to minimize user interaction, funcX to run user-defined functions on supercomputers, and Globus Flows to define and execute workflows. We describe the application of this system to ptychography, an ultra-high-resolution coherent diffraction imaging technique that can produce 100s of gigabytes to terabytes in a single experiment. When deployed on the DGX A100 ThetaGPU cluster at the Argonne Leadership Computing Facility and a microscopy beamline at the Advanced Photon Source, our system performs analysis as an experiment progresses to provide timely feedback.

Keywords: Ptychography · High-performance computing ·
Synchrotron light source · Scientific computing · Federation

1 Introduction

Synchrotron light sources are used by thousands of scientists from a wide variety of communities, such as energy, materials, health, and life sciences, to address

© Springer Nature Switzerland AG 2022
J. Nichols et al. (Eds.): SMC 2021, CCIS 1512, pp. 173–189, 2022.
https://doi.org/10.1007/978-3-030-96498-6_10

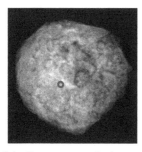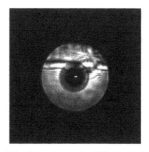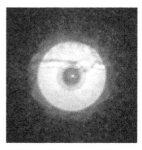

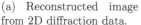

(a) Reconstructed image from 2D diffraction data.　(b) 2D cropped diffraction pattern.　(c) Visualization of pixels with log(b)

Fig. 1. (a) shows a sample ptychographic reconstruction of a catalyst particle view. The red circle shows the location of an X-ray measurement. The corresponding (cropped) diffraction pattern of this measurement is shown in (b). During a ptychography experiment, many of these diffraction patterns are collected. (c) shows the same diffraction pattern after taking its log, highlighting the distribution of the pixel values. The outer values of the diffraction pattern carry information about the sharpness/corners of the sample features. (Color figure online)

challenging research problems [3,8] by providing unique tools for materials characterization. A subset of these tools includes coherent imaging techniques which enable *in-situ* and *operando* studies of functional, structural, and energy materials at high-spatial resolution.

A nanoscale imaging technique of increasing importance to both x-ray and electron microscopes is ptychography [21,35,47]. This non-invasive 2D imaging technique is widely used at synchrotron light sources to study functional, structural, biological, and energy materials at extremely high spatial resolutions. During a ptychography experiment, a sample is continuously raster-scanned using a focused X-ray beam and the corresponding diffraction patterns are acquired on a photon-counting pixelated detector. These diffraction patterns are then processed using an iterative ptychographic reconstruction method to generate 2D real-space projection images (Fig. 1.) Although ptychography involves high photon cost, it can deliver extremely high spatial resolutions, enabling imaging of (bio)samples, for example, trace elements of green algae at sub-30-nm [24], bacteria at 20-nm [60] and diatoms at 30-nm resolution [57]. Ptychography is already used at many synchrotron light source beamlines, including Advanced Photon Source (APS) and National Synchrotron Light Source II (NSLS-II), and is expected to be yet more common at next generation light sources [1,6] where the required photon budget is easier to meet.

Ptychography experiments can generate data at high rates over extended periods. For example, detectors currently used in ptychographic experiments at synchrotron light sources can generate 1030×514 12-bit pixel frames at 3 kHz, yielding a 19.5 Gbps data generation rate. Next-generation light sources, such as the APS upgrade (APSU) [1], are expected to increase X-ray beam brightness by more than two orders of magnitude, an increase that will enable lensless imaging techniques such as ptychography to acquire data at MHz rates [29], potentially increasing data acquisition rates to Tbps. Such dramatically greater data acquisition rates are scientifically exciting but also pose severe technical challenges for data processing systems. It is expected that a single ptychography experiment will soon be able to generate many PBs of raw and reconstructed data, pushing the limits of I/O and storage resources even for high-performance computing resources and superfacilities [16,27,33,58].

Greatly increased data rates and volumes also pose major challenges for the reconstruction computations used to recover real-space images from the diffraction pattern data obtained via ptychographic imaging. The ptychographic reconstruction process is typically data-intensive, requiring hundreds of iterations over diffraction patterns and the reconstructed object. Moreover, if the goal is to recover a 3D volumetric image, then tomographic (or laminographic) reconstruction techniques need to be performed after ptychographic reconstruction [30,56], further increasing the computational demand and execution time of the processing pipeline [10,43].

Today's state-of-the-art ptychographic data analysis workflows mostly utilize locally available compute resources, such as high-end beamline workstations, or small clusters due to the difficulties in accessing remote HPC resources and/or scaling algorithms on large-scale systems. Further, the workflows are typically executed only after the data acquisition is finalized. This type of offline data analysis is not feasible for experiments that generate massive measurement data, and will generally be impossible to perform with the next generation light sources. Increasingly, therefore, the need arises to run data analysis workflows on specialized high-performance (HPC) systems in such a way that data can be analyzed *while an experiment is running*. However, effective federation of instrument and HPC system introduces many technical problems, from user authentication to job scheduling and resource allocation, transparent data movement, workflow monitoring, and fault detection and recovery. Robust solutions to these problems require sophisticated methods that for widespread use need to be incorporated into advanced software systems.

We present here a system that we have developed to implement solutions to these problems. This system unifies HPC and experimental facilities to enable on-demand analysis of data from a ptychographic experiment while the experiment is running. Its implementation leverages a suite of cloud-hosted science services provided by the Globus platform: Globus Auth for authentication, so as to avoid the need for repeated user authentication [52]; Globus transfer for rapid and reliable data movement between light source and HPC [19]; funcX for remote execution of user-defined functions on remote compute resources [20]; and Globus Flows to coordinate the multiple actions involved in collecting and analyzing data [5].

The rest of this paper is organized as follows. In Sect. 2, we briefly explain data acquisition and analysis steps for ptychography. In Sect. 3, we present components of our system and their interaction. We evaluate our system and its end-to-end performance in Sect. 4, discuss related work in Sect. 5, and conclude in Sect. 6.

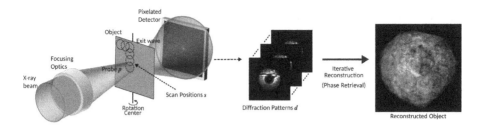

Fig. 2. Ptychography experiments and ptychographic reconstruction

2   Background

Figure 2 illustrates the experimental setup for ptychography and the basic steps for the 2D reconstruction. During a ptychography experiment, an object is placed on top of a rotation stage and scanned by a focused X-ray beam (probe p). As the object is being illuminated by an X-ray beam, the far-field diffraction patterns (d) are collected from a series of overlapping positions (s) using a pixelated detector. This allows large objects to be scanned and imaged with a higher resolution than the beam size.

At the end of a ptychography experiment, a 3D experimental dataset, which consists of 2D diffraction pattern images from a fixed rotation, is generated. The size of the dataset depends on many factors, such as target resolution, size of the object, overlapping area, and size of the detector. The data acquisition rates of ptychography experiments are typically proportional to the beam intensity. For example, while lab systems require significant scanning time over a small area to meet the photon requirements [12] (e.g., "16 h for $400\,\mu m^2$ area at 400 fps"), synchrotron light sources can provide bright beams and enable imaging cm^2 area at several kHz (and MHz in the future) with much higher resolutions.

Ptychographic reconstruction takes a set of diffraction patterns, d, with their corresponding scanning positions, probe information p, and the initial guess of the object (ψ^i), and then tries to iteratively converge an object, ψ^{i+1}, that is consistent with the measurement data while solving the phase retrieval problem as shown in Eq. 1. This process typically requires hundreds of iterations on a large dataset, therefore it is an extremely data-intensive process. Most state-of-the-art implementations rely on accelerators such as GPUs.

$$\psi^{i+1} = F(d, p, \psi^i) \tag{1}$$

Ptychographic reconstruction aims to recover a single 2D real-space projection using a set of diffraction patterns that are collected from a fixed rotation angle. This data acquisition scheme can be repeated for different angles, adding angle dimension to d, which, in turn, extends the 2D ptychography imaging technique to 3D ptychography (or ptychographic tomography) [32]. This compound technique can image 3D volumes of samples at extremely high spatial resolutions, for example, integrated circuits at sub-10-nm [34] and nanoporous glass at

16-nm [32]. However, the new ptychography dataset is typically more than two orders of magnitude larger compared to the single 2D ptychography dataset (d), which results in a significant increase in both storage and compute requirements of the analysis tasks.

Ptychographic tomography problem can be solved with several approaches, including the *two-step* and more advanced *joint* approaches [10,17]. The two-step approach treats ptychography and tomography as sequential problems, first recovering a 2D real-space projection for each rotation angle and then performing tomographic reconstruction on all projections to generate a 3D object volume. Joint approaches, on the other hand, consider the ptychography and tomography problems as one problem and continuously use information from both ptychography and tomography during reconstruction. The tomography problem can be solved by using high-performance advanced reconstruction techniques [18,55]; however, in both two-step and joint approaches, the added 3D reconstruction operations translate to additional compute resource requirements for the workflow [43].

3   Ptychography Workflow with Federated Resources

We now introduce our system and the ptychography workflow that is executed. Our system aims to automate workflow execution on geographically distributed facilities and resources using Globus services and performs high-performance ptychographic reconstruction. We describe the main components of our workflow system and how they interact with each other in the following subsections.

3.1   Automated Light Source Workflow Execution and Coordination

The ptychography workflows start with the data acquisition step as mentioned in the previous sections. The diffraction pattern data is collected at the detector and continuously streamed to the data acquisition machine. This process is illustrated with step (1) in Fig. 3.

We use *Globus Flows* to describe and execute ptychography workflows [5]. This cloud-based service is designed to automate various data management tasks such as data transfer, analysis, and indexing. Workflows in Flows are defined with a JSON-based state machine language, which links together calls to external *actions*. Flows implements an extensible model via which external *action providers* can be integrated by implementing the Globus Flows action provider API. At present, Flows supports ten actions (e.g., transfer data with Globus Transfer, execute functions with funcX, or associate identifiers via DataCite) from which users can construct workflows. Flows relies on Globus Auth [52] to provide secure, authorized, and delegatable access to user-defined workflows and also the Globus-auth secured action providers.

We specify the ptychography workflows as a Flows flow definition. This flow consists of three main *actions*: (i) *transfer* data from data acquisition machine (edge) at light source to compute cluster, e.g., ThetaGPU at Argonne Leadership Computing Facility; (ii) initiate *reconstruction process* via remote function call;

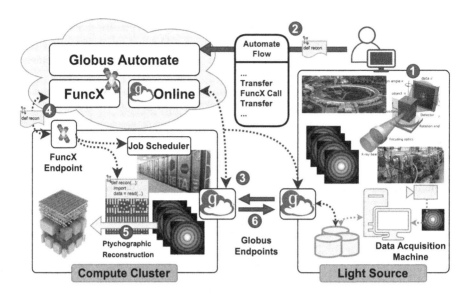

Fig. 3. System components and execution flow

and (iii) *transfer* reconstructed images from compute cluster back to light source. This flow definition is submitted to the Flows cloud service as shown in step (2) in Fig. 3. Once the flow definition is deployed to the Flows service, any number of flows can be initiated with workflow-specific input parameters.

Recall that ptychographic reconstruction process takes 2D diffraction patterns collected from a specific angle/view and recovers the corresponding 2D projection image. For 3D ptychography, the sample is rotated many times. The diffraction patterns collected from each angle can be reconstructed independently. Thus, we can write a single (generic) flow definition and reuse it with different reconstruction parameters for different angles. Therefore, a 3D ptychography workflow typically consists of many independent sub-workflows, each executing the same flow definition. A sample ptychography workflow definition can be found at DOE-funded Braid project [7].

3.2   Transparent Remote Function Calls and Data Transfers

The ptychography flow uses Globus transfer for efficient cross-facility data transfers. We deployed a Globus transfer endpoint to the beamline data acquisition machine. During the ptychography experiment, each scan is saved into a folder with a unique id, e.g., `scan100` or `flyscan100`. Our system reads these folder names, extracts the unique ids, and generates corresponding input and output folders at the beamline and the compute resource endpoints. For example, if ptychography data is stored in `<prefix>/input/scan100` at a beamline endpoint, our system will create `<prefix>/input/100` and `<prefix>/recon/100` directories at compute resource endpoint for transferring measurement data and saving (intermediate) reconstructed images.

After relevant folders are created and ptychography data is transferred to the compute endpoint, the ptychographic reconstruction tasks are initiated at the compute cluster. We use funcX for executing ptychographic reconstruction operations on remote computing clusters. funcX is a function as a service (FaaS) platform for secure and distributed function execution while supporting dynamic provisioning and resource management. funcX uses Globus Auth for secure access to remote computing systems and thus interoperates seamlessly with Globus Flows. In a similar manner to Globus transfer, funcX relies on endpoints deployed on remote computing systems to enable function execution.

We implemented the ptychographic reconstruction task as a Python function and registered it with the funcX cloud service. This operation serializes the reconstruction code, stores it in the cloud-hosted funcX service, and returns a unique identifier which can then be used to invoke the function. The reconstruction function can be invoked on-demand on any accessible funcX endpoints, providing flexibility for running any funcX function on any active endpoint the user has permission to use. If there are insufficient resources for the reconstruction task, the funcX endpoint dynamically requests additional resources (e.g., via Cobalt job scheduler at the ThetaGPU, ALCF). funcX automatically deploys *worker daemons* to newly allocated resources. These workers receive serialized reconstruction tasks and execute them.

Our ptychographic reconstruction code uses GPUs to perform analysis. If more than one reconstruction task is executed on a compute node, for example when a node has more than one GPU and each task requires only a single GPU, then each task needs to be pinned to a different GPU to maximize resource utilization. funcX functions can scale efficiently on CPU-based compute resources since operating systems handle load balancing. However, accelerator-based compute resources, e.g., GPUs, are typically managed by device drivers such as CUDA. One way to perform load balancing between tasks is to use inter-process communication, but this is nontrivial for stateless (lambda-like) funcX functions. We implemented a file-based synchronization mechanism on shared memory `tmpfs` to track available GPUs on allocated compute nodes. Specifically, when a worker starts executing a reconstruction task, it first tries to acquire an exclusive lock using `fcntl` on a predefined file (e.g., `/dev/shm/availgpus`), that keeps track of the GPUs. Once the lock is acquired, the reconstruction task checks the available GPUs from the file and updates them (setting a set of GPUs busy) according to its resource requirements. Since the number of GPUs and workers are limited on a compute node, the contention on the file is minimal and the performance bottleneck due to the (un)lock operations is negligible. Step (4) in Fig. 3 shows the interaction between compute cluster and the funcX service.

3.3 Accelerated Ptychographic Image Reconstruction

Ptychographic reconstruction is an iterative process that can be extremely data-intensive, depending on the dataset and reconstruction method. Efficient reconstruction of ptychography data and timely feedback are crucial for relevant data acquisition, early detection of experimental errors, and steering experiments.

Our ptychographic reconstruction workflows rely on our in-house developed parallel ptychographic reconstruction code [2,64]. Specifically, we implemented several parallel solvers, including multi-GPU conjugate-gradient and least-squares gradient descent solvers, to use in reconstructions. Our advanced parallelization methods provide efficient topology-aware communication between reconstruction threads, while mapping communication (synchronization) intensive threads to GPUs connected with high-performance interconnects, such as NVlink pairs and switch [63]. These parallelization techniques enable us to efficiently scale a single reconstruction task to multiple GPUs. We evaluate the scalability performance in the following section.

After the reconstruction task is completed, the funcX endpoint informs the Flows service, which then executes the next state, and initiates another Globus transfer operation to retrieve reconstructed images from compute cluster to beamline at synchrotron light source. The reconstruction and final data transfer steps are shown in steps (5) and (6), respectively.

4   Experimental Results

We evaluated the performance of our ptychographic reconstruction workflow in a configuration that connected the 2-ID microscopy beamline at the APS synchrotron light source facility and the ALCF HPC facility, located $\sim$1 km from APS at Argonne National Laboratory. To permit detailed and repeated evaluations, we did not perform actual ptychographic experiments in these studies but instead ran a program on the 2-ID data acquisition computer that replayed images at an appropriate rate. The data acquisition machine has a $\sim$30 Gbps connection to the detector and a 1 Gb Ethernet connection to outside.

We used four datasets to evaluate our system: a real-world catalyst particle dataset, and three phantom datasets: two coins and a Siemens star, respectively. The datasets have different dimensions and thus different computational requirements. Specifically, the catalyst particle dataset is a 3D ptychography dataset of 168 views/angles, each with $\sim$1.8K diffraction patterns with dimensions 128 $\times$ 128, for a total size of $168 \times 1800 \times 128 \times 128 \times 4B = 20$ GB. The coin and Siemens star datasets are 2D ptychography datasets with 8K, 16K, and 32K diffraction patterns, respectively, all of size (256, 256), for total dataset sizes of 2 GB, 4 GB, and 8 GB, respectively.

The datasets are reconstructed on the ThetaGPU cluster at ALCF, which consists of 24 DGX A100 nodes, each with eight NVIDIA A100 accelerators connected with NVSwitch. Each A100 GPU has 40 GB memory. The host machine has two AMD Rome CPUs and 1 TB DDR4 memory. The ThetaGPU nodes are connected to Grand, a 200 PB high-performance parallel file system. Since allocation of compute nodes from shared resources (using job scheduler) can introduce significant overhead, we reserved the compute nodes in advance. Our reconstruction jobs still use the job scheduler, however the queue wait time is minimized due to reserved nodes.

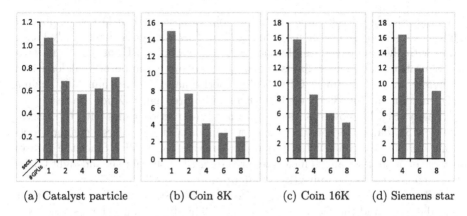

(a) Catalyst particle   (b) Coin 8K   (c) Coin 16K   (d) Siemens star

Fig. 4. Reconstruction times for different ptychography datasets on an eight-GPU DGX A100 node on the ThetaGPU cluster. The x-axis shows the number of GPUs used for reconstruction, and the y-axis shows the per iteration execution time in seconds. We reconstructed only a single view/angle from each dataset. The dimensions of datasets are (1.8K, 128, 128), (8K, 256, 256), (16K, 256, 256), and (32K, 256, 256) for catalyst particle, coin 8K, coin 16K, and Siemens star, respectively. Catalyst particle is a real experimental dataset collected at APS, whereas the others are synthetically generated.

The reconstructions are performed by using the Tike library [2], which provides parallel ptychographic reconstruction capabilities in multi-GPU settings [63,64]. We used a conjugate gradient solver and reconstructed both object and probe. The object is partitioned in grid cells and the neighboring cells are synchronized at the end of each iteration.

4.1 Optimum GPU Configuration

We first conduct experiments to determine the optimum GPU configuration for the reconstruction computation. We perform a 50-iteration reconstruction for each of our four datasets on each of $\{1, 2, 4, 6, 8\}$ GPUs. We present the *per iteration* reconstruction time with respect to corresponding GPU configuration in Fig. 4.

Reconstruction of catalyst particle, as shown in Fig. 4a, can (sub-optimally) scale up to four GPUs, then the inter-GPU communication becomes the bottleneck and starts introducing overhead. The speedups for the two and four-GPU configurations relative to the one-GPU configuration are only 1.56 and 1.88, respectively. The catalyst particle is a small dataset, where each view is ~113 MB, therefore its computational demand is minimal (~1 s per iteration). This results in sub-optimal scaling efficiency and favors single-GPU reconstruction.

Figure 4b shows scaling results for the synthetic coin dataset (with 8K diffraction pattern). We observe good scaling efficiency on up to four GPUs, achieving speedups of 1.96 and 3.6 on two and four GPUs, respectively. On more GPUs, we see diminishing returns due to communication and observe lower scaling efficiencies, ranging from 72–82%.

Figure 4c shows the same synthetic coin dataset with a larger number of diffraction patterns. The memory footprint of this dataset is significantly larger than with the previous datasets and cannot fit on one GPU; hence the missing configuration. The larger dataset translates to more computational load and therefore we see improved GPU scaling performance: more than 90% scaling efficiency for the four-GPU configuration and more than 80% for the rest.

Lastly, Fig. 4d shows the per iteration reconstruction times with the largest dataset. Similar to the previous dataset, this dataset has a large memory footprint and can be reconstructed only with more than four GPUs. Since the dataset is large enough, its scaling efficiencies are larger than 90% for six and eight GPUs when compared to the four-GPU configuration.

When we perform a cross-comparison between 8K and 16K versions of the coin datasets, and the Siemens star dataset (32K diffraction patterns), we see a good weak scaling performance for the reconstruction tasks. Specifically, comparing the two-GPU configuration of 8K and four-GPU configuration of 16K coin datasets, and the eight-GPU configuration of 32K Siemens dataset, shows >90.5% weak scaling efficiency.

4.2   End-to-End Workflow Evaluation

In these experiments, we evaluate the end-to-end execution of ptychography workflows using our system. We configure the number of GPUs according to our single-node performance results in Sect. 4.1.

Our initial experimental setup focuses on ptychographic reconstruction workflow for single (2D) view datasets on single-GPU. Our workflow consists of several (potentially overlapping) steps. Specifically, our workflow consists of the following stages: (i) a user-defined Globus Flows script is deployed to the Flows service; (ii) the Flows service initiates a Globus transfer from the beamline data acquisition machine to the ThetaGPU parallel file system; (iii) once the transfer is complete, the Flows service executes the next state, triggering a user-defined ptychographic reconstruction funcX function via the funcX service. At this point, if the funcX endpoint has insufficient compute resources, it interacts with the resource management system, i.e., the job scheduler, to allocate additional resources. Last, when the funcX function is finalized, (iv) the Flows service initiates another data transfer to return reconstructed images to the beamline data acquisition machine at APS.

Figure 5a shows the execution of this workflow. The `compute` column shows the reconstruction time, and `incoming` and `outgoing` columns represent the transfers between data acquisition machine and ThetaGPU. Finally, `others` shows the additional overheads, including initial resource allocation (job submission and queue wait time) and cloud service calls (interacting with Globus Flows, Transfer, and funcX services). Recall that we reserve the compute nodes in advance in order to minimize the overhead due to the queue wait time, however our system still requests compute resources from scheduler and this introduces a delay. The name of the configurations shows the dataset name and the number of GPUs used for reconstruction, e.g., Siemens-8GPU refers to the workflow of

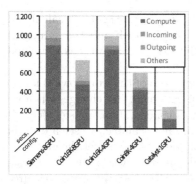

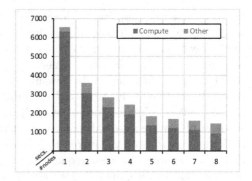

(a) Single node workflows   (b) Multi-node catalyst particle workflow

Fig. 5. End-to-end performance of ptychographic reconstruction workflows. (a) shows the performance (y-axis, in seconds) for different datasets (x-axis) on a single DGX A100 node (up to eight GPUs.) The performance information is broken down according to the stages of workflows. (b) shows the execution times for the 3D catalyst particle dataset. This workflow consists of 168 independent sub-workflows that can be executed concurrently. The x-axis shows the number of nodes (up to eight nodes or 64 GPUs) and the y-axis shows the total execution time (in seconds) for reconstructing all sub-workflows.

the Siemens star dataset where eight GPUs are used for reconstruction. We set the total number of iterations to 100 for these experiments.

Our first observation is the consistent reconstruction times among datasets. Specifically, we see more than 85% weak scaling performance among Siemens, Coin8K and Coin16K datasets, which follow our results in the previous section. Our second observation is the overhead due to **other** operations in the workflows. Since the system interacts with many external (cloud) services and the job scheduler, there is a significant noise during the execution. The effect of this overhead drops as the dataset sizes increase. We observe 10–30% overhead from **others** for Siemens, Coin16K and Coin8K datasets, and close to 50% overhead for Catalyst (which is the computationally least demanding dataset.) Lastly, we see the highest data transfer time for the Siemens star since it is the largest dataset. The data transfer times take 2.9–6.7% of the end-to-end execution times.

In Fig. 5b, we present the multi-node workflow performance results for the catalyst particle dataset. This dataset consists of 168 views, which translates to 168 independent workflows that can be executed concurrently. We use up to eight ThetaGPU nodes (or 64 total GPUs). Each view is reconstructed using a single GPU.

The concurrency between sub-workflows enables overlapping aforementioned workflow steps and therefore partially hides the overhead of the steps. Since each view is being reconstructed using one GPU, the maximum depth of the concurrency is 64 (from eight GPU nodes.) Although this concurrency provides better performance, it also complicates the breakdown of execution times. Therefore, we only show the `compute` and `other` in our figure. The `compute` is calculated according to the beginning of the first reconstruction task and the ending of the last, whereas the `other` column includes data transfer as well as the cloud service and resource allocation times.

The scaling efficiency of the `computing` component of the workflows is larger than 81% relative to the one-node configuration. However, this changes when we consider `other` column. Since most of the operations, e.g., data transfer, (cloud) service calls and resource allocation, in `other` are not scalable, we see a drop in performance gain with the increasing number of nodes. Also, we set the granularity of the resource allocation request to one node, in other words, funcX requests only one node after exhausting all the available GPUs. This improves resource utilization while decreasing idle time, however it also introduces additional queue and resource initialization time during the execution. Overall, the `other` column contributes 3–37% to the end-to-end execution time of the workflows, where we observe the worst case in eight-node configuration (mostly because of the shortest `compute` time.) The eight-node configuration still results in the shortest execution time with $3.9\times$ speedup over one-node configuration. If we try to execute the same workflow using a local beamline workstation that has a single A100 Nvidia GPU, the total execution time would exceed 14 h. Therefore, for large experimental datasets, e.g., hundreds of TBs, end-to-end execution times using local workstation can take weeks to finish. When we compare one-GPU configuration and eight-node configuration (64 GPUs), the speedup of using eight-node would be close to $29.8\times$ (or under 30 min).

5   Related Work

Ptychography has become one of the popular imaging techniques over the last decade [26,32,49]. Several advanced reconstruction algorithms and parallelization techniques have been developed in order to address the computational requirements of ptychography workflows [28,40,41,43,63]. However, when coupled with complementary 3D imaging techniques, such as tomography or laminography, ptychography experiments can generate massive amounts of experimental data. Many efficient and scalable 3D reconstruction techniques have been developed [14,31,59], but these techniques require high-performance computing resources that can only be accessed remotely, such as leadership computing facilities or large-scale user facilities.

Data analysis workflows at synchrotron light sources have been an active research area [11,15,37,46,48]. CAMERA, an interdisciplinary project led by Lawrence Berkeley National Laboratory, investigates data analysis problems and workflows relevant to light sources [25,45,54]. Similarly, Brookhaven National Laboratory initiated several programs that focus on NSLS-II facility and its workflows [4,22]. Jesse et al. from Oak Ridge National Laboratory uses a big data analysis framework to perform systematic analysis of ptychography [35]. These activities aim to provide efficient workflows and algorithms for analysis of imaging data at DOE facilities. Scientific workflows have also been extensively studied in other areas by DOE, universities and other institutions [13,42,44, 50,53,61]. Deelman et al. developed Pegasus workflow management system for transparent execution of scientific workflows, where workflows defined as directed acyclic graphs [23]. In this work, we implemented a workflow system that utilizes Globus services to enable execution of ptychographic reconstruction tasks on federated facilities and resources. Our system takes advantage of the Globus authentication infrastructure to manage identities [52] and eases remote task execution and resource management [5,20].

Many machine learning (ML) techniques have been successfully used and integrated to light source and electron microscopy data analysis workflows to enhance and improve the quality of images and reconstructions [9,36,56], including image denoising [39,62], artifact reduction[65] and feature extraction [51]. These techniques can also be used for accelerating the performance of workflows and data acquisition [38]. We plan to incorporate some of these advanced ML techniques in our workflow in the future.

6 Conclusion

We presented a system that unifies different facilities and resources to perform ptychographic data analysis. Our system establishes automated data analysis pipelines between (edge) instruments at synchrotron light sources and compute and storage resources in leadership computing facilities. Our system builds on several cloud-hosted services: funcX, a federated FaaS platform for remote execution of user-defined functions and resource management; Globus Flows, a workflow definition and execution service, for automation and definition of data analysis pipeline; and Globus, for efficient high performance and secure wide-area data transfers. We use high-performance ptychographic reconstruction software to maximize compute resource utilization.

We evaluated our system at APS and ALCF. Specifically, we simulated ptychographic data acquisition from a ptychography beamline at APS and reconstructed this data using the ThetaGPU cluster at ALCF. We observed significantly higher speedups and scalability efficiencies for large ptychography datasets compared to smaller ones. Since, our system utilizes Globus authentication service to integrate facilities, resources and services, data analysis pipelines can execute with little interference.

Acknowledgments. This material is based upon work supported by the U.S. Department of Energy, Office of Science, Basic Energy Sciences and Advanced Scientific Computing Research, under Contract DE-AC02-06CH11357. This research used resources of the Argonne Leadership Computing Facility and Advanced Photon Source, which are U.S. Department of Energy (DOE) Office of Science User Facilities operated for the DOE Office of Science by Argonne National Laboratory under the same contract. Authors acknowledge ASCR funded Braid project at Argonne National Laboratory for the workflow system research and development activities. Authors also acknowledge Junjing Deng, Yudong Yao, Yi Jiang, Jeffrey Klug, Nick Sirica, and Jeff Nguyen from

Argonne National Laboratory for providing the experimental data. This work is partially supported by the Office of the Director of National Intelligence (ODNI), Intelligence Advanced Research Projects Activity (IARPA), via contract D2019-1903270004. The views and conclusions contained herein are those of the authors and should not be interpreted as necessarily representing the official policies or endorsements, either expressed or implied, of the ODNI, IARPA, or the U.S. Government.

References

1. APS Upgrade. https://www.aps.anl.gov/APS-Upgrade. Accessed May 2021
2. Tike toolbox. https://tike.readthedocs.io/en/latest/
3. Advanced Photon Source, Argonne National Laboratory: Research and Engineering Highlights, APS Science (2020). https://www.aps.anl.gov/Science/APS-Science. Accessed May 2021
4. Allan, D., Caswell, T., Campbell, S., Rakitin, M.: Bluesky's ahead: a multi-facility collaboration for an a la carte software project for data acquisition and management. Synchrotron Radiat. News **32**(3), 19–22 (2019)
5. Ananthakrishnan, R., et al.: Globus platform services for data publication. In: Proceedings of the Practice and Experience on Advanced Research Computing, pp. 1–7 (2018)
6. APS: Early science at the upgraded Advanced Photon Source. Technical report, Advanced Photon Source, Argonne National Laboratory (2015). https://www.aps.anl.gov/APS-Facility-Documents
7. Argonne National Laboratory: Braid: Data Flow Automation for Scalable and FAIR Science. https://github.com/ANL-Braid/Flows. Accessed Jun 2021
8. Argonne National Laboratory: Advanced Photon Source, An Office of Science National User Facility. https://www.aps.anl.gov. Accessed May 2021
9. Aslan, S., Liu, Z., Nikitin, V., Bicer, T., Leyffer, S., Gursoy, D.: Distributed optimization with tunable learned priors for robust ptycho-tomography. arXiv preprint arXiv:2009.09498 (2020)
10. Aslan, S., Nikitin, V., Ching, D.J., Bicer, T., Leyffer, S., Gürsoy, D.: Joint ptycho-tomography reconstruction through alternating direction method of multipliers. Opt. Express **27**(6), 9128–9143 (2019)
11. Basham, M., et al.: Data Analysis WorkbeNch (DAWN). J. Synchrotron Radiat. **22**(3), 853–858 (2015). https://doi.org/10.1107/S1600577515002283
12. Batey, D.J., et al.: X-ray ptychography with a laboratory source. Phys. Rev. Lett. **126**(19), 193902 (2021)
13. Ben-Nun, T., Gamblin, T., Hollman, D.S., Krishnan, H., Newburn, C.J.: Workflows are the new applications: challenges in performance, portability, and productivity. In: 2020 IEEE/ACM International Workshop on Performance, Portability and Productivity in HPC (P3HPC), pp. 57–69. IEEE Computer Society, Los Alamitos (2020). https://doi.org/10.1109/P3HPC51967.2020.00011
14. Bicer, T., Gursoy, D., Kettimuthu, R., De Carlo, F., Agrawal, G., Foster, I.T.: Rapid tomographic image reconstruction via large-scale parallelization. In: Träff, J.L., Hunold, S., Versaci, F. (eds.) Euro-Par 2015. LNCS, vol. 9233, pp. 289–302. Springer, Heidelberg (2015). https://doi.org/10.1007/978-3-662-48096-0_23
15. Bicer, T., et al.: Real-time data analysis and autonomous steering of synchrotron light source experiments. In: IEEE 13th International Conference on e-Science (e-Science), pp. 59–68. IEEE (2017)

16. Bicer, T., Gürsoy, D., Kettimuthu, R., De Carlo, F., Foster, I.T.: Optimization of tomographic reconstruction workflows on geographically distributed resources. J. Synchrotron Radiat. **23**(4), 997–1005 (2016)
17. Chang, H., Enfedaque, P., Marchesini, S.: Blind ptychographic phase retrieval via convergent alternating direction method of multipliers. SIAM J. Imag. Sci. **12**(1), 153–185 (2019)
18. Chantzialexiou, G., Luckow, A., Jha, S.: Pilot-streaming: a stream processing framework for high-performance computing. In: 2018 IEEE 14th International Conference on e-Science (e-Science), pp. 177–188. IEEE (2018)
19. Chard, K., Tuecke, S., Foster, I.: Globus: recent enhancements and future plans. In: XSEDE16 Conference on Diversity, Big Data, and Science at Scale, pp. 1–8 (2016)
20. Chard, R., et al.: FuncX: a federated function serving fabric for science. In: 29th International Symposium on High-Performance Parallel and Distributed Computing, pp. 65–76 (2020)
21. Chen, Z., et al.: Electron ptychography achieves atomic-resolution limits set by lattice vibrations. Science **372**(6544), 826–831 (2021). https://doi.org/10.1126/science.abg2533
22. Computational Science Initiative, Brookhaven National Laboratory. https://www.bnl.gov/compsci/c3d/programs/NSLS.php. Accessed Jun 2021
23. Deelman, E., et al.: Pegasus, a workflow management system for science automation. Future Gener. Comput. Syst. **46**, 17–35 (2015). https://doi.org/10.1016/j.future.2014.10.008
24. Deng, J., et al.: Simultaneous cryo X-ray ptychographic and fluorescence microscopy of green algae. Proc. Natl. Acad. Sci. **112**(8), 2314–2319 (2015)
25. Donatelli, J., et al.: Camera: the center for advanced mathematics for energy research applications. Synchrotron Radiat. News **28**(2), 4–9 (2015)
26. Dong, Z., et al.: High-performance multi-mode ptychography reconstruction on distributed GPUs. In: 2018 New York Scientific Data Summit (NYSDS), pp. 1–5 (2018). https://doi.org/10.1109/NYSDS.2018.8538964
27. Enders, B., et al.: Cross-facility science with the superfacility project at LBNL, pp. 1–7 (2020). https://doi.org/10.1109/XLOOP51963.2020.00006
28. Enfedaque, P., Chang, H., Enders, B., Shapiro, D., Marchesini, S.: High performance partial coherent X-ray ptychography. In: Rodrigues, J.M.F., et al. (eds.) ICCS 2019. LNCS, vol. 11536, pp. 46–59. Springer, Cham (2019). https://doi.org/10.1007/978-3-030-22734-0_4
29. Hammer, M., Yoshii, K., Miceli, A.: Strategies for on-chip digital data compression for X-ray pixel detectors. J. Instrum. **16**(01), P01025 (2021)
30. Hidayetoğlu, M., et al.: MemXCT: memory-centric X-ray CT reconstruction with massive parallelization. In: International Conference for High Performance Computing, Networking, Storage and Analysis, pp. 1–56 (2019)
31. Hidayetoglu, M., et al.: Petascale XCT: 3D image reconstruction with hierarchical communications on multi-GPU nodes. In: SC20: International Conference for High Performance Computing, Networking, Storage and Analysis, pp. 510–522. IEEE Computer Society (2020)
32. Holler, M., et al.: X-ray ptychographic computed tomography at 16 nm isotropic 3D resolution. Sci. Rep. **4**(1), 1–5 (2014)
33. Huang, P., Du, M., Hammer, M., Miceli, A., Jacobsen, C.: Fast digital lossy compression for X-ray ptychographic data. J. Synchrotron Radiat. **28**(1), 292–300 (2021)

34. Intelligence Advanced Research Projects Activity: Rapid Analysis of Various Emerging Nanoelectronics. https://www.iarpa.gov/index.php/research-programs/raven. Accessed May 2021
35. Jesse, S., et al.: Big data analytics for scanning transmission electron microscopy ptychography. Sci. Rep. **6**(1), 1–8 (2016)
36. Kalinin, S.V., et al.: Big, deep, and smart data in scanning probe microscopy (2016)
37. Klein, M., Martinasso, M., Leong, S.H., Alam, S.R.: Interactive supercomputing for experimental data-driven workflows. In: Juckeland, G., Chandrasekaran, S. (eds.) HUST/SE-HER/WIHPC - 2019. CCIS, vol. 1190, pp. 164–178. Springer, Cham (2020). https://doi.org/10.1007/978-3-030-44728-1_10
38. Liu, Z., Bicer, T., Kettimuthu, R., Foster, I.: Deep learning accelerated light source experiments. In: 2019 IEEE/ACM Third Workshop on Deep Learning on Supercomputers (DLS), pp. 20–28. IEEE (2019)
39. Liu, Z., Bicer, T., Kettimuthu, R., Gursoy, D., De Carlo, F., Foster, I.: TomoGAN: low-dose synchrotron X-ray tomography with generative adversarial networks: discussion. JOSA A **37**(3), 422–434 (2020)
40. Marchesini, S., et al.: SHARP: a distributed GPU-based ptychographic solver. J. Appl. Crystallogr. **49**(4), 1245–1252 (2016)
41. Nashed, Y.S.G., Vine, D.J., Peterka, T., Deng, J., Ross, R., Jacobsen, C.: Parallel ptychographic reconstruction. Opt. Express **22**(26), 32082–32097 (2014)
42. Naughton, T., et al.: Software framework for federated science instruments. In: Nichols, J., Verastegui, B., Maccabe, A.B., Hernandez, O., Parete-Koon, S., Ahearn, T. (eds.) SMC 2020. CCIS, vol. 1315, pp. 189–203. Springer, Cham (2020). https://doi.org/10.1007/978-3-030-63393-6_13
43. Nikitin, V., et al.: Photon-limited ptychography of 3D objects via Bayesian reconstruction. OSA Continuum **2**(10), 2948–2968 (2019)
44. Ossyra, J.R., Sedova, A., Baker, M.B., Smith, J.C.: Highly interactive, steered scientific workflows on HPC systems: optimizing design solutions. In: Weiland, M., Juckeland, G., Alam, S., Jagode, H. (eds.) ISC High Performance 2019. LNCS, vol. 11887, pp. 514–527. Springer, Cham (2019). https://doi.org/10.1007/978-3-030-34356-9_39
45. Pandolfi, R.J., et al.: *Xi-cam*: a versatile interface for data visualization and analysis. J. Synchrotron Radiat. **25**(4), 1261–1270 (2018). https://doi.org/10.1107/S1600577518005787
46. Peterka, T., Goodell, D., Ross, R., Shen, H.W., Thakur, R.: A configurable algorithm for parallel image-compositing applications. In: Proceedings of the Conference on High Performance Computing Networking, Storage and Analysis, pp. 1–10. IEEE (2009)
47. Pfeiffer, F.: X-ray ptychography. Nat. Photonics **12**(1), 9–17 (2018)
48. Salim, M., Uram, T., Childers, J.T., Vishwanath, V., Papka, M.: Balsam: near real-time experimental data analysis on supercomputers. In: 2019 IEEE/ACM 1st Annual Workshop on Large-scale Experiment-in-the-Loop Computing (XLOOP), pp. 26–31 (2019). https://doi.org/10.1109/XLOOP49562.2019.00010
49. Shapiro, D.A., et al.: Ptychographic imaging of nano-materials at the advanced light source with the nanosurveyor instrument. In: Journal of Physics: Conference Series, vol. 849, p. 012028. IOP Publishing (2017)
50. da Silva, R.F., et al.: Workflows community summit: bringing the scientific workflows community together. In: Workflows Community Summit: Bringing the Scientific Workflows Community Together (WorkflowsRI). Zenodo (2021)

51. Somnath, S., et al.: Feature extraction via similarity search: application to atom finding and denoising in electron and scanning probe microscopy imaging. Adv. Struct. Chem. Imag. **4**(1), 1–10 (2018). https://doi.org/10.1186/s40679-018-0052-y

52. Tuecke, S., et al.: Globus Auth: a research identity and access management platform. In: 12th International Conference on e-Science, pp. 203–212. IEEE (2016)

53. Turilli, M., Balasubramanian, V., Merzky, A., Paraskevakos, I., Jha, S.: Middleware building blocks for workflow systems. Comput. Sci. Eng. **21**(4), 62–75 (2019)

54. Ushizima, D.M., et al.: Ideal: images across domains, experiments, algorithms and learning. JOM **68**(11), 2963–2972 (2016)

55. Venkatakrishnan, S.V., et al.: Robust X-ray phase ptycho-tomography. IEEE Signal Process. Lett. **23**(7), 944–948 (2016)

56. Venkatakrishnan, S., Mohan, K.A., Ziabari, A.K., Bouman, C.A.: Algorithm-driven advances for scientific CT instruments: from model-based to deep learning-based approaches. arXiv preprint arXiv:2104.08228 (2021)

57. Vine, D.J., et al.: Simultaneous X-ray fluorescence and ptychographic microscopy of Cyclotella meneghiniana. Opt. Express **20**(16), 18287–18296 (2012)

58. Wang, C., et al.: Deploying the Big Data Science Center at the Shanghai Synchrotron Radiation Facility: the first superfacility platform in China. Mach. Learn.: Sci. Technol. **2**(3), 035003 (2021)

59. Wang, X., et al.: Consensus equilibrium framework for super-resolution and extreme-scale CT reconstruction. In: Proceedings of the International Conference for High Performance Computing, Networking, Storage and Analysis, SC 2019. Association for Computing Machinery, New York (2019). https://doi.org/10.1145/3295500.3356142

60. Wilke, R., et al.: Hard X-ray imaging of bacterial cells: nano-diffraction and ptychographic reconstruction. Opt. Express **20**(17), 19232–19254 (2012)

61. Wolstencroft, K., et al.: The Taverna workflow suite: designing and executing workflows of web services on the desktop, web or in the cloud. Nucl. Acids Res. **41**, W557–W561 (2013). p. gkt328

62. Wu, Z., Bicer, T., Liu, Z., De Andrade, V., Zhu, Y., Foster, I.T.: Deep learning-based low-dose tomography reconstruction with hybrid-dose measurements. arXiv preprint arXiv:2009.13589 (2020)

63. Yu, X., Bicer, T., Kettimuthu, R., Foster, I.: Topology-aware optimizations for multi-GPU ptychographic image reconstruction. In: International Conference on Supercomputing, ICS 2021, pp. 354–366. ACM (2021)

64. Yu, X., Nikitin, V., Ching, D.J., Aslan, S., Gursoy, D., Bicer, T.: Scalable and accurate multi-GPU based image reconstruction of large-scale ptychography data (2021)

65. Ziabari, A., et al.: Beam hardening artifact reduction in X-ray CT reconstruction of 3D printed metal parts leveraging deep learning and cad models. In: ASME International Mechanical Engineering Congress and Exposition, vol. 84492, p. V02BT02A043. American Society of Mechanical Engineers (2020)

Machine-Learning Accelerated Studies of Materials with High Performance and Edge Computing

Ying Wai Li[1]([✉]), Peter W. Doak[2], Giovanni Balduzzi[3], Wael Elwasif[2], Ed F. D'Azevedo[2], and Thomas A. Maier[2]

[1] Los Alamos National Laboratory, Los Alamos, NM 87544, USA
yingwaili@lanl.gov
[2] Oak Ridge National Laboratory, Oak Ridge, TN 37931, USA
[3] ETH Zurich, 8093 Zurich, Switzerland

Abstract. In the studies of materials, experimental measurements often serve as the reference to verify physics theory and modeling; while theory and modeling provide a fundamental understanding of the physics and principles behind. However, the interactions and cross validation between them have long been a challenge even to-date. Not only that inferring a physics model from experimental data is itself a difficult inverse problem, another major challenge is the orders-of-magnitude longer wall-clock time required to carry out high-fidelity computer modeling to match the timescale of experiments. We envisage that by combining high performance computing, data science, and edge computing technology, the current predicament can be alleviated, and a new paradigm of data-driven physics research will open up. For example, we can accelerate computer simulations by first performing the large-scale modeling on high performance computers and train a machine-learned surrogate model. This computationally inexpensive surrogate model can then be transferred to the computing units residing closely to the experimental facilities to perform high-fidelity simulations at a much higher throughout. The model will also be more amenable to analyzing and validating experimental observations in comparable time scales at a much lower computational cost. Further integration of these accelerated computer simulations with an outer machine learning loop can also inform and direct future experiments, while making the inverse problem of physics model inference more tractable. We will demonstrate a proof-of-concept by using a quantum Monte Carlo application, Dynamical Cluster Approximation (DCA++), to machine-learn a surrogate model and accelerate the study of quantum correlated materials.

Keywords: Correlated materials · Quantum Monte Carlo · Machine learning · Edge computing

This manuscript has been authored in part by UT-Battelle, LLC, under contract DE-AC05-00OR22725 with the US Department of Energy (DOE). The publisher acknowledges the US government license to provide public access under the DOE Public Access Plan (http://www.energy.gov/downloads/doe-public-access-plan).

J. Nichols et al. (Eds.): SMC 2021, CCIS 1512, pp. 190–205, 2022.
https://doi.org/10.1007/978-3-030-96498-6_11

1   The Scientific Question: Correlated Quantum Materials

The study of correlated quantum materials and their emergent behavior remains at the forefront of condensed matter science. These materials exhibit a plethora of fascinating phenomena, including magnetism, superconductivity, quantum criticality, and topologically protected states, many of which promise to revolutionize energy-related applications. But the optimization of these properties requires a detailed understanding of the underlying microscopic mechanisms leading to their observed behavior. Without this knowledge, the deliberate design of new materials is impossible, revolutionary new advances only occur serendipitously, and developments in materials science remain mostly incremental.

Many powerful experimental and theoretical tools are routinely used to gain insight into the behavior of these materials. Neutron scattering, angular resolved photoemission and scanning tunneling spectroscopy provide a detailed characterization of a material's phenomenology in addition to other more basic experimental probes. For theory, the proper treatment of the strong electron correlations in these materials presents one of the most challenging problems in condensed matter physics. The strong correlations cannot be treated in a mainstream mean-field or single-particle description, but rather require sophisticated quantum many-body approaches that accurately treat the interactions between many electrons. Over the last few decades, many powerful and complementary numerical techniques have been developed that properly address this complexity, including sophisticated techniques such as the density matrix renormalization group [32,36], determinant quantum Monte Carlo [3,4] as well as quantum cluster theories [10,11,13,17].

Experimental and theoretical studies of these systems have historically been carried out relatively isolated. For example, inelastic neutron scattering is performed on a material to determine the dynamic magnetic structure factor $S(Q,\omega)$ in order to identify interesting regions in reciprocal (Q) and frequency (ω) space where the material shows a large response and to provide detailed information on the material's magnetic excitations. Subsequently, calculations of $S(Q,\omega)$ are carried out in a simple model that contains the electronic degrees of freedom deemed relevant, and the results are compared, usually at a qualitative level, through visual inspection of the corresponding plots of the experimental and theoretical data. *This process could be much more efficient if theory and experiment were more tightly integrated.* For example, experiments would follow the lead of simulations, which may be used to predict the interesting regions in reciprocal and frequency space, thereby greatly conserving beam time. In turn, the simulation results are validated by real data at an early stage, allowing necessary corrections and improvements to the models, thus enhancing the effectiveness of computing cycles. Clearly, a tight link between simulations and experiments would greatly accelerate the discovery process and is crucial for a capability that can deliberately guide the discovery and design of new materials.

Edge computing, i.e. low-latency computing that is done near the source of the data, offers a powerful strategy to enable a tight integration between experiments and simulations. In such a setup, simulations could be done on-the-fly, simultaneously with the experiments, allowing for an immediate feedback loop. However, performing the computations directly on the edge computing device is severely hampered by the fact that high-fidelity simulations of correlated quantum materials are computationally highly demanding. For example, state-of-the-art dynamic cluster approximation (DCA) [17] quantum Monte Carlo (QMC) simulations of a simple Hubbard model, a generic model of a correlated electron system, using ORNL's highly optimized DCA++ code [2,8,9], run on thousands of nodes on ORNL's Summit supercomputer for several hours. This model, however, is far too basic to quantitatively describe a material's specific features for all but very few compounds, and the computational requirements increase rapidly with the complexity of the models and the fidelity of the simulations. Clearly, these type of simulations are prohibitively expensive for any type of edge computing setup, and without significant acceleration, cannot be deployed in a rapid feedback setting.

Here we discuss a vision that enables the future deployment of high-fidelity simulations of correlated quantum materials on edge computing devices, thereby allowing to establish a tight integration and feedback loop between experiments conducted on these systems and simulations. The general idea is based on the observation that these type of simulations can be significantly accelerated by first performing large scale modeling on high-performance supercomputers and using the data generated in those simulations to train a machine-learned (ML) surrogate model. The computationally inexpensive surrogate model may then be deployed on the edge computing device as an efficient simulation tool that enables rapid interpretation and guidance on the time-scales of the experiment. Here we demonstrate a proof-of-concept for such a framework, using the DCA++ application as an example.

The rest of the paper is organized as follows: Sect. 2 introduces the theoretical background of the DCA quantum Monte Carlo method and its computational complexity; Sect. 3 describes the current practice of our machine-learning accelerated simulations and how it can be connected to experimental studies; Sect. 4 outlines the challenges we are facing when building and executing such a workflow connecting HPC and experimental facilities through edge technologies. We provide our insights in Sect. 5 on further developments that will streamline our current scientific workflow to enable an interactive feedback mechanism between theoretical and experimental material studies.

2   The Dynamic Cluster Approximation Quantum Monte Carlo Method, DCA

For the purpose of this discussion, we will illustrate the DCA/QMC method for the two-dimensional single-band Hubbard model, a standard model of strongly correlated electron systems. Its Hamiltonian

$$H = \sum_{ij,\sigma} t_{ij} c_{i\sigma}^{\dagger} c_{j\sigma} + U \sum_{i} n_{i\uparrow} n_{i\downarrow}. \tag{1}$$

is divided into a non-interacting part H_0 given by the first term and an interacting part H_{int} given by the second term. Here $c_{i\sigma}^{(\dagger)}$ destroys (creates) an electron on site i with spin σ and $n_{i\sigma} = c_{i\sigma}^{\dagger} c_{i\sigma}$ is the corresponding number operator. The first (H_0) term describes the hopping of electrons between sites i and j with amplitude t_{ij}, and the second (H_{int}) term raises the energy by the Coulomb repulsion U when two electrons with opposite spin reside on the same site. If not otherwise noted, we consider the sites in this model to form a two-dimensional (2D) square lattice with a hopping $t_{ij} = -t$ if i and j are nearest-neighbor sites. Despite its simplicity, this model is commonly believed to provide a description of the generic physics of the cuprate high-temperature superconductors, in which photoemission experiments find a single electronic band crossing the Fermi energy.

The single-particle dynamics of electrons with spin σ, momentum $\mathbf{k}$ and energy ω in the Hubbard model at finite temperatures is described by the thermodynamic Green's function $G_\sigma(\mathbf{k}, \omega)$. It may be written in terms of a Dyson equation, $G_\sigma^{-1}(\mathbf{k}, \omega) = G_{0,\sigma}^{-1}(\mathbf{k}, \omega) - \Sigma_\sigma(\mathbf{k}, \omega)$, where $G_{0,\sigma}$ is the Green's function of the non-interacting model, i.e. Eq. (1) with $U = 0$, and Σ_σ is the self-energy, which describes energy renormalization and lifetime effects due to the interaction U.

Calculating the Green's function and self-energy for large enough lattices to obtain a meaningful approximation for the thermodynamic limit (infinite system size) is prohibitively expensive, as the problem size grows exponentially with the number of degrees of freedom (number of lattice sites in the model (1)). The DCA [17] is a quantum cluster method that has been used successfully to study superconductivity in Hubbard models [15–25]. It reduces this complexity considerably by dividing the full problem into two parts: A small cluster of N_c lattice sites for which the many-body problem is solved exactly, and the remaining sites in the lattice that are coupled with the cluster sites at a mean-field level. This partitioning creates a self-consistency condition, which determines the mean-field from the solution of the cluster problem. This partitioning is enabled by making the assumption that the self-energy is only weakly momentum dependent, $\Sigma_\sigma(\mathbf{k}, \omega) \approx \Sigma_\sigma(\mathbf{K}, \omega)$ and well represented by a coarse-grid of cluster $\mathbf{K}$-points that are centered on N_c patches, which divide the domain of $\mathbf{k}$, the first Brillouin zone. Then, one can set up an effective cluster problem to calculate the self-energy $\Sigma_\sigma(\mathbf{K}, \omega)$ by first coarse-graining (averaging) the Green's function over the patches, $\bar{G}(\mathbf{K}, \omega) = \frac{1}{V_\mathbf{K}} \int_{\mathcal{P}_\mathbf{K}} d\mathbf{k}\, G(\mathbf{k}, \omega)$. Here $V_\mathbf{K}$ is the size of the patch denoted by $\mathcal{P}_\mathbf{K}$. Given the coarse-grained Green's function $\bar{G}(\mathbf{K}, \omega)$, one can then set up a quantum Monte Carlo algorithm to determine the Green's function of the effective cluster problem and its corresponding self-energy $\Sigma_\sigma(\mathbf{K}, \omega)$.

The continuous-time auxiliary field (CT-AUX) QMC algorithm [5–7] that is used in the DCA++ code starts with an auxiliary field decomposition of the interaction term in Eq. (1)

$$1 - \frac{\beta U}{K} \sum_i \left[n_{i\uparrow} n_{i\downarrow} - \frac{1}{2}(n_{i\uparrow} + n_{i\downarrow}) \right] = \frac{1}{2N_c} \sum_{i, s_i = \pm 1} e^{\gamma s_i (n_{i\uparrow} - n_{i\downarrow})}, \qquad (2)$$

with $\beta = 1/T$ the inverse temperature, $\cosh(\gamma) = 1 + \frac{U\beta N_c}{2K}$ and K a positive constant. With this, the problem of dealing with the original interaction term is replaced by an additional sum over auxiliary "spins" s_i. The CT-AUX algorithm then performs a perturbative expansion of the partition function $\mathcal{Z}$ in the interaction term and use Monte Carlo to sample the terms in this expansion. Specifically, $\mathcal{Z}$ is expressed as an expansion in terms of N-matrices that are related to the Green's function through $G_\sigma = N_\sigma G_{0,\sigma}$

$$\mathcal{Z} \propto \sum_{k=0}^{\infty} \sum_{s_1 \ldots s_k = \pm 1} \int_0^\beta d\tau_1 \ldots \int_{\tau_{k-1}}^\beta d\tau_k \left(\frac{K}{2\beta N_c}\right)^k \prod_\sigma |N_\sigma^{-1}(\{x, \tau, s\}_k)|. \quad (3)$$

Here, τ is an imaginary time that runs from 0 to β, $\{x, \tau, s\}_k$ is a configuration of k vertices with cluster site x, imaginary time τ and auxiliary spin s, and N_σ is a $k \times k$ matrix that represents the weight (probability) of that configuration. The Monte Carlo algorithm then samples the partition function $\mathcal{Z}$ by randomly creating and removing auxiliary spins s at random times τ and locations x according to their weights and updating the N_σ matrices using fast update formulas. Along this Markov chain, measurements of the Green's function G and other observables are periodically performed. This algorithm scales as $\mathcal{O}[(N_c U \beta)^3]$ in the number of sites N_c, the strength of the Coulomb interaction U and the inverse temperature β. Details of its implementation in the DCA++ code can be found in [2, 6, 8, 9, 33, 34].

3   ML-Accelerated Simulations and Feedback Loop Between Simulations and Experiments

3.1   Current Practices

To realize a tight integration and feedback loop between experiments and simulations, the key is to be able to carry out the DCA simulations on edge computing devices close to where the experimental data are collected, such as the Spallation Neutron Source (SNS) facility at ORNL. This requires that the simulation workload to be light-weight and fast, so that the simulation time is comparable to the experimental time scale. Our current strategy is to train a computationally inexpensive ML surrogate model to replace the computationally intensive QMC solver in DCA simulations. Training and deploying such a model involves a number of stages:

1. Generation of simulation/training data on Summit.
   The DCA++ code is run on thousands of nodes on the Summit supercomputer to perform the QMC simulations to generate the training data, which contain the reference for a mapping from the input parameters (which includes the diagram expansion order k, the imaginary time τ, the Ising auxiliary spin s and the electron spin σ) to an output log weight that determines the

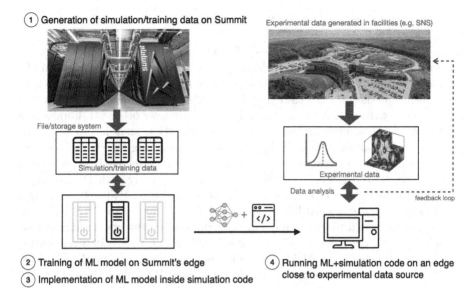

Fig. 1. An illustration of the current practices of a machine-learning-accelerated simulation developed and deployed on edge computers, connecting to HPC and experimental data sources, respectively. See text for details for the different numbered stages in the HPC and ML workflow. Photos and graphics merits: [27, 28, 31, 35].

acceptance probability. The data are written out as a Hierarchical Data Format (HDF5) file to the General Parallel File System (GPFS) scratch space at the end of the simulation. While the ML training task will be carried out by importing the data from the scratch space, the data would later be transferred to elsewhere such as the High Performance Storage System (HPSS) for long term storage.

2. Training of ML model on Summit's edge.

   The ML training task is performed on the "edge computer" platforms at OLCF. At the time of this writing, these resources are the data analysis cluster Andes and the newly launched Jupyter notebook service through the JupyterHub server, which is hosted by a small cluster providing both CPU and GPU flavors for different data analysis needs. These hardware are traditional computing clusters in their own right and are not typical edge devices. But in practice they have been serving the same purpose as an "edge" for data pre- and post-processing around Summit. Also, these clusters share the same NFS and GPFS file systems as Summit, so there is no need for data transfer and data analysis is done directly at the same place as where the data reside.

   The ML codes are developed using the Python programming language for its relatively mature ML libraries and ecosystems. Jupyter notebooks also provide an interactive programming and visualization environment, which makes it easier and more intuitive for the training and optimization ML models, and tuning of hyperparameters.

3. Implementation of ML model inside DCA++ production code.

Once a surrogate ML model is developed and trained, it needs to be implemented inside the DCA++ simulation code so that the ML model can be used to output predictions and the expensive QMC solver can be bypassed. Because DCA++ is written in C++, we chose PyTorch [30] over other ML libraries for the ML implementation based on the consideration that it provides relatively easier and more flexible Application Programming Interfaces (APIs) to incorporate with existing C++ production codes. In principle it is possible to interface the Python code developed in Stage 2 directly with DCA++ using the "just-in-time" compilation mechanisms provided by PyTorch, or using a static-compiler extension language as an interface layer like Cython. But in order to maintain programming language uniformity and ensure high performance in the production code, we opted for a pure C++ ML implementation using the PyTorch C++ API that largely resembles the Python API, instead of mixing C++ and Python programming languages. We linked DCA++ against the PyTorch C++ distribution and the LibTorch library by adding it to the package requirements in DCA++'s CMake build configuration.

4. Running ML accelerated simulation code on another edge close to experimental data source.

With the QMC solver substituted in DCA++, the ML-accelerated code can then be built and run on the edge devices close to the experimental facilities. These edge devices can be, for example, the NVIDIA's DGX servers at CNMS in our particular use case. This enables rapid theoretical calculations using much reduced computational resources. As experimental beamtime is usually allocated within a certain time frame, being able to run simulations in parallel with experiments is crucial for forming a feedback loop between them. Theoretical calculations are extremely useful for understanding and analyzing experimental observations, but traditionally they have usually been performed separately from the experiments at a different time for reasons already discussed. By bringing the simulation time down to a time-scale comparable to the experiments time frame, it is possible to provide real-time interpretation, and even guidance on future experiments with the combination of ML techniques.

3.2   Proof of Principles

We develop and implement a neural network (NN) that takes an input configuration, which includes the diagram expansion order k, the imaginary time τ, the Ising auxiliary spin s, and the electron spin σ. The NN outputs the log weight, which is a number, as a prediction. We also examine modifications to the neural network architecture that allow for variable input nodes, which accommodate different expansion orders k that exist in different input auxiliary spin configurations (work in progress)[1].

The NN predicted log weight is then used to calculate the acceptance probability in a MC step. As many of these MC steps will be discarded to obtain uncorrelated samples, it is computationally efficient to have a fast prediction of the log weights that scales roughly as $\mathcal{O}(N)$ for these intermediate MC steps in a Markov chain. At intervals where the algorithm determines whether to take a sample into statistics, the true acceptance weights would be calculated from QMC (computational complexity of $\mathcal{O}(N^3)$) to ensure accuracy in the acceptance. This procedure is similar to the one adopted in the earlier self-learning Monte Carlo methods [14,26].

Using a 2D single-band Hubbard model we collected training data as described above using the DCA++ code for system sizes 2×2, 4×4, 6×6 clusters on Summit at $\beta = 2$. This results in an expansion factor of $k \sim 32$ for 2×2, $k \sim 100$ for 4×4, $k \sim 256$ for 6×6. These data were then used to train the neural network surrogate model. We compare the performance of the CT-AUX algorithm and the trained ML model on a single core of a Power9-based workstation for the same Hubbard model system, and profiled the execution time of the ML forward prediction versus the equivalent code in the CT-AUX algorithm it will replace. Approximately 20000 measurements are taken in each case and the average execution times are compared. For the 2×2 system the ratio of execution time between CT-AUX and the ML method is $1 : 8$, for the 4×4 system the ratio is $1 : 1$, for the 6×6 system the ratio is $5 : 1$.

Note that these preliminary measurements were performed only for very small systems. For larger system sizes, the NN prediction cost only increases slightly with a bigger neural network model, where the input node count scales linearly as the expansion order k. However, the cost of the CT-AUX QMC solver will grow much more rapidly as it is cubic in the number of sites N_c, the strength of the Coulomb interaction U and the inverse temperature β, i.e., $\mathcal{O}[(N_c U \beta)^3]$. Therefore, we take our preliminary measurements as an indication that for larger systems that result in larger expansion factors, the ML model can significantly reduce the amount of computation needed instead of using DCA to simulate the systems directly.

4   Challenges in Current Workflow

While working towards building the ML/AI workflow connecting high performance and edge computing as described in Sec. 3.1, we came across a number of challenges and identified some limitations with the tools available at present. These limitations have either prevented the different stages of the workflow from interacting with each other, or have made building the workflow difficult. Here

---

[1] The development of machine-learning and neural-network surrogate models to speed up QMC simulations is an active research area in condensed matter physics. The method and model described here is an ongoing research effort and will be published elsewhere upon completion.

we share some observations on the limiting factors, and our visions of how to resolve these problems will be presented in Sec. 5.

4.1   An Observation: Two Data Sources and Two Edges

Very often in a discussion about developing edge technology to guide experiments with the aid of AI/ML, the edge computing aspect would be focused on the one sitting close to the experimental instruments (Step 4 in Fig. 1). This view is in line with some typical commercial applications of edge technology, for example, the voice and speech recognition services provided by smart phones, laptops, or personal assistant devices. However, in a scientific application like the one we are demonstrating in Sec. 3.1, this is only half of the story. Our scientific workflow involves *two* different data sources, hence two edge computing platforms: one edge resides close to the HPC, another edge resides close to the experimental instruments.

Why the difference? It depends on where the AI/ML surrogate models are trained before putting into an edge device, as well as the source of the data. In a commercial application such as the voice recognition example, the ML model development step is carried out and managed by the edge device provider, the resulting ML model is deployed in the cloud or shipped with the edge device, and everything is hidden from the user. The ML model does not change much once it is trained. Additionally, the data used to train the ML model are the same type of data as the one to be analyzed, such as real human voices and speeches. That also means that it is possible to acquire more data from the users to enrich the dataset for retraining and updating the ML model. In this case data are usually collected and sent back to the edge device provider intermittently.

On the contrary, in a scientific application such as ours, the ML model development is no longer opaque to users. ML models are developed by the scientists before their deployment on the experimental edge for analyzing or guiding experiments. Developing and training surrogate models is itself a scientific research activity that involves determining and investigating different neural network architectures, optimizing hyperparameters, etc. The training data come from a *different* data source than experiments – simulations on Summit or HPC. When a new material is being studied, new ML surrogate models models are devised and trained, with new simulations "customized" and performed to obtain very different set of training data. To minimize data transfer, these steps are brought close to Summit and are carried out on Summit's edge or Summit itself. Therefore, to achieve our scientific goal, we are actually bringing together two workflows involving two data sources (simulations and experiments) and two edge computing platforms serving HPC and experimental instruments respectively. As we shall see, this introduces challenges that are unique to scientific workflow of this sort.

4.2 Programming Languages Inconsistency for Different Tasks in the Workflow

Besides the ease of use and its powerful automatic differentiation, we chose PyTorch for our application also because it hits the sweet spot for two purposes: its native Python API enables efficient and interactive development and training of the ML model prototype with the use of Jupyter notebooks, while its relatively well-designed C++ counterpart and API allows for a uniform C++ implementation to integrate the ML models into the DCA++ source code without having to mix multiple programming languages.

Nevertheless, it still does not solve a fundamental problem that different programming languages must be used separately for different coding tasks, especially when incorporating ML workflow into traditional HPC applications. Traditional scientific applications are mostly written in Fortran and C++ for their high performance, and mature protocols such as MPI and OpenMP that support distributed and shared memory parallelization for scalability on HPC. Whereas ML applications are largely written in Python, sometimes Matlab or other languages, because of their ease to program, as well as the availability of a wide selection of well-developed and adopted ML libraries and functionalities – although Python and Matlab are not usually regarded as high performance programming languages and are seldom used to develop HPC applications. Bringing these two worlds together is difficult and requires compromises. In our application, even with the use of PyTorch for which the Python and C++ APIs greatly resemble each other, the ML surrogate model implementation in DCA++ was still a total code rewrite, particularly to ensure that the ML code is compliant with DCA++'s code design, classes, and data structures.

4.3 Lack of Standardized ML Model Specification Format

A related problem arises from the integration of ML models into scientific HPC applications is how to systematically transfer and incorporate the trained ML model from the Python prototype into the C++ production code, which should also allow for flexibility in specifying the ML model, code re-use and generality. This is probably easier to achieve by allowing Python and C++ codes to co-exist in the source code. Still, regardless of the programming language issue, the fundamental problem here is that the trained ML model has to be embedded in another application and is not used directly in the same code as where the ML model is trained. Therefore the ML model, in our case it is specified by the neural network architecture, weights, and hyperparameters, has to be saved into a file and then loaded into DCA++. Most ML libraries provide this capability and API so it is generally not a problem when the same ML library is used for model construction and in the scientific code. But different ML libraries use different formats to specify and save a ML model; how and what should a standardized procedure and data format look like to specify and transfer ML models across different ML libraries is still an open question. This is not an ideal situation from an science research point of view. Different researchers might want to develop the ML models with their choice of programming languages and ML libraries, or using different computer architectures to train and run the models; enabling reproducibility of scientific results should be one of the priorities. The lack of a standardized medium to specify and transfer ML models means that one can either re-implement and re-train the ML models from scratch using the information described in the literature, or they will have to use the existing ML code and model provided by the original developer without an option to change the ways to execute the project.

4.4   Heterogeneity in Hardware and Software Architectures on Different Edge Devices

During our workflow development, the largest challenge was the portability of the ML training code and ML-enabled DCA++ onto different computer hardware architectures. Part of the portability problem is similar to the "usual" performance portability we face with HPC applications, where the goal is to write a single code base that could run on various parallel and heterogeneous architectures. Indeed, modern ML libraries have pretty well-designed APIs and made it more accessible for users to run on different computer architectures. Making use of the GPU for acceleration only requires a few lines of code changes, instead of having to develop GPU-specialized kernels. This side of the portability problem, at least from a code developer's stance, has largely been alleviated in ML applications because the handling of various computer architectures is outsourced to the library developers.

Here, the major issue is that even with a single code base, it is still not trivial to port the application and run on different hardware architectures. The problem comes from that Python libraries and software support from different repositories, or channels, might or might not support certain hardware. For example, the software stacks on the HPC edge and Summit are centrally-managed by OLCF, the Python programming environment and ML libraries management tools are provided through Anaconda [1] and also a proprietary Open Cognitive Environment (OpenCE) module developed by IBM specially for Summit. However, the same programming environment and software stack are specific to the hardware and are not compatible with other machines. Additionally, the whole Python and ML ecosystem and library dependencies have always been complicated and fragile, which makes building codes and ensuring portability additionally difficult.

As an example, in proceeding to different steps in our workflow, we went through three computer hardware architectures as well as three different operating systems (OS) and software stacks: Summit's IBM Red Hat Enterprise Linux (RHEL), Andes's commodity-type linux, and DGX's proprietary Ubuntu-based OS. Every time we need to build the HPC and ML libraries from scratch and differently on different machines. As mentioned, our application uses the PyTorch C++ distribution for the ML implementation. On Summit, the LibTorch header files and libraries are provided by OpenCE, which are ensured to work with Summit's architecture. However on the edge systems, the Anaconda installed

PyTorch does not come with the C++ distribution. We had to download it from the source manually and put it somewhere available to our code. This procedure is error-prone and introduces compatibility issues. For example, we ran into software and compiler incompatibility problems between the Magma linear algebra library and the Libtorch ML library; the problem is still unsolved as of the time of this writing. This portability problem could arise not only across different edge devices, but also among code developers and users, when different versions of compilers and libraries might be used and preferred.

5   Opportunities and Needs for Development

As technologies continue to mature, we anticipate that some of the challenges discussed in Sec. 4 will be overcome. We highlight a few areas in different hardware and software aspects that are relevant to our application, in which advances will greatly facilitate and accelerate the development of a workflow that connects AI and HPC with edge computing.

5.1   A Unified Edge Capable of Serving both HPC and Experimental Data Sources

If it is possible to realize an edge device that can simultaneously connect to the HPC and experimental data sources, it will create a middle ground where the ML model can be developed, trained, and deployed at the same place, reducing the need for porting the ML-accelerated code between devices. This is less error-prone and reduce the repetitive work of building suitable programming environment on different edge devices for running the application. A major obstacle might be how to ensure the unified edge is still residing "somewhat close" to the data sources, and in turn will require new cyberinfrastructure technologies in networking, data transfer and storage, perhaps connection security between data sources.

5.2   Compatibility of HPC and ML Software Stack; Package Management Tools for *Both* HPC and ML Library Dependencies

For both HPC and ML applications, it remains that code developers and users are responsible for maintaining the library and package dependencies of the codes. Both the HPC world and the ML world have mature solutions for dealing with dependencies respectively. In HPC, build system like CMake provides a means for dealing with libraries, versions, and dependencies; HPC centers such as OLCF also provide users with pre-built libraries as modules to ensure compatibility with the computer architecture; it is also possible to use package managers such as Spack for building software. On the ML side, python package managers such as Anaconda or pip provide similar functionalities where package dependencies are automatically sorted out. Unfortunately, the interoperability and compatibility between HPC and ML package managers is often questionable. It would be desirable to have a package management tool that is able to handle both HPC libraries and ML libraries dependencies, i.e., having combined functionalities from Spack and Anaconda, and make it possible to specify software and library dependence and versions. A tool such as this will also alleviate the (in)compatibility problem, make porting applications between different computer hardware or edge architectures more standardized and less error-prone.

5.3   Workflow Tools and Policies on Edge Computers

Current workflow are mainly performed and shepherded manually, as data and ML models are moved from one computing resource to another at every stage. While this is unavoidable when the ML model is being researched and developed at the initial stage, the procedure can be automated at a later stage when the ML model/NN architecture is established and only needs to be refined by obtaining additional data. Also, at the experimental data analysis and guiding stage, the procedure should be fully automated to obtain a quick turnaround and feedback to the experimentalists. This will require a flexible job scheduling policy on the edge systems different from the current practices on leadership-class resources or commodity clusters, such that the application and workflow can be run on-demand and at the same time as when the experiment is performed. One possibility is to allocate a reserved time frame and node resources that align with the experimental beam time, for example.

Also, a workflow tool would need to be up and running continuously to monitor and orchestrate data collection and analysis. On HPC, workflows are related to job submissions and output monitoring, and are usually implemented with Python or shell scripts because of their abilities to interact with the OS and queuing system. In a workflow involving experimental components, we envisage that some degrees of interactions with the instruments might be needed. It is possible that Python might suffice in many cases in the development of workflow. For the experimental side or users who might not be familiar with programming, a tool similar to LabVIEW [12] that is more intuitive and can be controlled though Graphical User interface (GUI) for specifying a workflow or dataflow might be desirable. It will be informative to solicit such workflow needs from experimentalists as well besides the HPC application side.

5.4   Standardized ML Model Specification Format

A standardized format for specifying ML model would be equivalent to the role HDF5 is playing in the data format for HPC applications. As discussed, a standardized format would facilitate the transfer of ML models between scientific applications, as well as between different computing or edge devices. It enables the use of different ML libraries or framework, helps scientific information exchanges, encourages reproducibility of scientific results. Recently, technology companies started to realize the needs for greater interoperability of ML tools and established the Open Neural Network Exchange (ONNX) platform [29], which defines an open format based on computation graphs for representing ML especially neural network models. The platform also provides tools to convert different ML models between the format for a specific framework and the ONNX format. This is an important step toward interoperability of ML tools from the technology industry. We further advocate that standardized ML model formats as such should be better supported and integrated in different ML frameworks. Also, since scientific applications, workflows, and needs are often different from commercial ones, it will be beneficial for the scientific communities in different research areas to review and converge on a set of requirements for defining an open format for scientific ML applications.

6   Conclusions and Outlook

We outlined our first attempt to combining high-performance computers, edge computing, and machine learning in the study of quantum materials. In our application, the large-scale DCA quantum Monte Carlo simulations are performed on leadership-class computers such as Summit at OLCF. Simulation results are used as training data for machine-learning a computationally inexpensive, neural network surrogate model, which is trained on the edge devices around Summit. This surrogate model is implemented within the simulation code for acceleration, and is later transferred to another edge device that is close to the experimental data sources. With the much lower computational cost of the ML-accelerated simulations on the edge devices, such approach is the first step to enabling real-time data analysis for experimental data, as well as forming a feedback loop for guiding experiments.

In executing our proof of principles, we came across a number of challenges when using current technologies, most of which arose when we transfer the ML workloads across different computing platforms including edge devices. Heterogeneity in hardware architectures, in addition to inconsistencies and incompatibilities in HPC and ML programming languages, software stack and support, are the major road-blockers for our application. We discussed a number of development opportunities that we believe would provide a smoother and more standardized workflow for executing scientific ML applications across HPC and edge technologies. These practices will also be robust to hardware and software heterogeneity, while facilitating reproducibility and interoperability that are often required for scientific applications.

Acknowledgement. This work was supported by the Scientific Discovery through Advanced Computing (SciDAC) program funded by U.S. Department of Energy (DOE), Office of Science, Advanced Scientific Computing Research and Basic Energy Sciences, Division of Materials Sciences and Engineering. This research used resources of the Oak Ridge Leadership Computing Facility, which is a DOE Office of Science User Facility supported under Contract DE-AC05-00OR22725.

References

1. Anaconda Data Science Package Manager. https://www.anaconda.com/
2. Balduzzi, G., et al.: Accelerating DCA++ (dynamical cluster approximation) scientific application on the summit supercomputer. In: 2019 28th International Conference on Parallel Architectures and Compilation Techniques (PACT), pp. 433–444 (2019)
3. Blankenbecler, R., Scalapino, D.J., Sugar, R.L.: Monte-Carlo calculations of coupled Boson-Fermion systems. Phys. Rev. D **24**(8), 2278–2286 (1981)
4. dos Santos, R.R.: Introduction to quantum Monte Carlo simulations for fermionic systems. Braz. J. Phys. **33**(1), 36–54 (2003)
5. Gull, E., Millis, A.J., Lichtenstein, A.I., Rubtsov, A.N., Troyer, M., Werner, P.: Continuous-time Monte Carlo methods for quantum impurity models. Rev. Mod. Phys. **83**(2), 349–404 (2011)
6. Gull, E., et al.: Submatrix updates for the continuous-time auxiliary-field algorithm. Phys. Rev. B **83**(7), 75122 (2011)
7. Gull, E., Werner, P., Parcollet, O., Troyer, M.: Continuous-time auxiliary-field Monte Carlo for quantum impurity models. Europhys. Lett. **82**(5), 57003 (2008)
8. Hähner, U.R., et al.: DCA++: a software framework to solve correlated electron problems with modern quantum cluster methods. Comput. Phys. Commun. **246**, 106709 (2020)
9. Hähner, U.R., Balduzzi, G., Doak, P.W., Maier, T.A., Solcà, R., Schulthess, T.C.: DCA++ project: sustainable and scalable development of a high-performance research code. IOP Conf. Ser. J. Phys. Conf. Ser. **1290**(1), 12017 (2019)
10. Hettler, M.H., Tahvildar-Zadeh, A.N., Jarrell, M., Pruschke, T., Krishnamurthy, H.R.: Nonlocal dynamical correlations of strongly interacting electron systems. Phys. Rev. B **58**(12), R7475–R7479 (1998)
11. Kotliar, G., Savrasov, S., Pálsson, G., Biroli, G.: Cellular dynamical mean field approach to strongly correlated systems. Phys. Rev. Lett. **87**(18), 186401 (2001)
12. Laboratory Virtual Instrument Engineering Workbench (LabVIEW). https://www.ni.com/en-us/shop/labview.html
13. Lichtenstein, A., Katsnelson, M.: Antiferromagnetism and d-wave superconductivity in cuprates: a cluster dynamical mean-field theory. Phys. Rev. B **62**(14), R9283–R9286 (2000)
14. Liu, J., Shen, H., Qi, Y., Meng, Z.Y., Fu, L.: Self-learning Monte Carlo method and cumulative update in fermion systems. Phys. Rev. B **95**(24), 241104 (2017)
15. Mai, P., Balduzzi, G., Johnston, S., Maier, T.A.: Orbital structure of the effective pairing interaction in the high-temperature superconducting cuprates. NPJ Quantum Mater. **6**, 26 (2021)
16. Mai, P., Balduzzi, G., Johnston, S., Maier, T.A.: Pairing correlations in the cuprates: a numerical study of the three-band Hubbard model. Phys. Rev. B **103**, 144514 (2021)
17. Maier, T., Jarrell, M., Pruschke, T., Hettler, M.: Quantum cluster theories. Rev. Mod. Phys. **77**(3), 1027–1080 (2005)
18. Maier, T., Scalapino, D.: Pair structure and the pairing interaction in a bilayer Hubbard model for unconventional superconductivity. Phys. Rev. B **84**(18), 180513(R) (2011)
19. Maier, T.A., Jarrell, M., Schulthess, T.C., Kent, P.R.C., White, J.B.: Systematic study of d-wave superconductivity in the 2D repulsive Hubbard model. Phys. Rev. Lett. **95**(23), 237001 (2005)

20. Maier, T.A., Jarrell, M.S., Scalapino, D.J.: Structure of the pairing interaction in the two-dimensional Hubbard model. Phys. Rev. Lett. **96**(4), 047005 (2006)

21. Maier, T.A., Karakuzu, S., Scalapino, D.J.: Overdoped end of the cuprate phase diagram. Phys. Rev. Res. **2**(3), 33132 (2020)

22. Maier, T.A., Mishra, V., Balduzzi, G., Scalapino, D.J.: Effective pairing interaction in a system with an incipient band. Phys. Rev. B **99**(14), 140504 (2019)

23. Maier, T.A., Poilblanc, D., Scalapino, D.J.: Dynamics of the pairing interaction in the Hubbard and t-J models of high-temperature superconductors. Phys. Rev. Lett. **100**(23), 237001–237004 (2008)

24. Maier, T.A., Scalapino, D.J.: Pairfield fluctuations of a 2D Hubbard model. NPJ Quantum Mater. **4**(1), 30 (2019)

25. Maier, T.A., Staar, P., Mishra, V., Chatterjee, U., Campuzano, J.C., Scalapino, D.J.: Pairing in a dry Fermi sea. Nat. Commun. **7**, 11875 (2016)

26. Nagai, Y., Shen, H., Qi, Y., Liu, J., Fu, L.: Self-learning Monte Carlo method: continuous-time algorithm. Phys. Rev. B **96**(16), 161102 (2017)

27. Oak Ridge Leadership Computing Facility. Media Flickr page. https://www.flickr.com/photos/olcf/albums

28. Oak Ridge National Laboratory's Spallation Neutron Source Homepage. https://neutrons.ornl.gov/sns

29. Open Neural Network Exchange. https://onnx.ai/

30. PyTorch Machine Learning Framework. https://pytorch.org/

31. Samarakoon, A.M., et al.: Machine-learning-assisted insight into spin ice $Dy_2Ti_2O_7$. Nat. Commun. **11**(1), 1–9 (2020)

32. Schollwöck, U.: The density-matrix renormalization group. Rev. Mod. Phys. **77**(1), 259–315 (2005)

33. Staar, P., Maier, T.A., Schulthess, T.C.: Efficient non-equidistant FFT approach to the measurement of single- and two-particle quantities in continuous time Quantum Monte Carlo methods. J. Phys. Conf. Ser. **402**, 12015 (2012)

34. Staar, P., Maier, T.A., Summers, M.S., Fourestey, G., Solca, R., Schulthess, T.C.: Taking a quantum leap in time to solution for simulations of high-Tc superconductors (2013)

35. The Noun Project. Graphic designs created by IconMark, Econceptive, Rabbit Jes, and DinosoftLab, under the Creative Commons license. https://thenounproject.com/

36. White, S.R.: Density matrix formulation for quantum renormalization groups. Phys. Rev. Lett. **69**(19), 2863–2866 (1992)

Advanced Computing Systems and Software: Connecting Instruments from Edge to Supercomputers

A Hardware Co-design Workflow for Scientific Instruments at the Edge

Kazutomo Yoshii[1]([✉]), Rajesh Sankaran[1], Sebastian Strempfer[1],
Maksim Levental[2]([✉]), Mike Hammer[1], and Antonino Miceli[1]

[1] Argonne National Laboratory, Lemont, IL, USA
kazutomo@mcs.anl.gov, amiceli@anl.gov
[2] University of Chicago, Chicago, IL, USA

Abstract. As spatial and temporal resolutions of scientific instruments improve, the explosion in the volume of data produced is becoming a key challenge. It can be a critical bottleneck for integration between scientific instruments at the edge and high-performance computers/emerging accelerators. Placing data compression or reduction logic close to the data source is a possible approach to solve the bottleneck. However, the realization of such a solution requires the development of custom ASIC designs, which is still challenging in practice and tends to produce one-off implementations unusable beyond the initial intended scope. Therefore, as a feasibility study, we have been investigating a design workflow that allows us to explore algorithmically complex hardware designs and develop reusable hardware libraries for the needs of scientific instruments at the edge. Our vision is to cultivate our hardware development capability for streaming/dataflow hardware components that can be placed close to the data source to enable extreme data-intensive scientific experiments or environmental sensing. Furthermore, reducing data movement is essential to improving computing performance in general. Therefore, our co-design efforts on streaming hardware components can benefit computing applications other than scientific instruments. This vision paper discusses hardware specialization needs in scientific instruments and briefly reviews our progress leveraging the Chisel hardware description language and emerging open-source hardware ecosystems, including a few design examples.

Keywords: Scientific instruments · Edge computing ·
Streaming/dataflow computing · Compression · Chisel hardware
construction language · ASIC

1 Introduction

As CMOS scaling is coming to an end, specialization and heterogeneity are becoming crucial factors for sustaining performance growth, increasing energy efficiency, and improving resource utilization of computing hardware. Until

J. Nichols et al. (Eds.): SMC 2021, CCIS 1512, pp. 209–226, 2022.
https://doi.org/10.1007/978-3-030-96498-6_12

recently, the shrinking of CMOS transistors has masked the performance overheads associated with general-purpose architectures. Additionally, a perpetually evolving rich software ecosystem has accelerated software development on general-purpose architectures. Together, these trends have delayed the need for custom hardware solutions, which tend to be relatively expensive. However, with the end of the era of exponential performance growth and with the inefficiency associated with general-purpose architecture becoming increasingly made manifest [1], more specialized hardware, particularly AI accelerators, are emerging to fill the gap in computing environments [2].

Most AI success stories thus far have been associated with high-volume, mission-critical applications or high-profile projects in "hyperscale" companies such as Google, Microsoft, and Amazon. On the other hand, in the U.S. Department of Energy (DOE) scientific space, hardware customization needs are highly domain-specific (e.g., X-ray detectors) and thus relatively low volume (e.g., single unit to hundreds of units manufactured). Unfortunately, such low-volume use cases are not commercially lucrative for hardware vendors. Moreover, in many cases, such domain-specific hardware development tends to produce one-off implementations that are unusable beyond the initial intended scope. What is needed is to identify common hardware building blocks (e.g., compressor, encryption blocks) that can broadly cover our scientific edge-compute needs. We envision the co-design of hardware and software algorithms that can efficiently generate such modular and reusable components, and we develop a rich set of highly parameterized open-source hardware libraries. While our idea bears some resemblance to "intellectual property" (IP) cores provided by ASIC and FPGA vendors in terms of reusability, our goal is to develop hardware libraries of algorithmically complex blocks that, by virtue of their parameterization, are vendor and architecture agnostic. To this end, it is paramount to investigate (1) a hardware design environment that can capture practical high-level hardware design patterns (i.e., hardware algorithms) and can flexibly express them, (2) a lightweight, open (no commercial license) environment, including fast simulation and verification, for hardware libraries (to accelerate the design loop and maximize distributed development), and (3) a lightweight resource estimation tool. While the end-to-end chip development cycle is important eventually, we focus primarily on the development cycle of front-end ASIC designs including digital circuit implementation, functional verification, and simulation. At the feasibility study phase, the crucial first step is to investigate the implementability of hardware algorithms for our hardware specialization needs (e.g., on-chip streaming processing logics). Additionally, many ongoing research efforts are working to reduce the complexity of ASIC backend design cycles using AI techniques such as floor planning [3].

This manuscript is organized as follows. In Sect. 2 we first discuss our motivation for edge hardware specialization. We then discuss the current status, challenges, and opportunities for hardware specialization; and we describe the challenges and opportunities in hardware specialization for the edge in the realm of scientific instruments. In Sect. 3 we discuss hardware abstraction and programming languages. In Sect. 4 we illustrate our proposed workflow for our hardware library approach with our X-ray pixel detector's data compressor block as an example.

2   Background

In a wide range of scientific applications, a data acquisition system (possibly CPU or FPGA) collects values from sensor systems through a low-level communication protocol (e.g., I2C, SPI, parallel and serial buses) and transmits them to high-performance computing (HPC) systems over traditional high-speed networks. The sensor systems can range from simple individual sensors to more complex sensors paired with some intelligence extended by microprocessors, for example, FPGAs and ASICs.

While various phases of sensor data analysis can be lossy, it is crucial to transfer data from sensors to cloud or HPC systems without any reduction in data quality. This seemingly straightforward constraint is becoming a stiff challenge for many scientific instruments because of the explosion in the volume of data produced by scientific instruments as their spatial and temporal resolutions have continued to increase. For example, the highest frame rate of X-ray pixel detectors will soon approach a megahertz, necessitating an interconnect capable of transferring a terabit of raw data off the chip. Such an interconnect is cost-prohibitive. Other scientific disciplines, such as high-energy physics, cosmology, and environmental remote sensing, are also facing the same data bottleneck challenge. General-purpose processors at or near sensor nodes are no longer able to keep up with this increase in data rate since they are burdened with unnecessary inefficiency [1] due to the nature of load-store architectures, highly complicated memory subsystems, and lack of directional I/O connectivity. Note that novel accelerators, such as neuromorphic architectures, will not solve such problems for similar reasons. Adding larger on-chip memories that store captured data temporarily can be an intermediate solution; however, memory capacity is finite, which limits the time of experiments, and ultimately the solution is cost-ineffective. Thus, we need streaming (ideally stall-free) data-processing hardware designs that rely less so on temporary storage.

We believe a higher degree of hardware specialization (e.g., dataflow architecture) will be required to enable and support future scientific instrument needs. For example, for X-ray pixel detectors, the goal is to develop on-chip data compression algorithms that compress data and can be placed directly adjacent to the internal sensors in the detector ASIC [4]. Since our hardware development resources are currently limited, we focus on co-designing a simple, yet effective, lossless compressor that leverages application-specific characteristics and hardware specialization. This reduces the complexity of implementation. Moreover, to minimize the hardware development efforts (particularly hardware verification), we employ stateless dataflow architecture techniques wherever possible.

In addition to being ideal with respect to both throughput and energy efficiency, such architectures are a natural fit in the case of scientific instruments at the edge. This work has led to several interesting and critical research questions. These include the following: Which hardware architectures or platforms (FPGA, ASIC, structured ASIC, coarse-grained reconfigurable architecture, etc.) are suitable for our future needs? Which hardware programming languages or models improve our productivity and support our innovations? Which architectural techniques and design patterns are effective? How many components can be expressed as stateless dataflow designs? Considerable research and development are required to answer the questions.

We are also conducting a feasibility study on embedding AI classification components directly in the detector chip, which can be seen as a form of maximally efficient data compression. While a full-fledged AI capability is impractical to implement on-chip, specialized, lightweight AI capabilities are worth consideration as a possible replacement for conventional methods such as data reduction by feature detection. Implementation of AI algorithms as hardware algorithms is a novel area of research, enabled by this growth in access to EDA tools. Work in this area can be partitioned into two subareas, roughly along the dimension of generality. The first, and more general, involves the design and testing of domain-specific accelerators (e.g., GEMM accelerators such as Gemmini [5] and NVDLA [6]) as custom instruction set architectures (ISAs). Their value proposition to users is that prioritization, leading to outsized efficiency and increased performance (on AI workloads). This work in the research community is mirrored in industry, where recently there has been a renewed "Cambrian explosion" in architecture companies (such as Cerebras, Groq, Habana, and Samba Nova) that aim to support the same such AI workflows. The second subarea involves the design and testing of particular use-case-specific circuits, wherein a circuit is in one-to-one correspondence with, for example, a particular neural network. These implementations differ from those of the former in that they are not reconfigurable and represent, essentially, in silico instantiations of neural networks. The purported advantage of this approach is the hyper-refinement possible due to the specificity of the datapath and compute workload. Research in this area traditionally has employed HLS tools as "compiler" intermediaries between high-level implementations and the actual hardware design [7,8], which suffer from unpredictable resource usage. Recently exploratory work has been done using Chisel as the high-level implementation language *and* the low-level description language [9]. While this still is in its initial stages, we have begun to explore and develop such a solution for the purposes of Bragg peak detection [10].

Historically, hardware design ecosystems for ASICs have been dominated by a few companies, and the licensing fees for their commercial tools can often be a significant barrier to entry for many organizations. Additionally, the DOE scientific community is bifurcated: either projects have little experience in hardware design, or they may have internal hardware designers as part of their larger team who focus on single-purpose and project-/scope-optimized designs. As we are entering the post-Moore era, we believe hardware specialization is the only practicable approach to dealing with scaling problems, irrespective of the challenges awaiting us. We stress, however, that the number of hardware designers, developers, and architects is considerably low—orders of magnitude smaller than that of software developers. We believe that a lightweight and ergonomic development environment may help attract more developers and students and enable cross-training of current software developers as hardware practitioners.

3   Hardware Programming Ecosystem

Hardware description languages [11], such as Verilog and VHDL, are used to describe digital circuits. Both Verilog and VHDL were initially developed (in the early 1980s) for digital circuit simulation. These languages eventually incorporated synthesis functionality and are currently ubiquitous in both industry and academia. Although HDLs still play a primary role in digital circuit designs, as the complexity of hardware algorithms increases, the productivity of these traditional HDLs is becoming a matter of huge concern because of their lack of expressive language features, such as those found in modern general-purpose programming languages.

One of the biggest problems with HDLs is that their mechanisms for generating recursive (or tile) structures are weak. Thus, designers have to manually "unroll" modules with manual labeling and thereby reduce the codes' conciseness, maintainability, and reusability. Examples of this kind of rolling can be seen in any standard Verilog or VHDL implementation of a large barrel shifter (i.e., a 2D array of multiplexers), systolic array [12], network-on-chip architecture [13], or variable-size and fixed-size data converter [14], the latter being critical for data compression. To compensate for the weakness in recursive generating capability, designers tend to use a general-purpose programming language, such as Python, C++, or TCL, to build generators that themselves generate HDL codes. Unsurprisingly, these kinds of toolchains are quite rigid (i.e., single-purpose), often brittle, and not scalable. Furthermore, since HDL design predates modern software paradigms such as functional programming and test-driven development, as the complexity of software references or models increases, so do the challenges associated with developing "testbenches" that precisely exercise designs implemented as HDL codes. Thus we seek a hardware description language that enables a highly productive development process such that we can use it to describe a circuit concisely, express recursive structure, and describe testbenches more flexibly, among other features.

3.1   Chisel Hardware Construction Language

Inspired by the RISC-V agile development approach [15], we chose an emerging hardware "construction" language named Chisel [16–18] for implementing our hardware libraries, performing functional simulations, and designing extensions of our data compression block. Chisel, which stands for *Constructing Hardware in a Scala Embedded Language*, is designed to accelerate the digital circuit design process. As the name implies, Chisel is an embedded domain-specific language implemented as a class library in Scala [19]. Chisel offers a zero-cost abstraction of digital circuits, which means the overhead in performance and resource usage induced by the abstraction is nearly zero compared with that of a native HDL. Several studies have confirmed that Chisel significantly reduces the code size, improves code reusability, and incurs little performance penalty compared with native Verilog implementations (i.e., for most cases, Chisel-generated register-transfer level and equivalent native Verilog implementation run at the same frequency [13,20,21]). We note that these results are in stark contrast to HLS tools that let developers specify design behavior in higher-level languages and then infer lower-level implementations. Such synthesis tools incur the cost of higher performance overheads, particularly in resource usage.[1]

Leveraging the power of Scala's modern programming language features, Chisel offers higher expressivity, which dramatically improves the productivity and flexibility for constructing synthesizable digital circuits. It also integrates cycle-accurate simulators seamlessly, aiming for lightweight test-driven development, which significantly reduces the barrier to entry for hardware development. In essence, Chisel has brought modern software paradigms to hardware development, which should attract more software developers to hardware development, thereby growing the community and ecosystem. Indeed, since Chisel's original release in 2012 [16], the Chisel community has grown steadily, with the number of Chisel-based open-source projects increasing every year. Chisel is being used for many real-world tape-out designs [22–25] such as SiFive's RISC-V cores and Google's TPU [26]. Chisel has also become popular in academia for architecture research [27–30]. Additionally, it has a rich ecosystem. For example, Chipyard [31], a framework for developing systems-on-chip (SoCs), encompasses an in-order core generator called Rocket Chip [22], an out-of-order core generator named BOOM [32], hardware accelerators such as Gemmini [5], and a systolic array generator [5]. Additionally, ChiselDSP [33], a library for generating more traditional signal-processing designs such as fast Fourier transforms, is also available. Furthermore, ChiselVerify [34] is a verification tool that employs industry-standard Universal Verification Methodology to verify Chisel designs formally.

To compare and contrast Chisel and Verilog, we first consider a simple counter circuit written in Verilog and Chisel. Listing 1.1 is a Verilog implementation of a counter that increments every cycle, counting from 0 to 9. Listing 1.2 is the same circuit written in Chisel. This example highlights some fundamental feature differences between Chisel and Verilog. First, the Chisel version has no clock, reset signals, or **always** blocks; it automatically incorporates clock and reset signals when generating Verilog codes. **RegInit** creates a register that is initialized on reset with a specified value (in this example, 0 as an **nbits**-wide unsigned integer); and thus, implicitly, a reset signal is generated. Assigning to the register value **cntReg** is translated to a nonblocking assignment via an **always** block in Verilog. Since the default policy of the state element provided by Chisel is a positive-edge register that supports synchronous reset, no **always** blocks are needed. Such a default policy in the state element enforces a design guideline transparently and makes Chisel syntax more concise, at the cost of flexibility. Chisel provides frequently used data types such as **Int**, **UInt**, and **SInt**, instead of a range of bits as in Verilog, which also improves readability. This Chisel code snippet also includes an example of parameterization; the **Counter** class

---

[1] The performance offered by a carefully optimized HLS implementation is comparable to that of an HDL implementation; however, resource usage is still in question.

accepts the maximum value of the counter when instantiating and calculates the required bit length for the counter using `log2Ceil`.

```verilog
module Counter
  #(parameter MAXCNT=9) (
  input clock,
  input reset,
  input enable,
  output [$clog2(MAXCNT+1)-1:0] out
);
  reg [$clog2(MAXCNT)-1:0] cntReg;
  assign out = cntReg;
  always @(posedge clock) begin
    if (reset) begin
      cntReg <= 0;
    end else if (enable) begin
      if (cntReg == MAXCNT) begin
        cntReg <= 0;
      end else begin
        cntReg <= cntReg + 1;
      end
    end
  end
endmodule
```

Listing 1.1. A simple counter in Verilog. Note that $clog2 is supported by SystemVerilog or Verilog-2005

```scala
class Counter(val max:Int = 10) extends Module {
  val nbits = log2Ceil(max+1)
  val io = IO(new Bundle {
    val enable = Input(Bool())
    val out = Output(UInt(nbits.W))
  })
  val cntReg = RegInit(0.U(nbits.W))
  cntReg := Mux(io.enable,
   Mux(cntReg === max.U, 0.U, cntReg + 1.U), cntReg)
  io.out := cntReg
}
```

Listing 1.2. A simple counter in Chisel

An essential aspect of Chisel is that it encourages test-driven development and offers fully integrated testing harnesses. This allows users to write testbench codes in Scala, and running testbenches requires no additional hardware. Listing 1.3 is a simple testbench for the counter circuit (Listing 1.2). Since the language for testbenches is Scala, we can leverage its general-purpose programming features. Chisel's peek-poke-expect-step test harness is powerful and intuitive to use. For example, testbenches for our data compression components directly read and analyze massive X-ray datasets and feed selected regions to our compressor designs running in a circuit simulator to verify expected functionality. Such ergonomic testing enables effective software/hardware co-design. Chisel simulates the behavior of generated circuits using either an internal Scala-based simulator or Verilator [35], which translates Verilog codes into cycle-accurate models (specified as C++ codes) for faster simulation. In our experience, Chisel's integrated test accelerates iteration of the design loop (coding, compiling, evaluating), which greatly aids our design exploration, even when I/O layout and parameters frequently change during the exploration.

```
class CounterUnitTester(c: Counter) extends PeekPokeTester(c) {
  val max = c.max
  var ref = 0 // software reference count
  def test(e : Int) {
    poke(c.io.enable, e)
    for (i <- 0 until max+2) {
      // comparing hardware with software reference
      expect(c.io.out, ref)
      step(1) // forward a single cycle
      if (e==1) if(ref < max) ref += 1 else ref = 0
    }
  }
  test(1) // enable counting
  test(0) // disable counting
}
```

Listing 1.3. Testbench for counter

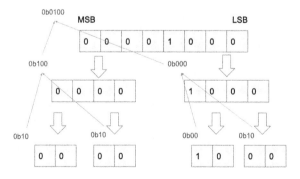

Fig. 1. Leading-zero counts divide-and-conquer algorithm.

A notably powerful feature of Chisel is its ability to construct recursive hardware in a traditional software-like manner, such as divide-and-conquer. As mentioned, many hardware algorithms are hierarchical and recursive. For example, leading zero counting can be implemented in a divide-and-conquer manner (Figure 1). If we recursively split a binary input stream into two-bit words, we can easily form the leading zero count with a look-up table (e.g., the leading zero count of 00 is 2). When two "conquered" blocks are merged, the leading zero counts of the merged block can be calculated from the leading zero counts of the conquered blocks, again with a simple bitwise XOR. One can implement the leading zero count in System Verilog using its "generated" primitive; however, conciseness and readability may be a concern. On the other hand, Chisel enables specifying such a divide-and-conquer algorithm directly and parameterizes the implementation. Listing 1.4 is a Chisel implementation example of leading zero counting.

```
class Clz(nb: Int = 64) extends Module {
  val lognb = log2Floor(nb)
  val io = IO(new Bundle {
    val in = Input(UInt(nb.W))
    val out = Output(UInt((lognb + 1).W))
  })
  if (nb == 1) io.out := !io.in
  else if (nb == 2) io.out := MuxLookup(io.in, 0.U, Array(0.U ->
      ↪ 2.U, 1.U -> 1.U))
  else {
    val largestPow2 = 1 << log2Ceil(nb) - 1
    val c0 = Module(new Clz(largestPow2))
    val c1 = Module(new Clz(nb - largestPow2))
    c0.io.in := io.in(nb - 1, nb - largestPow2)
    c1.io.in := io.in(nb - largestPow2 - 1, 0)

    io.out := Mux(c0.io.out(c0.lognb), largestPow2.U +& c1.io.out,
        ↪ c0.io.out)
  }
}
```

Listing 1.4. Recursive structure: counting leading zeros

3.2 Open-Source Hardware Development Ecosystems

The exploration of hardware programming ecosystems (e.g., programming models, tools) has been gaining significant attention in the field of computer architecture [36,37] recently. This trend has also been the catalyst for an open-source hardware ecosystem boom, including instruction sets such as RISC-V [38], hardware implementations [23,39], and hardware tools [16,35,40,41]. Indeed, Google recently announced an open-source foundry PDK for SkyWater's 130 nm node [42]. Furthermore, with the advent of innovative companies such as efabless[2], even a small R&D unit can now tape-out a chip with significantly lower cost, benefiting from a fully open-source and end-to-end ASIC design flow [43]. Additionally, we have been observing an interesting connection between software and hardware in terms of abstraction. Although no single abstraction can capture all features of a solution, multiple abstraction layers, with each layer bridging adjacent layers, are needed for developing a complex system efficiently. While abstraction is, in general, well studied in the software world, such has not been the case in the hardware world—but we observe that this now changing. Indeed, the hardware community is learning and incorporating ideas from software. Thus, we believe that now is the best and most exciting time to participate in and contribute to the open-source hardware ecosystem.

Productivity, which may include debugability, maintainability, and reusability, is of the utmost concern for the DOE scientific community. Therefore, investigation and development of efficient hardware abstractions and productive hardware languages are of utmost importance to the community [36]. Many research groups in DOE have explored high-level synthesis (HLS), which translates software codes into hardware description language (HDL) codes, such as OpenCL [44], in order to run high-performance computing kernels on FPGAs. This approach does attract software developers and has shown promising results on particular kernels or parameters. The downside of HLS is that optimization still requires hardware knowledge and offers no control over the generated HDL codes. Small changes in the HLS source code will often lead to large changes in the generated HDL codes, making debugging almost impossible. It also incurs tighter dependencies on the underlying platforms and tool versions, which negatively affect maintainability and reusability. HDL, particularly Verilog, is still the main workhorse for I/O designs and other low-level hardware designs. A possible practical compromise may be to develop a domain-specific hardware language for scientific instruments at the edge, stitching HDL, HCL, and HSL together and providing a higher-level domain-specific abstraction. While we primarily discuss Chisel in this paper, several other modern HDLs do exist and merit further investigation: MyHDL [45] and Migen [46] for Python, and CλasH [47] for Haskell. Even in the Scala language, there are other HDLs: SpinalHDL [48], which is essentially a "fork" of Chisel, and Spatial [49], whose chief improvement over Chisel is its incorporation of polyhedral compilation functionality.

4   Co-design Workflow for Hardware Libraries

In this section we first describe our current design workflow for developing hardware libraries. Next, we explain how we apply the workflow to our scientific instrument edge-computing using a data reduction stage for an X-ray pixel array detector ASIC chip. One of our requirements is that the workflow be easy to deploy to a typical development environment, such as a Linux server or laptop,

---

[2] An open community for analog and mixed-signal IC and IP development and commercialization https://efabless.com/.

without requiring special software licensing. Other than for philosophical reasons, the additional motivation for the easy-to-install and open-source workflow is to attract more hardware developers and students and to enable the training of software developers in hardware design. This is due to the fact that conventionally trained hardware developers remain scarce and there is no guarantee that this situation will improve in the near to medium term.

As we described, Chisel is fully open-source software that offers sufficient features for efficiently describing algorithmically complex hardware designs and provides a flexible testbench framework that is seamlessly integrated with a typical workflow. At this point, however, Chisel lacks lightweight resource estimation functionality (e.g., counting the number of logic gates, wires). Since both ASIC and FPGA are spatially constrained, the resource usage of a hardware design must be bounded by available resources. Unlike software platforms, hardware in general offers no dynamic memory allocation, time sharing or context switching, or virtualization of hardware logic. Thus, estimating resource usage for the target range of hardware parameters is crucial for hardware libraries and is one the most important steps of co-design.

Accurate estimation of hardware resource usage can be complicated, however, requiring domain expertise; moreover, depending on the platforms or technology, it may require prohibitively expensive commercial tools. For our purposes of estimating realistic resource usage for ASICs[3] we need only count the number of basic components such as wires, flip-flops, logic gates, and multiplexers efficiently. Several open-source digital circuit simulators or synthesis tools can give us such a resource estimate. We found that Yosys [40], an open-source synthesis tool for ASICs and FPGAs, provides a statistical report on resource usage for both ASIC and FPGA. Since Yosys is a full-featured register-transfer level (RTL) synthesis tool, it can also perform synthesis-level optimizations, such as removing redundant multiplexers, which can give us a more realistic resource usage estimation (since, in fact, all synthesis tools perform optimizations).

To illustrate our co-design workflow, we present a conceptual overview of our data compressor hardware designs for X-ray detectors, which will be placed in our X-ray detector chip that we are currently developing. To simplify and focus on the main points, we exclude the details of our hardware design that are specific to our X-ray array detector and its I/O characteristics. The pixel array generates data every cycle, where the total number of pixels generated per cycle depends on the hardware design parameters (e.g., 1,024 pixels or 8 columns × 128 rows of pixels). Data from an X-ray pixel array is generally sparse and contains few nonzero pixels. Our previous analysis of real datasets showed that a large percentage (e.g., 80% or greater) of X-ray pixel data have zeros (or even lower values) that occupy only the lower few bits. Hence, the purpose of our compressor block is to compress sparsely populated input data into a densely packed stream that includes a header and compressed data without stalling, in order to reduce the total amount of data that needs to be sent to the I/O block (Fig. 2). For our

---

[3] Currently, only a select few technology nodes can be targeted with open-source EDA tools.

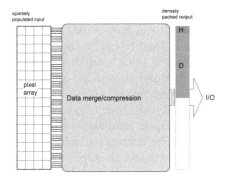

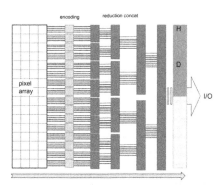

Fig. 2. Stream compressor concept (converts a sparsely populated input into densely packed, compressed data)

Fig. 3. Our design approach (concatenates variable-sized encoded outputs with hierarchical reduction stages).

detector chip, we must minimize the size of the internal buffer to temporarily store pixel data because of two factors: (1) the size of temporary memory limits the duration of experiments, and (2) memory is scarce on the detector ASIC chip. Additionally, since the cost of validation is large, dataflow designs with minimum state elements are preferable. For this reason, any compression approach based on an entropy algorithm such as Huffman coding [50] may be unsuitable for our on-chip compressor.

Figure 3 shows our data compression dataflow architecture consists of an encoding stage and reduction stages [51]. Since zero (or lower) values dominate the majority of the input data, we employ a bit-shuffling scheme in the encoding stage, which resembles a matrix transpose operation and increases the co-occurrence of zero pixels, to filter out unused higher bits. The bit-shuffling operation can be expressed simply as a set of wires between the input bits and the output bits in the correct order and requires no logic circuit in ASIC; hence it is inexpensive to implement and verify [4]. The output from the encoding stage is variable in size, and multiple encoding blocks generate variable-sized data simultaneously, so no I/O can handle such inputs directly. We employ a reduction stage to concatenate variable-sized data into a single continuous block in a hierarchical manner.

Figure 4 illustrates a baseline implementation, which uses multiple-input multiplexers to select input pixels. The input consists of two fixed data arrays, where the size is N and the length of the content is L_a and L_b, respectively. The size of the output array is $2N$, and the length of the concatenated content is L. This implementation approach requires $\left(N^2 + N\right)/2$ multiplexers. The baseline approach is straightforward to implement and can be implemented only with combinational logic for ASICs,[4] but the resource consumption could be prohibitive for

---

[4] FPGA deployments may require pipelining for the sake of achieving low latency.

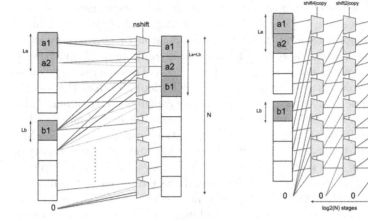

Fig. 4. Concat baseline implementation.   **Fig. 5.** Concat optimized implementation.

larger inputs. Figure 5 shows an optimized implementation that shifts the second input using a series of shifting stages, where each stage shifts only a specific power of 2. The required number of shifting stages is $\log(N)$, where N is the size of each input array. If the size of each input array is 4, for example, three shifting stages are needed (shifting 4 pixels, 2 pixels, and 1 pixel). The expected number of multiplexers in this implementation is $N \log(N)$. Both hardware algorithms can be easily implemented in Chisel and fully parameterized, including the testbenches, thanks to the power of modern language features such as functional programming.

The concision of the Chisel implementation improves the maintainability and helps other developers understand the fundamentals of the design, a crucial concern for hardware libraries. Table 1 includes the number of lines of code (LOC) for each algorithm in Chisel and the LOC of a generated Verilog code with a specific target size. Since the Chisel implementation is fully parameterized, including testbenches, the number of the LOC[5] is the same for any input size.

Table 1. Number of lines: Chisel and generated Verilog code

	Chisel	Verilog ($N=8$)	Verilog ($N=32$)	Verilog ($N=128$)
Baseline	54	432	3864	52152
Optimized	97	432	2250	11628

One important co-design criterion is resource usage. With a resource estimate, we can discuss the feasibility of an RTL code generated from a hardware

---

[5] Significant lines of code, i.e., excluding comments.

library generator or the number of copies we can fit on a target hardware platform. For the above example designs, the resource usage can be easily computed analytically, although in general this may not be possible or may require extra effort. As a demonstration, Figs. 6 and 7 include a comparison of analytically predicted resources and a statistical report from Yosys. They compare the number of ASIC multiplexers and the number of FPGA lookup tables (LUTs) for the two designs. The analytical method reasonably captures the trendline of the resource usage for both ASIC and FPGA. Depending on the algorithms or underlying architecture, however, the room for optimizations varies. For the baseline algorithm, the gap between the analytical prediction and the Yosys report is large. The reason is that synthesis tools, including Yosys, optimize multiplexer usage by removing unnecessary multiplexers and the redundancy of multiplexers in the baseline implementation artificially inflates multiplexer usage. FPGA-configurable logic blocks are also primitive building blocks and generally contain flip-flops, multiplexers, and LUTs with multibit inputs, which are much more complex than in the case of simple multiplexers (e.g., 1-bit, 2-input). In terms of estimation time, Yosys takes only up to a couple of seconds to report the resource usage for fairly large implementations. Since Yosys is a command-line tool, it is straightforward to integrate into our workflow.

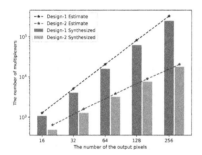

Fig. 6. ASIC multiplexer usage estimation with Yosys.

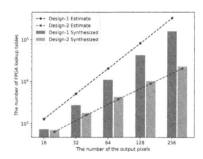

Fig. 7. FPGA lookup table usage estimation with Yosys.

5   Conclusion

Hardware specialization is poised to play a critical role in the post-Moore era, in improving both the performance and energy efficiency of computing in general. In scientific edge computing in particular, since the volume of data generated by sensors is expected to increase exponentially, placing computing power as close as possible to the data sources—where general-purpose processors or accelerators fail to meet our requirements— is becoming a crucial enabling factor for future scientific experiments. Custom hardware development needs tend to be confined to low-volume applications, with designs having low reusability. To address these issues, we employed the Chisel hardware construction language and other open-source design tools to create a co-design workflow for exploring hardware algorithms and developing reusable hardware libraries that can capture the design patterns of common hardware components. In particular, dataflow components can accelerate our specialized hardware development for future scientific edge-computing applications. We described our open-source-tools-based co-design workflow and delineated the development of our data compression block for our X-ray detector ASIC chip. Productive hardware ecosystems could shape future hardware innovation, and we believe that we are entering the golden age of hardware programming. We continue to investigate cutting-edge hardware ecosystems to improve the productivity of hardware algorithms and libraries development on data compression, encryption, and AI classification, for scientific instrument edge-computing.

Acknowledgments. We thank Ian Foster and Kyle Chard for supporting this exciting collaboration between Argonne National Laboratory and the University of Chicago Department of Computer Science. We thank Pete Beckman and Alec Sandy for encouraging this multidisciplinary collaboration between the X-ray Science Division (XSD) and the Mathematics and Computer Science (MCS) Division at Argonne National Laboratory. We also thank two anonymous referees for their useful comments. We thank Gail Pieper for editing this manuscript. The material is based upon work supported by Laboratory Directed Research and Development (LDRD 2021-0072) funding from Argonne National Laboratory, provided by the Director, Office of Science, of the U.S. Department of Energy under contract DE-AC02-06CH11357.

References

1. Hameed, R., et al.: Understanding sources of inefficiency in general-purpose chips. In: Proceedings of the 37th Annual International Symposium on Computer Architecture, pp. 37–47 (2010)
2. Ovtcharov, K., Ruwase, O., Kim, J.-Y., Fowers, J., Strauss, K., Chung, E.S.: Accelerating deep convolutional neural networks using specialized hardware. Microsoft Res. Whitepaper **2**(11), 1–4 (2015)
3. Kahng, A.B.: AI system outperforms humans in designing floorplans for microchips. Nature **594**(7862), 183–185 (2021)
4. Hammer, M., Yoshii, K., Miceli, A.: Strategies for on-chip digital data compression for X-ray pixel detectors. J. Instrum. **16**, P01025 (2021)
5. Genc, H., et al.: Gemmini: an agile systolic array generator enabling systematic evaluations of deep-learning architectures (2019)
6. Farshchi, F., Huang, Q., Yun, H.: Integrating NVIDIA Deep Learning Accelerator (NVDLA) with RISC-V SoC on FireSim. In: 2019 2nd Workshop on Energy Efficient Machine Learning and Cognitive Computing for Embedded Applications (EMC2), pp. 21–25 (2019)
7. Zhang, Y., Pan, J., Liu, X., Chen, H., Chen, D., Zhang, Z.: FracBNN: accurate and FPGA-efficient binary neural networks with fractional activations. In: The 2021 ACM/SIGDA International Symposium on Field-Programmable Gate Arrays (2021)

8. Duarte, J., et al.: Fast inference of deep neural networks in FPGAs for particle physics. J. Instrum. **13**(07), P07027 (2018)
9. Eldridge, S., Waterland, A., Seltzer, M., Appavoo, J., Joshi, A.: Towards general-purpose neural network computing. In: 2015 International Conference on Parallel Architecture and Compilation, PACT 2015, San Francisco, CA, USA, 18–21 October 2015, pp. 99–112 (2015)
10. Liu, Z., et al.: BraggNN: fast X-ray Bragg peak analysis using deep learning. arXiv preprint arXiv:2008.08198 (2021)
11. Golson, S., Clark, L.: Language wars in the 21st century: verilog versus vhdl-revisited. Synopsys Users Group (SNUG) (2016)
12. Kung, H.T., Leiserson, C.E.: Systolic arrays for (VLSI). Technical report, Department of Computer Science, Carnegie-Mellon University, Pittsburgh, Pennsylvania (1978)
13. Kwon, H., Krishna, T.: OpenSMART: single-cycle multi-hop NoC generator in BSV and Chisel. In: 2017 IEEE International Symposium on Performance Analysis of Systems and Software (ISPASS), pp. 195–204. IEEE (2017)
14. Ueno, T., Sano, K., Yamamoto, S.: Bandwidth compression of floating-point numerical data streams for FPGA-based high-performance computing. ACM Trans. Reconfigurable Technol. Syst. **10**, 1–22 (2017)
15. Lee, Y., et al.: An agile approach to building RISC-V microprocessors. IEEE Micro **36**(2), 8–20 (2016)
16. Bachrach, J., et al.: Chisel: constructing hardware in a Scala embedded language. In: DAC Design Automation Conference, pp. 1212–1221 (2012)
17. Bachrach, J.J., Asanović, K.: Chisel 3.0 tutorial. Technical report, EECS Department, UC Berkeley (2017)
18. Schoeberl, M.: Digital Design in Chisel. Kindle Direct Publishing, Seattle (2020)
19. Odersky, M., Spoon, L., Venners, B.: Programming in Scala. Artima Inc., Walnut Creek (2008)
20. Mosanu, S., Guo, X., El-Hadedy, M., Anghel, L., Stan, M.: Flexi-AES: a highly-parameterizable cipher for a wide range of design constraints. In: 2019 IEEE 27th Annual International Symposium on Field-Programmable Custom Computing Machines (FCCM), p. 338. IEEE (2019)
21. Arcas-Abella, O., et al.: An empirical evaluation of high-level synthesis languages and tools for database acceleration. In: 2014 24th International Conference on Field Programmable Logic and Applications (FPL), pp. 1–8. IEEE (2014)
22. Asanović, K., et al.: The rocket chip generator. Technical report, UCB/EECS-2016-17, EECS Department, University of California, Berkeley (2016)
23. Celio, C., Chiu, P.-F., Nikolic, B., Patterson, D.A., Asanovic, K.: BOOMv2: an open-source out-of-order RISC-V core. In: First Workshop on Computer Architecture Research with RISC-V (CARRV) (2017)
24. Bailey, S., et al.: A 28nm FDSOI 8192-point digital ASIC spectrometer from a Chisel generator. In: 2018 IEEE Custom Integrated Circuits Conference (CICC), pp. 1–4. IEEE (2018)
25. Cass, S.: Taking AI to the edge: Google's TPU now comes in a maker-friendly package. IEEE Spectr. **56**(5), 16–17 (2019)
26. Lockhart, D., et al.: Experiences building edge TPU with Chisel. In: 2018 Chisel Community Conference (2018)
27. Di Tucci, L., Conficconi, D., Comodi, A., Hofmeyr, S., Donofrio, D., Santambrogio, M.D.: A parallel, energy efficient hardware architecture for the merAligner on FPGA using Chisel HCL. In: 2018 IEEE International Parallel and Distributed Processing Symposium Workshops (IPDPSW), pp. 214–217. IEEE (2018)

28. Serre, F., Püschel, M.: A DSL-based FFT hardware generator in Scala. In: 2018 28th International Conference on Field Programmable Logic and Applications (FPL), pp. 315–3157. IEEE (2018)
29. Nowatzki, T., Gangadhar, V., Ardalani, N., Sankaralingam, K.: Stream-dataflow acceleration. In: 2017 ACM/IEEE 44th Annual International Symposium on Computer Architecture (ISCA), pp. 416–429. IEEE (2017)
30. Prabhakar, R., et al.: Plasticine: a reconfigurable architecture for parallel patterns. In: 2017 ACM/IEEE 44th Annual International Symposium on Computer Architecture (ISCA), pp. 389–402. IEEE (2017)
31. Amid, A., et al.: Chipyard: integrated design, simulation, and implementation framework for custom SoCs. IEEE Micro **40**(4), 10–21 (2020)
32. Asanovic, K., Patterson, D.A., Celio, C.: The berkeley out-of-order machine (BOOM): an industry-competitive, synthesizable, parameterized RISC-V processor. Technical report, University of California at Berkeley Berkeley United States (2015)
33. Wang, A.: Agile design of generator-based signal processing hardware. Ph.D. thesis, EECS Department, University of California, Berkeley (2019)
34. Dobis, A., et al.: Open-source verification with Chisel and Scala (2021)
35. Snyder, W.: Verilator: open simulation-growing up. DVClub Bristol (2013)
36. Truong, L., Hanrahan, P.: A golden age of hardware description languages: applying programming language techniques to improve design productivity. In: 3rd Summit on Advances in Programming Languages (SNAPL 2019), Schloss Dagstuhl-Leibniz-Zentrum fuer Informatik (2019)
37. Hennessy, J., Patterson, D.: A new golden age for computer architecture: domain-specific hardware/software co-design, enhanced. In: ACM/IEEE 45th Annual International Symposium on Computer Architecture (ISCA) (2018)
38. Asanović, K., Patterson, D.A.: Instruction sets should be free: the case for RISC-V. Technical report UCB/EECS-2014-146, EECS Department, University of California, Berkeley (2014)
39. Fatollahi-Fard, F., Donofrio, D., Michelogiannakis, G., Shalf, J.: OpenSoC fabric: on-chip network generator: using Chisel to generate a parameterizable on-chip interconnect fabric. In: Proceedings of the 2014 International Workshop on Network on Chip Architectures, pp. 45–50 (2014)
40. Wolf, C., Glaser, J., Kepler, J.: Yosys - a free Verilog synthesis suite. In: Proceedings of the 21st Austrian Workshop on Microelectronics (Austrochip) (2013)
41. Izraelevitz, A., et al.: Reusability is FIRRTL ground: hardware construction languages, compiler frameworks, and transformations. In: 2017 IEEE/ACM International Conference on Computer-Aided Design (ICCAD), pp. 209–216. IEEE (2017)
42. Ansell, T., Saligane, M.: The missing pieces of open design enablement: a recent history of Google efforts (invited paper). In: 2020 IEEE/ACM International Conference on Computer Aided Design (ICCAD), pp. 1–8. IEEE (2020)
43. Edwards, R.T., Shalan, M., Kassem, M.: Real silicon using open-source EDA. IEEE Des. Test **38**, 38–44 (2021)
44. Czajkowski, T.S., et al.: From OpenCL to high-performance hardware on FPGAs. In: 22nd International Conference on Field Programmable Logic and Applications (FPL), pp. 531–534. IEEE (2012)
45. Decaluwe, J.: MyHDL: a python-based hardware description language. Linux J. **127**, 84–87 (2004)
46. Migen, a python toolbox for building complex digital hardware. https://github.com/m-labs/migen

47. Baaij, C.: CλAash: from Haskell to hardware (2009)
48. Charles, P.: SpinalHDL (2016). https://github.com/SpinalHDL/SpinalHDL
49. Koeplinger, D., et al.: Spatial: a language and compiler for application accelerators. In: Proceedings of the 39th ACM SIGPLAN Conference on Programming Language Design and Implementation, pp. 296–311 (2018)
50. Hashemian, R.: Design and hardware construction of a high speed and memory efficient Huffman decoding. In: IEEE International Conference on Consumer Electronics, pp. 74–75. IEEE (1994)
51. Strempfer, S., Yoshii, K., Hammer, M., Bycul, D., Miceli, A.: Designing a streaming data coalescing architecture for scientific detector ASICs with variable data velocity. arXiv preprint arXiv:2008.08198 (2021)

NREL Stratus - Enabling Workflows to Fuse Data Streams, Modeling, Simulation, and Machine Learning

David Rager and Aaron Andersen[✉]

NREL, Golden, CO, USA
{David.Rager,Aaron.Andersen}@nrel.gov

Abstract. Integrating cloud services into advanced computing facilities provides significant new capabilities and offers several advantages over focusing solely on traditional high performance computing (HPC) workloads. The integration of cloud services is especially potent for workflows that fuse data streams, modeling and simulation ("modsim"), and machine learning. A key challenge to adopting a hybrid edge-cloud-HPC model is aligning optimal capability, data, and user intent on the right resources for each step in a workflow. The National Renewable Energy Laboratory (NREL) Stratus service provides a basis for this alignment. Stratus layers the capabilities needed to make cloud services accessible to a lab-based scientific community on commercial offerings, and currently supports upward of 200 projects, ranging from Internet of Things (IoT) integration to traditional modeling and simulation. This provides a real-world inventory of scientific workflow elements, which enables placing these elements appropriately between the edge, cloud, and traditional HPC. This paper outlines a vision via reference architecture and the application of that architecture in a typical workflow. We highlight multiple components, including sensor data intake, cleaning and transforming (edge/cloud suitable), generation of synthetic data through modsim, computationally heavy machine learning training and hyperparameter optimization (HPC suitable), and inference and deployment (cloud ideal). Every step in such a workflow involves a cost-benefit analysis of the data movement, computational efficiency, availability, latency, and resource capabilities. The reference architecture and examples outlined in this paper allow for better understanding of new opportunities in the context of emerging workflows that combine IOT, cloud, and HPC to bolster scientific productivity.

Keywords: HPC · Cloud · Computing · Edge · Data streams · Modeling simulation · Machine learning · NREL

1 Introduction

Service cloud providers bring a unique set of capabilities when integrated with traditional high performance computing (HPC) to form large, dynamic, and highly effective computing ecosystems for some of the most challenging research problems. Cloud computing offers, and has successfully commoditized, highly reliable services for receiving

© Springer Nature Switzerland AG 2022
J. Nichols et al. (Eds.): SMC 2021, CCIS 1512, pp. 227–246, 2022.
https://doi.org/10.1007/978-3-030-96498-6_13

data streams from the edge, which is essential for systems dependent on Internet of Things (IoT) devices. These services can be leveraged to optimize throughput, cost, and reliability for complex distributed ecosystems that are not well serviced by traditional scientific computing alone. However, the cloud is not cost competitive for running large, computationally intensive workloads. HPC provides access to highly efficient computing resources for large, computationally intensive workloads. HPC systems typically include single points of failure, and are often heavily subscribed, resulting in scheduling contention, which is not an appropriate basis for servicing real-time or near real-time data systems. However, a hybrid of HPC and cloud computing systems provides a unique basis for handling large scale computational workflows efficiently.

At the National Renewable Energy Laboratory (NREL), the Stratus cloud computing environment, which is provided by Amazon Web Services (AWS) enables a wide array of tools and services that work in concert with the Eagle supercomputer in the HPC Data Center. Some use cases include the generation of hundreds of terabytes of data on Eagle, which is transferred to Stratus for data distribution and analysis. In other cases, Stratus manages queues or provides the source data for larger modeling jobs. NREL is at the forefront of building the computational ecosystem needed to manage grid-connected or community-based field studies for large scale energy security or energy efficiency studies. These use cases do not fit the patterns of either HPC or cloud computing alone, so further effort is needed to bring this wealth of resources in alignment to optimize these complex workflows.

2 Advanced Computing at the National Renewable Energy Laboratory

NREL has merged HPC and cloud computing together under a single banner of "advanced computing" to address the compelling need to provide researchers with access to the tools best aligned for the work at hand. Traditionally, cloud computing was focused on outreach and knowledge transfer, whereas HPC did the heavy lifting for research. Over time, however, cloud computing at NREL has become an increasingly valued resource for the laboratory. More analysis and computational workloads are being deployed into the Stratus environment—substantially expanding the role cloud computing now plays at the laboratory—providing tools not previously available to researchers and analysts. As laboratory computing requirements and demands change, NREL's vision for the future of computing is receiving greater focus. The reference architecture and use cases presented here elaborate on NREL's vision for advanced computing [9].

In an idealized scenario, the advantages of agility, performance, and cost- or risk-avoidance would determine which computing environment to leverage. However, optimization and application of complex systems are far more dependent on expertise, experience, and continuity at the leading edge. In order to apply this type of vision to a strategic alignment of resources, it is useful to understand the systems' capabilities, apply them to different workflow scenarios that NREL's Advanced Computing Operations team is currently building support for, and invest in developing supporting expertise.

2.1 ESIF High Performance Computing Data Center

The Energy Systems Integration Facility's (ESIF's) HPC data center, which NREL has operated since 2013, demonstrates best practices in data center sustainability and serves as an exemplar for the community. The facility utilizes a holistic systems approach to the data center, focusing on three critical aspects of data center sustainability:

- Efficiently cooling the IT equipment using direct, component-level liquid cooling with a power usage effectiveness (PUE) design target of 1.06 or better
- Capturing and re-using the waste heat produced
- Minimizing the water used as part of the cooling process.

The Eagle supercomputer, in production since 2019, enhances NREL's leadership role in addressing the nation's renewable energy concerns. Eagle is an 8.9 petaflop Hewlett Packard Enterprise SGI 8600 system with Intel Skylake processors; 2,114 compute nodes; 296 terabytes of total memory; 14 petabytes of high-speed data storage; and a hypercube based 100 Gb/s Enhanced Data Rate (EDR) Infiniband network. Eagle is installed in the ESIF on NREL's campus—which is highly instrumented—and the facility, computing, and built environment are an experiment in energy usage and optimization, currently achieving regular PUE of 1.03 or better.

2.2 NREL Stratus Cloud Computing

The NREL Stratus cloud computing environment was launched over 10 years ago, when cloud computing was nascent. As an early adopter of cloud computing, NREL now provides expertise that continues to benefit a wide array of projects that support NREL's mission [9]. As cloud computing matures, the range of specialized, highly available and scalable services increases, providing compelling functionality that can be applied to specific use cases and needs. NREL's Stratus environment and the Computational Science Center's Cloud Operations Team (CSC Cloud Team) invest time in understanding these services, then help apply them to the needs of researchers throughout the lab. These needs include receipt and processing of data from field studies or equipment outside of the laboratory, big data analysis, publishing websites, and publishing web applications used by industry or the public. Currently, Stratus supports:

- Analysis on large modsim projects
- Data collection from edge devices for

  o field studies
  o power generation experiments

- Data processing workflows
- Public web applications
- Publication of large open data sets.

Recent growth trends in the Stratus environment are indicative of successful implementations in big data analytics utilizing data warehousing and big data management tools; multi-schedule containerized applications, deploying Docker containers at the edge or in serverless functions; and in IoT support for field experiments and grid management studies.

3 Competitive Positioning

HPC, cloud, and edge environments have differing value propositions, cost models, and staffing requirements. HPC traditionally excels at numerically intensive, parallelized, and tightly coupled simulations, with large fixed costs and low variable costs. Stratus cloud computing is composed of specialized services that provide application support and a framework for management and governance, as well as commodity computing and storage services. The edge has developed into an ideal target environment for computing, where very low latency controls, on-site alerts, and machine learning decision support are required. Cloud providers have multiple services to help with edge computing management and receipt of data. NREL is continuing to build on its vision for ideal synergies between HPC and cloud environments to provide efficient and reliable support for our researchers while lowering the barrier for ambitious computing and data intensive research projects. Jobs that require large core counts for hours or days are most efficiently served by Eagle, while jobs with small core counts of high intensity and short duration are often most cost effective when served by the cloud. NREL continues to research both cost and performance optimization for supporting traditional HPC workloads with Eagle and targeted support in the cloud. Recurring scheduled work, analysis, and highly available management of near real-time data streams are typically handled with cloud computing.

3.1 HPC

Eagle, like many HPC systems, can be viewed as a very large, high performance, optimized compute engine that can be molded to fit different workloads. It excels at numerically intensive, parallelized, and tightly coupled simulations. With years of supercomputing experience, the research staff at NREL typically have a higher comfort level with building and scheduling jobs for supercomputing schedulers. However, NREL also has a small but growing staff of highly proficient cloud computing developers, but the overwhelming expertise is with HPC.

Operating an HPC class data center involves significant expertise, labor, and capital investment, not only in the compute resources, but also in power infrastructure, networks, and the power dense data centers and buildings that host the compute resources. The end result is an optimized computing infrastructure that provides a very low cost per floating-point operation (flop) to run compute intensive workloads. As capabilities advance during the lifetime of an HPC facility, these advancements are incorporated into the supercomputing infrastructure with incremental capital investments.

3.2 Cloud Computing

Stratus cloud computing can largely be viewed as a scalable set of reliable microservices, each tuned to process a specific workload, that are accessible via highly available interfaces with a wide array of configurations available. Internally, cloud implementations are approached using best practices for software development. Infrastructure is leveraged as code to standardize how that infrastructure is defined in Python, and then best practices are applied through to launch, via agile software development processes. NREL's CSC Cloud Team manages the Stratus cloud computing enclave, security, application operations, and much of the education for use of the cloud at the laboratory. Pricing of resources in the cloud spans a wide range, depending on what services a customer can commit to using. The published on-demand pricing in AWS can be substantially reduced with pre-purchases or use of excess computing inventory, which AWS makes available as spot instances. The pre-purchased compute instances, or "reserved instances," can provide roughly a 40% savings over on-demand prices, with spot instances providing up to an 80% savings. Spot instances come with the agreement that the excess capacity can still be sold to other customers by AWS at higher prices, and removed from service with short notice, making the reliability of spot instances a challenge [12, 14]. This results in considerable planning complexity. The CSC Cloud Team assists NREL researchers in managing this complexity by working to leverage the most value for the laboratory from cloud services.

The approach to computing in Stratus differs from traditional HPC, as Stratus capabilities generally target a wide array of application support services. The cloud also provides a strong basis for analysis, serving near real-time data with highly reliable, 24/7/365 availability [7]. As an example, AWS provides 12 different database management system services for online analytical processing (OLAP) or online transactional processing (OLTP), and has an ecosystem that comprehensively supports big data management and analysis. The CSC Cloud Team introduced big data capabilities by leveraging cloud services, scaling from terabyte to petabyte datasets for researchers at NREL. This capability became a key enabler for teams to identify patterns of use and to develop cloud capabilities in order to move large datasets that in the past required HPC. Those projects can now be curated within the cloud environment.

Another area where Stratus provides complimentary services to the laboratory (that are not appropriately served in the HPC data center) is through support for IoT environments [3]. The Stratus cloud environment leverages the following advantages for IoT support [8]:

- Highly available endpoints used to receive device data delivered to highly available data streams, which auto-scale to meet variable load demands at minimal cost
- Transparent high availability across multiple cloud provider data centers in cases of equipment failure or other communication issues at the receiving end
- Highly available data stores for analysis that have scaling capabilities available to serve highly dynamic or growing workloads
- Highly available data pipelines and workflow systems that are capable of reliably scheduling machine learning pipelines, data processing, and transformations using scalable compute resources.

Cloud providers continue to rapidly expand their capabilities to better support computing at the edge. Recent service additions include placing AWS managed compute into third party data centers enhancing broad geographic coverage, including topologies running inside cellular networks. These computing installations allow research teams to compute in specified geographic or network locations meeting low latency requirements, while utilizing common cloud computing interfaces and support for the deployed infrastructure regardless of where it is located.

To support edge computing requirements in remote locations where cloud providers do not operate, AWS provides software solutions such as GreenGrass or the Real-time operating system for microcontrollers (FreeRTOS) that run on edge devices or gateways. These provide some basic capabilities for the edge systems to leverage and secure connections to highly available endpoints, facilitating transmission of data to the cloud for processing and analysis.

3.3 Edge Computing

Edge computing involves deploying computing resources geographically or topologically close to the IoT devices being monitored and controlled. Edge computing is often an important consideration for applications that have stringent real-time or data reduction requirements at the edge. In most cases, operating IoT environments at the edge have limiting compute capabilities or other constraints, such as space constraints, barriers to installing additional equipment, and prohibitive costs of supporting remote resources. Because of these constraints, latency requirements may need to be relaxed and mitigated so that equipment can be placed in higher latency locations [6, T13].

Edge computing brings a highly dynamic environment with challenges around fault tolerance that are not often encountered in the well-managed HPC and cloud infrastructure environments [5]. Decisions are required when deploying IoT resources in edge environments; these include adoption of proprietary management or data handling systems; appropriate environmental controls; methods for remote management; data retention and collection requirements; investments in network availability; and power management requirements. In many cases, these decisions are dictated by the working environment. In most cases, multiple single points of failure should be expected, which impact operations or communications in remote devices.

4   Hybrid Support of Real-Time Data Vision at Scale

To optimally support the growing demands and new capabilities needed to meet the U.S. government's ambitious renewable energy goal of creating a carbon-pollution-free power sector by 2035 [15], NREL envisions a hybrid environment that optimizes the use of edge, cloud, and HPC computing. This real-time data vision supports several efforts that will be discussed in more detail in the following sections, including data generation/intake, data cleaning, machine learning, and machine learning training.

4.1 Overview of the Workflow

The workflow in Fig. 1 provides a reference architecture for an IoT environment, illustrating the application of a well-supported hybrid ecosystem composed of edge, cloud and HPC components. In this case, the combined capabilities of HPC and cloud are leveraged to host highly available components used to manage IoT devices and the data

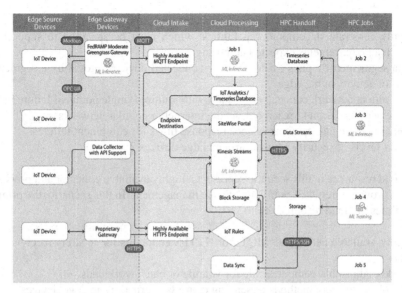

Fig. 1. A reference architecture with edge, cloud, and HPC components.

streams they produce. This architecture supports both very large compute workloads as well as small scheduled workloads within a secured enclave.

To best illustrate NREL's vision of an optimized edge, cloud, and HPC ecosystem, we present a theoretical architecture of field studies and large scale energy modeling that leverages the reference architecture and workflow. For the edge, the architecture should support experimental and field studies for the operation and optimization of smart devices in a residential neighborhood, or a "smart neighborhood." Goals include reducing energy consumption and supporting the use of renewable energy on the existing energy grid infrastructure with no or minimal negative impact on the residents. The architecture will support large scale modeling of simulated data ("modsim"), which then, via simulations, propagates the effects of smart neighborhood management across a larger scale—in particular, the surrounding areas affected by changes to power grid management and power consumption. In turn, those effects affect power generation and transmission schemes for typical residential, industrial, and commercial uses of energy. At both ends of this interaction, we will analyze experiments, trends, and effects to best understand how to optimize the larger ecosystem.

Edge devices are part of the system being optimized, monitored, and controlled. At the edge, some of the primary capabilities to be deployed or leveraged include:

- Very low latencies between edge devices and edge operational systems
- Smart aggregation of device data, leveraged to reduce the amount of data the overall ecosystem needs to manage
- Low latency machine learning inference, applied to device or data management
- Low latency data inspection and stream management
- Low latency controls of devices at the edge.

At the edge, some of the primary concerns include:

- Highly constrained compute capabilities, which must be specified to support the workload requirements expected at the edge
- Data segmented by physical location or connected devices, providing a segmented view of activity at the edge
- Intermittent network connectivity issues, with multiple single points of failure in line for devices that want to reach out via the internet or cellular networks
- Higher operational and maintenance response times for equipment failures
- Lower levels of security controls around edge devices.

Cloud resources in this scenario represent a highly available collector and processor of data, providing remote control and device management. In this scenario, the primary capabilities of cloud resources are:

- Highly available and secure MQTT or HTTPS endpoints for securely receiving IoT data
- Quickly adjustable compute scale for volatile or batch workloads
- Reliable and secure methods of sending controls instructions to edge devices
- Reliable and secure methods of deploying code or machine learning models to edge devices
- An array of data streaming, data storage, and data analysis tools.

Some of the primary concerns with using cloud resources are as follows:

- Cloud computing introduces complexity into any ecosystem by following a microservices architecture.
- Variable costs introduce risk and unpredictability.
- Complex deployments can introduce security risks.
- Data transfer costs and challenges can occur between the HPC data center and the cloud.

HPC resources in this scenario provide the tightly coupled parallel processing capabilities that require prolonged computation. In the HPC data center, the primary capabilities to be leveraged include:

- Efficient, high performance large scale compute job support
- Large scale modeling support, machine learning training, and inference support
- The capability to work with and generate very large datasets.

Some of the primary concerns with using HPC resources are as follows:

- Work must be scheduled well in advance of run dates.
- Scheduling contention may limit resources available to run the HPC jobs.
- Operational outages may interrupt planned scheduling.
- Wall time for job completion could potentially shut down jobs that have not fully completed.

4.2 Workflow Components and Positioning

The workflow that supports the smart neighborhood and large scale modsim work will be a synthesis of the following components:

- Improving smart controls of devices in the homes within smart neighborhoods
- Measuring satisfaction of smart neighborhood residents
- Measuring changes to energy usage and demand in the smart neighborhood
- Simulating the effects of efficiently run smart neighborhoods on large scale energy consumption and production trends.

The goals of the work include:

- Optimizing energy usage for current and future power generation infrastructure
- Improving the overall energy usage profile for adoption of more renewable energy resources, which are naturally less predictable.

Data Generation and Intake. In this overarching workflow, the real-time data of interest is delivered from smart neighborhoods. These data consist of timeseries from power meters, thermostats, or other sensors. Additionally, state information from different smart devices, such as appliances, heaters, washers, or even solar power distribution infrastructure, is collected. Many smart devices also emit events tied to their status or to sensor readings, such as occupancy sensor events or temperature limit violation events, that need to be collected. In addition to these real-time data streams, historical data on energy usage for the area would be identified and collected.

To support the modsim work, the smart neighborhood data, and an aggregate representation of the data from the surrounding areas, needs to be available to the HPC data center. In addition, the operators of the smart neighborhood experiment, who are attempting to optimize the controls for the neighborhood within the larger footprint, will want to issue controls by reacting to data in the real-time data streams. The reactions may require low to modest latencies (milliseconds to minutes). At the millisecond level, device alerts could identify possible safety hazards. In other cases, near real-time data streams and latencies of minutes or more may be acceptable—for example, when controlling a schedule for a washer based on current or near-term predicted energy use or cost trends. As such, we need multiple mechanisms in place:

- Edge device consumers of very low latency data to send alerts or activate controls
- Highly available cloud-based consumers of data that feed into decision support for controls informed by larger ecosystem datasets, and supplemental datasets collected form smart device operators
- Data collectors at the edge or in the cloud that aggregate data at a sufficient frequency to then deliver, or make available to HPC workloads, before they are scheduled to run.

The pairing of edge IoT devices and gateways with cloud-based, highly available endpoints for data collection provides a robust mechanism for handling data collection.

This pairing works around the low storage and compute capabilities in the smart neighborhood. It also provides researchers with live access to the data streams [6]. Because the data streams are live, the HPC data center is not used to poll the data or publish endpoints for device data collection. Its primary function is to perform batch work efficiently, without the overhead of providing highly available endpoints. Thus, we instead rely on the cloud for this architectural support. Details of the integration of this type of workflow are shown in Fig. 2.

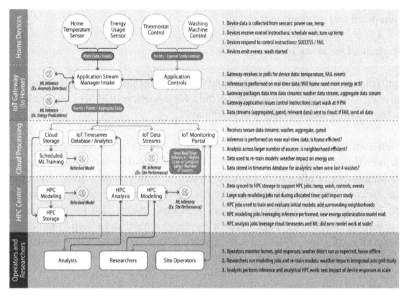

Fig. 2. Workflow illustration for data generation and intake based on a smart neighborhoods example.

Data Cleaning/Transformation. Data cleaning and transformation are a core component of any data processing system, especially when live device data from a disparate range of sources is brought together to form the basis for analysis and decision support. Typically, devices from multiple manufacturers are integrated, and as a result, the data is subject to varying signals, units, metric definitions, and proprietary information, which take some effort to homogenize and make useful. High frequency data may not be needed at all points of analysis and decision support, so aggregation points should be introduced to reduce the cost of data management tasks throughout the system. Aggregation as early as possible in the data flow lowers the impact of costs and complexity. Care does need to be taken, as aggregation can introduce an element of risk into the effectiveness of the analysis and decision support layers as information is lost.

In our scenario, the following data cleaning and transformation items could be configured at or near the edge:

- Simple checks on data quality for expected values
- Simple but smart aggregations to reduce data being operated on in the downstream systems
- Minimum required sample rates at the edge to reduce data being operated on in the downstream systems
- Replacement datasets for missing or corrupted data.

For simpler data manipulation, gateways are provided in line at the edge, as this is the earliest point in data processing. The gateways can assist in providing usable data for decision support at the edge. These devices also provide a software platform for the integration of machine learning or configurable algorithms, which operate on the devices. The options for how to place this software vary from location to location. Ideally, if there is some type of physical collection hub in the neighborhood that is being monitored, a device would be selected or added to handle the gateway software at this location. If that is not available, the next best options should be considered. The following options can help place the gateway system closer to the edge components [16]:

- Smart mobile devices – gateway software that can run on devices at the edge and perform inference or apply custom code/algorithms to data or processes
- Mobile cloud computing – installations of cloud infrastructure for customer use at third party data centers, providing a physically closer computing system to host the gateway
- Mobile edge computing – installations of cloud infrastructure within cellular networks, improving the network topological proximity to the edge systems when cellular networks are used to transmit data
- Cloud computing regions – the cloud provider's primary data centers, which are distributed across different physical regions; these can improve both physical and topological proximity by selecting the geographical region closest to the edge devices.

In all but the first case, the computing power provided can be significant enough for sophisticated processing and data management, so the requirements for data cleaning and transformation may be expanded. In the case of smart mobile devices, however, the compute power relies on what can be installed or leveraged in the smart neighborhood. To help overcome the limitations of managing edge computing, the AWS-provided GreenGrass mobile device software provides the following flexibility:

- Data streams management, including a cache of data per stream when outbound communications issues arise, preventing data from being handed off to the cloud
- A deployment target for custom gateway code that can be deployed from the cloud
- A deployment target for machine learning inference models that can be deployed from the cloud
- FedRAMP moderate certification, with secure communications back to AWS IoT services [1]
- Multiple methods to deliver data to the cloud for different scenarios, such as operations monitoring, archival storage of data, data streaming environments, and analysis environments.

Often, raw data is retained in a compressed form as a means of capturing the source of truth for the system. While this may result in duplication of captured data in the cloud, the data is handled in a less costly manner, typically being sent directly to block storage as an archive.

Synthetic Data/Modeling. The larger modeling efforts provide a basis for making strategic decisions on energy management that incorporate the future development of smart neighborhoods. This would typically be managed in the HPC environment, where performance and efficiency are maximized, supporting larger scale work at lower costs. The data collected from the edge is a critical input for tuning the larger strategic model. The model itself is used to simulate data, which becomes the basis for the analysis efforts used to determine efficiency gains, strategic direction for energy production, priorities for smart neighborhood capabilities or incentives, and how changes to elements in the larger ecosystem would propagate.

The larger, coordinated modeling effort combines the specialized skills of different groups. These groups generate their simulated datasets, which may then become a basis for the integrated work of other groups. In this environment, compute time is scheduled, and critical paths are developed. Once a data simulation effort is completed, that data is typically transferred up to the cloud for analysis purposes. It is also made available to other HPC jobs or ad hoc/scripted work efforts from the laboratory via big data storage and analysis tools in the cloud.

Machine Learning Inference. There are many opportunities for integrating machine learning capabilities into this workflow, taking into account the scope of the effort, the devices being controlled, the types of data being received from the field studies, and the amount of data being generated via HPC jobs. Opportunities for machine learning include supporting smart controls, data cleaning, data validation, anomaly detection, data simulation, predicting energy use, and scenario simulations. As with other processing work, the placement of inference endpoints and management of the models behind them needs to be determined based on each use case. On this topic, the questions we need to consider include:

- Who is the consumer of the inference endpoint?
- Are there low latency requirements for the inference endpoint?
- Are there availability requirements for the inference endpoint?
- What are the compute requirements for the inference endpoints?
- Are the compute requirements volatile or predictable?

One example of machine learning is anomaly detection at the edge for smart neighborhood field studies. The use of the generated anomalous behavior events will help in determining where the inference is performed. If the behavior is used to clean data before it is sent to the cloud, or if there is a notification mechanism at the edge that is intended to immediately alert people on site, then inference should be deployed to the edge gateway that is collecting the data for transmission to the cloud. In this case, the consumer who is notified of the event is at the edge, there are low latency requirements, the possibility of loss of network availability to the cloud interrupting notification of the event is too risky, and the event, while not predictable, would likely only need low computing requirements to handle, so a gateway device at the edge makes sense.

In these cases, by leveraging the Stratus environment, GreenGrass would be installed on the edge gateway, and AWS IoT deployments would be used to deploy the machine learning model and the code that performs inference on the related incoming data to the gateway [2]. Although the processing requirements go up with the addition of machine learning inference, it is likely that they would fall in line after the edge data reduction efforts and just prior to transmission to the cloud, limiting the amount of data being processed through inference. Depending on the scope of data collection and the number of smart neighborhoods being evaluated, the overall ecosystem may include multiple gateway devices that need to be updated. AWS's IoT Core allows Stratus operators to define a class of devices to receive the model updates as they are released, so that deployments are centrally managed for multiple gateways.

Another use case for machine learning at the edge is handling incorrect or missing data and performing corrective action. One example of this is via use of multiple weather stations at a particular location. It is reasonable to assume that temperature changes would result in somewhat predictable patterns of power usage, such that if two outdoor thermometers' temperature readings significantly disagreed on what the current temperature was in a smart neighborhood, inference on the incoming sensor, modeled in part on meter data, would likely be able to decide which thermometer was correct for use. This has the effect of cleaning the data used and recorded by the active systems and creating an event indicating that the other sensor may need service.

If anomalous behavior is instead based on aggregate data streams or on activity from multiple sources, then the cloud is typically an appropriate host for the inference endpoints. Data from multiple sources at larger aggregate throughputs will be available in the cloud. One key benefit of data processing in the cloud is the ability to implement auto-scaling to meet variable demands at minimal cost. Multiple streams from disparate sources can similarly be processed via a centrally managed endpoint, which is much simpler to update, monitor, and configure. In the Stratus cloud environment, inbound data from the edge is received via IoT Core endpoints, resulting in data streams that are configured in a manner that enables sending the data immediately through an inference endpoint.

To support the modsim evolution, machine learning is included to (1) assist with modeling future behaviors and the effects of changes to the overall ecosystem, (2) detect anomalous data in the simulated datasets, and (3) assist with the creation of simulated data used for analysis. Large scale effects in the simulations would result in recreating the detailed simulated data for the entire ecosystem, so the machine learning environment must be tuned to be responsive while data generation is performed to avoid bottlenecks in the compute work. Additionally, all the near real-time data being generated in the field is collected and available for inspection via the cloud Database Management System (DBMS) systems. The HPC data center at the ESIF is connected via VPN endpoints to the compute and data systems in Stratus, so the ability to inspect and use this data without transferring it all to the data center is supported. In other cases, the data systems may be available via AWS Application Programming Interface (API)s, which allows for direction interaction with data queued in a highly available, scalable, and low-cost AWS Kinesis stream [10], or placed in AWS data services such as DynamoDB or S3. While the rate of processing in the HPC data center can lead to contention in the cloud because of the high throughput rates, the auto-scaling capabilities of the cloud will often be able to correct these issues during HPC job executions. AWS also sets soft limits intended to protect customers from steep rises in costs; these limits also allow AWS to ensure they have provisioned enough resources to meet the limits set by its customers, so a review of these limits is required.

Machine Learning Training. Machine learning models often require retraining and tuning as the environment changes to address model drift. Typically, this is supported by data pipelines, which use a portion of the historical operational data as training and testing data sets. Again, the environment chosen for training will depend on the purpose or scope of the machine learning.

In the case of temperature sensors, the metered power usage will likely vary significantly with the seasons, so as the seasons progress, the historical data can be used to update the models to recognize newer scenarios.

Similarly, with the COVID-19 pandemic dramatically altering how and where energy is used, more recent data will provide the patterns needed to correct the drift in the model.

It is common for regular batch computing jobs to perform training on collected datasets at regular intervals. The jobs themselves are compute intensive and can require access to larger datasets, so this type of work is not performed at the edge, but instead in the Stratus or HPC environment. In the case of the temperature sensors, it is likely that a regular cadence would be beneficial. The cloud computing tools in Stratus make regular scheduling of training jobs simple. In contrast, scheduling repeating work in the HPC data center is less reliable due to maintenance periods and contention with other work being performed. As such, training jobs for these data sets or any other recurring training based on schedule or events will be part of a data pipeline run in the cloud. The pipeline may run the training jobs, publish the updated models, and then deploy those models to inference endpoints in the cloud or at the edge. For large or particularly intensive training jobs that are not reliant on repetitive scheduling, HPC jobs on Eagle would be an appropriate forum. The models could then be pushed to the cloud for further distribution if they are needed in the real-time data systems.

Edge Device Management. Devices at the edge will typically be provided by multiple manufacturers, and many will have proprietary interfaces that do not use industry standard protocols. Some of these devices may publish secure APIs for local access, or in other cases, the manufacturer may collect data that can be retrieved from a centrally managed API available on the internet. That said, others may use Modbus, OPC Unified Architecture (OPC-UA), or other standard interfaces and protocols to interact with the device. In most of these cases, a gateway device should be capable of interfacing with multiple devices installed at the edge. AWS provides GreenGrass with native Modbus and OPC-UA support as a means of interfacing with a large array of IoT devices. In the Stratus environment, AWS IoT supports the creation of shadow devices, which digitally represent the known and desired state of devices in the field [4]. With the understanding that remote connectivity is often unreliable, when controls or configuration updates are issued to field devices, the shadow's state is updated. Devices that are offline during the control or configuration events will receive the event when they come back online, and it is recognized that the desired state represented in the shadow device diverges from the running state of the device. The key components in this scenario are shown in Fig. 3.

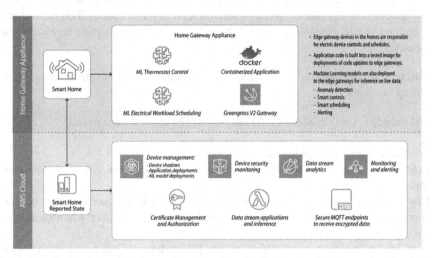

Fig. 3. Details of edge computing and machine learning integration based on smart home data and integration

As noted before, the IoT services in Stratus hosted by AWS also support code and machine learning model deployments to the edge. These deployments can be released to fleets of devices, thus enabling the management of a large footprint from a centralized service. The state of each deployment is available for review.

Another service available in the Stratus environment is provided by SiteWise, an AWS service that provides methods to monitor streams and provide live dashboards of activity. The streams from SiteWise become the source for data streams into other areas of AWS, supporting machine learning and analysis in the cloud.

Finally, cloud providers such as AWS are experts in security automation, and understand the controls needed to certify their service with different security schemes. At the national laboratories, sensitive data (in this case, data that contains details about homes in smart neighborhoods), is often classified as moderate level data, and ideally would require services to be certified under the Federal Risk and Authorization Management Program (FedRAMP) process. In the Stratus environment, the GreenGrass software, IoT Core endpoints and rules engine [11], and IoT Device Management services are FedRAMP moderate certified.[1]

---

[1] GreenGrass, IoT Core and IoT Device Management are also certified under the Payment Card Industry (PCI), System and Organization Controls (SOC 2) and Department of Defense Cloud Computing Security Requirements Guide (CC SRG) [1].

Feedback and Tuning Mechanisms. The Stratus environment provides a very reliable and robust method of logging and auditing systems, both in the cloud and externally. Nearly every activity in the cloud is based on an API call, and AWS provides a robust events system based on those API calls, which can also be augmented with custom events. For instance, a scheduled event could trigger a data pipeline supporting machine learning. Alternatively, that same pipeline could be triggered by an event signaling the arrival of a file in S3, a threshold being hit in a data stream, an alert being received from an IoT gateway, or an event triggered by inference on a related dataset. This flexibility is also built on highly available systems that span data centers supporting highly reliable processes.

Summary. To summarize, the architecture supports the following services at the specified locations:

At the edge, via GreenGrass software, we will have these capabilities:

- Low latency data collection from IoT devices
- Low latency controls of IoT devices, such as adjusting thermostats or setting wash schedules
- Low latency algorithmic or machine learning inference informed decision support, supporting decisions such as when to schedule certain events or when to alert on anomalies
- Low latency notification of safety events to residents or operators of the smart neighborhood
- Integration with AWS IoT to receive deployments of code or machine learning models from the cloud as a means to improve operations of the smart neighborhood
- FedRAMP moderate certified secure software and communications with AWS IoT endpoints for delivery of data [1]
- Data aggregation, validation, and cleaning, based on algorithmic or machine learning informed models, to help ensure downstream systems are operating efficiently
- Delivery of compressed, raw data for archival purposes.

Near the edge, when more compute power is needed, larger and more disparate holistic views of the data processing environment are needed, and latency requirements can be relaxed, AWS WaveLength or Local Zones provide the following capabilities:

- Processing of large data streams from more distributed sources, such as aggregate power consumption profiles across multiple neighborhoods or power distribution events
- Integration of more compute intensive machine learning inference engines that run models developed by HPC systems for larger scale coordination of controls affecting energy consumption in a region
- More intensive data cleaning routines, taking into account variables from surrounding areas, such as temperature readings from sensors in close proximity
- Large storage capacity for in-transit data streams or for archival data preparation.

In the cloud, we have the following services and capabilities:

- Scalable data collection via IoT endpoints or transfers to S3 to support real-time data streams and receipt of archival data
- Rules engines to send different datapoints to different services for processing, such as sending anomaly events directly to an operator via AWS notification services, or triggering a machine learning training when a particular dataset arrives
- Multiple DBMS systems available for analysis, such as timeseries databases for the incoming IoT timeseries data, columnar storage data warehousing for analysis of large datasets generated by HPC, and graph databases for digital things representations and APIs
- Services to manage remote IoT devices and gateways, including use of shadow devices, monitoring for tampering of devices, and deployment mechanisms for machine learning models and custom code
- A robust, highly available events system to reliably trigger services or processes, such as notifying operators when a remote device goes offline
- Secure communication, authorization, and authentication with the HPC data center and data center processes for providing or receiving data.
- Integration of AWS backed capabilities in HPC jobs, such as queue management, inference support, or workflow support.

In the HPC data center, the following capabilities are supported:

- Large processing jobs to simulate modeled energy usage and production data based on scenarios provided by researchers and guided by actual behaviors measured in the field
- Large machine learning jobs leveraging real or simulated data to train models to be deployed to the cloud or edge, to help improve energy efficiency and user satisfaction.

5   Challenges to Supporting the Vision

As with any larger scale ecosystem, the complexity and operational requirements of the deployed infrastructure and code create a significant challenge on many levels. The management of the Stratus environment has been incrementally built upon highly available and scalable services, such that simple services created by NREL or provided by AWS serve single purposes in a highly available and scalable manner. This allows for the development of patterns and practices, largely captured in code, that initially focus on smaller, focused deployments but that can be repurposed for scenarios of much higher scale or complexity. Developers need to be mindful of the potential costs and the AWS limits that will play a part in a large-scale deployment. The ability to fully define the environment their applications run in, as well as the applications themselves, should improve service levels overall, as the infrastructure can be tuned and tested per the software's requirements.

Data flow and data management are also a primary concern for systems such as this, where edge data and HPC modsim data are feeding into processes in the cloud used to augment the system or provide analysis, and edge data is being pulled into HPC jobs to augment the modeling being done. To fully support the environment, Stratus can publish data streams that can be consumed by any consumer connected to the internet with proper permissions, assigned using AWS APIs. It can also make available compressed files to the same consumers, query access to multiple data stores via the same API method or provide VPN access to DBMS systems hosted in the virtual private cloud in AWS.

6   Building Toward the Vision at NREL

The HPC data center at NREL has long been the computing engine driving innovation and research at the laboratory. In the decade since the introduction of cloud computing at NREL, the services provided to NREL by the CSC Cloud Team continue to expand as more specialized services are launched by the team, AWS, and other cloud providers. The expansion of computing at the edge provides additional opportunities and challenges as NREL begins to support power generation experiments, field studies, mobile fleet management, and other IoT supported work, and looks to further enhance and optimize power systems on both the production and consumption sides. As new research opportunities arise that leverage the broad range of capabilities now available to the laboratory, NREL continues to strategically invest in its advanced computing capabilities.

One of the recent steps taken was merging the cloud computing team, who manage the Stratus environment, with the HPC operations team, who manage Eagle and the ESIF HPC data center, under the banner of Advanced Computing Operations. Strategic initiatives have allowed the laboratory to fully leverage the hybrid environments unique to integrated HPC work. The HPC team continues to grow, improve, and expand HPC via dedicated efforts to launch private cloud tools on OpenStack and define and install the next generation of powerful and efficient supercomputers. The Stratus team is expanding support for specialized, highly available and flexible tools for deploying applications, machine learning models, data collection, and data analysis. Projects are underway to investigate the use of cloud computing to improve the efficiency of Eagle by moving inefficient work to the cloud, where it can be run at a lower cost, as well as by developing methods to simplify data transfer and data management between the edge, cloud, and HPC, and by developing methods to make machine learning inference available from multiple environments via centralized deployment mechanisms in the cloud.

The Advanced Computing Operations team continues to support education at the lab on using the various computing systems in support of our mission [9]. This now includes introducing concepts around high availability and scalability best practices to properly leverage cloud computing application support. The Advanced Computing Operations team has decades of cloud computing experience used to help augment the already successful processes in the ESIF data center supporting computationally intensive work. By merging the new cloud computing capabilities with the established, growing HPC capabilities, NREL is suddenly able to successfully support a much wider range of ambitious initiatives that could not be addressed by either computing capability alone.

As these efforts progress, the architectural vision supporting the scenario described in this paper moves much closer to reality. Currently, this vision depends on workloads that NREL is ready to implement; the necessary compute and infrastructure capabilities are currently available. The challenges are now primarily composed of education, process definition, governance and implementation of security controls, and work to support integrations with proprietary interfaces or protocols. While these challenges can still be substantial, they are being addressed with typical risk management strategies and process improvements, and as NREL continues down this path, the risk in those areas will become more manageable and better understood. In essence, the sky, full of clouds, is the limit.

References

1. AWS Services In Scope. https://aws.amazon.com/compliance/services-in-scope/. Accessed 26 May 2021
2. Bennett, K., Robertson, J.: Remote sensing: leveraging cloud IoT and AI/ML services. Proceedings of the SPIE 11746, Artificial Intelligence and Machine Learning for Multi-Domain Operations Applications III, 117462L, 12 April 2021. https://doi.org/10.1117/12.2587754
3. Borge, S., Poonia, N.: Review on Amazon web services, Google cloud provider and Microsoft windows Azure. Advance and Innovative Research, p. 53 (2020)
4. Botez, R., Strautiu, V., Ivanciu, I., Dobrota, V.: Containerized application for IoT devices: comparison between balenaCloud and Amazon web services approaches. In: 2020 International Symposium on Electronics and Telecommunications (ISETC), pp. 1–4 (2020). https://doi.org/10.1109/ISETC50328.2020.9301070
5. Javed, A., Malhi, A., Främling, K.: Edge computing-based fault-tolerant framework: a case study on vehicular networks. In: 2020 International Wireless Communications and Mobile Computing (IWCMC), pp. 1541–1548 (2020). https://doi.org/10.1109/IWCMC48107.2020.9148269
6. Liu, Y., Yang, C., Jiang, L., Xie, S., Zhang, Y.: Intelligent edge computing for IoT-based energy management in smart cities. IEEE Netw. 33(2), 111–117 (2019). https://doi.org/10.1109/MNET.2019.1800254
7. Mesbahi, M.R., Rahmani, A.M., Hosseinzadeh, M.: Reliability and high availability in cloud computing environments: a reference roadmap. HCIS 8(1), 1–31 (2018). https://doi.org/10.1186/s13673-018-0143-8
8. Muhammed, A., Ucuz, D.: Comparison of the IoT platform vendors, microsoft Azure, Amazon web services, and Google cloud, from users' perspectives. In: 2020 8th International Symposium on Digital Forensics and Security (ISDFS), pp. 1–4 (2020). https://doi.org/10.1109/ISDFS49300.2020.9116254
9. National Renewable Energy Laboratory's Mission. https://www.nrel.gov/about/mission-programs.html#:~:text=NREL%20advances%20the%20science%20and,integrate%20and%20optimize%20energy%20systems. Accessed 24 May 2021
10. Nguyen, D., Luckow, A., Duffy, E., Kennedy, K., Apon, A.: Evaluation of highly available cloud streaming systems for performance and price. In: 2018 18th IEEE/ACM International Symposium on Cluster Cloud and Grid Computing (CCGRID), pp. 360–363 (2018). https://doi.org/10.1109/CCGRID.2018.00056
11. Pflanzner, T., Kertesz, A.: A survey of IoT cloud providers. In: 2016 39th International Convention on Information and Communication Technology Electronics and Microelectronics (MIPRO), pp. 730–735 (2016). https://doi.org/10.1109/MIPRO.2016.7522237
12. Pham, T., Ristov, S., Fahringer, T.: Performance and behavior characterization of Amazon EC2 spot instances. In: 2018 IEEE 11th International Conference on Cloud Computing (CLOUD), pp. 73–81 (2018). https://doi.org/10.1109/CLOUD.2018.00017

13. Mohammed Sadeeq, M., Abdulkareem, N.M., Zeebaree, S. R. M., Mikaeel Ahmed, D., Sai-fullah Sami, A., Zebari, R. R.: IoT and cloud computing issues, challenges and opportunities: a review. Qubahan Acad. J. 1(2), 1–7 (2021). https://doi.org/10.48161/qaj.v1n2a36

14. Singh, V., Dutta, K.: Dynamic price prediction for Amazon spot instances. In: 2015 48th Hawaii International Conference on System Sciences, pp. 1513–1520 (2015). https://doi.org/10.1109/HICSS.2015.184

15. White House FACT SHEET: President Biden Sets 2030 Greenhouse Gas Pollution Reduction Target Aimed at Creating Good-Paying Union Jobs and Securing U.S. Leadership on Clean Energy Technologies. https://www.whitehouse.gov/briefing-room/statements-releases/2021/04/22/fact-sheet-president-biden-sets-2030-greenhouse-gas-pollution-reduction-target-aimed-at-creating-good-paying-union-jobs-and-securing-u-s-leadership-on-clean-energy-technologies/. Accessed 31 Aug 2021

16. Zhang, J., et al.: Energy-latency tradeoff for energy-aware offloading in mobile edge computing networks. IEEE Internet Things J. 5(4), 2633–2645 (2018). https://doi.org/10.1109/JIOT.2017.2786343

Braid-DB: Toward AI-Driven Science with Machine Learning Provenance

Justin M. Wozniak$^{(\boxtimes)}$, Zhengchun Liu, Rafael Vescovi, Ryan Chard, Bogdan Nicolae, and Ian Foster

Argonne National Laboratory, Lemont, IL 60439, USA
woz@anl.gov
https://github.com/ANL-Braid

Abstract. Next-generation scientific instruments will collect data at unprecedented rates: multiple GB/s and exceeding TB/day. Such runs will benefit from automation and steering via machine learning methods, but these methods require new data management and policy techniques. We present here the **Braid Provenance Engine (Braid-DB)**, a system that embraces AI-for-science automation in how and when to analyze and retain data, and when to alter experimental configurations. Traditional provenance systems automate record-keeping so that humans and/or machines can recover how a particular result was obtained—and, when failures occur, diagnose causes and enable rapid restart. Related workflow automation efforts need additional recording about model training inputs, including experiments, simulations, and the structures of other learning and analysis activities. Braid-DB combines provenance and version control concepts to provide a robust and usable solution.

Keywords: Provenance · Machine learning · Version control · Database

1 Introduction

Modern science must increasingly deal with high data rates and volumes; as a consequence, machines are supplementing humans as decision makers: for example, concerning how and when to analyze and retain data, and when to alter experimental configurations. Thus it becomes essential to automate also record keeping so that humans and/or machines can determine how a particular result was obtained—and, when failures occur, diagnose causes. Such records must frequently be recursively structured, for example when raw data are supplemented by ML model predictions that depend on training data. These factors, plus highly automated, dynamic, and adaptive execution, make capture of provenance information essential. We need methods for capturing sufficient information about all data products produced, both to *enable inspection of workflow progress* and to *make data findable, accessible, interoperable, and reusable* (FAIR).

© Springer Nature Switzerland AG 2022
J. Nichols et al. (Eds.): SMC 2021, CCIS 1512, pp. 247–261, 2022.
https://doi.org/10.1007/978-3-030-96498-6_14

Interpreting such automatic decisions to understand progress or performance and to validate scientific results will require new provenance concepts and systems to capture not just the data obtained, but also the models produced, which may be more important in the era of artificial intelligence (AI) for science.

Traditional provenance systems automate record-keeping so that humans and/or machines can recover how a particular result was obtained—and, when failures occur, diagnose causes and enable rapid restart. Such systems are typically built to handle static workflow patterns and capture predictable forward progress.

The Braid Provenance Engine (Braid-DB), introduced herein, provides specific features for use in an environment dominated by externally-produced data, such as experiment instruments, and machine learning (ML) data access patterns, as depicted in Fig. 1. It develops recursive and versioned provenance structures to capture how models may be constructed via other models (e.g., estimators and surrogates) and frequent model updates, allowing the user to track past decisions as models make decisions and are retrained. This paper will also survey partner applications for more detailed use cases and requirements. Braid-DB is a component of a larger effort within Argonne's Braid project to support experimental science workflows.

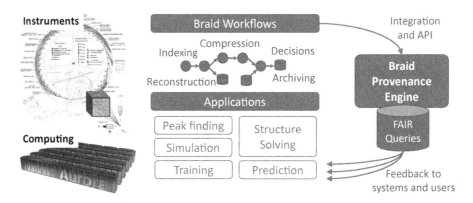

Fig. 1. Braid workflows and their connection to Braid-DB. Center top shows an example Braid workflow with various actions. The Braid provenance engine captures events from Braid tools or its API and provides a FAIR interface for the provenance of data products in the context of experiment, simulation, and learning.

Organization. The remainder of this paper is as follows. In Sect. 2, we provide background on provenance systems and other related efforts. In Sect. 3, we describe our approach in more detail, with its intended benefits. In Sect. 4, we describe the software architecture of our system. In Sect. 5, we outline several motivating case studies in experimental science that drove our design. In Sect. 6, we measure the performance of our system on a workload meant to stress all of its capabilities. In Sect. 7, we outline future work. In Sect. 8, we summarize the paper and provide concluding comments.

2 Background

Computer scientists have developed many provenance systems and related tools [20]. There is a significant body of prior work in provenance for scalable computing workflows, but additional developments are needed to address the needs of AI for Science workflows coupled with experimental science infrastructure. The need to capture not only data and associated metadata but also derived models in ways that are Findable, Accessible, Interoperable, and Reusable (FAIR) [26] is also highly relevant to this topic.

2.1 Provenance Needs in AI for Science

A 2020 DOE AI for Science report [22] offered a broad depiction of the future of AI-supported scientific studies. Data management and provenance were identified as critical to enabling real-time adaptation in simulation and experiment workloads. The report noted the "need for enhancements in data storage, access, and management that would facilitate rapid identification of relevant data, transformations between different data representations, and capture of relevant provenance to assist in reproducibility of results." The report also noted that provenance is critical to making AI/ML workflows effective when coupling experiment, AI/ML, and HPC, including for the purpose of managing uncertainty and validation in results.

Another DOE report, on Data and Models for AI [10], identified provenance as a critical component of the AI for Science effort. The report noted that "[w]hen used for control or autonomous decision making in a scientific workflow, the trained model may be an important digital artifact for reproducibility of the results." This need to capture trained models is precisely why the conception of provenance needs to be expanded in the the context of ML and experiment-in-the-loop computing efforts. More broadly, the report considered the challenges faced by scientists attempting to use popular tools for scientific problems, and the need to manage data in AI for Science contexts in ways that satisfy FAIR principles. The report also stressed the importance of human oversight of science workflows; as we describe in the following, the Braid-DB effort stresses human interpretability as a key driver.

A report on Scientific Machine Learning [5] stressed the importance of changes to the types of scientific questions that can be asked of computing systems. The report considered the question of how to perform data acquisition, a mode of operation which creates complex data provenance structures. The report also noted the importance of being able to interpret results of ML-driven studies. Another report [8] noted the difficulties of creating data that are useful for humans and machines, and of defining and measuring FAIR.

Overall, the AI for Science paradigm emphasizes the need for increased automation at all levels of experimental science and the resulting need to reuse data analysis techniques and systems in new ways.

2.2   Developments in Provenance Concepts for Machine Learning

Traditional provenance models are designed to capture key aspects of a dataset, including its derivation history from other data, quality, and ability to be replicated or reproduced [20]. The derivation history of a dataset is a description of the computational processes that produced it, and the input data consumed by those processes. It is generally assumed that provenance captures a coarse-grained view of dataset production; fine-grained information such as delineating particular predictions in a model are not captured. Conventionally speaking, we are interested in capturing provenance data at a file and version level, not at the record level, to reduce the overheads associated with storing records about such small data.

The Open Provenance Model [17] defines provenance concepts without regard to the underlying technologies or systems used to represent them. These concepts include "artifacts", or data objects in the system; "processes", actions caused by artifacts that produce new artifacts; and "agents", the contexts that control processes. For example, artifacts could be files, processes could be running programs, and agents could be computer systems running programs and managing files. These concepts are connected with various kinds of edges that represent various types of dependencies. For a particular workflow, the result is an *OPM graph* that captures the causal dependencies among all data products.

Souza et al. [21] considered provenance management for ML workloads in sciences. They defined human actors in the ML work cycle, and integrated model training data and other ML-specific concepts, such as ML hyperparameters, into the provenance model. This study, however, did not consider the evolving versions of an ML model that may be produced during an iterative study, in which different ML predictions are produced over time by varying versions of a model. This is a key contribution of the Braid-DB model and is critical for the integration of provenance techniques in experiment-oriented computing.

Polyzotis et al. [18] similarly identified human factors as critical in the ML pipeline. This study considered aspects of raw data manipulation needed for ML training, including cleaning and enriching datasets for training. The paper also touches on privacy-sensitive and limited-access datasets. Metadata tracking schemes for ML workloads have been proposed previously. In ModelDB [24], a ML metadata and training data architecture is easily accessible from within ML-oriented programming environments, including a graphical front-end. Notably, ModelDB, like our Braid-DB, uses a branching history model to track changes over time. An Amazon prototype [19] develops a formal database schema for tracking models and their training data, based on previous but more narrowly defined models [15]. This schema allows for the creation of graphs of data transforms in the ML workflow. Neither system, however, explicitly tracks versions of models in model-model interactions or after iterations of model-experiment iterations. Additionally, neither explicitly mentions the hardware used for ML training and inference, an increasingly important factor for flows that include deep learning and heterogeneous systems [2,12].

2.3 Globus Flows

The Braid project within which Braid-DB is developed uses *Globus Flows* to describe and execute workflows [3]. This cloud-based service is designed to automate various data management tasks such as data transfer, analysis, and indexing. Flows are defined with a JSON-based state machine language which links together calls to external *actions*. Flows implements an extensible model via which external *action providers* (e.g., for transferring data with Globus Transfer, executing functions with funcX, associate identifiers via DataCite) can be integrated by implementing the Globus Flows action provider API. Flows relies on Globus Auth [23] to provide secure, authorized, and delegatable access to user-defined flows and to action providers.

3   Approach

We now describe how the Braid Provenance Engine capture various aspects of the computing-experiment loop for inspection and analysis.

3.1   Contributions

Our work in this area is motivated by two goals: to enable inspection of workflow progress and to produce workflow data products that are FAIR. To this end, we design Braid-DB data structures to be comprehensive, by which we meant that they capture information about not only those outputs that are eventually associated with publications, but also intermediate products that may or may not ultimately prove to be important [9,16]. Braid-DB captures metadata about not only static data, such as well-established experimental data, but also live experimental data, which are treated separately before being promoted to static data.

   Braid-DB, like traditional provenance systems (Sect. 2), captures simulation inputs and outputs and model training inputs and outputs. Importantly, it integrates provenance records with model version history so as to record how a possibly complex ensemble of variably-accurate models were trained and updated over time. As training data may come from experiment, simulation, or other models (e.g., a higher-accuracy, higher-cost model, or an ensemble of lower-cost models) Braid-DB includes structures that allow a user to ask how a model inference result was obtained, in the form of a defensible *statement*. The provenance structure is designed to be portable so that provenance histories can be merged with other records from collaborating teams, as when a user borrows a model from another team.

We intended that the continuous generation and collection of records concerning inputs, code versions, locations, progress, and outputs of both individual actions and complete flows enable the construction of externally visible dashboards for monitoring application progress, and tools for tracking and reporting on, for example, the locations and sizes of data produced to date. These same records can also be leveraged to synthesize metadata records for loading into catalogs. The system is designed to integrate with external capabilities such as those provided by the Materials Data Facility [6] and associated data ingest tools [7].

Realizing our goal of policy-driven automation demands machine-level understanding of flows (Subsect. 2.3). We investigate what metadata representations and relationships are needed to maintain this understanding so as to enable automatic decisions, such as those to be made by workflow policy engines that are being developed within the Braid project (Sect. 4). Second, analyses often involve ML modules that are updated continuously by new data from multiple sources. This is a challenging provenance and version control problem. Thus in designing Braid-DB, we consider how to mix and match concepts from the provenance literature (Sect. 2) with popular version control concepts to provide a robust and usable solution to this model management problem.

3.2 Provenance Structure

We design Braid-DB data structures and implementation to enable automatic generation of identifiers [9,11], collection of descriptive metadata, and construction of provenance records to enable reproducibility, post-mortem analysis, and auditing of computations. We show the provenance structure of our system in Fig. 2. Inside the "Braid Provenance Engine" box, all boxes are Braid Records, and the arrows indicate Braid Dependencies. At the base of the structure, shown in green, are static Records, such as quantities from the literature, outputs from physical experiment runs, and methods encoded in software. The objects included in the Braid-DB model include:

1. **BraidRecord:** A super-class for Braid-DB provenance records. Each such entity has a unique ID, a (possibly not unique) string name, a list of dependencies, and a dictionary of user-specified, string-keyed metadata tags,
2. **BraidFact:** A simpler object consisting of static data: for example, preexisting trusted data or software, etc. BraidFacts may have a provenance outside the Braid-DB system.
3. **BraidData:** The Braid-DB representation of traditional provenance-tracked data, with traditional conceptions of its derivation history from other Braid-Data and/or BraidFacts. A Braid-DB containing only BraidData and Braid-Facts would be functionally indistinguishable from a traditional provenance database.
4. **BraidModel:** An ML model tracked by Braid-DB. A BraidModel has the additional capability **update()**, which represents model exposure to other BraidRecords, possibly including other models. This includes the possibility

of dependency cycles that capture complex interactions among models and data as experiment workflows progress.

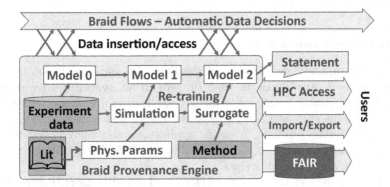

Fig. 2. Braid provenance internals and interfaces. Static records include experimental observations, data from literature, and algorithm definitions. Updateable records include simulation runs, surrogates, and models derived from other records. Small arrows indicate data accesses recorded as provenance information (e.g., model inputs).

4   Architecture

We now describe the software implementation of the Braid-DB system. The software-level goals of Braid-DB are to develop a system that implements the provenance structure described in Sect. 3 in a way that is easy to use and integrate with existing systems, and thus to provide a toolkit that can be rapidly adopted, shared, and extended.

4.1   Software Performance Targets

We design the Braid-DB prototype to be flexible and compatible with existing techniques and file formats, rather than a prescriptive framework. An HPC access module will be available via a MPI4Py library so that records can be rapidly ingested during an HPC run, and later merged with other records; this module will be used by our HPC features. The system will be scalable to the needs of an ML training-based workload. For reference of scale, we consider a challenge problem workflow from the ECP CANDLE project [28]. In this workflow, one training epoch is completed per node every five minutes. On an exascale system of 10K nodes, that is 33 records/second. Over one week of facilities experiment time, that would record 20M records. Achieving these rates will be the target of our database and HPC module.

We record metadata from Braid Flows in the provenance component in the form of structured metadata regarding data flows as they relate to objects represented in external storage, that is, reads and writes to/from flows. Thus, the provenance of an flow object in the store is the metadata history of the flows that have affected it, and so on.

4.2   Software Components

We show the principal components of the Braid-DB implementation in Fig. 3. At the top level, **applications and/or workflow systems** drive usage of Braid-DB. These components could include application workflows written using workflow systems such as Parsl [4] or Swift/T [27], which make it easy to call directly into Python libraries. Scientific applications and analysis systems such as NeXpy [1] could also access the system directly. A shell script library will also be provided to support such scripts.

Supporting the top layer are the **HPC cache** and **import/merge tools**. The *HPC cache*, a system component to support scalable Braid-DB workloads on exascale-class machines, will use a combination of database operation forwarding and aggregation to prevent overloading the underlying databases during bursty workloads. The *import/merge tools* will enable data slicing and extraction from Braid-DB instances so that subsets of data can be shared with others. These tools will also allow users to import external database records as a basis for the provenance of future experiments, to support use cases that involve reproducing and/or extending other experiments.

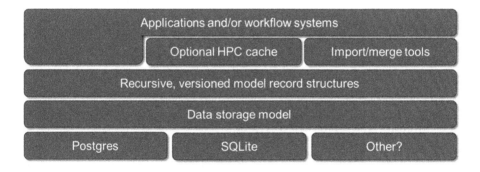

Fig. 3. Software architecture of the Braid Provenance Engine.

The **recursive, versioned model record structures** implement the abstraction described in Sect. 3. They provide Python access to Records and Dependencies and allow for these objects to be easily created, searched, loaded, manipulated, and stored. The **data storage model** persists the record structures in a non-volatile, consistent way, mapping Records and Dependencies, along with typical metadata such as timestamps and user tags, into a database schema.

Our current implementation uses a standard SQL-based approach for capturing this information. In this model, given a record ID, its dependencies and other metadata can quickly be traced back to original static Records with minimal complexity.

4.3 Software Implementation

We have developed a Braid-DB prototype [29] as an object-oriented Python library in which Braid-DB objects such as Records and Dependencies can be constructed, manipulated, and persisted to a data storage backend. A high-level API allows existing workflows to construct these objects persistently with just one or two additional lines of Python code.

We are developing methods for capturing sufficient information about all data products produced by flows to enable regeneration in supported workflow systems. To this end, we are working to combine existing and new capabilities to architect auto-documentation methods that collect provenance data automatically, with automated recording of identifiers, descriptive application-level metadata, and data access and dependency records to enable both reproducibility and post-mortem analysis and auditing of computations. Open questions include how to associate sufficient identifiers and metadata with the data, code, and resources involved in a computation, including dynamically updated ML models, automatically from workflow systems. The broader Braid project will orchestrate data flows using modular actions and integrate them with HPC resources, while enforcing data policies, e.g., to data capture quality and performance.

5 Case Studies

We briefly describe two of the experimental science case studies that are guiding Braid-DB development, and one synthetic Braid-DB application workflow that we are using to evaluate the performance of Braid-DB implementations.

5.1 Provenance Flow Capture for Training DNNs in X-Ray Science

Extremely high data rates at modern synchrotron and X-ray free-electron laser light source beamlines motivate the use of ML methods for data reduction, feature detection, and other purposes. Regardless of the application, the basic concept is the same: data collected in early stages of an experiment, data from past similar experiments, and/or data simulated for upcoming experiments are used to train a deep neural network (DNN) model that, in effect, learns specific characteristics of those data; this model is then used to process subsequent data more efficiently than would general-purpose models that lack knowledge of the specific dataset or data class [13]. In many cases, the DNN needs to be updated (retrained and fine-tuned) frequently to keep up with changes in experiment setup and sample conditions. Thus, a key challenge is to train models with sufficient rapidity that they can be deployed and applied within useful timescales. There are two common approaches to rapid DNN training: 1) using more powerful systems, such as purpose-built AI accelerators: e.g., TPU, Cerebras, SambaNova, GraphCore; and 2) use new data to fine-tune a similar model trained in the past.

Although purpose-built AI accelerators can train ML models much more rapidly than the computing clusters that may be deployed within an experiment facility, such accelerators must commonly be deployed within a data center due to their cooling, power supply, ventilation, and fire suppression requirements. Thus, a distributed workflow is needed to automate DNN training with remote AI systems deployed at data center. The workflow commonly comprises the following six basic operations: 1) Collect a datum; 2) Simulate an experiment to generate a datum, d, without an experiment; 3) Analyze the datum using a conventional algorithm (e.g., Bragg peak extraction), generating an analysis (e.g., Bragg peak locations) [14], a; 4) Train (or retrain) a ML model with some number of $\{d, a\}$ pairs, generating a new model, m; 5) Deploy the new model m on an edge-AI device; and 6) Apply the model m to a new experimental datum, generating an estimated analysis, $\hat{a}$.

Provenance information is needed for such geographically distributed workflows in order to make their performance interpretable ("on what basis did we conclude that experimental data record r included feature $f1$?") and to enable troubleshooting ("why did we not detect feature $f2$ in r?"). Another straightforward use for provenance records is to support locating a pre-trained model in the repository to be fine tuned with new data. To support such applications, we need to record DNN models as they are generated, along with their training dataset, the convergence curve of the training process, and validation performance. Each model trained by the workflow must be discoverable by using information about its training, such as the training data and experiment metadata. Similarly, users must be able to query a model in the workflow history and obtain its training data and parameters.

5.2   Serial Synchrotron X-Ray Crystallography

Serial synchrotron x-ray crystallography (SSX) enables novel studies of protein and enzyme dynamic processes by imaging small crystal samples 1–2 orders of magnitude faster than traditional crystallography techniques. SSX offers new opportunities for biologists to manage sensitive conditions such as time resolution by using light activation for change in conformation or change in pH, very low x-ray doses for sensitive samples, maintaining room temperature for more biologically-relevant environments, controlling radiation sensitivity for metalloproteins, and observing redox potentials in active sites. However, the increased data collection rates in SSX make it untenable for humans to manage experiments, because individual samples often result in hundreds of thousands of distinct images that must be analyzed, organized, and cataloged to deduce protein structures. Further, solving a protein structure is dependent on the configurations and thresholds used during the analysis and refinement process, necessitating fine-grained provenance tracking to associate structures with the raw data and analysis inputs used to create them.

At Argonne's Structural Biology Center at the Advanced Photon Source (APS) scientists have developed a Braid-compatible pipeline to process raw data, catalog and report interim results, and attempt to refine and solve protein structures [25]. This process captures sample information (including protein, preparation technique, exposure, and temperature) and feeds it into the analysis and publication pipeline. We are now working to extend these efforts to capture and record fine-grained provenance information regarding the sample, beamline configuration, data, analysis inputs, and results, in order to track how specific protein structures are derived during an experiment. The development of a complete Braid workflow for the experiment will then simplify the data acquisition and processing of new samples by tuning the analysis parameters based on previous experiments. Furthermore, it will allow the experiment control algorithms to decide what are the next steps to complete the acquisition, for example, acquire more data and/or move on to the next sample.

5.3 The Mascot Workflow

Application workflows such as the two just described tend both to use just a subset of Braid-DB capabilities and to incorporate numerous application complexities. Thus to illustrate Braid-DB capabilities and to permit flexible testing and performance evaluation (Sect. 6), we have developed the **Mascot workflow**, which exercises all Braid-DB capabilities in a synthetic setting.

The Mascot workflow starts with C configurations, each representing a static data record such as an instrument control script or some initial model training data. Each such configuration is stored in Braid-DB. Then, M models are instantiated, each depending on one configuration. These may be any kind of ML model that consumes training data and makes inferences. Then, N experimental cycles are run, each consisting of E experiment runs. Each run simulates the use of an experimental instrument that consumes configuration data and produces experiment data records. After each cycle, each model is exposed to all of the new experiment data, producing an updated model version and new provenance records, all of which are stored in Braid-DB. Each data record in the system, a configuration $c \in [0, C - 1]$ or experiment $e \in [0, E - 1]$ produces U URIs, representing an external data item referred to by the system.

A specific Mascot workflow can thus be configured by specifying the nature of the ML model used and by varying the values of the parameters C, M, N, E, and U (Fig. 4).

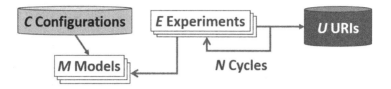

Fig. 4. Simplified depiction of Mascot workflow.

6 Performance

We describe an initial performance study of the Braid-DB system implementation (Sect. 4). In this study, we ran the Mascot workflow on a local workstation with an Intel i7-8700 running Ubuntu 20.04.0 and Python 3.8.2, using the Braid-DB SQLite backend. The Mascot workflow was configured to run using the parameterization described in Subsect. 5.3. The workflow swept over a range of model counts $M \in [10, 100]$ and experiment counts $C \in [10, 100]$ with step 10. For each run, we fixed $M = C$, and set $N = 5, U = 3$.

Each experiment ran on a fresh SQLite database file. We ran two batteries of tests, one with SQLite automatic commits enabled and one with that feature disabled. We measured execution times internally by Python and counted the number of database entries (SQL rows) generated to obtain a database insert rate. Each (count, time) pair was run for five trials and the average was computed.

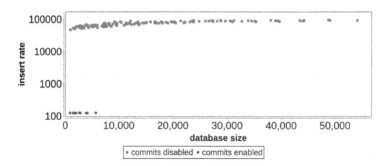

Fig. 5. Performance results for data insertion workflow

The results, plotted in Fig. 5, show that the database insert rate for runs without commits converges to just under 100 000 inserts per second (the maximum is 97 166). The run with commits enabled reached a maximum of only 128 inserts/second. Clearly, it will be infeasible to rely on SQLite to handle concurrency in this mode, and we will use the integration with the workflow systems to ensure consistent multiprocess access to the database, as has been done with prior Swift/T applications.

Additionally, we created a Braid-DB instance with 20 146 000 entries by setting $E = 4000$ and $M = 1000$. Constructing this database with the Mascot workflow took only 169.9 s, and thus indicates that the performance goal based on the CANDLE example (Subsect. 4.1) is easily achievable at this level of functionality. As we move forward we intend to maintain conformance with these rate targets as we add additional features and interfaces.

7 Future Work

We have reported here on just the initial aspects of the development of a comprehensive system for managing provenance data from self-driving experiments. Remaining challenges include:

1. Deeper integration with experiment management systems
   (a) Capturing experiment-level details about conditions
   (b) Ability to replay experiment conditions and alternative scenarios
2. Deeper integration with data systems
   (a) Capturing resource availability and pressures
   (b) Ability to evaluate scenarios under different loads and system-level performance capabilities
3. Deeper integration with learning modules.
   (a) Capturing why decisions were made
   (b) Capturing available alternatives to decisions that were made
4. Deeper integration with scientific software abstractions
   (a) Investigating potential portable provenance abstractions for a range of scientific software
   (b) Developing APIs for use by a wider range of programming models, including zero-programming-effort integration via interception of other activity.

8 Conclusion

We have argued that modern science workflows require new provenance methods to meet the needs of machine learning-driven experimental science. Autonomous experimental science experiments challenge traditional approaches to experiment workflow reproduction and interpretation. New provenance structures are needed to capture not just the progress of workloads mandated by the software developer or experimental user, but also the choices made by ML modules, which may be based on subtle data variations or changes in underlying computing resources.

The development of ever-increasing automation poses new questions about the role of humans in experimental science. Initially, the goal of experimental automation will be to enable experimentalists to focus on higher-level problems in these workflows. In these cases, provenance will allow users to correct and improve experimental studies more quickly. Forward-looking replay and scenario evaluation will maximize the value obtained from time consumed on valuable infrastructure. A future goal will be to enable human users to specify much higher-level scientific questions and receive justifiable answers. The goals of the Braid Provenance Database is to accelerate progress toward these high-level question-and-answer specifications.

Acknowledgments. This work was supported by the U.S. Department of Energy, Office of Science, Advanced Scientific Computing Research, under contract number DE-AC02-06CH11357.

References

1. NeXpy: A Python GUI to analyze NeXus data. http://nexpy.github.io/nexpy
2. Abeykoon, V., Liu, Z., Kettimuthu, R., Fox, G., Foster, I.: Scientific image restoration anywhere. In: IEEE/ACM 1st Annual Workshop on Large-scale Experiment-in-the-Loop Computing (XLOOP), pp. 8–13. IEEE (2019)
3. Ananthakrishnan, R., et al.: Globus platform services for data publication. In: Proceedings of the Practice and Experience on Advanced Research Computing, pp. 1–7 (2018)
4. Babuji, Y., et al.: Parsl: pervasive parallel programming in Python. In: Proceedings of the HPDC (2019)
5. Baker, N.: Basic research needs workshop for scientific machine learning, core technologies for artificial intelligence (2019)
6. Blaiszik, B., Chard, K., Pruyne, J., Ananthakrishnan, R., Tuecke, S., Foster, I.: The materials data facility: data services to advance materials science research. J. Mater. **68**(8), 2045–2052 (2016)
7. Blaiszik, B., et al.: A data ecosystem to support machine learning in materials science. MRS Commun. **9**(4), 1125–1133 (2019). https://doi.org/10.1557/mrc.2019.118
8. Borycz, J., Carroll, B.: Implementing FAIR data for people and machines: impacts and implications - results of a research data community workshop. Inf. Serv. Use **40**(1–2), 71–85 (2020)
9. Chard, K., et al.: I'll take that to go: big data bags and minimal identifiers for exchange of large, complex datasets. In: International Conference on Big Data (Big Data), pp. 319–328. IEEE (2016)
10. Fagnan, K., Nashed, Y., Perdue, G., Ratner, D., Shankar, A., Yoo, S.: Data and models: a framework for advancing AI in science. Report of the Office of Science Roundtable on Data for AI (2019). https://www.osti.gov/servlets/purl/1579323
11. Juty, N., et al.: Unique, persistent, resolvable: identifiers as the foundation of FAIR. Data Intell. **2**, 30–39 (2020)
12. Li, J., Zhang, C., Cao, Q., Qi, C., Huang, J., Xie, C.: An experimental study on deep learning based on different hardware configurations. In: 2017 International Conference on Networking, Architecture, and Storage (NAS), pp. 1–6. IEEE (2017)
13. Liu, Z., et al.: Bridge data center AI systems with edge computing for actionable information retrieval. arXiv preprint arXiv:2105.13967 (2021)
14. Liu, Z., et al.: BraggNN: fast X-ray Bragg peak analysis using deep learning. arXiv preprint arXiv:2008.08198 (2020)
15. Machine Learning Schema Community Group: W3C machine learning schema (2017). https://github.com/ML-Schema/
16. Madduri, R., et al.: Reproducible big data science: a case study in continuous fairness. PLoS ONE **14**(4), e0213013 (2019)

17. Moreau, L., et al.: The open provenance model core specification (v1.1). Future Gener. Comput. Syst. **27**(6), 743–756 (2011)
18. Polyzotis, N., Roy, S., Whang, S.E., Zinkevich, M.: Data management challenges in production machine learning. In: 2017 ACM International Conference on Management of Data, SIGMOD 2017, pp. 1723–1726. Association for Computing Machinery, New York (2017). https://doi.org/10.1145/3035918.3054782
19. Schelter, S., Böse, J.H., Kirschnick, J., Klein, T., Seufert, S.: Automatically tracking metadata and provenance of machine learning experiments. In: Machine Learning Systems Workshop at NIPS (2017)
20. Simmhan, Y.L., Plale, B., Gannon, D.: A survey of data provenance in e-science. ACM SIGMOD Rec. **34**(3), 31–36 (2005)
21. Souza, R., et al.: Provenance data in the machine learning lifecycle in computational science and engineering. In: Workshop on Workflows in Support of Large-Scale Science at SC, pp. 1–10 (11 2019). https://doi.org/10.1109/WORKS49585.2019.00006
22. Stevens, R., Nichols, J., Yelick, K.: AI for Science Report on the Department of Energy (DOE) Town Halls on Artificial Intelligence (AI) for Science (2020)
23. Tuecke, S., et al.: Globus auth: a research identity and access management platform. In: 12th International Conference on e-Science, pp. 203–212. IEEE (2016)
24. Vartak, M., et al.: ModelDB: a system for machine learning model management. In: Proceedings of the Workshop on Human-In-the-Loop Data Analytics, HILDA 2016. Association for Computing Machinery, New York (2016). https://doi.org/10.1145/2939502.2939516
25. Wilamowski, M., et al.: 2'-O methylation of RNA cap in SARS-CoV-2 captured by serial crystallography. Proc. Natl. Acad. Sci. **118**(21) (2021). https://doi.org/10.1073/pnas.2100170118. https://www.pnas.org/content/118/21/e2100170118
26. Wilkinson, M.D., et al.: The FAIR guiding principles for scientific data management and stewardship. Sci. Data **3**(1), 1–9 (2016)
27. Wozniak, J.M., Armstrong, T.G., Wilde, M., Katz, D.S., Lusk, E., Foster, I.T.: Swift/T: scalable data flow programming for distributed-memory task-parallel applications. In: Proceedings of the CCGrid (2013)
28. Wozniak, J.M., et al.: CANDLE/Supervisor: a workflow framework for machine learning applied to cancer research. BMC Bioinform. **19**(18), 491 (2018). https://doi.org/10.1186/s12859-018-2508-4
29. Wozniak, J.M., et al.: Braid-DB GitHub repository. https://github.com/ANL-Braid/DB

Lessons Learned on the Interface Between Quantum and Conventional Networking

Muneer Alshowkan$^{(\boxtimes)}$, Nageswara S. V. Rao, Joseph C. Chapman$^{(\boxtimes)}$, Brian P. Williams, Philip G. Evans, Raphael C. Pooser, Joseph M. Lukens, and Nicholas A. Peters

Oak Ridge National Laboratory, Oak Ridge, TN 37831, USA
{alshowkanm,chapmanjc}@ornl.gov

Abstract. The future Quantum Internet is expected to be based on a hybrid architecture with core quantum transport capabilities complemented by conventional networking. Practical and foundational considerations indicate the need for conventional control and data planes that (i) utilize extensive existing telecommunications fiber infrastructure, and (ii) provide parallel conventional data channels needed for quantum networking protocols. We propose a quantum-conventional network (QCN) harness to implement a new architecture to meet these requirements. The QCN control plane carries the control and management traffic, whereas its data plane handles the conventional and quantum data communications. We established a local area QCN connecting three quantum laboratories over dedicated fiber and conventional network connections. We describe considerations and tradeoffs for layering QCN functionalities, informed by our recent quantum entanglement distribution experiments conducted over this network.

Keywords: Quantum network · Efficient networks · Conventional network · Quantum key distribution · Control plane · Teleportation · Entanglement distribution

1 Introduction

Quantum networks promise fundamentally new capabilities for scientific discovery empowered by accelerator and reactor facilities, quantum computing, and cybersecurity. The highly anticipated Quantum Internet (QI) [29] is expected to enhance the role of the conventional Internet by quantum connectivity with integrated security. Indeed, quantum networks are known to play an important role in secure communications [8,23], distributed computing [15], blind computing [7,11], and enhanced sensing [9,21,22]. Their full potential, however, can only be realized by focused research and development efforts in novel quantum network technologies including quantum repeaters, entanglement sources, photon detectors, and powerful infrastructures with capabilities to test, deploy, and transition to production environments.

© Springer Nature Switzerland AG 2022
J. Nichols et al. (Eds.): SMC 2021, CCIS 1512, pp. 262–279, 2022.
https://doi.org/10.1007/978-3-030-96498-6_15

Practically and fundamentally, *quantum* networking is inextricably tied to *conventional* networking: (i) conventional fiber infrastructure and control-plane technologies are critical to support quantum network deployments, since the construction of a separate quantum infrastructure will likely prove prohibitively expensive; and (ii) all quantum networking protocols require some form of classical communications for their execution. Thus both networking capabilities must operate in concert to realize a successful QI.

In this work, we propose a quantum–conventional network (QCN) harness that enables a quantum network to operate its devices in concert with a conventional network, using a control plane for management and orchestration of services and a data plane as core for quantum information transfer. We describe an implementation of a QCN harness over a state-of-the-art quantum network connecting three quantum laboratories at Oak Ridge National Laboratory (ORNL). We summarize entanglement distribution experiments conducted over its connections provisioned using a wavelength-selective switch (WSS). Our network spanning three buildings uses eight independent entanglement channels (16 wavelengths), in the lowest loss telecommunications band, that are remotely and dynamically reconfigurable. This use case provides a rich scenario to explore the conventional networking needs of a deployed quantum network both in terms of the overall architecture and individual component capabilities and their implementations.

The organization of this paper is as follows. First, we lay out our framework for the network architecture of QCN harness in Sect. 2. Then in Sect. 3, we present a scientific use case that requires QCN control plane to assist the quantum network. Following that, we discuss our prototype network deployment and entanglement distribution experiments in Sect. 4 and lessons learned in Sect. 5. Finally, we conclude in Sect. 6.

2   Generic Quantum-Conventional Network Harness

Software-Defined Networking (SDN) [20] provides a flexible architecture in which the network control and data traffic are separated, and often carried over separate logical or physical planes. In the control plane, configuration signals are distributed from a central unit known as a controller to the network devices, including the routers and switches, to manage the data plane that carries the network traffic. The network devices feature a standardized programming interface for monitoring and forwarding network traffic based on the controller's choices. Because the control and data planes are separated, the management process in SDN networks is modular and streamlined, thereby simplifying network administration and security policy enforcement.

There is a natural separation in quantum networks between the quantum data being handled and the classical control and management signals required for the quantum services, which lends itself to an architecture similar to SDN. Furthermore, quantum networks require many specialized components at present, including nonclassical photon sources and single-photon detectors, that do not readily interface with conventional network components. For greater utilization of these resources, a dynamic network configuration can provide the flexibility needed to establish quantum services between several nodes, enabling the data plane to be reconfigured temporarily to provide a particular service. Moreover, this approach can be used for network segmentation to offer different network services to different network nodes using the same resources. A similar approach is currently being constructed in quantum computing services, where dedicated access to quantum computers is offered on the cloud.

In general, an SDN network consists of three planes: data, control, and application. The **data plane** is the lowest plane and comprises network equipment, including routers and switches (physical and virtual) and access points. Data plane devices are most commonly maintained and accessed via the SDN Control-Data-Plane Interface (CDPI) available in OpenFlow [36] via classically encrypted connections, such as Transport Layer Security (TLS). The **control plane** is the middle plane between the data and application planes, consisting of a group of software-based SDN controllers that enable network forwarding operations via the CDPI. It enables communications between different controllers and the Application-Control-Plane Interfaces (ACPIs). There are two main elements in a controller, which are either functional or logical. The functional component includes coordination and virtualization, and the logical component converts the application's requirements to executable instructions. The **application plane** is the top plane in the SDN architecture, comprising one or more applications that interact with the controllers to make internal decisions via an abstract representation of the network.

Our proposed QCN architecture builds extensively on the principles of SDN, whose well-defined planes not only provide a direct path to establish quantum services within the existing Internet Protocol (IP) infrastructure, but also enable flexible allocation and connection of heterogeneous quantum systems. In particular, the ability to configure the data plane for routing allows us to segment the QCN design and create customized services in the same network. QCNs are expected to be composed of (i) quantum devices such as switches, repeaters, photonic qubit sources, quantum processing or computing systems, and other end-node measurement systems; (ii) quantum links that support communications within and between these devices over local- and wide-area connections; (iii) conventional networking for classical data and control transport; and possibly (iv) classical analog control signals for quantum-device management. From an infrastructure perspective, the QCN data plane is where quantum communications take place. Indeed, the quantum part of the QCN data plane is somewhat akin to the dedicated optical data plane in conventional IP networks [42]. To be effective in U.S. Department of Energy (DOE) science infrastructures, such a quantum data plane must span various geographically distributed sites that house scientific instruments, and also integrate with existing IP networks, including DOE's Energy Science Network (ESnet). Certainly, dedicated data plane connections have been found to be very effective in provisioning high bandwidth optical connections in science environments, for example, OSCARS circuits over

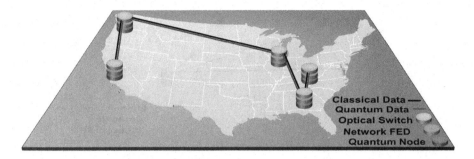

Fig. 1. Conceptual view of a QCN data plane supporting provisioning of conventional and quantum channels. Node locations are illustrative and modeled after USN.

ESnet [37] and dedicated wavelengths over UltraScienceNet (USN) [41]. The control plane design in this paper is based on USN, which implemented a cross-country encrypted control plane using firewalls over a separate IP network, about a decade prior to a full SDN framework development in [20].

QCN solutions for quantum connections for DOE science environments entail solving challenges including the development of control (both conventional digital and analog physical layer) and management planes for quantum devices, as well as scalable frameworks for jointly developing and testing QCN hardware devices and associated software. We address both these areas here by building upon previous DOE projects in high-performance networking for science infrastructures that consist of a small number of sites with stringent bandwidth requirements. In the next few paragraphs, we provide an overview of the data plane, control plane, and application plane designs envisioned for a QCN.

QCN Data Plane: The QCN data plane is expected to be composed of quantum and conventional network devices. Conventional network devices include routers, switches, and firewalls—either physical or virtual as in Palo Alto firewall and encryption devices (FEDs). On the other hand, the quantum part includes all-optical switches, nodes with quantum resources, and (in the future) quantum repeaters, as illustrated in Fig. 1. Its architecture and layered stack are specific to quantum signals and protocols as described in Sect. 3.2. In particular, quantum computing systems may be connected over quantum links to support quantum computations over a distributed quantum computer, and furthermore, they can be directly connected to a storage system comprised of quantum and classical memories. For quantum data transfers, these connections promise inherent security since eavesdropping on quantum channels is precluded by the no-cloning theorem [53]. Further, quantum key distribution (QKD) can be used with one-time-pad encryption to protect *classical* data transfers as well [42]. By integrating computing, communications, and storage devices, a distributed quantum computer, with each function carried out by specialized hardware, may be able to attain performance well beyond that possible with a single quantum computer—not unlike current high-performance computing architectures based on interconnected GPUs and CPUs. Furthermore, the required quantum

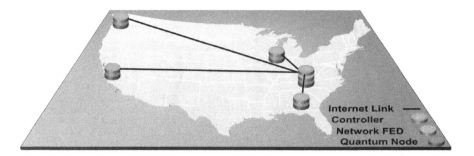

Fig. 2. The QCN control and management plane provides wide-area connections for configuration and management. (Node locations modeled after USN.)

connections between these devices can be established effectively using control plane technologies that exploit the softwarization of quantum devices [40], further described below. In the ultimate case of a continental quantum network, the QCN data plane will consist of repeaters in the core which are connected over fiber paths to other repeaters and end nodes.

QCN Control Plane: As noted above, recent advances in SDN control and management plane technologies [3,25] can be leveraged to provision quantum connections between nodes on demand. In USN specifically, a separate control plane was deployed to configure high-bandwidth optical connections between sites, wherein encrypted tunnels between firewalls carried the control and management traffic. Similar control planes can be developed for quantum networks to protect against cyberattacks while providing the security features of authentication and encryption using FEDs [41] as shown in Fig. 2, ideally secured with quantum keys. This solution requires softwarization wrappers for quantum devices so that they can be managed using SDN technologies over the IP control plane. One such method is based on using Virtual Machines (VMs) to implement an Open vSwitch as a frontend and custom communication channels to a quantum switch such that it can be controlled through OpenFlow. Such a solution for local connections is described in [25]. This approach is applicable to generic quantum connections, and additionally provides security features needed for wide-area deployments using FEDs.

QCN Application Plane: Even though there is not yet widespread quantum network deployment, there are already several proposed quantum applications which rely on network-aware capabilities. For example, quantum-enhanced telescopy [27,28] will need entanglement provisioning for its memories which will be dependent on the image brightness and will have precision timing delay requirements that will vary from other applications. Thus, we propose a quantum application plane on top of the secure control plane for the purpose of providing requests and constraints on the control plane for such applications, similar to conventional SDN where the application layer can request network functionality [1]. In our prototype, we execute a simple bandwidth provisioning application, testing various bandwidth allocation configurations for our network.

In the following sections, we show through example how the QCN structure introduced here can be applied to the use case of entanglement distribution in a deployed QLAN, highlighting the challenges encountered and lessons learned in our initial research.

3   Scientific Use Case

3.1   Entanglement Distribution

One of the most basic quantum networking capabilities is the support of on-demand entanglement between multiple parties. Currently, quantum network implementations can be classified at the logical level into four categories: point-to-point [44], trusted-node [14,17–19,35,38,43,47,50], point-to-multipoint [31, 48], and fully connected [6,26,32,51].

For quantum networks to be practical and useful, they must have nodes that are spatially separated and independent, ideally supporting heterogeneous quantum resources (stationary qubits, detectors, photon sources, etc.). Furthermore, the network architecture needs to be suitable for interconnecting with other network topologies to form larger, more complex networks. Classical networking capabilities, e.g., a control plane for management and a parallel data plane for node-to-node classical communications, will also be needed. Fully connected entanglement networks with dense wavelength-division-multiplexed allocation show promise but have been limited so far to demonstrations where all detection events occur at the same physical site [6,26,32,51]. While an important preliminary step, the time synchronization and data management requirements are, in these cases, excessively simplified: high-quality local connections or fiber loop-backs sidestep difficult issues that arise when detection systems are tied to different local clocks, for example. Our prototype testbed is designed to address the above needs by leveraging the QCN architecture to enable a dynamic, fully connected QLAN with adaptive bandwidth provisioning and simultaneous remote detection.

3.2   Prototype Network Architecture

Our vision for a layered network stack, introduced in [5], is outlined in Fig. 3(a). Drawn from the Transmission Control Protocol/Internet Protocol (TCP/IP) stack [10,12], this network stack includes not only the physical medium and routing but also the protocols and applications which define the node behavior in the network. Our stack specifically leverages spectral multiplexing, so that the physical layer consists of fiber links connected with WSSs. According to the QCN control and QCN data plane distinction described in Sect. 2, this layered stack can be viewed primarily as an elaboration of the quantum part of the QCN data plane that carries quantum signals using quantum protocols; by contrast, the QCN control plane and the conventional part of the QCN data plane follow the conventional TCP/IP stack. Thus in our case, for example, the instructions

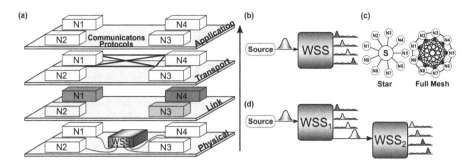

Fig. 3. (a) QCN quantum data plane layers and services. The physical layer includes the optical components where the quantum photons travel and are manipulated, the link layer slices the spectrum and routes each slice to a particular user, the transport layer is the quantum-correlated network where a pair of users shares entanglement, and the application layer uses the entangled pairs to perform a service. (b) Single WSS configuration: the input spectrum is sliced and routed to the output ports. (c) Comparison of physical (star) and logical (fully connected mesh) topologies in network design. (d) Nested WSSs where a portion of the spectrum is routed from the first to the second WSS, thereby expanding the number of nodes connected by the entanglement source [5].

sent to the WSS for configuration fall under the QCN control plane, while the photon detection timestamps are the purview of the conventional networking part of the QCN data plane.

In this architecture, each node/user is directly connected to the WSS by deployed fiber [Fig. 3(b)], corresponding to the star topology in Fig. 3(c). The link layer uses the WSS to partition the bandwidth of the entangled photon source and dynamically route the allocated spectral channels to their assigned user. The transport layer is characterized by a logical fully connected mesh topology shown in Fig. 3(c). In this way, the nonlocal potential of quantum entanglement provides greater flexibility for network topologies beyond restrictions of the physical layer alone. Indeed, as shown here, a star *physical* topology (all N nodes connected to a central source) can result in a fully connected *logical* mesh that gives entanglement connections between all $N(N-1)/2$ user pairs. These logical connections are then used in the application layer for quantum services/protocols between the nodes/users, e.g., QKD, quantum teleportation, and remote state preparation.

In our stack, we have purposely omitted an internet layer for connecting several networks since this is not needed in our single-network testbed to illustrate the QLAN concept. However, building on previous work for quantum access networks [4,16], this architecture could be expanded to include multiple nested WSSs [Fig. 3(d)] for future connectivity between multiple QLANs in larger, more complex networks. Regardless, quantum networks are in their early stages, so any network stack we propose is indeed tentative, with future refinements and modifications expected as development continues.

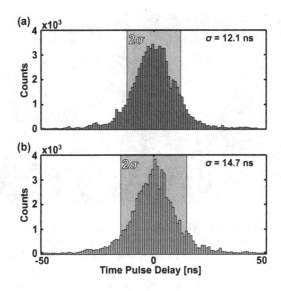

Fig. 4. Histogram of relative delays between time pulses from two GPS receivers [5]. (a) Alice and Bob. (b) Charlie and Alice.

4   Deployed Network

4.1   Time Synchronization

Distributed timing synchronization is crucial for extending tabletop quantum networking experiments to the field. Timing requirements for quantum networks are usually much stricter than for conventional LANs. In particular, the ubiquitous standard for synchronization over ethernet, the precision time protocol (PTP), is designed to attain only sub-μs jitter [2], whereas sub-ns precision is often sought for distributed photon-counting experiments. White Rabbit [33], a major improvement to PTP that uses synchronous ethernet to reach ps-level precision, thus offers considerable promise for future quantum network designs. Alternatively, previous quantum communications experiments have used fully optical approaches to compensate for clock drift between nodes, including direct tracking of pulsed quantum signals [13,24] or photon coincidence peaks [30,39,45,46].

For our QLAN [5], we use synchronization based on the Global Positioning System (GPS) due to its cost-effectiveness, simplicity, and availability (a GPS antenna was already located in one lab). The GPS signals allow us to derive two clocks from our Trimble Thunderbolt E receivers: a 10 MHz tone and a pulse per second (PPS). Multi-hour characterization of the timing jitter for independent receivers returned the histograms shown in Fig. 4. The relative-delay distributions have standard deviations of about 10 ns, which is a significant improvement over PTP.

Fig. 5. Map of QLAN on ORNL campus [5]. The receiver configurations at each node are shown as insets. APD: avalanche photodiode. CW: continuous-wave laser. FPC: fiber polarization controller. FPGA: field-programmable gate array. GPS: Global Positioning System. HWP: half-wave plate. MC: motion controller. Panel: fiber-optic patch panel. BS: beamsplitter. PBS: polarizing beamsplitter. PPLN: periodically poled lithium niobate. PPS: pulse per second. Source: entangled photon source. QWP: quarter-wave plate. RFoF Rx: RF-over-fiber receiver. RFoF Tx: RF-over-fiber transmitter. RPi: Raspberry Pi microprocessor board (to control MCs). SNSPD: superconducting-nanowire single-photon detector. WSS: wavelength-selective switch.

4.2   Experimental Implementation

Our prototype network is set up across three buildings at ORNL, as shown in Fig. 5. The entangled photon source used is a fiber-coupled periodically poled lithium niobate (PPLN) crystal phase-matched for type-II spontaneous parametric down-conversion (SPDC) [5]. The state produced is then split into frequency bands which are distributed to the network users. Using the WSS, we partition 8 pairs of frequency-correlated channels, each having bandwidth $\Delta\omega/2\pi = 25\,\mathrm{GHz}$ and aligned to the International Telecommunication Union (ITU) grid (ITU-T Rec. G.694.1). The channels are centered at $\omega_n = \omega_0 \pm \Delta\omega(n - \frac{1}{2})$ for the signal (idler). These channels span $\sim$3 nm in the C-band (1557.3–1560.5 nm).

Alice and the entangled photon source are within the same lab; meanwhile Bob and Charlie are in separate buildings, each connected to the source through approximately 250 m and 1200 m fiber path lengths, respectively. The WSS connects the entangled photon source and each user by a direct fiber link. The WSS outputs are directed to fiber-based polarization controllers (FPC) for passive polarization drift compensation: Alice's FPC output goes directly to her polarization analyzer, while Bob's and Charlie's connections include inter-building transmission fibers. The polarization analyzers are connected to single-photon detectors; Alice and Charlie are connected to highly efficient (but polarization sensitive) superconducting nanowire detectors and Bob is connected to an InGaAs avalanche photodiode (APD).

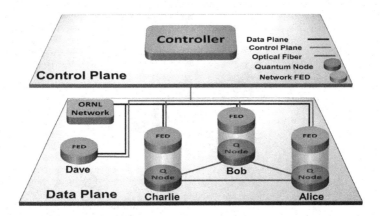

Fig. 6. Overview of the QCN control and data planes for the ORNL QLAN. Commands from the QCN control plane define routing connections for both the ethernet (black lines) and optical (red lines) traffic of the QCN data plane, the former carrying digital information such as timestamps while the latter carries photonic qubits.

Although each user could use their own GPS antenna, it is simpler and cheaper for us to distribute the GPS signal from Bob's location to the other nodes using RF over fiber (RFoF). Using the 10 MHz and 1 Hz (PPS) clocks, we synchronize the FPGA-based time-to-digital converter (TDC) at each node, which bins the photon detection events at 5 ns resolution according to the FPGA's internal 200 MHz clock. This approach is scalable for increasing network size since the resources can be readily duplicated for additional nodes.

To manage the measurement and instrument information flow between nodes, we employ a QCN control plane that establishes encrypted tunnels between the three quantum labs (Alice, Bob, and Charlie). As summarized in Fig. 6, a virtual router in each device enables each node to communicate with the other devices over these QCN data and control planes. QCN conventional control and data planes are implemented using Palo Alto 220 FEDs as shown in Fig. 7, that provide encrypted tunnels between the three quantum labs (Alice, Bob, and Charlie) and the conventional networking node (Dave). Multiple conventional subnets are supported behind each FED, to which devices including instruments, microprocessors, computing systems, and TDCs are connected. In the QCN data plane, photon detection events are time-tagged by the TDCs and then transferred to a central computer at Alice for coincidence counting and analysis. To ensure experimental integrity, it is critical that the conventional communications of the QCN data plane have access to sufficient bandwidth to handle the conventional data needs of the quantum network. For example, our photon counting experiments produce up to about 3 Mb/s of 32-bit timestamps which are handled easily by our ~1 Gb/s conventional data plane.

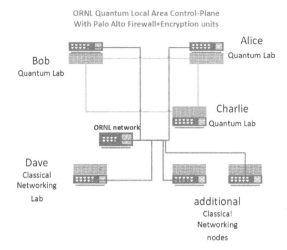

Fig. 7. Implementation of QCN conventional control and data planes using Palo Alto 220 FEDs. Secure tunnels (orange lines) between three quantum labs provide conventional network connectivity to support quantum experiments. Multiple conventional subnets are supported on secure sides of FEDs, which are in turn connected over the secure tunnels. The virtual router and timing exchange devices of quantum nodes are connected to these subnets for control and data conventional communications.

4.3   Bandwidth Allocation

Our eight-channel polarization-entangled photon source allows for a plethora of bandwidth allocations that can be optimized for a desired network configuration. The WSS enables dynamic real-time bandwidth provisioning without changing any fiber connections. Entanglement distribution with this approach was realized recently in a tabletop experiment [32], and here we summarize some of the key results extending this approach to our deployed QLAN [5].

The link efficiencies are highly imbalanced due to different deployed-fiber link loss and heterogeneous detector technology. In decreasing order of combined efficiency are Charlie and Alice (C–A), Alice and Bob (A–B), and Bob and Charlie (B–C). For Allocation 1, we choose to balance entanglement distribution rates as closely as possible, which in our case amounts to assigning the lowest-flux Ch. 8 to C–A, the highest flux Ch. 1 to A–B, and the remaining Ch. 2–7 to B–C. For Allocation 2, we seek to improve the average state fidelity between all channels, which can be degraded due to multipair emission and frequency-dependent polarization transformations. Specifically, we assign Ch. 1–2 to B–C, Ch. 3 to A–B, and Ch. 4 to C–A, which leaves the remaining channels available for future network expansion.

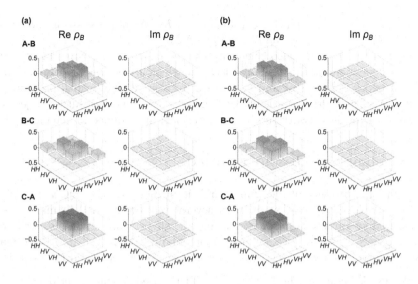

Fig. 8. Density matrices estimated by polarization tomography for each pair of users for (a) Allocation 1 and (b) Allocation 2 [5].

Figure 8 shows results of polarization state tomography for all pairs of users under these allocations, using a 10 ns coincidence window, 60 s integration time, and Bayesian mean estimation [34]. These measurements were conducted with only the logical link being measured passing through the WSS which provides equivalent results to spectrally resolved detection. The state fidelities with respect to the ideal maximally entangled Bell state are shown in Table 1; these data are without accidental coincidence subtraction.

The reconstructed density matrices provide complete information for protocol performance prediction at a per-photon-pair level, but do not offer insight into important aspects such as the rate. Therefore, we consider an "entanglement bandwidth" metric [5], which combines log-negativity $E_{\mathcal{N}}$ [49] and the coincidence rate to provide a measure of the entangled bits (ebits) per second (R_E). This metric, along with the supporting log-negativity, is shown for both

Table 1. Link data for both bandwidth allocations [5].

Alloc.	Link	Ch.	Fidelity	$E_{\mathcal{N}}$ [ebits]	R_E [ebits/s]
1	A–B	1	0.75 ± 0.03	0.70 ± 0.08	56 ± 6
	B–C	2–7	0.55 ± 0.06	0.4 ± 0.2	30 ± 10
	C–A	8	0.90 ± 0.01	0.89 ± 0.03	206 ± 6
2	A–B	3	0.75 ± 0.03	0.70 ± 0.09	57 ± 7
	B–C	1–2	0.69 ± 0.04	0.6 ± 0.1	26 ± 4
	C–A	4	0.84 ± 0.02	0.82 ± 0.05	320 ± 20

bandwidth allocations in Table 1. Fidelity and R_E are not necessarily positively correlated as evidenced by the B–C and C–A links in Allocations 1 and 2 due to the photon flux that R_E also considers. Consequently, optimal bandwidth allocation is dependent on the desired objectives, which are not necessarily known at initial network deployment and are subject to change. Bandwidth provisioning using a WSS provides remarkable flexibility to accommodate future objectives without disrupting network service with physical interconnection changes.

5 Summary of Lessons Learned

Through the process of designing and implementing the QCN paradigm within a deployed QLAN, we learned several important—and in many cases, unanticipated—practical lessons regarding the efficient operation of distributed quantum networks. Here we summarize our findings, classified into three main categories: (i) wired vs. wireless, (ii) timing synchronization, and (iii) security.

Wired vs. Wireless: The FPGA-based TDCs used in this experiment host a minimal operating system (OS) for limited hardware resources and optimization. Often, it is challenging to integrate them with third-party devices, especially if there is no support from the OS kernel or the manufacturer. Admittedly, this leads to unoptimized devices and limited capabilities, and can result in overall device performance that is highly dependent on the available network.

In general, there exist two options for network interfaces to share data between devices: wired via ethernet and wireless over an access point. The wired connection requires a network infrastructure that may not be easy to deploy. Even if a network exists, device OS, model, firmware, and vendors must be approved in the networking policies, which presents unique challenges for research prototypes in particular. The alternative to the wired connection is to set up a wireless access point with greater flexibility and a lower deployment cost. Yet although wireless networking is an attractive solution, we found in practice that its implementation led to unreliable data transfer. The lack of specialized wireless hardware support in the FPGA hardware resulted in a lower transfer rate and loss of timestamps experimentally. Accordingly, we found that the native and widely supported ethernet connection in our TDCs offered greater reliability for data transfer. Importantly, the QCN control plane enables a transparent connection between the network nodes using existing research network infrastructure—without impacting the business network. This advantage of the control plane design was one we did not fully appreciate when we began this project: it allows us to realize the speed of wired ethernet while simultaneously shielding our devices from the management requirements of an enterprise network.

Timing Synchronization: The photon counts collected to validate entanglement between the network nodes require precise timing, which can be subdivided into two categories: nonlocal clock distribution and instruction coordination. The former defines the absolute limits of site-to-site jitter, and was discussed in detail in Sect. 4.1, whereas the latter proves critical for collecting and organizing data—e.g., matching results with corresponding measurement device settings at each location. While much less stringent from the perspective of raw time, we found this latter point to pose interesting challenges distinct from clock distribution.

Instruction timing to start and stop a measurement play a crucial role in the expected quality of the distributed entanglement. Ideal timing helps optimize coincidence counting and reduce the processing time spent comparing out-of-detection window events. In our experiment, we observed issues when network delays prevented a timely arrival of measurement instructions. Because we depend on the GPS PPS to define a specific measurement period, any network delays greater than a second resulted in a discrete shift of timestamps between two locations, which needed to be corrected through additional post-processing. The dedicated links between the nodes provided by the control plane enabled us to send parallel instructions to each pair of nodes using script files which configured the instruments and helped minimize such network-induced offsets in the time records to 1 s or less.

Security: Current security measures in conventional networking devices such as firewalls employ public-key encryption. Because exchanging secret keys over long distances is difficult, a digital certificate or pre-shared secret key is used for initial authentication and encryption. Then, session keys are exchanged using public-key cryptography. While our current QLAN utilizes these principles for securing the control plane firewalls, a more secure system can be implemented by utilizing secret keys pulled from QKD. It is possible to configure the control plane firewall to utilize external symmetric keys for encryption and authentication within the same network infrastructure. Upgrading our QLAN to full-QKD security thus forms a major goal of future work to ensure the long-term integrity of all classical information on the QCN.

6 Conclusion

We have proposed a method to enable a quantum network to operate its devices in concert with a conventional network, showing how this QCN harness was able to support reconfigurable entanglement distribution in our prototype network. The QCN control plane harmonizes the network by configuring devices on-demand including end-to-end data transfer, thus maximizing utilization of available quantum resources. Multiple controllers in future designs will be essential to manage different and specialized services analogous to commercial quantum computing services on the cloud. Future work involves assessing and integrating additional synchronization and timing requirements of control-plane QI devices and deployments.

We note that the polarization entanglement used in our prototype is well suited for quantum networks, especially ones with short and environmentally protected fibers that minimally disturb the quantum state over time. Even submarine fibers show enough stability for polarization encoding to be used successfully over ∼100 km without active compensation [52]. Finally, it should be possible to extend our work to a larger, more complex network of networks, by subdividing the biphoton spectrum and sending different parts to several WSSs [5].

Acknowledgments. This research used resources of the Oak Ridge Leadership Computing Facility at the Oak Ridge National Laboratory, which is supported by the Office of Science of the U.S. Department of Energy under Contract No. DE-AC05-00OR22725. This research is supported by the U.S. Department of Energy, Office of Science, Office of Advanced Scientific Computing Research, through the Early Career Research Program and Transparent Optical Quantum Networks for Distributed Science Program (Field Work Proposals ERKJ353 and ERKJ355).

References

1. Open Newtorking Foundation. SDN Architecture Overview (2013). https:// opennetworking.org/wp-content/uploads/2013/02/SDN-architecture-overview-1. 0.pdf
2. IEEE-SA Standards Board. IEEE Standard for a Precision Clock Synchronization Protocol for Networked Measurement and Control Systems. IEEE Std 1588-2008 (2008). https://standards.ieee.org/ieee/1588/4355/
3. Aguado, A., López, V., Brito, J.P., Pastor, A., López, D.R., Martin, V.: Enabling quantum key distribution networks via software-defined networking. In: 2020 International Conference on Optical Network Design and Modeling (ONDM), pp. 1–5. IEEE (2020). https://doi.org/10.23919/ONDM48393.2020.9133024
4. Alshowkan, M., Elleithy, K.: Quantum entanglement distribution for secret key establishment in metropolitan optical networks. IEEE International Conference on Networking, Architecture and Storage, pp. 1–8 (2016). https://doi.org/10.1109/ NAS.2016.7549416
5. Alshowkan, M., et al.: Reconfigurable quantum local area network over deployed fiber. PRX Quantum **2**, 040304 (2021). https://doi.org/10.1103/PRXQuantum.2. 040304
6. Appas, F., et al.: Flexible entanglement-distribution network with an ALGaAs chip for secure communications. npj Quantum Inf. **7**, 118 (2021). https://doi.org/10. 1038/s41534-021-00454-7
7. Barz, S., Kashefi, E., Broadbent, A., Fitzsimons, J.F., Zeilinger, A., Walther, P.: Demonstration of blind quantum computing. Science **335**(6066), 303–308 (2012). https://doi.org/10.1126/science.1214707
8. Bennett, C.H., Brassard, G.: Quantum cryptography: public key distribution and coin tossing. Theor. Comput. Sci. **560**, 7–11 (2014). https://doi.org/10.1016/j.tcs. 2014.05.025
9. Bollinger, J.J., Itano, W.M., Wineland, D.J., Heinzen, D.J.: Optimal frequency measurements with maximally correlated states. Phys. Rev. A **54**, R4649–R4652 (1996). https://doi.org/10.1103/PhysRevA.54.R4649
10. Braden, R.: Requirements for internet hosts - communication layers. RFC 1122 (1989). https://datatracker.ietf.org/doc/html/rfc1122
11. Broadbent, A., Fitzsimons, J., Kashefi, E.: Universal blind quantum computation. In: Proceedings of the 50th Annual IEEE Symposium on Foundations of Computer Science, pp. 517–526 (2009). https://doi.org/10.1109/focs.2009.36

12. Cerf, V., Kahn, R.: A protocol for packet network intercommunication. IEEE Trans. Commun. **22**(5), 637–648 (1974). https://doi.org/10.1109/TCOM.1974.1092259

13. Chapuran, T.E., et al.: Optical networking for quantum key distribution and quantum communications. New J. Phys. **11**(10), 105001 (2009). https://doi.org/10.1088/1367-2630/11/10/105001

14. Chen, T.Y., et al.: Metropolitan all-pass and inter-city quantum communication network. Opt. Express **18**(26), 27217–27225 (2010). https://doi.org/10.1364/OE.18.027217

15. Cirac, J.I., Ekert, A.K., Huelga, S.F., Macchiavello, C.: Distributed quantum computation over noisy channels. Phys. Rev. A **59**, 4249–4254 (1999). https://doi.org/10.1103/PhysRevA.59.4249

16. Ciurana, A., Martin, V., Martinez-Mateo, J., Schrenk, B., Peev, M., Poppe, A.: Entanglement distribution in optical networks. IEEE J. Sel. Top. Quantum Electron. **21**(3), 37–48 (2015). https://doi.org/10.1109/JSTQE.2014.2367241

17. Dynes, J.F., et al.: Cambridge quantum network. npj Quantum Inf. **5**(1), 101 (2019). https://doi.org/10.1038/s41534-019-0221-4

18. Elliott, C.: Building the quantum network. New J. Phys. **4**, 46 (2002). https://doi.org/10.1088/1367-2630/4/1/346

19. Evans, P., et al.: Demonstration of a quantum key distribution trusted node on an electric utility fiber network. In: IEEE Photonics Conference, p. 8908470 (2019). https://doi.org/10.1109/ipcon.2019.8908470

20. Feamster, N., Rexford, J., Zegura, E.: The road to SDN. ACM SIGCOMM Comp. Commun. Rev. **44**(2), 87–98 (2014). https://doi.org/10.1145/2602204.2602219

21. Giovannetti, V.: Quantum-enhanced measurements: beating the standard quantum limit. Science **306**(5700), 1330–1336 (2004). https://doi.org/10.1126/science.1104149

22. Giovannetti, V., Lloyd, S., Maccone, L.: Advances in quantum metrology. Nat. Photon. **5**(4), 222–229 (2011). https://doi.org/10.1038/nphoton.2011.35

23. Gisin, N., Thew, R.: Quantum communication. Nat. Photon. **1**(3), 165–171 (2007). https://doi.org/10.1038/nphoton.2007.22

24. Hughes, R.J., et al.: A quantum key distribution system for optical fiber networks. Proc. SPIE **5893**, 589301 (2005). https://doi.org/10.1117/12.615594

25. Humble, T.S., Sadlier, R.J., Williams, B.P., Prout, R.C.: Software-defined quantum network switching. Proc. SPIE **10652**, 72–79 (2018). https://doi.org/10.1117/12.2303800

26. Joshi, S.K.: A trusted node–free eight-user metropolitan quantum communication network. Sci. Adv. **6**(36), eaba0959 (2020). https://doi.org/10.1126/sciadv.aba0959

27. Khabiboulline, E.T., Borregaard, J., De Greve, K., Lukin, M.D.: Optical interferometry with quantum networks. Phys. Rev. Lett. **123**(7), 070504 (2019). https://doi.org/10.1103/PhysRevLett.123.070504

28. Khabiboulline, E.T., Borregaard, J., De Greve, K., Lukin, M.D.: Quantum-assisted telescope arrays. Phys. Rev. A **100**(2), 022316 (2019). https://doi.org/10.1103/PhysRevA.100.022316

29. Kimble, H.J.: The quantum internet. Nature **453**(7198), 1023–1030 (2008). https://doi.org/10.1038/nature07127

30. Krenn, M., Handsteiner, J., Fink, M., Fickler, R., Zeilinger, A.: Twisted photon entanglement through turbulent air across Vienna. PNAS **112**(46), 14197–14201 (2015). https://doi.org/10.1073/pnas.1517574112

31. Lim, H.C., Yoshizawa, A., Tsuchida, H., Kikuchi, K.: Wavelength-multiplexed distribution of highly entangled photon-pairs over optical fiber. Opt. Express **16**(26), 22099 (2008). https://doi.org/10.1364/oe.16.022099

32. Lingaraju, N.B., Lu, H.H., Seshadri, S., Leaird, D.E., Weiner, A.M., Lukens, J.M.: Adaptive bandwidth management for entanglement distribution in quantum networks. Optica **8**(3), 329–332 (2021). https://doi.org/10.1364/OPTICA.413657

33. Lipiński, M., Włostowski, T., Serrano, J., Alvarez, P.: White rabbit: a PTP application for robust sub-nanosecond synchronization. In: IEEE International Symposium on Precision Clock Synchronization for Measurement, Control and Communication, pp. 25–30 (2011). https://doi.org/10.1109/ISPCS.2011.6070148

34. Lukens, J.M., Law, K.J.H., Jasra, A., Lougovski, P.: A practical and efficient approach for Bayesian quantum state estimation. New J. Phys. **22**(6), 063038 (2020). https://doi.org/10.1088/1367-2630/ab8efa

35. Mao, Y., et al.: Integrating quantum key distribution with classical communications in backbone fiber network. Opt. Express **26**(5), 6010 (2018). https://doi.org/10.1364/oe.26.006010

36. McKeown, N., et al.: OpenFlow. ACM SIGCOMM Comput. Commun. Rev. **38**(2), 69–74 (2008). https://doi.org/10.1145/1355734.1355746

37. On-demand secure circuits and advance reservation system (OSCARS). http://www.es.net/oscars

38. Peev, M., et al.: The SECOQC quantum key distribution network in Vienna. New J. Phys. **11**(7), 075001 (2009). https://doi.org/10.1088/1367-2630/11/7/075001

39. Peloso, M.P., Gerhardt, I., Ho, C., Lamas-Linares, A., Kurtsiefer, C.: Daylight operation of a free space, entanglement-based quantum key distribution system. New J. Phys. **11**(4), 045007 (2009). https://doi.org/10.1088/1367-2630/11/4/045007

40. Rao, N.S.V., Humble, T.: Control plane and virtualized development environment for softwarized quantum networks. In: DOE ASCR Quantum Networks for Open Science Workshop (2018). https://www.osti.gov/biblio/1468059

41. Rao, N., Wing, W., Carter, S., Wu, Q.: Ultrascience net: network testbed for large-scale science applications. IEEE Commun. Mag. **43**(11), S12–S17 (2005). https://doi.org/10.1109/MCOM.2005.1541694

42. Runser, R.J., et al.: Progress toward quantum communications networks: opportunities and challenges. Proc. SPIE **6476**, 147–161 (2007). https://doi.org/10.1117/12.708669

43. Sasaki, M., et al.: Field test of quantum key distribution in the Tokyo QKD network. Opt. Express **19**(11), 10387–10409 (2011). https://doi.org/10.1364/OE.19.010387

44. Scarani, V., Bechmann-Pasquinucci, H., Cerf, N.J., Dušek, M., Lütkenhaus, N., Peev, M.: The security of practical quantum key distribution. Rev. Mod. Phys. **81**, 1301–1350 (2009). https://doi.org/10.1103/RevModPhys.81.1301

45. Shi, Y., Moe Thar, S., Poh, H.S., Grieve, J.A., Kurtsiefer, C., Ling, A.: Stable polarization entanglement based quantum key distribution over a deployed metropolitan fiber. Appl. Phys. Lett. **117**(12), 124002 (2020). https://doi.org/10.1063/5.0021755

46. Steinlechner, F., et al.: Distribution of high-dimensional entanglement via an intra-city free-space link. Nat. Commun. **8**(1), 15971 (2017). https://doi.org/10.1038/ncomms15971

47. Stucki, D., et al.: Long-term performance of the SwissQuantum quantum key distribution network in a field environment. New J. Phys. **13**(12), 123001 (2011). https://doi.org/10.1088/1367-2630/13/12/123001

48. Townsend, P.D.: Quantum cryptography on multiuser optical fibre networks. Nature **385**(6611), 47–49 (1997). https://doi.org/10.1038/385047a0

49. Vidal, G., Werner, R.F.: Computable measure of entanglement. Phys. Rev. A **65**, 032314 (2002). https://doi.org/10.1103/PhysRevA.65.032314

50. Wang, S., et al.: Field and long-term demonstration of a wide area quantum key distribution network. Opt. Express **22**(18), 21739–21756 (2014). https://doi.org/10.1364/OE.22.021739

51. Wengerowsky, S., Joshi, S.K., Steinlechner, F., Hubel, H., Ursin, R.: An entanglement-based wavelength-multiplexed quantum communication network. Nature **564**(7735), 225–228 (2018). https://doi.org/10.1038/s41586-018-0766-y

52. Wengerowsky, S., et al.: Entanglement distribution over a 96-km-long submarine optical fiber. PNAS **116**(14), 6684–6688 (2019). https://doi.org/10.1073/pnas.1818752116

53. Wootters, W.K., Zurek, W.H.: A single quantum cannot be cloned. Nature **299**(5886), 802–803 (1982). https://doi.org/10.1038/299802a0

Use It or Lose It: Cheap Compute Everywhere

Taylor Groves[(✉)], Damian Hazen, Glenn Lockwood, and Nicholas J. Wright

Lawrence Berkeley National Laboratory, NERSC, Berkeley, USA
{tgroves,dhazen,glock,njwright}@lbl.gov

Abstract. Moore's Law is tapering off, but FLOPS per dollar continues to grow. Inexpensive CPUs are emerging everywhere from network to storage as an effective way of managing and deploying hardware and firmware as well as providing services close to the data path. Examples of this include ARM cores within Mellanox Bluefield, Broadcom Stingray DPUs, switches, and compute in storage. This additional processing power can be useful for (1) enabling higher throughput, (2) decreasing or hiding latency, (3) increasing power/cost efficiency, (4) alleviating contention for oversubscribed resources. In order to make these additional resources available to a wide range of services and applications we must first develop: (1) an understanding of the strengths and weaknesses of the hardware, (2) an understanding of how portions of a workload might be decomposed into tasks for offload, (3) abstractions to allow code portability on the heterogeneous components. We take a look at existing hardware trends through a survey of existing and original work to examine how new compute-in-network show promise, where they fall short and how HPC might evolve to take advantage of them.

Keywords: Data processing unit · Smart NIC · Infrastructure Processing Unit · Compute-in-network

1 Introduction

Facilities deploy high-end systems for a variety of reasons, including (1) faster time to solution, (2) higher-precision support (3) better power efficiency (4) difficulty of problem decomposition (as seen in the ML landscape) and (5) achieving unprecedented simulation scale. Given the coming ubiquity of cheap computational resources,

---

This manuscript has been authored by an author at Lawrence Berkeley National Laboratory under Contract No. DE-AC02-05CH11231 with the U.S. Department of Energy. The U.S. Government retains, and the publisher, by accepting the article for publication, acknowledges, that the U.S. Government retains a non-exclusive, paid-up, irrevocable, world-wide license to publish or reproduce the published form of this manuscript, or allow others to do so, for U.S. Government purposes.

© Springer Nature Switzerland AG 2022
J. Nichols et al. (Eds.): SMC 2021, CCIS 1512, pp. 280–298, 2022.
https://doi.org/10.1007/978-3-030-96498-6_16

the question naturally arises - how can ancillary services and infrastructure be profitably offloaded to these compute resources?

Over the last 10 years compute power has continued to become more affordable. The cost of a transistor and FLOPS per dollar have continued to decrease in recent years. However, at any point in time there is a range of performance per dollar that can be obtained. At one end, high-end (premium) hardware offers greater density, additional I/O connectivity and more sophisticated error correction, albeit at a higher price. On the other end of the spectrum, lower-end (freemium) components provide moderate computation at a value price point. And while they may not have all of the features of the high-end parts (e.g. increased failure rates, decreased memory capacity, or reduced precision) we are seeing a proliferation of these compute resources scattered throughout HPC systems, including in networking and storage.

Traditionally, everything was run on a homogeneous CPU system. As Moore's Law slowed down, and Dennard scaling ended, this was followed by systems that offloaded portions of codes to accelerators like GPUs. The next logical step is to push the code and software that can effectively use them onto these lower performance components. This will leave the premium hardware to the applications and software that can leverage the most benefit.

In this paper we begin by reviewing the current landscape providing background and further comparing the qualities of premium vs. freemium components. We begin with a focus on Data Processing Units (DPUs)[1] and how cheap compute is creating new opportunities. We discuss hardware design points, uses of the hardware, the perceived strengths and weaknesses as well as open challenges. We follow this with a brief discussion of the memory market and potential solutions for addressing the growing cost of system memory. Last, we summarize how cheap compute everywhere may alter the HPC landscape as we must orchestrate distributed heterogeneous resources for complex workflows.

2 Motivation

2.1 Premium and Freemium

In today's hardware landscape there is often a breadth of choice when it comes to balancing power, density, performance and cost. More capable processor SKUs command a premium, but typically don't provide the most efficient value in $/FLOP. In some cases the lower-end (or freemium) components may have started as premium components that encountered a defect in manufacturing. The manufacturers then disable the defective portions of the unit and sell the remainder at a discount. Customers that purchase these models are, in effect, riding on the coat tails of the customers purchasing premium SKUs. In other examples we see how economies of scale (such as the cell phone and gaming market) have led to massive increases in performance per dollar. We see these price-to-performance gaps across both GPU and CPU architectures.

---

[1] DPU, Smart NIC, and IPU are used interchangeably.

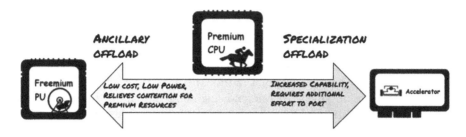

Fig. 1. In the spectrum of offload, HPC has pivoted towards specialization offload such as GPUs to provide additional capability to a subset of the workloads. Moving in the opposite direction is the possibility of ancillary offload which isolates performance critical workloads from those that could run on less capable hardware.

The price premium for top-tier performance provides motivation for offloading ancillary software and infrastructure. If we can offload these workloads, the remaining code running on the premium hardware benefits by reducing contention for shared resources. An ancillary offload makes sense, when the workload is either (1) not in the critical performance path or (2) does not make use of premium hardware capabilities (e.g. 64 bit precision, or vector and tensor units). This ancillary offload may be on the same CPU as the Premium CPU (e.g. big.LITTLE) or distributed more broadly, such as on a NIC. The benefit of having the ancillary services on the same CPU is tighter coupling. The downside is that this takes up chip area on the high density premium CPU and there are challenges of having multiple clock and power domains within an integrated circuit (Fig. 1).

2.2   Data Movement

Another reason to distribute cheap compute throughout the system is to reduce the cost of data movement, which can improve both throughput and latency [56]. Placing computation throughout the data path reduces the need for additional transfers and hops across the network and through complex memory hierarchies, resulting in improved latency. By placing the compute next to the data we may be able to take advantage of higher throughput links while reducing the load on shared network resources.

Though, just because the compute is closer physically to the data does not guarantee it will achieve improved performance. Even if positioned closer to the data, low power, cheap cores running a full OS may not be able to provide enough processing power to facilitate increased throughput and lower latency. From a throughput perspective, a single core does not have enough cycles to keep up with 100, 200, 400 Gbps or greater network speeds we are seeing in HPC [19,38]. Because of the deep memory hierarchy on the host CPU, it would take many cores to saturate the NIC peak message rate (IB HDR is 5 ns per message). Figure 2 illustrates how a single Broadwell core is unable to come close to saturating the Mellanox EDR 100 GBps NIC. Furthermore the lower power

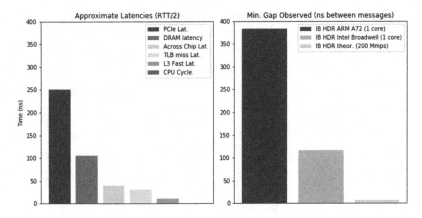

Fig. 2. Approximate latencies (half round trip) for different interconnects and memory alongside the time (gap) between sending consecutive messages over an Infiniband network with different CPUs. Latency values are approximates from [8,45]. Best case gap was recorded for single core ib_write_bw tests using Arm A72 and Intel Broadwell E5-2697A CPUs connected to an IB HDR NIC.

and cheaper A72 incurs an additional delay of around 250 ns per message. The penalty of using lightweight cores may not provide a data locality benefit since link latency is approximately 5 ns per meter of fiber plus an additional 100–200 ns per switch. For this reason, many approaches targeting throughput and latency improvements are built around lightweight and specialized line-rate offload [27].

However, offload hardware need not be devoted entirely to line rate processing. Cheap cores may be part of a data pipeline in DPUs that allows for variable performance offload as seen in work by Lin et al. [35]. In their design, separate paths in the switching fabric of the NIC allow for line rate traffic to proceed through a lightweight reconfigurable match table. Depending on the match/action, traffic may (1) forwarded directly out the NIC or (2) proceed to a buffer and scheduling unit where more complex and potentially non-line rate offload chains may be composed on the NIC. Additionally, if we look at current trends for hardware such as the Mellanox Bluefield [46], Xilinx Alveo [60] and Broadcom Stingray [14] series DPUs, we see that there is a set of inexpensive Arm cores on the NIC (ancillary offload) as well as a set of accelerator units (e.g. compression, encryption, regular expression engines or FPGAs) which provide specialization offload.

In summary, the benefits of reduced data movement can provide a benefit as both (1) a direct performance benefit by reducing latencies and providing greater throughput and (2) indirect performance benefit by reducing contention for shared network resources. In some cases it may create opportunities for performance gains, but the other benefit is from freeing premium resources.

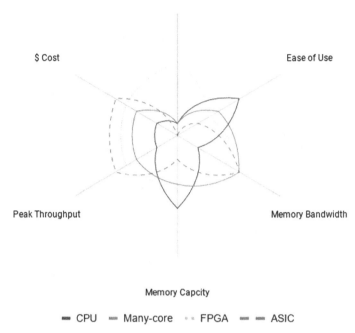

Hardware Reconfigurability

$ Cost

Ease of Use

Peak Throughput

Memory Bandwidth

Memory Capcity

— CPU   — Many-core   ·· FPGA   — — ASIC

Fig. 3. Summary of different strengths and weaknesses of varied DPU architectures.

3 Hardware Design Points

NICs began as a card to provide a connection between the computer and an external network. Historically, a substantial amount of network processing was done on the host CPU, but over time more functionality shifted onto the NIC, such as protocol offload [51], Remote Direct Memory Access (RDMA) and programmable match and action engines [28]. Smart NICs have been a part of the HPC vocabulary for over twenty years [18,51], but recently there has been a revival of interest in the topic with Smart NIC, or in vogue data processing units (DPU) and Infrastructure Processing Unit (IPU), being announced by a variety of vendors and hyperscalers. While many of these cards include a mixture of CPU, many-core, Field Programmable Gate Array (FPGA) or Application Specific Integrated Circuit (ASIC) components we must understand the strengths and weaknesses of each approach.

In Fig. 3 we map the attributes of FPGA, CPU, many-core and ASIC hardware used in DPUs to their strengths and weaknesses. We provide rough guidelines regarding Peak Throughput, Memory Bandwidth, Ease of Use, Cost (in terms of hardware and design time), and Hardware Reconfigurability.

3.1   FPGA

A large proportion of DPUs rely on line-rate packet processing with fast turn around times using FPGAs [15,17,19,30,43,59,60]. This class of hardware expanded on traditional Smart NIC use cases offloading hypervisor functionality, multi-tenant Software Defined Networking (SDN), and application-specific functionality such as portions of a web search engine [53]. The strengths of these architectures are focused around high peak throughput, hardware reconfigurability and memory bandwidth. The downsides of this these cards are the absolute cost (though they may provide good performance per dollar value), the DRAM memory capacity and ease of use.

FPGAs are a common architectural choice for processing packets at line rate. This is accomplished by allowing developers to construct application-specific assembly lines that can fully leverage pipelining and parallelism inherent to a particular workload. This contrasts with a CPU where data moves between deep memory hierarchies and stalls incurred are hidden by pipelining and scheduling. FPGAs have a large amount of extremely fast SRAM. As a reference point, the Xilinx Alveo U250 targets memory bandwidth-bound code and features 38 TB/s of internal SRAM bandwidth (54 MB capacity).

Regarding ease of use, these cards require a significant investment in software and programming, but have a faster development cycle than an ASIC. These approaches target specialization offload but have an emphasis on use cases that require iterative hardware design and deployment.

3.2   Many-Core

Other approaches utilize a mixture of many packet and flow processing cores combined with specialized hardware blocks to perform processing for a variety of different network and data-centric flows [23,44]. By leveraging many cores these platforms provide good peak throughput, but the hardware is not reconfigurable. These approaches still target line-rate processing, but may focus on a subset of targeted use cases (e.g. disaggregated storage platform [24]). As a reference point, the Fungible F1 DPU [23] is divided into multiple data cluster of 200 threads with full cache coherency. All of this is connected to a scheduling block, network units and host units by an on chip network. Again, there is a higher absolute cost than cheap CPUs, though the performance per dollar can be great if the application can leverage the parallelism of the architecture. Memory bandwidth is often favored in lieu of memory capacity. For this reason, these approaches typically target specialization offload.

One of the challenges of building out a many-core approach is the on-chip network that ties it all together. As the number of cores and endpoints increases, it becomes increasingly difficult to scale a non-blocking full bisection network that can facilitate line rate processing on the chip [19,35]. Another challenge of many-core architectures is extracting sufficient parallelism from the workload to fully leverage collections of threads in a SIMD architecture.

3.3 Cheap CPUs

A third class of DPUs [14,39,46,50] combine general purpose, but relatively weak, inexpensive and low power Arm cores with network and storage centric acceleration blocks. These often run a Linux operating system. In the Blue-field [46] architecture these CPUs are connected to the NIC over a PCIe switch that treats the CPU the same as the host CPU, while in other cases the CPU is more tightly integrated [50]. The benefits of these CPUs are that they are extremely cheap and easy to integrate. This means that they are commonly added to other varieties of FPGA DPUs [60] to handle exceptions, errors and non-conventional control plane functions. However, this style of CPU provides lower throughput than alternatives [36] and they may need to provide greater memory capacity for data buffering and storage with relatively modest memory bandwidth compared to many-core and FGPA architectures. **This third class of NIC is the optimal choice for ancillary offload, since they provide a minimal of specialized and costly resources.**

3.4 ASICs and ASIC-Hybrid

Throughout all of these design points are many heterogenous ASIC components such as encryption, compression and regular expression engines. These are specialized hardware units that provide excellent performance and value but only for a subset of fixed functionality. The fixed function blocks are designed around static workloads that don't change frequently. To create a good value proposition the speedups of an ASIC must offset one-time design and verification costs (both time and money). It is likely that many DPU architectures will take a hybrid approach combining ASICs for well understood, slow-to-change acceleration and flexible, lightweight cores or FPGAs for rapidly evolving use cases.

4 Target Market and Use Cases

4.1 Opportunities Better Suited for Specialization Offload

Protocol Offload, Load Balancing, Security and Encryption: Things that used to be considered *smart* such as TCP/IP acceleration and virtualization offload (e.g. SR-IOV) are now commonplace in NICs. Newer Smart NICs have expanded the role of what is offloaded and added additional functionality for networks and packet processing [9,31,32,51]. This may include things such as RDMA protocol acceleration, traffic monitoring, programmable match+action engines and HPC targeted protocol offload such as MPI tag-matching.

Virtualization Offload and Multi-tenancy: Hyperscalers have embraced DPU solutions to free up premium CPU cores on the host for applications and customers. Publicly announced platforms include Microsoft Catapult [19], Amazon Web Services Nitro [10], and Alibaba X-Dragon [16]. On these platforms there is an emphasis on providing as close to bare metal performance, while enabling the efficiency, security and flexibility that virtualization offers. Offload challenges here include scheduling [57], multi-tenant QoS [54], and security [10]. All of these have an emphasis on line rate processing and a majority of them rely on FPGAs for implementation/prototyping, this is because the lightweight hypervisor being offloaded is in the critical path for accessing resources and application performance.

The initial work using FPGAs at Microsoft for the Catapult Project was motivated primarily by finding alternative pathways to performance in light of the slowdown of Moore's Law. In the Catapult work [53], the authors chose FPGAs to provide a layer of computation to accelerate a search ranking engine between the host CPU and the network. FPGAs were selected because they could provide price/performance benefits in latency and throughput at line rate, while being reconfigurable as the datacenter workloads evolved. In later work, FPGAs were used to both offload and accelerate the software defined networking (SDN) that ran on the host hypervisor [19]. For Microsoft the deployment of FPGAs makes sense, given the fleet of more than a million nodes, the development cost is easily amortized. However the HPC environment has different economies. Top HPC centers have significantly lower node counts and rather than focusing on a small number of workloads (such as search) our centers contain thousands of unique workloads with application developers running on bare-metal systems.

Virtualization and resource isolation has not been a focus in the HPC space because workloads are designed to run across multiple nodes and utilize the full node for each node allocated. However machine learning is pushing node sizes bigger, with more GPUs and resources tied up in a single node. The economics of this have bled into many recent HPC designs which now feature nodes with fatter architectures. As future systems grow even larger and more heterogeneous, we may need to leverage multi-tenancy techniques similar to cloud providers, but it is unlikely to be a job suited for cheap cores and ancillary offload.

4.2 Opportunities for Ancillary Offload

Compared to cases leveraging specialization offload, relatively little work has been done to motivate ancillary offload on the DPU. However there are several areas where DPUs have found success by being able to alleviate pressure for host resources.

Key Value Stores: In work by Liu et al. [38] a range of microservices were evaluated comparing, the Marvell CN78XX DPU with 12 MIPS cores, against more powerful host based CPUs. The work showed that complicated workloads performed poorly on the DPU, but was unique in that it highlighted the potential energy savings cheap DPU cores could provide. One of the microservices the DPU provided greater energy efficiency for was key value stores. Key value stores are fundamentally (1) a hash evaluation which provides a memory location and (2) a memory access to read/write or perform atomics on the data, both of which can be adequately handled by cheap cores. In work by [36] using the *stress-ng* benchmark, memory focused benchmarks such as mcontend performed better on Bluefield Arm cores than compared to a range of host CPUs. In work by Phothilimthana et al. [52], a DPU was used as a write-back cache for a host-based key-value store (KVS) and observed a 28–60% performance improvement. By offloading to portions of a KVS, host applications may experience less pollution of the cache due to network-induced memory contention [25]. Despite the benefits, a challenge of utilizing the DPU as a cache is maintaining a consistent state between the data that resides on the DPU and host memory.

Simple Analytics: A number of simple analytics functions can be implemented on a DPU where a powerful host CPU would otherwise be overkill. These include things like K-nearest neighbor, and Spike [38], or portions of the Apache Storm [21] like multiplexing and demultiplexing operations. In the case of the latter, a 76% improvement was observed when multiplexing and demultiplexing was offloaded to the DPU compared to running the workload entirely on the host CPU [52]. In cases where analytics are sufficiently independent of host workloads, such that they can tolerate the extra hop over PCIe or network interfaces, cheap compute on DPUs can be leveraged successfully. If the DPU processor and host memory could be more tightly coupled, additional avenues for analytics would be possible as often the penalty for moving memory across PCIe is several times greater than local memory accesses (as shown in Fig. 2).

Communication and Computation Overlap: A third avenue for ancillary offload is providing communication and computation overlap by leveraging cheap cores on DPUs to manage complex communications on the host's behalf. In work by Bayatpour et al. [11], non-blocking all-to-all collectives are delegated to Arm cores on the Bluefield 2 DPU. In this model the host simply provides metadata information about the collective to threads on the DPU. These threads then read and write host memory using Remote Direct Memory Addressing (RDMA) to complete the iterations of the all-to-all algorithm. Because of the extra latency incurred transferring data to and from host memory to DPU cores this approach focused on message sizes greater than 16KiB. In this range, four A72 Arm cores were able to deliver performance similar to that of the host CPU. However, the real benefit of this approach is that the all-to-all operation is offloaded and the host is left able to focus on other more demanding work.

Node-Local IO Virtualization. The proliferation of AI and other non-traditional I/O workloads on HPC systems has resulted in a tension in storage systems design between traditional parallel file systems and node-local storage. Node-local NVMe (Non-volatile Memory Express) has been shown to dramatically accelerate some workloads by localizing metadata-intensive and high-frequency accesses to the PCIe data paths within nodes, sparing the global network and parallel file system from disruption that would otherwise adversely affect other users of those shared network and file system resources. Not every HPC workload can use node-local storage because they collectively lack the coherence required by shared-file I/O. As a result, the decision of whether to provision hinges on balancing the cost of adding new components to every compute node against the fact that those components may be poorly utilized.

NVMe over Fabrics (NVMeoF) allows compute nodes to mount NVMe devices over the network, offering the benefits of localizing many expensive metadata and high-frequency I/O operations to a compute node by fully delegating namespace coherence and I/O buffering to each compute node. Using NVMeoF, it is possible to provision only a subset of nodes with node-local NVMe, and letting any node "borrow" an unused NVMe drive from a neighboring compute node on-demand. As such, systems designers can provision only a subset of compute nodes with NVMe drives to keep costs commensurate with utilization but still achieve the effect of any compute node having a node-local NVMe when needed.

The biggest challenge with this disaggregated NVMeoF model is that the node "loaning" its NVMe to another node still has to service interrupts triggered by NVMeoF activity, and its memory bandwidth must be shared between its local computational workload and the I/O workload targeting its loaned NVMe drive. SNAP [42] holds promise to break this tradeoff by allowing the entire NVMeoF stack to run entirely on the loaner node NIC, fully shielding the host from interrupts and memory contention associated with serving up NVMeoF. A borrower node uses the NVMe drive loaned by a DPU, and the "loaner" node can be completely unaffected by I/O targeting its physically local NVMe and compute its local workload without interruption.

Machine Learning Inference: By sitting on the network data path, DPUs provide an opportunity for deploying ML inference at the edge. A typical inference workload will load relevant features of the data, apply the weights of the model and then perform multiply-accumulate operations on the result. Many neural networks may only need 8 bit precision compared to 64 bit precision of many scientific workloads. This means that the host CPU is mismatched with the workload. A standalone GPU may provide much greater efficiency than the host CPU, but may be overkill for modest inference workloads. The standalone GPU often contains a large volume of costly on-package memory that is critical for training but less for inference. In this scenario having a less powerful GPU on the DPU may provide an opportunity for ancillary offload and leave premium GPU resources for more intensive workloads. Nvidia has recently announced the Bluefield-X [6] line of DPUs which include an A100 GPU integrated into the DPU. While this is a premium GPU it may make sense to explore future offerings with less power-hungry GPUs – similar to the approach taken with Nvidia Jetson [7]. Other companies may begin to incorporate functionality of the ARM Ethos NPUs [1] into their DPU. This is an exciting area to look forward to in the future of DPUs.

Specialization offload often receives most of the attention when researchers evaluate the benefits of DPUs. However, given the premium paid for HPC systems and the proliferation of cheap CPUs appearing on NICs we believe ancillary offload deserves greater consideration. However, in order to accelerate this development there are open questions that must be addressed.

5   Open Questions

5.1   Balancing Power, Performance and Cost

One such question is, how powerful a CPU should reside on the DPU? Current studies show that the Arm A72 on the Bluefield 2 DPU and Marvell CN913X are incapable of driving line rate speeds of 100 Gbps. This means that products relying on CPUs-on-NIC for pushing the network will need to shift towards more cores. Additionally, newer architectures may increase the number of memory channels and bandwidth. This has the downside of adding increased power and cost to the DPU. For example, Bluefield 3 is anticipated to have a 5X increase in SPECint performance over the previous-generation Bluefield 2 [47]. Similar upgrades to the Marvell line of DPUs required moving from four to thirty-two cores with the transition to the latest generation of processors. This requires increasing the TDP by 70–110 W [41]. How much processing power to shift over to the DPU from the host is an open question that requires the community to engage in successive evaluations to determine whether future DPUs are best suited for ancillary or specialization offload. Determining exactly where the delineation will fall between host CPU, NIC, DPU and GPU is difficult to predict.

5.2   The Right Level of Abstraction

One of the biggest hurdles of developing code for a DPU is the interfaces for programming them. One of the reasons for this is the breadth of architectural design points that DPUs span and the range of use cases. Many interfaces are low-level, focused on processing packets, designed to be stateless and perform at line rate, such as P4 [12]. A number of efforts have attempted to ease the development burden by providing abstraction layers on top [34,52]. Interfaces such as the Data Plane Development Kit (DPDK) [4] abstract common packet processing functions in a run-to-completion model. Other efforts introduce abstract machine models to allow for portability across varying architectures. In sPIN [27] different header, payload and completion handlers are associated with different connections to facilitate flexible offload, but has the constraint that the workload must not obstruct line rate processing. The INCA model [55] supports additional functionality by removing the deadline constraints of line-rate processing, but requires the code running on the DPU be preemptable. In an environment where cheap cores are everywhere, the INCA model facilitates ancillary offload and allows for more varied types of computation than prior approaches.

There is a huge gap between these abstractions and a fully featured Linux environment on a Bluefield DPU, where process scheduling is provided by the operating system and codes are written at a higher level. In order to encompass the total range of functionality possible, we are seeing the continued evolution and layering of abstraction on top of performance-focused, lower-level interfaces. This will allow systems and communication library designers to develop powerful tools that can be composed and leveraged by higher level user applications.

Work by Liu et al. [37] developed the iPipe framework to provide an actor-based model that supports multi-tenancy, scheduling and hardware heterogeneity. Cloud-focused DPU company, Pensando has proposed portable APIs that target popular cloud services, but has noted that there is a lack of standardization for controller interfaces, operating systems, and data paths [49]. Within the Unified Communication Framework there is an effort to create a Smart NIC API (OpenSNAPI) [22] which will allow developers to leverage compute cores in the network. Nvidia is developing the DOCA SDK [48]. With the DOCA SDK Nvidia's goal is to create a single portal for harnessing the DPU in a manner akin to CUDA for GPUs. We see similar approaches from Broadcom [13] and Marvell [40] where each of these SDKs consolidates lower level functionality. **Two of the questions around this are how much will these SDKs differ as products try to differentiate themselves and what will the hurdles be for program portability?**

Other companies take more of an appliance-based approach, where services are accessed via REST APIs [24] or blocks of functionality can be downloaded from product specific app-stores [61]. While this approach may provide great performance it isn't necessarily a good fit for ancillary offload in an HPC environment where the emphasis is on ease of programming and portability rather than raw performance.

When considering which approaches are likely to gain traction with ancillary offload, DPUs that contain cheap CPUs are attractive because they provide one of the simplest programming environments. Since they run a full Linux OS, it is possible to log onto and compile code much like any other node in the system. The downside of running a full system software stack means that cheap cores incur greater overheads on performance. However, this is not as much of a concern for ancillary offload.

Finally, DPUs create an additional domain for computation, which creates additional challenges for memory interfaces and migration of data in much the same way GPUs and CPUs experience today with unified virtual memory. Adding in a third processing unit to the mix will require additional coordination between the CPU, GPU and DPU.

5.3 The Memory Problem

While FLOPS per dollar has continued to become more affordable over time, memory prices per byte have been relatively flat or occasionally spiked depending on demand as shown in Fig. 4. 3D technologies such as HBM have raised the cost of memory even further for the workloads that require greater bandwidth than traditional DDR can provide.

Exacerbating this problem is the fact that each time an accelerator such as a GPU is added into a system we are paying for extra memory in addition to the host memory. This is because host DRAM often serves as a launching point for GPU kernels before data is transferred to HBM, but then may go unused during the execution of the GPU kernel. DPUs threaten to create another instance

Memory Price History

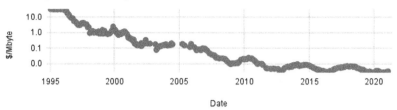

Date

Fig. 4. Historic memory prices per byte. Memory prices per byte have not continued to drop as the same rate of computation, resulting in memory taking up larger percentages of system budgets. Data was originally from John C. McCallum of http://jcmit.net.

where additional memory is required. Furthermore, having multiple memory spaces complicates programming and necessitates additional data movement.

One idea would be to create a unified memory space between the DPU, CPU and GPU with coherency supported in hardware. This would allow for a reduction of device attached memory, but the interfaces to support this efficiently are (1) still under development and (2) the market has not yet chosen a standard. PCIe is insufficient for these goals since it suffers substantial latency overheads [29] compared to a local memory access and the protocol does not provide the abstractions necessary for complex interactions across multiple memory domains. In work by Li et al. [33], PCIe presented a number of challenges to implementing a key-value cache on DPUs such as a limited number of requests due to credit-based flow control, and a limited number of PCIe tags to differentiate between DMA read response that may arrive out of order.

The need for a coherent interface between processors and accelerators has been identified in the past. Coherent Accelerator Processor Interface (CAPI) [58] is the protocol supported by IBM. CAPI provides coherency and virtual addressing capabilities that more tightly couple the accelerator to IBM Power Processors. In joint development between Nvidia and IBM, ORNL's Summit [26] system leveraged a tighter coupling between its Power 9 CPUs and Nvidia GPUs by having multiple NVLink [20] connections going directly on-die. Nvidia has bypassed the limitations of PCIe by utilizing NVLink for its DGX products. NVLink provides high bandwidth and low latency between Nvidia devices with hardware coherency and load/store semantics. NVLink is a central component of enabling machine learning training by composing multiple GPUs and creating large memory spaces for problems that are difficult to decompose. As companies expand their offerings to cover greater breadth we would like to see tighter integration between CPU, GPU and future DPUs.

Two other technologies, Compute Express Link (CXL) [3] and Cache Coherent Interconnect for Accelerators (CCIX) [2], both provide opportunities to address problems with managing memory by building on PCIe. CXL has three different levels of capabilities that hardware may support: CXL.io, CXL.cache and CXL.mem. CXL.io is similar to PCIe with a few extensions for initialization, device discovery and memory mapped register access. CXL.cache targets applications that require basic coherency protocols between a CXL compliant accelerator's cache and host-attached memory. This is beneficial for applications that want to leverage CXL supported atomic operations, and allow for flexible ordering models. CXL.mem provides additional functionality to CXL.cache by allowing the host to access device memory without incurring overheads that offset the benefit of having an attached device or DPU. This relies on host CPU to provide management of device memory and manage coherency via a *Home Agent* and *Coherency Bridge*. Ownership of memory can favor the host or device depending on different *bias* assigned. The downside to this approach is that it is host-centric and doesn't readily facilitate device to device memory transactions. CCIX is a competing standard that differs by allowing the Home Agent to reside on the accelerator rather than limiting that location to solely the host. In either case having the reduced latency and coherency that CXL and CCIX support greatly increases the variety of work that could be offloaded to a DPU and reduces the number of required transactions over PCIe.

One of the biggest hurdles is that there are many competing standards today which limit portability between future CPUs and devices which must provide mutual support for a standard.

5.4   Tying It All Together

In Fig. 5, we provide an example of the different places that compute-in-network may be applied throughout a HPC center such as NERSC. Green stars indicate where offload may be placed and text pop-outs exemplify types of offload that could be enabled. Determining how these resources are accessed and shared across hundreds of workloads creates new challenges for HPC workflows. In contrast to typical HPC applications running on a single system such as Perlmutter [5], these workflows may span (1) a larger variety of heterogeneous hardware, (2) multiple networks, and (3) may sit beyond the reach of traditional resource management and scheduling systems. One solution is to implement these offload units as appliances with user interaction limited to specific purposes similar to data-transfer nodes on today's systems. But the more interesting discussion is focused on how we can make these programmable, flexible and accessible to a wide ranger of users and workflows, bridging the HPC-to-workflow gap. New methods for orchestrating and facilitating data-flow and communication may be necessary and we may need to leverage best practices from cloud environments for this. For example we may need a stable definition for Quality of Service (QoS) throughout the data center, so that an urgent HPC workload may run at a higher priority as it traverses the many locations of compute-in-network. This will require efforts in scheduling, program portability, and multi-tenancy. If we do this successfully we reduce the number of non-compute and service nodes, while opening up new possibilities for scientific workflows and machine learning.

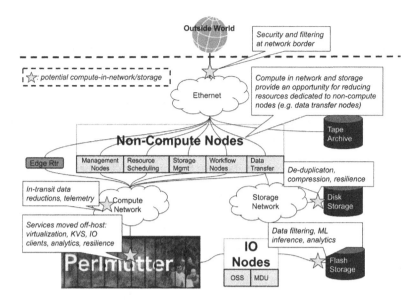

Fig. 5. Opportunities for compute-in-network/storage to offload tasks (both ancillary and accelerated) in a typical HPC datacenter. Green stars represent different points where compute-in-NIC, fabric or storage could be applied with example uses called out. Potential benefits include a (1) reduced data movement, (2) reduction of required non-compute nodes, IO nodes and (3) reduced contention for premium resources on the compute cluster. (Color figure online)

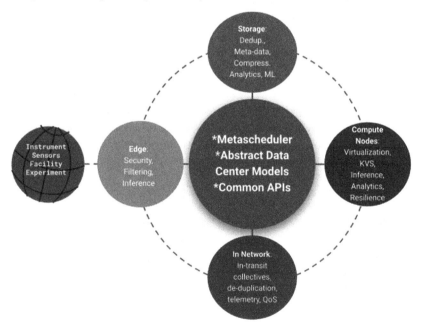

Fig. 6. Abstract view of cheap compute in the data center (edge, storage, traditional compute nodes and in-network) and the functionality needed (center) to tie it all together.

6 Conclusions

Heterogeneity and specialized units are now part of the HPC landscape. In the future we want to reserve premium resources for high priority workloads, while taking advantage of the cheap compute that is being distributed throughout the network. For these types of resources we propose ancillary offload, and an effort should be made in the HPC community to identify the opportunities in hardware and software to leverage this strategy. Ancillary workloads are the types of workloads that can tolerate the performance penalty that may occur because of (1) lower frequency or fewer cores, (2) reduced memory capacity/bandwidth and (3) additional latency across an on-node interconnect. Already identified opportunities include: key-value stores, node-local storage virtualization, analytics and inference, but many more exist. We show in Fig. 6, that to fully leverage the hardware we must expand beyond abstract machine models and develop abstract data center models that enable center-wide scheduling and runtimes. Abstract data center models must efficiently represent heterogenous hardware characteristics and match them to appropriate portions of a workflow with an understanding of the quality of service required by the workload. In order to make this vision a reality we must address future challenges of developing programming abstractions that support a multitude of architectures and use cases, multi-tenancy, and the memory problem. If we do this successfully, we can reduce the number of non-compute and service nodes, alleviate the noise on premium compute units and enable new possibilities for scientific workflows and machine learning.

References

1. Arm Ethos. https://developer.arm.com/ip-products/processors/machine-learning/arm-ethos-n
2. Cache coherent accelerator interface. https://www.ccixconsortium.com/
3. Compute express link. https://www.computeexpresslink.org/
4. Data plane development kit. https://www.dpdk.org/
5. NERSC perlmutter. https://www.nersc.gov/systems/perlmutter/
6. Nvidia DPU. https://www.nvidia.com/en-us/networking/products/data-processing-unit/
7. Nvidia embedded systems. https://www.nvidia.com/en-us/autonomous-machines/embedded-systems/
8. AnandTech: AMD 3rd generation Milan review. https://www.anandtech.com/show/16529/amd-epyc-milan-review/4
9. Arashloo, M.T., Lavrov, A., Ghobadi, M., Rexford, J., Walker, D., Wentzlaff, D.: Enabling programmable transport protocols in high-speed NICs. In: 17th {USENIX} Symposium on Networked Systems Design and Implementation ({NSDI} 20), pp. 93–109 (2020)
10. AWS: AWS Nitro. https://aws.amazon.com/ec2/nitro/
11. Bayatpour, M., Sarkauskas, N., Subramoni, H., Maqbool Hashmi, J., Panda, D.K.: BluesMPI: efficient MPI non-blocking Alltoall offloading designs on modern Blue-Field smart NICs. In: Chamberlain, B.L., Varbanescu, A.-L., Ltaief, H., Luszczek, P. (eds.) ISC High Performance 2021. LNCS, vol. 12728, pp. 18–37. Springer, Cham (2021). https://doi.org/10.1007/978-3-030-78713-4_2

12. Bosshart, P., et al.: P4: programming protocol-independent packet processors. ACM SIGCOMM Comput. Commun. Rev. **44**(3), 87–95 (2014)
13. Broadcom: Broadcom SmartNIC SDK. https://docs.broadcom.com/doc/5880X-UG30X
14. Broadcom: Stingray PS225. https://docs.broadcom.com/doc/PS225-PB
15. Cisco: Cisco Nexus SmartNIC+ V9P data sheet. https://www.cisco.com/c/en/us/products/collateral/interfaces-modules/nexus-smartnic/datasheet-c78-743830.html
16. Cloud, A.: X-dragon. https://www.alibabacloud.com/blog/introducing-the-sixth-generation-of-alibaba-clouds-elastic-compute-service_595716
17. Data, A.: ADM-PCIE-9V3. https://www.alpha-data.com/pdfs/adm-pcie-9v3.pdf
18. Dufey, J.P., Jost, B., Neufeld, N., Zuin, M.: Event building in an intelligent network interface card for the LHCB readout network. In: 2000 IEEE Nuclear Science Symposium. Conference Record (Cat. No. 00CH37149), vol. 3, pp. 26–50. IEEE (2000)
19. Firestone, D., et al.: Azure accelerated networking: SmartNICs in the public cloud. In: 15th {USENIX} Symposium on Networked Systems Design and Implementation ({NSDI} 18), pp. 51–66 (2018)
20. Foley, D., Danskin, J.: Ultra-performance Pascal GPU and NVLink interconnect. IEEE Micro **37**(2), 7–17 (2017)
21. Foundation, A.S.: Apache Storm. https://storm.apache.org/
22. Framework, U.C.: OpenSNAPI. https://www.ucfconsortium.org/projects/opensnapi/
23. Fungible: Fungible F1 data processing unit. https://www.fungible.com/wp-content/uploads/2020/08/PB0028.01.02020820-Fungible-F1-Data-Processing-Unit.pdf
24. Fungible: Fungible storage cluster. https://www.fungible.com/wp-content/uploads/2020/12/PB0020.04.02021214-Fungible-Storage-Cluster-FSC-Disaggregated-Storage-Platform.pdf
25. Groves, T.L., Grant, R.E., Gonzales, A., Arnold, D.: Unraveling network-induced memory contention: deeper insights with machine learning. IEEE Trans. Parallel Distrib. Syst. **29**(8), 1907–1922 (2017)
26. Hanson, W.A.: The coral supercomputer systems. IBM J. Res. Dev. **64**(3/4), 1:1–1:10 (2019)
27. Hoefler, T., Di Girolamo, S., Taranov, K., Grant, R.E., Brightwell, R.: sPIN: high-performance streaming processing in the network. In: Proceedings of the International Conference for High Performance Computing, Networking, Storage and Analysis, pp. 1–16 (2017)
28. Ibanez, S., Brebner, G., McKeown, N., Zilberman, N.: The P4-> NetFPGA workflow for line-rate packet processing. In: Proceedings of the 2019 ACM/SIGDA International Symposium on Field-Programmable Gate Arrays, pp. 1–9 (2019)
29. Ibanez, S., Shahbaz, M., McKeown, N.: The case for a network fast path to the CPU. In: Proceedings of the 18th ACM Workshop on Hot Topics in Networks, pp. 52–59 (2019)
30. Intel: Intel FPGA programmable acceleration card N3000. https://www.intel.com/content/www/us/en/programmable/products/boards_and_kits/dev-kits/altera/intel-fpga-pac-n3000/overview.html
31. Kaufmann, A., Peter, S., Sharma, N.K., Anderson, T., Krishnamurthy, A.: High performance packet processing with FlexNIC. In: Proceedings of the Twenty-First International Conference on Architectural Support for Programming Languages and Operating Systems, pp. 67–81 (2016)

32. Le, Y., et al.: UNO: uniflying host and smart NIC offload for flexible packet processing. In: Proceedings of the 2017 Symposium on Cloud Computing, pp. 506–519 (2017)
33. Li, B., et al.: KV-direct: high-performance in-memory key-value store with programmable NIC. In: Proceedings of the 26th Symposium on Operating Systems Principles, pp. 137–152 (2017)
34. Li, B., et al.: ClickNP: highly flexible and high performance network processing with reconfigurable hardware. In: Proceedings of the 2016 ACM SIGCOMM Conference, pp. 1–14 (2016)
35. Lin, J., Patel, K., Stephens, B.E., Sivaraman, A., Akella, A.: {PANIC}: a high-performance programmable {NIC} for multi-tenant networks. In: 14th {USENIX} Symposium on Operating Systems Design and Implementation ({OSDI} 20), pp. 243–259 (2020)
36. Liu, J., Maltzahn, C., Ulmer, C., Curry, M.L.: Performance characteristics of the BlueField-2 SmartNIC (2021)
37. Liu, M., Cui, T., Schuh, H., Krishnamurthy, A., Peter, S., Gupta, K.: Offloading distributed applications onto smartNICs using iPipe. In: Proceedings of the ACM Special Interest Group on Data Communication, pp. 318–333 (2019)
38. Liu, M., Peter, S., Krishnamurthy, A., Phothilimthana, P.M.: E3: energy-efficient microservices on smartNIC-accelerated servers. In: 2019 {USENIX} Annual Technical Conference ({USENIX}{ATC} 19), pp. 363–378 (2019)
39. Marvell: Marvell CN913X. https://www.marvell.com/content/dam/marvell/en/public-collateral/embedded-processors/marvell-infrastructure-processors-octeon-tx2-cn913x-product-brief-2020-02.pdf
40. Marvell: Marvell Octeon SDK. https://www.marvell.com/content/dam/marvell/en/public-collateral/embedded-processors/marvell-octeon-tx2-sdk-solutions-brief.pdf
41. Marvell: Marvell Octeon TX2 press deck. https://www.marvell.com/content/dam/marvell/en/company/media-kit/infrastructure-processors/marvell-octeon-tx2-press-deck.pdf
42. Mellanox: NVMe SNAP. https://www.mellanox.com/files/doc-2020/sb-mellanox-nvme-snap.pdf
43. NetFPGA: NetFPGA SUME. https://netfpga.org/site/#/systems/1netfpga-sume/details/
44. Netronome: Netronome NFP-4000 flow processor. https://www.netronome.com/media/documents/PB_NFP-4000-7-20.pdf
45. Neugebauer, R., Antichi, G., Zazo, J.F., Audzevich, Y., López-Buedo, S., Moore, A.W.: Understanding PCIe performance for end host networking. In: Proceedings of the 2018 Conference of the ACM Special Interest Group on Data Communication, pp. 327–341 (2018)
46. Nvidia: Nvidia Bluefield-2 DPU. https://www.nvidia.com/content/dam/en-zz/Solutions/Data-Center/documents/datasheet-nvidia-bluefield-2-dpu.pdf
47. Nvidia: Nvidia Bluefield-3 DPU. https://www.nvidia.com/content/dam/en-zz/Solutions/Data-Center/documents/datasheet-nvidia-bluefield-3-dpu.pdf
48. Nvidia: Nvidia DOCA SDK. https://developer.nvidia.com/networking/doca
49. Pensando: the need for standardization. https://pensando.io/the-need-for-standardization-in-a-thriving-network-ecosystem/
50. Pensando: Pensando DSC-100. https://pensando.io/wp-content/uploads/2020/03/Pensando-DSC-100-Product-Brief.pdf

51. Petrini, F., Feng, W., Hoisie, A., Coll, S., Frachtenberg, E.: The quadrics network (QsNet): high-performance clustering technology. In: HOT 9 Interconnects. Symposium on High Performance Interconnects, pp. 125–130 (2001). https://doi.org/10.1109/HIS.2001.946704

52. Phothilimthana, P.M., Liu, M., Kaufmann, A., Peter, S., Bodik, R., Anderson, T.: Floem: a programming system for NIC-accelerated network applications. In: 13th {USENIX} Symposium on Operating Systems Design and Implementation ({OSDI} 18), pp. 663–679 (2018)

53. Putnam, A., et al.: A reconfigurable fabric for accelerating large-scale datacenter services. In: 2014 ACM/IEEE 41st International Symposium on Computer Architecture (ISCA), pp. 13–24. IEEE (2014)

54. Radhakrishnan, S., Geng, Y., Jeyakumar, V., Kabbani, A., Porter, G., Vahdat, A.: {SENIC}: scalable {NIC} for end-host rate limiting. In: 11th {USENIX} Symposium on Networked Systems Design and Implementation ({NSDI} 14), pp. 475–488 (2014)

55. Schonbein, W., Grant, R.E., Dosanjh, M.G., Arnold, D.: INCA: in-network compute assistance. In: Proceedings of the International Conference for High Performance Computing, Networking, Storage and Analysis, pp. 1–13 (2019)

56. Shi, H., Lu, X.: TriEC: tripartite graph based erasure coding NIC offload. In: Proceedings of the International Conference for High Performance Computing, Networking, Storage and Analysis. SC 2019. Association for Computing Machinery, New York, NY, USA (2019). https://doi.org/10.1145/3295500.3356178

57. Stephens, B., Akella, A., Swift, M.: Loom: flexible and efficient {NIC} packet scheduling. In: 16th {USENIX} Symposium on Networked Systems Design and Implementation ({NSDI} 19), pp. 33–46 (2019)

58. Stuecheli, J., Blaner, B., Johns, C., Siegel, M.: CAPI: a coherent accelerator processor interface. IBM J. Res. Dev. **59**(1), 7:1–7:7 (2015)

59. Accolade Technology: ANIC host CPU offload features overview. https://accoladetechnology.com/whitepapers/ANIC-Features-Overview.pdf

60. Xilinx: Alveo SN1000 data sheet. https://www.xilinx.com/support/documentation/data_sheets/ds989-sn1000.pdf

61. Xilinx: Xilinx app-store. https://www.xilinx.com/products/app-store/alveo.htm

Deploying Advanced Computing Platforms: On the Road to a Converged Ecosystem

Enabling ISO Standard Languages for Complex HPC Workflows

M. Graham Lopez$^{(\boxtimes)}$, Jeff R. Hammond, Jack C. Wells, Tom Gibbs, and Timothy B. Costa

NVIDIA, Santa Clara, CA 95051, USA
glopez@nvidia.com

Abstract. Parallel processing is increasingly important in scientific software, not only for supercomputer simulations, but also for edge computing applications and intelligently processing experimental data in real time. Due to this expansion in the diversity of hardware being used for next-generation and fused experimental/HPC facilities, productively writing code that performs well across these diverse environments is an increasing concern. To meet this challenge, NVIDIA is working in the Standard C++ Committee to develop a roadmap for C++ Standard Parallelism, a parallel programming model that is portable to all platforms, from massively parallel HPC to many-core embedded systems, while preserving the defining goals of C++: performance and efficiency for most use cases.

Our vision of C++ Standard Parallelism consists of three key components: (1) Common parallel algorithms that dispatch to vendor-optimized parallel libraries; (2) Tools to write your own parallel algorithms that run anywhere; (3) Mechanisms for composing parallel invocations of algorithms into task graphs.

In this paper, we'll dive into this roadmap and how it fits into NVIDIA's broader strategy that also includes parallelism in ISO Standard Fortran and highly optimized library APIs to enable full-platform scientific productivity. We'll discuss what we already have that you can use today across a wide variety of deployed systems, what's coming down the line, and where the future may lead us.

Keywords: Programming languages · Performance portability

1 Introduction

Effectively programming HPC systems has been continually increasing in complexity along several dimensions over the years. HPC systems where large-scale simulations are performed have become larger which has led to a variety of network topologies, nodes have become more dense and more complex, and the processor architectures and memory hierarchies have become more diverse. In reaction to these trends and to try to mitigate some of the resulting loss in developer productivity, large parts of the HPC community have become interested in so-called performance-portable programming models, with a focused DOE workshop series starting in 2016 [1], and it is still a current topic of ongoing research in leadership computing facilities [2].

© Springer Nature Switzerland AG 2022
J. Nichols et al. (Eds.): SMC 2021, CCIS 1512, pp. 301–309, 2022.
https://doi.org/10.1007/978-3-030-96498-6_17

Indeed, research and development of performance-portable solutions has become its own cottage industry, even with larger scale efforts being directly funded independently of any direct connection to any particular systems, applications, or basic science efforts. However, similarly to how intense focus on advancing the state of the art of parallelism methods can sometimes obscure their ultimate goal of reducing execution time, the exact definition of performance portability isn't as important as developer productivity and reducing time-to-science. This includes giving the developer the ability to both performantly adapt to or ignore with minimal impact corner cases in platform features, depending on the continually changing needs of their workload.

And now, besides performance portability across leadership-class machines being used for traditional HPC simulation applications, the desire for edge-connected and federated instruments further complicates the platform space that HPC developers are targeting. As hardware diversifies, hardware and software stack implementers need to meet developers where they are already working, in the languages they are used to such as ISO Standard C++ and ISO Standard Fortran which have been the languages of choice in HPC for decades.

This paper discusses the role that ISO Standard languages play in performance portability for HPC workloads targeting the increasingly diverse platforms available today and that are currently under development.

1.1 The Role of Standards in HPC

When looking for past successes in the area of performance portability for HPC applications, a small set of programming languages and models clearly stand out. Technologies like Fortran, C++, and MPI dominate the stack of almost every single HPC application running on today's systems. Indeed, there was a period where these were the only ingredients dominating the makeup of HPC applications, and the successes of these programming models seem to correlate well with the strength of the standard behind each.

Almost by definition, ISO standard languages are the most productive programming models available to HPC developers, as the primary justification for the effort of standardization is the promise of consistency and portability. "ISO was founded with the idea of answering a fundamental question: 'what's the best way of doing this?'" [3] In order to achieve all of these goals, the standards are designed to be slow-moving so that they can standardize existing practice. Community solutions like libraries, frameworks, and language extensions such as directives are critical in the exploration and development of these existing practices, but working to incrementally integrate the best ideas into standards is the goal [4], rather than indefinitely developing non-standard solutions. For the same reasons, standards that are meant to provide consistency and portability are not appropriate vehicles for the exploration and research of new solutions; good standards require implementation and substantive usage experience of candidate proposals. In this context, it makes sense that parallel features are seemingly "only just now" making their way into the ISO standards, since parallelism first had to achieve a certain amount of mainstream usage for the best practices to emerge after the wider community had gained significant experience with it.

Finally, it is worth pointing out that C++ is a bit of an outlier amongst the other most influential standards in HPC. Unlike MPI, OpenACC, OpenMP, and even ISO Fortran to a large extent, C++ standardization gets most of its participation from outside of the HPC community. Of course, C++ development is motivated by performance [5], having been used for a variety of high-performance applications [6] over the years. But having participation from experts in diverse other fields is an advantage as HPC attempts to expand beyond traditional simulation on distributed systems. For example, C++ is thriving in the embedded space where edge computing interests could take current HPC practitioners and applications, with active progress continuing through things like proposals to improve support for freestanding implementations [7].

1.2 Performance and Programming Models

On the other end of the spectrum from portability lies one of main interests of HPC, runtime performance. It is useful to remind ourselves that no programming model can obviate the need for parallelism or the efforts that often come along with it. Data often needs to be restructured for more performant usage via things like caching efficiency, coalesced access, and serialization for network communications. Exposing parallelism or even adopting new algorithms that allow for higher performance by reducing the need for communication and/or synchronization and increasing data locality and reuse, possibly even at the expense of duplicated work, are common practice in HPC.

Similarly, platform specialization will typically be necessary for achieving the highest-possible performance on any given machine; accessing the full and often unique hardware characteristics of a given architecture is usually required to realize its peak capability. It is common for performance-oriented programming to use non-portable assumptions, regardless of if the programming model tries to abstract it for the user or not. Architecture-specific programming models help the programmer more efficiently express these optimizations in a way that fully utilizes the hardware. Because the very point of these performance-oriented programming models is to leverage the newest hardware advancements as they become available, it is inappropriate to ask the user to wait for these features to become mainstream enough for standardization, thereby losing the advantages of diverse architectural innovations as they are developed.

These kinds of optimizations that are so common in HPC can also be a bit transient, only applying to one or a few hardware generations. However, the fundamental expression of the science and the parallelism inherent in those algorithms is usually longer-lived and platform-agnostic. ISO standard languages continue to serve as the most flexible and stable base from which HPC practitioners can dial in as much or as little extra optimizations as their use-case calls for, depending on the tradeoff between runtime performance and developer productivity that allows them to reach their scientific goals the quickest.

Portability, stability, and innovation are fundamentally at odds. The domain of HPC thrives on hardware that changes and improves rapidly, and on applications that live over multiple hardware generations. ISO standards provide the most stable and portable foundation for applications upon which platform-specialized solutions can be added in order to keep up with hardware innovations.

2   ISO Standard C++ Parallelism for HPC Workloads

The ISO Standard C++ committee has grown fairly large during the course of the last standard releases, with all processor vendors participating, as well as regular participation from several DOE laboratories including LLNL, LANL, SNL, ORNL, and ANL. Despite growing participation from the HPC community, the C++ committee is not dominated by domain-specific interests, and everyone remains focused on providing general abstractions that achieve high performance for a diverse set of platforms and workloads.

Generally aiming for more abstraction and expressiveness than the Fortran community, experts on the C++ committee are advocating for three classes of features needed for parallelism as demonstrated by the papers that are currently moving through the committee: (1) common parallel algorithms that dispatch to vendor-optimized parallel libraries [8, 9], (2) tools to write your own parallel algorithms that run anywhere [10], and (3) mechanisms for composing parallel invocations of algorithms into task graphs.

2.1   ISO C++ Today

Although the most user-visible changes that directly exposed parallel features came to the ISO C++ Standard in the C++17 revision, necessary groundwork was being laid in the C++11 and C++14 revisions that strengthened the language's memory model and forward-progress guarantees. The so-called "parallel algorithms" were introduced in C++17 (and augmented in C++20), which allow the user to optionally specify an execution policy for most existing C++ standard algorithms that indicates to the implementation the strength of the forward progress needed by the algorithm. Given sufficiently weak requirements, the implementation can then choose to execute the algorithm with varying amounts of parallelism.

These existing standard algorithms fall into the first category of parallel features listed above, and they are somewhat more rigid by their nature. Because of this relative lack of ultimate expressiveness, some state-of-the-art parallel algorithms that require complex hierarchies or fine-grained control might be difficult to use. But it turns out that many of these existing standard algorithms with weakened forward progress requirements implement bandwidth-bound kernels and are well-suited to saturating the memory controllers and bandwidth of today's massively parallel machines, so they are a great fit for many bandwidth-bound areas of code. The variety of compute-bound algorithms commonly in use by HPC applications is somewhat less diverse than their bandwidth-bound counterparts, and they have been the subject of much existing research and development. As such, most compute-bound algorithms have found their way into optimized libraries that are provided as a matter of course with each new HPC architecture. With the combination of the C++ parallel algorithms and vendor-optimized numerical libraries, a wide swath of HPC application use cases can be covered.

In Fig. 1, we show performance results using the LULESH [11] mini-app comparing the standard C++ parallel algorithms across different compilers including the GNU GCC compiler, the Intel compiler, and the NVIDIA HPC compiler. We use the OpenMP threading model for CPUs of each compiler as a baseline comparison.

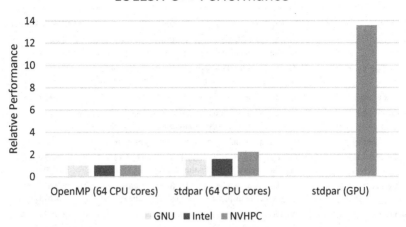

Fig. 1. Performance results for the LULESH mini-app using the C++17 parallel algorithms and OpenMP using the GNU, Intel, and NVIDIA HPC compilers. Results were collected on a system with an AMD EPYC 7742 CPU (64 cores) and an NVIDIA Ampere A100 GPU. The "stdpar" results were obtained using the same unmodified ISO-standard C++ code recompiled by the different compilers, and in the case of the NVHPC compiler, targeting both CPU and GPU.

We note also the results reported by Jonas Latt et al. for the open-source stlbm code [12]. From the conclusions of the article [13], the authors observe a performance loss of only approximately 20% compared to an optimized version of the code using a domain-specific language, and comment on the advantages of the performance portability of the standard C++ approach: "While it is traditionally thought that GPU development is substantially more time consuming than CPU development, but more rewarding thanks to performance gains of one to two orders of magnitude, the stlbm library presented in this article paints rather the opposite picture. Indeed, the same effort leads to a code that compiles to a CPU and a GPU binary without changes." with a speedup of 11.12x for a single A100 GPU compared to 64 core AMD EPYC 7742 CPU [12].

2.2 Evolving ISO C++

ISO Standard C++ has not finished developing features for performant and portable parallel programming. While the present facilities already allow for HPC programmers to achieve portable performance in production, new features being proposed will both expand these capabilities as well as making them easier to use and more productive. Table 1 gives an overview of some of the features that are of greatest interest to HPC developers.

Table 1. Roadmap of parallel features in the ISO C++ standard.

Parallel feature	Description	C++ standard (paper)
Memory model	Clarifications allow for future work on progress guarantees for algorithms, precise definitions for atomics, etc.	C++11
Forward progress	Abstract machine defines guarantees for multithreaded execution	C++11
Atomics extensions	2.1 Printing area	C++14
Parallel algorithms	Execution policies to standard algorithms allow programmers to relax forward-progress requirements on the compiler	C++17
Concurrency library	New library facilities provide concurrency primitives	C++20
Multi-dim. array abstractions	Library types for flexible multidimensional storage and indexing, compile- and run-time extents [8]	C++2x (p0009)
Linear algebra	Standard algorithms interface for BLAS routines; designed to allow efficient mapping to existing vendor libraries [9]	C++2x (p1673)
Executors	Abstraction of execution resources including heterogeneity and asynchrony [10, 14]	C++2x (p0443)
Extended floating-point types	Native-language support for new data types, e.g. reduced-precision floating point [15]	C++2x (p1467)
Range-based parallel algorithms	More natural expression of hierarchical multi-loop parallel algorithms [16, 17]	C++2x

While we don't expect the entire community to provide speculative implementations of standard wording from draft proposals, NVIDIA has plans to provide preview support in our HPC toolchain for at least the executors [10], linear algebra [8], and mdspan [9] proposals to further increase productivity for HPC developers who want to use ISO Standard C++ features.

Finally, the ISO C++ committee has freestanding, numerics, and machine learning working groups among others. If HPC wants to expand beyond scale-out simulation to areas such as integrated machine learning and connected edge compute, the C++ standard is already working towards providing a reliable way to move across these diverse domains of computation.

3   ISO Standard Fortran Parallelism for HPC Workloads

Besides C++, Fortran is the other base programming language that dominates today's HPC applications, and its development is also governed by an ISO standards committee. Unlike C++, Fortran is a smaller language overall having no standard library, and its usage is dominated by much smaller, HPC-focused community when compared with C++.

Fortran first integrated parallel features like co-arrays and 'do concurrent' in Fortran 2008 Standard, almost ten years before C++17. These are language-level features, unlike the library-based parallel algorithms of C++17. While C++ as a community is focused on providing abstractions over common tasks and mechanisms for generic customization of computations, Fortran is typically more focused on providing simpler and direct exposure of features, and these philosophies apply appropriately to each Standard's approach for integrating parallelism.

3.1 ISO Fortran Today

The primary parallel features in the ISO Fortran Standard available to developers today are co-arrays and 'do concurrent.' Co-arrays are typically used for coarse-grained and distributed parallelism in applications and have features comparable to MPI-3 one-sided communication (RMA), while 'do concurrent' allows for expressing the fine-grained and node-level parallelism – similar to OpenMP parallel "do" – that causes portability and productivity problems for today's HPC developers. For this reason, we focus more on the discussion of 'do concurrent' and enhancements to fine-grained parallelism facilities, but that should not be interpreted as implying that co-arrays are any less useful. We also note that several ISO Fortran language intrinsics that act on arrays such as matmul, transpose, reshape, spread, conjg, abs, etc. are amenable to parallel execution as well, which is supported by the NVFORTRAN compiler.

In Fig. 2, we show several kernels from the NWChem application that use the parallel capabilities of 'do concurrent' and the array intrinsics to execute standard Fortran in parallel on an NVIDIA A100 GPU.

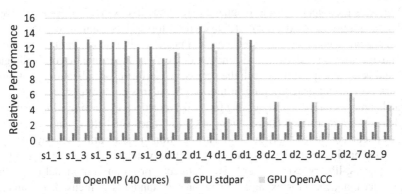

Fig. 2. Performance results for NWChem using the parallel 'do concurrent' feature in standard Fortran along with accelerated standard intrinsics. The relative speedup is displayed normalized to running on all 40 cores of a dual-socket Xeon Gold 6148 with 20 cores per socket. The performance of the ISO standard Fortran version of each kernel is shown running on a single NVIDIA A100 GPU, along with their OpenACC versions for reference.

3.2 Evolving ISO Fortran

One of the obvious shortcomings of the current Fortran parallelism features is the lack of a reduction operation for do concurrent. This is being addressed by the working draft

[18] of the next ISO Fortran standard and will be prototyped in the NVHPC compiler. Beyond reductions, many HPC applications use atomic operations in parallel loops for updating shared tables, e.g. as in particle-in-cell (PIC) codes. Adding an atomic locality specifier to do concurrent is one way to address this.

We also observe that HPC applications are increasingly interested in task parallelism, which is more coarse-grained than what is supported by do concurrent and has a very different character from what can be implemented with co-arrays. Shared-memory task parallelism is available in OpenMP [19] and existing in distributed-memory contexts for C++ users in Charm++ [20], HPX [21], Legion [22], and other projects. Eventually, bringing shared-memory task parallelism into the Fortran language would provide an opportunity for well-defined composability with the other parallel features and eliminates the temptation for application developers to abandon the Fortran language in order to reap the benefits of task parallelism.

4 Conclusion

For HPC applications, two things are always required: a base language and some kind of platform specialization. By separating the concerns of performance and portability, but composing them to complement each other appropriately for each application's needs we arrive at the optimal solution for productive performance-portability. Neither programming model is asked to tackle conflicting goals, and focusing the responsibility of each allows it to fully excel. Minimizing the number of moving pieces allows them to better compose together.

Directives like OpenMP, and language extensions like SYCL/DP C++ are disjoint parallel programming models that are layered on top of base languages, and in some cases are contradictory or divergent (e.g. atomics). Having native parallel features in the language allows for better consistency with the style and semantics of the language itself, and better composability with the necessary platform specialization solutions.

Work on parallel programming in the ISO Standards committees for the C++ and Fortran languages has been progressing for well over a decade, starting with the memory model and forward progress clarifications in C++11, and even before that with co-arrays and 'do concurrent' in ISO Fortran 2008. Participation in these committees by HPC practitioners and hardware vendors continues to increase, with NVIDIA alone sending compiler engineers, library experts, hardware architects, programming model researchers, and product managers, for example. Work on the standards is focused on enhancing concurrency and parallel programming for all platforms, with open collaboration taking place between partners and competitors alike [8–10].

Even higher-level languages can provide are being explored for use in HPC, such as Rust, Julia, and especially Python. These languages can provide even more expressiveness and access to parallelism than ISO C++ and ISO Fortran which give more fine-grained control to the programmer. However, the strategy for these languages should remain consistent: the place for portability for scientific computing developers is in the language itself. To take Python as an example, this would mean providing high quality, parallelized, and scalable implementations of the PyData ecosystem.

As the ISO standards continue to evolve, NVIDIA encourages developers to begin to phase-out non-ISO standard constructs in favor of standard language parallel capabilities.

Using the NVIDIA HPC compilers, we are seeing evidence that this strategy is viable in real-world algorithms and applications and that the time is now to focus on implementing ISO standard parallelism into HPC application codes. Some of this evidence is presented in Sects. 2 and 3 of this paper.

References

1. COE PP meeting 2016 final report. https://asc.llnl.gov/sites/asc/files/2020-09/COE-PP-Meeting-2016-FinalReport_0.pdf. Accessed 25 May 2021
2. DOE computation facilities research workshop report February 2020. https://publications.anl.gov/anlpubs/2020/02/158604.pdf. Accessed 25 May 2021
3. ISO - Benefits of standards. https://www.iso.org/benefits-of-standards.html. Accessed 25 May 2021
4. Trott, C.R., Hollman, D.S., Sunderland, D., Hoemmen, M.F., Edwards, C., Adelstein-Lelbach, B.: mdspan in C++: a case study in the integration of performance portable features into international language standards. United States (2019)
5. Stroustrup, B.: The essence of C++. https://youtu.be/86xWvb4XIyE. Accessed 25 May 2021
6. C++ applications. https://www.stroustrup.com/applications.html. Accessed 25 May 2021
7. Craig, B.: Freestanding proposal. http://www.open-std.org/jtc1/sc22/wg21/docs/papers/2019/p0829r4.html. Accessed 25 May 2021
8. A free function linear algebra interface based on the BLAS. http://www.open-std.org/jtc1/sc22/wg21/docs/papers/2021/p1673r3.pdf. Accessed 26 May 2021
9. MDSPAN. http://www.open-std.org/jtc1/sc22/wg21/docs/papers/2021/p0009r12.html. Accessed 06 June 2021
10. A unified executors proposal for C++. http://www.open-std.org/jtc1/sc22/wg21/docs/papers/2020/p0443r14.html. Accessed 26 May 2021
11. Karlin, I., Keasler, J., Neely, R.: LULESH 2.0 updates and changes, August 2013, pp. 1–9. LLNL-TR-641973 (2013)
12. UniGeHPFS/stlbm. https://gitlab.com/unigehpfs/stlbm. Accessed 06 May 2021
13. Latt, J., Coreixas, C., Beny, J.: Cross-platform programming model for many-core lattice Boltzmann simulations. PLoS ONE **16**(4), 1–29 (2021)
14. STD::execution. http://www.open-std.org/jtc1/sc22/wg21/docs/papers/2021/p2300r1.html. Accessed 27 Sept 2021
15. Extended floating point types and standard names. http://www.open-std.org/jtc1/sc22/wg21/docs/papers/2020/p1467r4.html. Accessed 27 Sept 2021
16. Ranges views as inputs to non-ranges algorithms. http://www.open-std.org/jtc1/sc22/wg21/docs/papers/2021/p2408r1.html. Accessed 27 Sept 2021
17. views::cartesian_product. http://www.open-std.org/jtc1/sc22/wg21/docs/papers/2021/p2374r1.html. Accessed 27 Sept 2021
18. WD 1539-1 J3/21-007 (Draft Fortran 202x). https://j3-fortran.org/doc/year/21/21-007.pdf. Accessed 05 June 2021
19. OpenMP API specification: version 5.1. https://www.openmp.org/spec-html/5.1/openmp.html. Accessed 06 June 2021
20. Charm++ parallel programming framework. https://charm.cs.uiuc.edu/. Accessed 06 June 2021
21. HPX 1.6.0 documentation. https://hpx-docs.stellar-group.org/latest/html/index.html. Accessed 06 June 2021
22. Legion overview. https://legion.stanford.edu/overview/. Accessed 06 June 2021

Towards Standard Kubernetes Scheduling Interfaces for Converged Computing

Claudia Misale[1], Daniel J. Milroy[2], Carlos Eduardo Arango Gutierrez[3],
Maurizio Drocco[1], Stephen Herbein[2], Dong H. Ahn[2(✉)], Zvonko Kaiser[3],
and Yoonho Park[1]

[1] IBM T. J. Watson Research Center, Yorktown Heights, NY, USA
{c.misale,maurizio.drocco}@ibm.com, yoonho@us.ibm.com
[2] Lawrence Livermore National Laboratory, Livermore, CA, USA
{milroy1,herbein1,ahn1}@llnl.gov
[3] Red Hat, Raleigh, NC, USA
{carangog,zkosic}@redhat.com

Abstract. High performance computing (HPC) and cloud technologies are increasingly coupled to accelerate the convergence of traditional HPC with new simulation, data analysis, machine-learning, and artificial intelligence approaches. While the HPC+cloud paradigm, or *converged computing*, is ushering in new scientific discoveries with unprecedented levels of workflow automation, several key mismatches between HPC and cloud technologies still preclude this paradigm from realizing its full potential. In this paper, we present a joint effort between IBM Research, Lawrence Livermore National Laboratory (LLNL), and Red Hat to address the mismatches and to bring full HPC scheduling awareness into Kubernetes, the *de facto* container orchestrator for cloud-native applications, which is being increasingly adopted as a key converged-computing enabler. We found Kubernetes lacking of interfaces to enable the full spectrum of converged-computing use cases in the following three areas: (A) an interface to enable HPC batch-job scheduling (e.g., locality-aware node selection), (B) an interface to enable HPC workloads or task-level scheduling, and (C) a resource co-management interface to allow HPC resource managers and Kubernetes to co-manage a resource set. We detail our methodology and present our results, whereby the advanced graph-based scheduler Fluxion – part of the open-source Flux scheduling framework – is integrated as a Kubernetes scheduler plug-in, KubeFlux. Our initial performance study shows that KubeFlux exhibits similar performance (up to measurement precision) to the default scheduler, despite KubeFlux's considerably more sophisticated scheduling capabilities.

Keywords: First keyword · Second keyword · Another keyword

1 Introduction

Economic factors are fragmenting computing into a "fast lane" and a "slow lane," with applications relegated to one or the other depending on their ability

© Springer Nature Switzerland AG 2022
J. Nichols et al. (Eds.): SMC 2021, CCIS 1512, pp. 310–326, 2022.
https://doi.org/10.1007/978-3-030-96498-6_18

to adopt market-leading technologies [25]. Since the early 2000s, computing has relied on increasing levels of parallelism together with Moore's Law to drive performance improvement. As Moore's Law now begins to taper, market forces are spurring development of heterogeneous and dynamic systems. As a dominant market force, the cloud is a prime source and benefactor of the development. Revenue from public cloud technologies is expected to exceed $397 billion by 2022 [7], while on-premises (excluding public cloud) High Performance Computing (HPC) spending is projected to reach $32 billion by 2022 [8]. The gap is anticipated to grow in the future.

To avoid being trapped in the "slow lane," HPC systems and applications are increasingly coupling with cloud technologies through *converged computing*, an environment that aims to offer the best features of HPC (performance, efficiency, and sophisticated scheduling) and the cloud (resiliency, elasticity, portability, and manageability). Large and complex HPC workflows and applications [11,14,17], which often integrate traditional HPC with new simulation, data analysis, Machine Learning (ML), Artificial Intelligence (AI) approaches, increasingly depend on converged computing to make scientific discovery. Furthermore, forthcoming exascale HPC machines such as Frontier at Oak Ridge National Laboratory (ORNL) and El Capitan at Lawrence Livermore National Laboratory (LLNL) will integrate the cloud technologies more tightly and at a greater scale [2].

Similarly, an urgent, market-driven need for accelerating the development of HPC technologies in the cloud itself is pulling the two environments closer. The growing demand for big data domain problems is blurring the line between HPC and cloud computing [16,20], and HPC technologies are being integrated into the cloud.

Despite a flurry of individual efforts, there remains a lack of studies on understanding the key interfaces between HPC and cloud that must be standardized to accelerate convergence. Containerization is rapidly gaining traction in HPC due to its ability to deliver portability and reproducibility and facilitate ML and AI analysis. Container orchestration, which provides fully-featured declarative management of lifecycles of sets of containers and their networks, fundamentally supports resource dynamism and elasticity, which is key to enabling next-generation HPC [27]. While traditional Resource and Job Management System (RJMS) for HPC such as Slurm can perform rudimentary container management, fully featured orchestration is only possible with purpose-built solutions like Kubernetes. Current RJMS are ill-suited to handle resource dynamism and elasticity which are fundamental capabilities of Kubernetes. On the other hand, Kubernetes is designed to manage a heterogeneous software environment, and it considers software to be a scheduling constraint. Unless we solve such a fundamental mismatch between Kubernetes and HPC schedulers in the standard interfaces, it will be extremely difficult to create a converged computing environment that is seamless, cost-effective, and sustainable.[1] Due to its increased

---

[1] While we use "RJMS" and "scheduler" interchangeably in the paper, a scheduler is one component of an RJMS.

popularity, customers are starting to use Kubernetes to manage their HPC workloads. Default Kubernetes schedules a job or many jobs in a sequence, which is good for most of the use cases, but this introduces challenges when, for instance, it is required to start+execute+stop all jobs on a GPU based hardware. To enable Kubernetes to run HPC workload, Red hat has invested in developing specialized schedulers [19] for HPC.

In this work, we target the problem of combining Kubernetes and HPC scheduling. We discuss various approaches to this. This paper makes the following contributions:

1. Conceptualization of HPC+Kubernetes scheduler composition models;
2. Definition of an augmented tight composition approach;
3. Identification of gaps in the current interfaces;
4. KubeFlux, our scheduler plug-in prototype for Kubernetes

Our preliminary results suggest that our proposed model provides a viable path that is sustainable, useful, and scalable, although critical deficiencies do exist in the current interfaces.

The paper is structured as follows. Section 2 covers three essential technology building blocks. Section 3 surveys the ways how Kubernetes scheduling can be extended, along with pros and cons of different approaches. Section 4 discusses the challenges we faced when designing KubeFlux and its integration with Node Feature Discovery (NFD) which provides information about hardware features important to HPC applications. Section 5 shows our preliminary experimental results. Section 6 discusses related work. Finally, we summarize and discuss future work in Sect. 7.

2   Technology Building Blocks

In this section, we describe the three basic building blocks that we used: 1. **Flux**, an HPC workload manager; 2. **Kube-scheduler**, the default scheduler within Kubernetes; 3. **NFD**, an open-source Kubernetes project that provides information about node hardware features.

2.1   Flux

Flux [4] is a fully hierarchical workload manager for HPC. It was born out of growing production computing needs for more sophisticated scheduling of larger, more heterogeneous and dynamic systems at large facilities such as U.S. Department of Energy (DOE) national laboratories.

Flux uses a graph-based approach to represent resources and their relationships. For instance, it models a *contains* relationship as an edge from rack to cluster resource nodes. Similarly, it can model a *conduit-of* relationship between, e.g., an InfiniBand (IB) core and edge switch. This scheme allows Flux to represent different type of resources and many distinct relationships within the same resource graph, organizing subsystems into subgraphs.

Symmetrically, Flux uses a graph-oriented, domain-specific language [21] based on YAML to specify each job's resource requirements. Figure 1 shows the graphical representations of the resource request of three simple job specifications. Each vertex, except for `slot`, represents a physical hardware resource type along with its requesting quantity. Edges represent relationships between two connected vertices. Box- and circular-shaped vertices denote resources to be allocated exclusively or shared between different jobs, respectively. The diamond-shaped `slot` specifies that its subtree must be exclusively allocated to those processes. Figure 1a, for instance, requests an exclusive allocation of 1 `slot` that contains 1 `socket` with 5 `cores`, 1 `gpu` and 16 `memory` units (e.g., GBs) within a compute `node` that can be shared with other jobs. Also note that this is an example where a simple resource affinity is specified. Because of the `socket` constraint, its contained resources like `cores` and `gpu` must come from the same socket. Figure 1b has a higher `rack`-level constraint, as it requests 4 `slots` each containing 2 compute `nodes` with at least 22 `cores` and 2 `gpus` per node. Because of this high-level constraint, those `slots` (and thus `nodes`) must be spread across 2 compute `racks`. Finally, Fig. 1c requests an exclusive allocation of 128 I/O bandwidth units (e.g., GB/s) within a parallel file system (`pfs`) which must be in the same `zone` as the `cluster` that contains these `nodes`.

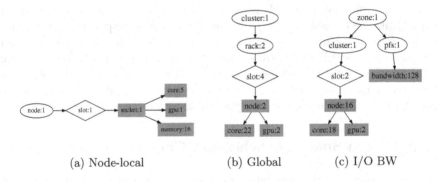

(a) Node-local   (b) Global   (c) I/O BW

Fig. 1. Resource request specification with multi-level constraints.

Flux uses its graph-based approach to perform many scheduling operations, mapping the problem of best resource selection to graph matching. Core operations include, e.g., checking resource states, scheduling allocations, adding or removing resources, and transforming representations. The majority of the graph functionality is implemented in the Fluxion advanced graph scheduler [5].

2.2   Kube-scheduler

Kube-scheduler looks for unscheduled pods, finds nodes for them, and binds the pods to the selected nodes. A pod is a Kubernetes object which has one or more containers along with configuration information. The node selection is performed within each scheduling cycle by applying *Predicates* and *Priorities* functions to every node from the pool of *schedulable* nodes. Predicates are boolean functions that act as filters, while Priorities score each node not filtered out by assigning a numeric value to indicate how well the pod can fit on that particular node. The node with the highest score will host the pod. Predicates and Priorities consider resource requirements, hardware/software constraints, affinity/anti-affinity, "taints" and "tolerations." Node affinity is a property of pods, while taints allow a node to refuse pods. Tolerations are applied to pods and make it possible to assign them to nodes with a matching taint.

Kubernetes schedules multiple pods *sequentially*, which is designated the *pod-by-pod* operating mode. By default, Kubernetes does not consider whether the pods belong to a group and/or must be scheduled together. The Kubernetes scheduling algorithm is optimized for microservices (either stateful or stateless) whose corresponding pods are typically independent.

2.3 Node Feature Discovery

NFD [15] is a software project that enables the detection of hardware features available on each node in the Kubernetes cluster, and advertises those features using node labels. The NFD project consists of two software components, a leader and a follower. The NFD leader provides a service running on privileged nodes (Kubernetes leader nodes). The leader service is responsible for communicating with the Kubernetes API server and receiving labeling requests from follower processes (via gRPC calls), and then updating node objects according to the requests. An NFD follower process is a daemon responsible for hardware detection at the node level. It creates an inventory of available resources and requests node object modifications from the leader service.

3   A Design Space for Scheduler Composition

Integrating an HPC scheduler into Kubernetes is not a new concept, and there are several HPC scheduler offerings with Kubernetes support. However, the existing offerings are midpoints in the design space spectrum of composing the default Kubernetes scheduler and another scheduler, each with a distinct scheduling objective. Figure 2 depicts our view on this space. As you move from left (Sect. 3.1) to right (Sect. 3.2) the schedulers are composed in a tighter and more controlled fashion. A looser composition is well-suited for ad hoc solutions but not standardization. One of the primary objectives of standardization is to make it easy and seamless to support and to sustain a wide array of HPC schedulers. Therefore, standardization should target the tighter composition model. In fact, we argue for a novel composition model called *augmented tight composition* that is at the far right of the design space in Fig. 2.

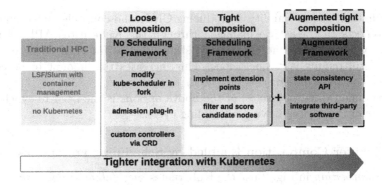

Fig. 2. A design space for integrating external schedulers (e.g., RJMS) into Kubernetes. From left to right, the approaches are sorted according to the "tightness" with the default Kubernetes scheduler in the corresponding integration model.

3.1   Looser Composition Provided by Custom Controllers

We refer to composition models as *loose* which consist of applications that run on top of Kubernetes and do not make use of any native extension capabilities to directly extend the scheduler. Within loose composition, we identify three ways to extend Kubernetes with capabilities provided by an external scheduler: 1. fork and change the Kube-scheduler; 2. implement an admission plug-in to assign a node name to a pod "in transit"; 3. write a complete scheduler operating on new resource API objects, namely Custom Resource Definitions (CRDs).

The advantage of option 1 is that developers have the entire scheduler infrastructure available to implement their own scheduling logic. This was the officially supported method to add scheduling logic before the Scheduling Framework was introduced. The disadvantage of option 1 is that developers need to keep their code up-to-date with the main code base in order to maintain compatibility with current and previous versions of Kubernetes. The Scheduling Framework aims to solve this problem.

Option 2 uses a Kubernetes extension point [26]. Admission plug-ins act at the user request level and can be extended by adding a *webhook* that implements logic to allow or deny a request to Kubernetes. In an admission plug-in it is possible to inspect each pod creation request and inject the node name provided by a third-party scheduler. Then the pod would be directly bound to that node. If no node is found for the pod, the request is rejected. Kubernetes would not try to reschedule it as there is no queuing mechanism in admission plug-ins. This methodology is also quite inefficient because the webhook is exposed through gRPC.

Option 3 allows custom external schedulers to be added by extending the Kubernetes API and implementing dedicated controllers to manage the objects to be scheduled. Examples of this approach include LSF-Kubernetes, Volcano, and Firmament which are discussed in Sect. 6. While this approach increases flexibility, there are several disadvantages with respect to performance, state reconciliation, and portability. Introducing CRDs and controllers translates into more objects that must be managed through the Kubernetes API. Although caching reduces shared access latency, state updates for both CRD and node objects still require API operations. This increases the amount of processing that the controller-based scheduler needs to perform.

A common drawback to all of the above options is the need to synchronize the state of the nodes at every scheduling cycle.

3.2 Tighter Composition Enabled by Scheduling Framework

Tight composition in Fig. 2 use the Kubernetes *Scheduling Framework* to introduce custom scheduling logic. We use "tight" to describe the integration because it reuses all of the preexisting components in the Kubernetes scheduler that are exported and used as packages. This, in turn, minimizes the amount of code required to implement a functional scheduler and it makes it easier to deploy schedulers built on top of the Framework, as it improves portability and compatibility with different Kubernetes versions. Also, the Scheduling Framework is maintained by the Kubernetes Scheduling Special Interest Group, and it gives an entry point to developers to contribute to Kubernetes directly. Schedulers implemented on top of the scheduling framework are referred to as *plug-in schedulers*.

The Kubernetes Scheduling Framework [22] defines several *extension points* to extend and customize the default Kubernetes scheduler to make it possible to convert existing features, such as Predicate or Priority functions, into plugins that are included at compile time. The main goals of the framework are to (1) make the scheduler easily extensible through extension points and (2) provide mechanisms to handle errors, continue or abort scheduling cycles. Figure 3 shows the extension points with green and yellow labels. A set of custom extension points defines a plug-in. A plug-in needs to implement at least one extension point between *Filter* and *Score*. The implementation of a plug-in scheduler is the Kube-scheduler imported as (Golang) packages that are initialized and augmented with the desired changes.

An unscheduled pod enters the *scheduling context*, which is the composition of scheduling cycle with the binding cycle. The scheduling cycle selects the node that can host the pod, and that decision is propagated by the binding cycle. Scheduling cycles are run serially pod-by-pod, while binding cycles may run concurrently.

3.3 Augmented Tight Composition Demands an API Extension

The spectrum in Fig. 2 culminates in a tighter integration model we refer to as *augmented tight composition*. With respect to the less tight approaches, this model would ideally make container orchestrators more consumable by the external schedulers (e.g., HPC RJMSs). To this aim, we identified two essential features that this approach needs to provide: unified resource representation and shared information about the state of cluster resources (e.g., node occupation). In Sect. 6, we show that no current approaches provide this level of integration,

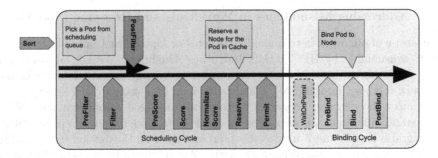

Fig. 3. Kubernetes Scheduling Framework infrastructure [22].

effectively identifying a gap at the end of the spectrum. The central contribution of this work is filling that gap with an example of the augmented tight composition model.

3.4 API Semantics Must Accommodate Fundamental Mismatches

Kubernetes is designed to use a declarative management model, where users describe the desired state and properties of the application and allows Kubernetes to transform the state to the desired configuration.

HPC RJMS more closely follows the imperative model, where the user describes how and where the application must run. The strategy is motivated by the user need to maximize application performance through detailed knowledge of node and network topology and process location. The model is not easily adapted to resiliency and elasticity because complex topological and hardware constraints make imperative state changes difficult to express.

The imperative-declarative mismatch manifests in two main ways. First, migration and elasticity that support the declarative Kubernetes model can interfere with the performance of imperative-model applications. For example, Kubernetes may decide to migrate a failed pod to resources used by a jitter-sensitive imperative-model workload. Second, the flexibility afforded Kubernetes by its declarative model paired with microservice workloads is reflected in its rudimentary default resource model. To achieve higher performance, HPC applications running in Kubernetes will need to fix the application-to-hardware mapping, which restricts Kubernetes' dynamic remapping and introduces significant complexity in maintaining the Kubernetes declarative model.

4 KubeFlux Design and Challenges

In this section, we show how we instantiated the augmented composition model by implementing the KubeFlux plug-in scheduler. We discuss how we addressed the challenges of unifying the resource representation (Sect. 4.1) and sharing information about cluster resources (Sect. 4.2). We also provide details about the design and implementation of KubeFlux (Sect. 4.3).

4.1   Addressing Mismatches in Workloads and Resource Models

The scope of our work is to make Kubernetes or OpenShift Container Platform more consumable by HPC RJMS and other schedulers. We aim at providing easy and standardized access to Kubernetes resources, enhanced by NFD and network topology information. The development of a standardized interface will help meet the demand across all sectors for converged computing jobs. With this standardization, we also seek to define a unified resource representation (i.e., graph-based) and a unified job representation and definition using YAML labels. This is very important to allow the plug-in schedulers to schedule native Kubernetes jobs like pods, daemonsets, deployments, and statefulsets, and therefore avoid forcing users to install and use custom objects they are not familiar with. An important consequence is that, by design, we support scheduling of resources that are part of upstream Kubernetes.

4.2   Resource Sharing

More than one scheduler can be deployed at the same time, and operators can make decisions about creating or deleting existing pods. Consistency and accessibility of worker nodes information is managed by Kubernetes which allows entities competing for the resources have access to correct information. Let us consider a Kubernetes cluster running the default scheduler and a custom plug-in scheduler implemented using the Scheduling Framework. On each scheduling cycle, the schedulers' nodes local state is updated, so that each scheduler has the current status of cluster utilization.

The KubeFlux scheduler, or any other plug-in scheduler utilizing third-party software to make scheduling decisions, needs to update its internal representation. This implies that unless a plug-in scheduler operates on dedicated nodes, the nodes states must be updated at least at every scheduling cycle. The internal update of the resource utilization at every cycle can cause performance degradation, so it is important to perform it outside of the critical path.

4.3   KubeFlux Plug-in Scheduler

We design KubeFlux as a plug-in scheduler implemented using the Scheduling Framework (see Fig. 4 below). KubeFlux is composed of a Golang binding to access Fluxion API and the implementation of the extension points from the Scheduling Framework. We implement the PreFilter and Filter extension points.

At KubeFlux startup, the binding is used to translate Kubernetes node objects into a Flux resource graph which is loaded by the Flux library running within the plug-in. We created a JSON Graph Format (JGF) writer, which reads the worker node API objects and parses them collecting the information provided by Kubernetes and by NFD, if deployed. With this representation, we can create an initial topology of the cluster.

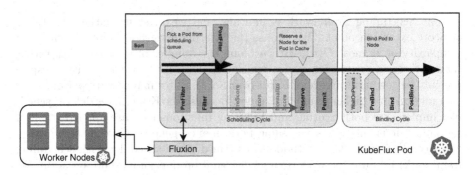

Fig. 4. KubeFlux design with Scheduling Framework [22].

In the *PreFilter* stage, a new pod manifest is parsed by a pod-to-jobspec converter, which creates a Flux job manifest (jobspec). For instance, in Listing 1.1 we create a pod requesting a cpu with Advanced Encryption Standard New Instructions (AESNI), and Listing 1.2 is the result of the pod-to-jobspec converter. Pods created with the label schedulerName: kubeflux, will be redirected to KubeFlux. Then we use the Golang binding to query Fluxion with *match_allocate*. If the pod can not be scheduled, it is marked as *unschedulable*. Otherwise, Fluxion will return a node name that is stored throughout the current scheduling cycle. Next, the Filter extension point is invoked on each node of the Kubernetes cluster. Once we hit the node name selected by Fluxion, we conclude the scheduling cycle. The pod is hence bound to the node and the new cluster state is saved in the Kubernetes etcd store, keeping the resource utilization information up-to-date for all the other controllers running in the cluster.

Listing 1.1. Pod manifest

```
apiVersion: v1
kind: Pod
metadata:
  name: hello
  labels:
    AESNI: "1"
spec:
  schedulerName: kubeflux
  containers:
  - name: hello
    image: busybox
    command: ["cmd"]
```

Listing 1.2. Flux JobSpec

```
version: 9999
resources:
- type: node
  count: 1
  with:
  - type: slot
    count: 1
    label: default
    with:
    - type: core
      count: 1
      with:
      - type: AESNI
  - type:
    count: 1
tasks:
- command: ["cmd"]
```

The Scheduling Framework is limiting, and we must use either the Filter or Score extension points. We choose the filtering extension point, which has a complexity of at most $O(n)$, with n being the number of worker nodes, rather than the scoring extension point, which has a fixed $O(n)$ complexity. Despite possibly better performance of Filter over Score, Filter may lead to performance degradation on a higher number of nodes. Because the Kubernetes default scheduler implements both Scoring and Filtering functions that are applied to all of the nodes, it is subject to the same performance penalty. Care must be taken when combining the two methodologies (third party scheduler with scheduling framework) because the performance degradation of each method are additive.

As a possible contribution, we could propose a more suitable extension point, which would prioritize a node and skip the Filter and Score extension points.

5   Experimental Work

In this section, we show the results for an initial evaluation of KubeFlux performance. First, we evaluate KubeFlux to Flux overhead (Sect. 5.1). Secondly, we compare the execution time between the default scheduler and KubeFlux to determine if the Scheduling Framework and KubeFlux introduce overhead with respect to plain Kubernetes scheduling (Sect. 5.2). The former aspect targets possible slowdowns due to the Kubernetes infrastructure, whereas the second aspect measures the impact of using KubeFlux to schedule microservices as opposed to plain Kubernetes scheduling.

We use a Kubernetes cluster on an x86 Virtual Private Cluster on AWS, composed of three master/control-plane nodes and six worker nodes. Each worker node is an instance of an m4.2xlarge type server, equipped with eight 2.4 GHz Intel® Xeon E5-2676 v3 Processor vCPUs, 32 GiB of memory, and network bandwith of 1000 Mbps. We use the Quay registry to store and share the KubeFlux container image. We run workloads with exclusive vCPU allocation and vCPU over-subscription. Pods requesting exclusive vCPU, are tested with properties exposed through NFD.

5.1   Overhead of KubeFlux over Flux

We analyze the overhead introduced by KubeFlux over plain Flux, by measuring the time Flux spends to run a `match_allocate` on the resource graph and the total execution time of the KubeFlux call. The difference between the two execution times, which is accountable to Golang bindings that KubeFlux uses to wrap Flux operations, represents the overhead.

First, we consider the *over-subscribtion* case, where we try to allocate the maximum number of pods a node can host (default is 110). We do not expect to reach the maximum number of pods with our workload because every worker node already hosts some load. For instance, some worker nodes runs Kube-Proxy, NFD, and core-dns in pods. We initialize KubeFlux with a graph of resources that can allow sharing of cores among more pods, therefore we create nodes with as many virtual cores (`vcore` in Flux resource graph terminology) as the number of maximum pods that can be hosted in a node. This is necessary to allow KubeFlux to handle regular cloud microservices as well, which may not require exclusive use of resources. Both KubeFlux and the Kubernetes default scheduler are able to find allocations for the same number of pods (471). Kubelets will then stop any further allocation on the nodes. Table 1 shows the overhead introduced by KubeFlux bindings with over-subscription is on average less then 10% of the Flux execution time.

Table 1. Golang binding and Scheduling Framework overhead as total KubeFlux execution times, compared to the portion spent in Flux's `match_allocate` function.

	Over-subscription				Exclusive vCPU			
	Average	Median	Min	Max	Average	Median	Min	Max
Total execution time (s)	0.0030	0.0027	0.0023	0.0089	0.0007	0.0007	0.0004	0.0018
Match-allocate time (s)	0.0027	0.0024	0.0020	0.0084	0.0003	0.0003	0.0001	0.0005

Secondly, we consider *exclusive vCPU* usage, where we initialize KubeFlux with a graph of resources that does not allow sharing of cores among pods, therefore enforcing exclusive usage of vCPUs. We create a graph with the exact mapping of a single virtual core (`vcore`) to a single vCPU. In the case of exclusive vCPUs utilization by the pods in our workload, we expect to get at most 48 pods (8 vCPU × 6 worker nodes). In the pod manifests, we instruct both the default scheduler and KubeFlux to select the cores with `AESNI` feature enabled. The right side of Table 1 shows the results. With respect to the over-subscription case, for exclusive vCPU reservation we provide a smaller graph to Flux and the execution times for the `match_allocate` is indeed lower than the total execution time in the over-subscription case, resulting in higher relative overhead. However, the overall execution phases are still several orders of magnitude smaller with respect to times needed for scheduling pods, as we detail in the following.

5.2   Overhead of KubeFlux over Kubernetes

The default scheduler does not provide any fine-grain information about the scheduling decision time, therefore we rely directly on the timestamps pod life-cycles. In this evaluation we look at a few key points in the pod lifecycle. In particular: pod object *Created* timestamp; the *PodScheduled* timestamp, meaning the pod has been scheduled to a node; and the *ContainersReady* timestamp, meaning the containers are ready to be executed [18]. Unfortunately, Kubernetes only provides timestamps with a granularity of seconds. Despite this coarse granularity, we can use the timestamps to check whether the Scheduling Framework introduces overhead. We dump timestamps in both experiments discussed above.

In Table 2, we show the time elapsed between the moment the pod is created and then scheduled (`created:sched`), the time elapsed between the pod being marked as scheduled and ready to be executed (`sched:ready`), and the total time elapsed between pod creation and containers ready to run (`created:ready`).

Table 2. Median, minimum and maximum execution times in seconds of various stages in the pod lifecycle. Timestamps mismatches are shown in the **sched:ready mismatch** row.

	Default excl			Default over			KubeFlux excl			KubeFlux over		
	Med	Min	Max	Med	Min	Max	Med	Min	Max	Med	Min	Max
created:sched	0	0	568	127	0	635	0	0	1	262	0	1252
sched:ready	1	1	2	1	0	2	1	0	2	286	0	847
sched:ready textbfmismatch	0	0	0	622	0	633	0	0	0	712	0	1234
created:ready	1	1	2	1	0	2	1	0	2	309	0	1281

Since timestamp resolution is in seconds, a value of 0 indicates that the difference is anywhere in $(0, 1)$; the same applies for values of 1 and 2. Interestingly, if we look at the average time elapsed in `created:sched` in KubeFlux, we see that times are not consistent with the actual execution times reported in Table 1. We also see very high values for the default scheduler. This suggests that these timestamps may be set with inconsistent delays. This can be seen in the `sched:ready` mismatch row where we report a mismatch for the *PodScheduled* and *ContainersReady* timestamps. Containers are marked as ready before the pod is marked as scheduled. In the exclusive use case, we do not see this discrepancy which is probably due to the reduced event load. In the over-subscription case, we see that the delay in setting timestamps can be extremely high, especially in the scheduler plug-in case. We hypothesize that this might be due to an increased load to the API server and requires additional investigation. Timestamp management is a clear area of improvement for Kubernetes. Despite the high variability, we observe that the `created:sched` median for both schedulers is 0 in the exclusive run and comparable in the over-subscription case. This is a good indicator that execution times in each scheduling cycle are similar and therefore performance are comparable.

6   Related Work

In this section, we describe work on multiple schedulers cooperatively schedule the same resources, with a particular focus on integrating HPC schedulers in container-based environments.

6.1   Cooperative Scheduling

When integrating multiple schedulers to cooperatively schedule resources, there are several general techniques that can be used to synchronize and coordinate their actions.

Shared State Scheduling has been popularized by Omega [23] and Kubernetes [3]. In shared state scheduling, multiple schedulers simultaneously schedule different sets of tasks onto the same resources. Concurrent conflicting scheduling decisions are rolled back, the work re-queued, and scheduling is re-attempted. In this technique, multi-scheduler throughput is a function of the frequency of shared state synchronization and conflicts, which increase with the number of concurrent schedulers. On the plus side, since every resource is available to every scheduler, there is the potential for high resource utilization.

Multi-level Scheduling has been popularized by Mesos [6] and Flux [1]. In multi-level scheduling (also called hierarchical), a top-level scheduler divides and delegates resources and jobs to sub-schedulers. In the case of Mesos, it acts as a meta-scheduler for other types of schedulers (e.g., Yarn, HPC schedulers) so it is limited to two levels. In the case of Flux, it can nest itself arbitrarily, forming a hierarchy of Flux schedulers, but it does not support other schedulers like Mesos does. Multi-level scheduling does not suffer from the same synchronization and conflict overheads as shared state scheduling, but the division of resources can result in reduced utilization due to resource fragmentation. The multi-level scheduling model is promising for converged computing.

Work and Resource Stealing was popularized as a technique for HTC scheduling by Slurm++ [29]. Resources and jobs are initially partitioned among concurrent schedulers. As the load balance between schedulers changes, idle schedulers attempt to steal work from busy schedulers and vice-versa. Additionally, resource stealing can starve large scale jobs and even result in livelock as the resources bounce between sub-schedulers with pending large jobs. More research must be done on this cooperative scheduling model before it can fully meet the needs of converged computing.

6.2   Integrating HPC Schedulers in Container-Based Environments

Several previous efforts for integrating HPC schedulers into container-based environments and Kubernetes exist. For each effort, we identify the closest match in our design space diagram.

Launching Containerized HPC Applications. Many HPC schedulers, including LSF [10] and Slurm [32] can perform parallel launches of containerized HPC applications. The integration between scheduler and container is limited to aiding the bootstrapping of the containerized parallel runtime (e.g., no container orchestration, elasticity or resiliency). This is the left-side *no Kubernetes* section of the Fig. 2.

Custom HPC Scheduler Controllers for Kubernetes. Several HPC schedulers (e.g., LSF [9], PBS [30], and Torque [33]) can integrate with Kubernetes through a custom controller. Users can submit batch jobs directly to the HPC scheduler and pods directly to Kubernetes, where the HPC scheduler select which nodes Kubernetes uses for the pod. For all of these controllers, it is assumed that every pod and HPC job placement is handled by the HPC scheduler, avoiding the need for state synchronization. This assumption simplifies the implementation but limits the capabilities of the Kubernetes cluster to those provided by the HPC scheduler. This cooperative scheduling is represented by the *loose composition* section of the diagram.

Batch Meta Scheduler. YuniKorn [31] is an ongoing effort to decouple scheduling from individual cloud-native Resource Managers (RMs) by creating a common scheduler interface. YuniKorn supports various RMs through a custom shim that translates requests, resources, and scheduling decisions between the RMs and the YuniKorn core. Currently, only a Kubernetes shim exists. The YuniKorn scheduler supports batch jobs, stateful services, hierarchical queues with resource fairness, and accelerators. YuniKorn is also represented by the *loose composition* section of the diagram. While YuniKorn can be used to implement KubeFlux, it is quite immature (still in incubation). In addition, the current architecture is limiting because all scheduler function must be implemented in YuniKorn core.

Custom Kubernetes Schedulers. Other efforts focused on extending Kubernetes through new schedulers designed to support both Cloud and HPC requirements. The topology-aware scheduler [24] for Kubernetes uses NFD to gather node Non-Uniform Memory Access (NUMA) information and a custom scheduler that ingests and schedules based on this NUMA information, avoiding *Topology Affinity Errors* for pods with the *single-numa-node* policy enabled. Kube Batch [12] is a custom scheduler that supports gang scheduling but it does not support data management, accelerators, isolation between tenants, job management or HPC-centric container runtimes. Volcano [13,28] builds on Kube Batch to add job and data management, accelerator support, and advanced scheduling algorithms. Volcano uses a *Cache Component* to provide an efficient state snapshot to the scheduler for all of the clusters. These schedulers are all a part of the *tight composition* part of the diagram, since they leverage the Kubernetes Scheduling Framework. While Kube Batch and Volcano do provide more advanced batch scheduling, both are Kubernetes Native while KubeFlux is aiming for convergence of HPC and Kubernetes and support for multi-level scheduling.

7   Summary and Future Work

In this paper, we show preliminary results of the integration of an HPC RJMS with Kubernetes as a scheduler plug-in, KubeFlux, targeting cloud and HPC convergence. We conceptualize HPC+Kubernetes scheduler composition models and identify gaps in the existing Kubernetes interfaces and infrastructure. We propose a composition model best suited for the scheduling interface standardization and explore it with KubeFlux. Preliminary results suggest that our initial prototype does not impact performance and compares well to the Kubernetes default scheduler. KubeFlux exhibits identical performance (up to measurement precision) to the default scheduler, despite KubeFlux's sophisticated scheduling capabilities. However, we found that the execution times and timestamps provided by Kubernetes infrastructure are not precise enough to allow performance comparisons and timestamps are often inaccurate.

In the future, we will investigate the Kubernetes timestamp issues we found. We will expand KubeFlux to provide richer semantics for pods that can be correctly parsed by the podspec-to-jobspec parser. Currently, we can parse some of the features exposed by NFD. We tested synthetic workloads in this first evaluation. We plan to test more representative HPC workloads and benchmarks in the near future to show how Kubernetes and KubeFlux can handle large job submissions.

Acknowledgements. This work was performed under the auspices of the U.S. Department of Energy by Lawrence Livermore National Laboratory under Contract DE-AC52-07NA27344 (LLNL-CONF-823344).

References

1. Ahn, D.H., et al.: Flux: overcoming scheduling challenges for exascale workflows. Future Gener. Comput. Syst. **110**, 202–213 (2020)
2. Cray announces Shasta software to power the Exascale Era. https://www.hpe.com/us/en/newsroom/press-release/2019/08/cray-announces-shasta-software-to-power-the-exascale-era.html. 13 Aug 2019. Hewlett Packard Enterprise (2019)
3. Ding, H.: Multi-scheduler in Kubernetes. https://stupefied-goodall-e282f7.netlify.app/contributors/design-proposals/scheduling/multiple-schedulers/. Accessed 20 June 2021
4. Flux framework: a flexible framework for resource management customized for your HPC site. http://ux-framework.org. Accessed 20 June 2021. Flux Framework Community
5. Fluxion: an advanced graph-based scheduler for HPC. https://github.com/ux-framework/ux-sched. Accessed 20 June 2021. Flux Framework Community
6. The Apache Software Foundation. Apache Mesos. http://mesos.apache.org/. Accessed 20 June 2021
7. Gartner, Inc.: Gartner forecasts worldwide public cloud end-user spending to grow 23% in 2021. https://www.gartner.com/en/newsroom/press-releases/2021-04-21-gartner-forecasts-worldwide-public-cloud-end-user-spending-to-grow-23-percent-in-2021. Accessed 20 June 2021
8. Hyperion Research. How cloud computing is changing HPC spending. https://hyperionresearch.com/wp-content/uploads/2021/01/Hyperion-Research-Special-Analysis-Clouds-and-HPC-December-2020.pdf. Accessed 20 June 2021
9. IBM LSF-Kubernetes. https://github.com/IBMSpectrumComputing/lsf-kubernetes. Accessed 20 June 2021. IBM
10. IBM Spectrum LSF. https://www.ibm.com/. Accessed 20 June 2021. IBM
11. Jacobs, S.A., et al.: Enabling rapid COVID-19 small molecule drug design through scalable deep learning of generative models. Int. J. High Perform. Comput. Appl. **35**, 469–482 (2021)
12. Kube Batch. https://awesomeopensource.com/project/kubernetes-sigs/kube-batch. Accessed 20 June 2021
13. Volcano Community Maintainer. Volcano: collision between containers and batch computing. https://www.cncf.io/blog/2021/02/26/volcano-collision-between-containers-and-batch-computing/. Accessed 20 June 2021
14. Minnich, A.J., et al.: AMPL: a data-driven modeling pipeline for drug discovery. J. Chem. Inf. Model. **60**(4), 1955–1968 (2020)
15. Node Feature Discovery. https://kubernetes-sigs.github.io/node-feature-discovery/master/get-started/index.html. Accessed 12 Sept 2021. The Kubernetes SIGs
16. Novella, J.A., et al.: Container-based bioinformatics with Pachyderm. Bioinformatics **35**(5), 839–846 (2019)
17. Peterson, J.L., et al.: Merlin: enabling machine learning-ready HPC ensembles. In: CoRR abs/1912.02892 (2019)
18. Pod lifecycle. https://kubernetes.io/docs/concepts/workloads/pods/pod-lifecycle/. Accessed 20 June 2021. The Kubernetes Authors

19. Red Hat Certified optional operator for secondary schedulers. https://github.com/openshift/secondary-scheduler-operator. 24 Sept 2021. Red Hat

20. Reed, D.A., Dongarra, J.: Exascale computing and big data. Commun. ACM **58**(7), 56–68 (2015)

21. RFC 14: Canonical job specification. https://ux-framework.readthedocs.io/projects/ux-rfc/en/latest/spec_14.html. Accessed 20 June 2021. Flux Framework Community

22. Scheduling Framework. https://github.com/kubernetes/enhancements/blob/master/keps/sig-scheduling/624-scheduling-framework/README.md. Accessed 20 June 2021. The Kubernetes Authors

23. Schwarzkopf, M., et al.: Omega: flexible, scalable schedulers for large compute clusters. In: SIGOPS European Conference on Computer Systems (EuroSys), Prague, Czech Republic, pp. 351–364 (2013)

24. Sehgal, S., et al.: Topology awareness in Kubernetes part 2: don't we already have a topology manager? https://www.openshift.com/blog/topology-awareness-in-kubernetes-part-2-dont-we-already-have-a-topology-manager. Accessed 20 June 2021. Topology-aware Scheduling Working Group

25. Thompson, N.C., Spanuth, S.: The decline of computers as a general purpose technology. Commun. ACM **64**(3), 64–72 (2021)

26. User Admission Controller. https://kubernetes.io/docs/reference/access-authn-authz/admission-controllers/. Accessed 20 June 2021. The Kubernetes Authors

27. Vetter, J.S., et al.: Extreme heterogeneity 2018 - productive computational science in the era of extreme heterogeneity: report for DOE ASCR workshop on extreme heterogeneity (2018). https://www.osti.gov/biblio/1473756. https://doi.org/10.2172/1473756

28. Volcano Kubernetes Native Batch System. https://volcano.sh. Accessed 20 June 2021

29. Wang, K., et al.: Towards scalable distributed workload manager with monitoring-based weakly consistent resource stealing. In: Proceedings of the 24th International Symposium on High-Performance Parallel and Distributed Computing. HPDC, Portland, Oregon, USA, pp. 219–222 (2015)

30. PBS Works. Kubernetes connector for PBS professional. https://github.com/PBSPro/kubernetes-pbspro-connector. Accessed 20 June 2021

31. Yang, W., et al.: YuniKorn: a universal resources scheduler. https://blog.cloudera.com/yunikorn-a-universal-resources-scheduler. Accessed 20 June 2021. Cloudera

32. Yoo, A.B., Jette, M.A., Grondona, M.: SLURM: simple linux utility for resource management. In: Feitelson, D., Rudolph, L., Schwiegelshohn, U. (eds.) JSSPP 2003. LNCS, vol. 2862, pp. 44–60. Springer, Heidelberg (2003). https://doi.org/10.1007/10968987_3

33. Zhou, N., et al.: Container orchestration on HPC systems through Kubernetes. J. Cloud Comput. **10**(1), 16 (2021)

Scaling SQL to the Supercomputer for Interactive Analysis of Simulation Data

Jens Glaser[1]([✉]), Felipe Aramburú[2], William Malpica[2], Benjamín Hernández[1], Matthew Baker[1], and Rodrigo Aramburú[2]

[1] Oak Ridge National Laboratory, 1 Bethel Valley Road, Oak Ridge, TN 37831, USA
glaserj@ornl.gov
[2] Voltron Data, Inc., Mountain View, USA
https://voltrondata.com/

Abstract. AI and simulation workloads consume and generate large amounts of data that need to be searched, transformed and merged with other data. With the goal of treating data as a first-class citizen inside a traditionally compute-centric HPC environment, we explore how the use of accelerators and high-speed interconnects can speed up tasks which otherwise constitute bottlenecks in computational discovery workflows. BlazingSQL is SQL engine that runs natively on NVIDIA GPUs and supports internode communication for fast analytics on terabyte-scale tabular data sets. We show how a fast interconnect improves query performance if leveraged through the Unified Communication X (UCX) middleware. We envision that future computing platforms will integrate accelerated database query capabilities for immediate and interactive analysis of large simulation data.

1 Introduction

Data-analytics driven scientific discovery is rapidly transforming the landscape of computational and experimental sciences. With the emergence of pre-exascale and exascale computing platforms, harnessing their capabilities for data analytics tasks is essential to address the need for the analysis of ever larger data sets [15]. These datasets, usually represented as numeric data arrays or tabular data, serve as an input to many operations (e.g. filtering, feature extraction, anomaly detection) that produce new arrays or tables. The database community has provided automatic query processing along with CPU and IO parallelism and more

This manuscript has been authored by UT-Battelle, LLC, under contract DE-AC05-00OR22725 with the US Department of Energy (DOE). The US government retains and the publisher, by accepting the article for publication, acknowledges that the US government retains a nonexclusive, paid-up, irrevocable, worldwide license to publish or reproduce the published form of this manuscript, or allow others to do so, for US government purposes. DOE will provide public access to these results of federally sponsored research in accordance with the DOE Public Access Plan (http://energy.gov/downloads/doe-public-access-plan).

© Springer Nature Switzerland AG 2022
J. Nichols et al. (Eds.): SMC 2021, CCIS 1512, pp. 327–339, 2022.
https://doi.org/10.1007/978-3-030-96498-6_19

recently, robust GPU support. These capabilities have been shown to be effective for the analysis of a large-scale molecular docking campaign, to identify potential drug candidates [12]. To explore chemical space, libraries containing billions of SMILES strings [29] and associated text and numerical data of small organic molecules are screened in a high-throughput manner, generating terabytes of data that need to be searched, sorted and merged with other data. Another, *in-situ* application of large-scale data analytics in plasma physics uses OpenPMD [24] to stream simulation data into `dask` distributed data frames [16], which can then further be analyzed with Python-based tools such as RAPIDS [19] and BlazingSQL, which we discuss below. Both examples demonstrate the need for fast manipulation of large-scale structured and semi-structured data close to where it is being produced, without the need for costly conversion, transformation or indexing of data, both in terms of time to solution as well as memory or compute footprint.

However, for distributed applications, data movement across the HPC interconnect is expensive and therefore the communication portion of an algorithm is often the bottleneck, particularly when the compute portion is already highly optimized and runs on GPUs. In distributed, GPU-accelerated data analytics tools, a high-performance communication layer is extremely important to leverage low-latency, high-bandwidth and overall scalability when transporting data across nodes and across GPUs [15]. Our contribution in this respect is the implementation of a high performance communication layer on top of the UCX library [25] to enhance BlazingSQL, a GPU accelerated database query engine.

Seminal work for scaling and optimizing database management systems dates back to the early 1990s [9], when foundations for efficient query algorithms, *e.g.* hash joins, were laid. In the early '2000s, the computer graphics community experimented with general-purpose computing on graphics processing units (GPGPU) as a way to accelerate computational workloads beyond graphics applications, and in particular, to speed up selections, aggregations, and semi-linear queries on GPUs [2,10,13,14] and co-processors [20]. Heterogeneous approaches to database query processing combine GPUs with multi-core CPUs or FPGAs [4,7,26] to make optimal use of the available hardware. Specific optimizations include the use of compression techniques [11], off-loading to the level of the storage engine [30], learning techniques for query optimization [5] and design of GPU-CPU heterogeneous query plans [17].

Several popular open-source frameworks for GPU-accelerated database query processing are under active development with contributions from the community: BlazingSQL [3], PG-Strom [23], and OmniSciDB [21]. In particular, we focus on BlazingSQL and the implementation of a new communication layer utilizing the UCX library [25].

2   RAPIDS and the BlazingSQL Software Architecture

RAPIDS is a suite of software libraries that provide data analytics and machine learning functionality on GPUs. From an end-user viewpoint, they generalize existing software offerings in the Python data ecosystem such as Pandas [27] and scikit-learn [22], maintaining the familiar Python-based API but offering accelerated primitives implemented in C++ and CUDA. On a lower level, RAPIDS' data processing routines are built on the Apache Arrow library, which is an industry standard that implements an efficient in-memory storage format for columnar data.

BlazingSQL builds on RAPIDS as a C++ library with a Python interface. The library provides a fast, *ad-hoc* query capability for terabyte-scale tabular data using GPUs, without the need for precomputed data structures such as hash tables. It implements out-of-core computation by optionally using unified memory and/or caching to disk (*e.g.*, NVME), and allows distributing the query processing on 10 s–100 s of GPUs for data that doesn't fit in single GPU memory. BlazingSQL is built on top of the RAPIDS ecosystem [19], and in particular, the RAPIDS cudf C++ library. It is thus different from dask-sql [1], which is a purely Python-based implementation of SQL with (currently) experimental support for RAPIDS. The library allows users to execute SQL queries against a variety of file formats, including text files with comma-separated values, Apache parquet and Apache ORC files, and in-memory data representations. Figure 1 depicts the architecture of the BlazingSQL software stack.

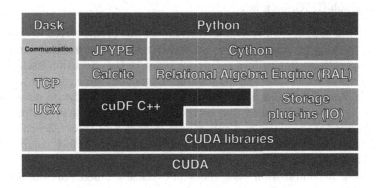

Fig. 1. Overview of the BlazingSQL software stack

The main user interface for BlazingSQL is its Python library blazingsql. Through this API, users register tables residing on one of the supported types of filesystems (such as, local or cloud bucket storage) as data sources, execute queries and obtain their results. BlazingSQL returns query results as single-GPU cudf DataFrames or distributed, multi-GPU dask-cudf DataFrames. When the engine processes an SQL query, it is converted into relational algebra using the Apache Calcite Java component. The BlazingSQL core relational algebra engine (RAL) then creates a query graph for optimized execution.

The result of the RAL is a directed acyclic graph (DAG), in which the nodes are kernels that take data as input, operate on it, and produce output. The edges are caches that connect producers and consumers of the data. The DAG is uniform across all parallel workers. Every kernel is connected to any other kernel only through a cache. The purpose of the caches is to take the output of a kernel and allow the engine to either leave that information in GPU memory, cache it in CPU, on disk, or on centralized storage. In this way the algorithm allows selective caching of individual query nodes and the processing of queries even when the intermediate tables do not simultaneously fit in memory (Fig. 2).

```
SELECT DISTINCT ss_item_sk, ss_ticket_number
    FROM store_sales s, item i
    WHERE s.ss_item_sk = i.i_item_sk
    AND i.i_category_id IN (1, 2, 3)
    AND s.ss_store_sk IN (10, 20, 33, 40, 50)
```

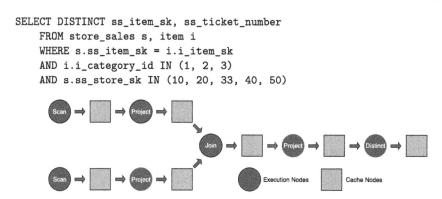

Fig. 2. The first sub-query of the GPU Big Data benchmark (top), and corresponding execution graph (DAG, bottom).

All kernels implement the `Kernel` interface or one of its derived classes. A kernel's purpose is to organize the flow and orchestration of performing complex distributed operations, but it does not perform any of the execution itself. Instead, it creates tasks which are sent to the `TaskExecutor`, which stores a queue of tasks to be completed and is responsible for managing hardware resources and rescheduling tasks that failed due to resource exhaustion. Kernels push information forward into caches and subsequent kernels pull those cached data representations to get inputs. They are decached only right before computation is about to take place.

The data decomposition uses the same coarse-grained partitioning as the distributed `dask-cuda` DataFrame, and the partitions can reside in GPU or CPU memory, on local file systems or on distributed file systems like HDFS. Individual kernels may decompose these partitions further using heuristics.

3   Implementation of Communications *via* UCX in BlazingSQL

An important aspect of performing relational algebra operations on distributed datasets is the need to send around messages of varying sizes between peers working on a problem with minimal latency and high bandwidth. BlazingSQL has supported communication *via* TCP sockets since its earliest releases. For high-speed communications, UCX is an open-source, production-grade communication framework for data-centric and high-performance applications. It therefore appears as a natural fit to leverage the native performance of the high-speed

Infiniband interconnect. UCX additionally supports accelerated transports such as GPUDirect RDMA and NVLINK. Here we describe an implementation of UCX in a user application that is only based on zero-copy host memory. UCX support is currently available in the `dask.distributed` data analytics framework *via* `ucx-py`. Our implementation, on the other hand, leverages a highly performant, native implementation of UCX on the C/C++ level.

3.1 False Starts for Implementing the UCX API in an Application Code

BlazingSQL uses Python as a user interface and `dask` to initialize the context on every compute node, which acts as an entry point to query execution. We first attempted to take advantage of `ucx-py` and `dask`'s UCX communication layer to perform the actual sending and receiving of messages. We defined the context, the workers, and performed all sending and receiving within Python. This first strategy exposed many problems. The GIL (Global Interpreter Lock) in Python prevented messages from being sent using several threads in parallel and the sending and receiving of messages quickly became the bottleneck and performed an order of magnitude worse than our original TCP implementation.

To optimize for latency in sending and receiving messages over UCX, we then kept `ucx-py` for the creation of the context and the workers, and implemented our own Python-based progress routine that needs to be executed to make sure that UCX is moving messages through its queues. Unfortunately this solution remained unstable when used with UCX in multi-threaded mode, and slow in both multi-threaded and single-threaded mode.

Leveraging UCX from `C++` instead of Python therefore suggested itself as the most versatile solution. We moved all code related to UCP workers, endpoints, and message transmission to leverage UCX's C APIs directly. Following the example found in the UCX documentation [28], our first `C++` implementation relied on C-only callbacks that could not receive additional scope variables. The code called `ucp_worker_progress`[1] on every message sent and received, from multiple threads. This approach turned out to be a performance anti-pattern with UCX.

3.2 Final Implementation of UCX Communications

We created a hierarchy of abstractions that would allow us to alternatively leverage TCP and UCX, and open up the possibility for additional interfaces in the future. We provided for this scenario by separating the sending and receiving of buffers from the actual serialization and deserialization of messages.

All data is placed into page-locked CPU memory before transmission. Even though the very fast GPU to GPU interconnects offer further opportunities for optimization through offloading the communication buffers to GPU memory, it does not make sense to persist data in GPU memory entirely because that

---

[1] https://openucx.github.io/ucx/api/v1.10/html/group__u_c_p__w_o_r_k_e_r.html

memory could rather be used for more performance sensitive applications. We opted to exclusively use GPU memory for the compute portions of the kernels. The greatly reduced GPU memory pressure resulted in satisfactory performance as more memory became available for processing. We implemented the following new C++ classes and abstractions.

OutputCache. This class is a cache that converts all incoming data sources to a structure that is ready for transmission. When data is cached onto CPU, we do so using fixed size chunks that are allocated by an arena allocator, see Fig. 3. If the data is already cached on CPU, adding to the cache does not incur extra costs. The cache chunks are page locked to ensure rapid movement between CPU and GPU. All messages exchanged are therefore of the same size, which is configurable. The default chunk size is 1 MB. In preliminary tests, we determined this to be close to the optimum value for Infiniband communication, balancing increased latency for too many small messages with wasted communication bandwidth for too large chunks. Data will stay in the OutputCache until there are threads in the sending thread pool.

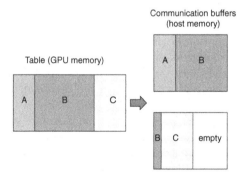

Fig. 3. Serialization of GPU-resident tables in host pinned memory buffers of constant size for communication. The arena allocator provides pinned memory buffers which hold chunks (columns) of the GPU table that is being sent *via* UCX or TCP.

MessageSender. The purpose of message sender is to poll the output cache for messages that need to be sent and then to create the appropriate BufferTransport class. The message sender is responsible for invoking the functions on the buffer transport.

```
transport->send_begin_transmission();
transport->wait_for_begin_transmission();
for(size_t i = 0; i < raw_buffers.size(); i++) {
    transport->send(raw_buffers[i], buffer_sizes[i]);
}
transport->wait_until_complete();
```

The class waits using a condition variable to allow us to limit the number of messages that are in transmission at any given point in time.

BufferTransport. All buffer transports implement the `BufferTransport` interface. The buffer transport is responsible for performing the work of sending buffers and metadata over a specific protocol. In the case of UCX it is the `UCXBufferTransport` that is responsible for calling `ucp_tag_send_nbr`[2] and dispatching buffers that belong to a message. It is not responsible for ensuring that the transmission is complete. We use the `tag` sending API and we split the tag into six bytes for the message id and two bytes which are used to indicate which part of the DataFrame is being transmitted.

MessageListener. The message listener is polling using the `ucp_tag_recv_nbr` API and when it receives a new request it is responsible for instantiating the `MessageReceiver` and then polling for any messages that are related to those incoming requests and adding them to the `MessageReceiver`.

MessageReceiver. The receiver accepts buffers from the `MessageListener`. The first buffer is the metadata and includes information about the number of buffers that will be received, the routing information of the message, the output location in the DAG, and information that allows us to convert the buffers back into GPU DataFrames when they are needed for further processing.

After all frames have been received, the receiver adds the data to the cache for the next kernel. There are also cases of intra-kernel messaging that usually include only very small payload, where messages might be placed into a more general input cache which is used to send messages that have unique and deterministic identifiers that allow kernels to retrieve them when they expect them. Figure 4 shows a complete example of a kernel sequence with communication.

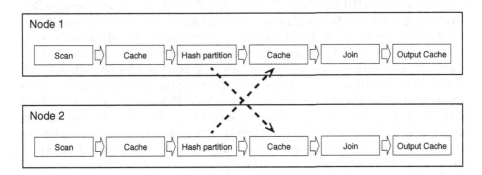

Fig. 4. A kernel is sending a message to the next kernel on another node during a hash join.

---

[2] https://openucx.github.io/ucx/api/v1.10/html/group___u_c_p___c_o_m_m.html.

4 Performance Results

4.1 Performance of UCX *vs.* IPoIB

We use the NVIDIA GPU Big Data benchmark (gpu-bdb[3]), an unofficial derivative of the TPC-BB benchmark[4] ported to RAPIDS and BlazingSQL. The gpu-bdb benchmark is a RAPIDS library based benchmark for enterprises that includes 30 queries representing real-world extract-transform-load (ETL) and Machine Learning (ML) workflows in the context of retailers with physical and online store presence. Each query is in fact a model workflow that can include SQL, user-defined functions, careful sub-setting and aggregation, and machine learning. Figure 5 shows a natural language description of one of the queries of the benchmark. The benchmark can be run at various scale factors: scale factor 1000 is 1 TB of data, scale factor 10 000 is 10 TB. In this contribution we run only 27 of the 30 queries, because three of the queries (Q22, 27 and 28) did not complete or had unmet dependencies for external libraries on the POWER9 architecture.

```
For a given product get a top 30 list sorted by number of views
in descending order of the last 5 products that are mostly viewed
before the product was purchased online. For the viewed products,
consider only products in certain item categories and viewed within
10 days before the purchase date.
```

Fig. 5. Example of a query (no. 2) from the GPU Big Data benchmark for retailers with a physical and an online store presence.

The standard nodes of Summit have six NVIDIA V100 GPUs with 16 GB of DDR5 memory, sharing 512 GB of DDR4 main memory. The high-memory nodes have six NVIDIA V100 GPUs with 32 GB of DDR5 memory, and 2 TB of DDR4 main memory. We performed all testing on the high-memory partition.

We compare the performance of the UCX *vs.* the TCP code path for scale factor 1000 in Fig. 6, both using the Infiniband interconnect as the low-level transport, using the median runtime of three repeated queries for each gpu-bdb query. As can be seen, the geometric average of the time per query is 13.82 s for IPoIB, and 12.06 s for UCX, which amounts to a 15% speed-up resulting from using UCX. However, the improvement is more clearly visible for the longest running queries, which leads us to speculate that the short-running queries involve less communication, and that a larger amount of input data would better expose the benefits of improved communication.

To investigate the query performance for larger data sets and its dependence on the communication protocol, we perform the same comparison for a ten times larger data set (scale factor 10 000). The results are shown in Fig. 7. Of note,

---

[3] https://github.com/rapidsai/gpu-bdb.
[4] http://tpc.org/tpcx-bb/default5.asp.

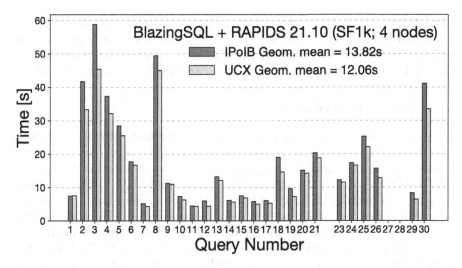

Fig. 6. GPU Big data benchmark at scale factor 1000 (1 TB dataset). Shown is the performance for the TCP code path (left/red bars) and the UCX code path (right/green bars). The benchmark was executed on four nodes of Summit (using six 32 GB V100 GPUs per node). (Color figure online)

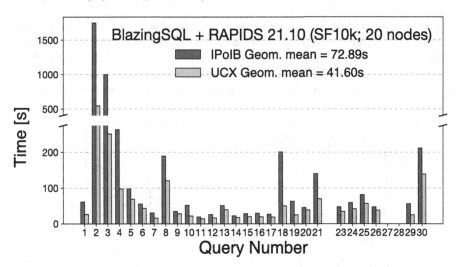

Fig. 7. GPU Big data benchmark at scale factor 10 000 (10 TB dataset). Shown is the performance for the TCP code path (left/dark shaded bars) and the UCX code path (right/light shaded bars). The benchmark was executed on 20 nodes of Summit (using six 32 GB V100 GPUs per node). (Color figure online)

the previously slowest query is still an outlier at this scale factor, however now by more than one order of magnitude compared to the geometric mean of all queries. Interestingly, the UCX code path clearly outperforms the TCP code path and delivers an average speed-up of 75%. Communication *via* UCX is therefore consistently superior to IPoIB for all queries. This result demonstrates that our optimizations were successful, and that communication indeed becomes the limiting factor for the performance of distributed queries on large data sets.

4.2 Multi-node Performance

To investigate the balance between compute- and communication-intensive parts of a query, we perform a strong scaling test at scale factor 10 000. Figure 8 shows the geometric mean for 27 queries as a function of the number of nodes. The performance is already optimal for the smallest node count that allows for successful benchmark completion, *i.e.*, 18 high-memory nodes of Summit. Adding more nodes degrades performance. The absence of strong scaling at this data set size indicates that the queries are strongly memory-bound, and that the available computational work likely fails to saturate the GPU. We believe this to be a general characteristic of GPU-based data analytics. We did not analyze weak scaling efficiency.

5   Implications for Future and Emerging HPC Platforms

With the availability of high-speed interconnects and accelerated transports supporting heterogeneous hardware such as GPUs comes the mandate of leveraging their superior performance in applications. However, the traditional API for fast communication on HPC platforms is the message passing interface (MPI), which is particularly suited for synchronous and regular problems involving only

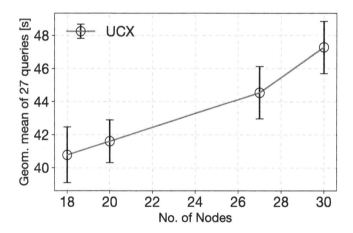

Fig. 8. Geometric mean of the query time of the GPU Big data benchmark at scale factor 10 000 (10 TB dataset) on different numbers $N = 18, 20, 27, 30$ of nodes (1 node $= 6 \times 32$ GB V100) on the Summit supercomputer at Oak Ridge National Laboratory, using UCX. The leftmost data point ($N = 18$) corresponds to the smallest number of nodes for which the benchmark completes successfully.

numerical data. The MPI stack on the Summit supercomputer uses the Parallel Active Messaging Interface (PAMI) for underlying accelerated transports, but also supports an experimental UCX option. Conversely, many data analytics methods have been developed outside the realm of traditional high-performance computing, and the focus has been on massively parallel compute with little or no communication [8,18]. Therefore, reconciling the world of HPC and data analytics requires communication middleware that combines aspects of commercial big data processing, such as fault-tolerance, with the reproducible performance of compute- and communication intensive HPC workloads. In our case, we found that UCX combines the best of both worlds: it is considerably more lightweight than a full MPI implementation, yet it includes hardware and system-specific backends for most (if not all) industry-standard interconnects. Nevertheless, the performance benefit and portability is offset by the higher implementation effort needed to program UCX compared to MPI or OpenSHMEM [6], due to the lower-level API.

With AI and deep learning entering the forefront of computational sciences, and with high-throughput workflows being executed on HPC platforms, we see an ever-increasing need for multi-node, multi-GPU database query processing. Data-centric workflows serve to organize, manipulate, search and combine massive datasets, which may have been produced by simulation or experiment, e.g., for preparing training data or processing results from large-scale inference. Moreover, workflows that can be expressed in high-productivity languages such as Python are composable, and the BlazingSQL library fills in a gap for high-performance database query processing. As database query processing becomes more commonplace in HPC, we also see a trend towards interactive use of HPC resources through Jupyter notebooks.

High-performance file systems at HPC facilities are a necessary prerequisite. However, since BlazingSQL supports both bucket storage and traditional POSIX file systems, it is compatible with future developments in HPC data center technology. We believe that gradual convergence between cloud computing and traditional HPC through the deployment of more service-oriented architectures at supercomputing facilities further enables processing of big data alongside traditional compute workloads.

6   Conclusion

We discussed the implementation of a new UCX-based communication layer in the open-source, GPU-accelerated database query engine BlazingSQL. The promise of fast communication over Infiniband lies in accelerating distributed queries that execute in seconds on tens or hundreds of GPUs on a super-computer to interactively query terabyte-scale datasets. We have shown that a performance-optimal implementation should make use of the low-level, C++ interface to the UCX library. We benchmarked BlazingSQL performance with UCX against the baseline implementation with IPoIB (TCP) on multiple nodes, and demonstrated superior performance of the UCX code path. In summary, we have shown how to incorporate UCX communication middleware into a library with a high-level user API. The improved communication layer brings about significance performance improvements for distributed database query processing, particularly of large data sets. In addition to performance improvements on the POWER9 platform, the library is portable and runs equally well on x86 architecture. The speed-ups should therefore also manifest themselves on NVIDIA DGX systems, and on workstations with multiple NVIDIA GPUs.

Acknowledgments. We are grateful to Oscar Hernandez (NVIDIA) for initial conceptualization of this research. We thank Arjun Shankar (ORNL) for support. This research used resources of the Oak Ridge Leadership Computing Facility (OLCF) at the Oak Ridge National Laboratory, which is supported by the Office of Science of the U.S. Department of Energy under Contract No. DE-AC05-00OR22725.

References

1. dask-sql. https://github.com/dask-contrib/dask-sql (2021). Accessed 5 Nov 2021
2. Bakkum, P., Skadron, K.: Accelerating SQL database operations on a GPU with CUDA. In: Proceedings of the 3rd Workshop on General-Purpose Computation on Graphics Processing Units, GPGPU-3, pp. 94–103. Association for Computing Machinery, New York, NY, USA (2010). https://doi.org/10.1145/1735688.1735706
3. BlazingSQL: high performance SQL engine on RAPIDS AI. https://blazingsql.com/ (2021). Accessed 08 Oct 2021
4. Breß, S., Saake, G.: Why it is time for a HyPE: a hybrid query processing engine for efficient GPU coprocessing in DBMS. Proc. VLDB Endow. **6**(12), 1398–1403 (2013). https://doi.org/10.14778/2536274.2536325
5. Bre, S., Beier, F., Rauhe, H., Sattler, K.U., Schallehn, E., Saake, G.: Efficient co-processor utilization in database query processing. Inf. Syst. **38**(8), 1084–1096 (2013). https://www.sciencedirect.com/science/article/pii/S0306437913000732
6. Chapman, B., et al.: Introducing OpenSHMEM: SHMEM for the PGAS community. In: Proceedings of the Fourth Conference on Partitioned Global Address Space Programming Model, pp. 1–3 (2010)
7. Chrysogelos, P., Sioulas, P., Ailamaki, A.: Hardware-conscious query processing in GPU-accelerated analytical engines. In: Proceedings of the 9th Biennial Conference on Innovative Data Systems Research. No. CONF (2019)
8. Dean, J., Ghemawat, S.: MapReduce: simplified data processing on large clusters. Commun. ACM **51**(1), 107–113 (2008)
9. DeWitt, D., Gray, J.: Parallel database systems: the future of high performance database systems. Commun. ACM **35**(6), 85–98 (1992). https://doi.org/10.1145/129888.129894
10. Fang, R., et al.: GPUQP: query co-processing using graphics processors. In: Proceedings of the 2007 ACM SIGMOD International Conference on Management of Data. SIGMOD 2007, pp. 1061–1063. Association for Computing Machinery, New York, NY, USA (2007). https://doi.org/10.1145/1247480.1247606
11. Fang, W., He, B., Luo, Q.: Database compression on graphics processors. Proc. VLDB Endow. **3**(1–2), 670–680 (2010). https://doi.org/10.14778/1920841.1920927
12. Glaser, J., et al.: High-throughput virtual laboratory for drug discovery using massive datasets. Int. J. High Perform. Comput. Appl. **35**, 452–468 (2021). https://doi.org/10.1177/10943420211001565

13. Govindaraju, N.K., Lloyd, B., Wang, W., Lin, M., Manocha, D.: Fast computation of database operations using graphics processors. In: Proceedings of the 2004 ACM SIGMOD International Conference on Management of Data. SIGMOD 2004, pp. 215–226. Association for Computing Machinery, New York, NY, USA (2004). https://doi.org/10.1145/1007568.1007594

14. He, B., Relational query coprocessing on graphics processors. ACM Trans. Database Syst. **34**(4) (2009). https://doi.org/10.1145/1620585.1620588

15. Hernández, B., et al.: Performance evaluation of Python based data analytics frameworks in summit: early experiences. In: Nichols, J., Verastegui, B., Maccabe, A.B., Hernandez, O., Parete-Koon, S., Ahearn, T. (eds.) SMC 2020. CCIS, vol. 1315, pp. 366–380. Springer, Cham (2020). https://doi.org/10.1007/978-3-030-63393-6_24

16. Huebl, A.: OpenPMD release 1.4.0 with support for data processing through dask. https://github.com/openPMD/openPMD-api/releases/tag/0.14.0 (2021)

17. Lee, S., Park, S.: Performance analysis of big data ETL process over CPU-GPU heterogeneous architectures. In: 2021 IEEE 37th International Conference on Data Engineering Workshops (ICDEW), pp. 42–47 (2021)

18. Lu, X., et al.: High-performance design of hadoop RPC with RDMA over InfiniBand. In: 2013 42nd International Conference on Parallel Processing, pp. 641–650 (2013)

19. NVIDIA: Open GPU data science-RAPIDS. https://rapids.ai (2021). Accessed 26 May 2021

20. Olsen, S., Romoser, B., Zong, Z.: SQLPhi: a SQL-based database engine for intel Xeon Phi coprocessors. In: Proceedings of the 2014 International Conference on Big Data Science and Computing. BigDataScience 2014. Association for Computing Machinery, New York, NY, USA (2014). https://doi.org/10.1145/2640087.2644172

21. OmniSciDB: OmniSciDB: open source SQL-based, relational, columnar database engine. https://github.com/omnisci/omniscidb (2021). Accessed 26 May 2021

22. Pedregosa, F., et al.: Scikit-learn: machine learning in Python. J. Mach. Learn. Res. **12**, 2825–2830 (2011)

23. PGStrom: PG-Strom: a GPU extension module of PostgreSQL. https://github.com/heterodb/pg-strom (2021). Accessed 26 May 2021

24. Poeschel, F., et al.: Transitioning from file-based HPC workflows to streaming data pipelines with openPMD and ADIOS2. arXiv preprint arXiv:2107.06108 (2021)

25. Shamis, P., et al.: UCX: an open source framework for HPC network APIs and beyond. In: 2015 IEEE 23rd Annual Symposium on High-Performance Interconnects, pp. 40–43. IEEE (2015)

26. Shehab, E., Algergawy, A., Sarhan, A.: Accelerating relational database operations using both CPU and GPU co-processor. Comput. Electr. Eng. **57**, 69–80 (2017). https://www.sciencedirect.com/science/article/pii/S0045790616310631

27. The pandas development team: pandas-dev/pandas: Pandas (2020). https://doi.org/10.5281/zenodo.3509134

28. UCX: UCX Client-Server. https://openucx.github.io/ucx/api/v1.10/html/ucp_client_server_8c-example.html (2021). Accessed 26 May 2021

29. Weininger, D.: SMILES, a chemical language and information system. 1. Introduction to methodology and encoding rules. J. Chem. Inf. Comput. Sci. **28**(1), 31–36 (1988)

30. Woods, L., István, Z., Alonso, G.: Ibex: an intelligent storage engine with support for advanced SQL offloading. Proc. VLDB Endow. **7**(11), 963–974 (2014). https://doi.org/10.14778/2732967.2732972

NVIDIA's Cloud Native Supercomputing

Gilad Shainer, Richard Graham$^{(\boxtimes)}$, Chris J. Newburn, Oscar Hernandez,
Gil Bloch, Tom Gibbs, and Jack C. Wells

NVIDIA Corporation, Santa Clara, USA
{shainer,richgraham,cnewburn,oscarh,gil,tgibbs,jwells}@nvidia.com

Abstract. NVIDIA is defining a High-Performance Computing system
architecture called Cloud Native Supercomputing to provide bare-metal
system performance with security isolation and functional offload capabilities. Cloud Native Supercomputing delivers a cloud-based user experience in a way that maintains the performance and scalability that is
uniquely delivered with supercomputing facilities. This new set of capabilities is being driven by the need to accommodate new scientific workflows that combine traditional simulation with experimental data from
the edge and combine it with AI, data analytics and visualization frameworks in an integrated and even real-time fashion. These new workflows
stress the system management, security and non-computational functions
of traditional cloud or supercomputing facilities. Specifically, workflows
that include data from untrusted (or non-local) sources, user experiences that range from Jupyter notebooks and interactive jobs to Gordon Bell-class capacity batch runs and I/O patterns that are unique to
the emerging mix of *in silico* and live data sources. To achieve these
objectives, we introduce a new architectural component called the Data
Processing Unit (DPU), which in early embodiments is a system-on-
a-chip (SoC) that includes an InfiniBand (IB) and Ethernet network
adapter, programmable Arm cores, memory, PCI switches, and custom
accelerators. The BlueField-1 and BlueField-2 devices are NVIDIA's first
DPU instances. This paper describes the architecture of cloud native
supercomputing systems that use DPUs for isolation and acceleration,
along with system services provided by that DPU. These services provide
enhanced security through isolation, file-system management capabilities, monitoring, and the offloaded support for communication libraries.

Keywords: Data processing unit · High performance computing ·
Cloud computing · Artificial intelligence · Storage

1 Introduction

Historically, high performance computing (HPC) has aimed predominantly at
serving the scientific simulation community. These users tend to come to simulation science from well-defined disciplines and access national-scale supercomputing resources through well-defined user programs (e.g. DOE's INCITE, ALCC,

© Springer Nature Switzerland AG 2022
J. Nichols et al. (Eds.): SMC 2021, CCIS 1512, pp. 340–357, 2022.
https://doi.org/10.1007/978-3-030-96498-6_20

ERCAP, or NSF's XSEDE, etc.), mission-critical programs, and the broader research community infrastructure. However, new trends are emerging as HPC changes to serve a broader range of application motifs. NVIDIA sees three trends that are changing the landscape of how supercomputers are being used. First, the use of machine learning (ML) and especially artificial intelligence (AI) is emerging in the scientific community [11,20] as an important category of new tools that is being applied with conventional simulation to improve the scale and time to solution for scientific discovery process. The use of AI/ML to improve the accuracy, scale, and time to solution for *in silico* models has been demonstrated across multiple scientific disciplines. Most recently, in 2020 the research that was done for the Gordon Bell ACM award and the special Gordon Bell Award for COVID-19 [4] both applied advanced AI concepts along with conventional simulation methods to achieve accuracy at scale and within practical time constraints more so than ever before. Second, the desire to use HPC capabilities in scenarios where user data protection is a non-negotiable requirement, without requiring special purposed systems, is elevating the need to include data protection as a first-class element in overall system architecture. Last, the need to use a range of HPC capabilities as part of large scale experimental workflows where some of the computational resources are shared and some remote adds another wrinkle. Examples include the real-time operation of a Tokamak reactor, the multi-messenger astrophysics campaigns, and the interpretation of data acquired by scientific instruments, e.g. SNS/VISION, electron microscopes, etc.

This paper introduces an HPC architecture under development that aims to address these requirements along with a description of the first instance of this architecture. The first release is expected in 2022, followed by regular updates. The proposed architecture is named Cloud Native Supercomputing [2], reflecting its target of serving both the traditional HPC segment as well as that of highly shared data centers. It brings HPC and AI side by side [18] by providing bare-metal performance for HPC modeling and simulation while meeting cloud services requirements [13]: least-privilege security policies [19] with isolation [14], data protection, and instant, on-demand AI services that can interact [15] with bare-metal performance HPC simulations [16]. This is achieved through an infrastructure to manage the workloads that is capable of providing isolation for jobs sharing compute resources, performance isolation [12] and hybrid mode where HPC applications can run on HPC compute nodes while other jobs like data processing, telemetry, and analytics services can run on a management infrastructure attached to the node. Subsequent sections describe this architecture and NVIDIA's implementation vision.

2   Solution: Cloud Native Supercomputing Design Principles

High-performance computing and artificial intelligence, with their thirst for ever-increasing performance, have driven supercomputers into wide commercial use as the primary data processing engines enabling research, scientific discoveries, and product development. Extracting the highest possible performance from supercomputing systems while achieving efficient utilization has traditionally been incompatible with the secured, multi-tenant architecture [10] of modern cloud computing. The Cloud Native Supercomputing architecture is designed to bridge this gap. A cloud-native supercomputing architecture aims at the goal of combining peak system performance expected from HPC systems in a shared environment, while driving toward zero trust [17] for security isolation and multi-tenancy.

Cloud Native Supercomputing systems have two main parts. The infrastructure control plane (iCP) owns the underlying control, network, and storage resources. It manages the data center. It is trusted and it enforces administrator policies. NVIDIA includes the iCP as part of its Base Command Manager (BCM) [5] product. The tenant control space manages the ordering and binding of tenants and jobs and makes requests of the iCP for services. Login and compute nodes are part of the tenant control space. Management of the tenant control space is performed by the Base Command Platform (BCP) [6] product.

A key element to implement a Cloud Native Supercomputing architecture is the Data Processing Unit (DPU) that resides on the data path and is separated from the host compute nodes. It is used by the infrastructure control plane to provide services typically provided by the host, network services, and application services.

The cloud-native design adheres to several design principles:

– **A scalable, balanced, and vetted node architecture.** The node design supports a mix of computational elements including CPUs and GPUs, which effectively supports a wide range of workloads. The architecture is flexible, and supports a range of CPUs and GPUs per node, such as a 1-to-many ratio of CPUs to GPUs, where GPUs are interconnected via a high-speed memory fabric (e.g. NVLINK2). There is a 1-to-1 ratio between GPUs and network adapters. Each node should have at least one DPU, reachable from the CPU and GPU via a PCIe bus, that can participate in infrastructure control plane. A reference node architecture is offered by the NVIDIA SuperPOD [8] design. Generalizations of this may be applied, such as using compute nodes from third-party OEMs.
– **A secured and trusted infrastructure control plane.** In a zero-trust architecture, the principle of least privilege is supported by shifting any activities that require trust outside of the compute nodes and into a trusted infrastructure control plane that is secure. The DPU is an agent within that trusted infrastructure control plane that is on the threshold of the compute node. The DPU implements the control path, which helps manage the shared compute resources within and across nodes, such as GPUs, file systems, and network resources. The CPU and GPU can readily communicate with the DPU because it sits on the PCIe bus of the compute node. This is true whether the compute node is part of a supercomputing data center or at the edge. Other elements in the trusted infrastructure control plane may include network switches, control nodes for policy management, and control nodes

for managing the infrastructure management plane, which may be based on Kubernetes. In initial embodiments, third parties will not be able to run code anywhere on the trusted infrastructure control plane, including the DPU, and only highly-vetted code is permitted to run there with least privilege.

Some of the control nodes accomplish provisioning, e.g. with Foreman [3] and Ansible [1] scripts.

- **Isolation from the tenant control space.** The tenant control space may include one or more tenant control planes (tCPs), perhaps one per institution where greater separation is desired. Each tCP can be driven by either a job scheduler like Slurm or an orchestrator like Kubernetes, such as in the BCP product. The choice of tCP implementation is independent of whatever is used in the infrastructure control plane. There is a recognition that different end users may have different needs and requirements for the tCP. That tCP may include a jump box for network entry, and login nodes such as those used by Slurm to accept user submissions and data management commands. The tCP informs and makes requests of the infrastructure control plane, but is not granted its privileged capabilities. Among the requests that the tCP makes are those that pertain to mounting file systems for use by the compute node (e.g. by a storage service in the DPU that is accessible to the compute node), and changes to the network connectivity to accommodate interactions among or cleanup after groups of compute nodes owned by the same tenant or job. Isolation among tenants in the tenant control plane may be accomplished using hypervisors, since the performance constraints there are more relaxed.
- **Network isolation.** Today, policies for controlling traffic tend to be enforced at fairly coarse granularity, e.g. at the granularity of whole nodes, enabling anything on node A to communicate with anything on node B. There is growing interest in making ingress and egress policies more fine-grained, by letting each container or service have its own network endpoint, and letting connectivity be explicitly permitted only among the desired subset of endpoints. For example, a given job may be allowed to either connect to the corporate network or the internet but not both, to inhibit exfiltration of data. A subset of allowable connections are configured when the data center starts up, and are relatively static. Other connections are changed with each new institution or even job, at the request of a scheduler like Slurm or orchestrator like Kubernetes. Network switches, and with this design, DPUs, manage the routing tables and establish both allowable connections and quality of service. Following the principle of least privilege, no endpoint, e.g. a user container, can communicate with another other job or service that isn't strictly required and enabled through scheduling and orchestration. Any packet that is not allowed gets dropped and reported, generally without a performance hit to other traffic. Protections may be manually managed or a subnet manager may be used. IB packets include PKeys, which are checked at switches or the DPU, and the programming for Pkeys are protected with 64-bit Management keys (Mkeys) that never go in the hands of users.

- **Support for in-network computing and communication offload.** The solution should include shifting communication management to the DPU, where control nearer to the network and less invasive to the CPU can both avoid performance bottlenecks and enjoy the benefits of specialized acceleration hardware that can transform, compress, and encrypt data. Operations may include offloading collectives, progress engines, and computing while data is moving through the network. It also includes data transformations, compression, and encryption services that can run on the DPU. It could also include checking that content from internet sources is properly signed.
- **Storage Access Isolation.** Making requests to a local or distributed parallel file system is inherent to the compute or edge node. Translating file requests to block or key-value requests, presenting mounts, and directly accessing the storage network endpoints need not be performed by the compute node itself, and can be conducted more securely within the trusted infrastructure control plane as a storage service running on the DPU. This is even true of local storage: an application user doesn't need to have direct access to disk sectors and shouldn't be able to tell the number of sizes of files (even if encrypted) owned by others. Presenting storage through a restricted file interface implements the principle of least privilege. Through an abstracted storage service, an implementation may be free to cache or prefetch data and manage its locality. The underlying implementation of the file system can still leverage current offerings such as Lustre, GPFS (IBM Spectrum Scale), NFSoRDMA, key-value stores, and object storage, once properly enabled.
- **Support for integration with the edge computing.** Computation in large systems is increasingly distributed and heterogeneous. It may include edge computing that manages data collection from science instruments or industrial controllers or robots, for example. Large amounts of data may be generated, which tend to need to be distilled into a smaller volume of higher-quality data before being sent on to a data center for further analysis. The computing elements at the edge may include a local cluster, a DGX, EGX or Jetson-based system. Accessing edge resources in a cloud native supercomputing should be transparent to any computational user or an instrumentalist/scientist working at the edge.

3   Implementation Principles and Technologies

The Cloud Native Supercomputing hardware architecture differs from traditional supercomputer designs with the insertion of a DPU between the node and the network, as shown in Fig. 1(a).

This DPU based infrastructure allows a cloud-native HPC and AI platform architecture that delivers native HPC performance without virtualization on an infrastructure platform that meets cloud services requirements. The implementation of the infrastructure comes from the open-source community and is driven by standards, similar as how some of the traditional HPC software stack that is maintained by a community including commercial companies, academic organizations, and government agencies.

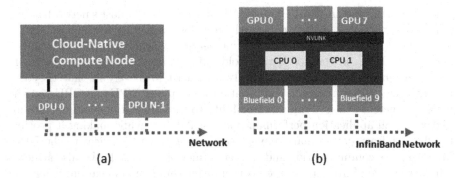

Fig. 1. The cloud native supercomputer node architecture. (a) Generic Cloud Native Supercomputing architecture (b) NVIDIA's reference architecture

Figure 1(b) gives a high level view of NVIDIA's implementation of the Cloud Native Supercomputing hardware architecture. A large number of GPUs each have their own connection to the network via a BlueField system-on-a-chip [7] DPU. Network connections may include InfiniBand for interconnection compute elements and attaching high-performance storage, and perhaps other networks connecting to the user management and slow storage planes.

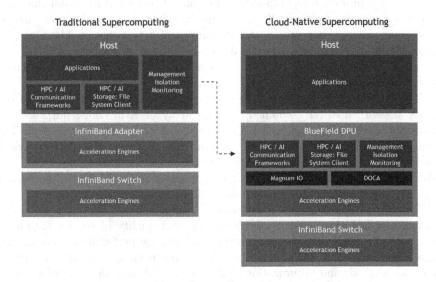

Fig. 2. System services perspective [2]: (a) Generic cloud-native supercomputer node (b) NVIDIA's cloud native supercomputer node

Figure 2 shows the node design of a cloud native supercomputer from a system services perspective and how it differs from traditional HPC system design from a system services perspective. NVIDIA's design choice for the DPU places the DPU and the Host Channel Adapter (HCA), the host's network access point, in a single system-on-a chip, with very close proximity to the host. As the figure shows, a portion of the application services workload is moved from the host to the DPU on the host's threshold, affinitizing those functions to where they run most efficiently, most securely, and least invasively in that they can interfere less with server-side computational resources. CPUs or GPUs on the node can increase their compute availability to the applications and operate for higher overall application performance and scalability, while making it possible to offload infrastructure management, storage, and cloud services to the DPU. Migrating the communication and storage frameworks to the DPUs also achieves a higher degree of overlap between computation and communication, delivering HPC supercomputing performance while improving resource utilization, node management, and a providing a secure environment for user sharing resources. The following sections describe design and implementation principles of the cloud native supercomputer in more detail.

3.1   Bluefield Data Processing Unit

The key element enabling the Cloud Native Supercomputing architecture transition is the Data Processing Unit. This is a fully integrated data-center-on-a-chip [7] platform that imbues each cloud-native supercomputing node with two new capabilities: First, offloading the control plane services from the main compute processor to the DPU and, thus, enabling bare-metal multi-tenancy. Second, an isolated data path with hardware acceleration that enables high performance data movement. As such, data path access to compute, network and storage is not required to be done via some virtualization layer, maintaining native performance characteristics.

The NVIDIA BlueField Data Processing Unit consists of an NVIDIA ConnectX network adapter combined with an array of Arm cores; purpose-built hardware acceleration engines for data processing and a PCIe subsystem. The combination of the acceleration engines and the programmable cores provides the flexibility to deploy complex cloud services from the host to the DPU, simplifying and eliminating compute overheads associated with them, as well as accelerating high-performance communication and storage frameworks.

When the infrastructure control plane is offloaded to a DPU, the DPU can provide the isolation, security, performance, and quality of service for multi-tenants while optimizing network traffic and storage performance. It can also help collect telemetry data on the host from various equipment in a supercomputer for analysis and optimization of the resource utilization. This information can be fed to a DPU-based infrastructure AI engines that can accelerate this analysis. These AI engines could also be used to assist in generating various system operational reports. In addition, DPUs supports protected data computing by securing data transfers between the storage unit and the supercomputer, and by executing data encryption on the DPU for user.

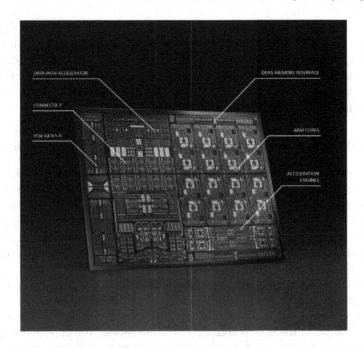

Fig. 3. NVIDIA's Bluefield-3 hardware components

Figure 3 highlights the main features of NVIDIA's next DPU, the BlueField-3 DPU. This is the device targeted for the first production release of NVIDIA's Cloud Native Supercomputing architecture.

The design choice placing the data processing elements in close proximity to the network data path, on the same die, with co-optimization opportunities, is preferable to inserting another host between a server nodes and the network for several reasons:

1. The close proximity and coordinated SOC design support processing data packets at close to wire speed. This enables maintaining the high-performance data transfers while providing services such as packet sniffing.
2. The inserted node lacks direct access to the memory of the server node, removing the ability of a user inaccessible resource to provide control plane services to the host.
3. The server node would need to use CPU cycles to handle control plane tasks, negating the benefits of offloading such tasks to the management CPU cores.
4. Inserting a server grade node in the control plane removes the ability to tailor its capabilities for services it is intended to provide. This includes hardware acceleration of specific tasks, such as regular-expression engines.
5. The data processing elements in the SOC provide a natural substrate for offloading communication library capabilities, supporting asynchronous communication.

The system on a chip approach provides the opportunity to select fitting grade CPU's for providing system and application level control plane needs and acceleration engines and the HCA core in a single device. This provides direct and secure management access to both the network resources to be used by the application as well as to host memory. This extends an existing system component and does not introduce new system level components.

3.2   Multi-tenant Isolation: Toward a Zero-Trust Architecture

In a data center in which resources like hosts, networks, and storage are shared, administrators and users tend to be forced to trust other users and the integrity of the overall infrastructure. In a zero-trust architecture, the principle of least privilege is applied wherever possible: don't give any agent any more privilege than they minimally need. The reason for the use of "toward" for a zero-trust architecture is obvious: no system is ever fully secure and we are striving to increase security over time.

While a host can run in kernel lockdown mode and only run user applications that are in containers, it is still possible for an application to break out of its container and wreak havoc with root privileges for long periods of time without being discovered. If the host is compromised and rooted, it can potentially access any network endpoint and any storage filer and potentially other hosts unless it is isolated. However, if the host's interaction with other nodes is limited to a well defined and constrained set of interfaces, and the services for reaching other resources are provided only by a trusted infrastructure control plane, then no one node needs to trust the potentially compromised host.

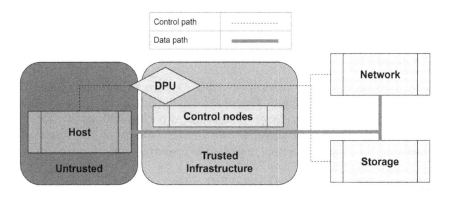

Fig. 4. Differentiation of trusted and untrusted components in a data center.

Consider an analogy. When you walk into a bank, you do not expect to put your hand on the money drawer. You speak nicely to an agent through a little window and if all goes well, lots of cash is briskly shuffled your way through the wide passage at the bottom of the glass. Similarly, agents running on an untrusted host are limited to restricted interfaces to agents running on the DPU, which is part of the trusted infrastructure, which can efficiently move data.

As shown in Fig. 4, the compute server can't directly "see" or address the network or storage without going through trusted infrastructure. The BlueField DPU is positioned on the threshold of the host. If permitted, it may share access to limited regions of CPU, GPU and DPU memory via the PCIe bus. The Blue-Field acts as a sheep's gate, inline with the control path to any connection outside of the CPU, but enabling direct and uninhibited RDMA on the data path. Thus, the DPU becomes a key mechanism for providing isolation of the untrusted host from the rest of the components in the network. The DPU can provide this isolation without the host CPU needing a hypervisor. Thus even if the DPU does some of the work, bare-metal performance is offered without having the cost of a hypervisor on the host.

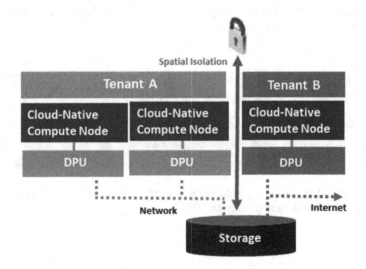

Fig. 5. Spacial isolation of cloud native hosts, where DPUs enforce network isolation and permit only selected connections. (Color figure online)

Consider the system with three nodes illustrated in Fig 5. Tenant A (green) uses nodes 1 and 2, while tenant B (red) uses node 3. There's a green network path between nodes 1 and 2 but not to 3. There's a green network path to storage from nodes 1 and 2 and a red path to storage from node 3. Node 3 has a red path to the internet but there's no green path. It's the DPUs by the three nodes that implement the routing tables that permit or deny network connectivity for the communication arrangement prescribed by the tenant control plane agent such as Slurm's prolog.

A remote server could also be at the edge of a network, intermittently connected to a central supercomputer or bigger data center. Just as the DPU manages the control path for interactions between a host and the rest of the data center, it can do the same between a host at the edge and a data center. It can also help with provisioning the edge node and with re-establishing a trusted network connection after disconnection, where the data center initiates the connection for greater security.

Spatial isolation within a node, where multiple users' jobs are isolated behind a single DPU, is something we'll aspire to in the longer term. But temporal isolation of one job from the next job to run on the same resources is the first step. Consider the compute node host as shown in Fig. 6, whether it is in a data center or at the edge. The DPU, as part of the trusted infrastructure, can help ensure a clean hand-off from one tenant to the next. The DPU can either be configured to make direct accesses to CPU and GPU memory, which is called introspection [21], or it can spur a process on the node to do its own inspection, albeit with potentially less security but less invasiveness. As part of this process, the BlueField DPU protects the integrity of the nodes, reprovisions resources as needed, clears states left behind, provides a clean boot image for a newly scheduled tenant, and more.

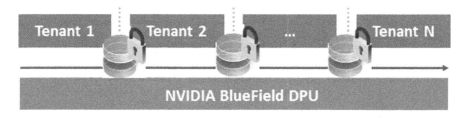

Fig. 6. Temporal multi-tenant isolation within the host enforced by Secure Compute Node Handoff services that involve the DPU.

3.3   Services

The DPU, in the trusted infrastructure control plane, can host several trusted services that span compute, networks, storage, and telemetry/logging. There are a few objectives in protecting activities in the data center. Data in memory, network, and storage should neither be snooped nor compromised. Compute should be what was intended and not perturbed by modifying the OS or libraries that the application calls. Finally, performance should be as expected and quality of service should be upheld. Each service conforms to an architecture that mandates discovery and enumeration, policy-based configuration, and telemetry (counters, e.g. to Prometheus) and logging (e.g. to Graylog) for activities executed or monitored as part of the service. Sample services are described below.

Secure Compute Node Handoff Service. Whether it is developing more efficient sources of energy, discovering new compounds for use in pharmaceutical compounds, or AI-based recommender systems, the value of outputs from computation is increasing rapidly. AI neural networks used for inference are a dense codification of the large data sets on which they were trained in actionable form. There is a growing interest in avoiding the cost of losing computation or having those valuable networks snooped, but also in avoiding running afoul of regulatory constraints on how data must be protected, e.g. for GDPR or HIPAA [9].

Attacks originating in host compute nodes leverage two forms of concurrency. The first is spatial, where two jobs execute at the same time on different hosts, where one node attempts to snoop on or corrupt another. The second is temporal, where one job's tenancy follows another on the same resources. A temporal attack may occur is the former tenant inadvertently leaves state behind, e.g. in uncleaned storage or memory, and the later job picks it up. Or, the first job may intentionally change persistent state in the node, e.g. corrupting the kernel or firmware or host platform application libraries, in ways that allow the later job to have its computation, data, or performance compromised.

There are two ways of avoiding these forms of attack. One is detection of corruption from the first job before the second executes. This is accomplished by examining relevant and vulnerable state. If the host is measured to be in a known-good condition, its state can be attested to in order to allow a confident transition to the next tenant. The other means of avoiding attacks is to scrub state at the end of a tenancy, for example by removing files and scrubbing memory.

Now consider that either attestation or scrubbing could itself be suppressed or corrupted by a malicious agent running on the corrupted host. One way around that is to do the work from the DPU. The DPU could initiate a DMA from host memory to DPU memory and conduct the examination there outside of the influence of a malicious host agent. The DPU could also measure the application doing the checking before and after it runs and check the kernel's tracking of running processes to be sure that it actually runs.

Secure Networks Service. Data centers may have a mix of networks. NVIDIA recommends InfiniBand (IB) for compute networks that connect hosts and edge nodes to the data centers, and for connections to high-bandwidth storage. Ethernet networks are commonly used for the user management planes that reach to the internet and to control nodes for Slurm, Kubernetes, subnet managers, etc. They may also be used to reach slower storage.

Isolation within IB networks is achieved at network adapters and switches using InfiniBand partition keys (PKeys) which are assigned by the InfiniBand Subnet Management (SM) utility. For network configuration purposes, each HCA port and optionally HCA-facing switch port is configured with the PKeys it is allowed to accept, and packets with mismatched PKeys are dropped. Corresponding PKey violation traps are generated and sent by HCA or switch firmware to the SM. The SM uses a unique Management Key (MKey) to configures switches and HCAs. Only management packets with the matching MKey are accepted. This programming can be done with inband communication rather than a separate network. Changing in permissible connections are made in responses to requests from the tenant control plane, such as the Slurm prolog and epilog at transitions of the specified granularity, e.g. among institutions or even among jobs.

Isolation on Ethernet networks is affected with routing tables. Those tables may be programmed and enforced in the top of rack (TOR) switch or in the DPU. In the DPU, more sophisticated mechanisms may be used that are accelerated by the DPU hardware, such as connection tracking. If these protections are not in place, one host might be able to ssh into another node and take control of it or otherwise interfere with it. Or one node might be able to direct traffic among nodes for another tenant to inspect or corrupt it.

Secure Storage Service. A file system client performs a mount operation to cause the files and directories of a remotely served volume to appear in the local file system namespace. The protocol used between the file system client and remote server may be a simple proxy of each local file system request; NFS is a good example of this. In such a model the role of access control is performed on either or both ends of the communication channel.

High-performance file system client access is enabled by offloading some of the storage access to the file system client as well. In such a mode, the server may merely coordinate with a file system client on where the client might directly read and write the data for a file. Restricting the operations required of the server to only metadata operations enables a scaling out of bandwidth-intensive workloads.

In either of these models, some level of trust is placed on the file system client. When the file system client executes in an untrusted CPU, unintended access by unauthorized clients will be a constant threat.

If the file system client were to run in the trusted DPU environment, much of the threat posed by the untrusted CPU will be thwarted. If access keys used to perform volume mounting are only exposed to the DPU, no entity in the CPU will ever need to have them. In addition, if the DPU is the only entity with a physical connection to the storage network hosting the servers, even a CPU in possession of the keys will be unable to access the storage.

Monitoring Service. There are generally two kinds of monitoring conducted. The first is telemetry, which counts a configured set of events. Event counts tend to be scraped in a pull model by tools like Prometheus. The second is logging, which accumulated a record of events of interest and pushes them to a remote entity like Graylog.

To summarize, every service running on the DPU conforms to an architecture. That architecture specifies capabilities that all services should conform to, including discovery and enumeration, configurability according to administrative policy, and support for monitoring interfaces such as Prometheus. The configurability includes settings that control what is counted by the service, and it enables Prometheus to know what and where to scrape.

3.4 In-Network Computing: Offloading Capabilities

DOCA. The Arm cores that are part of the DPU enable users to add their own offloaded application-specific capabilities. The NVIDIA DOCA software development kit (SDK), shown in Fig. 7, enables infrastructure developers to rapidly create software-defined, hardware-accelerated network, storage, security, telemetry and management services on top of the NVIDIA BlueField DPU, leveraging industry-standard APIs such as Open Smart Network API (OpenSNAPI). It provides a highly-flexible environment for developing applications and services that run on DPUs while seamlessly leveraging NVIDIA's In-Network Computing acceleration engines and Arm programmable engines to boost performance and scalability. In the future, embedded GPU cores will also be leveraged to execute AI algorithms on network workloads to gain increased security and performance. DOCA-based services are exposed in the hosts as industry-standard input/output interfaces, enabling infrastructure virtualization and isolation.

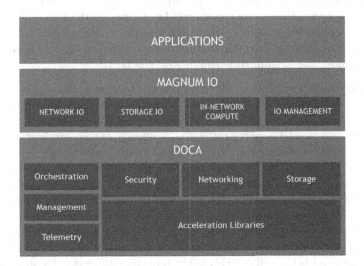

Fig. 7. The NVIDIA communications software stack includes the multi-GPU/multinode (Magnum IO) set of technologies, and the Data Center On a Chip (DOCA) SDK. HPC and AI applications may use employ programming models like MPI, NVSHMEM, UCX/UCC frameworks, and NCCL built on Magnum IO. Infrastructure developers may develop applications to work with the DPU using DOCA. This stack supports a range of operating systems, and it includes drivers, libraries, tools, documentation, and example applications.

Communication Library Offload. To enable fast and efficient development of new capabilities, the DOCA SDK provides a feature set required to enable new capabilities on the DPUs.

This includes:

- **Secure service provisioning.** Once a new service (e.g., acceleration engine, communication offload engine) is designed, providing the service to user processes requires some provisioning. There are multiple use cases supported to allow the required flexibility. Provisioning of a new service on a DPU can be implemented in several ways:

  - Software update for the DPUs in the system by the infrastructure administrator. In such a case, the service can be authenticated before it is installed. Once installed it can be available to all users on the system.
  - Dynamic provisioning for specific nodes based on tenant node allocation. The service is provisioned by the system administrator and can be authenticated. It allows a service to a specific tenant/user based on requirements and a service level agreement.
  - Run-time shipping of the service from the host. In this mode, the service can be compiled with the application in a way that when running on a system with DPUs, the service will be shipped to the DPU. In this mode, the service is not authenticated and this mode might be disabled in some embodiments to keep maximum isolation between user code running on the host and system code running on the DPU.

- **Service registration and discovery.** Any application running on the server or host can discover all services available on a local and remote DPU. This way, an application can decide which services it can get from the DPU and use the best available accelerations and offloads. These services can also be used for performance, or access of a resources in a secure way.

- **Secure communication channel.** An application using a service on the DPU might require communication between the processes running on the CPU/GPU in the host compute node and the service process running on the DPU. The communication channel might be used for control and configuration as well as for the data path moving user data between the user process and the service process. DOCA provides secure and high performance message queue APIs that efficiently enable data communication for short and long messages. When the service-user communication requires even more sophisticated and high performance communication, the user can set a UCX channel on top of the DOCA message queue.

- **Secure memory management and zero copy.** A service running on the DPU might want to send or receive data from a remote node (over the InfiniBand network) on behalf of a user process. While the DPU services are completely isolated from the host, it is of a great benefit to enable the service to send and receive data directly from the user memory on the host. A new API is provided to enable secure memory access delegation from the host user process to the service running in the DPU. Using those APIs, a host process can grant access to specific parts of its virtual memory to the DPU, allowing an efficient communication orchestration by the DPU service without the need to copy data to and from the DPU.

This support may be used to move the desired portion of the communication libraries implementations from the main host to the DPU. This allows communication algorithms to progress independently of the computational activity occurring on the host, supporting asynchronous progress. This is required for application computation-communication overlap, to improve applications performance and scalability.

Some functionality, like hardware tag matching and SHARP, have already been offloaded to the HCA or switch. The DPU creates opportunities to supplement these with new forms of offload, and retains the abilities to leverage features in the HCAs and switches.

The MVAPICH team at Ohio State University (OSU) has created a version of the nonblocking MPI allgather algorithm that uses the DPU capabilities. As shown in Fig. 8, this improves the performance of the algorithm by over 36% with large messages. Currently, work to take advantage of the DPU's capabilities for accelerating communication libraries, such as MPI and OpenSHMEM, is in progress.

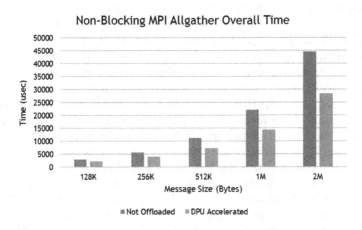

Fig. 8. Non-blocking Allgather MPI performance.

Application and Systems Software Offload. While the DPU is normally used to run code created by infrastructure developers, it could also be used by developers of application and systems software. The programmable Arm cores and the familiar host-side program development tool chain can be used for this purpose. As the new Cloud Native Supercomputer architecture is being developed, application developers are starting to explore these new capabilities, looking at ways to improve their workflows using the DPU.

One challenge with allowing more than a small, carefully-vetted set of code to run inside the trusted infrastructure control plane on the DPU is that doing so increases security risks and compromises the principle of least privilege. So one alternative is to run such code in a VM on the DPU, and another is to use an additional DPU for unrestricted application offload.

4 Summary

The state of the art with HPC is evolving from a near-singular focus of large capacity simulation runs, where data analytics is generally independent from the simulation and from interaction with live data, toward new workflows that integrate these functions in a way that is stressing previous system management and designs. To address these new requirements, NVIDIA is introducing a Cloud Native Supercomputing Architecture focused on providing bare-metal performance and scalability with a cloud-based user experience for interactivity, security, and resource elasticity. A cloud-native supercomputing platform provides the best of both worlds by combining peak performance and cluster efficiency while driving toward a modern zero trust model for security isolation and multi-tenancy. The key element enabling this architecture transition is the data processing unit. The DPU is a fully integrated data-center-on-a-chip platform that imbues each supercomputing node with two new capabilities: First, an infrastructure control plane processor that secures user access, storage access, networking, and life-cycle orchestration for the computing node, offloading the main compute processor from running the data center operating system, and enabling bare-metal multi-tenancy. Second, an isolated line-rate data path with hardware acceleration to offload data processing to the DPU to enable bare-metal performance on the compute node. To help enable the development and innovation of new tools to provide system software management that can leverage these new capabilities, NVIDIA has introduced a product called Base Command Manager (BCM) to enable HPC data centers to enjoy the benefits of comprehensive management of resources with greater trust and an SDK for Data Center management on Chip Architecture (DOCA). The BCM and DOCA software along with the DPU hardware are intended to accelerate the development and adoption of the Cloud Native Supercomputing Architecture.

Today, no one is offering public access to cloud native bare-metal multi-tenancy supercomputers, and you certainly can't buy the systems and software yourself. We anticipate an explosion of end users needing scaled systems for AI on HPC infrastructure to solve a range of problems for ground-breaking science and commercial applications. NVIDIA believes that these technologies should be democratized and is working to make them broadly available in data centers with HPC infrastructure.

References

1. Ansible: drive automation across open hybrid cloud deployments. https://www.ansible.com/overview/how-ansible-works
2. Cloud Native Supercomputing Website. https://www.nvidia.com/en-us/networking/products/cloud-native-supercomputing/
3. Foreman is a complete lifecycle management tool for physical and virtual servers. https://theforeman.org/
4. Gordon Bell prize winners embrace summit to advance COVID-19 research. https://www.hpcwire.com/off-the-wire/gordon-bell-prize-winners-embrace-summit-to-advance-covid-19-research/

5. NVIDIA base command: AI workflow and cluster management software. https://docs.nvidia.com/base-command/index.html
6. NVIDIA base command platform
7. NVIDIA unveils new data center chips to speed pace of AI. https://www.datacenterknowledge.com/machine-learning/nvidia-unveils-new-data-center-chips-speed-pace-ai
8. The world's first cloud-native supercomputer. https://www.nvidia.com/en-us/data-center/dgx-superpod/
9. Annas, G.J.: HIPAA regulations – a new era of medical-record privacy? N. Engl. J. Med. **348**(15), 1486–1490 (2003). PMID: 12686707
10. 0 Bezemer, C.-P., Zaidman, A.: Multi-tenant SaaS applications: maintenance dream or nightmare? In: Proceedings of the Joint ERCIM Workshop on Software Evolution (EVOL) and International Workshop on Principles of Software Evolution (IWPSE), IWPSE-EVOL 2010, pp. 88–92. Association for Computing Machinery, New York, NY, USA (2010)
11. Fagnan, K., Nashed, Y., Perdue, G., Ratner, D., Shankar, A., Yoo, S.: Data and models: a framework for advancing AI in science (2019)
12. Gupta, D., Cherkasova, L., Gardner, R., Vahdat, A.: Enforcing performance isolation across virtual machines in Xen. In: van Steen, M., Henning, M. (eds.) Middleware 2006. LNCS, vol. 4290, pp. 342–362. Springer, Heidelberg (2006). https://doi.org/10.1007/11925071_18
13. Kumar, M.: An incorporation of artificial intelligence capabilities in cloud computing. Int. J. Eng. Comput. Sci. **5**, 19070–19073 (2016)
14. Mansfield-Devine, S.: Security through isolation. Comput. Fraud Secur. **2010**(5), 8–11 (2010)
15. Peterka, T., et al.: ASCR workshop on in situ data management: enabling scientific discovery from diverse data sources (2019)
16. Rad, P., Chronopoulos, A.T., Lama, P., Madduri, P., Loader, C.: Benchmarking bare metal cloud servers for HPC applications. In: 2015 IEEE International Conference on Cloud Computing in Emerging Markets (CCEM), pp. 153–159 (2015)
17. Rose, S., Borchert, O., Mitchell, S., Connelly, S.: Zero trust architecture. NIST Special Publication 800-207 (2020)
18. SAIC. Report on HPC trends for federal government (2019)
19. Schneider, F.B.: Least privilege and more [computer security]. IEEE Secur. Priv. **1**(5), 55–59 (2003)
20. Stevens, R., Taylor, V., Nichols, J., Maccabe, A.B., Yelick, K., Brown, D.: AI for Science. U.S. Department of Energy Office of Science Report (2019)
21. Win, T.Y., Tianfield, H., Mair, Q.: Virtualization security combining mandatory access control and virtual machine introspection. In: 2014 IEEE/ACM 7th International Conference on Utility and Cloud Computing, pp. 1004–1009 (2014)

Scientific Data Challenges

Smoky Mountain Data Challenge 2021: An Open Call to Solve Scientific Data Challenges Using Advanced Data Analytics and Edge Computing

Pravallika Devineni[1]([⊠]), Panchapakesan Ganesh[1], Nikhil Sivadas[1],
Abhijeet Dhakane[1], Ketan Maheshwari[1], Drahomira Herrmannova[1],
Ramakrishnan Kannan[1], Seung-Hwan Lim[1], Thomas E. Potok[1],
Jordan Chipka[2], Priyantha Mudalige[3], Mark Coletti[1], Sajal Dash[1],
Arnab K. Paul[1], Sarp Oral[1], Feiyi Wang[1], Bill Kay[1], Melissa Allen-Dumas[1],
Christa Brelsford[1], Joshua New[1], Andy Berres[1], Kuldeep Kurte[1],
Jibonananda Sanyal[1], Levi Sweet[1], Chathika Gunaratne[1], Maxim Ziatdinov[1],
Rama Vasudevan[1], Sergei Kalinin[1], Olivera Kotevska[1], Jean Bilheux[1],
Hassina Bilheux[1], Garrett E. Granroth[1], Thomas Proffen[1], Rick Riedel[1],
Peter Peterson[1], Shruti Kulkarni[1], Kyle Kelley[1], Stephen Jesse[1],
and Maryam Parsa[4]

[1] Oak Ridge National Laboratory, Oak Ridge, TN, USA
devinenip@ornl.gov
[2] Telemetry Sports, Noblesville, USA
[3] General Motors, Detroit, USA
[4] George Mason University, Fairfax, USA

Abstract. The 2021 Smoky Mountains Computational Sciences and Engineering Conference enlists scientists from across Oak Ridge National Laboratory (ORNL) and industry to be data sponsors and help create data analytics and edge computing challenges for eminent datasets in a variety of scientific domains. This work describes the significance of each of the eight datasets and their associated challenge questions. The challenge questions for each dataset were required to cover multiple difficulty levels. An international call for participation was sent to students, asking them to form teams of up to six people and apply novel data analytics and edge computing methods to solve these challenges.

Keywords: Scientific data · Data analytics · Machine learning · Edge computing

This manuscript has been co-authored by UT-Battelle, LLC, under contract DE-AC05-00OR22725 with the US Department of Energy (DOE). The US government retains and the publisher, by accepting the article for publication, acknowledges that the US government retains a nonexclusive, paid-up, irrevocable, worldwide license to publish or reproduce the published form of this manuscript, or allow others to do so, for US government purposes. DOE will provide public access to these results of federally sponsored research in accordance with the DOE Public Access Plan http://energy.gov/downloads/doe-public-access-plan).

J. Nichols et al. (Eds.): SMC 2021, CCIS 1512, pp. 361–382, 2022.
https://doi.org/10.1007/978-3-030-96498-6_21

1   Introduction

This year's Smoky Mountains data challenge consists of two categories of challenges - data analytics and edge computing. All the challenges we host represent real world problems in different areas of research. While data analytics is a well known to researchers, edge computing is an emerging field that is especially useful in scientific domains requiring real-time feedback. Unlike traditional computing, edge computing devices are placed closer to the data source and take on the task of carrying out preliminary data processing instead of transmitting raw data to data centers for processing [10]. This greatly reduces the latency and computational complexity, enabling the edge computing nodes to perform tasks such as real-time signal and image processing, combinatorial optimization, agent-based modeling, big data analytics etc. The 2021 challenge solutions could impact unsolved questions in ferroelectric materials science, identifying new links in COVID-19 knowledge graphs, autonomous driving, designing sustainable cities, improving efficiency in supercomputing resources, effective sampling for electron microscopy scanning, resolving spatial features in neutron radiography and high dimensional active learning[1].

By requiring the challenge questions for each data set to cover multiple difficulty levels and by allowing students and experts to compete in separate categories we hope to draw in a diverse set of researchers and perspectives to help solve these questions. The call for participation was broadly advertised and open to all interested parties. It appeared in scientific and engineering newsletters such as HPCWire, and was spread by social media and via mailing lists. Invitations to participate were also sent to several university computer science department professors and users of Oak Ridge Leadership Computing facility.

In addition to providing and serving the datasets for the challenges, organizers and data sponsors held an interactive webinar to explain the relevance of each challenge task and describe the size and composition of its associated dataset, to which the video is publicly available[2]. Subsequently, the participants were able to interact with the data sponsors and other participants via a dedicated Slack channel during months before solutions were due, so participants could post questions about the tasks and get answers from each other and the data sponsors. Lastly, to especially provide direction to young researchers, the organizers provided the participants with resources on better scientific paper writing and presenting effective lightening talks.

In this paper, each challenge has its own section wherein the authors of the challenge describe the motivation and science behind the challenge, the data and its origins, and the reasoning behind the individual challenge questions.

---

[1] https://smc-datachallenge.ornl.gov/data-challenges-2021/.
[2] https://www.youtube.com/watch?v=e6gqWr0Ly4g.

2 Challenge 1: Unraveling Hidden Order and Dynamics in a Heterogeneous Ferroelectric System Using Machine Learning

2.1 Background

Ferroelectrics are materials that have spontaneous electric polarization that can be reversed by the application of an external electric field. Existence of a spontaneous polarization implies that the ferroelectric material shows a hysteretic response to the applied field, ideal for use as a memory function, in a ferroelectric random-access memory (FeRAM) device.

Real materials are not pure - they have point-and extended-defects, buried-interfaces as well as domain-walls (i.e. spatial discontinuity in the local polarization vector). In the presence of heterogeneities, in addition to the global order-parameter (i.e. overall spontaneous polarization of the material) there are additional manifestations on the local order parameter (local polarization), that lead to 'hidden' order in the material. As an example, interfaces of different ferroelectric thin-films can show chiral polarization loops, whose formation, stability and motion are not only governed by material properties, but also topological properties. We find that the shape as well as the area of the hysteresis loops are strongly modified by such 'hidden' order. Further, the dynamics of ferroelectric switching are also significantly modified in the presence of such 'hidden' order in heterogeneous ferroelectrics.

We are specifically interested in discovering such 'hidden' order from molecular dynamics simulations and correlate them with the type of heterogeneities present in the simulation, and ascertain how this order influences not just the memory function, but also its 'dynamics' under externally applied field. Dynamic control of memory is the basis of ferroelectric based neuromorphic materials.

We provided the files with local polarization for a length of time for all datasets. Local polarization P_u of each unit cell shown in Fig. 1 was calculated using:

$$P_u(t) = \frac{1}{V_u}\left(Z^*_{Ti} r_{Ti}(t) + \frac{1}{8}Z^*_{Ba}\sum_{i=1}^{8} r_{Ba,i}(t) + \frac{1}{2}Z^*_o\sum_{i=1}^{6} r_{o,i}(t)\right) \tag{1}$$

where V_u is the volume of the unit cell, Z^*_{Ti}, Z^*_{Ba}, Z^*_o are the charges of the Ti, Ba and O atoms obtained using the Electron Equilibration Method (EEM) approach using a reactive force field (ReaxFF), and $r_{Ti}(t)$, $r_{Ba,i}(t)$, $r_{O,i}(t)$ are the positions of Ti, Ba and O atoms of each unit cell at time t [1].

2.2 Dataset Description

We provide two batches of datasets:

- **Batch-A:** Equilibrium dynamics at a constant temperature at zero electric-field, with one trajectory each for 4-different defect structures (i.e. SETs 1 to 4). Each trajectory has a time-step of 0.25 fs, and is run for 7775000 time-steps, with snapshots written out every 4 time-steps (i.e. every $1fs$);

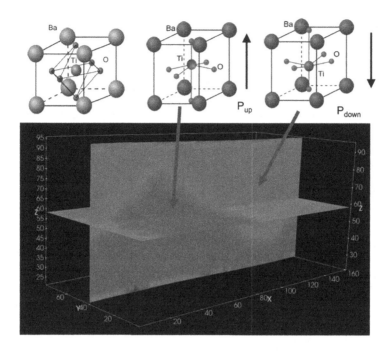

Fig. 1. Unit cell schematic of the BaTiO$_3$ (top), for the case with zero-polarization, polarization pointing UP and polarization pointing DOWN, respectively. The bottom figure, generated by PARAVIEW, is a snapshot from the molecular dynamics (i.e. time-series data of local polarization), where the UP regions show up as orange, and DOWN regions as blue. The domain-wall i.e. the interface between the UP/DOWN region should have different dynamics than the rest. (Color figure online)

- **Batch-B:** Non-Equilibrium dynamics at a constant temperature with the same 0.25 fs time-step, but data dumped every 500 times-steps (i.e. every 125fs) for each of the SETs. The total trajectory of each defect structure (i.e. each SETs 1 to 4) is 2800000 time-steps (5600 snapshots), with stepping of electric-field by 0.01 $V/A°$, after every 100,000 time-steps (i.e. every 200 snapshots), from E = 0 to E = 0.05 $V/A°$ to E = -0.05 $V/A°$ to E=0.05 $V/A°$.

One can visualize the dynamics of the given dataset by using the uploaded VTKFILES using the PARAVIEW software. LOCAL_DIPOLE_FILES snippet below contains co-ordinate of Ti atoms and local polarization for each snapshot (Fig. 2 and Table 1).

```
#TIMESTEP 250000 0.000000   0.000000   0.000000 162.462759 81.229598 120.800000
2.079   2.043 20.809        0.00505805        -0.00416993       -0.00028926
2.059   2.028 25.018       -0.00045007        -0.00058029        0.00758195
2.085   2.019 29.146        0.00016893         0.00004470        0.00600944

1 #TIMESTEP <timestep> <xlow> <ylow> <zlow> <xhigh> <yhigh> <zhigh>
2 <x>    <y>    <z>    <Px>    <Py>    <Pz>
```

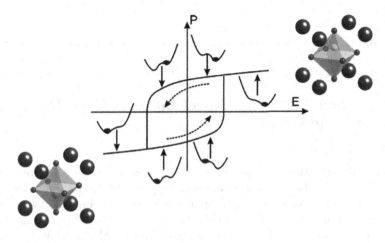

Fig. 2. Shows the hysteric response of BaTiO$_3$ to an applied electric field. It is not clear how domain wall dynamics differ for different heterogeneities, and control the shape of this loop

Table 1. Representation of the two subsets in the dataset, each containing different types of defects.

Subset		File name	Files
A	Equilibrium Dynamics	SET1 (no defects)	VTKFILES, LOCAL_DIPOLE_FILES
		SET2 (with O defect)	VTKFILES, LOCAL_DIPOLE_FILES
		SET3 (with Ba defect)	VTKFILES, LOCAL_DIPOLE_FILES
		SET4 (with Ba-O defects)	VTKFILES, LOCAL_DIPOLE_FILES
B	Non-Equilibrium Dynamics	SET1 (no defects)	VTKFILES, LOCAL_DIPOLE_FILES
		SET2 (with O defect)	VTKFILES, LOCAL_DIPOLE_FILES
		SET3 (with Bav defect)	VTKFILES, LOCAL_DIPOLE_FILES
		SET4 (with Ba-O defects)	VTKFILES, LOCAL_DIPOLE_FILES

First line represents the header, where unit of timestep is (fs), xlow-xhigh determines the cartesian min/max of the simulation box along the x-direction. Similarly, for y- and z-directions. The first three columns in line 2 are cartesian co-ordinates of Ti atoms (in $A\circ$) while next three columns are the cartesian coordinates of the local polarization vector (in micro-Coulomb/cm2).

2.3 Challenges of Interest

1. How to extract and represent dynamical states from a molecular dynamics simulation using graph-based methods?
2. How do these dynamical states evolve under an applied electric-field?
3. How are these dynamical states modified in the presence of heterogeneities thereby leading to a change in the hysteretic response?

Notes

- ML algorithms to be implemented in one of the following languages: Python, C/C++, Julia.
- Preference for ML framework: PyTorch/Pytorch Geometric, Tensorflow.

3   Challenge 2: Finding Novel Links in COVID-19 Knowledge Graph

3.1   Background

The scientific literature is expanding at incredible rates, which were recently estimated to be in the millions of new articles per year. Extracting information from such vast stores of knowledge is an urgent need, as exemplified by the recent open release of materials relevant to the current SARS-CoV-2 pandemic. In this context, this challenge seeks to develop algorithms for the analysis and mining of knowledge graphs. The main task in this challenge is to leverage a graph of biomedical concepts related to COVID-19 and the relations between them to try to discover novel, plausible relations between concepts. For this challenge, the participants are provided with a graph dataset of biomedical concepts and relations between them extracted from scientific literature, along with all-pairs shortest path information between the concepts in the graph. They will be asked to analyze the data and use it to predict which concepts will form direct novel relations in the future. In addition, they will be asked to rank the predicted links according to the predicted importance of each relation.

3.2   Introduction

The scientific literature is expanding at incredible rates, which were recently estimated to be in the millions of new articles per year [7]. Extracting information from such vast stores of knowledge is an urgent need, as exemplified by the recent open release of materials relevant to the current SARS-CoV-2 pandemic [8]. Given that the volume of information is easily beyond the capacity of any one person, analysts have been strongly motivated to develop automated knowledge-mining methods and extraction tools [2,14,17].

In this context, this challenge seeks to develop algorithms for the analysis and mining of *knowledge graphs*. More specifically, this challenge is based on the process of literature-based discovery [12]. It has been shown that previously unknown relationships exist in the scientific literature that can be uncovered by finding concepts that link disconnected entities [12,13,15]. This process, called *Swanson Linking*, is based on the discovery of hidden relations between concepts A and C via intermediate B-terms: if there is no known direct relation A-C, but there are published relations A-B and B-C one can hypothesize that there is a plausible, novel, yet unpublished indirect relation A-C. In this case the B-terms take the role of bridging concepts. For instance, in 1986, Swanson applied this concept to propose a connection between dietary fish oil (A) and Raynaud's disease (C) through high blood viscosity (B), which fish oil reduces [11]. This connection was validated in a clinical trial three years later.

3.3 Dataset Description

The main task in this challenge is to leverage a graph of biomedical concepts related to COVID-19 and the relations between them to try to discover novel, plausible relations between concepts.

The participants will be provided with the following data:

- **Training data:**
  - Graph representing biomedical concepts and relations between them constructed from PubMed[3], Semantic MEDLINE[4], and CORD-19[5]. This graph will represent a historic snapshot of the data (e.g., a version of the knowledge graph built from papers published up until June 2020). An explanation of the graph is shown in Fig. 3.
  - Data representing the shortest path between all pairs of concepts in the above graph.
- **Validation data:**
  - A version of the above graph and shortest path information that includes all available data (e.g., all data up until February 2021).
  - List of concept pairs representing novel relations that have formed since the year captured in the above graph, e.g., all novel relations between the concepts in the graph that have formed between June 2020 and February 2021.
  - Additionally, each concept pair will be assigned several ranks representing the importance of the relation. These ranks will include rank according to the moth and year the connection has been formally established (approximated using the date of publication of the associated research article), number of citations received by the relevant article, and other relevant ranks.

The participants will be asked to use the graph and the all-pairs shortest paths information provided (training data) to predict which concepts will form a direct connection in the future (validation data). This process is depicted in Fig. 4.

A detailed description of the dataset including the format and the process used to produce the dataset is provided in [5]. The dataset that will be provided for this competition represents an updated version of the dataset[6] described in [5]. The updated version includes concepts that were extracted from articles published since the first release of the dataset.

The participants are allowed to leverage external data, particularly data from PubMed and Semantic MEDLINE that are not included in the provided dataset.

---

[3] https://pubmed.ncbi.nlm.nih.gov/.

[4] https://skr3.nlm.nih.gov/SemMedDB/.

[5] https://www.semanticscholar.org/cord19.

[6] https://dx.doi.org/10.13139/OLCF/1646608.

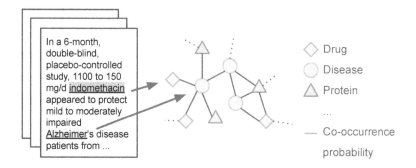

Fig. 3. Depiction of the challenge data for Challenge 2.

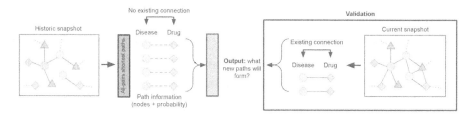

Fig. 4. Depiction of the challenge task for Challenge 2.

3.4   Challenges of Interest

1. Analyze and visualize the provided graph and all-pairs shortest paths (APSP) data and provide statistics such as, betweenness centrality, average path length and frequency of concept occurrence in different paths.
2. Compare APSP path statistics with the future connections – are the length of a path between two concepts or other path statistics indicative of whether the concepts will form a connection in the future?
3. Develop a classification or a model that uses the APSP data or other relevant data as input and predicts which concepts will form a connection in the future.
4. Develop ranking model/function for ranking the predicted links according to their importance.

4   Challenge 3: Synthetic-to-Real Domain Adaptation for Autonomous Driving

4.1   Background

The ultimate ambition of autonomous driving is that it would be able to transport us safely to every corner of the world in any condition. However, a major roadblock to this ambition is the inability of machine learning models to perform well across a wide range of domains. For instance, a computer vision model trained on data from sunny California will have diminished performance when tested on data from snowy Michigan. The goal of this challenge is to develop innovative techniques to enhance domain adaptation capabilities. The accompanying dataset spans both synthetic and real-world domains to present a unique challenge to the participant.

State of the art autonomous driving technology relies on robust artificial intelligence (AI) models. These models require vast amounts of diverse, high-quality driving data to be collected and annotated for training. Although these AI models demonstrate good performance in local environments, they often fail when met with new data from a different distribution. This problem, also known as distribution shift, can occur due to changes in lighting, weather, and sensor hardware/configuration.

A more drastic form of distribution shift is encountered when the AI model is trained on synthetic data but tested with real-world data. Although this is a very appealing strategy for AI model development, as it eliminates the need to collect and annotate large amounts of costly real-world driving data, distribution shift remains a difficulty that must first be resolved. Consequently, the research community has put considerable emphasis on domain adaptation techniques to resolve difficulties such as these.

4.2   Dataset Description

The dataset is comprised of both real and synthetic images from a vehicle's forward-facing camera. Each camera image is accompanied by a corresponding pixel-level semantic segmentation image.

The training data is split into two sets. The first set consists of synthetic RGB images collected with a wide range of weather and lighting conditions using the CARLA simulator [4]. The second set includes a small pre-selected subset of data from the Cityscapes training dataset - which is comprised of RGB-segmentation image pairs from driving scenarios in various European cities [3].

The testing data is split into three sets. The first set contains synthetic images with weather/lighting conditions that were not present in the training set. The second set is a subset of the Cityscapes testing dataset. Finally, the third set is an unknown testing set which will not be revealed to the participants until after the submission deadline.

4.3   Challenges of Interest

1. Data augmentation: Determine the most effective data augmentation strategies to enhance the model's performance on the testing sets.
2. Model development: Determine novel model architectures or training methodology that can be used to enhance performance on the testing sets.

Performance will be measured by the mean intersection-over-union (mIOU) across all classes for the segmentation results on all three testing sets.

Note: Participants are permitted to perform data augmentation by transforming the given training data (e.g. crop, mirror, brighten, etc.). However, they are not permitted to use additional data outside of the provided training data - either real or synthetic - to augment training (e.g. use additional Cityscapes training data outside of the pre-selected subset).

5   Challenge 4: Analyzing Resource Utilization and User Behavior on Titan Supercomputer

5.1   Background

Resource utilization statistics of submitted jobs on a supercomputer can help us understand how users from various scientific domains use high-performance computing (HPC) platforms and better design a job scheduler. We explore to generate insight regarding workload distribution and usage patterns domains from job scheduler trace, GPU failure information, and project-specific information collected from Titan supercomputer. Furthermore, we want to know how the scheduler performance varies over time and how the users' scheduling behavior changes following a system failure. These observations have the potential to provide valuable insight, which is helpful to prepare for system failures. These practices will help us develop and apply novel machine learning algorithms in understanding system behavior, requirement, and better scheduling of HPC systems.

5.2   Dataset Description

This challenge has two datasets[7]. Each dataset directory has a `ReadMe` document that has information on all the features.

- *RUR*: This dataset is the job scheduler traces collected from the Titan supercomputer from 01/01/2015 to 07/31/2019 (2015.csv–2019.csv). These were collected using Resource Utilization Report (RUR), a Cray-developed resource-usage data collection and reporting system. It contains the usage information of its critical resources (CPU, Memory, GPU, and I/O) of each running job on Titan during that period [16].
  Project Areas: Every job is associated with a project ID. The ProjectAreas.csv dataset provides a mapping of the project ID to its domain science.
- *GPU*: There have been some hardware-related issues in the GPUs in Titan that caused some GPUs to fail, sometimes irrecoverably during some job runs. This dataset provides information regarding these failures during the execution of the submitted jobs. Each GPU on Titan has a unique serial number (SN), and they are installed in a server location. A GPU can be installed in a location, then removed from that location following a failure, and then re-installed in a different location after fixing the problem. If the

---

[7] https://doi.ccs.ornl.gov/ui/doi/334.

failure can't be recovered, the GPU might be removed entirely from Titan. Two prominent types of failures resulted in the removal of GPUs from Titan: *Double Bit Error (DBE)* and *Out of the Bus (OTB)*. The dataset has the following fields:

1. SN: Serial number of a GPU
2. location: The location where it is installed
3. insert: The time when it was inserted into that location
4. remove: The time when it was removed from that location
5. duration: Amount of time the GPU spent in this location
6. out: If the device was taken out entirely w/o a re-installment into a new location
7. event: If the GPU was taken out entirely, the reason for its removal.

To learn more about this dataset, please refer to the Github repository[8] and the related publication [9].

5.3   Challenges of Interest

There are four challenges with varying degrees of difficulty and openness of the scope. The participants are encouraged to explore the problems in-depth and refine the challenge objectives.

1. Perform exploratory data analysis on the RUR dataset to summarize data characteristics. Is there any relationship between client CPU memory usage, GPU memory usage, and the job size (number of compute nodes)?
2. For every job, extract the project information from the command feature given in the RUR dataset. Use clustering methods to see if there are similarities in the resource usage patterns among jobs based on projects.
3. Given a month's data, can you predict the next seven days' usage (memory, CPU hours (stime and utime), GPU hours (gpu secs), etc.)? Is there any seasonal impact on such predictions? The predictive model should consider various domains, user, season, system failure, etc.
4. (a) Can you characterize the time-lagged relationship between the GPU dataset and the RUR dataset? How does the change in pattern in the RUR dataset affect any change in pattern in the GPU dataset?
   (b) Provide a predictive analysis on how the change in GPU dataset has impacted the user behaviors in terms of submitted number of jobs and job sizes. Verify and validate your predictive analysis with the RUR dataset. You can consider GPU data and the RUR data from early 2015 to build and train your predictive models and verify and validate your predictive models with the GPU and RUR data from 2015–2017.

---

[8] https://github.com/olcf/TitanGPULife.

6   Challenge 5: Sustainable Cities: Socioeconomics, Building Types, and Urban Morphology

6.1   Background

In urban environments, demographic, and infrastructural characteristics co-evolve and together determine risks, vulnerability and resilience. Infrastructure systems such as energy and water determine many environmental risks and provide access to various essential services. These risks and benefits are transferred across long distances and differentially across demographic and socioeconomic subgroups. Additionally, urban environments have significant effects on public health and population level resilience, especially to extreme events such as heat waves. However, interactions among urban microclimate, urban morphology, socioeconomic heterogeneity, and anthropogenic activities are not well understood. To begin to understand these interactions, our team has developed three new datasets for the Las Vegas Metropolitan Statistical Area, and we challenge the participants to combine these data sets (and other relevant data of participants' choosing) to answer our challenge questions.

We look forward to presentations using novel methods for interpreting and visualizing this data that draw on machine learning and other big data techniques, and we welcome new collaborations to complement the work of understanding how current and future neighborhood morphological patterns can contribute to the development of smart and sustainable cities.

6.2   Dataset Description

- Microsoft building shapefile dataset[9]. Data type: ESRI shapefile (size: 4378 MB).
- Building archetypes for the city based on an open-source aggregation scheme that reflects the statistical occurrence of each building type in the city including estimates of building use type, number of stories or building height, total floor area, and year built for each building/parcel. Data type: csv (size: 160 MB). Please find the pertaining dataset[10] and visualization[11].
- Census block group summaries of building characteristics pertaining to construction type and quality, parcel layout, lot value, and numerous home characteristics, i.e., economic characteristics associated with building size and shape in each block group. Data type: csv (size: 6.69 MB). Data is publicly available with a DOI[12].
- Census tract level files containing 100 m resolution urban parameters for each 5m vertical level. Parameters include frontal area density, plan area density, roof area density, mean building height, building surface to plan area ratio, complete aspect ratio, height to width ratio, and many more. Data type: csv (size 22.7 MB).

---

[9] https://www.arcgis.com/home/item.html?id=3b0b8cf27ffb49e2a2c8370f9806f267.
[10] https://zenodo.org/record/4552901.YY6zXL3MIcB.
[11] https://evenstar.ornl.gov/autobem/virtual_vegas/.
[12] https://doi.ccs.ornl.gov/ui/doi/328.

6.3   Challenges of Interest

1. How does the number and arrangement of buildings, along with the building surface to plan area ratio in a given block group relate to building construction quality and value?
2. What is the distribution of commercial, industrial, and residential buildings within each block group? Do these distributions correlate with building age? Building value? Building size?
3. Using temperature data from a source of the participant's choosing, are there locations within the city that tend to be warmer than others? How does this relate to building density and building type?
4. How does the built environment and the local scale experience of heat co-vary with socio-economic and demographic characteristics of residents?
5. Using additional data on urban landscaping, how does green space vary with urban temperature and demographic distribution? Find an example here[13].

7   Challenge 6: Where to Go in the Atomic World

7.1   Background

Scanning Probe and Electron microscopes are the tools that opened the atomic world for exploration by providing the beautiful images of metals, oxides, semi- and superconductors with atomic resolution. Currently, both the scanning probe and transmission electron microscopy (SPM and STEM) fields almost invariably rely on classical rectangular raster scans in which the beam or the probe rapidly traverses the surface in the fast scan direction, and slowly shifts in the perpendicular direction forming the slow scan direction. This scanning mode offers both the advantage of easy implementation and yields data in the form of 2D maps that can be readily interpreted by a human eye.

However, the rectangular scanning is inefficient from the information theory point of view, since the interesting information is often concentrated in a small number of regions on the sample surface. Hence, beyond rectangular scanning becomes a key prerequisite for the AE aimed at structural discovery, minimizing the surface damage, or attempting controlled modification of the surface. The possible paradigms for AE in this case are summarized in Fig. 5. Ultimately, we can envision the freeform scanning approaches, where the direction and velocity of the probe motion are updated based on previously detected information. However, given the latencies of SPM and STEM imaging, this will necessitate development of specialized light algorithms and edge computations, as discussed below. On a shorter time frame, adapting the parameters of the predefined waveform, e.g., pitch of the spiral or line density in rectangular sub scans offers a more practical alternative.

---

[13] https://koordinates.com/layer/97329-las-vegas-nv-trees/.

7.2   Dataset Description

'Graphene_CrSi.npy' contains a scanning transmission electron microscopy (STEM movie from graphene monolayer. The movie is a sequence of atom-resolved images from the same sample region that undergoes chemical and structural transformations due to interaction with electron beam (which is used to perform imaging). 'topo_defects.npy' contains coordinates of some of the objects of interest (topological defects in graphene). It is a dictionary, where keys are frame numbers and values are xy coordinates. These objects are usually localized in relatively small areas of the image and we are interested in identifying them without having to scan an entire grid (which leads to fast degradation of the sample).

The dataset is publicly available using its DOI[14].

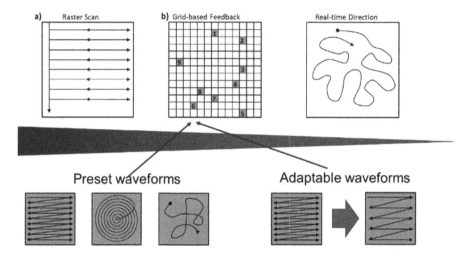

Fig. 5. Possible scanning paradigms in SPM and STEM. Shown are (a) classical scan, (b) sub-scan-based images for structural discovery, based either on preset or adjustable scan-forms, or (c) freeform scanning. The selection of image regions in (b) or scanning direction and velocity in (c) are guided by a suitable ML algorithm.

7.3   Challenges of Interest

The challenges are

1. Given the provided ground truth images of graphene with atomic resolution, formulate the algorithm for efficient exploration of the surface looking for elements of interest. These can be predefined (e.g., identification of the topological defects in graphene whose ground truth coordinates are provided as a part of the submission), or algorithm can optimize the discovery (e.g., curiosity in RL methods).

---

[14] https://doi.ccs.ornl.gov/ui/doi/326.

2. Assume that the given images are "virtual microscope", and the algorithm can address the specific regions on the sample surface. Note that natural constraint that imaging is performed via moving the probe, rather than just selecting pixels at random.
3. Explore the approach based on sub-image scanning with preset scanform, variable scanform, and freeform scanning.

   Hint: This can be based on the Bayesian Optimization or Reinforcement Learning where the objective could be trying to visit a maximal number points of interests in the shortest amount of time.

8 Challenge 7: Increased Image Spatial Resolution for Neutron Radiography

8.1 Background

Neutron radiography (nR) is a technique that is used for a broad range of applications such as energy materials, engineering, geomaterials (rocks, plants and soil), biology, and archeology. A sample placed in front of a 2D detector is illuminated with neutrons and a shadowgraph is measured based on the neutrons that transmitted through the sample. Like most imaging techniques, domain applications require increased spatial resolution beyond what is currently and routinely achievable today. New detector technologies offer the possibility to increase spatial resolution by reducing the effective pixel size. More specifically, advanced analysis is used to precisely locate the position of impact of a detected neutron (also called neutron event). The challenge here is to develop a novel method to better resolve the neutron position for the Timepix3 detector, hence increasing the spatial resolution of the radiograph. Specifically, the goal of this challenge it to resolve features that are smaller than 25–50 µm.

8.2 Dataset Description

Neutron Radiography Principle
Neutron radiography is a technique that measures neutrons transmitted through an object placed in front of a two-dimensional pixelated detector. The radiograph is often called the transmission radiograph as it corresponds to the ratio of the transmitted beam, I, over the incident beam, I_0. The Lambert-Beer law defines the transmission, T, as

$$T = I/I_0 = e^{-\mu x} \tag{2}$$

where μ is the linear attenuation coefficient and x is the object thickness.

Neutron radiography is complementary to X-ray radiography. Since neutrons have no charge, they can deeply penetrate into materials, such as steel, which are often difficult to access with X-rays. Moreover, neutrons are sensitive to light elements such as hydrogen and lithium. Examples of domain applications that frequently utilize neutron radiography are the measurements of lithium distribution in batteries used for electronics such as a cellphone, water uptake in plant roots, hydrocarbons in vehicle particulate filters, inner structures of archaeological materials or planetary objects such as meteorites.

Since neutrons have no charge, their measurement is non trivial. Most detection methods involve their capture and conversion into a charged particle that can then be detected. In the case of this challenge, the pixelated detector is called a multi-channel plate (MCP) timepix3 detector. Neutrons are first absorbed in the ^{10}B in the MCP and subsequently a charged alpha particle is released, which creates an avalanche of electrons. See Fig. 7 for details. The Timepix3 chip is reading the electron signal. More specifically, advanced analysis is used to precisely locate the position of impact of a neutron (also called neutron event) from the avalanche of electrons.

Because spatial resolution is key in measuring small features such as defects in objects, there is a continuous pursuit to reach higher spatial resolution. The resolution of a detector is defined by its ability to measure fine details in a radiograph. Spatial resolution can be measured using a resolution mask called a SIEMENS star. A SIEMENS star is a flat object that is composed of concentric bright lines, through which most neutrons transmit, surrounded by an opaque background with little to no neutron transmission. The lines become more separated as they move away from the center, as illustrated in Fig. 6. At the center of the star, the lines are spaced at 25 µm and at the outside the spacing is 500 µm. Varying continuously from the center outwards.

 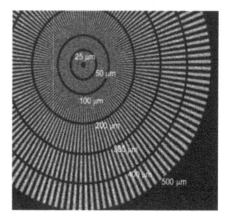

Fig. 6. (left) Photograph of the SIEMENS star affixed to the MCP Timepix 3 detector, (right) Neutron radiograph of the SIEMENS star measured with a previous detector (Color figure online)

Timepix 3 Detector

The novel generation of nR detector, called the Timepix 3 detector, presents a new and exciting opportunity to increase spatial resolution beyond today's 25–50 µm limit. These detectors run in event mode, i.e., the position (x and y axes), the time, and time-over-threshold (TOT) of each neutron event are recorded in a data file. The 3rd generation of these detectors was, for the first time, tested at the Spallation Neutron Source, and the data it produced are available for this challenge. The rate of acquisition can reach 150 MB/s. The large size of the data arises from the fact that each neutron event causes an avalanche of electronic events or in other words lots of electronic events per neutron. These electronic events occur around where the neutron interacted with the detector so we call each one a cluster of events. In practice, each cluster is analyzed to determine its centroid which determines the position of the neutron event. The maximum spatial resolution of the nR detector is directly dependent upon the accuracy of the method used to determine the centroid of each cluster.

Cluster Analysis

When a neutron is captured by the detector, a series of chain events, or hits, takes place. Each neutron event can create up to 60 or more of these hits. All hits produced by the same initial neutron capture is known as a cluster.

The main properties of hits from a given cluster is the fact that occur at approximately the same time and the same place in the detector. The time window and the location window are generally considered free variables in the analysis of the pixel hits. But one must keep in mind that two or more clusters may be recorded at the same time if two neutron captures are very close in time and even in space as well. Other parameters that can be used to associate such or such hit to a particular cluster are the total number of hits in a cluster, the total energy of the cluster (given by the sum of the time over threshold (TOT) values for each pixel hit), and the shape of the cluster (typically elongation and whether missing pixels in the geometry are allowed). The information we are seeking is the position of the incident neutron, which can be determined by either centroiding (center of mass of the discretized TOT function as calculated using the TOT values for each pixel hit) or using other fitting algorithms. It will be up to the challenge candidates to determine the optimum algorithm to use. By optimum we mean the algorithm that will allow to reach the highest spatial resolution.

Working with the Data Stream

As mentioned above, pixel hits associated with a cluster do not necessarily come in order. For this reason, the algorithm must keep a log of pixel hits that start to form a cluster and when a new pixel hit is seen, the software must decide if it belongs to a currently forming cluster or if one must start a new cluster.

8.3   Challenges of Interest

The goal of this challenge is to be able to resolve the lines as close to the center of the circle as possible (see yellow arrow in Fig. 6 (right)). The dataset is publicly available with a DOI[15]. With the ultimate goal to increase the spatial resolution of the new Timepix3 detector, the following sub-challenges need to be addressed:

---

[15] https://doi.ccs.ornl.gov/ui/doi/330.

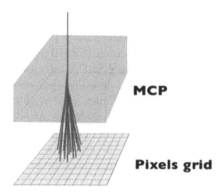

Fig. 7. Incident neutron (red) creates multiple hits when going through the multichannel plate (MCP) and creates a cluster of hits registered over several pixels. (Color figure online)

1. Using a limited data section (imaging_small.h5)
   (a) Extract data from the HDF5
   (b) Show a 2D color map image of the clusters, i.e., plot x, y of the cluster footprint using TOT as the color variable
   (c) From this 2D image
      i. Identify the average cluster shape and spread across x and y pixels.
      ii. Use standard statistical methods to quantify the goodness of fit of various standard curves to cluster shape (centroiding, gaussian, …).
      iii. Provide a statistical analysis of cluster shape variations.
      iv. Determine the extent to which the x and y variables are separable.
      v. Isolate each individual cluster.
      vi. Determine the center of each cluster as precisely as possible.
      vii. Provide an uncertainty for each cluster (the spatial resolution).
2. Using the full data set (*imaging_large1.h5* and *imaging_large2.h5*):
   (a) Utilize your algorithm to demonstrate how fine of features it can resolve by showing a reconstructed SIEMENS star radiograph.
   (b) Extra consideration is given if:
      i. a resolution of 25 microns (inner dot) or better is achieved.
      ii. The algorithm operates at a speed to handle a 150 MB/s data rate.
3. Additional challenge: See how your algorithm perform with not fully formed clusters such as on the edge of the detector or around the gap between the chips (see Fig. 8).

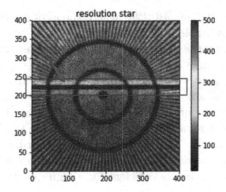

Fig. 8. Horizontal gap between two chips is highlighted here. Full detector contains an array of 4 (2 × 2) chips

9 Challenge 8: High Dimensional Active Learning for Microscopy of Nanoscale Materials

9.1 Background

Atomic force microscopy (AFM) is a premiere research tool utilized to explore material behavior at the nanoscale and has been a mainstay of nanoscience in the past three decades. It consists of a tip at the end of a cantilever that interacts with a sample to derive information on the sample properties and correlate the functional properties to microstructural features of the sample. Usually, in addition to regular raster-based scanning for high-resolution images of topography, the AFM enables individual point-based spectroscopy, where stimulus is applied to the tip or sample or environment and the response of the material is measured locally. Typically, the spectroscopy can be time consuming, as each pixel can take from 0.1 to 10 s to acquire, and this has to be repeated across a grid of points to determine the response variability on spatially heterogeneous samples. One example is in measuring the relaxation of piezoelectric response in ferroelectric materials, as shown in our recent work [6].

9.2 Dataset Description

In this data, we acquired the piezoelectric response as a function of voltage, time and space in a 200 nm thick ferroelectric film of $PbTiO_3$. Such data is critical to understanding the role of domain walls in enhancing the piezoelectric and dielectric properties of ferroelectric materials. The results are provided as a h5 file with tensors for the response and vectors for the applied voltage. These measurements are time consuming and difficult. One method to reduce the time is to instead explore active learning strategies, where only specific voltages and/or spatial locations are measured, and then the full response 'reconstructed' from this subset of measurements. Determining where to sample to optimize the reconstruction becomes an optimization problem which lies at the heart of this challenge.

The dataset is of size (60, 60, 16, 128) where the axes are (x, y, Voltage, time). The full details are available in the manuscript. Please access the Colaboratory notebook[16] provided by the data sponsor to explore the dataset.

The data challenge questions revolve around developing and implementing a machine learning (ML) or statistical learning algorithm to best guide the instrument as to where to sample based on an existing subset to optimize the reconstruction, i.e., 'active learning'. Here, some subset of data is first captured, and then a set of new measurement conditions (e.g., certain spatial pixels) are given by the algorithm to sample next. The microscope captures that data, the new data is fed back into the algorithm to guide the next points, and so on until enough data is captured that is sufficient for a high quality reconstruction with sparse sampling.

9.3   Challenges of Interest

The challenges are:

1. Perform reconstruction of the dataset based on different image reconstruction techniques (e.g., Gaussian process regression) in high dimensional spaces, to observe how redundant the information in the dataset is.
2. Develop an ML algorithm for optimized sequential sampling of the multidimensional dataset.
3. Implement the algorithm in a workflow, as if the microscope was actually taking datapoints, to showcase the method.
4. Ensure that the method
   (a) reconstructs the true dataset to some tolerance (e.g., 90%), and
   (b) that there is at least a 25% gain in efficiency (i.e., less number of spatial and or voltage/time points that need to be measured).

Note

- The preference is for the code to be written in Python, but other languages are not forbidden. Please use the Colaboratory notebook provided to get started on the challenge.
- For challenge questions 1, explore how much of the voltage, time and spatial data can be eliminated safely without dramatic loss in reconstruction accuracy.
- Note that the efficiency gain needs to take into consideration algorithm running time on a DGX-2 machine for every iteration, because algorithms that take longer than several iterations of the actual full spectroscopy will not be useful to the instrument user.
- The successful algorithm will be deployed at the CNMS for a real experiment. Note that high use of GPU acceleration is desired given the availability of the GGX-2 system at the CNMS.

---

[16] https://colab.research.google.com/drive/1ioa9kwibwJcwZkFrw3tW_oAI3Wnwg1Ev.

10   Conclusions

The data challenge contributes towards exploring solutions to open scientific research questions. We hope these challenges gave participants a taste of the types of data and research problems in each of the scientific areas featured in the 2021 Data Challenge. We also hope these challenges got researchers thinking about how important and difficult it is to account for uncertainty and probability in large scientific datasets. In total, 55 teams competed to solve the eight data challenges. Of those, 21 teams submitted solution papers. The best solutions were selected for publication by a peer review. About 80% of the finalists identified themselves as students. Events like the SMC Data Challenge can be highly motivating and promote deeper engagement in tasks and lead to longer-term persistence in pursuits like research and entrepreneurship.

Acknowledgment. Dataset generation for Challenge 1 was supported by the Center for Nanophase Materials Sciences, which is a DOE Office of Science User Facility. Through the ASCR Leadership Computing Challenge (ALCC) program, this research used resources of the Oak Ridge Leadership Computing Facility at the Oak Ridge National Laboratory which is supported by the Office of Science of the U.S. Department of Energy under Contract No. DE-AC05-00OR22725. Dataset generation for Challenge 2 was supported by the U.S. Department of Energy, Office of Science, Office of Advanced Scientific Computing Research, Robinson Pino, program manager, under contract number DE-AC05-00OR22725. Dataset generation for Challenge 3 used resources from General Motors.

Dataset generation for Challenge 4 used resources of the Oak Ridge Leadership Computing Facility at the Oak Ridge National Laboratory, which is supported by the Office of Science of the U.S. Department of Energy under Contract No. DE-AC05-00OR22725. Dataset generation for Challenge 5 was completed by researchers at Oak Ridge National Laboratory sponsored by the DOE Office of Science as a part of the research in Multi-Sector Dynamics within the Earth and Environmental System Modeling Program as part of the Integrated Multiscale Multisector Modeling (IM3) Scientific Focus Area led by Pacific Northwest National Laboratory. The dataset for Challenge 7 was acquired at the Spallation Neutron Source which is sponsored by the User Facilities Division of the Department of Energy. The research for generating datasets for challenges 6 and 8 was conducted at and partially supported by the at the Center for Nanophase Materials Sciences, a US DOE Office of Science User Facility.

References

1. Akbarian, D., et al.: Understanding the influence of defects and surface chemistry on ferroelectric switching: a ReaxFF investigation of BaTiO 3. Phys. Chem. Chem. Phys. **21**(33), 18240–18249 (2019)
2. Biomedical Data Translator Consortium, et al.: Toward a universal biomedical data translator. Clin. Transl. Sci. **12**(2), 86 (2019)
3. Cordts, M., et al.: The cityscapes dataset for semantic urban scene understanding. In: Proceedings of the IEEE Conference on Computer Vision and Pattern Recognition, pp. 3213–3223 (2016)

4. Dosovitskiy, A., Ros, G., Codevilla, F., Lopez, A., Koltun, V.: CARLA: an open urban driving simulator. In: Conference on Robot Learning, pp. 1–16. PMLR (2017)
5. Herrmannova, D., et al.: Scalable knowledge-graph analytics at 136 petaflop/s – data readme. DOI (2020)
6. Kelley, K.P., et al.: Tensor factorization for elucidating mechanisms of piezoresponse relaxation via dynamic Piezoresponse Force Spectroscopy. npj Comput. Mater. **6**(1), 1–8 (2020)
7. Landhuis, E.: Scientific literature: information overload. Nature **535**(7612), 457–458 (2016)
8. Office of Science and Technology Policy: Call to action to the tech community on new machine readable COVID-19 dataset. Online (2020). Accessed 18 Apr 2020
9. Ostrouchov, G., Maxwell, D., Ashraf, R.A., Engelmann, C., Shankar, M., Rogers, J.H.: GPU lifetimes on Titan supercomputer: survival analysis and reliability. In: SC20: International Conference for High Performance Computing, Networking, Storage and Analysis, pp. 1–14. IEEE (2020)
10. Passian, A., Imam, N.: Nanosystems, edge computing, and the next generation computing systems. Sensors **19**(18), 4048 (2019)
11. Swanson, D.R.: Fish oil, Raynaud's syndrome, and undiscovered public knowledge. Perspect. Biol. Med. **30**(1), 7–18 (1986)
12. Swanson, D.R., Smalheiser, N.R.: An interactive system for finding complementary literatures: a stimulus to scientific discovery. Artif. Intell. **91**(2), 183–203 (1997)
13. Swanson, D.R., Smalheiser, N.R., Torvik, V.I.: Ranking indirect connections in literature-based discovery: the role of medical subject headings. J. Am. Soc. Inform. Sci. Technol. **57**(11), 1427–1439 (2006)
14. Thilakaratne, M., Falkner, K., Atapattu, T.: A systematic review on literature-based discovery: general overview, methodology, & statistical analysis. ACM Comput. Surv. (CSUR) **52**(6), 1–34 (2019)
15. Tshitoyan, V., et al.: Unsupervised word embeddings capture latent knowledge from materials science literature. Nature **571**(7763), 95–98 (2019)
16. Wang, F., Oral, S., Sen, S., Imam, N.: Learning from five-year resource-utilization data of titan system. In: 2019 IEEE International Conference on Cluster Computing (CLUSTER), pp. 1–6. IEEE (2019)
17. Yang, H.T., Ju, J.H., Wong, Y.T., Shmulevich, I., Chiang, J.H.: Literature-based discovery of new candidates for drug repurposing. Brief. Bioinform. **18**(3), 488–497 (2017)

Advanced Image Reconstruction for MCP Detector in Event Mode

Chen Zhang[1]([✉]) and Zachary Morgan[2]([✉])

[1] Computer Science and Mathematics Division, Oak Ridge National Laboratory, Oak Ridge, USA
zhangc@ornl.gov
[2] Neutron Scattering Division, Oak Ridge National Laboratory, Oak Ridge, USA
morganzj@ornl.gov

Abstract. A two-step data reduction framework is proposed in this study to reconstruct a radiograph from the data collected with a micro-channel plate (MCP) detector operating under event mode. One clustering algorithm and three neutron event back-tracing models are proposed and evaluated using both example data and a full scan data. The reconstructed radiographs are analyzed, the results of which are used to suggest future development.

Keywords: DBSCAN · Image reconstruction · MCP detector

1 Introduction

Neutron radiography is a neutron-based technique where an object is placed in front of a neutron or photon sensitive detector while being radiated with neutron beam [1]. As neutrons are highly penetrative and more sensitive than X-ray to some light elements such as hydrogen due to its interaction with the nuclei, it is often used to distinguish elements of different isotopes [2] and image components that are opaque to X-rays. The unique nature of neutron radiography makes it an important imaging technique that can characterize materials where standard X-rays fails due to lack of sufficient penetration or contrast.

5th Annual Smoky Mountains Computational Sciences Data Challenge (SMCDC21).

© Springer Nature Switzerland AG 2022
J. Nichols et al. (Eds.): SMC 2021, CCIS 1512, pp. 383–397, 2022.
https://doi.org/10.1007/978-3-030-96498-6_22

A new neutron imaging instrument is being constructed at Oak Ridge National Laboratory (ORNL) which is expected to accelerate advanced discovery in energy-related, engineering, and natural materials [3]. The new instrument, named VENUS, will be located at the Spallation Neutron Source (SNS), aiming to provide measurements with high temporal resolution to the scientific community by integrating neutron imaging with time-of-flight technique. The enabling technology behind this new capability is a combination of a well established boron-doped micro-channel plate (MCP) detector [4] with the Timepix3 chip that drives the data collection at extremely high speed [5]. This new type of MCP detector is expected to increase the spatial resolution beyond the current $20\,\mu m$ to $50\,\mu m$ limit [6].

When the new MCP detector operates in event mode, the incident neutron hitting the front panel generates an alpha particle, which is converted to an electron cloud within the micro-channel. The electron cloud is continuously accelerated when travelling towards the sensor array at the back panel of the MCP detector. Upon hitting the sensor array, each electron will generate a signal, which is recorded by the Timepix3 chip as an event consisting of time-of-arrival (TOA), time-over-threshold (TOT), and position of the corresponding sensor. The data acquisition rate can approach $170\,\mathrm{MB\,s^{-1}}$, which poses a serious challenge due to the shear quantity of collected data.[1] Supposing that the commissioned VENUS instrument collects data continuously for 24 h at this rate, it alone will produce tenfold of data compared to all other 31 instruments combined at High Flux Isotope Reactor (HFIR) and SNS. Quickly and efficiently processing the neutron event data collected with the new detector is key to enabling the full capabilities of VENUS.

The challenge is to identify the cluster of events in the data so as to obtain the position of the neutron event from the distribution of the cluster. These neutron event locations can be used to reconstruct the image, the spatial resolution of which is tied to the accuracy of these neutron event positions. As mentioned before, the high data acquisition rate, $150\,\mathrm{MB\,s^{-1}}$, requires the reconstruction method to be both accurate as well as efficient. Bearing these requirements in mind, This study proposes a data reduction framework that can reduce the raw data collected with the new MCP detector to a standard radiograph. The proposed reduction framework consists of both automatic clustering of electron clouds as well as backtracing the neutron event. The evaluation of the proposed framework is performed with data sets of a SIEMENS star resolution mask [8], the line spacing of which ranges from $500\,\mu m$ at the outer edge to $25\,\mu m$ at the center.

2   Image Reconstruction

The data reduction framework proposed in this study[2] to transform the event data collected with MCP detector into a standard radiograph consists of two

---

[1] To put things into perspective, current ORNL neutron scattering instruments produce $1.2\,\mathrm{TB\,d^{-1}}$ [7], and the full operation of the new MCP detector will add another $12.96\,\mathrm{TB\,d^{-1}}$ on top of it.

[2] https://github.com/KedoKudo/MCPEventModeImageReconstruction.

major components: event clustering and incident neutron back-tracing. During the event clustering, events recorded by the Timepix3 chips are grouped into different clusters such that events within the same cluster are caused by the same incident neutron. Upon the completion of the clustering, the spatial and intensity distribution of each cluster will be analyzed such that the associated incident neutron can be back-traced and translated into the radiograph of interest.

2.1 Event Clustering

As described in Sect. 1, the interaction between the incident neutron and the front panel of the MCP detector leads to a cloud of electrons travelling towards the sensor array, the generated signals of which are recorded by the Timepix3 chip operating at a clock speed of 640 MHz. Since Timepix3 operates at a much higher speed than the incident neutron (about 60 MHz), the recorded events tend to cluster both spatially and temporally as demonstrated in Fig. 1. Furthermore, the number of events within each cluster can vary with respect to the incident neutron energy and the interaction between neutron and the front panel. Given these two unique features of the event data, density-based spatial clustering of applications with noise algorithm, also known as DBSCAN is selected to be the clustering engine for the proposed framework [9]. For better clustering results, the temporal axis is adjusted to match the resolution of the two spatial axes. More specifically, the TOA of each event is re-scaled by a factor of 0.04 such that every 25 ns is considered as one unit of time, denoted as a packet in this study. One packet of time is roughly within the vicinity of both the Timepix3 internal step clock speed (40 MHz) as well as the aforementioned neutron speed, simplifying the cluster identification along the temporal axis.

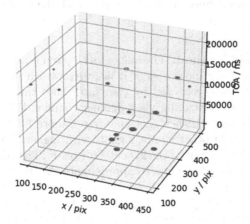

Fig. 1. Three dimensional view (x, y, TOA) of the first 1500 events (out of total 16 000 000 events) in the example data set. The shape of each cluster represents the spatial and temporal spread whereas the opacity of each cluster denotes the corresponding density of events for each cluster.

In this study, the search radius used during DBSCAN clustering is set to $2\sqrt{3}$, which is the diagonal distance of two voxels connected via a single vertex. The minimum number of events required to qualify as within the same cluster is set to four, which is the number of the first order neighbors in a discrete 2D grid. Since the clustering is performed in a hybrid 3D parameter space (two spatial and one temporal), the criteria above is a relaxed one, ensuring that events near the edge of the clusters are included in the final results. As a typical three-minute scan can yield around 4 000 000 000 events, it is impractical to process the entire scan in one run even with a modern high-performance computing environment. Therefore, the scan is sliced into smaller chunks along the temporal axis with 10% overlap prior to event clustering.

2.2   Incident Neutron Back-Tracing

The alpha particles generated by the interaction between the incident neutron and the MCP front panel cannot be directly measured by the sensor array. Therefore, a series of micro-pillar channels are used to convert the alpha particles into a cloud of electrons followed by consecutive amplification such that the electron cloud becomes visible to the sensor array in the back panel. Due to the chaotic nature of the signal amplification process inside the micro-channels, there is no explicit formula one can use to calculate the location where neutrons interact with the detector. For the purpose of investigating the design and performance of the detectors, it is common to use a forward modeling approach where all possible cluster formation trajectories are simulated with a physics-based model [10,11]. However, such forward modeling approach is not suitable for production due to its intrinsic low efficiency. Consequently, this study proposes three different statistic models, all of which provide direct and efficient ways to approximate the location where the incident neutron interact with the front panel of the MCP detector.

Weighted Centroid Method. The longer an electron is accelerated within the micro-pillar channels, the more energy it acquires, which in turn is translated into a higher TOT value recorded by the chip. Since the MCP detector can effectively prevent back-scattering via a angular channel design [4], it is safe to assume that the electrons with higher energy are more likely generated closer to the neutron event. In other words, signals with higher TOT provide better estimates of the neutron event in the 2D detector plane. Therefore, one could use a simple weighted centroid formula to approximate the location of the neutron event, i.e.

$$\bar{\mathbf{x}} = \sum_i (w_i \mathbf{x}_i), w_i = \frac{I_i}{\sum I} \tag{1}$$

where $\mathbf{x}_i$ denotes the position vector of event i in the 2D detector plane, I_i is the corresponding TOT value, and $\bar{\mathbf{x}}$ denotes the approximated neutron event position in the 2D imaging plane.

Two Dimensional Gaussian Fitting. Assuming the cluster follows a normal distribution, a straightforward method for obtaining the location of the neutron event is to fit the cluster using a Gaussian function:

$$I_{xy} = Ae^{-[(x-x_0)^2+(y-y_0)^2]/(2w^2)} \tag{2}$$

Here, I_{xy} is the TOT, A is the height, w is the standard deviation, and $\bar{x} = (x_0, y_0)$. Since variables of interests are located in the exponent, an implicit iterative optimization is often necessary to acquire the best results. In this study, the 2D Gaussian fitting is carried out by LMFIT [12], an open source software package dedicated for n-dimensional peak fitting with various peak shapes.

Fast Gaussian Fitting Using Least-Square Approximation. Although the Gaussian peak fitting offers detailed information such as the height and standard deviation of the cluster, the implicit iterative fitting process provided by LMFIT incurs computational cost too high for cases with extremely high data throughput. Therefore, a more efficient approach based on least-square regression is proposed in this study to explicitly compute the approximated neutron event location. More specifically, with the background subtracted, Eq. (2) can be rewritten as

$$x^2 + y^2 = 2x_0 x + 2y_0 y - 2w^2 \ln I_{xy} + 2w^2 \ln A - x_0^2 + y_0^2. \tag{3}$$

Provided the known TOT and position vector of each signal, it is possible to use linear least-squares regression directly to obtain estimates of the neutron event and width. Lumping the common terms together gives equation

$$x^2 + y^2 = a_1 x + a_2 y + a_3 \ln I_{xy} + a_4 \tag{4}$$

with only four unknowns. From a mathematical point of view, a cluster with more than four signals will ensure that the corresponding system is over-determined, therefore offering deterministic results with strong resistance to random noise. The formula of the approximated linearized Gaussian function is adapted from Anthony and Granick's work [13], and is realized with Numba [14] for better computing efficiency. In addition, the fitting is weighted according to the square of TOT to help suppress the influence of noise.

3 Results

The data reduction framework proposed in this study consists of two major components: event clustering and the subsequent incident neutron back-tracing. The resulting 2D positions of the incident neutron, also known as the neutron events can then be directly populated into a 2D grid to form the final radiograph of interest. Due to the indirect nature of the reconstruction process, optional super-resolution can be applied when populating the approximated neutron events into the image grid, which can help highlight features that are difficult to identify with the native resolution of the sensor array.

Before reconstructing a full scan, a smaller data set with about 16 000 000 events was tested with the proposed data reduction framework, the clustering results of which was visualized and analyzed in Sect. 3.1. This provides insight of the characteristics of the electron clouds as well as the necessary data pruning criteria to facilitate the cluster pruning prior to incident neutron back-tracing. The findings of the aforementioned analysis help guide the event clustering of a full three-minute scan, the results of which were fed to three different incident neutron back-tracing methods to generate the corresponding reconstructed radiographs shown in Sect. 3.2.

3.1   Clustering Results

The example data set contains 15 646 982 individual events, which was grouped into 169 357 clusters using the proposed DBSCAN based clustering engine. There are about 0.17% events that cannot be assigned to any cluster using the proposed clustering engine. Therefore, these events were deemed as noise and removed from the final clustering results. Figure 2 presents a three dimensional view of the clustering results for the first 1500 events used in Fig. 1, demonstrating that the proposed clustering engine can successfully group events into clusters without any prior knowledge of the data.

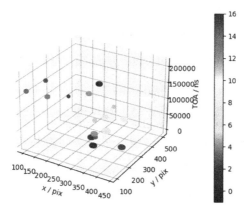

Fig. 2. Clustering results of the first 1500 events shown in Fig. 1, with mark size increased for better visualization. The color represents the assigned cluster ID, ranging from −1 to 16 where −1 denotes events that were deemed as noise. (Color figure online).

In most physics-based model developed for analyzing the MCP detector, the electron cloud is often assumed to follow a standard Gaussian distribution, and the resulting signal profile should also be of a Gaussian nature. However, this is rarely true with the real data as demonstrated in Fig. 3. More specifically, the distribution of events in the hybrid 3D parameter space can have various artifacts (top row in Fig. 3), including fracture, ring-shape near the edge of cluster as well as many others not shown here. Due to these various artifacts, it is difficult to categorize these cluster to be of standard Gaussian distribution characteristics. On the other hand, the time-over-threshold (TOT) value represented as color in Fig. 3 does posses a Gaussian like distribution, especially when we combine TOT and TOA together[3] to form the z-axis (middle row in Fig. 3). The similar conclusion can also be drwan by analyzing the cumulative density distribution (CDF) plot of TOA and TOT for these clusters, which are drawn at the bottom of Fig. 3.

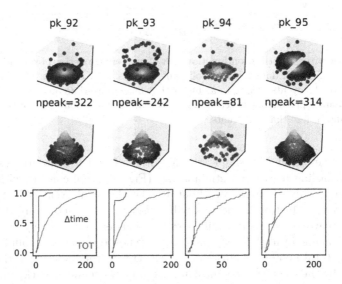

Fig. 3. Four selected cases to demonstrate the shape (x, y, TOA) and intensity (TOT) of the resulting clusters. The label npeak denotes the number of events included in each cluster, and the cumulative density distribution function at the bottom row indicates that the four clusters have very distinct characteristics. (Color figure online).

Given the fact that the shape and size varies greatly from one cluster to another, it is important to prune out clusters that do not have a well defined shape or sufficient statistics for incident neutron back-tracing. In the meantime, it is also important to keep as many clusters as possible such that at least 262144 (512^2) clusters are available to be evenly distributed across the native sensor array grid (512×512). To balance the contradictory requirements above, visual inspections as well as statistical analysis were performed on the clustering results of the example data set. The visual inspection of all the clusters reveals that clusters with a segmented CDF of TOA (Δtime) tends to exhibit

---

[3] $z_i = TOT_i + TOA_i$ where i denotes each signal.

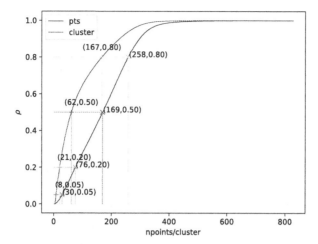

Fig. 4. Cumulative distribution function plot of cluster size derived from the clustering results of the example data set. The solid line denotes a per point based analysis where about 95% of the events belong to a cluster that have more than 30 events. The dashed line represents a per cluster based analysis, revealing that about 20% of the identified clusters contain less than 21 events.

a severely skewed cluster shape, the majority of which contains less than 50 events. According to the statistic analysis (Fig. 4), these clusters with severely skewed shape only accounts for about 10% of the total events. Therefore, the proposed data reduction framework will conservatively remove any cluster with less than 30 events as it is most likely to be a cluster that can negatively impact the back-tracing results. Interestingly, the removed clusters accounts for over 20% of the total number of clusters, indicating that the majority of the clusters generated by the clustering engine contains too few events for back-tracing. To a certain extent, this is a natural outcome of the relaxed cluster criteria described in Sect. 2.1, and the proposed framework can correct the false positive via data pruning described above.

3.2 Image Reconstruction

The clustering engine verified in Sect. 3.1 was applied to a full scan containing 3 839 200 000 events collected over three minutes. The clustering results was pruned using the criteria consolidated in previous section, then fed to three different back-tracing models detailed in Sect. 2, resulting in the final reconstructed radiographs in Fig. 5. The images in the top row are the full field of view whereas the images in the bottom row zoom in on the SIEMENS star located close to the cross section of the 2×2 sub-panels. Additionally, the exposures of the full field of view images are adjusted so that the background chips are visible for visual inspection.

Weighted Centroid   LMFit Gaussian   Fast Gaussian

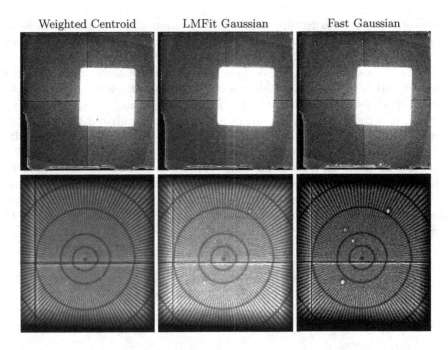

Fig. 5. Radiographs reconstructed from data set frame20 using three different methods. Images on the top are full field of view with the SIEMENS star region over exposed and the zoomed views of the reconstructed SIEMENS star are in the bottom row.

4   Discussion

4.1   Event Clustering Analysis

The proposed DBSCAN based clustering engine can successfully identify clusters automatically as demonstrated in Sect. 2.1. However, the identified cluster tends to have very distinct shape with various artifacts.

For instance, most well formed clusters have a halo ring when using TOA as the z-axis, indicating that the electrons near the edge of the cluster arrive at a much later time when compared with the rest of the electrons from the same cloud. One could attribute this feature to recording errors on the electronics end. However, the consistent appearance of this halo feature among the inspected clusters strongly suggests that a critical scattering angle exists where electrons excited beyond that will have a much smaller initial speed or need to travel a much longer distance before hitting the sensor array. It is possible to verify this hypothesis by reducing the gap between the front and back panel in the MCP detector, which should reduce the occurrence of these halo rings as it effectively eliminates the distance required to distinguish these special electrons. Unfortunately, such a MCP detector has not been constructed and further exploring the physics behind these halos is out of the scope of this study.

Nevertheless, this halo feature should have minimum impact on the incident neutron back-tracing thanks to its circular shape and relatively low TOT value.

Another type of artifact worth discussing is the fractured cluster as shown in the right most cluster in Fig. 3. This type of fracture often occurs near the center of cluster, and it is most likely a out-of-sync error. More specifically, the fracture lines tend to form a straight line or a right angle shape, indicating that the underlying reading electronics might be temporally out of sync as the Timepix3 chip used in this study is operating at its maximum clock speed. Its associated negative impact on the reconstructed can be negated by ignoring TOA entry during the back-tracing. In other words, these electronic error induced artifacts have minimum impact on the performance of the MCP detector during static imaging. However, these artifacts will need to be suppressed for dynamic imaging where the synchronization among sensors within the same chip is of great importance.

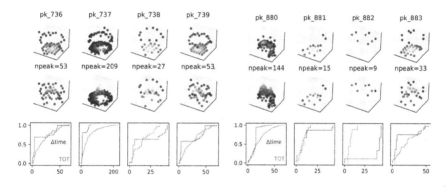

Fig. 6. Examples where the identified the cluster contains a hole in the middle (pk_{737}) and connected clusters (pk_{880}) formed due to multiple neutrons arrive at the same time (highly unlikely) or gamma radiation from incident beam.

The two types of artifacts discussed above generally have negligible negative impact on the reconstruction results. However, the artifacts discussed in this paragraph will have a visible negative impact on the reconstruction. In most clusters, the events are evenly distributed with the exception of the regions where halo ring or fracture occur. However, there are some cases where the formed cluster contains a hole in the middle (second column in Fig. 6). Depending on the location and quantity of the missing events, the back-traced neutron event can have different levels of error. Peak fitting based methods are generally more resistant to missing events, however when the amount of missing events passing a certain threshold as seen in the third column in Fig. 6, the only solution would be excluding the cluster from the back-tracing as it will almost certainly generate an incorrect neutron event that reduce the quality of the reconstruction. Another type of artifacts that could negatively impact the reconstruction quality is the connected peaks as shown in Fig. 6. These kind of clusters cannot be automatically separated by DBSCAN as they often form a cluster that are similar to a regular cluster with multiple events with unusually high TOT. Although it is possible that these artifacts can be caused by multiple neutrons arrive at the same location at the same time, it is more likely that these clusters are caused by interaction between gamma rays with the MCP front panel. Given that these type clusters accounts for less than 0.001% of the total number of clusters, no special action was taken to address this type of artifacts in the current reduction framework.

4.2   Image Reconstruction with Different Models

All three methods can successfully reconstruct the radiograph from the pruned clustering results as shown in Fig. 5. However, the reconstruction quality varies among three different methods as seen in Fig. 7. More specifically, the reconstruction result from weighted centroid method has a smooth, glossy appearance with less details, especially near the edge of the chip where the blurring leads to a much wider gap. In contrary, peak fitting based methods (both Gaussian fitting and fast Gaussian fitting) generates a much sharper edge of the chip while showing different artifacts and revealing some unknown bright features that are located near the top and bottom left. These bright features are more pronounced in the fast Gaussian method. For the Gaussian fit, the image appears sharper, but there is a grainy, grid-like artifact that covers the entire image. Contrarily, the fast Gaussian method shows a ripple-like feature that covers much of the image especially near the center ring. With weighting, the linear approximation may introduce these ripples. Different fitting weights can be explored to improve the sensitivity of the fitted result to the ripple like and bright features. For both fitting methods, these artifacts could potentially be suppressed or even removed via post imaging processing.

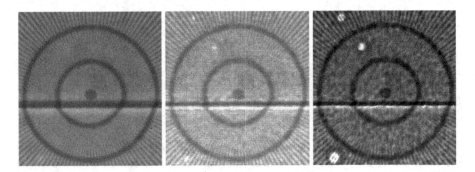

Fig. 7. Center ring comparison of three methods (left: weighted centroid; middle: lmfit-based Gaussian; right: fast Gaussian).

Another way to quantify the reconstruction results for the SIEMENS star is to calculate the modulation transfer function (MTF) [15]. This function captures the fraction of the contrast in the image as a function of frequency. For the

SIEMENS star, the intensity in the image along arcs ranging from 50 to 200 μm are converted to modulation. Figure 8 shows a comparison of the MTF among the three methods. The results indicate a similar performance between the weighted centroid and fast Gaussian method. However, the Gaussian fit shows slightly worse performance. Although the image looks sharper, the grainy texture may suppress the amount of contrast captured by the reconstruction. Despite the ripple like features introduced in the fast Gaussian method, the MTF appears to be insensitive to these artifacts. Care must be taken to visually inspect the reconstruction results for artifacts when comparing the MTF.

At the 10% point (MTF = 0.1), the resolution of each three methods are nearly the same at 100 μm (10 lines pairs mm^{-1}). This is confirmed visually in Fig. 7 as the spokes of the SIEMENS star transition from discernible by eye from the 100 μm partition (outer dark ring) to indistinguishable at the 50 μm partition (inner dark ring). The MTF drops off to near 5% all the way past 16 line pairs mm^{-1} which is equivalent to about 60 μm. The image reconstruction resolution is just above the desired target of 50 μm.

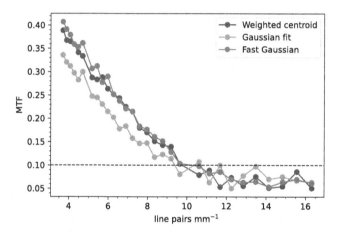

Fig. 8. Comparison of the MTF for each of the three methods. Each MTF is calculated using the same radial arcs centered at a common pixel in the images. The spacial frequency is given in number of line pairs per mm.

One interesting observation of the reconstruction results is the phantom sensor effect where very fainted feature of the SIEMENS star can be observed in the chip gap where no actual sensor resides (Fig. 9). This is because the final reconstruction result is an indirect measurement where the information collected in the back panel (electron clouds distribution) is interpreted into the radiograph on the front panel, therefore disconnecting the final image with physical sensor array. Taking advantage of this effect, one could potentially develop a new type of detector with a sparse detector array and a high resolution front panel. The sparse sensor array reduces the data load and thermal pressure on the hardware whereas the high density micro-channels in the front panels can further improve the image resolution. Naturally such design would require an accurate interpretation model that can faithfully translate the sparse cluster into the image on the front panel. With the help of modern physics-based forward modeling as well as the recent development in the deep convoluted neural network, such a novel MCP detector might be very well within reach for the scientific community.

Fig. 9. Demonstration of phantom sensor effect appear in all three methods.

Table 1. Computation efficiency evaluation of the proposed Python-based reduction framework using an example data set of 1 000 000 events.

Category	Time in sec (mean ± std)
IO	2.645772 ± 0.134921
DBSCAN	214.238336 ± 3.387800
Weighted Centroid	152.728930 ± 1.542076
Fast Gaussian	164.590848 ± 1.556662
LMFit Gaussian	277.697482 ± 9.697102

Table 1 shows the computation efficiency evaluation results of the proposed Python-based reduction framework. The evaluation was performed on a single workstation[4] using an example data set of 1 000 000 events. The statistics of each category listed in Table 1 is estimated from 100 cases, using a Python toolkit *line_profiler*. Generally speaking, IO only accounts for about 0.2% of the total time whereas the DBSCAN and the cluster center finding (Weighted Centroid, Fast Gaussian, LMFit Gaussian) account for the rest. Due to the implicit peak finding implemented in LMFit, it takes significantly longer for LMFit Gaussian to locate the cluster center when compared with the other methods. Overall, the DBSCAN based clustering step accounts for about 50% of the total time, and future development should focus on finding a more effective implementation of the DBSCAN to improve the overall efficiency.

---

[4] The workstation has a Intel(R) i7-8565U @ 1.80 GHz CPU and 32 GB of memory, running Ubuntu 20.04.3 LTS.

5 Summary

A new data reduction framework consisting of clustering and back-tracing provides a new way to reduce the data collected with MCP detector under event mode into a static radiograph. The clustering process used in this study is based on DBSCAN with a relaxed criteria, the results of which need to be pruned before feeding to the subsequent image reconstruction. Among the three image reconstruction models proposed in this study, both weighted centroid method and fast Gaussian method can reduce a full scan with nearly 4 000 000 000 events within 48 h at the cost of either resolution (less details) or ripple-like artifacts. The standard Gaussian fitting based method provides the most visually appealing reconstruction results, however its iterative nature renders unsuitable for production purpose. Given the indirect measurement nature of this detector, the future development can focus on both reducing the data throughput via sparse sensor array as well as improving the interpretation process where the electron distribution can be more efficiently transformed into the radiograph of interest.

Acknowledgements. A portion of this research used resources at the SNS, a Department of Energy (DOE) Office of Science User Facility operated by ORNL. ORNL is managed by UT-Battelle LLC for DOE under Contract DE-AC05-00OR22725.

References

1. Thewlis, J.: Neutron radiography. Br. J. Appl. Phys. **7**(10), 345–350 (1956)
2. Sears, V.F.: Neutron scattering lengths and cross sections. Neutron News **3**(3), 26–37 (1992)
3. Rumsey, J.: US begins construction of unique neutron imaging instrument to accelerate materials discovery. MRS Bull. **44**(10), 748–749 (2019)
4. Leskovar, B.: Microchannel plates. Phys. Today **30**, 9 (1977)
5. Bilheux, H., Herwig, K., Keener, S., Davis, L.: Overview of the conceptual design of the future VENUS neutron imaging beam line at the Spallation Neutron Source. Phys. Proc. **69**, 55–59 (2015)
6. Poikela, T., et al.: Timepix3: a 65K channel hybrid pixel readout chip with simultaneous ToA/ToT and sparse readout. J. Instrum. **9**(05), C05013–C05013 (2014)
7. Godoy, W.F., Peterson, P.F., Hahn, S.E., Billings, J.J.: Efficient data management in neutron scattering data reduction workflows at ORNL. In: 2020 IEEE International Conference on Big Data (Big Data), pp. 2674–2680 (2020)
8. Grünzweig, C., Frei, G., Lehmann, E., Kühne, G., David, C.: Highly absorbing gadolinium test device to characterize the performance of neutron imaging detector systems. Rev. Sci. Instrum. **78**(5), 053708 (2007)
9. Ester, M., Kriegel, H.-P., Sander, J., Xu, X.: A density-based algorithm for discovering clusters in large spatial databases with noise. In: A Density-Based Algorithm for Discovering Clusters in Large Spatial Databases with Noise, pp. 226–231. AAAI Press (1996)
10. Kruschwitz, C.A., Wu, M., Rochau, G.A.: Monte Carlo simulations of microchannel plate detectors. II. Pulsed voltage results. Rev. Sci. Instrum. **82**(2), 023102 (2011)

11. Wu, M., Kruschwitz, C.A., Morgan, D.V., Morgan, J.: Monte Carlo simulations of microchannel plate detectors. I. Steady-state voltage bias results. Rev. Sci. Instrum. **79**(7), 073104 (2008)
12. Newville, M., Stensitzki, T., Allen, D.B., Ingargiola, A.: LMFIT: non-linear least-square minimization and curve-fitting for Python, opt11813 (2014)
13. Anthony, S.M., Granick, S.: Image analysis with rapid and accurate two-dimensional Gaussian fitting. Langmuir: ACS J. Surf. Colloids **25**(14), 8152–8160 (2009)
14. Lam, S.K., Pitrou, A., Seibert, S.: Numba: a LLVM-based Python JIT compiler. In: Proceedings of the Second Workshop on the LLVM Compiler Infrastructure in HPC, pp. 1–6 (2015)
15. Loebich, C., Wueller, D., Klingen, B., Jaeger, A.: Digital camera resolution measurements using sinusoidal Siemens stars. In: Digital Photography III, vol. 6502, p. 65020N. International Society for Optics and Photonics (2007)

An Study on the Resource Utilization and User Behavior on Titan Supercomputer

Sergio Iserte[(⊠)]

Universitat Jaume I, Castellón de la Plana, Spain
siserte@uji.es

Abstract. Understanding HPC facilities users' behaviors and how computational resources are requested and utilized is not only crucial for the cluster productivity but also essential for designing and constructing future exascale HPC systems.

This paper tackles Challenge 4, 'Analyzing Resource Utilization and User Behavior on Titan Supercomputer', of the 2021 Smoky Mountains Conference Data Challenge. Specifically, we dig deeper inside the records of Titan to discover patterns and extract relationships.

This paper explores the workload distribution and usage patterns from resource manager system logs, GPU traces, and scientific areas information collected from the Titan supercomputer. Furthermore, we want to know how resource utilization and user behaviors change over time.

Using data science methods, such as correlations, clustering, or neural networks, our findings allow us to investigate how projects, jobs, nodes, GPUs and memory are related. We provide insights about seasonality usage of resources and a predictive model for forecasting utilization of Titan Supercomputer. In addition, the described methodology can be easily adopted in other HPC clusters.

Keywords: HPC · Workload · GPU · Data science · Scheduling

1 Introduction

High-performance computing (HPC) systems are facilities composed of large amounts of computational resources interconnected. This architecture allows computers to collaborate in the solution of a particular problem. Moreover, these systems are not expected to have a single user. Instead, HPC facilities are shared among hundreds or thousands of users coming from very different areas of knowledge.

Next-generation of HPC clusters is expected to reach exascale performance, which implicitly implies an unprecedented growth in the number of computational resources. Probabilistically, the more resources the higher rate of hardware failures. Moreover, increasing the pool of resources enables the submission of more jobs and larger requests.

© Springer Nature Switzerland AG 2022
J. Nichols et al. (Eds.): SMC 2021, CCIS 1512, pp. 398–410, 2022.
https://doi.org/10.1007/978-3-030-96498-6_23

For these reasons, understanding how HPC clusters are utilized is not only crucial to detect productivity issues but also to improve the design of both job scheduling policies and future HPC systems [1].

Each year, Oak Ridge National Laboratory (ORNL) and the Smoky Mountains Computational Sciences and Engineering Conference (SMC) publishes a series of data science challenges, known as the SMC Data Challenge. In the 2021 edition, Challenge 4 *Analyzing Resource Utilization and User Behavior on Titan Supercomputer* [2] put the spotlight on how a particular HPC system has been utilized. In this regard, the challenge presents two datasets with data from the year 2015 to 2019 of the Titan supercomputer, which remained in the top 10 of the TOP500 list for a long time [3]. Titan was a Cray XK7 system composed of 18,688 nodes AMD Opteron 6274 16-core with 32 GB of DDR3 ECC memory and each one equipped with an Nvidia Tesla K20X GPU with 6GB of GDDR5 ECC memory [4]. The first dataset (RUR dataset) contains the scheduler traces of submitted jobs which bring information about users' requests [5], while the second (GPU dataset) compiles GPU hardware-related failures [6].

Resource utilization statistics of submitted jobs on a supercomputer can help us understand how users from various scientific domains use HPC platforms, in turn, design better job scheduling policies. Thanks to the data gathered from schedulers, hardware, and users, we can analyze resources utilization and how the behavior of users may change over time adapting to given circumstances.

Concretely, in this paper, a thorough analysis of Titan's log is performed to provide a better understanding of user behaviors and how resources are used in this facility. The rest of the paper is structured as follows: Sect. 2 presents a preliminary datasets exploration which helps to understand which information is available, and how to make the most of it. This section tackles tasks 1 and 2 from the proposed challenge. Section 3 explores the data over time and studies behaviors in different year seasons and front of system failures. The section also includes a predictive model trained on Titan data. This section addresses tasks 3 and 4 from the proposed challenge. Finally, in Sect. 4 most remarkable conclusions are highlighted.

2   Exploratory Data Analysis

This section deals with tasks 1 and 2 from the challenge. On the one hand, an exploratory data analysis on the RUR dataset to summarize data characteristics is performed. We also investigate if there are relationships between client CPU memory usage, GPU memory usage, and the job size (number of compute nodes). On the other side, using clustering methods we will see if there are similarities in the resource usage patterns among jobs based on the projects to which they belong.

2.1   Data Preprocessing

The job scheduling dataset (RUR) has the traces of 12,981,186 jobs submitted by a total of 2,372 users. To begin with, raw data is preprocessed and loaded into a clean dataset. For this purpose, from the RUR dataset we leverage the following fields:

- node_count: Number of nodes requested by the job.
- max_rss: Estimation of the maximum resident CPU memory used by an individual compute node through the lifespan of a job run.
- start_time: The timestamp when the job started.
- end_time: The timestamp when the job ended.
- alps_exit: Job status upon completion.
- command: The executable path from where the information about the area of knowledge and project of the job can be extracted.
- gpu_maxmem: Maximum GPU memory used by all the nodes of the job.
- gpu_summem: Total GPU memory used by all the nodes of the job.
- gpu_secs: Time spent on GPUs by the job.

The preprocessing method will remove incomplete, as well as not relevant, traces in order to reduce noise or outliers, which is translated into a higher quality dataset. For this purpose, the preprocessing consists of the following actions:

1. Filter our jobs that did not run successfully (alps_exit value different from zero). This involves canceled or failed jobs, among other causes that prevented jobs to be completed with success.
2. Job duration calculation from the difference between end time and start time.
3. Dismiss jobs without GPU time assigned. In other words, jobs that did not use GPU acceleration.
4. Remove jobs shorter than 13 min. Short jobs may be understood as tests or debugging jobs. This action can be understood as a noise remover that highlights interesting correlations. Thus, by dropping those jobs the correlations (direct or indirect) following depicted are stronger.
5. Extract the project and area identifiers from command field.
6. Filter out incomplete job traces without information about the project or area.

After the sanitation, the clean dataset contains 685,101 rows, in other words, jobs.

2.2   Data Correlation

To study relationships among the target fields, we have opted to visualize them with a heat map that highlights the strengths of their correlations.

Since our clean dataset contains numerical and nominal values the correlation mechanisms have to discriminate between types: numerical and nominal. Thus, although the project identifier is an integer, it is treated as a nominal field.

On the one hand, we have leveraged Person's R between numerical-numerical (continuous) values. With Pearson's R we measure the linear correlation between sets. The coefficient ranges from -1 to 1, indicating the positive value a strong correlation, while the negative values an indirect correlation. On the other hand, between numerical-nominal values, we have used the correlation ratio. The correlation ratio of two sets is defined as the quotient between their standard deviations. It ranges from 0 to 1, being 1 the highest correlation, and 0 no correlation at all.

Figure 1 showcases the correlation matrix with the ratios between tuples of the fields under study.

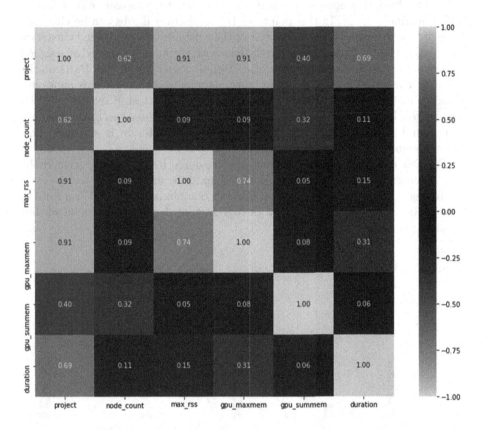

Fig. 1. Correlation matrix after the data preprocessing.

This study considers a *strong correlation* those tuples with ratio values above 0.5. In this regard, we can see that the job project is highly correlated to the CPU and GPU memory. Likewise, the project identifier is related to the job duration and the number of nodes assigned to the job. This can be understood as that long or large jobs are associated with the same projects.

Putting aside the project identifier, the CPU-GPU job memory relationship shows a meaningful direct correlation. Nevertheless, the number of nodes field does not show an important correlation with memory usage.

Since only maximums data of memory were used, the sum of GPU memory is included in the study. However, the ratios with the number of nodes or the project are still not significant enough to be accepted as significantly correlated.

2.3   Data Clustering

Thanks to the data preprocessing performed in Sect. 2.1, jobs can be classified by their scientific domain. In this point, we try to discover if jobs can be clustered by their resource usage and, in the case of the existence of well-defined clusters if those groups present similarities or relations with the area of knowledge assigned to their jobs. For this purpose, clustering techniques are leveraged. Particularly, K-means clustering [7] is one of the most popular methods for this endeavor. K-means methodology is: given an initial point for each cluster, relocate it to its new nearest center, update the centroid by calculating the mean of the member points, and repeat the process until a convergence criterion is satisfied. This process is done for each cluster centroid.

For this clustering study, the following resource usage metrics seemed the most interesting: `node_count`, `max_rss`, and `gpu_maxmem`.

To begin with, the distribution of jobs per domain is analyzed. For a total of 30 scientific areas, Fig. 2 contains a histogram that depicts the number of jobs belonging to each of them.

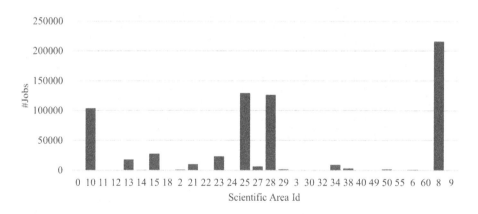

Fig. 2. Number of jobs assigned to each area.

Among the 30 areas, four of them stand out with a higher number of jobs. These four predominant areas correspond to *Chemistry* (10), *Lattice Gauge Theory* (25), *Materials Science* (28), and *Biophysics* (8), respectively in the figure from left to right.

Coincidentally, when using the *elbow method* to get an insight into the number of possible clusters in which the data could be grouped, we obtain the same number of clusters, four.

However, when applying the K-means algorithm to the dataset, the clustering is not conclusive enough since 99.95% of the samples are clustered together. Leaving the 0.05% to the three remaining clusters.

In conclusion, the heavy unbalance share of jobs among areas, and the apparent similarities in their usage make clustering not helpful enough to search for relationships.

3   Time Series Analysis

Challenges 3 and 4 are tackled in this section. Initially, we study if there is any seasonal impact on resources utilization. Furthermore, GPU dataset with hardware-related issues is aligned to the RUR dataset information, in order to characterize relationships between them. Finally, research on the time series extracted from the datasets is conducted with the help of a predictive model.

3.1   Seasonality

This study aims to detect recurrent patterns through the seasons of the year. For this purpose, we initially start the study by understanding how many jobs Titan has run in each month. Figure 3 showcases this metric. Although there is no certain pattern along with the time series, last year shows spikes in the number of running jobs during July–August.

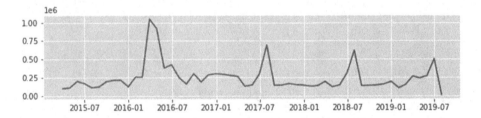

Fig. 3. Count of run jobs (y-axis) per month (x-axis).

Seasonality is studied with the technique of Season-Trend decomposition using LOESS (STL) [8], grouping data by months. Furthermore, depending on the analyzed metric, the aggregation method will vary within the mean, maximum, or sum.

Regarding the number of nodes assigned to jobs, we have opted for aggregating with sum. Since the number of nodes in the cluster is known, with this sum we can estimate the aggregated load per month of the cluster. However, as it is depicted in Fig. 4, CPU memory and time also show a seasonal pattern.

In Figs. 4a and c we can appreciate an increase of nodes assigned to jobs and CPU time, respectively during the first semester of the year. For the second semester, the trend decreases.

The CPU memory (see Fig. 4b) presents spikes of usage at the end of the summer season. Furthermore, CPU time and memory peaks correspond to running job count spikes (see Fig. 3). Likewise, the drop of the spikes coincides with the decrease in the node count.

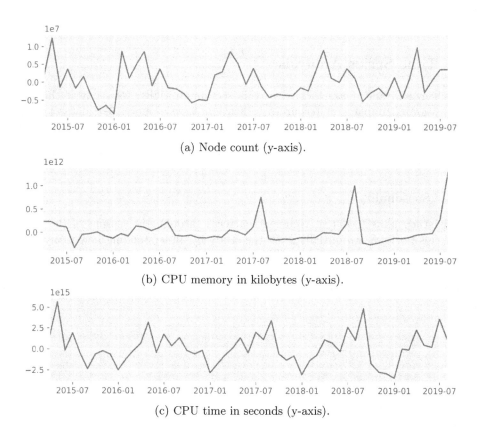

(a) Node count (y-axis).

(b) CPU memory in kilobytes (y-axis).

(c) CPU time in seconds (y-axis).

Fig. 4. Seasonality per month aggregated by sum.

In parallel with the sum, mean aggregation (see Fig. 5) shows the same seasonal patters in CPU time (see Fig. 5b) and memory (see Fig. 5a).

When grouping data by months aggregated with maximum values, we find the seasonal patterns showcased in Fig. 6. Figure 6a illustrates that very long jobs are usually executed in August and Christmas, probably corresponding to vacation periods, where the job queue is less overloaded.

Figure 6b discovers that long GPU-enabled jobs tend to be executed at the end and in the middle of the year.

Notice that depicted drops in running jobs count, assigned nodes, memory usage, or computation time, may correspond to maintenance shutoffs or power outages.

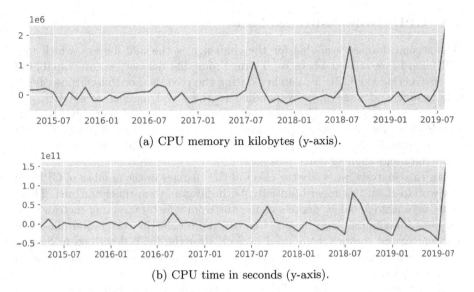

(a) CPU memory in kilobytes (y-axis).

(b) CPU time in seconds (y-axis).

Fig. 5. Seasonality per month aggregated by mean.

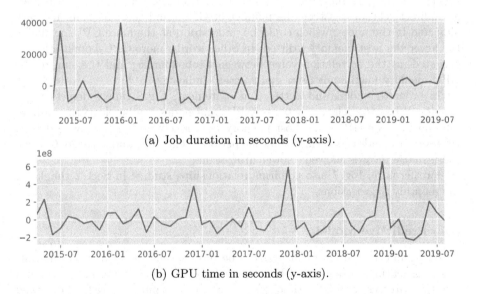

(a) Job duration in seconds (y-axis).

(b) GPU time in seconds (y-axis).

Fig. 6. Seasonality per month aggregated by maximum.

3.2 GPU Hardware-Related Issues

The second dataset available for the challenge is the GPU dataset which logs
GPU hardware-related issues on Titan. From this dataset, we are capable of
reconstructing the GPU availability during the records. For this purpose, fields
SN, insert and remove, corresponding to the serial number of a GPU, and
times when it was inserted/removed into/from the cluster, respectively, are studied. Besides, the GPU dataset presented a time-lagged relationship with the RUR
dataset, corrected during the preprocessing stage, particularly, removing incomplete data and aligning dates (see Sect. 2.1).

In this analysis, we study the effect of the changes in the number of GPUs in
the workload. In this regard, initially, both datasets were timely aligned. Then,
data were aggregated in periods of months from which extracting metrics such
as sums, maximums, and means. Figure 7 represents the correlation matrix of
the aggregated metrics introduced in Sect. 3 for the fields described in Sect. 2.
This matrix also includes the count of maximum available GPUs, the count of
executed jobs, and the count of failed jobs per month.

Regarding the GPUs availability, we appreciate a relation with the count of
maximum nodes available per month, probably because a node shutdown (or
breakdown) implies relocation of its GPUs. Curiously, this matrix also reveals
an indirect relation between the number of GPUs and the maximum memory
allocated in the nodes, which could be understood as the more GPUs available
the lower the host memory utilized. In other words, more GPU-bound jobs are
executed, as the correlation value between #jobsRunning and the sum of the
GPU memory maximums (sum gpu_maxmem) indicates.

In order to understand better that statement, Fig. 8 timely depicts those
metrics. While the relation between GPUs and nodes can be clear, the indirect
relation between GPUs and host memory (max_max_rss) is not easy to detect.
However, it could be determined by the period of late 2015 and early 2016, when
the memory records showed a lower utilization.

Furthermore, Fig. 7 also confirms relationships studied in Sect. 2 thanks to
the monthly aggregations.

3.3 Predictive Model

Given a month's data we can predict the next seven days' values of the four
following features: usage of CPU memory (max_rss), CPU system (stime)and
user time (utime), and GPU time (gpu_secs). For this purpose, we have designed
a predictive model based on a recurrent neural network (RNN). Particularly, it
is based on the Long Short Term Memory (LSTM) implementation of the RNN.

Figure 9 represents the network architecture. It expects the data of the four
features for 30 days. And it returns the features for the seven following days.
The model is composed of an LSTM layer with 200 neurons that feeds four
parallel double dense layers, one for each feature. This behavior is achieved
thanks to repeating the output vector from the recurrent layer (LSTM) with the
"RepeatVector" layer. The result of this operation is four predictions, one for

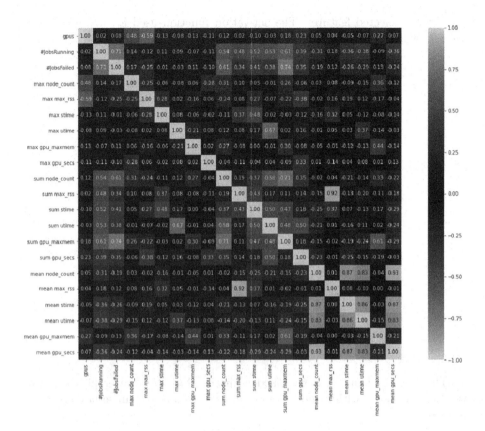

Fig. 7. Correlation matrix for aggregated data.

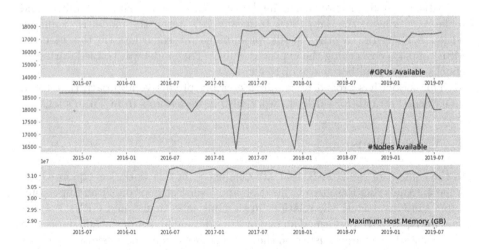

Fig. 8. Evolution in time of the resources.

each of the selected features. The activation function used for non-linearity is the *relu* which stands for "Rectified Linear Unit".

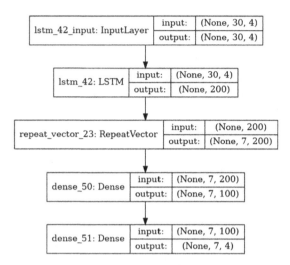

Fig. 9. Neural network architecture.

The presented model is compiled with the *Adam* optimizer [9] to update weights and biases within the network, and relies on the mean square error loss function:

$$MSE = \frac{1}{n} \sum_{i=1}^{n} (y_i - y_i')^2, \tag{1}$$

After normalizing, preparing the data for supervised learning, shuffling, and make partitions of the data (80% train and 20% test), the model is evaluated with a 0.4% error. In other words, predictions present a loss (in this case the MSE) of 0.4% concerning the expected values. The model was trained during 11 epochs with a mini-batch size of 16 elements.

This model has proved to be an interesting predictive approach that could be extended straightforwardly to work with more features from Titan's logs.

4   Conclusions

In the context of the 2021 SMC Data Challenge, in this work, we explore Challenge 4, 'Analyzing Resource Utilization and User Behavior on Titan Supercomputer', and investigate the relationships among jobs, nodes, and GPUs.

Firstly, we have performed an exploratory data analysis on the RUR dataset to summarize data characteristics on the, a priori, some of its most relevant features for the development of this challenge. Then, we have studied the seasonality of the data. For this purpose, we load the original RUR dataset without the previous preprocessing since time series is also dependant on job bad terminations, no GPU jobs, or test and debug jobs, among the rest of logged circumstances. Nevertheless, we have extended this dataset with the job duration time calculated subtracting the end time from the start time.

As part of this investigation, the provided datasets are systematically characterized and prepared to be analyzed. We have devised a methodology to understand seasonal usage patterns and methods to study the relationships. Finally, we provide open-source scripts for conducting the associated analysis and visualizations. For this purpose, scripts and instructions can be found in https://github.com/siserte/SMC2021-Challenge4.git.

From the results of our analysis, we can conclude that the available data help to understand user behaviors and resource utilization, as it has been documented through the paper. However, data depicts two well-differentiated stages in the use of Titan split in mid-2017. For this reason, provided data may be insufficient at some points, particularly if the data is timely aggregated.

All in all, the study shows the strong relationship between the projects and how users of those projects reflect similar usage of GPU and CPU memory. Moreover, projects also provide a well-understanding of node counts and job durations.

We have also detected seasonality patterns that are periodically repeated in the mid and end of the year. Nevertheless, as usual in these types of studies, more quality data means more accurate results and predictions. For this reason, new HPC systems are expected to count with more reliable monitoring and logging mechanisms.

The presented work may be easily adopted in other HPC facilities since many of them periodically record their users' actions. In fact, some insights described in this paper were applied to Cori Supercomputer of NERSC at Lawrence Berkeley National Laboratory (LBNL)[1].

Future resource management systems of HPC facilities will benefit from these kinds of studies, providing their scheduling policies with the experience of past events that are likely to be reproduced. For instance, since jobs that request large amounts of resources tend to wait for long in the queue, systems may schedule their execution taking into account seasonality low peaks where users traditionally submit fewer jobs. In addition, as we have also seen, the indirect relationship in the number of available GPUs and the host memory usage may make the schedulers collate GPU-enabled jobs with memory-bound jobs to exploit better the resources.

Acknowledgements. S. Iserte was supported by the postdoctoral fellowship APOSTD/2020/026 from Valencian Region Government and European Social Funds[2]. The study on Cori supercomputer was carried out during an internship funded under

---

[1] https://www.nersc.gov/assets/Uploads/NERSC-2019-Annual-Report-Final.pdf.

[2] https://innova.gva.es/va/web/ciencia/a-programa-i-d-i/-/asset_publisher/ jMe1UDRYZMHO/content/iv-subvenciones-para-la-contratacion-de-personal- investigador-en-fase-postdoctor-2.

HiPEAC Collaboration Grant H2020-ICT-2017-779656[3]. Finally, the author wants to thank the anonymous reviewers whose suggestions significantly improved the quality of this manuscript.

References

1. Patel, T., Liu, Z., Kettimuthu, R., Rich, P., Allcock, W., Tiwari, D.: Job characteristics on large-scale systems: long-term analysis, quantification, and implications. In: SC20: International Conference for High Performance Computing, Networking, Storage and Analysis, pp. 1–17 (2020)
2. Dash, S., Paul, A.K., Wang, F., Oral, S., Technology Integration, SMC Data Challenge 2021: Analyzing Resource Utilization and User Behavior on Titan Supercomputer (2021). https://smc-datachallenge.ornl.gov/wp-content/uploads/2021/05/C4-SMC_DataChallenge_2021.pdf
3. Top500 the list. https://www.top500.org. Accessed 04 Aug 2021
4. Oak Ridge National Laboratory, ORNL Debuts Titan Supercomputer (2012). https://www.olcf.ornl.gov/wp-content/themes/olcf/titan/Titan_Debuts.pdf
5. Wang, F., Oral, S., Sen, S., Imam, N.: Learning from five-year resource-utilization data of Titan system. In: Proceedings - IEEE International Conference on Cluster Computing, ICCC 2019, September (2019). https://doi.org/10.1109/CLUSTER.2019.8891001
6. Ostrouchov, G., Maxwell, D., Ashraf, R.A., Engelmann, C., Shankar, M., Rogers, J.H.: GPU lifetimes on Titan supercomputer: survival analysis and reliability. In: International Conference for High Performance Computing, Networking, Storage and Analysis, SC 2020, November (2020)
7. Jin, X., Han, J.: K-means clustering. In: Sammut, C., Webb, G.I. (eds.) Encyclopedia of Machine Learning, pp. 563–564. Springer, Boston (2010). https://doi.org/10.1007/978-0-387-30164-8_425
8. Cleveland, R.B., Cleveland, W.S., McRae, J.E., Terpenning, I.: STL: a seasonal-trend decomposition. J. Off. Stat. **6**(1), 3–73 (1990)
9. Kingma, D.P., Ba, J.L.: Adam: a method for stochastic optimization. In: 3rd International Conference on Learning Representations, ICLR 2015 - Conference Track Proceedings, pp. 1–15 (2015). arXiv:1412.6980

---

[3] https://cordis.europa.eu/project/id/779656.

Recurrent Multi-task Graph Convolutional Networks for COVID-19 Knowledge Graph Link Prediction

Remington Kim[1]([✉])[iD] and Yue Ning[2]([✉])[iD]

[1] Bergen County Academies, Hackensack, NJ 07601, USA
[2] Stevens Institute of Technology, Hoboken, NJ 07030, USA
yue.ning@stevens.edu

Abstract. Knowledge graphs (KGs) are a way to model data involving intricate relations between a number of entities. Understanding the information contained in KGs and predicting what hidden relations may be present can provide valuable domain-specific knowledge. Thus, we use data provided by the 5th Annual Oak Ridge National Laboratory Smoky Mountains Computational Sciences Data Challenge 2 as well as auxiliary textual data processed with natural language processing techniques to form and analyze a COVID-19 KG of biomedical concepts and research papers. Moreover, we propose a recurrent graph convolutional network model that predicts both the existence of novel links between concepts in this COVID-19 KG and the time at which the link will form. We demonstrate our model's promising performance against several baseline models. The utilization of our work can give insights that are useful in COVID-19-related fields such as drug development and public health. All code for our paper is publicly available at https://github.com/RemingtonKim/SMCDC2021.

Keywords: Recurrent graph convolutional networks · Multi-task learning · COVID-19 knowledge graph · Link prediction

1 Introduction

In recent years, the amount of data in a variety of domains has skyrocketed. Amidst this vast collection of information, there exist entities and relationships that can be modelled as a knowledge graph (KG) in which the entities are the nodes and the relationships are the edges. Although KGs can be extremely illuminating, the quantity of data contained in many KGs makes them prohibitively vast for manual review. Thus, a computational model that predicts novel connections in these KGs can provide valuable insight without time-consuming labor and reveal relationships unapparent to humans.

A relevant example of a KG is a COVID-19 KG of biomedical concepts and research papers formed using the scientific literature. Predictions of novel links in a COVID-19 KG may be helpful in areas such as drug development, public health, etc. To this end, we make the following contributions in this paper:

© Springer Nature Switzerland AG 2022
J. Nichols et al. (Eds.): SMC 2021, CCIS 1512, pp. 411–419, 2022.
https://doi.org/10.1007/978-3-030-96498-6_24

1. We construct a COVID-19 KG using data provided by the Oak Ridge National Laboratory Smoky Mountains Computational Sciences Data Challenge and auxiliary data processed with natural language processing techniques. We then analyze this network and its properties.
2. We propose a multi-task recurrent graph convolutional network (MTL-Recurrent GCN) that predicts the existence of novel links in a COVID-19 KG as well as the time at which a link will form.
3. We compare the performance of our model to several baselines and evaluate each model's performance using accuracy, AUC, precision, recall, and F1 score.

2   Related Work

2.1   COVID-19 Knowledge Graphs

In response to the COVID-19 crisis, several KGs centered around COVID-19 have been formed. A cause-and-effect COVID-19 KG was constructed from the scientific literature that contains 10 node types, including proteins and genes, and 10,232 edge types, including increases and association [4]. For ease of access, this KG was made available on a public web application. Wise *et al.* [14] built a COVID-19 KG of research papers and trained a model that utilizes KG embeddings for retrieving similar papers. Giarelis *et al.* [5] developed a method for predicting future research collaboration links in a COVID-19 KG that incorporates structured and unstructured text data using a graph-of-docs representation.

2.2   Temporal Link Prediction

Temporal link prediction is the task of predicting the formation of links in the future state of a dynamic network [3]. Peddada and Kostas [11] performed temporal link prediction on a Pinterest network using temporal feature extraction of proximity measures and machine learning models. Li *et al.* [8] developed a self-attention and graph convolutional network-based temporal link prediction model that outputs the probability of a link between every pair of nodes at the next timestep given a sequence of graphs. They apply their model to a private message, an interaction, and two email networks. Their model focuses on the sole task of link prediction, unlike our work which predicts the time of link formation as well.

3   Methodology

3.1   Problem Formation

We assume that $G_t = (V_t, E_t, X_t)$ is an undirected graph at time t, where V_t is the set of nodes, E_t is the set of edges, $N_t = |V_t|$ is the number of nodes, and $X_t \in \mathrm{R}^{N_t \times F}$ is the matrix containing the F features for each node. Every edge in E_t has an associated r, which is its relation type. Let $S_{t,j} = \{G_{t-j-(\alpha-1)l}, \ldots, G_{t-j-l}, G_{t-j}\}$ represent a sequence of graphs where j is the leadtime, l is the time length between two consecutive graphs in $S_{t,j}$, and α is the number of graphs in $S_{t,j}$.

The task of the model is to predict the existence of a link between target nodes u and v that forms at time t as well as j given $(S_{t,j}, u, v)$. In other words, the model predicts whether or not a link will form and *when* a link will form. As there are two objectives, this can be modeled as a multi-task learning problem.

3.2   Model

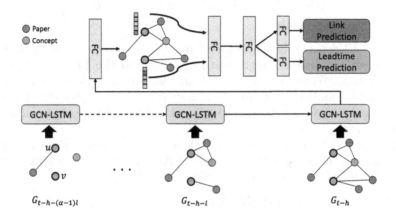

Fig. 1. Architecture of MTL-Recurrent GCN. GCN-LSTM represents a Chebyshev Graph Convolutional Long Short Term Memory cell and FC represents a fully connected layer. u and v are the target nodes.

The architecture of our model, MTL-Recurrent GCN, is displayed in Fig. 1. We utilize a Chebyshev Graph Convolutional Long Short Term Memory cell (GCN-LSTM) [13] for the recurrent unit of our model. A GCN-LSTM employs a Chebyshev Graph Convolutional operator to learn graph features and a Long Short Term Memory cell to learn temporal dependencies within the sequence of input graphs [13].

Given X, the node feature matrix of graph G, Chebyshev Graph Convolutional operator [2] computes

$$X' = \sum_{k=0}^{K-1} T^{(k)} \cdot W^{(k)}$$
$$T^{(0)} = X \qquad\qquad (1)$$
$$T^{(1)} = \hat{L} \cdot X$$
$$T^{(k \geq 2)} = 2 \cdot \hat{L} \cdot T^{(k-1)} - T^{(k-2)}.$$

Here, $W^{(k)}$ is a learnable weight matrix, and $\hat{L} = \frac{2(I - D^{\frac{-1}{2}} A D^{\frac{-1}{2}})}{\lambda_{\max}} - I$ is the normalized Laplacian where I is the identity matrix, D is the diagonal degree matrix of G, A is the adjacency matrix of G, and $\lambda_{\max}$ is the largest eigenvalue of $I - D^{\frac{-1}{2}} A D^{\frac{-1}{2}}$.

A GCN-LSTM [13] builds upon this Chebyshev Graph Convolutional operator with an Long Short Term Memory cell. Given X_t, the node feature matrix of graph G_t, it computes

$$
\begin{aligned}
i_t &= \sigma(\zeta(W_{xi}, X_t) + \zeta(W_{hi}, h_{t-1}) + w_{ci} \odot c_{t-1} + b_i) \\
f_t &= \sigma(\zeta(W_{xf}, X_t) + \zeta(W_{hf}, h_{t-1}) + w_{cf} \odot c_{t-1} + b_f) \\
c_t &= f_t \odot c_{t-1} + i_t \odot \tanh(\zeta(W_{xc}, X_t) + \zeta(W_{hc}, h_{t-1}) + b_c) \qquad (2) \\
o &= \sigma(\zeta(W_{xo}, X_t) + \zeta(W_{ho}, h_{t-1}) + w_{co} \odot c_t + b_o) \\
h_t &= o \odot \tanh(c_t).
\end{aligned}
$$

Here, $\zeta(W, X)$ denotes the Chebyshev Graph Convolutional operator where W is the tensor of learnable weight matrices utilized in (Eq. 1) and X is a node feature matrix. Weights w and biases b are also learnable parameters. h and c are the hidden and cell state matrices, respectively. $\odot$ denotes the Hadamard product, and σ and tanh denote the sigmoid and hyperbolic tangent activation functions, respectively.

In the case of MTL-Recurrent GCN, the input is $(S_{t,j}, u, v)$. First, the graphs in $S_{t,j}$ are sequentially inputted into the GCN-LSTM to produce a final output of h_{t-j}. Then, MTL-Recurrent GCN computes

$$
\begin{aligned}
h_{t-j} &= \text{ReLU}(h_{t-j}) \\
h_1 &= \text{ReLU}(W_1 \cdot h_{t-j} + b_1) \\
h_2 &= \text{ReLU}(W_2 \cdot (h_1[u] \oplus h_1[v]) + b_2) \\
h_3 &= \text{ReLU}(W_3 \cdot \text{Dropout}(h_2) + b_3) \qquad (3) \\
\hat{y}^b &= \sigma(W_4 \cdot \text{Dropout}(h_3) + b_4) \\
\hat{y}^m &= \text{Softmax}(W_5 \cdot \text{Dropout}(h_3) + b_5).
\end{aligned}
$$

Here, $\hat{y}^b$ and $\hat{y}^m$ are the outputs of the link prediction and leadtime prediction tasks, respectively. $\oplus$ denotes the concatenation operator, and weights W and biases b are learnable parameters. Note that leadtime prediction is a multiclass classification task where each class is a possible leadtime window or the negative class. The negative class denotes that the link will not form in the future. The link prediction task is a binary classification task. We use hard parameter sharing multi-task learning, meaning the fully connected (FC) layers for both tasks are shared before the output layer, as it prevents overfitting [12].

This multi-task learning architecture has two advantages: performance improvements [1] and computational efficiency, as only one model is needed even though there are multiple prediction tasks.

Finally, we define a custom loss function (Eq. 4) for training MTL-Recurrent GCN that combines binary cross entropy and categorical cross entropy losses via a weighted average:

$$L = \beta[y^b \cdot \log(\hat{y}^b) + (1 - y^b) \cdot \log(1 - \hat{y}^b)] + (1 - \beta)[\sum_{i=0}^{p} y_i^m \cdot \log(\hat{y}_i^m)], \quad (4)$$

where β is the weight hyperparameter and p is the number of possible leadtime values.

In summary, MTL-Recurrent GCN learns graph features and temporal dependencies from a sequence of a graphs and performs the classification tasks with FC layers.

4 Experiments

4.1 Datasets

We conduct our experiments on a COVID-19 KG with three auxiliary datasets. The main KG dataset is provided by the Oak Ridge National Laboratory as a part of their 5th Annual Smoky Mountains Computational Sciences Data Challenge 2. This dataset contains a network of biomedical concepts nodes and research paper nodes formed using the PubMed, Semantic MEDLINE, and CORD-19 databases. The three relations present in the network are paper-concept edges (paper references concept relation; e_{pc}'s), paper-paper edges (citation relation; e_{pp}'s), and concept-concept edges (paper links two concepts relation; e_{cc}'s). The existence of e_{cc}'s and when they will form are to be predicted.

The three auxiliary datasets we utilize are the Unified Medical Language System (UMLS) API - for retrieving the names of the biomedical concepts in the network - and the CORD-19 metadata dataset and the PubMed NCBI E-utilities API - for retrieving the abstracts of the scientific papers in the network.

4.2 Preprocessing

We first drop all papers that are missing a valid publication date or a valid abstract. We then drop all concepts that have zero associated papers as a result. We remove e_{pc}'s and e_{pp}'s that stem from an invalidated paper node as well as e_{pc}'s and e_{cc}'s that stem from an invalidated concept node. We also remove e_{cc}'s that have no valid papers linking the two relevant concepts.

As only the publications dates of the papers are given, we assign dates to the edges in the following manner: the date of a e_{pc} is the publication date of the relevant paper, the date of a e_{pp} is the publication date of the citing paper, and the date of a e_{cc} is the publication date of the paper that links the two relevant concepts (if more than one paper linking the concepts exists, the earliest publication date is used).

We then create node feature vectors using a pretrained Google News Word2Vec model with the papers' abstracts and concepts' names as input. For each document, we generate a 300-dimensional Word2Vec [10] embedding for every one of its words and take the term frequency-inverse document frequency (TF-IDF) weighted average of them to get the document embedding. We then perform dimensionality reduction using principal component analysis (PCA) to get a 32-dimensional feature vector for each node.

Finally, due to the network's prohibitively large size, we employ the Forest Fire sampler with a burning probability of 40% and an 85% reduction in the number of nodes because of its ability to retain the original properties of the graph [7].

4.3   Analysis

The final network contains $42,062$ nodes and $1,744,025$ edges. There are $11,741$ concept nodes and $30,321$ paper nodes. e_{pc}'s are the most prevalent with a total of $1,502,372$ of them in the network, followed by e_{cc}'s with $146,704$ and e_{pp}'s with $94,967$.

The disparity between the number of e_{pc}'s and the number of e_{cc}'s is explained by the fact that a paper referencing multiple concepts does not necessarily mean that all the referenced concepts are linked to each other by e_{cc}'s. For example, a paper references both "RNA" and "degrees Celsius"; however, there does not exist an e_{cc} between these two concepts as there is no substantial association between them. Additionally, there are papers that only reference a single concept, which makes extracting an e_{cc} from them impossible.

The average node degree of the network is 41.46. Concept nodes have a much higher average degree (152.95 ± 496.50) than paper nodes (55.81 ± 29.03); however, their degrees vary more. Additionally, a concept is referenced by an average of 127.96 ± 456.17 papers while a paper references an average of approximately 49.55 ± 22.54 concepts. Figure 2a displays the degree distribution of the network, and Fig. 2b plots the formation dates of all the links in the network. The majority of new links were formed in 2020, which is expected due to the influx of COVID-19 research.

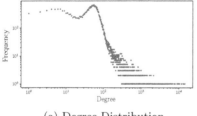
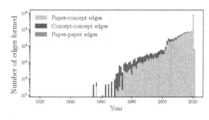

(a) Degree Distribution   (b) Distribution of Link Formation Dates

Fig. 2. Distributions of network

4.4   Baseline Models

We compare the performance of MTL-Recurrent GCN to several link prediction baseline models.

Heuristic Algorithms. We utilize the following link prediction heuristic algorithms: Common Neighbors, Jaccard Coefficient, Preferential Attachment, Adamic-Adar, and Resource Allocation [9,15]. For a node pair between which a link is formed at time t with leadtime j, we extract the heuristics for the node pair from G_{t-j}. For a node pair between which a link is not present with leadtime j, we extract the heuristics for the node pair from G_{T-j}, where T is the last available timestep. We then train a logistic regression model on each heuristic.

N2V. node2vec (N2V) generates node embeddings by feeding random walks sequences on the graph into a word2vec model [6]. We generate 128 dimensional node embeddings on the training graph G_c, where c is the cutoff date between training and validation/testing dates, using node2vec and take the Hadamard product of node pairs' embeddings to train a 2-layer neural network model.

GCN. We utilize two different graph convolutional neural network (GCN) models as baselines: GCN and MTL-GCN. Both are standard GCN models with one Chebyshev spectral graph convolutional layer. GCN performs a single task while MTL-GCN performs multi-task learning using MTL-Recurrent GCN's custom loss function. For these models, the only graph inputted for predicting a link formed at time t with leadtime j is G_{t-j}.

Recurrent GCN. Recurrent graph convolutional network (Recurrent GCN) has the same architecture as MTL-Recurrent GCN; however, it forgoes the multi-task learning and performs a single task only.

4.5 Experimental Setup

In our experiments, we set Chebyshev filter sizes $k = 3$, and manually set $\beta = 0.6$ (Eq. 4). For our input graph sequences $S_{t,j}$, the leadtime $j \in \{1, 12, 24, 36\}$ months, the length of time between graphs $l = 12$ months, and the number of graphs $\alpha = 3$.

All e_{cc}'s formed between January 2019 and July 2020 are training, formed in August 2020 are validation, and formed between September 2020 and May 2021 are testing sampled. Negative node pairs (i.e., concept nodes pairs without a link by May 2021) are randomly sampled in equivalent numbers. In total, there are $45,922$ samples and a train:validation:test split of 82.3:7.4:10.3%. Every sample is randomly assigned a leadtime j.

Our GCN and Recurrent GCN models are trained for 10 epochs with AUC early stopping using the Adam optimizer, a learning rate of 0.001, and a dropout value of 0.5 on a NVIDIA TITAN V GPU server. All models are implemented using PyTorch.

4.6 Results

Table 1 summarizes the link and leadtime prediction performance of MTL-Recurrent GCN along with the baseline models. Note that two separate models are trained for all non-multi-task learning baselines: one for each task.

Table 1. Prediction Results. Best results for each metric are bolded.

Model	Link prediction					Leadtime prediction	
	Accuracy	AUC	Precision	Recall	F1	AUC	Accuracy
Common Neighbors	0.6682	0.7380	0.8173	0.4333	0.5664	0.5983	0.6192
Jaccard Coefficient	0.6880	0.7415	0.7984	0.5030	0.6171	0.6176	0.6257
Preferential Attachment	0.5276	0.5469	0.5627	0.2477	0.3440	0.4864	0.6274
Adamic-Adar	0.6608	0.7332	0.7983	0.4303	0.5592	0.5984	0.6194
Resource Allocation	0.5489	0.7071	0.6448	0.2175	0.3253	0.5909	0.6249
node2vec	0.7326	0.8043	0.8249	0.5905	0.6883	N\A	N\A
GCN	0.8137	0.8994	0.8545	0.7562	0.8023	0.7640	0.5423
MTL-GCN	0.7802	0.9051	**0.9019**	0.6287	0.7409	0.7661	0.5516
Recurrent GCN	0.8141	0.9149	0.8890	0.7179	0.7944	**0.8839**	**0.6653**
MTL-Recurrent GCN	**0.8335**	**0.9193**	0.8508	**0.8088**	**0.8293**	0.7770	0.5603

MTL-Recurrent GCN achieves that best link prediction performance out of all the models in terms accuracy, AUC, recall, and F1 score; however, MTL-GCN exhibits the best precision. This suggests that forcing the model to learn *when* a link will form via a multi-task learning architecture also improves the model's ability to predict *if* a link will form.

Additionally, although the link prediction performance of Recurrent GCN is slightly worse than that of MTL-Recurrent GCN, both give 1–2% AUC performance gains compared to GCN and MTL-GCN, which suggests the effectiveness of the recurrent architecture in learning temporal dependencies for link prediction. In general, all four GCN models give appreciable link prediction AUC and F1 score performance gains of 11–13% and 7–19%, respectively, compared to the best non-GCN baseline: node2vec.

Lastly, Recurrent GCN exhibits the best leadtime prediction AUC and accuracy out of all the models. We suspect that this is due to the model's recurrent architecture and its loss function being comprised solely of categorical cross entropy loss.

5   Conclusions

In this paper, we present MTL-Recurrent GCN, a recurrent graph convolutional neural network model for temporal link prediction that utilizes a multi-task learning architecture. We also construct and analyze a COVID-19 KG of biomedical concepts and research papers using data provided by the Oak Ridge National Laboratory Smoky Mountains Computational Sciences Data Challenge and auxiliary textual data. Finally, we demonstrate MTL-Recurrent GCN's ability to outperform several baseline models at predicting novel links between biomedical concepts within this KG.

Currently, the leadtime prediction is limited to a set number of classes. Therefore, future works involves altering the multi-task learning models to allow for leadtime regression. Additional future work involves grid searching β for our custom loss function.

References

1. Caruana, R.: Multitask learning: a knowledge-based source of inductive bias. In: Proceedings of the Tenth International Conference on Machine Learning, pp. 41–48. Morgan Kaufmann (1993)
2. Defferrard, M., Bresson, X., Vandergheynst, P.: Convolutional neural networks on graphs with fast localized spectral filtering (2017)
3. Divakaran, A., Mohan, A.: Temporal link prediction: a survey. N. Gener. Comput. **38**(1), 213–258 (2019)
4. Domingo-Fernández, D., et al.: COVID-19 knowledge graph: a computable, multimodal, cause-and-effect knowledge model of COVID-19 pathophysiology. Bioinformatics **37**(9), 1332–1334 (2020)
5. Giarelis, N., Kanakaris, N., Karacapilidis, N.: On the utilization of structural and textual information of a scientific knowledge graph to discover future research collaborations: a link prediction perspective. In: Appice, A., Tsoumakas, G., Manolopoulos, Y., Matwin, S. (eds.) DS 2020. LNCS (LNAI), vol. 12323, pp. 437–450. Springer, Cham (2020). https://doi.org/10.1007/978-3-030-61527-7_29
6. Grover, A., Leskovec, J.: node2vec: scalable feature learning for networks (2016)
7. Leskovec, J., Faloutsos, C.: Sampling from large graphs. In: KDD 2006, pp. 631–636. Association for Computing Machinery, New York (2006)
8. Li, J., Peng, J., Liu, S., Weng, L., Li, C.: TSAM: temporal link prediction in directed networks based on self-attention mechanism (2020)
9. Liben-Nowell, D., Kleinberg, J.: The link prediction problem for social networks. In: Proceedings of the Twelfth International Conference on Information and Knowledge Management, CIKM 2003, pp. 556–559. Association for Computing Machinery, New York (2003)
10. Mikolov, T., Chen, K., Corrado, G., Dean, J.: Efficient estimation of word representations in vector space (2013)
11. Peddada, A.V., Kostas, L.: Users and pins and boards, oh my! temporal link prediction over the Pinterest network (2016)
12. Ruder, S.: An overview of multi-task learning in deep neural networks (2017)
13. Seo, Y., Defferrard, M., Vandergheynst, P., Bresson, X.: Structured sequence modeling with graph convolutional recurrent networks. In: Cheng, L., Leung, A.C.S., Ozawa, S. (eds.) ICONIP 2018. LNCS, vol. 11301, pp. 362–373. Springer, Cham (2018). https://doi.org/10.1007/978-3-030-04167-0_33
14. Wise, C., et al.: COVID-19 knowledge graph: accelerating information retrieval and discovery for scientific literature (2020)
15. Zhou, T., Lü, L., Zhang, Y.C.: Predicting missing links via local information. Eur. Phys. J. B **71**(4), 623–630 (2009)

Reconstructing Piezoelectric Responses over a Lattice: Adaptive Sampling of Low Dimensional Time Series Representations Based on Relative Isolation and Gradient Size

Michael R. Lindstrom$^{(\boxtimes)}$, William J. Swartworth$^{(\boxtimes)}$, and Deanna Needell

University of California Los Angeles, Los Angeles, USA
{mikel,wswartworth,deanna}@math.ucla.edu

Abstract. We consider a $d-$dimensional lattice of points where, at each lattice point, a time series can be measured. We are interested in reconstructing the time series at all points of the lattice, to a desired error tolerance, by adaptively sampling only a subset of lattice points, each over a potentially short time interval. The method we develop is tailored to atomic force microscopy (AFM) data where time series are well-represented by constant functions at each lattice point. Through a convex weighting of a point's relative isolation and relative gradient size, we assign a sampling priority. Our method adaptively samples the time series and then reconstructs the time series over the entire lattice. Our adaptive sampling scheme performs significantly better than sampling points homogeneously. We find that for the data provided, we can capture piezoelectric relaxation dynamics and achieve a relative ℓ_2 reconstruction error of less than 10% with a 47% reduction in measurements, and less than 5% with a 25% reduction in measurements.

1 Introduction and Background

Atomic force microscopy (AFM) is an imaging paradigm used to study materials at the nanoscale [9]. The method is often costly in terms of the time it takes to measure each pixel, and thus efficient sampling and reconstruction approaches are desired. The example we consider here arises in the study of ferroelectric materials and involves the measurement of the piezoelectric response as a function of time, space and voltage. Piezoelectricity refers to an electric charge that collects in solid materials, such as the ferroelectric film of the compound lead titanate (PbTiO3), which motivates the challenge posed by the *2021 Smoky Mountains Computational Sciences and Engineering Conference Data Challenge* that we address in this paper.

The challenge (problem 8) amounts to reconstructing the piezoelectric response of a ferroelectric film as a function of time, measured at points (x, y)

M. R. Lindstrom and W. J. Swartworth—Equal contributions.

© Springer Nature Switzerland AG 2022
J. Nichols et al. (Eds.): SMC 2021, CCIS 1512, pp. 420–429, 2022.
https://doi.org/10.1007/978-3-030-96498-6_25

on its surface at various voltages V by taking as few measurements as possible. Measurements are taken over some time duration (on the order of seconds) at a fixed (x, y, V) to obtain the piezoelectric response $p(t; x, y, V)$ representing the surface deformation [12] as a function of time. The method should quickly determine the next set of (x, y, V)-values at which to measure p. These problem data are based on ferroelectric polarization dynamics measured with dynamic piezoresponse force microscopy [7].

2 Proposed Solution

In solving this problem, we have developed Relative Isolation and Gradient Size Sampling (RIGS Sampling), a simple active learning method that can "fill in" the piezoelectric response from incomplete data—specifically, we work with a subset of points on the surface with corresponding voltages to reconstruct the piezoelectric response at unmeasured position-voltage pairings. While active learning typically focuses upon an algorithm selecting unlabelled points from which to learn in classification tasks [4,10], it can be used in contexts where measurements of complicated systems can only be applied sparsely such as in air quality measurements [1]. Here, RIGS Sampling learns the piezoelectric response by choosing positions and voltages at which to take measurements to improve its reconstruction accuracy.

At a high level, RIGS builds intermediate constructions, by using the simple and fast k-nearest neighbors regression [3]. It then uses these reconstructions to bias towards sampling points with large gradients. Importantly, we demonstrate that adaptive sampling substantially outperforms non-adaptive sampling.

We begin with some notation and assumptions. We assume the surface locations and voltages at which measurements can be taken belong to a lattice with x−values $0 \leq x_0 < x_1 < \ldots < x_{N_x-1} \leq L_x$, y−values $0 \leq y_0 < y_1 < \ldots < y_{N_y-1} \leq L_y$, and V−values $V_{\min} \leq V_0 < V_1 < \ldots < V_{N_V-1} \leq V_{\max}$ for some positive integers N_x, N_y, and N_V with lengths $L_x, L_y > 0$ and voltages $V_{\min} < V_{\max}$. Furthermore, the piezoelectric responses can be measured at time points $0 \leq t_0 < t_1 < \ldots < t_{N_t-1} \leq T_{\max}$ with $N_t > 0$ an integer and $0 < T_{\max}$. In the original dataset, x, y, V, t, and the piezoelectric response p had physical units but they are not directly relevant for our study. Here, we work with dimensionless x, y, and V: $x_0 = 0$ and $x_{N_x-1} = N_x - 1$ with regular spacings of 1 between x's and similarly for y. The voltages are made dimensionless by dividing physical voltages by 1 Volt. The times are measured in seconds and the piezoelectric responses are measured in picometers.

We define a sample point as a point of the lattice $(x, y, V) \in [0, L_x] \times [0, L_y] \times [V_{\min}, V_{\max}]$ and assume that at each sample point, measurements are taken at times $t_0, t_1, \ldots, t_{n_t-1}$ for some positive integer $n_t \leq N_t$. With a point (x, y, V) of the lattice, we denote $p(t; x, y, V)$ to be the piezoelectric response as a function of time t and $\hat{p}(x, y, V)$ to be a constant approximation of the piezoelectric response. Now for $i \in \{0, \ldots, N_x - 1\}, j \in \{0, \ldots, N_y - 1\}, k \in \{0, \ldots, N_V - 1\}$ and $m \in \{0, \ldots, N_t\}\}$, we let $\mathcal{E}_{ijkm} = p(t_m; x_i, y_j, V_k)$ be a tensor of the full experimental measurements at all lattice points and all times and $\widehat{\mathcal{E}}_{ijkm}$ reconstructions at all lattice points and times. Much of our notation is summarized in Table 1.

Table 1. Parameters used in this study.

Symbol	Value	Type	Meaning
N_x/N_y	60 each	Given	Number of x-values/y-values
N_V	16	Given	Number of voltage values
N_t	128	Given	Number of time values that can be measured
$\mathcal{E}$	Full dataset	Given	Tensor of response over lattice points and times
f	Varies	Hyperparameter	Fraction of lattice points sampled for reconstruction
n_t	Varies	Hyperparameter	Number of time values used in sampling
w	Varies	Hyperparameter	Weighting in $[0, 1]$ to give to gradient vs isolation
n_r	2000	Fixed hyperparemeter	Number of steps between full reconstructions
n_n	4	Fixed hyperparameter	Number of nearest neighbors for reconstructions
k	$k(u, s) = \exp(-|u - s|^2)$	Fixed hyperparameter	Kernel for local density
$\hat{p}$	Not set	Computed from method	Time-constant approximation to response
$\widehat{\mathcal{E}}$	Not set	Computed from method	Tensor of response predictions over lattice points and times

With these notations set up, we formulate our objective as follows: given a tolerance $0 < \tau$, we seek to find $n_t \leq N_t$ to generate a collection of sample points $\mathcal{S}$ with $|\mathcal{S}| < N_x N_y N_V$ with which we can accurately reconstruct the piezoelectric responses over the entire lattice and over the full time window $[0, T_{\max}]$ to within a relative ℓ_2-error of τ. We define both the relative ℓ_2-error r by

$$r = ||\widehat{\mathcal{E}} - \mathcal{E}||_F / ||\mathcal{E}||_F \tag{1}$$

where the F-subscript denotes the Frobenius norm, i.e., the square root of the sum of squared differences running over all 4 dimensions.

In deriving our methodology, we first seek to understand the innate dimension of the data. We begin by considering what the piezoelectric response looks like as a function of t. In sampling approximately 1% of (x, y, V)−values and performing a Principal Component Analysis [6], we find that over 98% of the total variance of the response time series $p(t; x, y, V)$'s can be expressed by the first principal component and that the first component is approximately constant as depicted in Fig. 1. This suggests the time series can be well described by constant functions $p(t; x, y, V) = \text{const}$. Based on other experiments of piezoelectric responses (see e.g. [8]) where the response had a correlation length on the order of ≈ 100 nm, we also expect that nearby points in space will have similar responses. This makes our later choice to fill in missing data through nearest neighbor regression seem plausible.

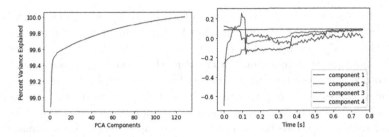

Fig. 1. Left: percentage of variance explained given number of principal components used in standardized samples of 1% of lattice points. Right: plots of first 4 principal components as a function of time.

At a high level, until some fixed fraction of lattice points have been sampled, RIGS Sampling does the following: (1) for each unsampled lattice point (x_i, y_j, V_k), compute a sampling priority based upon its distance to nearby sampled points and estimated gradients (with respect to x, y, and V) of the piezoelectric response at that point; (2) from the priorities assigned, identify lattice points (x, y, V) at which to to measure $p(t; x, y, V)$; then (3) take measurements up to a time t_{n_t} and approximate $p(t; x, y, V)$ by a constant $\hat{p}(x, y, V)$. Periodically, for use in computing the gradients, and at the end when all sampling has been done, a full reconstruction is done to generate $\widehat{\mathcal{E}}$ with a nearest-neighbor regression either by (a) using the time-constant approximates $\hat{p}$ (always done in intermediate steps and can be done as the final step) or (b) using the full time series at all sampled lattice points and reconstructing each fixed time slice separately (only as final step). We shall refer to (a) as a constant reconstruction and (b) as a full-time reconstruction.

3   Approach

Python code implementing our sampling scheme is available at this Github repository [11]. Algorithm 1 provides the full details of RIGS Sampling and makes use of the helper routines specified by Algorithms 2 and 3. In Algorithm 2, we wish to score how isolated a point is from other points that have been sampled. To do so, we ascribe a proxy for local density at each point by summing radially symmetric, decaying kernel functions centered at each sampled point and its reflections (to be explained later in this paragraph). Then unsampled points with the largest inverse density are deemed more isolated and should be sampled with higher priority. We find that with using the sampled points alone, points on the boundary will be scored as being more isolated even when they are not since they have fewer neighbors. To address this, we add reflection points in computing the density, i.e., to compute the density proxy, we use not only the sampled points but also their reflections $\mathcal{R}$ across each face of the cube. When gradient weight is not considered, this tends to give reasonably uniform samplings of points as can be seen in Fig. 2. For simplicity, our kernel function is $k(u,s) = e^{-|u-s|^2}$ but in the future we could consider choosing kernels based on Kernel Density Estimation [5]. In Algorithm 3, we score points based on how large $|\nabla \hat{p}|$ (computed in (x, y, V)-space) is relative to other points.

We note here that more sophisticated methods, such as those often used in image processing, could be used in place of a simple weighted average of nearest neighbors. However, we found such methods, like the Biharmonic Inpainting [2] approach, to be much slower while yielding comparable results. As another comment, it seems quite natural that instead of using constant approximations, we could instead compute the principal component representation of $p(t; x, y, V)$ at a sample of (x, y, V)-points and then use the first few principal components to reconstruct the piezoelectric response (with suitable adaptations such as using only n_t values to estimate the projections onto the components). This is especially appealing given that higher principal components have a nontrivial time-dependence; however, with regards to reconstruction errors, we did not find better performance in doing so and thus opt for the more simple approach. As a result, our method uses constant approximations, which is more or less equivalent to using only the first principal component.

Algorithm 1. Relative Isolation and Localized Gradient (RIGS)

1: |**Input**| the averaging window width n_t; an initially empty list of position-voltage points that have been sampled; a list of unsampled position-voltage points $\mathcal{U}$, initially including all lattice points; a gradient weight $0 \leq w \leq 1$; a sampling fraction threshold $0 < f \leq 1$; a reconstruction frequency n_r; a number of nearest neighbors for image reconstruction n_n; and whether or not to do a full time reconstruction, $full$.

2: $step = 0$

3: $m = (x_{round((N_x-1)/2)}, y_{round((N_y-1)/2)}, (V_{round((N_V-1)/2)})), \mathcal{S} = \{m\}, \mathcal{U} \leftarrow \mathcal{U} \setminus \{m\}$

4: Measure $p(t_0; m), p(t_1; m), ..., p(t_{n_t-1}; m)$ and set $\hat{p}(m) = \frac{1}{n_t} \sum_{j=0}^{n_t-1} p(t_j; u)$

5: **while** $|\mathcal{S}|/(|\mathcal{S}| + |\mathcal{U}|) < f$. **do**

6:    **if** $step$ is a multiple of n_r **then**

7:        Compute a reconstruction $\widehat{\mathcal{E}}$ over the entire lattice using the n_n nearest neighbors applied to the points in $\mathcal{S}$ with their constants $\{\hat{p}(s)|s \in \mathcal{S}\}$ using Python's KNeighborsRegressor from the sklearn module.

8:        Compute the gradient score at each point according to Algorithm 3.

9:    **end if**

10:   Make a list of sampling priorities $\mathcal{P}$ corresponding to each unsampled point with scores given by $wg + (1 - w)i$ where $g \in \mathcal{G}$ is the corresponding gradient score of the unsampled point and $i \in \mathcal{I}$ is the corresponding isolation score of the unsampled point—see Algorithms 2 and 3.

11:   At the $u \in \mathcal{U}$ with highest priority, measure $p(t_0; u), p(t_1; u), ..., p(t_{n_t-1}; u)$ and approximate the piezoelectric response at u by $\hat{p}(u) = \frac{1}{n_t} \sum_{j=0}^{n_t-1} p(t_j; u)$.

12:   $U \leftarrow \mathcal{U} \setminus \{m\}, \mathcal{S} \leftarrow \mathcal{S} \cup \{m\}$.

13:   Run Algorithm 2.

14:   $step \leftarrow step + 1$.

15: **end while**

16: **if** $full == true$ and $n_t == N_t$ **then**

17:   Compute the full-time reconstruction $\widehat{\mathcal{E}}$ over the entire lattice using the nearest neighbor algorithm as before in each time slice separately.

18: **else**

19:   Compute the constant reconstruction $\widehat{\mathcal{E}}$ over the entire lattice using the nearest neighbor algorithm as before using a constant-in-time approximation.

20: **end if**

21: |**Output**| $\widehat{\mathcal{E}}$

Algorithm 2. Density Algorithm: each unsampled point is ascribed an isolation score on $[0, 1]$. The set of reflecting functions $\mathcal{R}$ reflect sampled points across all 6-boundaries of the lattice.

1: |Input| a list of sampled lattice points $\mathcal{S}$, a list of unsampled lattice points $\mathcal{U}$ with corresponding isolation
    scores $\mathcal{I}$ all initially 0, a symmetric $k(u, s) = K(|u - s|)$ a decreasing function, and reflecting functions
    $\mathcal{R}$.
2: **for all** $u = (x, y, V)$ in $\mathcal{U}$ **do**
3:     $density = 0$
4:     **for all** $s = (x', y', V')$ in $\mathcal{S}$ **do**
5:         $density \leftarrow density + K(u, s) + \sum_{r \in \mathcal{R}} K(u, r(s))$.
6:     **end for**
7:     Set isolation score in $\mathcal{I}$ corresponding to u to $1/density$.
8: **end for**
9: $TotalIsolationSqd = 0$
10: **for all** i in $\mathcal{I}$ **do**
11:     $TotalIsolationSqd \leftarrow TotalIsolationSqd + i^2$
12: **end for**
13: **for all** i in $\mathcal{I}$ **do**
14:     $i \leftarrow i/\sqrt{TotalIsolationSqd}$
15: **end for**
16: |Output| $\mathcal{I}$

Algorithm 3. Gradient Algorithm: each point is ascribed a gradient score on $[0, 1]$.

1: |Input| a list $\mathcal{L}$ of all lattice points with corresponding gradient scores $\mathcal{G}$ all initially set to 0.
2: **for all** ℓ in $\mathcal{L}$ **do**
3:     Assign the corresponding gradient score of $\mathcal{G}$ to be the magnitude of the gradient at ℓ using Python's
        gradient from the numpy module.
4: **end for**
5: $TotalGradSqd = 0$
6: **for all** g in $\mathcal{G}$ **do**
7:     $TotalGradSqd \leftarrow TotalGradSqd + g^2$
8: **end for**
9: **for all** g in $\mathcal{G}$ **do**
10:     $g \leftarrow g/\sqrt{TotalGradSqd}$
11: **end for**
12: |Output| $\mathcal{G}$

4   Results

Here we focus on investigating how the method performs at reconstructing the complete dataset $\mathcal{E}$ by sampling only a subset of lattice points or time series over a shorter duration. In sequence: we begin by observing how the gradient weight affects the lattice points being sampled; then, we study how the constant reconstructions fare under the choice of various hyperparameters; finally, we repeat the previous line of investigation for the full-time reconstruction.

We first see that as the relative weight ascribed to the gradient increases, the set of sampled points chosen changes from almost uniform to highly focused on areas with rapid changes in the piezoelectric response (see Fig. 2). We speculate some of the circular sampling patterns with $w = 1$ stem from the gradients only being estimated every n_r iterations. Qualitatively, we also note that for a fixed time slice, a constant reconstruction accurately captures key features of the piezoelectric response. In Fig. 3, we see that with only $n_t = 30$ time points used and by only sampling a fraction $f = 0.4$ of all lattice points, the constant approximation we obtain accurately depicts the response at time slice 64, which is beyond the range of times used in sampling. In particular we note that the reconstruction captures sharp edges from the original image quite well.

Among the hyperparameters we deem most important, we wish to study how the overall reconstruction error (Eq. 1) varies as we change the gradient weight w, number of time samples used n_t, and fraction of lattice points sampled f. We wish to identify which combinations of hyperparameters reduce the reconstruction error to within various tolerances. In the case of using constant reconstructions, Fig. 4 shows these results. With $w = 0.8$, $n_t = 50$ time points, and $f = 0.6$ lattice points sampled, the relative error is less than 15%, corresponding to measuring only 23% of all $N_x N_y N_V N_t$ possible lattice-time points. However, this fails to capture time-dynamics as the responses are constant in time for each fixed (x, y, V).

In Figs. 5 and 6 we consider the full-time reconstruction, which yields our highest quality results. Figure 5 shows the relative ℓ_2-loss for various fractions of points sampled and gradient weights. Unsurprisingly, the quality of the reconstruction strictly improves with the fraction of sampled points. More interestingly, we often observe improvement as the gradient weight w increases. This implies that our algorithm benefits from adaptivity. When $w = 0$ our algorithm samples non-adaptively, while adaptivity plays a progressively greater role as w increases. When only a small fraction of points are sampled, setting w to be too large damages the reconstruction accuracy. We suspect this is due to our algorithm leaving large low-gradient patches almost completely unsampled. For large fractions of sampled points f this effect is less significant as it is difficult to avoid sampling large patches. Notably we achieve less than 10% error by sampling only 53% of points, and achieve less than 5% error by sampling 75% of points. In addition Fig. 6 shows that reconstructing time slices individually allows our reconstruction to capture the piezoelectric response as a function of time.

As a final remark, a `Python` implementation of RIGS Sampling for this dataset takes on average 2.7 ms per iteration with $n_r = 2000$ and $n_n = 4$, making it a viable choice in computing the optimal subsequent lattice sampling points.

5   Contributions

Our method is capable of reducing the number of experimental measurements necessary to describe the piezoelectric response measured at various positions and voltages. Notably, we have shown that in the example data, we can reconstruct the full dataset to within a relative ℓ_2-error of 10% with 47% fewer measurements than done to obtain the data. Additionally, we demon-

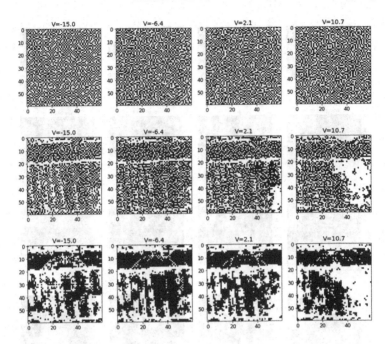

Fig. 2. The set of set of sampled points (shown in white) generated by sampling the first time series component ($n_t = 1$) from 50% of grid points, using gradient weights 0 (top row), 0.5 (middle row), 1.0 (bottom row). The dataset included 16 different voltages but for compactness only 4 are shown.

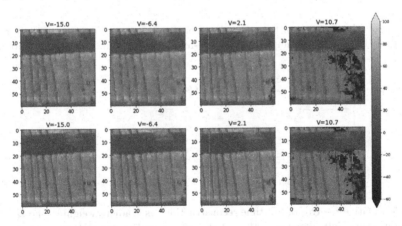

Fig. 3. Top row: The reconstructed piezoelectric response at time slice 64 using the first 30 time series points, sampling from 40% of the lattice, and with a gradient weight of 0.81. Bottom row: The true piezoelectric response at time slice 64.

strate that adaptive measurements can significantly reduce the measurement capacity required for piezoelectric microscopy, as compared to non-adaptive measurements.

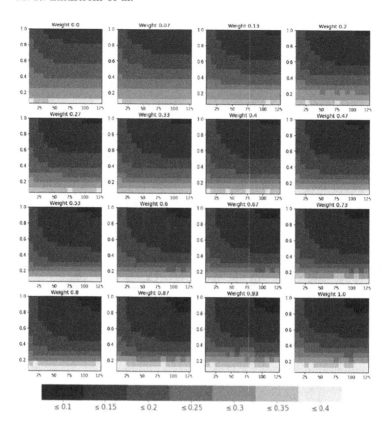

Fig. 4. Relative ℓ_2-error of the constant reconstructions as a function of the gradient weight w, the fraction of sampled points f (y-axes), and the number of time components n_t used (x-axes).

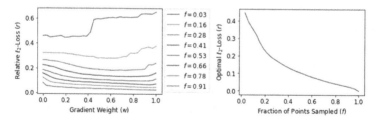

Fig. 5. Relative ℓ_2-error of full-time reconstructions as gradient weight w and sampling fraction f vary (left) along with the optimal reconstruction error attainable for a given sampling fraction f (right).

Our work demonstrates that active learning based on gradient information is beneficial and that time series may have a low dimensional representation (constant in this case), which could be useful for other large multidimensional datasets.

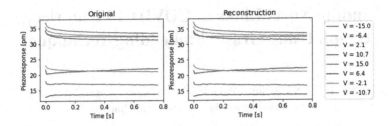

Fig. 6. Plots of the experimental and reconstructed piezoelectric responses vs time at 50% sampling, averaged over all (x, y)-lattice values at various voltages.

Acknowledgments. WJS and DN acknowledge funding from NSF BIGDATA #1740325 and NSF DMS #2011140.

References

1. Chang, H., Zhiwen, Y., Zhiyong, Y., Qi, A., Bin, G.: Air quality estimation based on active learning and kriging interpolation. Big Data Res. **4**(6), 2018061 (2018)
2. Damelin, S.B., Hoang, N.: On surface completion and image inpainting by biharmonic functions: numerical aspects. Int. J. Math. Math. Sci. **2018** (2018). https://doi.org/10.1155/2018/3950312. Article ID 3950312
3. Fix, E., Hodges, J.L.: Discriminatory analysis. Nonparametric discrimination: consistency properties. Int. Stat. Rev./Revue Internationale de Statistique **57**(3), 238–247 (1989)
4. Hu, Y., Zhang, D., Jin, Z., Cai, D., He, X.: Active learning via neighborhood reconstruction. In: Proceedings of the Twenty-Third International Joint Conference on Artificial Intelligence, pp. 1415–1421. Citeseer (2013)
5. Hyndman, R.L., Zhang, X., King, M.L., et al.: Bandwidth selection for multivariate kernel density estimation using MCMC. In: Econometric Society 2004 Australasian Meetings, no. 120. Econometric Society (2004)
6. Jolliffe, I.T., Cadima, J.: Principal component analysis: a review and recent developments. Philos. Trans. R. Soc. A Math. Phys. Eng. Sci. **374**(2065), 20150202 (2016)
7. Kelley, K.P., et al.: Tensor factorization for elucidating mechanisms of piezoresponse relaxation via dynamic Piezoresponse Force Spectroscopy. npj Comput. Mater. **6**(1), 1–8 (2020)
8. Kiselev, D., Bdikin, I., Selezneva, E., Bormanis, K., Sternberg, A., Kholkin, A.: Grain size effect and local disorder in polycrystalline relaxors via scanning probe microscopy. J. Phys. D Appl. Phys. **40**(22), 7109 (2007)
9. Rugar, D., Hansma, P.: Atomic force microscopy. Phys. Today **43**(10), 23–30 (1990)
10. Settles, B.: Active learning literature survey (2009)
11. Swartworth, W., Lindstrom, M., Needell, D.: RIGS Code. https://github.com/wswartworth/active_imaging
12. Xu, T.B.: Energy harvesting using piezoelectric materials in aerospace structures. In: Structural Health Monitoring (SHM) in Aerospace Structures, pp. 175–212. Elsevier (2016)

Finding Novel Links in COVID-19 Knowledge Graph Using Graph Embedding Techniques

Ankit Patel[1(✉)], Saeel Shrivallabh Pai[2(✉)], Haresh Rengaraj Rajamohan[3],
Manohar Bongarala[2], and Rajanala Samyak[4]

[1] Blue Wave AI Labs, West Lafayette, IN 47906, USA
[2] School of Mechanical Engineering, Purdue University, West Lafayette, IN 47906, USA
pai15@purdue.edu
[3] Center for Data Science, New York University, New York, NY 10003, USA
[4] Department of Statistics, Stanford University, Stanford, CA 94305, USA

Abstract. With the rapid proliferation of scientific literature, it has become increasingly impossible for researchers to keep up with all published papers, especially in the biomedical fields with thousands of citations indexed every day. This has created a demand for algorithms to assist in literature search and discovery. A particular case is the literature related to SARS-CoV-2 where a large volume of papers was generated in a short span. As part of the 2021 Smoky Mountains Data Challenge, a COVID-19 knowledge graph constructed using links between concepts and papers from PubMed, Semantic MEDLINE, and CORD-19, was provided for analysis and knowledge mining. In this paper, we analyze this COVID-19 knowledge graph and implement various algorithms to predict as-yet-undiscovered links between concepts, using methods of embedding concepts in Euclidean space followed by link prediction using machine learning algorithms. Three embedding techniques: the Large-scale Information Network Embedding (LINE), the High-Order Proximity-preserved Embedding (HOPE) and the Structural Deep Network Embedding (SDNE) are implemented in conjunction with three machine learning algorithms (logistic regression, random forests, and feed forward neural-networks). We also implement GraphSAGE, another framework for inductive representation on large graphs. Among the methods, we observed that SDNE in conjunction with feed-forward neural network performed the best with an F1 score of 88.0% followed by GraphSAGE with F1 score of 86.3%. The predicted links are ranked using PageRank product to assess the relative importance of predictions. Finally, we visualize the knowledge graphs and predictions to gain insight into the structure of the graph.

Keywords: COVID-19 knowledge graph · Link prediction · Graph embeddings · PageRank · Supervised learning

1 Introduction

Scientific literature is expanding at an ever-increasing rate, with an estimated 8% annual growth in publications over the past few decades [1]. It is humanly impossible to keep

© Springer Nature Switzerland AG 2022
J. Nichols et al. (Eds.): SMC 2021, CCIS 1512, pp. 430–441, 2022.
https://doi.org/10.1007/978-3-030-96498-6_26

track of all new developments in a field of study. This is especially significant in biomedical fields, which are broad and vast; where there were more than 1.5 million new citations indexed in the PubMed database in 2020 [2], almost three every minute. As a result, automated tools for knowledge mining have become increasingly relevant to obtain useful information from data that is too large to be analyzed by any individual. In this context, we implement methods to analyze and mine knowledge from a COVID-19 knowledge graph provided as part of the 2021 Smoky Mountains Data Challenge [3]. The COVID-19 knowledge graph is constructed using relations between biomedical concepts and papers from PubMed, Semantic MEDLINE, and CORD-19 [4]. Our aim is to discover as-yet-undiscovered links between concepts, leveraging other connections in the graph, also called Swanson linking, first described in Swanson and Smalheiser in 1997 [5].

Given a graph, several heuristic methods exist for link prediction among different nodes, often building on various proximity measures which are computed directly from the graph structure. For example, the Adamic/Adar index [6] uses the sum of the inverse logarithm of the degrees of common neighbors; PageRank [7] invokes the global structure of the graph by assigning weights to the nodes according to the stationary distribution of a random walk on the graph and links are predicted between nodes with high PageRank scores. A review of various approaches based on such graph characteristics can be found in Nowell et al. [8].

In this paper, we explore link prediction using embeddings of the graph in fixed-dimensional Euclidean space obtained in different ways, with nodes close or similar in the graph being in close proximity in the embedding. Such embeddings allow us to use established Machine Learning (ML) methods by framing the link prediction problem in the standard supervised learning setup. In such approaches, selecting a good embedding method is essential for better overall performance in the downstream ML model. A survey of various graph embedding structures is in Goyal et al. [9]. We explore embedding methods such as the Large-scale Information Network Embedding (LINE) [10], the High-Order Proximity-preserved Embedding (HOPE) [11], and the Structural Deep Network Embedding (SDNE) [12]. These different methods are engineered to harness different aspects of the graph structure including various first, second, or higher order proximities. We evaluate the quality of these embeddings for link prediction using popular ML techniques including logistic regression, random forests, and feed-forward neural networks. These results are further compared with those obtained from GraphSAGE [13], which is a new framework for inductive representation learning on large graphs.

In Sect. 2.1, we discuss dataset curation of the COVID-19 knowledge graph including a time stamping procedure for splitting the data into a training and a test set. We visualize the given data using Graphia [14], an open-source graph visualization platform in Sect. 2.2, and present exploratory results including various node summary statistics in Sect. 2.3. Subsequently, we describe methods for link prediction and their implementation, and describe a method to quantify the importance of the predicted links. In the next section, we evaluate the performance of our methods on the data provided, and qualitatively discuss the reasons for the trends observed. We finally conclude with a discussion on topics for future work.

2 Methodology

2.1 Dataset Curation

Three subgraphs with links between pairs of concepts (C-C), between papers and concepts (P-C), and between pairs of papers (P-P) are provided as the dataset for the challenge. In addition, some metadata is provided for some of the papers in a file called "papers.csv". For training and testing of link prediction algorithms, a train-test split data is essential and the challenge description [3] indicated that these two versions of the data would be made available, one with connections only until June 2020 for training data, and an updated one with connections till February 2021 for validation data. However, this split data was not provided and therefore an artificial dataset for validation is created from the given dataset by replicating the challenge description. The process used to obtain the train-test-validation data splits is described below.

The distribution of the publication year and month were obtained from the paper.csv file, and this distribution was used to randomly assign a year and month to the C-C links such that the distribution of the years and months assigned are consistent with the paper.csv file. Based on these assigned time stamps, the C-C data was split into train, test and validation data sets. The data set consisting of links after June 2020 is called the validation data (as mentioned in the challenge description), and the data set consisting of links before June 2020 has been further split into two more sets, the training and the testing data sets. In our context, because the data after June 2020 was called the validation data in the challenge description, the terminologies of validation data and testing data have been interchanged from their usage in common machine learning terminology. Thus, the models developed to predict future links have been trained on the training set, their hyperparameters tuned based on their performance on the test set, and then the final performance of the models have been evaluated on the validation set. The flow chart of this process is shown in Fig. 1.

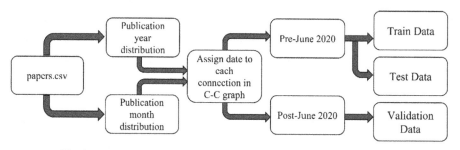

Fig. 1. Flowchart for data generation from papers.csv and the C-C graph

A more accurate method to trace back the dates for C-C links would be to identify all papers associated with both concepts (using the P-C graph) followed by identifying pairs of paper where one cited the other (using the P-P graph). For all such pairs, publication date of citing paper is found (using papers.csv) and the earliest date among all is assigned to the C-C link. However, this method was not feasible as the connections between alphanumeric paper ID are not present in the P-P graph making the data incomplete.

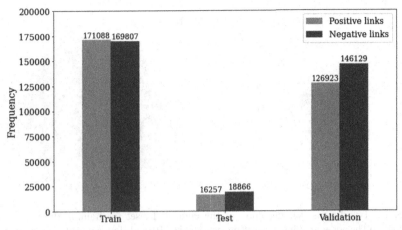

Fig. 2. The distribution of positive and negative samples in the train, test and validation data sets

Training models require negative and positive links. Here, the pair of nodes between which a connection exists is called a positive link and pair of nodes between which a connection does not exist is called a negative link. We generate an approximately equal number of negative links between pairs of nodes and append to our train, test and validation datasets. The negative links required for training were sampled randomly from the adjacency matrix. Once these data sets were generated, it was also ensured that there was no duplication of links or any data leakage between the datasets before the different prediction models were trained and evaluated on the data. The final distribution of the train, test and validation data is shown in Fig. 2.

2.2 Data Visualization

Depiction of a network graph in a 2- or 3-dimensional space allows for proper interpretation and insight into the nature of the data. Visualizing a huge network such as the COVID-19 knowledge graph involves placing interconnected nodes in 2- or 3-dimensional space; the locations of which are determined by layout algorithms. The depicted graphs in the present work are generated using a force directed layout algorithm where the connected nodes attract, and the disconnected nodes repel each other with a certain force. The final visualization is the output of an optimization problem minimizing the energy of the system. An open-source graph visualization platform called Graphia is used for visualization. Graphia provides 2D and 3D depictions of the network graph with robust control over graph attributes and provides inbuilt metrics and clustering algorithms for assessment of the output visualizations.

A 2D graph of the training data set is shown in Fig. 3(a). The central nodes are highly interconnected with the highest degree and the peripheral nodes are the least connected. Figure 3(b) further highlights into the nodes with the degree greater than 10. The node sizes here are proportional to their degree.

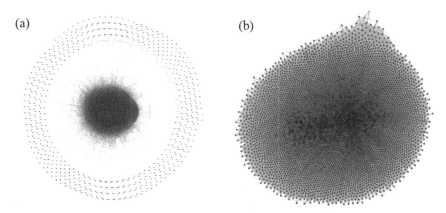

Fig. 3. (a) Two-dimensional depiction of the curated dataset for training (train_test) using Graphia, (b) The nodes are filtered based on the degree (> 10) and plotted with the size proportional to their degree.

2.3 Exploratory Data Analysis

The COVID-19 knowledge graph consists of nodes representing various medical concepts and the connection between them as undirected edges. Concepts are indexed terms/phrases in biomedical research. The links between them are obtained by text mining the abstracts of papers from the PubMed database maintained by the US National Library of Medicine, and further enriched with data from the new COVID-19 Open Research Dataset (CORD-19) [4]. Exploratory data analysis was performed on the train plus test data without looking into the validation data. For convenience, the train plus test set will be called as "train_test" in the rest of the work.

The train_test data set consists of a total of 40,313 nodes (concepts) in 374 disconnected sub graphs. The major subgraph consists of 39,555 nodes, and the rest of the nodes are distributed in smaller sub graphs with mostly 2–4 nodes each, as seen in Fig. 3(a). The major subgraph has an average node degree of 9.49 and a median degree of 2. The node degree distribution is skewed with only a few nodes exhibiting a very high degree, while the rest have relatively lesser degrees. The highest degree of node observed is 7648, the second highest is 3,974 and the lowest is 1. This demonstrates that there are only a few nodes with very high degrees, which is consistent with the graph visualization in Fig. 3(b), where the size of the node is indicative of its degree.

The PageRank values of the nodes, the node betweenness centrality, the Katz centrality index and the node degree were calculated for all the nodes in train_test and their correlation with the PageRank is depicted in Fig. 4. All node metrics were found to have a very strong positive correlation with each other. The Spearman's correlation coefficient between PageRank and degree, PageRank and Katz centrality, PageRank and betweenness of the nodes were found to be 0.939, 0.878 and 0.916 respectively. Since all the metrics are positively correlated to each other, there does not seem to be a particular advantage of using one over the other. In this work, the PageRank values of the nodes are used to assess the importance of the nodes.

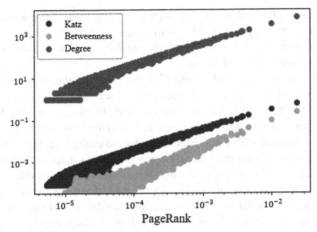

Fig. 4. The correlation between different nodal metrics (PageRank, Katz and Betweenness Centralities, and degree)

2.4 Methods for Link Prediction

Traditional methods to predict links based on graph theory concepts (such as Adamic Adar index, preferential attachment, etc.) have been explored widely in the past. In this work, we explore novel embedding based machine/deep learning methods for link prediction. These embeddings-based methods use different algorithms to map the nodes of the graph onto a Euclidean space with the aim of preserving graph structure in the embedded space. Following embedding techniques are explored:

- Large-scale Information Network Embedding (LINE) [10]: In this method, an objective is optimized that preserves both local and global network structures. The local structure is dependent on first order proximity, which is the local pairwise similarity between nodes linked by edges. On the other hand, second-order proximity between nodes depends on number of shared neighbors and thus captures global network structure. The first-order proximity is captured by minimizing the Kullback-Leibler (KL) divergence of the joint probability distribution and empirical probability distribution between pair of nodes. In this method, nodes sharing similar connections or similar distribution of "context" nodes are deemed to be similar. For second-order proximity, probability of a "context" node generated by a node in consideration is calculated using the softmax function. The empirical probability for same pair of nodes is calculated using existing edges and out-degree of the nodes being considered. The minimization of KL-divergence between the above two probability distributions gives the second-order proximity. The representations obtained from each objective (first order and second order proximity) are concatenated to obtain final embeddings.
- High Order Proximity preserved Embedding (HOPE) [11]: This method extends LINE by preserving asymmetric transitivity in directed graphs through approximation of high order proximities using methods that are scalable to large graphs. To learn the asymmetry in graph edges, this embedding technique finds two embedding vectors,

source and target, for each node. Although the HOPE technique has been developed for directed graphs, it is applicable to all graphs as any type of graph (directed or undirected) can be represented as a directed graph by replacing each undirected edge with two oppositely-directed edges.

- Structural Deep Network Embedding (SDNE) [12]: Similar to LINE, this method also captures both first and second order proximities in the graph. This method uses an autoencoder approach to calculate embeddings by preserving both first and second order similarity simultaneously, thus characterizing both local and global network structure. As mentioned earlier, the second order proximity is related to neighborhood similarity of nodes. Each row of the adjacency matrix of a graph depicts the neighbors of a particular node. SDNE preserves the second-order proximity through an autoencoder approach whereby each row of adjacency matrix of the graph is reconstructed and one of the intermediate outputs in the autoencoder are obtained as embeddings. Further, to preserve first-order proximity, the embedding space representations of nodes that are linked are constrained to be similar. SDNE is thus different from LINE in the aspect that first and second order proximities are preserved simultaneously in the former.

- GraphSAGE [13]: The aforementioned methods are suited for static graphs, as they cannot facilitate inference on any unseen nodes. GraphSAGE uses node features such as text information and other attribute information to generalize to unseen nodes. In this approach, a set of aggregator functions learn to combine feature information from a node's local neighborhood and the aggregated feature vector is concatenated to the embedding vector of the node. Each aggregator function aggregates information from a different number of hops, search depth, etc. so that the learned embeddings can encode neighborhood information at different scales. These embeddings can be used directly for the downstream task (node classification, link prediction etc.) and this whole pipeline can be trained end-to-end making the method fully supervised and the embeddings optimized specially for the task at hand. Although the GraphSAGE framework is more suited for dynamic graphs, we employ it on a static graph to see how the results obtained from its end-to-end training framework compare against those obtained from the other methods where the embeddings generated are not optimized for the specific prediction task.

The embeddings are used to train and test a supervised learning problem, and obtain metrics such as accuracy, precision, recall, and F1-score. Three supervised learning algorithms, namely logistic regression, random forests and feed-forward neural networks are implemented. For random forests, we used 25 decision trees with a maximum depth of 10. While for neural networks, two hidden layers with 32 and 8 neurons were chosen. The network was trained with Adam optimizer with a learning rate of 0.001. The above hyperparameters were optimized through a process of trial and error by monitoring performance on the test data. The code is available in the GitHub repository[1].

---

[1] GitHub repository: https://github.com/SaeelPai/GraphVizards2.

2.5   Importance of Predicted Links

For each of the embedding techniques, predictions from the algorithm with the best F1-score are chosen as the final predictions. The importance of these predictions is empirically defined as product of PageRank of pair of nodes in each connection. Intuitively, this makes sense because PageRank is a measure of importance of a node and a link between two important nodes must be significant. The obtained product for each predicted link is sorted in descending order and connections at the top are identified as being the most important links.

3   Results and Discussions

Table 1 shows performance on validation dataset by various supervised algorithms utilizing four different embedding techniques discussed in previous section. F1-score, which is the harmonic mean of precision and recall is used as a comparison metric between different approaches and algorithms. SDNE embeddings with feedforward neural network obtained overall best result with an F1-score of 88%. GraphSAGE achieves the second highest F1-score of 86.3%, while LINE and HOPE embeddings could only achieve best F1-scores of 84.6% and 83.4%, respectively. Figure 5 shows the F1-scores of the various supervised learning algorithms on LINE, HOPE and SDNE embeddings. While both SDNE and LINE embedding frameworks preserve first and second order proximities, the former performs better since the latter adopts a sub-optimal approach of preserving first and second order proximities separately and then concatenating the obtained representations. On the other hand, SDNE's optimization framework is superior whereby both proximities are preserved in a combined objective. Secondly, SDNE's autoencoder approach involves multiple layers of non-linear functions that can capture the complex structure of a graph better.

Table 1. Performance on validation dataset.

Method	Algorithm	Accuracy	Precision	Recall	F1-Score
LINE	Logistic regression	82.0	88.1	70.8	78.5
	Random forest	85.9	88.8	79.6	84.0
	Feedforward NN	85.4	82.9	86.3	**84.6**
HOPE	Logistic regression	70.1	99.6	35.8	52.7
	Random forest	86.4	96.8	73.2	**83.4**
	Feedforward NN	85.6	94.9	72.9	82.5
SDNE	Logistic regression	86.9	90.0	80.7	85.1
	Random forest	87.6	85.3	89.0	87.1
	Feedforward NN	88.7	86.6	89.4	**88.0**
GraphSAGE	Feedforward NN	87.1	85.5	87.1	**86.3**

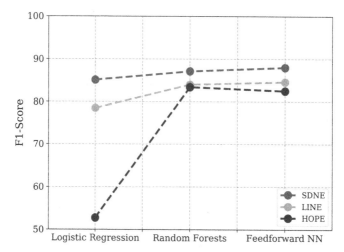

Fig. 5. Comparison of F1-scores across different embeddings for three different ML algorithms

From Table 1, it is evident that the precision values of HOPE are high while the recall values are low. This may be attributed to the fact that HOPE is an embedding technique for directed graphs. Before calculating the embeddings for the nodes of an undirected graph, the graph is first converted into a directed graph [11] by replacing every existing edge with two oppositely-directed edges. This would result in having twice the number of positive links as the number of negative links in our training set. The positive links are more strongly reinforced, and the nodes which are connected to each other are placed much closer than the other nodes in embedding space. ML algorithms learn this bias whereby a link between two nodes is predicted only when the proximity in embedding space is extremely high leading to conservative positive link predictions. Hence, with these embeddings the precision value is high but recall value is low. This is also evident from Fig. 6 in which HOPE is seen to have the least number of false positives, and in Fig. 7 where the link importance of the positive links of HOPE is the highest.

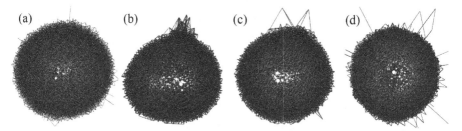

Fig. 6. Visualization of positive predictions from (a) LINE embeddings with feedforward NN, (b) HOPE embeddings with random forest, (c) SDNE algorithms with feed forward NN, and (d) GraphSAGE. The edges in blue indicate true positives and the edges in red indicate false positives. Only nodes of degree >5 are represented. (Color figure online)

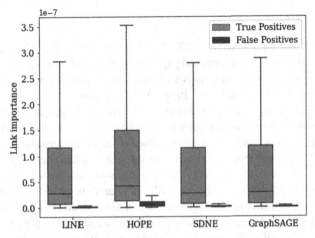

Fig. 7. Box and whisker plots of link importance based on PageRank for the true positives and false positives for the different methods employed

Table 2. Average PageRank-based importance of positive predictions.

	LINE ($\times 10^{-9}$)	HOPE ($\times 10^{-9}$)	SDNE ($\times 10^{-9}$)	GraphSAGE ($\times 10^{-9}$)
True positives	184.87	217.85	180.58	184.24
False positives	2.66	12.88	3.56	2.66

GraphSAGE approach performs well on all the metrics on the final validation set with an F1-score of 86.3%. The network was trained with two aggregators that aggregate information from five nodes in the neighborhood. Further tuning with more aggregators and using neighborhoods of different scale could help learn more robust representations and improve the test performance.

The positive predictions using each of the embedding techniques and best performing algorithm as well as positive predictions from GraphSAGE are visualized in Fig. 6. The blue links represent the true positives while the red edges depict false positives. For all predictions, the false positives are mainly located at the boundary of the graph where the nodes have low degree and are thus not important, as mentioned earlier. Thus, falsely predicted links are in general less important. The importance of links is quantified by taking the product of PageRank values of the respective nodes. Thereafter for validation, all positive links are identified as false and true positives and average link importance within each group is calculated as shown in Table 2. The corresponding box and whisker plots are shown in Fig. 7 for all embeddings and GraphSAGE. As can be observed, predicted true positives are two orders more important on average compared to false predictions.

4 Conclusion

In this work, we have analyzed the COVID-19 knowledge graph constructed using relations between biomedical concepts and papers from PubMed, Semantic MEDLINE, and CORD-19. We used node embeddings and machine learning methods to predict future concept-concept links (formed after June 2020) by training on the graph of concept-concept links prior to June 2020. Multiple embedding techniques including LINE, HOPE, and SDNE were implemented using a training dataset followed by link prediction through logistic regression, random forests, and feed-forward neural networks. GraphSAGE framework with neural networks was also implemented. SDNE with neural networks outperformed all other combinations of embeddings and algorithms with an F1-score of 88%. This is be attributed to SDNE's capability to exploit simultaneously both first- and second-order proximities to characterize the local as well as global structure of the network. Further, the predicted links are assigned an importance score based on the product of the PageRank of the nodes involved. We observed that false positives are assigned extremely low importance under this framework, around two orders of magnitude lower than the importance assigned to true positives. This is crucial in our context where a decision to conduct new research to identify potential links between pairs of concepts can be determined based on the assigned importance.

For future work, the proposed methods can be extended to optimize hyperparameters of embedding techniques as well as supervised algorithms. For example, the size of the embeddings, the number, and the depth of decision trees in random forest, and number of neurons in neural network layers can be optimized. Further, we observe a bias towards nodes with high degrees in our results when assigning link importance score based on PageRank. Often, such high degree nodes may represent generic concepts like virus, protein, etc. Knowledge about the mapping of nodes to their respective concepts could help reduce the bias towards them. Additionally, since the scientific literature is rapidly expanding and new concepts are introduced frequently, it may help to treat existing knowledge graphs as dynamic. Methods such as GraphSAGE can generalize to dynamic graphs if we have text/feature embeddings available for the concepts. These embeddings can also be learned in a self-supervised manner from the text of the papers and can help make the models more robust and improve their performance.

References

1. Landhuis, E.: Scientific literature: information overload. Nature **535**, 457–458 (2016). https://doi.org/10.1038/NJ7612-457A
2. MEDLINE PubMed Production Statistics. https://www.nlm.nih.gov/bsd/medline_pubmed_production_stats.html. Accessed 13 Sept 2021
3. Herrmannova, D., Kannan, R., Lim, S., Potok, T.E.: Finding novel links in COVID-19 knowledge graph; smoky mountains data challange (2021). https://smc-datachallenge.ornl.gov/2021-challenge-2/. Accessed 13 Sept 2021
4. Kannan, R., et al.: Scalable knowledge graph analytics at 136 Petaflop/s. In: SC20, pp. 1–13. IEEE (2020)
5. Swanson, D.R., Smalheiser, N.R.: Artificial intelligence an interactive system for finding complementary literatures: a stimulus to scientific discovery. Artif. Intell. **9**, 183–203 (1997)

6. Adamic, L.A., Adar, E.: Friends and neighbors on the web. Soc. Netw. **25**, 211–230 (2003). https://doi.org/10.1016/S0378-8733(03)00009-1

7. Page, L., Brin, S., Motwani, R., Winograd, T.: The PageRank Citation Ranking: Bringing Order to the Web. Stanford InfoLab, Stanford (1999)

8. Liben-Nowell, D., Kleinberg, J.: The link-prediction problem for social networks. J. Am. Soc. Inf. Sci. Technol. **58**, 1019–1031 (2007). https://doi.org/10.1002/ASI.20591

9. Goyal, P., Ferrara, E.: Graph embedding techniques, applications, and performance: a survey. Knowl.-Based Syst. **151**, 78–94 (2018). https://doi.org/10.1016/J.KNOSYS.2018.03.022

10. Tang, J., Qu, M., Wang, M., Zhang, M., Yan, J., Mei, Q.: LINE: large-scale information network embedding. In: WWW 2015 - Proceedings 24th of International Conference World Wide Web, pp. 1067–1077 (2015). https://doi.org/10.1145/2736277.2741093

11. Ou, M., Cui, P., Pei, J., Zhang, Z., Zhu, W.: Asymmetric transitivity preserving graph embedding. In: Proceedings 22nd ACM SIGKDD International Conference *Knowledge Discovery* Data Mining (2016). https://doi.org/10.1145/2939672

12. Wang, D., Cui, P., Zhu, W.: Structural deep network embedding. In: Proceedings 22nd ACM SIGKDD International Conference *Knowledge Discovery* Data Mining (2016). https://doi.org/10.1145/2939672

13. Hamilton, W.L., Ying, R., Leskovec, J.: Inductive representation learning on large graphs. In: 31st Conference Neural Information Processing Systems (2017)

14. Graphia—visualisation tool for the creation and analysis of graphs. https://graphia.app/. Accessed 13 Sept 2021

Exploring the Spatial Relationship Between Demographic Indicators and the Built Environment of a City

Ridhima Singh[1]([✉]) [iD] and Melissa Allen Dumas[2] [iD]

[1] Farragut High School, Knoxville, TN 37934, USA
[2] Computational Science and Engineering Division,
Oak Ridge National Laboratory, Oak Ridge, TN 37830, USA
allenmr@ornl.gov

Abstract. In addition to global and regional drivers of urbanization, neighborhood development in urban areas across the United States has been shown to be influenced by various local socio-economic factors. These factors, despite varying across socio-economic groups, have large implications regarding a population's vulnerability to extreme climate events, including heat waves resulting in adverse health impacts. Additionally, the demographics of an urban area can shape its infrastructural characteristics, causing different populations groups to face varying levels of risks and benefits. As a result, the urban morphology and socio-economic characteristics of a city are deeply intertwined; however, their interactions on a finer scale are not yet fully understood. This research aims to better understand the relationships between various socio-economic factors and the built environment of a city, considering variability in building types, and temperature patterns. This research focuses on the city of Las Vegas, NV, and uses spatial data analysis to understand the correlation between of socio-economic characteristics, building morphology, building characteristics, and temperature data to understand the correlation between these various factors. Results of these research shows there is a distinct pattern of clustering of socio-economic characteristics with the city and there is a distinct correlation between age and cost, socio-economic characteristics, and locations of high heat distribution within the city.

Keywords: Urbanization · Socio-economic indicators · Social equity · Environmental justice

1 Background

1.1 Introduction

Currently, more than 55% of the world's population live in urban areas, and by 2050, this number is expected to increase to 68% [1]. The rapid urbanization in recent years have

© Springer Nature Switzerland AG 2022
J. Nichols et al. (Eds.): SMC 2021, CCIS 1512, pp. 442–454, 2022.
https://doi.org/10.1007/978-3-030-96498-6_27

greatly shaped neighborhood development across the United States, with local socio-economic factors proving to be a strong influence. These factors, despite varying across demographic groups, have large implications regarding a population's vulnerability to extreme climate events, including heat waves and illnesses. In fact, recent research has shown that areas with a higher proportion of minorities and lower income and education levels are disproportionately impacted by higher temperature [2]. This is because such neighborhoods have less green space, causing these groups to become exposed to higher heat stress [3].

Additionally, the demographics of an urban area can also shape its infrastructural characteristics. It has been proven that neighborhoods varying socio-economic characteristics have different spatial structures, with socio-economic factors being the main influencers of urban development, housing patterns, and accessibility to essential services [4]. Moreover, urban expansion has continued to develop in a way that pushes disadvantaged communities into more tightly packed neighborhoods. As a result, neighborhoods that have a higher population density, large portions of undeveloped land, many roads with dead-ends, and more uniform street patterns tend to exhibit higher levels of deprivation [5].

Therefore, the urban morphology and socio-economic characteristics of a city are deeply intertwined; however, their interactions on a finer scale are not yet fully understood. Thus, this research aims to better understand the relationships between various demographic factors and the built environment characteristics of a city, considering variability in building types, and temperature patterns.

1.2 Study Area and Data Sources

The city of Las Vegas, Nevada was the study area for this research. Located in Clark County, Las Vegas is the largest city in Nevada in terms of population, with over 600,000 residents, and has an area of 218 square kilometers [6]. As per the Department of Energy, Las Vegas falls within the hot-dry climate zone, meaning it receives less than 20 inches (50 cm) of precipitation each year and has a monthly mean temperature greater than 45 °F (7 °C) throughout the year [7]. The 2016 National Land Cover Data (NLCD) for Las Vegas was downloaded from the United States Geological Survey (USGS), and the NCLD map showing the urban areas is displayed in Fig. 1. Figure 1 also displays the block groups in Las Vegas. Block groups are divisions of Census tracts, which are subdivisions of a county used for statistical purposes during the decennial census [8].

Fig. 1. National Land Cover Data for Las Vegas. The urbanized areas are show in various shades of red. (Color figure online)

2 Methodology

This research addresses the following data challenges and most of the data used in the analysis are at the block group level.

2.1 Challenge 1: What is the Distribution of Commercial, Industrial, and Residential Buildings Within Each Block Group? Do These Distributions Correlate with Building Age? Building Value? Building Size?

Building data for the city of Las Vegas at the block group [9] was used in this analysis. This tabular data contains various characteristics of buildings aggregated across each block group, such as parcel quantity, year built, building size, building price, and other interior characteristics for both residential and commercial buildings. Nevada block group outline shapefile was obtained from the US Census Bureau for spatial analysis. QGIS was used to spatially join this shapefile with the building data to visualize the parcel distributions along with distribution of building price, size, and age at the block group level across Las Vegas. This data helped in understanding the spatial distribution of commercial, and residential buildings within each block group, and the correlations between these distributions with building age, value and size.

2.2 Challenge 2: Using Temperature Data from a Source of the Participant's Choosing, Are There Locations Within the City That Tend to Be Warmer Than Others? How Does This Relate to Building Density and Building Type?

Two sources of temperature data for Las Vegas were used in this analysis. One was the Daymet data [10] from Oak Ridge National Laboratory's Distributed Active Archives Center (ORNL DAAC). Daymet is a gridded data product consisting of various daily weather parameters, including maximum and minimum temperatures, precipitation, vapor pressure, radiation, snow water equivalent, and day length. For this analysis, the maximum temperature (in degrees Celsius) for September 6th, 2020, was used since September 6th was the hottest day in 2020. Additionally, daytime land surface temperature for Las Vegas derived from the MODIS satellite was also used for this analysis [11]. Both the datasets helped to visualize the distribution of temperature across the city. The LST data helped to understand if the urbanization of the city plays a role in the spatial pattern of temperature. Temperature data from each product was also aggregated at the block group level to understand the correlation with block group level building densities and building type.

2.3 Challenge 3: How Does the Built Environment and the Local Scale Experience of Heat Co-vary with Socio-economic and Demographic Characteristics of Residents?

Socio-economic data developed by the US Environmental Protection Agency's (EPA) Environmental Justice Screening and Mapping Tool (EJSCREEN) was downloaded for Las Vegas [12] and used in this analysis. EJSCREEN is a tool that the EPA uses to relate environmental and demographic indicators [13]. In this study, the following demographic indicators were considered: housing unit density, percent of minority populations, percent of low-income households, percent of adults without a high school diploma, percent of individuals over the age of 64, and percent of vulnerable populations. The percent of vulnerable populations was defined as the average of percent minority and percent low income in the block group. This data was visualized for each block group using QGIS.

These variables were also correlated against building characteristics and temperature, and the Pearson correlation coefficient (or R value) and the degree of significance (or p values) at a 95% confidence interval for each of the correlations were derived. The relationships that had a R value of greater than 0.45 or less than −0.45 and a p value of less than .00001, were considered important and plotted.

3 Results

3.1 Challenge 1: Distribution of Building Types and Their Correlation with Building Characteristics (Age, Value and Size)

Spatial distribution of residential parcels, residential building values, residential building sizes and residential building ages are shown in Fig. 2. There are more residential parcels in the southern and western parts of the city. The most expensive residential buildings are mostly concentrated in the southern part of the city, while the least expensive buildings are slightly northeast of the center. Interestingly, the least expensive buildings are also some of the oldest.

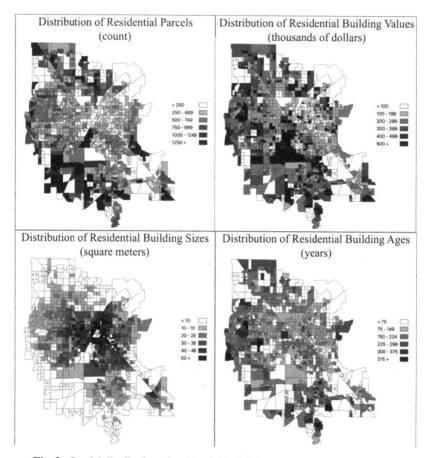

Fig. 2. Spatial distribution of residential building parameters across Las Vegas

Correlation between the spatial distribution of residential buildings within each block group, and the distributions with building age, value and size were plotted in Fig. 3. There is no significant correlation between residential parcel count and residential building value and size. However, there is a strong correlation between residential building age and residential parcel count.

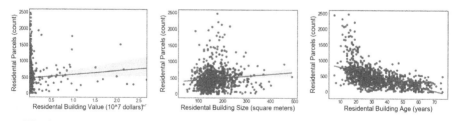

Fig. 3. Correlations between residential parcel count and residential building parameters

Spatial distribution of commercial parcels, commercial building values, commercial building sizes and commercial building ages are shown in Fig. 4. It can be observed that most of the commercial parcels are located along a central diagonal of the city spanning from the northeast corner to the southwest portion. The highest concentration of commercial parcels is located directly to the southwest of the center, and this area is famously known as "The Strip." This area also has the more expensive and bigger commercial buildings. Additionally, most of the commercial buildings are also relatively new, with the oldest ones located in the direct center of Las Vegas.

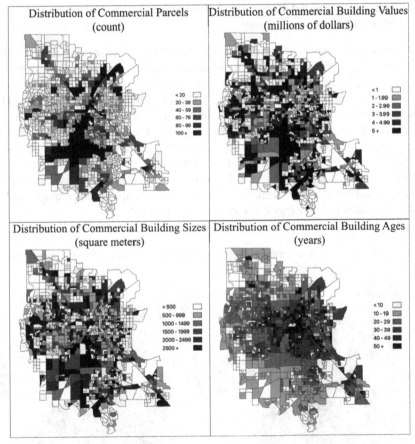

Fig. 4. Spatial distribution of commercial building parameters across Las Vegas

Correlation between the spatial distribution of commercial buildings within each block group, and the distributions with building age, value and size were plotted in Fig. 5. There was no significant correlation between commercial building parcel count and commercial building age, size and value.

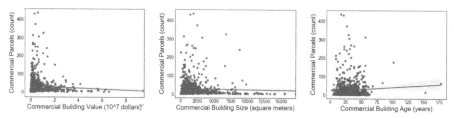

Fig. 5. Correlations between commercial parcel count and commercial building parameters

3.2 Challenge 2: Spatial Pattern of Temperature and Its Correlation with Building Type and Density

Spatial pattern of temperature across the city of Las Vegas is visualized in Fig. 6. There is a distinct gradient in the maximum air temperature from west to east with the city with eastern part being hotter. However, the pattern of the land surface temperature does not follow this same gradient. But there is a spatial relationship between the building density and the land surface temperature as seen in Fig. 7. The areas with higher building densities tends to have higher land surface temperature. Therefore, this pattern of the land surface temperature distribution clearly shows that the built environment can change the weather patterns of an area. Moreover, the difference between air temperature and land surface temperature in the city of Las Vegas can be as high as 10 °C as seen in Fig. 7 and can be attributed to urbanization. This significant change in temperature can have serious implications for energy costs and health impacts.

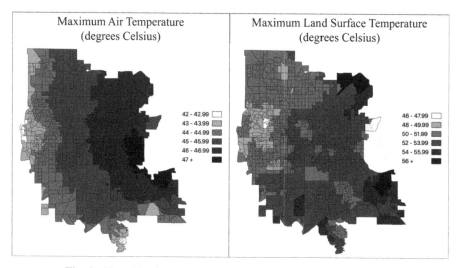

Fig. 6. Air and land surface temperature distributions across Las Vegas

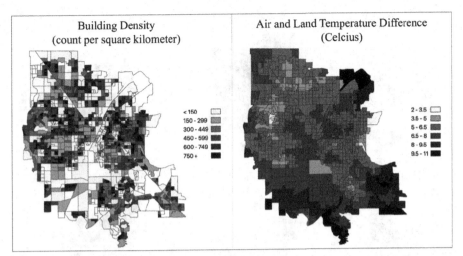

Fig. 7. Building distributions and difference between air temperature and LST across Las Vegas

3.3 Challenge 3: Correlation Between Socio-economic and Demographic Characteristics and the Built Environment

A detailed analysis of socio-economic factors and its correlation temperature data and building characteristics was performed for the city of Las Vegas. Socio-economic factors considered were (a) housing unit density (b) percent of minority populations (c) percent of low-income individuals (d) percent of adults without a high school diploma (e) percent of individuals above the age of 64 and (f) percent of vulnerable populations. Vulnerable population is defined as the average of percent minority and percent low income in the block group. The spatial distribution of the socio-economic factors is displayed in Fig. 8. It can be observed that the northeast part of the city has the highest percentages of minorities, low-income individuals, people without a high school diploma, and vulnerable populations. The northeast part also has a higher housing unit density. Additionally, the northeastern areas also are the hottest part of the city as can be seen from Fig. 6. Due to higher building densities these areas also show a higher difference in the air temperature and land surface temperature as seen in Fig. 7. The same areas also have residential parcels with mainly older and cheaper buildings as seen from Fig. 2. Conversely, the western part of Las Vegas has a predominantly white population, fewer numbers of low-income individuals, and more people with a high school diploma. This portion also has more expensive, newer houses, and both the air and land temperatures are relatively cooler here.

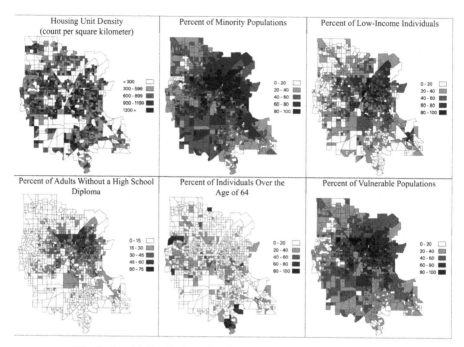

Fig. 8. Spatial distribution of socio-economic data across Las Vegas

Correlations between the 5 socio-economic indicators (percent of minority popula-tions, percent of low-income individuals, percent of adults without a high school diploma, percent of individuals above the age of 64 and percent of vulnerable populations) with 3 temperature variables (maximum air temperature, maximum LST and difference in the air temperature from the LST) and 10 building characteristics (residential/commercial parcel count, residential/commercial building value, residential/commercial building size and residential/commercial building age, housing unit density and building density) resulted in 95 combinations. To quantify the significant relationships between the socio-economic indicators with temperature and building characteristics, only the correlations with Pearson correlation coefficient (or R value) with R > 0.45 or R < −0.45 and the degree of significance (or P values) with p < .00001 at a 95% confidence interval are tabulated in Table 1. Out of the 95 combinations, only 16 relationships were deemed to be significant. The highest R value of 0.6 was seen between percent of vulnerable populations with maximum air temperature, and percent of adults without a high school diploma and maximum air temperature, followed by R value of 0.59 between adults with-out a high school diploma and residential building age. In fact, percent of vulnerable populations showed significant correlation with maximum air temperature, maximum LST, residential building age and residential building size. The high correlation values indicates that a significant proportion of the vulnerable population are forced to inhabit older structures and reside in parts of the city which are significantly hotter.

Table 1. Significant correlations in socio-economic variables with temperature and building characteristics

Significant correlations			
Metric 1	Metric 2	R Value	P Value
Percent of vulnerable populations	Maximum air temperature	0.60	1.21E−56
Percent of adults without a high school diploma	Maximum air temperature	0.60	5.48E−58
Percent of minority populations	Maximum air temperature	0.56	9.41E−50
Percent of low-income individuals	Maximum air temperature	0.53	3.853E−43
Percent of vulnerable populations	Maximum land surface temperature	0.49	5.84E−36
Percent of adults without a high school diploma	Maximum land surface temperature	0.49	3.45E−36
Percent of minority populations	Maximum Land Surface Temperature	0.46	1.15E−31
Percent of Adults Without a High School Diploma	Residential building age	0.59	6.89E−56
Percent of low-income individuals	Residential building age	0.53	3.20E−43
Percent of vulnerable populations	Residential building age	0.51	3.32E−39
Maximum air temperature	Residential building age	0.50	2.02E−38
Percent of low-income individuals	Commercial building age	0.45	5.40E−30
Percent of low-income individuals	Residential parcel count	−0.45	2.24E−30
Percent of low-income individuals	Residential building size	−0.46	2.49E−31
Percent of vulnerable populations	Residential building size	−0.47	1.23E−32
Residential parcel count	Residential building age	−0.54	9.98E−46

Scatter plots of the 16 significant relationships between the socio-economic indicators with temperature and building characteristics, with Pearson correlation coefficient (or R value) with $R > 0.45$ or $R < −0.45$ and the degree of significance (or p values) with $p < .00001$ at a 95% confidence interval are shown in Fig. 9. The scatter plots show the direction, form, and strength of the relationships along with the outliers in the data. It is seen that 12 of the significant relationships have a strong positive correlation whereas 4 relationships have a strong negative correlation. Percentage of low-income individuals correlated negatively with residential parcel count, residential building size; percentage of vulnerable population also correlated negatively with residential building size and residential parcel count also had a negative correlation with residential parcel age.

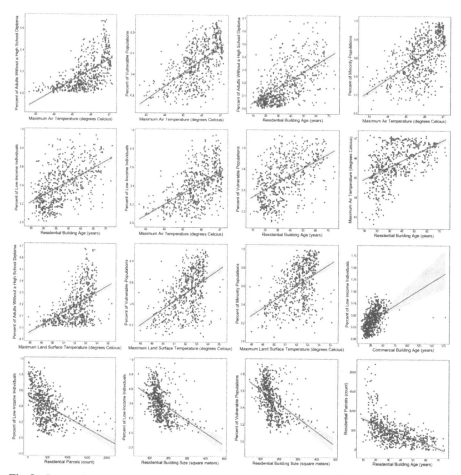

Fig. 9. Scatterplots of the significant correlations in socio-economic variables with temperature and building characteristics

4 Conclusion

The findings of this research have notable implications regarding the relationship between the built environment of Las Vegas and its socio-economic indicators. Through data analysis and visualization this study identified that the northeastern part of Las Vegas as an area of concern for social equity and environmental justice. This area is characterized by a high building density consisting largely of older and less expensive buildings. In addition, the same area contains the highest percentage of minorities, low-income households, and individuals without a high school diploma, causing it to also have the largest percentage of vulnerable populations. Vulnerable population being pushed into older, hotter parts of the city has serious implications for social equity and environmental justice. Furthermore, the correlation analysis also found that both air temperature and land surface temperature have significant correlation with the vulnerable populations.

Moreover, residential building age is also highly correlated with air temperature and vulnerable populations. As a result, the energy cost of older buildings will be generally higher as compared to newer building [14] and therefore residents have to pay higher costs for heating and cooling which will be a challenge for vulnerable populations. Thus, it would benefit Las Vegas if more funds were allocated to this portion of the city to mitigate issues relating to social equity and environmental justice. Nevertheless, in the upcoming years, scientists, urban planners, and legislators alike must determine ways to help ensure environmental justice and social equity for the entire population.

Appendix

Open-source code and visualizations can be accessed via the Github page: https://git hub.com/ridhima-singh/smcdc2021_challenge5.

References

1. UN Department of Economic and Social Affairs (UNDESA). 68% of the world population projected to live in urban areas by 2050, says UN (2018). Accessed https://www.un.org/dev elopment/desa/en/news/population/2018-revision-of-world-urbanization-prospects.html
2. Hoffman, J.S., Shandas, V., Pendleton, N.: The effects of historical housing policies on resident exposure to intra-urban heat: a study of 108 US urban areas. Climate **8**(1), 12 (2020)
3. Mishra, V., Ganguly, A. R., Nijssen, B., Lettenmaier, D.P.: Changes in observed climate extremes in global urban areas. Environ. Res. Lett. **10**(2), 024005 (2015)
4. Boampong, E., Çubukçu, K.: The organization of urban space and socio-economic characteristics: a graph theory-based empirical study using hierarchical cluster analysis. Planlama **29**(3), 259–270 (2019). https://doi.org/10.14744/planlama.2019.61687
5. Venerandi, A., Quattrone, G., Capra, L.: A scalable method to quantify the relationship between urban form and socio-economic indexes. EPJ Data Sci. **7**(1), 1–21 (2018). https://doi.org/10.1140/epjds/s13688-018-0132-1
6. US Census Bureau. QuickFacts: Las Vegas City, Nevada (n.d.). Accessed https://www.census.gov/quickfacts/lasvegascitynevada
7. US Department of Energy and Pacific Northwest National Laboratory. Guide to determining climate regions by country. In: Building America Best Practices Series, vol. 7.3 (2015). Accessed https://www.energy.gov/sites/prod/files/2015/10/f27/ba_climate_region_guide_7.3.pdf
8. US Census Bureau. Glossary (n.d.). Accessed https://www.census.gov/programs-surveys/geography/about/glossary.html
9. Brelsford, C.: Las Vegags Block Group Buildings Data (2021). Accessed https://doi.ccs.ornl.gov/ui/doi/328
10. Thornton, M.M., Shrestha, R., Wei, Y., Thornton, P.E., Kao, S., Wilson, B.E.: Daymet: daily surface weather data on a 1-km grid for North America, Version 4. ORNL DAAC, Oak Ridge, Tennessee, USA2020). https://doi.org/10.3334/ORNLDAAC/1840
11. Hengl, T.: Long-term MODIS LST day-time and night-time temperatures, sd and differences at 1 km based on the 2000–2017 time series (1.0). Zenodo (2018). https://doi.org/10.5281/zenodo.1435938

12. US Environmental Protection Agency. EJSCREEN (2020). Accessed https://www.epa.gov/ejscreen/download-ejscreen-data

13. US Environmental Protection Agency. EJSCREEN technical documentation (2019). Accessed https://www.epa.gov/sites/default/files/2021-04/documents/ejscreen_technical_document.pdf

14. Aksoezen, M., Daniel, M., Hassler, U., Kohler, N.: Building age as an indicator for energy consumption. Energy Build. **87**, 74–86 (2015)

Atomic Defect Identification with Sparse Sampling and Deep Learning

Michael C. Cao[1]([✉]), Jonathan Schwartz[2], Huihuo Zheng[3], Yi Jiang[4], Robert Hovden[2,5], and Yimo Han[1]

[1] Department of Materials Science and NanoEngineering, Rice University,
Houston, TX, USA
`mc133@rice.edu`
[2] Department of Material Science and Engineering, University of Michigan,
Ann Arbor, MI, USA
[3] Argonne Leadership Computing Facility, Argonne National Laboratory,
Lemont, IL, USA
[4] Advanced Photon Source, Argonne National Laboratory, Lemont, IL, USA
[5] Applied Physics Program, University of Michigan, Ann Arbor, MI, USA

Abstract. Scanning Transmission Electron Microscopy (STEM) is a high-resolution characterization technique that can resolve atomic lattices. Recent advances in high-brightness sources enable in-situ STEM experiments with acquisition rates reaching 20 frames per second. However, high-doses of electron radiation damage the atomic lattice and limit frame-rates. Thus the real-time visualization of lattice transformations with sub-angstrom resolution requires innovative tools to track defect evolution while limiting electron radiolysis. Here we present a trained deep learning model that automatically tracks lattice defects in graphene while scanning around 60% of the total area for an in-situ experiment. Our approach extracts relevant physical information from STEM movies without requiring any knowledge of the lattice symmetry. Atomic defect identification using sparse sampling and deep learning was demonstrated on a multi-image dataset of defects in graphene as part of the 2021 Smoky Mountains Data Challenge.

Keywords: Scanning transmission electron microscopy · Machine learning · Defects · Convolutional neural network

1 Introduction

Structural analysis at atomic resolution is commonly used to understand the functionality and properties of materials. Scanning transmission electron microscopy (STEM) uses sub-angstrom probes for high-resolution analysis of interfaces, defects or strain fields. Conventionally for STEM imaging, the focused probe follows a rectangular raster path across the specimen, which inherently results in uneven distribution of dose due to scan flyback corrections [1]. STEM imaging often suffers from radiation damage that modifies or even destroys the

© Springer Nature Switzerland AG 2022
J. Nichols et al. (Eds.): SMC 2021, CCIS 1512, pp. 455–463, 2022.
https://doi.org/10.1007/978-3-030-96498-6_28

specimen [2,3]. Moreover, key specimen information is often constrained on small regions of interest rather than the full scan area. This is especially prevalent when searching for lattice defects, which requires imaging below 2–3 unit cells with high signal-to-noise ratio (SNR). Various strategies can be employed to minimize electron dose, such as shorter dwell times or reduced beam current. However these solutions could impose significant image distortions and significantly degrade SNR-limited resolution.

As part of the 2021 Smoky Mountains Data Challenge No. 6, we were tasked with finding a more efficient scanning path for exploring defects in a graphene lattice [4]. The data provided was a STEM movie of graphene lattice transformations. In this experiment, the graphene system evolves with time and an emerging number of electron beam induced defects results in the production of carbon vacancies. To determine optimal dose-efficient scans, we modified an existing neural network [5,6], which automatically identifies defects in lattice images, to additionally determine a sparser scan. Within the graphene dataset tested, our neural network can successfully (>90% accuracy) identify defects and develop sparse sampling strategies when trained on the entire time-series experiment. On the other hand, the prediction accuracy becomes worse when the model is trained on a portion of the dataset, which is possibly due to a limited number of images (only 100) and poor SNR. This work suggests sparse sampling, optimistically as low as 50%, can still allow atomic defect identification when a convolutional nueral network is used.

2   Background

We used a convolutional neural network (CNN) to identify defects and develop efficient sampling strategies. A CNN is composed of a series of abstract mathematical steps, typically referred as layers, most commonly applied to analyze visual imagery (e.g. classification or segmentation) [5,7–9]. While the sequence of discrete mathematical operations (e.g. convolutions) are decided by the coder, the weights are "learned" by the machine. Rather than implementing a linear CNN which uses a series of convolutions in a encoder-decoder setup, we modified an existing neural network [6] into a U-Net [10] architecture which keeps track of encodings at various length scales and then passes them forward to the decoder at matching scales, creating a U-shaped schematic (Fig. 1). The U-Net architecture is a more sophisticated model that excels for image segmentation applications. CNNs have been successfully demonstrated in the past to identify interstitial and vacancy defects in $WSe_{2-2x}Te_{2x}$ for low SNR raw STEM images [11]. In addition, similar U-Net CNNs identified atomic-scale defects in a WS_2 STEM movie [12]. However in both these cases, these networks required fully sampled micrographs for lattice feature localization. It is also worth pointing out that previous works perform extensive simulations to generate diverse training datasets with various structures, orientations, and SNRs. This is key to achieving high accuracy during the inference step.

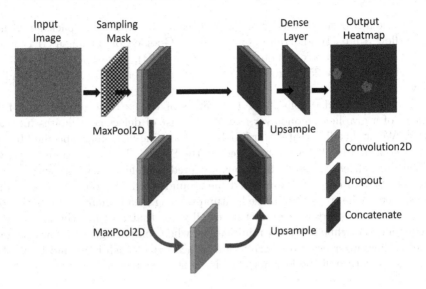

Fig. 1. Schematic of the U-Net architecture used for atomic defect identification in STEM image data. The final output is a heatmap made by placing gaussians at the given defect coordinates.

3   Methods

Here, we extend the CNN model's functionality and investigate whether the neural network can learn a sparse scan pattern that efficiently distributes dose for the entire experiment. The network is based on a U-Net architecture as shown in Fig. 1 with a preceding sampling layer after the input image. The sampling layer is similar to a dense layer, with a trainable weight composed of float values. To transform the sparse sampling layer into a binary mask of 1's and 0's, we apply a sharp sigmoid function to the weights. In general, a mask of all 1's is optimal for identifying defects and achieving a minimal loss since the entire image is visible to the network. Therefore, to encourage sparsity, the sparse sampling layer as well as the convolutional layers have an additional loss based on its L2-norm, weighted by some regularization weight. The total loss is then represented as:

$$L = E + \sum_i \lambda_i N_i, \tag{1}$$

where E is the loss incurred by the error between truth and prediction and N is the L2 norm of a layer weighted by its respective λ weight. This presents a trade-off in prediction accuracy and weight sparsity in the convolutional layers as well as the sparse sampling layer. The larger the regularization weights, the more the neural network is willing to make the sampling and convolutional layers more sparse at the cost of possibly worse defect identification. These regularization weights form a set of hyperparameters that are automatically optimized by the Adaptive Experiment (AX) Platform package [13].

The neural network was implemented using the Keras [14] package with a Tensorflow [15] backend. Training was done on Google Colab using a GPU accelerated python notebook. Due to RAM limits (10 GB), we restricted the training on a cropped 256×256 pixel area rather than the entire 1024×1024 field of view.

The data provided consists of 100 frames of 1024×1024 annular dark field images of a graphene monolayer as well as a list of defect coordinates for each frame. We artificially created our labels by producing heat maps specified by the defect coordinates that were provided by the SMDC. To create these maps, we added normalized Gaussian functions centered at defect locations with $\sigma = 5$ pixels to blank images and evaluated the ground truth with our network predictions. Due to the sparsity of these heatmaps, using mean square error as the loss metric tends to produce a prediction of all zeros that matches the majority of the label pixels while incurring minimal loss when comparing to the few non-zero pixels. Thus, we chose cross-correlation, which avoids such issue and better fits the true structure of the heatmap labels, as the loss metric.

4   Results

We explored various data partitioning strategies and whether frame order affects the training process. Specifically, we used the initial 75 movie frames for training/validation and the final 25 for testing. The model was first trained on the ascending frames, since the movie and defect evolution progresses in chronological order. We observed our modal almost perfectly predicted defects in the training dataset, achieving over 90% accuracy (Fig. 2a, b). Unfortunately, performance poorly translated for the test frames as prediction accuracy was merely 66% (Fig. 2d, e). Moreover, we tried shuffling the frame order and found the network actually performed worse. Shuffling the frames made the model 20% less accurate than when they were in chronological order. This reduction in performance is most likely because the model was learning the beam-induced structural evolution along with identifying defects. Refer to Table 1 to observe the evaluation statistics for all the training strategies.

Beyond evaluating prediction accuracy against the provided ground truth, we measured the frequency of false-positives. We mapped predicted defects with the ground truth and plotted a distance histogram between these correlated pairs (Fig. 2c, f). Paired points must be within a 3 pixel distance for defects to be considered predicted correctly. However, we see a significant number of extraneous prediction points as shown in the unpaired prediction % column. While some extraneous points may be actual defect locations that were previously unidentified in the dataset we were provided, the majority of cases are most likely false positives. Future efforts would seek improved identification strategies to suppress the prediction of false positives by training on frames beyond the first 37.

Lastly, we trained a neural network on the entire dataset (i.e. all 100 frames were in the training dataset) to seek an optimal scan for the entire experiment. Both qualitatively and quantitatively our network perfectly trained over the

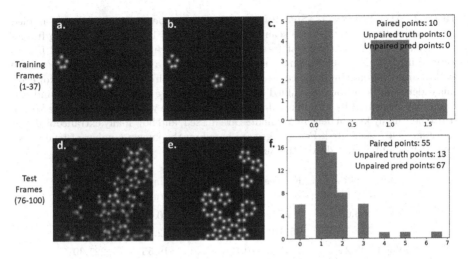

Fig. 2. Ordered training results of atomic defect identification. (a, b) The neural network prediction and the ground truth respectively for frame 1 of the training set. (c) Histogram of distances between paired neural network predictions and ground truth shows that predictions are very close to the ground truth. (d, e, f) Performance of the neural network vs. ground truth for frame 76, which is part of the test set.

entire dataset indicating an optimal solution exists. As demonstrated in Fig. 3a, b, d, e, both model predictions are nearly identical to the ground truth and the overall accuracy was over 94%. However, when our CNN model was trained with 98 out of 100 frames with 1 validation frame and 1 test frame, the test accuracy was only 50% despite training accuracy above 90%. This failure to converge to the ideal model indicates a lack of convexity in the solution space, which can be solved either with more training data diversity or a more robust regularized model.

We visually observe the neural network properly generating masks that use roughly 50% to 60% of the available field of view (highlighted in Table 1 as percent sparsity). However, the distribution appears mostly random with only the full training set showing a discrete region with markedly less sampling. Since our model determined this scanning strategy with full knowledge of all the frames, it determined that lower-left quadrant required less attention as its defect density was significantly smaller throughout the experiment. The more predictive sampling masks from the ordered and shuffled training sets have roughly uniform sparsity and suggest that the original data was oversampled for defect detection. While the lack of structure in the sampling masks is disappointing, the sparsity percentage is always lower than the defect matching percentage even for the test frames, so these masks are arguably more dose efficient than the full raster scan.

While we located a sparser set of points to sample, the data challenge tasked us to find a contiguous scanning path for exploring the sample. Seeking the shortest path through a series of points of interest is commonly referred as

Table 1. Averaged results. Sparsity % represents the percentage of points sampled compared to the total 256×256 scanning points. Frames 1–37 are the training frames and frames 76–100 were the test frames, except for the full dataset where all frames were trained on. Numbered frames between the ordered and the full training sets are in the same original chronological order, so results are directly comparable. However, this order is not kept for the shuffled dataset. Performance across the training and test frames are measured by how many defect coordinates are within 3 pixels of the known truth, how many known defect coordinates are missed, and how many extraneous defect coordinates are generated. Percentages are based on the known number of true defect coordinates and averaged over the number of frames.

Training	Sparsity %	Frames	Good match %	Unpaired truth %	Unpaired Pred. %
Ordered	53.65	1–37	91.22	0.67	136.31
		76–100	66.77	22.78	163.29
Shuffled	49.24	1–37	70.18	19.55	227.30
		76–100	59.30	35.29	59.51
Full	62.19	1–37	89.97	1.88	49.10
		76–100	96.97	2.87	1.32

the Traveling Salesman Problem (TSP), a non-deterministic polynomial-time (NP-hard) problem in combinatorial optimization [16]. There are many existing packages that generate adequate paths through a series of coordinates. We used OR-Tools [17], an open source package developed by Google, to generate a path through the 40,759 points generated by our sparse sampling layer. The resulting path is has a path length of 50,203.59 pixels compared to the 65,536 pixels of a traditional raster (not including the flyback), reducing scan time by approximately 25%. Figure 5 highlights a subsection (40×40 area) of the mask from Fig. 4b. Solving TSP is extremely time-consuming and expensive optimization, the calculation took over 24 h to complete for a 256×256 mask. Currently available tools for solving the TSP would require significant computational resources to calculate for the full 1024×1024 field of view (FOV).

However, the resulting scan path requires extremely precise controls of the scan coils and minimal sample drift. Furthermore, as shown in the path length, connecting the various sampling points necessitates sampling extraneous points and lowering the scan sparsity. If the goal is ultimately to limit dosage and radiation damage, using a standard rectangular raster along with a rapid shuttering system and blanking the beam at unnecessary points in the sample is a more practical implementation of a sparse sampling strategy than a contiguous path.

Overall, we found our CNN model significantly outperformed conventional algorithms that measured local discrepancies from a pristine graphene lattice. We used AtomNet [5] to locate atom coordinates and measure the angle and distance from its nearest-neighbors. While this traditional approach successfully found unlabeled defects, its average prediction across all frames was 40%. Even worse, the algorithm performance exponentially degraded as we increased the sparsity

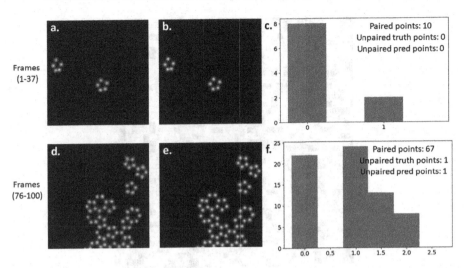

Fig. 3. Full training results of atomic defect identification. Results are shown for frames 1 and 76 for comparison to the ordered training, but there are no test frames as the whole dataset was used for training.

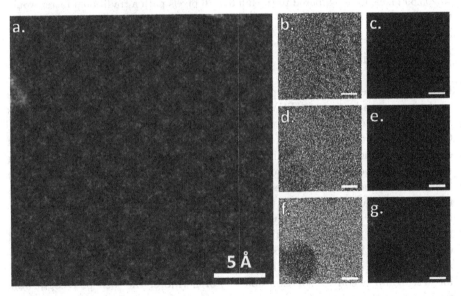

Fig. 4. Sparse sampling masks and the resulting masked data. (a) Frame 1 of the dataset. (b, d, f) The sparse sampling masks generated from the ordered, shuffled, and full training sets respectively. (c, e, g) The resulting masked frame 1.

in our images. Ideally, future efforts would fully sample the first 5-frames to identify sub-domains of interest consisting of <150 pixels^2 and constrain future frames within those cropped regions.

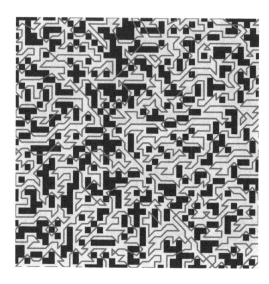

Fig. 5. 40×40 top left corner of the full path generated through all 40,759 sampled points from the 256×256 sparse sampling mask shown in Fig. 4f. The resulting path is 50,203.59 pixels long compared to the full 65,536 pixels path a traditional raster would take.

5   Conclusion

In summary, we present a deep learning approach to identify atomic defects in the graphene lattice of STEM images while also seeking dose efficient scans after training a CNN on data provided by the Smoky Mountain Data Challenge. Our CNN architecture contains an initial sparse sampling layer that represents electron beam locations on which to probes a sample. These sparse sampling strategies can be integrated into electron microscopes by either seeking a path that connects the pixels of interest, or blanking a raster scan at appropriate times to match the map. We can tune the sparsity of these sampling strategies to cover half the FOV while still identifying defects with high accuracy. We found that training on the full dataset indicates that there is an optimized sampling and defect strategy for the entire experiment. Unfortunately, our inability to approach that solution indicates either the model or the training data is insufficient for setting up a convex solution space. Furthermore, the lack of recognizable structure in the sampling strategies suggests we can make better use of our knowledge of the lattice structure. One can expect with larger STEM datasets for training, learning methods could lead to more robust sampling strategies that extend beyond the imaging of graphene lattices.

Acknowledgments. M. C. and Y. H. are supported by start-up funds provided by Rice University. J.S. and R.H. acknowledge support from the Army Research Office, Computing Sciences (W911NF-17-S-0002). H.Z. acknowledges support the Argonne Leadership Computing Facility, which is a DOE Office of Science User Facility supported under Contract DE-AC02-06CH11357.

Code. A Google Colab notebook with the code used in the project can be found at https://colab.research.google.com/drive/1H_o5DZf5ECbrBhIJ5lGY0kWx8uPav1L k?usp=sharing.

References

1. Sang, X., et al.: Dynamic scan control in STEM: *spiral scans*. Adv. Struct. Chem. Imaging **2**(6), 1–8 (2016)
2. Meyer, J.C., et al.: Accurate measurement of electron beam induced displacement cross sections for single-layer graphene. Phys. Rev. Lett. **108**(19), 196102 (2012)
3. Kretschmer, S., Lehnert, T., Kaiser, U., Krasheninnikov, A.V.: Formation of defects in two-dimensional MoS_2 in the transmission electron microscope at electron energies below the knock-on threshold: the role of electronic excitations. Nano Lett. **20**(4), 2865–2870 (2020)
4. Smokey Mountains Data Challenge (SMCDC). https://smc-datachallenge.ornl. gov/. Accessed 01 Sept 2021
5. Ziatdinov, M., et al.: Deep learning of atomically resolved scanning transmission electron microscopy images: chemical identification and tracking local transformations. ACS Nano **11**(12), 12742–12752 (2017)
6. Ziatdinov, M.: Convolutional neural networks for classification and localization of atomic defects. https://github.com/pycroscopy/AICrystallographer/blob/master/ Tutorials/DefectLocalization_ClassActivationMaps.ipynb (2019)
7. Sommer, C., Straehle, C., Koethe, U., Hamprecht, F.A.: Ilastik: interactive learning and segmentation toolkit. In: 2011 IEEE International Symposium on Biomedical Imaging: From Nano to Macro, pp. 230–233. IEEE (2011)
8. Arganda-Carreras, I., et al.: Trainable Weka Segmentation: a machine learning tool for microscopy pixel classification. Bioinformatics **33**(15), 2424–2426 (2017)
9. Schnitzer, N., Sung, S.H., Hovden, R.: Optimal STEM convergence angle selection using a convolutional neural network and the Strehl ratio. Microsc. Microanal. **26**(5), 921–928 (2020)
10. Ronneberger, O., Fischer, P., Brox, T.: U-Net: convolutional networks for biomedical image segmentation. In: Navab, N., Hornegger, J., Wells, W.M., Frangi, A.F. (eds.) MICCAI 2015. LNCS, vol. 9351, pp. 234–241. Springer, Cham (2015). https://doi.org/10.1007/978-3-319-24574-4_28
11. Lee, C.-H., et al.: Deep learning enabled strain mapping of single-atom defects in two-dimensional transition metal dichalcogenides with sub-picometer precision. Nano Lett. **20**(5), 3369–3377 (2020)
12. Maksov, A., et al.: Deep learning analysis of defect and phase evolution during electron beam-induced transformations in WS_2. npj Comput. Mater. **5**(12), 1–8 (2019)
13. Ax - adaptive experiment platform. https://ax.dev/ (2021)
14. Chollet, F., et al.: Keras. https://keras.io (2015)
15. Abadi, M., et al.: TensorFlow: large-scale machine learning on heterogeneous systems (2015). Software Available From tensorflow.org
16. Flood, M.M.: The traveling-salesman problem. Oper. Res. **4**(1), 61–75 (1956)
17. Perron, L., Furnon, V.: Or-tools. https://developers.google.com/optimization/ routing/tsp (2019)

Author Index

Printed in the United States
by Baker & Taylor Publisher Services